1973

ADULT DEVELOPMENT AND AGING

ADULT DEVELOPMENT AND AGING

MARGARET H. HUYCK
ILLINOIS INSTITUTE OF TECHNOLOGY

WILLIAM J. HOYER
SYRACUSE UNIVERSITY

Wadsworth Publishing Company
Belmont, California
A Division of Wadsworth, Inc.

Psychology Editor: Kenneth King
Production Editor: Sally Schuman
Designer: Cynthia Bassett
Manuscript Editor: Susan Weisberg
Technical Illustrators: Joan Carol and Ginny Mickelson
Cover Design: Stephen Rapley
Photo Researcher: Kay James
Signing Representative: Tom Orsi

Printed in the United States of America

1 2 3 4 5 6 7 8 9 10—86 85 84 83 82

Library of Congress Cataloging in Publication Data
Huyck, Margaret Hellie.
  Adult development and aging.

  Bibliography: p.
  Includes index.
  1. Adulthood. 2. Aging. 3. Life cycle,
Human, I. Hoyer, William J. II. Title.
HQ799.95.H88   305.2′4   81-16477
ISBN 0-534-01013-X   AACR2

Cover Photo Credits

For their inspiration and example, I dedicate this book to

My husband Tom
My children Elizabeth and Karin
My parents Ole, Elizabeth, Bill, and Bettie
I enjoy growing older with you all.

Margaret Hellie Huyck

For their love and spirit, I dedicate this book to

My wife Joan
My children Molly, Emily, Jane, Michael, and David
My parents Ann and Bill
You are each a vision in this book.

William J. Hoyer

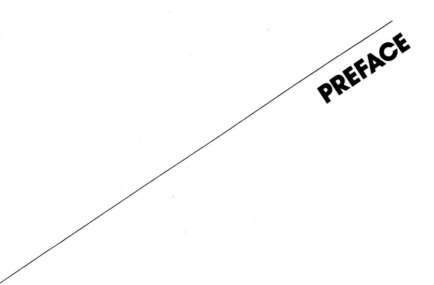

PREFACE

The study of adulthood and aging is a complex field, and in this book we have tried to capture this complexity rather than presenting a simplified version. Many disciplines are involved; we have drawn on the contributions of biologists, sociologists, psychologists, and other scientists. Because of the newness of the field, the state of theorizing and research inquiry is not highly systematic, and we often found ourselves in the process of creating new organizations of the material. Nonetheless, our goal from the outset was to provide a clear and comprehensive presentation of the current state of knowledge about adult development and aging.

Approach and Organization

Developmental psychologists are interested in changes in behavior over time. The analyses of these concerns can be organized by emphasizing either dimension—time or behavior. Organization by time makes good sense in child development, and many books report changes in terms of characteristics at birth, toddlerhood, early childhood, and other periods. The use of *stages, eras, seasons,* or other such terms to organize our analysis of adult years would make sense if we had similarly distinct and recognizable periods of adulthood to work with. The existence, number, naming, and salient characteristics of phases of adult life are not yet clear, however. For the purposes of general organization, it's possible to distinguish young adulthood, middle age, and old age; some research, however, identifies much more specific periods of seven to ten years each (Levinson, 1978), whereas other researchers essentially deny that such characterizations are useful or legitimate.

We have chosen the alternative approach, organizing the evidence in terms of basic areas of adult behavior familiar to psychologists. Part One is our *introduction* to the basic frameworks for understanding adult development: the life-span perspective in adult development; information about age groups, models, and designs used to study adult development; and the ways personal characteristics of sex, socioeconomic status, ethnicity, and age determine the individual's place in the social structure and thus influence development. Part Two presents evidence about changes from young adulthood to old age in behavior: psychobiological changes; sensory and perceptual processes; memory and information processing; intelligence and cognition; and concepts, theories, and changes in psychosocial behavior. These chapters provide the *foundation* for understanding adult development. On the basis of such understanding, Part Three considers various *applications* of such knowledge. This section of the book discusses adaptation, mental health and psychopathology, kinds of interventions in adulthood, and death and dying. Finally, the epilogue summarizes our perspective on adult development and points out how this perspective can be used to anticipate personal aging.

Acknowledgments

We undertook this project about four years ago. Many people helped us along the way, and we are grateful to each and all. Because this book has two authors, it is only fitting that we heartily thank each other for constructive criticism and much encouragement. Both of us have had extensive experience in teaching courses in adult development and aging, and we tried hard to create a book that was an honest synthesis of our interests, knowledge, and orientation. Out of a great deal of dialogue and work, we believe that something better than us both has emerged. We take full responsibility for any shortcomings and errors in the finished product.

We also wish to express gratitude to the many writers and researchers, colleagues, students, friends, and mentors who have supplied us with information, ideas, and inspiration. We thank David Bebko, M. Elliott Familant, D. Lynn Gotas, Emily B. Hoyer, Jane E. Hoyer, Cheryl L. Raskind, Linda A. McNally, and Marcia L. Shank for editorial and clerical assistance. We acknowledge the Norwegian Institute of Gerontology for its hospitality to Margaret H. Huyck during her sabbatical year of writing. Our special thanks go to Joseph M. Fitzgerald, Kathy Gribbin, and Carol A. Nowak for their detailed reviews of our manuscript, and we also thank reviewers Irene M. Hulicka, Paul Kaplan, Daniel P. Keating, Eugene A. Lovelace, and Marion Perlmutter. A grateful bow goes to Ken King, Sally Schuman, Susan Weisberg, Mary Arbogast, and other Wadsworth staff for their patience, thoroughness, and support.

Margaret H. Huyck
William J. Hoyer

BRIEF CONTENTS

PART ONE **INTRODUCTION 1**

Chapter One   Identifying the Issues   2
Chapter Two   Social Status and Individual Development   38

PART TWO **FOUNDATIONS 71**

Chapter Three   Psychobiology   72
Chapter Four   Sensation and Perception   104
Chapter Five   Memory and Information Processing   134
Chapter Six   Intelligence and Cognition   162
Chapter Seven   Models of Adult Psychosocial Development   196
Chapter Eight   Personality   228
Chapter Nine   Loving: Between Generations   264
Chapter Ten   Loving: Marriage and Friendship   296
Chapter Eleven   Working and Relaxing   330

PART THREE **APPLICATIONS 375**

Chapter Twelve   Adapting to Change   376
Chapter Thirteen Psychopathology: Maladaptive Behavior   412
Chapter Fourteen Interventions   450
Chapter Fifteen   Death, Dying, and Mourning   490
Chapter Sixteen   Epilogue   520

References   537

Index   591

CONTENTS

PART ONE **INTRODUCTION 1**

Chapter One Identifying the Issues 2
  Why Study Adult Development and Aging? 2
  Life-Span Developmental Psychology 4
    Conceptual Paradigms 5
    Ages and Stages 8
    Rate and Direction of Development 12
  Research in Adult Development 13
    Cohort Factors 13
    Some Common Approaches to Research 15
    Intraindividual Change and Individual Differences 17
    Research Methods 19
  The Study of Aging: Status and Scope 23
    The Development of Gerontology 23
    Classifying Gerontology 24
    The Concept of Age 25
  The Aging Population 27
    Demographic Characteristics 27
    Changes in Life Expectancy 29
    Factors Contributing to Longevity 30
  The Consequences of Aging 31
    Consequences for Individuals 31
    Consequences for Societies 32
  Summary 36

Chapter Two Social Status and Individual Development 38
  Social Status 40
    Stratification Systems 40

Stereotypes and Discrimination   41
Status Mobility   42
Sex as a Status Characteristic   43
Models of Masculinity-Femininity   45
Consequences of Sex Differentiation   46
Explanations for Sexual Differentiation   49
Changes over the Life Span   51
Social Policies   52
Socioeconomic Status   54
Perceptions of Social Strata   55
Qualifications for Membership   55
Mobility   56
Changing Social Class Systems   57
Women and Status   58
Social Policies   58
Ethnicity   59
Assessment   59
Stereotypes and Discrimination   61
Consequences   62
Social Policies   62
Age as a Status Characteristic   63
Life Periods   64
Social Class and Sex Differences with Age   65
Age Norms and Behavior   65
Consequences of Age Stratification   66
Social Policy Perspectives   67
Group Patterns and Individual Behavior   68
Summary   68

PART TWO   **FOUNDATIONS   71**

Chapter Three   Psychobiology   72
Senescence   74
What Is Senescence?   74
Senescence Versus Senile Dementia   75
Senescence of the Brain   76
Neuronal Loss   76
Brain Size   79
Accumulation of Lipofuscan and Other Matter   80
Neurofibrillary Tangling   80
Changes at the Synapse   81
Levels of Senescence   81
Theories of Senescence   82
Cellular Theories   82
Genetic Theories   84
Wear-and-Tear Theories   86

Senescence and Disease   87
    Heart Disease and Aging   88
    The Ecology of Disease   91
    Preventive Health Care   91
    Physical Fitness and Aging   92
Sexuality and Aging   93
Sleeping, Dreaming, and Senescence   96
Reversing Senescence   97
Bioethics and Sociobiology   100
Summary   101

Chapter Four   Sensation and Perception   104
Sensory Processes and Aging   106
Vision   108
    Visual Acuity   108
    Accommodation   109
    Cataracts   110
    Dark Adaptation   110
    Critical Flicker Frequency   111
    Illusions   111
Hearing   113
Taste and Smell   115
Touch   117
Thermoregulation   119
Pain   119
The Practical Implications of Sensory Loss   121
The Processing of Sensory and Perceptual Information   122
    Information Processing   122
    Attention   123
    Other Models of Perception   125
    Studying Age-Related Changes in Perception   125
    Response Persistence   127
    Perceptual Rigidity   127
    Perceptual Preference   128
Perception and Cognition   130
Summary   132

Chapter Five   Memory   134
A Sociohistorical Perspective   136
Some Models of the Structure of Memory   138
    Sensory, Short-Term, and Long-Term Memory   138
    Semantic Memory and Episodic Memory   141
    Depth of Processing   142
Memory and Learning   143
Age Changes in Memory   146
    Encoding and Retrieval   146

Encoding Specificity and Cue Overload   147
Interference   149
Reconstructive Memory   150
Reminiscence   152
Metamemory   153
Clinical Aspects of Memory   155
Korsakoff's Syndrome   156
Senile Dementia   156
Memory Loss and Depression   157
Intervention   158
Summary   158

Chapter Six   Intelligence and Cognition   162
Defining and Measuring Intelligence   164
What Is Intelligence?   164
Guilford's Structure of Intellect Model   166
The General Factor Theory   168
The Primary Mental Abilities Model   168
Current Factor Analytic Models   169
Reliability and Validity   172
Modifiers of Intelligence   174
Intelligence and Cohort   174
Intelligence and Educational Level   175
Intelligence and Occupation   176
Intelligence and Anxiety   177
Intelligence and Plasticity   178
Intelligence and Terminal Drop   179
Some Conclusions   180
Development of Cognition in Adulthood   181
The Stages of Cognitive Development   182
Some Aspects of Adult Cognitive Development   183
Intelligence in Context   184
Environmental Taxonomies   185
The Competence-Performance Distinction   186
Problem Solving and Concept Learning   187
Testing Problem-Solving Ability   188
Evidence of Age-Related Deficits   189
Creativity, Flexibility, and Curiosity   190
Creativity   190
Flexibility   191
Curiosity   192
Summary   193

Chapter Seven   Models of Adult Psychosocial Development   196
David Gutmann: Parenting as a Key to the Species Life Cycle   198
Concepts   198
Human Development   200

    Critique of the Theory   202
   Erik Erikson: The Psychosocial Life Cycle   204
    Concepts   205
    Human Development: The Eight Ego Challenges   207
    Critique of the Theory   216
   Robert Havighurst: The Age-Graded Life Cycle   217
    Concepts   217
    Tasks in Human Development   218
    Critique of the Theory   219
   Dialectical Perspectives on Change   220
   Daniel Levinson: The Seasons of a Man's Life   221
    Concepts   221
    Human Development: Eras and Transitions   222
    Critique of the Theory   224
   Summary   225

Chapter Eight   Personality   228
   Challenges in the Study of Personality   228
   Personality Variables That Show No Relationship to Age   231
    The Normative Aging Study and the Baltimore Study of Aging   231
    The Berkeley Guidance Study and the Oakland Growth Studies:
      From Adolescence to Middle Age   233
    Growing Old in a Community   235
    Actual and Remembered Continuity   236
   Personality Characteristics Showing Changes with Age   237
    Decreased Sex-Typed Qualities   237
    Further Questions   242
   Ego Functioning   243
    Adaptiveness   243
    Maladaptiveness   244
   Moral Development   245
    Moral Behavior   245
    Kohlberg's Stages of Moral Development   246
   Self-Concept and Age   247
    Age Identification   247
    Self-Esteem   249
   Crisis or Continuity? The Case at Mid-life   252
    The Crisis-for-All Position   252
    The Continuity Position   254
    The Differential Position   255
    Some Conclusions   261
   Summary   261

Chapter Nine   Loving: Between Generations   264
   What Is This Thing Called Love?   264
    The Capacity to Love   266
    Developmental Changes in Affiliation   267

Families: Myths and Realities   268
   Family Functions   268
   Family Structure   272
   The Family Life Cycle   272
   Contact Among Family Members   273
   Affection and the "Generational Stake"   274
   Cultural Variability   275
   The Family as Caregivers   275
   Factors Strengthening and Weakening the Family   276
Developmental Issues in Parent-Child Relations   278
   Phase I: Immature Child and Responsible Adult   278
   Phase II: Adult Child and Adult Parent   283
   Phase III: Older Adult Child and Elderly Parent   289
Summary   293

Chapter Ten   Loving: Marriage and Friendship   296
Some Perspectives on Marriage   296
   Strain in Marriage   298
   Marriage as Process   298
Developmental Issues in Marriage   300
   Young Adulthood   301
   Middle Adulthood   311
   Old-Age Partnerships   319
Other Relationships and Lifestyles   321
   The Never-Married   321
   Brothers and Sisters   322
   Friends   323
   Lovers   325
Summary   326

Chapter Eleven   Working and Relaxing   330
Motivations for Working   332
   Meanings of Work   332
   Satisfactions and Burdens in Working   333
The Worlds of Work   335
   Social Stratification of the Work Force   335
   Sexual Division of Labor   338
   Historical and Cohort Differences   340
Work Involvements Throughout Adulthood   343
Men and Work   346
   Early Socialization for Work   346
   Vocational Development   346
   Retiring from Employment   349
Women and Work   353
   Early Socialization   353
   Vocational Development   354

Male Responses to Women Achievers   363
Retiring from Employment   364
Relaxation and Leisure   365
Theories of Leisure Behavior   365
Leisure Involvements over Adulthood   367
Age Changes in Leisure   369
The Challenge: Balancing the Whole Life   371
Summary   372

PART THREE   **APPLICATIONS   375**

Chapter Twelve   Adapting to Change   376
Defining and Assessing Adaptation to Change   378
The Nature of Changes in Adulthood   378
Defining "Successful" Transitions   378
Examples of Changes Requiring Adaptation   380
Menopause   381
Understanding the Changes   381
Outcomes: From Symptoms to Zest   382
Factors Explaining Variable Symptom Reports   382
Men's Responses to Menopause   385
Facilitating Adaptation to Menopause   386
The Male Climacteric   387
Widowhood   388
Understanding the Changes   389
Resources for Widows   389
Other Factors Affecting the Impact of Widowhood   392
Outcomes of Widowhood   394
Coping with Transient Life Crisis: Mastectomy   396
Phases of Adjustment   396
Coping with Other Transient Life Crises   399
Factors Affecting Adaptation to Change   399
Cognitive Processes and Adaptation   399
Personality and Adaptation: Type A and Type B Personalities   401
Personality and Aging: The Kansas City Studies   401
Coping with Change   404
Coping Strategies   404
Social Resources and Adaptation   408
Summary   409

Chapter Thirteen   Psychopathology: Maladaptive Behavior   412
Some Definitions and Examples   412
Developmental Perspectives on Psychopathology   415
Explanations of Abnormal Behavior   418
Biological Explanations   418
Psychosocial Explanations   419

Assessing Behavior: Does the Diagnosis Describe the Population?   422
    Reasons for Assessing Mental Health   422
    Classifying Abnormal Behavior   423
Major Forms of Abnormal Behavior During Adulthood   424
    Neurosis   424
    Anxiety Disorders   424
    Psychosexual Disorders   430
    Affective Disorders and Suicide   431
    Somatoform Disorders   435
    Substance Use Disorders: Alcoholism and Drug Abuse   437
    Psychotic Disorders   438
    Organic Mental Disorders: General Characteristics   440
    Dementias: Nonreversible Brain Syndromes   441
    "Acute"/Reversible Brain Syndromes   445
Summary   447

Chapter Fourteen   Interventions   450
A Developmental Perspective on Intervention   450
    Intervention in Young Adulthood   452
    Intervention in Middle Adulthood   453
    Intervention in Late Adulthood   454
Defining the Problem Requiring Intervention   456
Identifying Probable Causes   457
    The Identified-Problem Group   458
    Comparison of Problem and Nonproblem Groups   458
    Epidemiological Studies   458
    Inferences from Treatment Effects   459
Understanding Intervention Options   459
    Goals of Intervention   459
    Areas of Intervention   462
Techniques of Intervention   463
    Pharmacotherapies   463
    Psychotherapy   465
    Education and Training   472
    Service Delivery   473
    Environmental Interventions   474
    Settings and Agents for Interventions   474
Evaluating the Outcomes of Intervention   475
    Reasons for Evaluation   475
    An Example of Evaluation: Drug and Psychotherapy
        Treatments for Depression   476
    An Alternative: Intensive Analysis of a Few Cases in
        Brief Psychotherapy   479
Establishing Intervention Policies   483
    The Mental-Health System   483

Age: Relevant or Irrelevant? 484
Need Versus Entitlement 485
Advocacy for All 486
Summary 486

Chapter Fifteen Death, Dying, and Mourning 490
What Is Death? 492
Some Definitions 492
Individual and Societal Views of Death 493
Mourning 495
The Challenge of Mourning 496
The Process of Mourning 496
Outcomes of Mourning 499
Factors Affecting the Mourning Process 500
Understanding Death 503
Time and Death 503
Death and Personal Causation 503
Confronting Death 506
Stages of Dying 506
Dying Trajectories 507
Death Anxiety 508
Life, Death, and Life after Death 510
Planning for Death 511
Looking Ahead 511
Euthanasia 514
Working with the Dying 516
Summary 518

Chapter Sixteen Epilogue 520
Some Basic Themes 520
Models of Development 522
General Models 523
Interpretations of Adult Developmental Research 525
Dimensions of Adult Development and Aging 526
Developmental Forecasting 528
Self-Development: Does Any of This Apply to You? 529
Self-Health 530
Personal Control 531
Do We or Can We Know How Society Will Change? 532
How Will Psychogerontology Change in the Future? 534
Conclusion 535

References **537**

Name Index **591**

Subject Index **611**

PART ONE

INTRODUCTION

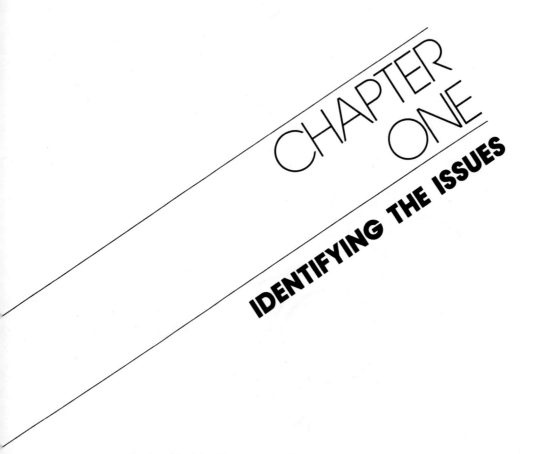

WHY STUDY
ADULT DEVELOPMENT AND AGING?

Until just a few years ago the term *adulthood* rarely appeared in the literature of the biological and social sciences. Now people in many fields of study have become interested in "life after 20," and their investigations have led to a growing body of knowledge. The purpose of this book is to describe this field of knowledge—the psychology of adult development and aging—and to look at some of the many questions we still need to answer about adulthood and aging. How do adults develop? What factors influence this development? Do we become our "self" as we grow older? Are we continuously learning and developing our cognitive abilities throughout life?

Even the concepts *childhood* and *adolescence* are of fairly recent origin. In medieval society there was no idea of a separate childhood, adolescence, and adulthood. To quote Philippe Ariès (1962):

In the Middle Ages, at the beginning of modern times, and for a long time after that in the lower classes, children were mixed with adults as soon as

they were considered capable of doing without their mothers or nannies. . . . They immediately went straight into the great community of men, sharing in the work and play of their companions, old and young alike. The movement of collective life carried along in a single torrent all ages and classes, leaving nobody any time for solitude and privacy. . . . The family fulfilled a function; it ensured the transmission of life, property, and names; but it did not penetrate very far into human sensibility. (p. 411)

Age differentiation has been a particular obsession of 20th-century historians.

At the same time, we are more concerned today than ever before about the quality of life for all individuals. Our society has heightened its sensitivity to the rights of minorities, the handicapped, women, children, the aged, and other distinct groups. We have come to recognize, accept, and perhaps even cherish human diversity. Human differences are greatest in adulthood—the largest and most significant portion of the life cycle—so that period is a rich subject of study.

A lengthened life span has resulted in a growing number and proportion of older people. These individuals have more leisure time, better health, and more education than in the past. We need to pay more attention to them—*to ourselves.*

LIFE-SPAN DEVELOPMENTAL PSYCHOLOGY

For many years developmental psychology emphasized early development—from conception through adolescence. The assumption was that the most dramatic and important changes occurred during these years; adult behavior was considered quite stable, and predictable from early behavior. It has become obvious, however, that many significant changes and new behaviors occur during adulthood, although the new behaviors that emerge during the adult years have many antecedents in earlier life. Development is now considered a continuous, dynamic, and lifelong process of change.

Any field of study that is concerned with time-associated or age-associated change is considered to be a developmental discipline. Psychology is defined as the scientific study of behavior, so, by extension, developmental psychology is the scientific study of age-associated behavior change. The *life-span developmental* approach emphasizes the lifelong nature of development and asserts that our understanding of any point in the life span is enhanced by taking into account the individual's past history and perhaps his or her future developmental expectations.

What behaviors do we study the development of? Obviously, researchers who are interested in infants and toddlers study different behavioral dimensions than people who do research with adolescents or adults. Yet sometimes the processes under investigation are very similar. *Psychological processes* are inner actions that are inferred from behavior. Someone interested in the developmental study of memory processes, for example, can study remembering and forgetting at any point in the life span.

One of the most important questions asked by the adult developmentalist is, "What are the basic processes of development, and how do these processes change with age in adulthood?" In this book we will be examining a wide variety of basic *behavioral, cognitive,* and *social* processes from a developmental perspective. Under what conditions is it more difficult for the older person to learn and to remember? Why is this so? How does the older person adapt to a changing world?

In these and many other areas of study the goals of the developmental psychologist are to describe, explain, predict, and modify age-associated behavior change (Goulet & Baltes, 1970).

Conceptual Paradigms

Nature and Nurture   Many factors influence development. Developmental determinants generally are classified as either external—that is, environmental—or internal—that is, biological or genetic—and developmental psychologists tend to emphasize one or the other when they try to describe, explain, and predict behavior. The issue of nature versus nurture is at the core of research and theory in developmental psychology (Lerner, 1976). The word *nature,* derived from the Latin root meaning birth, is used to refer to the innate or genetically carried characteristics and dispositions of an organism. *Nurture,* in contrast, refers to the environmental factors that affect the individual from conception onward. The relative influence of nature and nurture in human development continues to be widely and often vigorously debated. For example, are there race differences in learning ability? Are age differences in intelligence biologically based and hence irreversible, or are they a product of educational factors and the way adults are treated at different ages in contemporary society?

Two important facts pertain to the nature–nurture issue. First, the relative contributions of nature and nurture are age-specific (Huston-Stein & Baltes, 1976). In other words, if we were to compare the developmental stages of infancy, adulthood, and senescence (say, over 90), we would find that genetic contributions were strongest at the beginning and end periods of the life cycle and environmental contributions strongest in the middle period.

Second, development cannot take place in the absence of either nature or nurture. Nature and nurture are not only determinants, they are requisites of development. To quote T. C. Schneirla (1957):

The critical problem of behavioral development should be stated as follows: (1) to study the organization of behavior in terms of its properties at each stage, from the time of egg formation and fertilization through individual life history, and (2) to work out the changing relationships of the organic mechanisms underlying behavior, (3) always in terms of the contributions of earlier stages in the developmental sequence, (4) and in consideration of the properties of the prevailing developmental context at each stage. (p. 80)

In spite of the fact that developmental psychologists know that both nature and nurture are required for development, and generally accept that their relative contributions depend on the age period being studied, the nature–nurture issue and its implications continue to be disputed. The debates have nothing to do with the facts; rather, they involve the way development is implicitly conceptualized. Consider the following hypothetical example:

Michael is 20 years old. He was born and grew up in New Jersey. In high school he maintained average grades and participated in two sports, wrestling and track. During the past two years he's been attending a medium-sized college in Pennsylvania. He is a B student, he enjoys some of his courses but not others, and he works hard in the courses that he likes. His social relationships throughout his development (thus far) have been plentiful, although not especially deep or enduring.

What will Michael be like at age 30? At 50? At 70? How we approach these questions, as well as how we interpret the information given, reflects our conception, or paradigm, of development. A *paradigm* is a model for interpreting events and the relationships among events (Achenbach, 1978). Paradigms have two main influences on the study of any subject. First, they guide the kinds of research questions that are asked. For example, should we emphasize environmental or intrapersonal factors in trying to understand Michael's academic and social development? Second, paradigms influence the interpretations we give to casual as well as systematic observations. Which specific environmental or intrapersonal factors have affected Michael's adult development?

It is important not to confuse paradigms with theories and to understand the relationship of paradigms to theory and research. *Research* is defined as the systematic, detailed, and often relatively prolonged attempt to discover knowledge or confirm facts that bear upon a certain problem (English & English, 1958). There are two main ways to do research: (1) historical research based on documents such as journal articles and books, and (2) firsthand, systematic observation. The purposes of *theory* are (1) to organize and integrate knowledge, and (2) to direct research aimed at increasing knowledge (Baltes, Reese, & Nesselroade, 1977). Paradigms are more comprehensive. They implicitly, and sometimes explicitly, govern what questions we choose to investigate and how we organize and interpret the results of our research. Theories and facts can be accepted or rejected, proven or falsified, but our view of the world, its people, and how they develop is at a higher level. Paradigms are superordinate to theories and facts.

In psychology, researchers currently use three main paradigms for understanding development: the *mechanistic, organismic,* and *dialectical* paradigms.

The Mechanistic Paradigm   According to this viewpoint, the developing individual is a machine-like entity whose parts are quantifiable and reduceable. The individual is acted upon by external forces, shaped by the environment. For example, Michael's behavior could be explained in terms of his past and present socially defined and socially reinforced roles, such as male youth, college student, and Easterner.

The Organismic Paradigm   This model characterizes the individual as an integrated organism. Organismic and mechanistic paradigms differ with regard to the use of *reductionism* in research, or the view that complex phenomena are best understood by analyzing their elementary components. The mechanistic view supposes that the analyzed parts are real and that the whole (that is, the organism) can be completely explained as made up of *only* the analyzed components. In contrast, the organismic model suggests that the whole organism is greater than the sum of its parts.

The mechanistic and organismic paradigms also differ in viewing development as a quantitative change or as a sequence of qualitative changes (Overton & Reese, 1973; Reese & Overton, 1970). Mechanistic theories emphasize the quantitative aspects of change, whereas organismic theories stress qualitative changes. Many developmental psychologists are interested in qualitative change, and they think of development as taking place in a series of stages. Erikson, Piaget, and Kohlberg are representative of this view. From the organismic perspective the developing individual is the *active* force who determines his or her own actions. The environment serves simply to trigger the internal "blueprints" that characterize each stage of human development. More will be said about developmental stage theories later in this chapter.

The Dialectical Paradigm   This paradigm has only recently emerged as an alternative to the mechanistic and organismic models. Dialectics refers to the interaction of conflicting or contradictory principles (Riegel, 1975a, b). The dialectical view is that any action (thesis) must inevitably lead to its counteraction (antithesis) and then be followed by integration (synthesis). Development is seen as an outgrowth of conflict or crisis. To quote Riegel (1975b):

. . . the thoughts, actions, and emotions of an individual, once generated and actualized, can transform those of others who live with him or come after him. At the same time, the thoughts, actions, and emotions of the other individuals can transform those of the single individual. In this dynamic interactionism of inner and outer dialectics, man not only transforms the outer world in which

he lives but is himself transformed by the world which he and others have created. (pp. 50–51)

Riegel (1975a) has also argued that the dialectical model resolves many of the discrepancies between the organismic and mechanistic paradigms (qualitative versus quantitative change; reductionism versus holism; active organism versus reactive organism; nature versus nurture). For example, according to the dialectical perspective, the influences of nature and nurture are continuously interacting in what Riegel referred to as the "developmental interdependence of organism and environment, individual and society" (1977, p. 72). Behavioral development reflects the mutual interactions between inner/biological and outer/physical influences that are never static.

Intervention   In addition to affecting how we describe, explain, and predict human actions, thoughts, and feelings, paradigms also influence our approach to intervention.

The fairly recent debates about the nature of intelligence and cognitive functioning can serve as an illustration. It was long assumed that intelligence was innate—that a child was "born bright" or "born average," and consequently little effort was made to intervene. In the past few years, however, it has been demonstrated that intelligence is relatively plastic, or modifiable throughout the life span (Baltes & Baltes, 1977; Labouvie-Vief, 1977). Psychologists have quite convincingly shown that intelligence is not "fixed" at conception—a stimulating, supportive social and intellectual environment can develop intellectual potential throughout life. Of course, there is some genetic/biological contribution, though there is no clear agreement on just how much. This changing conception of the nature of intelligence logically leads to a changing attitude toward intervention.

For many years it was assumed that old age brings "natural" deterioration of intellectual functioning, and that nothing could be done to prevent this—a frightening possibility that certainly contributed to anxieties about aging. However, researchers are now exploring the biological and environmental factors associated with decline and maintenance of intellectual functioning in old age. The relative contributions of nature and nurture are far from clear, but this is one of the exciting areas of developmental psychology today (Fozard & Popkin, 1978).

Ages and Stages

People have been noticing commonalities in behavioral development for centuries. The notion that the life course can be separated into predictable phases is very old. For example, we have old pictures from Sweden (Figures 1–1 and 1–2) showing the ten ages of man and woman, from infancy to old age. Shakespeare immortalized his own vision of seven periods in life. The question for psychologists interested in development over the course of life is to what extent "stage" concepts describe and explain the changes that we observe. Scientists use the term *stage* in a different way than Shakespeare did.

All the world's a stage.
And all the men and women merely players.
They have their exits and their entrances.
And one man in his time plays many parts,
His acts being seven ages. At first the infant,
Mewling and puking in the nurse's arms.
Then the whining school-boy, with his satchel
And shining morning face, creeping like snail
Unwillingly to school. And then the lover,
Sighing like a furnace, with a woeful ballad
Made to his mistress' eyebrow. Then a soldier,
Full of strange oaths, and bearded like the pard,
Jealous in honour, sudden, and quick in quarrel,
Seeking the bubble reputation
Even in the cannon's mouth. And then the justice,
In fair round belly with good capon lin'd,
With eyes severe and beard of formal cut,
Full of wise saws and modern instances;
And so he plays his part. The sixth age shifts
Into the lean and slipper'd pantaloon,
With spectacles on nose and pouch on side;
His youthful hose, well sav'd, a world too wide
For his shrunk shank; and his big manly voice,
Turning again toward childish treble, pipes
And whistles in his sound. Last scene of all,
That ends this strange eventful history,
Is second childishness and mere oblivion,
Sans teeth, sans eyes, sans taste, sans everything.

As You Like It (II, vii, 139–166)

Anyone proposing a stage model of development must make several assumptions. It is important to understand these assumptions in order to use stage models accurately. One assumption is that there is, in fact, an underlying, biologically based "blueprint" for development, which unfolds in a fairly predictable fashion. The blueprint, or structure, of the individual is genetically determined. With such a blueprint we would expect changes to be universal; that is, we could find the same kinds of changes in Oslo, in Chicago, and in

Bangladesh. In addition, a stage theory assumes that there are identifiably different stages, and that each individual proceeds through all of the stages in sequence. While the duration of each stage may vary from individual to individual, a person may not skip any stage in the series.

Flavell (1971) summarized some characteristics common to the various stage conceptualizations of development. First, each individual's behavior is considered to reflect some kind of underlying structure. The underlying structure changes at different stages of development, promoting the different observed behavior.

Second, the changes in behavior are qualitative, not merely quantitative, changes. For example, an increase in the number of words that a child knows represents merely a quantitative change; the ability to speak and communicate with words, however, represents a qualitative change from nonverbal communication or babbling.

Figure 1–1 The ages of man.

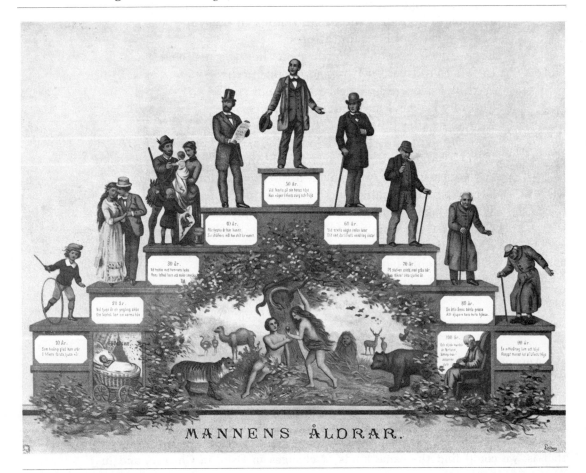

Third, most stage theories postulate some kind of reasonably abrupt change in behavior. The caterpillar becomes a butterfly; the infant becomes a toddler, then a child. There is some transition from one stage to another, but the beginning of one stage and the ending of another stage should be identifiable. For example, most 15-year-olds can be clearly identified as adolescents, and their behaviors are primarily, if not exclusively, typical of that stage. This characteristic is related to the assumption that many aspects of behavior are assumed to change together; that is, a number of changes occur in a short period of time, and the individual actually shifts to a different level of development.

Do successive stages represent higher levels of functioning? The issue is a debatable one. Not all stage theories postulate the direction of development. On the other hand, popular images of the stages of life, such as that represented in Figures 1-1 and 1-2, clearly have the 50s as the pinnacle of life: We ascend the pyramid to the 50s; life is a descent after that.

Figure 1–2   The ages of woman.

There are several current stage theories of human development. One of the most famous is Erik Erikson's theory of psychosocial development. Erikson discusses psychosocial functioning throughout the life span, with an emphasis on people's strategies for dealing with environmental tasks (Erikson, 1963). More will be said about Erikson's stages of development in Chapter 7.

A more recent and widely popularized stage theory of adulthood is that of Daniel Levinson. On the basis of interviews with middle-class men in their middle years, Levinson and his colleagues have postulated a stage theory of development for the young adult and the middle years. They see development as proceeding in periods of roughly seven years, separated by transitional periods of three to six years; they have identified, named, and characterized each of these periods (Levinson, 1978). Recently, Gail Sheehy (1976) has expanded on Levinson's model by including information based on interviews with women.

Bromley (1966) proposed a stage conceptualization of the life cycle that emphasized both biological and social factors. Bromley's framework included three stages prior to birth, three childhood stages, two adolescent stages, and seven stages of adulthood and old age. Table 1-1 summarizes the last seven stages of Bromley's theory.

Such conceptualizations are valuable because they impose some order on what often seem to be chaotic, complex life experiences. However, many psychologists do not accept the assumptions of stage theories. Are stage theories useful once we go beyond the general characterizations of the kind offered by Shakespeare? One of the questions to which we will return is indeed to what extent the adult life course can be characterized in terms of stages.

Rate and Direction of Development

Developmental changes are perhaps most visible as the infant becomes the adult. During these years the direction of change seems to be clear: toward

Table 1-1   Bromley's Stages of Adulthood and Senescence

Stage	Age range	Main characteristics
Early adulthood	21 to 25 years	Acquisition of adult roles; economic responsibilities; marriage; employment; children; professional training; total involvement in adult activities; athletic achievements.
Middle adulthood	25 to 40	Consolidation of social and occupational roles; intellectual achievements; some decline in physical and mental functions.
Late adulthood	40 to 55	Departure of children; reduction in sexual activity; further decline in physical and mental functions.
Preretirement	55 to 65	Continued decline of physical and mental functions; partial disengagement from social and occupational roles.
Retirement	65	Disengagement from social and occupational roles; heightened vulnerability to physical and mental illness; greater importance given to family ties.
Old age	70	Dependency; full disengagement; physical and mental decline.
Terminal illness and death	to 110	Senility; breakdown of critical biological functions.

Adapted from D. B. Bromley, *The Psychology of Human Aging.* Copyright © 1966, 1974 by D. B. Bromley. Reprinted by permission of Penguin Books Ltd.

greater complexity and increased function. After maturity, changes over time may lead to enhanced functioning (for example, increased verbal skill, the "wisdom" of advanced age) or to decrements (for example, losses of visual acuity, slower response speed). On the other hand, people may show little change over most of the adult years. We will accept Neugarten's (1977) assertion that we should call developmental "those changes demonstrated to vary in an orderly way with age, regardless of the direction of change" (p. 630).

The rate of developmental change varies over the life course. Changes are most rapid during the early months after conception and the first few years of life, whereas the rate of change over most of adulthood is slow and relatively steady. Variations are particularly evident in biological functioning, where puberty, menopause, and dying in old age mark periods of relatively rapid change. When several changes occur in a short space of time, the pace of developmental change seems quickened. For example, young men and women typically leave home, complete formal education, become financially self-supporting, marry, and assume parental responsibilities in a relatively short space of time (five to seven years or less); the two decades after that are marked by a slower rate of change. Postretirement changes may proceed at a moderate rate until the predeath period of disintegration begins and the rate of decline accelerates.

The rate of developmental change also varies greatly from individual to individual during adulthood. It varies as well by historical periods: For example, as general health and nutrition improve, the rate of biological aging is slowed, and when older people are prohibited from continuing their earlier activities (such as work), the rate of aging is accelerated.

RESEARCH IN
ADULT DEVELOPMENT

To find out how individuals change (or how they stay the same) during the adult years, special methods of study are necessary. In this section we will discuss some of the general research methods for investigating adult development.

Cohort Factors

Aging takes place along a multitude of psychological, social, biological, and functional dimensions. There are also numerous nature and nurture factors that influence or determine the course of behavioral development. Both the outcomes and determinants of development need to be considered in relation to the time when the individual lives. *Cohort* is a term that identifies persons born or entering a particular system at a given point in historical time. Clearly, people's experience is determined in good part by when they live. For instance, being 17 in 1900 was different from being 17 in 1980, and the person who attended college in 1900 was not the same as the college student of today. In 1900 there were approximately 1.5 million people who were 17 years old. Only about

3 percent of this cohort completed high school; 57 percent of the high school graduates were women. Only 27,410 people graduated from college in 1900; 81 percent were men. In comparison, about 75 percent of the 17-year-olds in 1976 graduated from high school. In that year there were over 3.1 million high school graduates and almost 1 million college graduates. Just over 50 percent of the high school graduates and 43 percent of the college graduates were women.*

People who were born around the same time and who share similar experiences over the life course are members of the same cohort. We cannot assume that these girls will grow old in the same ways as have the women who are now old, because they belong to different cohorts.

The importance of cohort factors in the study of adult development should not be underestimated. Schaie (1965) and Baltes (1968) were among the first writers to draw attention to the problem of comparing individuals who represent different cohorts. Schaie's (1965, 1970) general developmental model, in which chronological age, cohort, and time of measurement are treated as distinguishable sources of influence, has been the departure point for much of the current methodological dialogue in developmental psychology (Adam, 1978; Baltes, Reese, & Nesselroade, 1977). Before we discuss Schaie's general developmental model, let us look at two basic developmental designs.

*Statistics from U.S. Department of Health, Education and Welfare, National Center for Education Statistics (*Information Please Almanac*, 1979).

Some Common Approaches to Research

The Cross-sectional Method   The cross-sectional and longitudinal methods are the most commonly used strategies for collecting developmental data. The *cross-sectional method* involves testing individuals or groups of individuals who differ in chronological age at one point in time. For example, we could test the personality or the intellectual performance of groups of individuals who are 20, 30, 40, 50, and 60 years old in 1980. Such a study would yield information about *age differences*. The cross-sectional method is probably the easiest way to study developmental trends, but the method has its limitations. The most serious problem is that actual age differences cannot be distinguished from cohort or generational differences.

Researchers say that data are *confounded* when it is not possible to assess separately the influences of the various factors in an investigation. In a cross-sectional study it cannot be determined just how much of the variation is due to the age of the participants and how much of it is due to cohort factors; in other words, age and cohort influences are confounded in the cross-sectional study. The 20- , 30- , 40- , 50- , and 60-year-olds who were tested in 1980 differ with regard to cohort (or year of birth) as well as age. Because they were born in 1960, 1950, 1940, 1930, and 1920, respectively, they have many experiences that are unique to their time of birth and development.

The Longitudinal Method   The second method, the *longitudinal method,* involves testing the same individuals at progressive points in time. One cohort is selected for study (for example, a sample of people born in 1900), and they are tested at selected intervals (such as every five years). Longitudinal studies provide information about *age changes*.

Ideally, the longitudinal method provides exactly the knowledge sought by the developmental psychologist. In reality, however, the longitudinal method has several limitations. First, age changes are confounded with *time of measurement* changes. The individual develops in a changing society, and circumstances at the time of testing may interact with age level and past experience to affect performance on whatever is being measured. For example, trends in art, music, and media may have more of an effect on the development of some age groups than others. The confounding of age and time of measurement can be compensated for by using sequential strategies (see p. 17).

Second, age changes obtained using the longitudinal method may be attributable to the effects of *repeated measurement*. Repeated exposure to the same or similar testing instruments often influences performance for a number of reasons, such as familiarity with the test content and testing situation, increased motivation, or reduced test anxiety. Such biases can be eliminated by testing new samples of people representative of the initial cohort (Schaie, 1972).

Third, age changes obtained by the longitudinal method may be affected by task characteristics that are different for different age groups. The same task requirements and a standardized testing situation may have different effects for younger and older adults. For example, lighting conditions, time pressure to answer, the size of the print to be read, and writing speed may be more deleterious to an older person than to a college student in an experiment (Hoyer, Labouvie, & Baltes, 1973).

Fourth, age changes may be confounded by the effects of *selective attrition*. For a variety of reasons (mobility, mortality, and motivation), some of the participants drop out of the longitudinal study as it progresses. Several investigators (for instance, Baltes, Schaie, & Nardi, 1971; Riegel & Riegel, 1972; Siegler & Botwinick, 1979) have shown that drop-out or attrition is not random but is related to test performance. Siegler and Botwinick, for example, examined attrition effects in a 20-year (1955–1976) longitudinal study of intelligence at Duke University (Buss, 1970). Scores from the Wechsler Adult Intelligence Scale (WAIS; Wechsler, 1955) were analyzed for 246 subjects ranging in age from 60 to 94. Consistent with previous studies of selective attrition, Siegler and Botwinick (1979) found that subjects who remained in the study were those who had higher mental ability scores than those who dropped out. In other words, as a longitudinal study progresses, the subject sample (1) may no longer be representative of the initial population from which it was drawn, and (2) may no longer be representative of the selected cohort at that time of measurement. This problem can be handled by making sure that the sample is representative at each time of measurement (see also Botwinick & Siegler, 1980).

Fifth, there are *practical limitations* to the longitudinal method. These include factors related to the length of time required to conduct the study, such as data storage and the investigator's mobility, motivation, and even mortality. Several of the current longitudinal investigations of the adult years are actually extensions of longitudinal studies of childhood development. For example, Maas and Kuypers (1974) reported a longitudinal analysis of the personality and lifestyle of adults ranging in age from approximately 30 to 70. The adults in the Maas and Kuypers study were the parents of children who were part of the Berkeley Growth Study, which has followed since childhood people who are now nearly 50. Information about the parents' personality was collected for the purpose of examining the effects of parent personalities on child development. Serendipitously, the investigators had also collected valuable descriptive information about adult personality development over a period of approximately 40 years. Adult developmental data have also been obtained as a by-product of a longitudinal study of psychological development from birth to maturity done by the Fels Research Institute (see Kagan & Moss, 1962).

In summary, both the cross-sectional and the longitudinal methods can provide erroneous information about developmental change. In addition, contradictions may be obtained when the results of cross-sectional and longitudinal studies are compared. For example, norms for the Wechsler Adult Intelligence Scale were based on cross-sectional comparisons of adult men and women. Typically, older people performed more poorly than younger adults on many of the intelligence subtests (Matarazzo, 1972; Wechsler, 1955). However, when the same adults were tested longitudinally, many of their subtest scores improved with advancing age (Kangas & Bradway, 1971). The age differences obtained by means of the cross-sectional method may have been due in part to such cohort-related factors as educational level and socialization rather than to "true" developmental differences in intelligence. Similarly, the age changes obtained by the longitudinal method may have been due in part to such factors as selective survival, repeated testing, and time-of-measurement influences.

Time-Lag Analysis   Sometimes psychologists are specifically interested in studying different cohorts at different times of measurement. For example, how are college students today different from the college students of the 1960s and 1970s? A method in which different cohorts are compared at different times of measurement, with chronological age constant, is called a *time-lag design*. Another example would be to compare and contrast the attitudes and interests of those who are now age 65 with those who were this age five years ago and with those who will be this age five years from now.

As we have seen, two of the three factors that must be considered in the study of development—chronological age, cohort, and time of measurement—are confounded in each of the three methods we have discussed. Age differences and cohort differences are confounded in the cross-sectional method, and age changes and time-of-measurement changes are confounded in the longitudinal method. The time-lag design confounds cohort differences with time of measurement.

Sequential Data Collection Strategies   Schaie (1965) introduced the *general developmental model* as a way of disentangling the contributions to development of age, cohort, and time of measurement. From this model he derived the three *sequential strategies* shown in Table 1-2. These are the *cohort-sequential, time-sequential,* and *cross-sequential* strategies. Basically, the researcher simultaneously conducts a series of longitudinal and cross-sectional studies, which permit the investigator to specify the relative influences of age, cohort, and time of measurement. Readers interested in these strategies are referred to Schaie (1965), Baltes (1968), or Baltes, Reese, and Nesselroade (1977) for further information.

Intraindividual Change and Individual Differences

Developmental psychology includes the study of two aspects of behavioral change (Baltes, Reese, & Nesselroade, 1977). One involves understanding the origins and development of behavior within any individual organism; this focus is known as *ontogeny,* or *intraindividual* change. Writing an autobiography or

Table 1-2 Comparison of Developmental Research Designs Corresponding to Schaie's (1965) General Developmental Model

Cohort	Time of measurement												
	'35	'40	'45	'50	'55	'60	'65	'70	'75	'80	'85	'90	'95
1895					60								
1900					55	60							
1905					50	55	60						
1910					45	50	55	60					
1915	20	25	30	35	40	45	50	55	60				
1920		20	25	30	35	40	45	50	55	60			
1925			20	25	30	35	40	45	50	55	60		
1930				20	25	30	35	40	45	50	55	60	
1935					20	25	30	35	40	45	50	55	60
1940						20	25	30	35				
1945							20	25	30				
1950								20	25				
1955									20				

Entries represent chronological ages corresponding to each combination of cohort (year of birth) and time of measurement (calendar year).

Columns represent *cross-sectional* designs, rows represent *longitudinal* designs, and (southeast) diagonals represent *time-lag* designs. The *cohort-sequential* design involves a comparison of rows, the *time-sequential* design is based on a comparison of columns, and the *cross-sequential* design is represented by a comparison of diagonals. (Adapted from Wohlwill, 1970.)

keeping careful notes on how your child changes from birth to marriage are examples of ways to study intraindividual change. Developmental psychologists also study *interindividual* variation, or how people develop in different ways. You might compare your child with her cousins, for example, and try to identify the ways their individual development was alike and different. Birren (1964) observed that individuals become more "like themselves" as they grow older; that is, they increasingly show individualized patterns of behavior and appearance.

One of the major challenges for developmental psychologists is to find ways to study both intraindividual change and individual differences. The research designs described in the last section involve the study of groups of individuals. However, as Hoyer (1974) and Kratochwill (1978) have pointed out, group data may be faulty for predicting individual development. For one thing, the group data may be misleading if we are studying reversible characteristics rather than irreversible characteristics. Individuals can marry, be widowed, divorced, and remarry, or not; thus conclusions about marriage based on comparing groups of people at different ages may be very misleading. In addition, the shifts over the life course of an individual may be concealed in cohort data if the shifts tend to counteract each other. For example, it might be true that an individual tends to read fewer books as he gets older. But if more recent cohorts read fewer books and watch more television than their grandparents did, cross-sectional age-group data would show little difference between age groups.

Changes in the kinds of people in a cohort at any given time may be interpreted, erroneously, as changes in life history. For example, reported higher job satisfaction among older workers may be due not to increasing job satisfaction over the life course but to the fact that the less satisfied workers leave the work force or are not available for testing for some reason. Survival within any cohort is selective. Differential survival affects cohort behavior but not the behavior of the individual. If the most alert, "engaged," healthy members are left available for study in the oldest cohort, the cohort as a whole may seem little different from younger cohorts.

It is important to remember these limitations of conclusions drawn from group data as we review the research in particular areas.

Research Methods

Regardless of whether we operate from a mechanistic, organismic, or dialectical perspective, or whether we choose to use cross-sectional, longitudinal, time-lag, or sequential data collection strategies, we need to know how to find out what we want to know. In developmental psychology, as in all sciences, systematic observation is the basic tool of research. *Systematic observation* involves the collection of facts by individuals trained to observe behavior and record what they have seen and heard as carefully, completely, and objectively as they can.

The common observational techniques used to study adult development vary in many ways, but especially in the amount of control the researcher has in the investigation. Generally, the ideal of science is to move toward the specification and control characteristic of *experimental* research. However, because not all research questions can be answered using experimental methods, we sometimes use *descriptive* research strategies. As we review what is known about various domains of adult functioning throughout this book, keep in mind the different research methods used to generate the findings. We must always ask: Was the method used the best one for the questions asked?

Descriptive Research   When we use systematic observation techniques to record the complexity of behavior as it occurs naturally, we are doing *descriptive* research. For example, we might go to a local community college and find out how many individuals enrolled in courses the past year, how many of those who registered completed the courses, and what percentage of the total community was enrolled in the community college. We might also contact ten individuals who registered for a course and interview them in depth about their reasons for enrolling, their experiences at the school, and their feelings about education.

The data we obtained would give some sense of formal learning behavior among the adults in that community. However, it would not give us much information about the sources of *variability*: Why are some adults enrolled and others not? Why do some finish a course and others drop out? Why do some report such enthusiasm for the experience and others convey such disappointment?

Because we are developmental psychologists, we are especially interested in age as a source of variability in adult behavior. We could begin by seeing if variation in formal learning experiences is related to age—that is, if these two variables are *correlated*. We may well find that, in this study, as age increases, school attendance decreases. Younger adults are more likely to enroll in courses, to complete them, and to report satisfaction with the experience. Does this mean that, as we grow older, we become less interested in formal educational opportunities? Does aging cause a decline in motivation to learn?

It is important to remember that correlation is *not* causation—even though correlations may suggest causal relationships. Other explanations for the results are possible. An obvious one is the cohort effect: Those people who are now older adults have less formal education and so are less likely than younger, better-educated adults to look to colleges for learning experiences. If the correlation reflects a cohort effect, we would expect that, as better-educated adults grow older, they will continue to use formal educational opportunities. If we want to explore further the relationships disclosed with descriptive research, we can use experimental research methods.

Experimentation   An *experiment* consists of a systematic arrangement of conditions under which observed behavior is to be objectively measured. The goal of experimentation is to establish causal relationships. The process of experimentation usually begins with the formulation of a hypothesis, which may come from systematic observations, from a formal theory, or from casual observation or a "hunch." It is very important that the hypothesis be stated clearly enough that we can decide whether the evidence collected supports the statement or not.

Suppose that we wish to design an experiment to test causal relationships between age and learning. In formulating the hypothesis, we can draw on research in related areas. We know, for example, that many formal learning programs require mastery of new materials at a fairly fast pace—a pace that seems reasonable for "most students." However, there is considerable evidence that general physical processes slow down with advancing age. Perhaps the reluctance of older students to enroll in courses is related to the difficulties they experience in responding as quickly as "most" (that is, younger) learners.

Following this line of reasoning, we can propose a hypothesis: If older adults are given sufficient time, they will learn new materials as well as younger adults. The hypothesis could be stated more formally: Age and learning performance will be related only in time-limited tests.

The next step in experimentation is to formulate *operational definitions* for the crucial terms in the hypothesis. In the hypothesis stated above, the important terms are *age, learning performance,* and *time-limited.* Our operational definition for each term could be, for example, chronological age for "age"; the recall of unfamiliar verbal material (word pairs) after an initial presentation to assess "learning performance"; and the number of seconds allowed to study the new material as our measure of "time limits."

Conducting the Study   Having formulated a hypothesis, the researcher must decide on a precise set of procedures. The *population* must be defined—in our case adults living in the community where the college is located. Research *subjects* must be representative of the population. Thus we do not want to test only old people who have attended the college or only those younger adults who attend daytime classes. We will consider the techniques for finding a cooperative representative sample more fully as we discuss particular kinds of research.

The variable manipulated by the researcher is the *independent variable.* The major independent variable in our experiment is time allowed to study new material. We are observing the effect of changes in study time on the *dependent,* or *outcome,* variable: amount of learning demonstrated.

Practically any behavior that can be reliably measured can serve as a dependent variable, but there are practical and ethical limitations on what conditions can serve as independent variables in an experiment. The independent variable has to be under the control of the experimenter in order for cause-effect relationships to be established, and not all variables can be brought under such control. Variables that are characteristic of individuals—such as age, cohort, race, and gender—are referred to as *subject variables.*

Experimental studies in developmental psychology examine the effects of age-related independent variables on selected dependent measures. In the simplest type of experimental study of age differences the effect of one independent variable on one dependent variable is assessed at two or more age levels. For example, we could examine the effects of altering study time on learning performance in groups of adults aged 20–30, 40–50, and 60–70. We could show the subjects ten slides, with two words on each slide, for a particular length of time. Each subject would be instructed to remember which word pairs went together. Recall would be tested later, and the number of correct responses would give a learning performance score. The experimental manipulation would be to vary the time each slide was shown and to compare recall for word pairs exposed for, say, 3, 5, 7, 9, and 11 seconds.

We would probably find that learning performance (correct recall) increased as exposure (study) time increased, but that the effect was much more evident for the oldest subjects than for the youngest subjects. Such a finding would be referred to as an *age-by-treatment interaction.* Could we then conclude that the better learning (recall) performance was related to time available for studying the new information? Not necessarily, since practice with the task could account for changes in performance. We might want to have a *control group,* who would have as many learning trials as the experimental group but all at the same study time.

On the basis of our research so far we might suspect that speed of learning was related to age. If we wished to pursue the question of whether speed of processing new information was related to enrollment in courses at the community college, we could use a *quasi-experimental design.* Such designs are used when random assignment of subjects to different groups is not possible, or when the experimenter lacks full control over the independent variable(s). Both these circumstances often pertain in investigations of adult development. For quasi-experimental designs we rely on naturally occurring variations rather than experimentally induced differences. For example, we could identify individuals in each age group who had relatively fast or relatively slow response times; their response times would be the independent variable, although it would not be manipulated (or controlled) by the researcher. The dependent variable would be enrollment and completion of a course at the college.

Reliable and Valid Data   Regardless of whether we use descriptive or experimental research designs, we must select techniques of assessing behavior that are credible and appropriate. Any assessment procedures should have two qualities: reliability and validity. *Reliability* refers to the stability of the measure. If we measure learning performance on Wednesday afternoon, will we get similar results if we take another measure the following Monday morning? *Validity* is more complex since it refers to the extent that the particular measure used actually assesses what it purports to measure. In the example study of age and learning we claimed to measure "learning" by obtaining recall of matched word pairs. We assumed that performance on this task is related to other, more meaningful, kinds of adult learning. It would be relatively easy to assess the reliability of this measure by testing some people several times. However, we would need also to demonstrate the validity of the particular measure for inferring more general learning abilities.

Issues of reliability and validity are especially problematic in the study of adult development, as we try to identify patterns of change over long time periods. We will return to the issue later. For now, try to think how you would interpret declines in "learning performance" scores of ten individuals at age 25 and later at age 30. Would you focus on the age changes or assume that the test lacked reliability? A more challenging question would be how to make a valid assessment of learning ability for 20-year-olds, for 50-year-olds, or for 80-year-olds. Could you use the same tests for all?

There are many strategies used to obtain reliable and valid data about adult behavior, all designed to serve the needs of scientific psychology to describe, explain, and modify human behavior. Informal observation, structured observation, structured precoded questionnaires, paper-and-pencil tests, in-depth interviews, examination of paintings and stories—all have been used to identify patterns of adult behavior. Some researchers use only a few techniques and reject others as invalid; some researchers use a wide variety of methods. Reliability and validity will be discussed further in Chapter 6.

As we review the research in particular areas of adult psychology throughout the book, the currently favored designs and techniques will become clearer. There are no intrinsically "bad" or "good" research designs or methods, but there are ways of approaching research that are more and less useful in terms of what we already know. Throughout our review the most crucial criterion for recognizing good research will be: Is the strategy used an appropriate one for the research questions asked?

Growing older may not be a particularly positive experience from a medical stance, but the more insidious problems are attitudinal and social. Societies have belief systems—attitudes that people within the culture know to be "true." However, there may be very little evidence for many such beliefs. For example, Shanas (1979) examined the popular belief that the aged in the United States are often alienated and isolated from their younger family members. She found that neglect of the old by the younger generation was in fact the exception rather than the rule in our society. Many of our views about aging and the aged are the creations of television and other media. Does intelligence decline with advancing age? What about memory? Does personality change during adulthood? How? The scientific study of aging involves separating fact from fiction, dispelling false stereotypes and myths.

The Development of Gerontology

Gerontology is the scientific study of aging, where aging is understood as involving "the regular changes that occur in mature, genetically representative organisms living under representative environmental conditions as they advance in chronological age" (Birren & Renner, 1977, p. 4).

The initial impetus for studying the later years was the identification of old age as a *social problem* (Maddox & Wiley, 1976; Riegel, 1977). As early as the

Scientific studies by gerontologists show that most older persons remain involved with their family. Elders share a personalized view of the past that provides family members with a sense of continuity over time.

1930s, social scientists were drawing attention to the problems of aging. The social and psychological consequences of retirement and the need for economic security and health care were the main topics of concern. Scientific interest, as distinct from the social aspects of aging, had its formal beginnings in the 1940s. The Gerontological Society of America was founded in 1945 to advance knowledge of aging. *The Journal of Gerontology,* which publishes scientific articles on the biological, clinical, psychological, and social aspects of aging, first appeared in 1946. In 1947 the Division of Maturity and Old Age (Division 20) was formed within the American Psychological Association. This group, now known as the Division of Adult Development and Aging, has approximately 1000 members.

The scope of gerontology has broadened considerably since its beginnings. The study of aging is no longer limited to the last fourth or the last third of life. As it has become evident that much of what occurs in the last decades of life reflects earlier life periods, gerontologists have broadened their field of vision to include the middle years. The gap is closing between traditional developmental studies ending at adolescence and gerontological research. Aging and development have no clear dividing lines—both begin at conception.

Classifying Gerontology

One of the current debates is whether the study of aging should be considered a discipline, a profession, or an orientation. The issue is complex and involves questions of the philosophy of science, the sociology of knowledge, and the appropriate design of educational and professional programs.

A field is usually considered a *discipline* when it involves a specialized body of knowledge and, often, special techniques of discovery. Modern universities reflect the current definitions of relatively "bounded" disciplines such as mathematics, philosophy, psychology, and economics. The fact that the names and content of such identified disciplines and subdisciplines shift (sometimes fairly frequently) is one clue that there is nothing intrinsic about each discipline.

We can now identify a considerable and increasing body of knowledge that informs us about the special characteristics of older adults. Those who argue that gerontology is, and should be recognized as, a discipline emphasize that understanding human aging is an endeavor that inherently and inevitably crosses existing disciplinary boundaries. The experience of aging cannot be understood without an appreciation of the ways in which biological, psychological, and sociological aspects interact over the course of life. To understand only one component is to risk misunderstanding the human complexities. Such a rationale has motivated the establishment of interdisciplinary programs in human development and gerontology at Duke University, The Pennsylvania State University, Syracuse University, University of Southern California, University of Chicago, and many other institutions.

A *profession* involves the application of specialized knowledge. Professionals decide—largely among themselves—what they should know and how to apply their expertise. Insofar as there is an acknowledged disciplinary base in gerontology, we may use the label *professional gerontologist.* However, there is relatively little agreement about what a professional gerontologist could or should do. In what settings and with what responsibilities should this special knowledge be applied? What ethical standards should pertain? The issue of preserving genuine expertise and still avoiding isolation from the complexities of whole human lives is serious; the professional identity for those interested in how humans change in the adult years is not fully established.

One option is to recognize gerontology as an *orientation*—a point of view that usefully applies to some of the already recognized disciplines and professions. "Gerontologizing" existing disciplines involves introducing or emphasizing age as a relevant dimension. Most disciplines have something to offer to the study of aging. For example, biologists investigating proliferation of cancer cells see how that process is affected by the age of the host organism; other biologists are searching for the mechanisms that control longevity (see Finch & Hayflick, 1977). Anthropologists have explored the ways people of different ages behave in varied cultural settings. They have begun to identify universal as well as culture-specific developmental trends in later life. Some cultures are stressful for older members; others offer much support. Economists have documented patterns of income, consumption, and saving over the life span (Kreps, 1976) and have identified several basic determinants of income in late life. Political scientists have been particularly interested in voting behavior by age; they find little evidence that age is a useful predictor of either political behavior or attitudes (Maddox & Wiley, 1976). Health professionals (such as nurses, physicians, recreation workers, dance therapists, and social workers) are learning how to adapt their skills to meet the special needs of different age groups. Architects and engineers are applying their talents to designing devices and buildings that can be used by those with the physical frailties of advanced age.

Psychologists, too, can focus their particular interests and skills on issues of change during adulthood in order to be able to describe, explain, predict, and modify age-related trends. Some cognitive psychologists might focus on how age-related biological changes affect cognitive functioning in later years. A personality researcher might investigate how various emotional defense strategies are adaptive or maladaptive at various life periods (for instance, see Lieberman, 1975). Clinical psychologists might try to adapt therapeutic techniques to the needs of older clients (Butler & Lewis, 1977; Levy, Derogatis, Gallagher, & Gatz, 1980).

Let us now look more specifically at some of the conceptual and research issues involved in the study of adult development and aging.

The Concept of Age

The basic dimension of our study is *age,* a concept that can be defined (or interpreted) in several ways. The answer to "How old are you?" is usually given in terms of *chronological age,* the time passed since birth. It is a convenient measure because there are standard units of time that are uniform from one individual to another. However, chronological age itself has little intrinsic meaning. It is, rather, an "index" of other aspects that vary with time.

Age can be measured in another way. Because the biological organism changes over time, we can develop measures of *biological age,* or "the estimate of the individual's present position with respect to his potential life span" (Birren & Renner, 1977, p. 4). We may be most interested in the condition of the biological organism: How healthy is the individual? At the beginning of the life span biological age is often used to assess the relative physical maturity of children, with height, skeletal age, or dental age frequent measures. In adulthood we can assess the functioning of various organ systems (circulatory, cardiovascular, excretory), rating an individual in comparison to most people at the same chronological age.

Since psychologists are primarily concerned with adaptive capacities, we may want to assess individual abilities to adapt to changing environments. *Psychological age* refers to the adaptive capacity of individuals relative to others of the same age (Birren & Renner, 1977). Learning, memory, intelligence, feelings, motivations, and emotions may be assessed for the purposes of predicting how well an individual can adapt to change. Unfortunately, psychological age does not provide an independent measure of adaptive functioning since biological status as well as social demands also affect the resources and requirements of adaptation.

Because of the difficulties in using chronological age to predict adult behavior, considerable emphasis has been given to developing yet a fourth measure: *functional age.* This would assess the level of ability to function in a given society, relative to others of the same chronological age. Often, when we want to know "how old" an individual is, we really mean: Can this man of chronological age 56 keep up on the assembly line? Can this woman of 78 continue living in her own apartment, doing her own cooking and shopping? How many individuals of 78 can do that? Could this person profit from formal education, work part time, or use support services? Functional age is a far better predictor than chronological age. However, it is still not an entirely satisfactory index.

A fifth measure—*social age*—reflects the fact that we have expectations about social participation, social habits, and social roles performed by individuals in various age groups and that, by and large, individuals conform to those expectations. Social age assesses the roles and social habits of an individual relative to other members of a society. For example, to understand the behavior of a young woman in contemporary America, it may be more important to know that she has a 3-year-old daughter than to know that she was born 24 or 35 years ago.

Given that any individual's age can be assessed in several ways, the answer to the question "How old are you?" can be very complex. It becomes even more complex when we ask a number of interesting questions that relate all the various ages to one another.

Some of these questions have been investigated in research. For example, we can compare biological age and chronological age, assessing the biological capacities of individuals who vary in chronological age at a particular time. The Baltimore studies of aging (see Chapter 8), which have been doing this for some time, have found that indeed some men at chronological age 70 have the biological capacities of most men who are 50 years of age, and that some 50-year-old men have the biological capacities of the average 78-year-old (Granick & Patterson, 1971). We can compare individuals of different social ages in terms of, say, relationships to parenting. Being pregnant with a first child, the mother of a young infant, mother of an 8-year-old, mother of a 15-year-old, mother of a 25-year-old, or mother of a 40-year-old are all different social ages, and we could compare the behavior of women of those different social ages. The mother who had her first child at 17 and her last child when the youngest entered college would be several social ages.

Another question involves the interrelation of the individual's location on all the ages and the consequences of different patterns. It is probably quite different to have the social age of "mother of a young child" at chronological age 20 than at age 40. The 70-year-old who is in fine physical condition (young biological age) and still employed (young social age) will have different experiences from the 70-year-old who is in poor biological health and unemployed and from the employed 55-year-old in poor health. In other words, we would have to explore the impact of relative positions in terms of various ages on the experience of aging. Chronological age as an index is often only a rough estimate of the development we would really like to assess.

THE AGING POPULATION

Before we go on to explore various aspects of aging in the chapters to come, it will be helpful to have some general information about the older U.S. population.

Demographic Characteristics

Americans like to think of themselves as young, and historically the average age of the American population has been young. In 1790, the year of the first census, half the people in the United States were 16 years of age or younger. In 1980 the median age was 29.7. When the United States declared its independence over 200 years ago, there were only about 50,000 Americans age 65 or over, and they represented about 2 percent of the total population. By 1900 there were approximately 3 million people age 65 or older, and they constituted approximately 4 percent of the population. Only 39 percent of those born in 1900 reached age 65, whereas it is expected that 72 percent of those born today will reach age 65 (Bouvier, Atlee, & McVeigh, 1975). In 1978, 24 million people over age 65 represented 11 percent of the population.

In the year 2000, it is expected there will be 30.6 million older Americans. If present demographic trends continue, half the population will be over 50 and a third will be over 65 in 2000 (Ostfeld & Gibson, 1975). Currently about 11.5 percent of the total population is age 65 or older.

Each day about 5000 Americans reach age 65, and about 3600 who are over 65 die—a net increase of 1400 per day (or 511,000 per year). The older population is continuously changing. People who will be reaching age 65 in the next decade will be different in many ways from people who are already over 65.

So far in our discussion we have been labeling as *the aged* or *the elderly* those people who are age 65 or older. However, age 65 is a relatively arbitrary chronological marker for entering old age. There is no psychological, biological, or social event that separates this point in the life span from any other for *all* individuals. People who are 65 or over differ from each other in many ways; in fact, there is greater diversity in the older population than there is in younger

People who are over 65 differ from one another in many ways. There is greater diversity in this age group than there is in younger population groups.

groups (Hoyer, 1974). Furthermore, the findings of a study may apply only to the people who were assessed—not to people who will be reaching old age in the future. Consequently, generalizations about the aged must be made cautiously.

Changes in Life Expectancy

Old age and old people used to be relatively rare because most people died fairly young. We have now succeeded in assuring that most individuals who are born will live to experience old age. However, we have not, contrary to popular belief, really increased the length of the normal expectable life span very much. *Life expectancy* describes the average number of years remaining for a person at any specified age. Analysis of death rates at each age makes it possible to construct a table showing the life expectancy at each age. The life expectancy at birth has increased substantially over the past century; this is due largely to the decrease in the mortality rate during the first few years of life. Although the average life expectancy has increased, longevity has not. *Longevity* is the normal expectable life span under good conditions. Eighty years has remained the normal human life span, and a century seems to be about as long as human beings are going to live. Far fewer than 1 percent of those who reach age 65 live to age 100; currently there are only about 7500 centenarians in the United States.

Changes in life expectancy from 1940 to 1977 in the United States are shown in Table 1-3. Sex differences, race differences, and life expectancies at birth, at age 20, at age 40, and at age 65 are compared. Several things are apparent. First, for every subgroup there are increases in the average life expectancy over the period 1940 to 1977. Secondly, females have higher life expectancies than males. Third, whites are favored in life expectancy at birth, though there is little or no racial difference in life expectancies for those who survive to later life.

Figure 1-3 shows the number of males and females in different age groups in the United States in 1978 and as estimated for the year 2000. The largest

Table 1-3 Life Expectancy by Age, Sex, and Race: 1940 and 1977

| | 1940* | | | | 1977 | | | |
| | White | | Nonwhite | | White | | Nonwhite | |
	M	F	M	F	M	F	M	F
At birth	62.8	67.3	52.3	55.5	70.0	77.7	64.6	73.1
At age 20	67.8	71.4	59.7	62.1	71.9	79.1	67.2	75.2
At age 40	70.0	73.3	65.2	67.3	73.4	79.8	70.2	76.7
At age 65	77.1	78.6	77.2	79.0	78.9	83.4	79.0	82.8

*Averages from 1939–41.

Source: Adapted from the U.S. Department of Commerce, *Statistical Abstract of the United States: 1979* (100th Edition). Washington, D.C.: 1980, p. 70.

increases are anticipated in the older age groups (35 years and over). If current demographic trends continue, by the year 2000 half the population will be over 50 (Offir, 1974). Many more women survive to old age. In 1980 there were 147 women over 65 for every 100 men over 65; by 2000 it is estimated that there will be 154 women for every 100 men. If the birth rate continues as it has been in recent years, there will be fewer 18-to-24-year-olds in 2000 than in 1978. This decrease in absolute numbers of "college age" individuals is one factor that is encouraging colleges to retrench and to develop alternate sources for students, such as older adults returning to school or resuming an education interrupted by family or career responsibilities.

Gains in life expectancy are primarily found in the early years of life. In earlier times individuals died from early childhood diseases, and many women died during the process of childbirth. The likelihood of early death has substantially lessened in recent years. For example, in 1920 the life expectancy at birth for whites was 54.4 years for men and 55.6 years for women; from 1920 to 1940 some 12 years were added to the expected life span for men and nearly 17 years for women.

Factors Contributing to Longevity

Whether you are thought of as "old" or "middle-aged" or even "young" at age 50 depends not only on *when* you live; it also seems to be related to *where*. In

Figure 1-3 United States population by age and sex: 1978 and projected to 2000 (in thousands). (Source: U.S. Department of Commerce, *Statistical Abstract of the United States: 1979* [100th Edition]. Washington, D.C., 1980, pp. 8–9.)

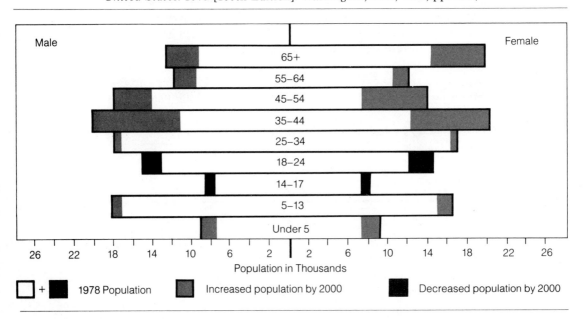

other words, there are cross-cultural differences in longevity. Table 1-4 shows that many countries have an average life expectancy longer than that of the United States.

Many of the factors related to longevity have been identified. One important factor is *heredity*. There's a better chance of your living to a ripe old age if your parents and grandparents did than if they did not. We cannot do anything about the selection of our parents, but we can change other factors that apparently affect our chances for a healthy long life. Heavy cigarette smokers have a life expectancy that is 12 to 14 years shorter on the average than nonsmokers. Lack of regular exercise, stress, obesity, and poor nutrition are also associated with shorter average life expectancies. More will be said about these and other factors in Chapter 3.

THE CONSEQUENCES OF AGING

Consequences for Individuals

Increased chances of survival have many consequences. The fact that old age is now a predictable part of the normal life experience means that we can more or less expect a period of old age for ourselves, for those we love, and even for those we dislike. In terms of our own individual life course it means that we should now plan on a *postparenthood* and a *postretirement* period of life. This very fact may alter our perception of other life periods. For example, we may feel less concerned about cramming all life experiences into the young adult years if we can feel assured that there is life after middle age and even life in old age. However, remember that these numbers are averages, not guarantees.

Another consequence of changes in life expectancy concerns family life. More relatives now survive to become old—sometimes very old. Traditionally, the elderly have been provided for within the family network. Patterns of mu-

Table 1-4 Average Life Expectancies at Birth for Different Countries (Based on 1970–1975 Data)

Years	Country	Years	Country
75.3	Sweden	70.6	United States
73.5	Norway	70.2	Jamaica
73.5	France	69.0	Finland
73.0	Israel	62.0	Peru
73.0	Ireland	59.1	Philippines
72.9	Japan	53.0	Iran
72.8	Italy	52.9	Egypt
71.6	Greece	46.8	Bolivia
71.3	West Germany	41.0	Ethiopia
70.9	Russia	37.3	Upper Volta (Africa)

Adapted from *United Nations Monthly Bulletin of Statistics* April, 1971.

tual exchange between older parents and their adult children gradually shift to provide the assistance needed by frail elderly. This was realistic when several adult children shared responsibility for the few surviving adults. Declining birth rates, increased longevity, and divorce–remarriage patterns may, however, make it difficult for the oldest and younger generations to negotiate the needed supports. For example, one woman of 48, an only child and married to an only child, is wondering how she can possibly be responsive to her aging mother (70), grandmother (89), unmarried aunts (72 and 68), and mother-in-law (76).

In the past such dilemmas have been the impetus for shifting part of the responsibility for the elderly to the society at large (Treas, 1977). The society as a whole must decide how to distribute resources fairly and appropriately in order to care for the needs of individuals at all stages of the life cycle.

Consequences for Societies

Age Structure   Every society has members of different ages. Given that groups differing in age also differ in some other important respects, the distribution of individuals by age is important.

The percentage of the population in successive age groups (0–4 years, 5–9 years, 10–14 years, and so on) gives the *age structure* of a population. Demographers construct graphs indicating the percentage of males and females in various age groups. These "population pyramids" can reveal interesting and important facts about populations. For example, the population pyramids for the United States for 1850 and 1950 are shown in Figure 1-4. These pyramids reflect births, deaths, and migration both in and out of the population at various periods. We can look at population pyramids for various historical periods, for different countries—as in Figure 1-4—or for any group we wish to understand. We can use these pyramids for social planning if we have some idea of the needs and assets of various age groups.

Dependency Ratio   A common index used by demographers and economists is called the *dependency ratio*. This, in its simplest form, is the sum of the number of individuals under the age of 15 and those over the age of 65, divided by the number of people age 15 to 65. This index presumably reflects the proportion of those in the working population who are available to support the needs of those who are out of the labor force and need care or support of some kind. The dependency ratio in the United States in 1945 was 35 to 1. In 1977 it was 3.2 to 1. By 2030 it is estimated to be less than 2 to 1. Obviously, such a ratio is very rough, particularly if we consider that young adults in our culture may well be "dependent," at least financially, on their working parents until they are 20–25 (or, in some cases, through advanced training until they are 30), and that retirement or exit from paid labor force participation comes earlier than 65 for some and later than 65 for some.

Figure 1-4 Population of selected countries, by age and sex. (Source: United Nations, Department of Economic and Social Affairs, *The Aging of Populations and Its Economic and Social Implications,* "Population Studies," No. 26 [New York: United Nations, 1956].)

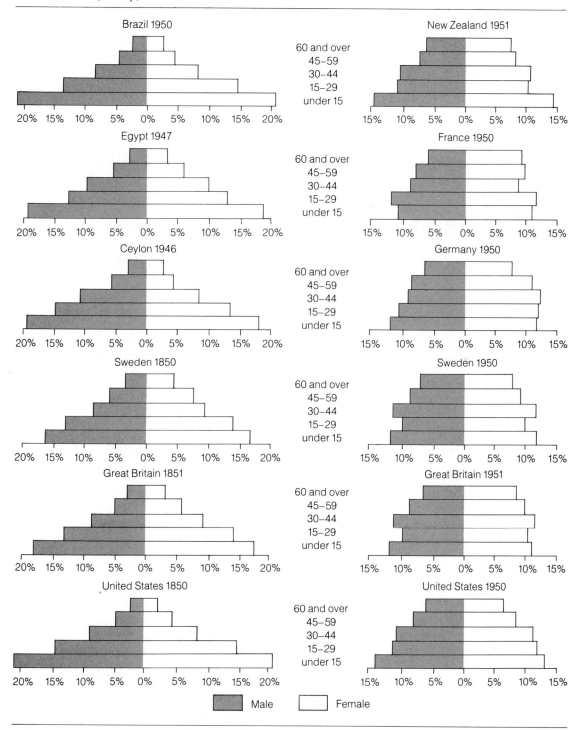

Dependency at both ends of the life span is expected to increase greatly during the next 50 years. It is very important to know whether the "dependents" are young or old. If there is a large dependency ratio with most of the dependents under 15, clearly social planners will plan for well-baby clinics, child-care facilities, elementary schools, and first-job training. If the majority of the dependents are older, we need to think about economic support, opportunities for continued social interaction, and, ultimately, the supplementary services that will maintain people in their own homes or compensate for declining health. To determine which end of the life span will produce the greatest burden on the working population in the future, demographers have calculated an *old-age dependency ratio*—the number of people age 65 and over divided by the number of people between the ages of 18 and 64. Table 1-5 gives the computed old-age dependency ratios from 1930 to 2030 (projected). Keep in mind that this ratio estimates the needs of the older population only crudely because not every old person is unemployed and not every young and middle-aged adult is employed.

"Old" and "Young" Populations　　An aging population is indicated by a relatively large percentage of older people. If we look at the population pyramids for different countries of the world, we find considerable variation in the extent to which the population could be termed "old" or "young." For example, the German Democratic Republic has the largest percentage of older people (those over 65)—15.6 percent; Mali has the lowest, with 1.6 percent; the United States has approximately 11 percent (Hauser, 1977).

A study commissioned by the United Nations defined population as *aged, mature,* and *young* on the basis of the proportions of people over 65 (Hauser, 1977). Among the nations included in the study 34 countries, including the United States, are termed aged, with 7 percent or more over 65. There are 13 mature countries, with 4 to 7 percent of the population over 65, and 34 countries with young populations—under 4 percent over 65. The young populations are mostly in the less-developed countries; in fact, one of the consequences of development is increased life expectancy (Hauser, 1977). Thus socioeconomic

Table 1-5　Old-Age Dependency Ratios in the United States

	Year	Old-Age Dependency Ratio
Actual	1930	.09
	1950	.13
	1970	.17
Projected	1980	.18
	1990	.19
	2000	.19
	2010	.19
	2020	.24
	2030	.29

Source: U.S. Bureau of the Census. *Demographic Aspects of Aging and the Older Population in the United States* (1978).

development and increased standard of living go hand-in-hand with aging of the population. And with that comes an increased necessity for understanding the issues of aging.

There are various explanations of an aging population. In the United States the aging of the population reflects a reduced birth rate, which means that there are fewer young people to keep the average age low. In other countries the aging of the population reflects a decrease in death rate or other factors. In some rural communities in the United States the population of the aged has greatly increased relative to the young because many younger adults move to metropolitan areas to find employment. Population pyramids can be constructed for towns, suburbs, or neighborhoods, as well as nations. Such information can be useful in planning services and for understanding the experiences of the people in those groups.

Implications of an Aging Population   There are several implications of having an aging population. For example, as shown in Figure 1–3, relatively fewer children were born between 1930 and 1940 in the United States than were born during succeeding decades. Throughout life this cohort born during the Great Depression has experienced and will continue to experience relatively less peer competition for education, jobs, and promotions. These people will reach old age when there are many large younger cohorts able to pay the Social Security benefits of the older generation. Individuals born from 1955 to 1960, on the other hand, have had to compete heavily with each other for resources such as nursery schools, colleges, entry-level jobs, promotions, and the like. If the birth rates continue to decline, they could reach old age when there are relatively few middle-aged and young adult workers to support them.

The age structure will influence allocation of resources. If one age group is relatively large, it can demand proportionally more resources. As the better-educated cohorts become old, they will articulate their needs and wishes, and they will have the expertise and experience to obtain important social resources. Younger cohorts will grant such access to resources for complex reasons such as regard and/or obligations toward their parental generation, public pressure, or a desire for the employment created by service provisions to the elderly. The increasing number of special facilities to serve the needs of the older population—including nursing homes, recreation programs, special continuing educational programs, special housing, and special banking—all reflect changes in the age structure.

The potential danger of *age politics*—advocating for a special age group—should be obvious to the life-span developmental psychologist who is, after all, concerned with the quality of life at all periods. Our primary concern must be enhancing the quality of life as we move from infancy to young adulthood to middle age and into old age, not enhancing life for one group at the expense of others. This is a most delicate challenge, one that we have hardly begun to meet.

SUMMARY

1 Development is a continuous and dynamic process of change that takes place throughout life. This book explores the changes in behavioral, cognitive, and social processes occurring during adulthood.

2 Development involves both nature and nurture. *Nature* refers to innate or genetically carried characteristics and dispositions of an organism. *Nurture* refers to the environmental features that affect the individual from conception onward. The relative contributions of nature and nurture depend on the age period studied; generally, nature has relatively more impact in the beginning and final periods of life.

3 Conceptual paradigms influence the questions that are asked and the interpretation of results in scientific research, as well as the approach to intervention. Researchers currently use three main paradigms in studying development. The *mechanistic* paradigm sees the individual as a machinelike entity. The *organismic* paradigm sees the individual as an integrated organism greater than the sum of its parts. The *dialectical* paradigm sees development as an outgrowth of conflict or crisis.

4 Models of development that emphasize common patterns of change are called *stage theories*. Stage theories assume that visible behavior reflects some underlying structure; that the underlying structures change and produce qualitatively different behaviors at different ages; that one can identify the end of one stage and the beginning of the next stage; and that all individuals proceed through all the stages in the same sequence.

5 Research on adult development most commonly uses cross-sectional or longitudinal methodology. *Cross-sectional* research involves testing individuals or groups of different ages at one point in time; this method yields information about age differences. The *longitudinal* method involves testing the same individuals at different points in time; this method yields information about age changes. Because both methods have limitations in providing information about developmental change, a variety of sequential data collection strategies may be used instead.

6 All scientific research on adult development and aging involves systematic observation to study both intraindividual and interindividual changes. *Descriptive research* records behavior as it occurs naturally. *Experimental research* involves the systematic arrangement of conditions under which observed behavior is objectively measured. Both methods are important sources of understanding how adults change over time.

7 The scientific study of aging is known as *gerontology*. Gerontologists focus on changes in mature organisms as they advance in chronological age. Gerontology may be thought of as a discipline, with a specialized body of knowledge, although many gerontologists cross traditional disciplinary boundaries (such as psychology, biology, and sociology). It can also be considered a profession, which applies specialized knowledge. Gerontology is also an orientation; that is, it involves introducing or emphasizing the issue of age as a relevant aspect within disciplines and professions.

8   Several measures of age are used in studying changes over time. The most common measure is *chronological age,* the time passed since birth. However, chronological age is not a very good predictor of adult behavior. *Biological age* estimates how close an individual is to the end of life. *Psychological age* assesses the individual's ability to adapt to changing environments. *Functional age* more specifically measures the ability to function compared to others of the same chronological age. *Social age* describes the roles and social habits of an individual with respect to other members of a society. Each measure is best for understanding some aspects of behavior; it is very important to use the appropriate measure for the particular questions under study.

9   The American population has been "aging" for some time. The aging of a population occurs when the proportion of older adults increases relative to the proportion of children. A population may age because of a low birth rate or because more people survive to become old. Both factors have contributed to the aging of the U.S. population.

10   The average life expectancy is increasing as more people live to experience old age. However, the normal expectable life span of a human being has not really increased; most people who survive to later life still die before they are 90.

11   The fact that most people in a society can expect to become old has important consequences for both individuals and social systems.

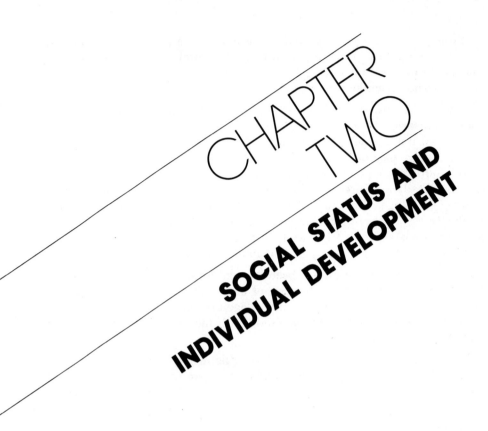

CHAPTER TWO

SOCIAL STATUS AND INDIVIDUAL DEVELOPMENT

As psychologists, we are especially interested in *patterns* of behavior. Patterned ways of doing things evolve in any group interacting over time. We look for variables that will help explain the differences we observe within and among groups of individuals. We must consider how individual or collective experiences may affect behavior over adulthood, and perhaps lead to differences in aging. More generally, as psychologists, we need to understand how individual life experience is shaped by interactions with the social system, how social status can affect individual development. An important concept to understand, in considering how individual characteristics become important, is that reality is socially constructed. This axiom of social science states essentially that, "if individuals believe something is true, then it will become real in its consequences" (Thomas & Znaniecki, 1918–1919).

In this chapter, we will consider four variables which are useful in predicting patterns of differences within any heterogeneous group: sex, socioeconomic status, ethnicity, and age. These variables reflect differentiation within a social structure and account for relatively large proportions of variance in behavior among adults living in the United States (Bengtson, Kasschau, & Ragan, 1977).

SOCIAL STATUS

The term *status* refers to the different positions an individual may hold within a social system. Traditionally an individual's status serves as a basis for assigning valued resources—material resources such as money, respect and prestige, and power over others. In addition, status forms a basis for channeling people into various social roles (Gerth & Mills, 1946). Thus, in effect, status predicts the life experience an individual is likely to encounter by virtue of membership in one social category and not another (Bengtson et al., 1977).

Sociologists who have studied social status often distinguish between two kinds of status: ascribed and achieved. *Ascribed status* is granted at birth on the basis of visible characteristics; the individual has no choice in the matter and does not have to demonstrate any special qualifications. Sex, ethnicity, family economic status, age, and position in the family (third son, first granddaughter) are all ascribed statuses. *Achieved status* requires some demonstration of willingness and ability to meet the requirements. Marital status and occupation (plumber, lawyer, homemaker) are two general types of achieved status in most societies. Within any organization there are many other more specific types of achieved status (secretary of the Elks, foreman, precinct captain, and the like).

Stratification Systems

Status defines one's position in a stratification system and determines one's rights and responsibilities relative to other people. *Stratification system* differentiates among the people in the system, usually giving some people more honorific status than others; the stratification system is, then, hierarchical.

Any stratification system is based on shared beliefs about differentiating people on the basis of identifiable characteristics. Most people hold implicit assumptions about the presumed "natural" distribution of human characteristics on the basis of biological attributes such as sex, ethnicity, and age. One model posits that groups such as males and females, Anglos and Latinos, old and young are so different from each other that they constitute almost separate "species." This view would draw the normal distribution curves for characteristics (such as body build, strength, energy, intellectual style, skills, interests, and so on) by this model:

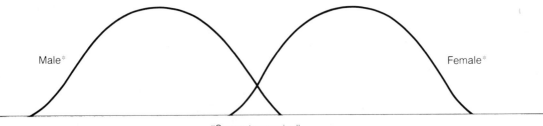

Male*   Female*

"Separate species"

Another model proposes some degree of differentiation but also considerable overlap or similarity. The characteristics that are shared, and the extent, will vary, depending on the groups compared. A third model views groups based on ascribed characteristics as basically similar; sex, race, age, and so on have no necessary relationship to activities or attributes. Observed differences in actual behavior may be explained in terms of learning or opportunity. Those who accept this view may emphasize, for example, that, while males and females differ in reproductive specialization, any other differences have been acquired in the process of socialization. A less restrictive social system would produce males and females who are very similar to each other; a social system in which males and females (or members of racial groups) are measurably distinct from each other must be providing substantially different developmental experiences for each group.

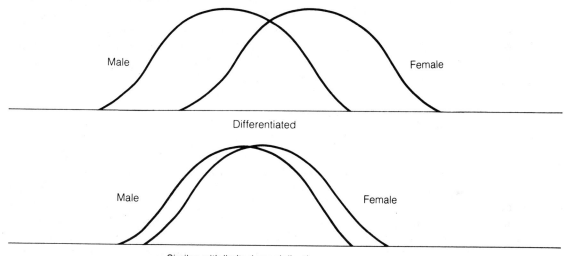

Members of a coherent, cohesive society would probably agree on one of the above models as representing the "natural truth" about a particular status characteristic and would probably evolve a status system reflecting their beliefs. A *coherent* society is one in which the various social institutions mesh with each other, and where the values and practices of one aspect of the society do not conflict with the values and practices of other aspects of the society. Contemporary American society is characterized by a relatively low degree of coherence; traditional folk or peasant societies are more coherent.

Stereotypes and Discrimination

Shared beliefs about characteristics associated with individuals in a particular social group are *stereotypes*. In this section we will review the stereotypes associated with sex, ethnicity, social class, and age.

Stereotypes in themselves are not necessarily bad. Some stereotypes accurately reflect unique characteristics of groups. Sometimes individuals can use stereotypes to their advantage. For example, a woman with grey hair and wrinkles may win a seat on the bus from a tired middle-aged man with back problems just after she has finished running a marathon. Stereotypes do become a problem when they prevent individuals from attaining a desired goal. For example, if grey hair or being over 55 had disqualified the woman from entering a marathon, she would have been deprived—arbitrarily—of reaching her goal. Thus stereotypes can reflect the allocation of rewards and roles of a status system and often form the basis of discrimination.

Discrimination is the systematic denial of opportunities or rewards on the basis of some ascribed characteristic. Discrimination reflects differential evaluation of characteristics. Sometimes discrimination is blatant, as in the saying "If you're white, you're all right; if you're black, stay back"; other times race, sex, and age discrimination is very subtle.

Many social systems, including that in the United States, have as an important ideology that social rewards should be allocated on the basis of achievement rather than ascription. Nevertheless, there is ample evidence of sexism, racism, and agism in contemporary society.

Status Mobility

Another important dimension of social stratification is the extent of mobility within the system. Some hierarchies allow individuals to change their position; one may finish high school, college, or technical training at any time during adulthood. Ascribed statuses (such as sex or ethnicity) are difficult or impossible to change. Individual mobility may be real—for example, when the daughter of a store clerk finishes medical school, or the electrician's helper marries the store owner's daughter. Individual mobility may also be apparent—as when a light-skinned black woman "passes" for white; a 67-year-old dyes his hair, jogs, and "passes" for 57; or a man curls his hair, practices his walk, and dresses to "pass" for a woman.

In each case, the individual has the challenge of being credible in the new status. Is the individual now treated in a way that is consistent with the new status? Is the individual comfortable with his or her new status? Individuals may be unsure how to behave, or they may have misjudged the opportunities, rewards, and costs now available to them. The task of adjustment is greatest when changing a status that affects many behaviors. For example, those few individuals who undergo sex-change operations and resume life as the "opposite" sex must adapt to subtle and obvious shifts in nearly every aspect of life (for example, see Morris, 1974). By contrast, becoming a lawyer may represent a rise in socioeconomic status for the son of a bricklayer, but—especially if the son remains in the same community—his life may remain much the same because of family, ethnic, and religious ties.

In some status systems mobility is deliberate and planned, usually involving some formal or informal training for the new status. Medical training, for example, includes the study of professional ethics and demeanor as well as anatomy and pharmacology. There is no formal training for downward mobility. A doctor who decides to "drop out" and become a part-time plumber will receive no formal preparation for his or her new lifestyle. Autonomy and freedom from constraints are usually considered compensation for the loss of prior status. However, even being "on the street" requires learning to adapt to the status system. Some have suggested that old age is downward social mobility and that lack of preparation for it contributes to negative experiences in aging (Rosow, 1977). Other researchers have focused on the disintegrative effects of sudden, prolonged unemployment or marked occupational status change, such as happens with many refugee immigrants who leave behind a thriving business or profession and start as unskilled laborers in a new land.

In addition to individual mobility, a devalued lower-status group may try to change its position collectively. Successful efforts to open up new social roles and increase the rewards may mean individuals in the social category will experience some mobility. For example, blacks and women have been campaigning against "second-class" status, and some older Americans fight against negative stereotypes of the elderly and for an improved guaranteed standard of living. Sometimes a social category will experience mobility accidentally, as part of other social changes. The Japanese-Americans incarcerated in U.S. detention camps during the hysteria of World War II were deprived of all their normal social statuses, simply on the basis of ethnicity. During that same war American women collectively experienced upward mobility. Largely because of the war effort, women became recognized as competent, competitive, hard workers; they were employed in traditionally male jobs, earned reasonable incomes, and shared child care with nurseries provided at the work place.

We will now look more closely at each of the four major variables that help to determine an individual's social status.

SEX AS A STATUS CHARACTERISTIC

Sex is an individual characteristic of universal significance. Every culture differentiates between males and females. How is this biological fact transformed into social and psychological reality? How much individual behavior can we predict on the basis of sex? How does sex interact with other variables to shape human development?

It is crucial to differentiate three aspects of sex: biological sex, gender identity, and social sex role.

Biological sex is coded genetically into every body cell, giving rise not only to visible differences in genitals and body build but also to differential hormonal characteristics. While the "intent" to develop a male or female is determined at conception, biological sex develops during the prenatal period. The "male" and "female" embryos are similar during the first six to eight weeks after conception; thereafter "normal" masculine development occurs only with the correct amounts of androgenic hormone production at the right times. When androgenic hormones are not sufficient, development reverts to a feminine form. Feminine development requires no special hormonal secretions prenatally. Usually this process is coordinated enough to produce a newborn with internal reproductive apparatus, external genitalia, and hormonal secretions appropriate to the initial chromosomal sex. On the basis of external cues (penis or vagina) the infant is declared male or female (Money & Ehrhardt, 1972). A small minority of infants do not have a good "match" between various aspects of biological sex (for example, an enlarged clitoris that is mistaken for a penis or an unclosed scrotum that resembles a vagina). Such cases are useful for studying the relationships between biological sex, sex of assignment and rearing, and gender identity (see Stoller, 1968).

Gender identity is the individual acceptance of belonging to one social category or another: male or female. Generally, basic gender identity agrees with the sex of assignment and rearing—the sex one is assigned by parents at birth. Money and Ehrhardt (1972) have shown in several cases that it is very difficult to reverse gender identity after age 2. They found that children who were

Gender identity is the acceptance of belonging to one social category or the other: male or female. It seems to be stable by age 6 or 7 and remains important throughout life.

"named," accepted, and treated as girls but who turned out to have the internal reproductive apparatus of a male identified themselves as female and showed "feminine" characteristics. Young boys and girls may think they could turn into the opposite sex, even though they claim membership in their own gender category. Kohlberg (1966) has indicated that gender identity is a stable self-attribute by age 6 or 7.

The term *sex role* has been used in diverse ways (Angrist, 1969), and the multiple uses are sometimes confusing. Anthropologists use the term to describe the positions men and women are expected to occupy—and do occupy—in the social system. Sociologists tend to use it to describe the sex-linked expectations about how men and women relate to each other. The psychological meaning emphasizes the characteristics that distinguish men and women in behavior, personality, preferences, intellect, and abilities. This section will summarize some of the research on psychological models of sexual differentiation and then examine evidence that sex is used as a stratification system.

Models of Masculinity–Femininity

As we indicated earlier, any stratification system is based on shared beliefs about differentiating among people on the basis of identifiable characteristics. There is currently little agreement about the nature and extent of differentiation possible—or desirable—on the basis of biological sex.

To begin with, researchers disagree on the meaning of *masculine* and *feminine*. Social scientists studying this issue have often regarded gender as a single continuum, with masculine at one end and feminine at the other. Any individual could be located on the continuum on the basis of observed behavior, psychological tests, and so forth.

1 ———————————————————————————— 1
Masculine   Feminine

On the basis of fairly extensive research trying to measure masculinity and femininity, most psychologists now regard masculinity and femininity as two separate dimensions (Constantinople, 1976). A particular individual may be placed anywhere along each continuum.

Low ————————————————————————— High
                          "Masculinity"

Low ————————————————————————— High
                          "Femininity"

Although there is not much agreement on how to measure masculinity and femininity scientifically, there are stereotypes associated with sex in every culture. As Margaret Mead (1949) has pointed out, the stereotypes vary from culture to culture. However, women are generally seen as more family-oriented, gentle, cooperative, and nurturant, and as providers of emotional resources. Men, in contrast, are generally regarded as more aggressive; more able to protect the family, tribe, or nation; more emotionally controlled; and as the providers of material resources.

These themes are well illustrated in Figures 1-1 and 1-2 (Chapter 1), which depict the ten ages of man and woman. The girl is brought to life by an angel; at 10 years she is playing independently; from 20 through 70 she is pictured with others primarily in nurturing or care-giving relationships to family members; at 80, cane in hand, she leans on a middle-aged man (presumably her son). She sits alone in her chair at 90 and is visited by angels at 100. The boy is "born" in a buggy, ready to roll; he steers a hoop at 10; at 20 courts a demure maiden; at 30 brings food from the hunt to his wife and two children; and thereafter is pictured standing alone, looking outward. His peak of vigor is at 50; after 60 he walks (alone) with a cane, and even at 90, though stooped, he does not sit idle.

In considering the evidence about sex-role differentiation, it is important to separate beliefs about what men and women actually do (sex-role *behaviors*) and what men and women should do (sex-role *norms*). These beliefs may be ascribed to "other people" but not necessarily accepted by individuals to whom society ascribes them. For example, Steinman and Fox (1966) surveyed hundreds of adult men and women about their sex-role expectations. Women thought men wanted a home-oriented, subordinate wife, whereas women themselves preferred to be equally balanced between self and home orientation. In fact, many men indicated they preferred the latter.

Consequences of Sex Differentiation

There are commonly held beliefs about the characteristics of men and women in all societies. On the basis of sex one is assigned at birth a place in a status system that has virtually no mobility between categories. Membership in one category and not another has been perhaps the single most important fact in regulating adult lives. "Men and women play different roles in society, and even when they are playing the same role they are exposed to different constraints and imperatives that shape their behavior" (Pearlin, 1975, p. 192). Both real and imagined differences contribute to observed differences in behavior.

We shall summarize some of the evidence about sex-typed behavior and differential access to social rewards; other evidence will emerge as we consider various behavioral domains. It is important to note, however, that it is difficult to assess the impact of sex itself separate from social class, ethnicity, age, circumstances, and personality. Such separation may, in fact, be impossible.

Power   Researchers have collected data from many different cultures to compare the "fates" of men and women collectively. The consequences of sex differentiation are usually studied in terms of how equal men and women are in power and privilege. *Power* in social status terms reflects the ability to carry out one's will even when opposed by others. Most stratification research assumes that power means economic power, political power, and the power of force (Lenski, 1966).

How do men and women compare with each other on the particular indices of power? Analysis of many cultures indicates that men regularly surpass women in political and forceful power. "There is no known society where women achieve even a fifty-percent share of political power" (Blumberg, 1979, p. 117). It is easy to see this pattern in the American political system.

Women rarely exercise the power of force, but they are frequently the victims of it. For example, in the United States wife beating is now admitted as a problem.

Economic power means the ability to control the means and fruits of production and to decide how surplus goods will be distributed. In some cultures (mostly preindustrial societies where women are hoe horticulturalists and/or market traders) women exercise more economic power than men. In other cultures the women have virtually no economic power relative to the men of their class or society (Blumberg, 1979).

Individual economic power in more complex societies is related to the ability to obtain education, to work for reasonable wages, and to decide how money will be spent. It seems clear that equality between men and women does not exist in the occupational world; women are nowhere distributed on a par with men in positions of power, authority, and prestige (Fogarty, Rapoport, & Rapoport, 1971; Youssef & Hartley, 1979). Occupations are sex-segregated: More men than women are found in some occupations (such as engineering, medicine, university-level teaching, heavy construction, military combat), and more women than men are found in others (secretary, household worker, bookkeeper, elementary school teacher, waitress); the extent of this sex segregation remained virtually unchanged in the United States from 1900 to 1970 (Blau, 1979). Furthermore, "women's jobs" pay lower wages. In an occupation that employs both men and women, men are more likely to reach the top positions, whereas women are more likely to stay at the lower salary and status levels.

Employed women earn less than employed men, even when comparisons are between men and women with similar education, occupation, experience, and hours worked. For example, in 1976 the annual median income or salary of women who worked full time, year round was $8,099, only 60 percent of the annual median earnings of working men (Blau, 1979, p. 280). This disparity has remained quite stable over the past two to three decades. According to research on male–female pay differences, pure sex discrimination accounts for between 29 and 43 percent of the differential earnings for men and women (Sawhill, 1973; Staines et al., 1976).

Privilege   How do men and women compare in regard to privilege? Blumberg (1979) has suggested that one very important privilege is the degree of control over one's own life. Men and women in a particular class or group can be compared in terms of freedom to control various options potentially open to both. These life options include, for example, decisions about (1) whether, when, and whom to marry; (2) engaging in premarital or extramarital sex; (3) regulating reproduction; (4) moving about without restriction; (5) exercising household authority; (6) taking advantage of educational opportunities; (7) whether, when, and what work to pursue; (8) military service, particularly in active combat. Overall, contemporary American women have relatively more freedom than men in some aspects (for example, employment and military service; men "must" work outside the home and are much more subject to active military duty). American women have less freedom in other areas, however.

Another index of sex differences is the amount of discretionary time available to men and women. Unemployed women, particularly those with older children or no children, have more discretionary time than do employed men. Evidence from surveys in 12 countries showed, however, that employed women have less nonpreempted time at their disposal than men—an average of an hour less daily than employed men on weekdays and 2.3 hours less on days off (Szalai, 1975, Table 2). These consequences reflect the dual job responsibilities of women employed outside the home. While employed women obtain some help in housekeeping and child care from husband, children, or paid workers, the responsibility for arranging it often remains theirs. The responsibility for household work does not seem to be significantly equalized when the wife has a full-time career (Rapoport & Rapoport, 1976; Holstrom, 1972), or when the husband retires from full-time employment (Troll & Turner, 1976). Among some groups of younger couples there may be more equalization of free time.

Mental Health   Since psychologists are often interested in mental health, we will explore the possible impact of sex differences on emotional well-being. Some researchers suggest that the stresses associated with female sex-role experiences account for higher rates of mental illness among women (for instance, Chessler, 1972; Gove, 1976; Gove & Tudor, 1973). Others have pointed out ways in which male role expectations contribute to distress for men (for instance, Fasteau, 1976; Goldberg, 1976).

However, the most reasonable position seems to be that presented by Dohrenwend and Dohrenwend (1976). On the basis of extensive reviews of research since 1900 in rural and urban settings in the United States and Europe, they concluded that there are no sex differences in overall rates of severe emotional illnesses (functional psychoses). Thus it does not seem useful to argue that one sex is under greater stress than the other. However, males and females do seem pushed to express stress in different deviant directions. Women consistently show higher rates of personality disorders characterized by depression and anxiety (neurosis and manic-depressive psychosis), whereas men show consistently higher rates of personality disorders reflected in irresponsible and antisocial behavior (alcohol and drug addiction, violence).

Explanations for Sexual Differentiation

Several kinds of explanations for observed patterns of sex differences are common in both scientific and popular thought.

Biological   The most conservative view of sex differences emphasizes the *biological* bases of behavior. Human interests, desires, abilities, and needs are seen as determined more by innate factors than by an individual's own efforts or the situation. Thus, while everyone is not equal in talents and abilities, the kinds of differences observed between men and women are considered both natural and relatively unchangeable. Goldberg (1976), for example, argues that, because the male child's brain receives far greater stimulation from the male hormone testosterone, males are more aggressive; the aggression alone is assumed to "explain patriarchy, male dominance, and male attainment of high status roles, for the male hormonal system gives men an insuperable head start toward attaining those roles which any society associates with leadership or high status as long as the roles are not ones that males are biologically incapable of filling" (Jaggar & Struehl, 1978, p. 93). Another version of the biological argument is offered by Erikson (1968), who suggested that there is a basic body "ground plan" that creates predispositions to respond in characteristically male or female ways.

Sociocultural   Another conservative explanation for sex differences assumes some fairly universal *sociocultural* mandates. The emphasis is on the ways sex-role socialization prepares men and women to respond to two common "emergency" situations—parenting small children and war. Gutmann (1975, 1977) has suggested that parenting is one activity that requires differentiation between the sexes. (This model of difference will be discussed more fully in Chapter 7.) The nurturance, sensitivity, flexibility, and accommodative qualities associated with good "mothering" are presumed to be antithetical to the qualities of competitiveness, emotional control, and goal-directedness required for either occupational success or success as a warrior.

Thus, according to Gutmann's thesis, sex differences in socialization, sex roles, and psychological characteristics reflect important sex-linked challenges in young adulthood. In this sense the observed differentiations are largely functional, both for the social system at large and for the individuals in family systems.

Others, however, emphasize the negative aspects of sex differences in parenting. For example, Dinnerstein (1977) has argued that observed psychological differences—and the uneasy relationships—between men and women reflect not so much biology as the unfortunate early experiences related to the nearly exclusive care of small children by women. These crucial experiences occur so early in life, she argues, that the results are profound, long-lasting differences that resist later experiences and efforts at change. According to this view, the fact that women care for small children means that boys develop a basic ambivalence toward all women: They desire the potential comfort and ecstasy from union with the "good mother" but fear her power to withhold or deny that comfort. Consequently, they must keep distance from women and exercise adult control over women. Girls also have the infantile experience of a seemingly all-powerful mother; as they grow older, they learn they are to be like her. However, even adult women are caught between striving to obtain the love and approval of the mother and feelings of profound inadequacy compared to the preconscious memories of the powerful mother of their childhood. Dinnerstein uses this experience to help account for women's concerns with love and approval and men's concerns with power and control. She suggests that male–female relationships will not change until parenting of small children is shared equally by men and women.

Functionalist   The arguments in favor of sexual differentiation rest, in part, on a *functionalist* argument. Functionalism assumes that observed differences contribute to the general well-being and functioning of the system as a whole. Conflicting qualities may be uncomfortable in the same person but easier to deal with if they exist within different actors in a social system. It may therefore be desirable to preserve contradictory qualities in the system as a whole, "assigning" to men or women distinct attributes that are, in actuality, shared by both sexes (Parsons & Bales, 1955).

Feminist   *Feminist* interpretations of sex differences stress the ways women are oppressed by social structure. Sex differences are assumed to reflect learned behavior, not innate differences, and the ideal society is considered one in which power, authority, and wealth are not disproportionately under male control (Freeman, 1979; Williams, 1977). *Radical feminists* tend to see sexism as the most fundamental—and most unfortunate—form of inequality in any society (see Firestone, 1970; Gornick & Moran, 1971). *Socialist feminists* place more emphasis on the interaction of social class and gender in shaping male and female experiences; the ideal society would be both classless and genderless (Jaggar & Struhl, 1978). Within the socialist model sex differences are seen as perpetuated largely by the forms of family and work life found in capitalist, private-wealth societies. In such systems women are "enslaved" by the assumption that they will labor as unpaid housewives and mothers in private households, leaving men free to control wage labor and wealth (Baude, 1979).

There is evidence that social structure does affect the allocation of rewards by sex role. In part, the degree of equality between men and women reflects the extent of economic development (Youssef & Hartley, 1979). After reviewing countries at different developmental levels, Safilios-Rothschild (1971) concluded that (a) in countries at medium levels of economic development women are provided the greatest opportunity to work, to work after marriage, and to enroll in college; and (b) in the least advanced economies women have the greatest opportunities to compete with men in professional employment. In fact, in the least advanced economies women are often an impressive proportion of all professional workers. Other research indicates that in highly competitive industrial systems, in which major sources of power and prestige are derived from achievement-based attributes, women have been denied equal access in the competition for highest educational, occupational, and income opportunities.

Changes over the Life Span

So far we have shared the common approach that the importance of sex as a status system is relatively static, at least after maturity. Although there has been much research on the early development of sex differences and gender identity, we have inadequate evidence about adulthood, and definite confounding of cohort and developmental differences during the adult years (Emmerich, 1973).

However, if we look at sex-role development over the entire course of life, the general patterns are fairly clear. The sense of self as male or female seems to develop in the first two years of life. We know this especially in cases of confused or mistaken sexual identification (Stoller 1968; Money & Erhardt, 1972). The socially prescribed patterns for males and females are identifiable by age 4 (Gadpaille, 1975). These patterns are usually reinforced at home, in books, in television, and in the street throughout childhood.

Adolescence is associated wtih increasing differentiation, as both boys and girls strive to establish some sense of sex-role identity and prepare for adult roles. If the prescriptions are that both adult men and women work outside the home, both will prepare for that. Nevertheless, the psychological differences associated with masculinity and femininity may persist and be emphasized, primarily in the dating and mating sphere. One factor in sex differences is that adolescent and young adult males are recognized as having more potential for aggression and violence. This potential seems biologically based, but a strong, coherent culture will provide ways the individual can use his aggressive impulses and energy in some constructive rather than destructive manner—usually to protect the society from outside enemies.

The young adult and early middle-age years seem to be characterized by sex differences in behavior for those who marry and become parents; as mentioned earlier, parenting is probably the more crucial experience. During the later middle years, men and women may shift toward less sexually stereotyped modes of responding, with shifts in covert personality styles that precede behavioral changes of later life (see Chapter 7 and Gutmann, 1977). These shifts may relate to changes in the hormonal balance—that is, the relative proportions of androgenic and estrogenic hormones. They may also reflect changes in parenting and other activities of adult lives. The later years are marked by less emphasis on sex differentiation. The old are regarded by others, and apparently by themselves, as least subject to sex-role norms and least identifiably masculine or feminine (Cameron, 1976; Gutmann, 1977), although sex-typed behavior may persist in structured situations where long-held norms and expectations are influential.

We will review the empirical evidence concerning sex-role norm perceptions and behavior for the second half of life in later chapters.

Social Policies

Three main perspectives determine social policies regarding sex differences and sex status systems. Pluralists emphasize differentiation and separation; assimilationists focus on helping the "lesser" group become more like the dominant one; and hybrid theorists want males and females to become more like each other and less distinctively gender-typed.

The particular policy followed—by an individual, group, or society—is very important in determining interventions. For example, what would be the approach within each orientation to a counseling program intended to help young adult men and women prepare to leave school? What would be recommended for men and women dealing with a "mid-life transition"?

Pluralism   The *pluralistic* ideology stresses separation and differentiation of the sexes. Some state clearly that the desired state is separate and unequal, with man as the chief and woman as his natural helper (for example, Morgan, 1973). Other proponents stress a separate but equal stance and would relieve current inequalities by "upgrading" women and valuing distinctive qualities equally. In the occupational realm this ideology would support sex typing of work (or at least minimize strenuous efforts to integrate already sex-typed fields). The focus is instead on creating home and work schedules that would mesh with the involvements of mothering and homemaking over the life course. In addition, the assumption is that, even when men and women do fill the same position (management trainee, nursery school teacher, PTA president), they will have a characteristically masculine or feminine style. Women and men will be "liberated" and "equal" only when they are free to follow their deepest, most instinctual, distinctive impulses in mothering and fathering (Erikson, 1974).

Pluralism is based on conservative biological or sociocultural explanations of human behavior. It is supported by the evidence that sex-role divisions tend to persist even when conscious ideology and social structure blur the differences (Spiro, 1900). Others argue for sex-typed activities on the premise that the social cost of a completely open merit system is too great; the concern is that the most crucial parenting roles would not be adequately performed.

The argument against the pluralistic position is that different is always unequal, and one set of characteristics inevitably comes to be valued—and rewarded—above others. In addition, men and women do not differ, systematically and predictably, beyond reproductive roles; thus sex typing inevitably leads to mismatching of many individuals. Finally, this position may be rejected on the basis of social cost: The social system cannot afford the undeveloped talents of scientific women and nurturant men.

Assimilationism   An *assimilationist* ideology focuses on helping the "lesser" group become more like the dominant. The refrain "Why can't a woman be more like a man?" is effectively, though perhaps more subtly, expressed in literature urging women to forgo mothering or to reallocate such duties to free them for "real work," and in articles celebrating women who "break through" to fill traditionally male jobs. In this view young women are urged to prepare for "masculine" work patterns, with full-time involvement; career success is assessed by how nearly it approximates masculine achievement. Women are encouraged to win success by developing "masculine" characteristics (rationality, emotional control, competitive assertiveness, and the like) and overcoming feminine "deficiencies" (such as emotionality, intuitive thinking, and "frills"). For example, a best-selling book (Malloy, 1977) tells women how to dress for success. Malloy based his advice on scientific research, testing how various groups reacted to standard modes of dress. According to his findings, women can succeed—especially in business—insofar as they can project an image of power and authority: "Dressing to succeed in business and dressing to be sexually attractive are almost mutually exclusive" (p. 21).

Assimilationism is based on the adage "If you can't beat 'em, join 'em." The assumption is that women *can* become very much like men and that, only by doing so, will they have access to the same rewards as men. Those favoring this position may stress the potential benefits for women in later life—primarily, an adequate personal income and more self-esteem.

Critics of this position (for instance, Williams, 1977) point out that women are not men and men are not women. A more serious argument against the assimilationist position is that it most devalues "feminine" qualities; whatever socially desirable characteristics are included in female sex roles would be lost,

An assimilationist ideology focuses on helping the "lesser" group become more like the dominant group. For example, women may be encouraged to win success by developing "masculine" characteristics.

upsetting a vital balance in the home and the workplace. Masculinity and male roles also have liabilities; in fact, many women may prefer traditional home-making, mothering, and limited employment to being responsible for economic support and defense.

Hybrid   A third ideology holds that most characteristics are not—and should not be—distributed on the basis of biological sex. Individuals differ from each other and should be encouraged to develop and use whatever talents and skills they possess, without the constraint of sex-role norms or sex typing. One possibility, then, is to find a compatible partner, of either sex, and share responsibilities on the basis of personal skill and preference. Divorced or wid-owed mothers and fathers might find parenting preferable with another person of the same gender. In later life it is easier for women to find other women to share life with. In the workplace neither jobs nor work assignments would be sex-typed; while women might want flexible or reduced-time jobs for mother-ing, men might want the same arrangements for parenting or other interests (see Lipman-Blumen & Bernard, 1979). This ideology stresses androgyny—the flexible combination of both masculine and feminine characteristics.

Those who favor this ideology regard it as the only viable solution to cur-rent sex status inequalities. They stress that both men and women will have to change if either changes. Change is necessary and inevitable because the cur-rent costs of differentiation are excessive. By reducing differences, inequalities based on sex will be lessened.

The primary arguments against this position are pragmatic and moral—that such blending won't work because it requires unrealistically rapid, inti-mately personal changes; or that it shouldn't work because it violates the "nat-ural plan" evolved over the centuries.

SOCIOECONOMIC STATUS

Every social system has some form of social class system—popularly known as the rich and the poor, the uppers and the lowers, the haves and the have-nots. These terms reflect implied inequalities: Some have more, and some have less. Generally speaking, those in the upper classes fill more socially valued roles and have more access to rewards such as power, esteem, and money. Thus members of different social classes have unequal *life chances*—opportunities to obtain whatever goods the society has to offer. The social classes are also differ-ent in lifestyles—the typical patterns of daily life reflected in occupation, hous-ing, clothing, use of leisure time, values, and morals.

Socioeconomic status tells us some things about probable access to income, prestige, and social services; something about the likely kind of occupation, use of leisure time, and resources people will carry into old age. At the bottom levels the incidence of poor health and low morale are greater; morale does not necessarily increase with additional status above the bottom. An individual's location in a particular social stratification system (a village, an urban neighborhood) may be a reasonably good predictor of individual lifestyle.

Socioeconomic status has profound impact on individual lives in some systems and minimal impact in others. Generally, the more differentiated the class system is, and the more unequal the access to social resources, the more socioeconomic status is important in understanding individual behavior.

Perceptions of Social Strata

Individuals differ in their perception of the social system. Obviously, one of the facts that influence one's perception of the social system is one's location in it. When Warner and Lunt (1941) made their classic analyses of social stratification in American towns, they found that those near the top identified several layers of upper statuses, then broadly lumped the middle and bottom. Classes below that of the informant were described in moralistic terms—as flawed in character and talent. Informants in bottom social classes distinguished several distinct groups at the lower end but lumped middle and upper classes together, and they ascribed their position in lower classes to bad luck rather than bad character. On the other hand, there was some agreement about which particular people in the town belonged to upper, middle, and lower classes; what each class typically did; and how they lived (Warner & Lunt, 1941).

Qualifications for Membership

A social class may be regarded as "real" if members accept each other as belonging and generally reject others as not belonging. This standard of personal acceptability is generally assessed by the willingness of members to associate with each other informally (for instance, at home parties or as members in private clubs) and as proper marriage partners. It is the patterns of mutual interaction and validation of values among those who "belong" and rejection of those who are outside the class that probably account most for the impact of social class on behavior.

The characteristics needed to qualify for different social classes vary. From both classic fairy tales and the modern fairy-tale television shows we are acquainted with royalty and aristocracy, where class membership is inherited, and its members have money and, sometimes, titles. The top status is generally based on heritage—"old money," "good breeding," and "respectability." In most towns in democratic countries the classes are identified on the basis of occupation, education, neighborhood, type of housing, and income. Even a small town distinguished the "ruling class" of wealthy persons, doctors, lawyers, business owners, and land owners; they lived in grander houses and partied together. Those working for wages, steadily employed and moderately educated, living in more modest but comfortable homes, constituted the middle class. The lower classes had little, although most distinguished between the "poor but honest" who tried to work, even though poorly educated and lacking in special skills valued by the community, and the "shiftless poor" who depended on welfare, lived in run-down housing, and seemed to have given up life's struggle. Life in such a social system has been most vividly described in novels such as *Main Street* by Sinclair Lewis (1948); the closed status system he described still characterizes some smaller communities around the world.

In such a system social class is highly visible: Everyone knows the status of everyone else. There are usually clear expectations about "proper" behavior, including styles of dress and home decorating, religious affiliation, eating patterns, forms of entertainment, reading matter, colleges, friendships, and general demeanor. These expectations are reinforced by a shared religious–cultural belief system and by continued social interactions. Children born in such a community learn the social class system—and their place in it—as they are growing up. Daily life routines are "natural" within social class boundaries.

Mobility

Lack of mobility within a system reflects the importance of family identity and heritage. However, even where individuals must demonstrate particular competencies and values in order to be accepted as members of a particular social class, it is most likely that the child born into that class will acquire them. Even in the American system, which places relatively high value on opportunities for social mobility and has policies of universal education, there is considerable social class inheritance, and even occupational inheritance. For example, doctors' children are likely to become doctors (or doctors' spouses), and children of business people are more likely to enter business than other fields. This reflects the cumulative impact of learning in the early years: Children learn, gradually, the lifestyle, values, work hours, leisure-time pursuits, and even the vocabulary of parental occupations.

Social class mobility has long been the American dream, and many immigrants were lured to this country partly on the belief that, with hard work and talent, they could rise above humble beginnings. Education and diligence were the paths to occupational and social success for many. Sons could be raised for upward mobility, with the whole family supporting the education, clothing, and social expenses. Often such men tried to marry a girl nearer to—if not actually in—the social class they aspired to. For example, research indicates that, even as adolescents, boys who eventually rose in social class had sexual habits closer to those of the higher social class than to those of their friends (Kinsey, Pomeroy, & Martin, 1948).

Daughters could also be raised for upward social mobility. Sometimes they concentrated on obtaining education and training for a higher-status occupation. In other cases young women worked on the personal skills (beauty, dress, grooming, homemaking, and "charm") presumed necessary to attract a husband from a higher social class. In fact, "marrying up" has been the most traditional path for women who wished to better their position in life.

Mobility often results in behavior that is a mixture of the class of origin and the adult social class. Marriages where the spouses are from different social classes are more subject to stress than within-class marriages, but particularly when the wife is of higher status. Individuals who are upwardly mobile may feel real pride in their accomplishment; they may also feel guilty about being more successful than their parents and implicitly "rejecting" those they grew up with.

Individuals may experience downward social mobility, where they occupy a lower social position than the family they grew up in or where a class position established in earlier adult years is not maintained. Downward mobility may occur because of social conditions or bad luck, as many people find during periods of economic depression. Downward mobility may also reflect the relative lack of ambition or skills required to maintain one's status; serious or prolonged illness, for example, may contribute to downward social mobility. Downward social mobility may be a source of shame and feelings of worthlessness, but at the same time there may be relief at not having to struggle to maintain a higher status.

Changing Social Class Systems

The social class system in a small community may be upset by migration, especially of newcomers who move in and, through ignorance or defiance, refuse to "follow the rules" of the original group. Sometimes a new class evolves—the "outlanders" or the "summer people"—and that group creates its own status system.

Such social class systems evolve in a community of any size. Generally, the status system reflects the class structure of the larger society; in a working-class suburb, for example, the steadily employed skilled laborers and supervisors will have higher status than unskilled or marginally employed workers. Sometimes, however, a new community establishes new criteria for elitism; for example, in some U.S. retirement communities, the upper class is defined in terms of current health and vigor, rather than previous occupational or family status.

The socioeconomic status system is less clearly elaborated in many modern urban areas. The traditional definitions of social class in terms of family, education, occupation, income, and residence, as translated into a visible lifestyle and informal acceptability by others in the same class, are more difficult to assess in an urban area, where many people are geographically mobile and are unlikely to know much about family background, social interactions, or daily lifestyle. Recent research indicates that occupation is the most important index of social class placement, particularly in urban areas. Occupational status ranking has remained remarkably stable in the United States over at least the past

30 years; there is remarkable consensus among the population as a whole in evaluating occupations as excellent to very poor. Supreme Court judges, physicians, university professors, business executives, and corporate lawyers consistently rank high; social workers, teachers, secretaries, nurses, salesmen, and skilled workers (electricians, plumbers) are in the middle; and unskilled laborers, grocery store clerks, and gas station attendants are at the bottom (see Duncan, 1961).

Women and Status

Traditionally, the socioeconomic status of a woman has been determined first by her father and then by her husband; her own occupational achievements—unless they were outstanding—were not considered. In part, of course, this reflected reality; when few women were employed outside the home after marriage, the husband was legitimately the source of status for the family. However, as women are more involved in work outside the home, higher education, and careers, it seems reasonable to consider the contributions of both husband and wife to the family status. Many wives work to increase the family status by supporting the family while the husband finishes specialized training or by working to help buy things for a working-class, middle-class, or upper-middle-class lifestyle. Those couples where both partners are professionals usually have a higher economic status and thus may have higher social status; their lifestyles and life chances are probably affected. However, sociologists have done little research on these issues so far.

The past two decades have seen an increase in the number of women preparing for lifetime work, with or without marriage and motherhood. This trend is most evident among upper-middle-class women, who have the most options and who aspire to the most rewarding jobs. It is not clear, however, to what extent women are—or will be—evaluated socially in terms of their own occupational status, or to what extent they will live a lifestyle comparable to a man in a similar position. Married women usually have an occupation of the same or lower status than their husbands; where the wife has a higher-status job, what is the lifestyle? Do women who are divorced or widowed carry their husband's social status or their own? Are unmarried women granted status equivalent to that of a man in the same occupation? These questions become increasingly important when we realize that many women will spend a substantial portion of adult life employed.

Social Policies

As in cases of sex difference, the social policies based on different points of view about socioeconomic differences can have profound consequences for life chances.

Pluralism   A pluralistic society recognizes distinct class differences, with distinct lifestyles and markedly unequal rewards. However, some systems are based on hereditary *castes,* clearly boundaried social statuses with little or no mobility between strata. An alternate version of the pluralistic model accepts unequal rewards but endorses opportunities for any individual to reach the status level he or she desires and "deserves." This may involve providing prenatal care and enhanced social-emotional experiences for young children, to help the disadvantaged overcome their background. It may also lead to providing opportunities for socialization and training during adulthood. According to this point of view, individuals are assumed to get the rewards their talents and diligence merit, and those at the bottom of the stratification system are granted a subsistence-level living. This policy partly accounts for much of the poverty in the United States.

Assimilationism   An assimilationist view leads to policies designed to decrease socioeconomic class difference. The extreme version is the classless society envisioned by some utopian writers. Some societies have implemented many specific acts to minimize class differences. Norway, for example, tries to guarantee a reasonable minimum standard of living and discourages wealth by substantial taxes on "excessive" income or overtime pay. Education can be designed to reduce, rather than accent, differences in talent; manual work may be emphasized and rewarded as fully as the professions. Services considered essential for general welfare—such as health care, education, recreation, and culture—are provided through central, tax-supported funding. Noncompetitive groups such as the elderly, the handicapped, and the young may be assumed to have as much "right" to social resources as those who run manufacturing plants or provide medical care.

ETHNICITY

In a society comprising a single ethnic group an individual's ethnicity will not predict much about individual differences. However, when comparing two or more social groups, or evaluating behavior within a heterogeneous society, ethnicity is often an important variable.

Assessment

Ethnicity is complex to define and to measure, which is one reason the data on ethnic differences in adult behavior are so inadequate. Ethnicity has a biological base in common genetic ancestry; however, any group of people who move out of their original setting are unlikely to be very "pure." (For example, a very small proportion of modern Afro-Americans have only African ancestry.) It is not clear to what extent or how genetic predispositions contribute to observed differences in health and habits betweeen ethnic groups. Biological factors may be primarily important insofar as they give visible cues about ethnicity—skin color, hair texture, body build, and so on—which in turn may provoke stereotyped social interactions.

Ethnicity is also assessed in terms of sociocultural heritage—the typical values, artifacts, and ways of meeting human needs. This heritage includes notions about what kinds of work are most honorable, what men and women do, how children are reared, how best to relate to the supernatural, what and when to eat, and what and who are worth knowing. A coherent culture provides for both sacred and secular concerns. The *sacred* realm defines what is most valued and honorable in that culture; by directing his capacity (and need) to idealize the culturally shared beliefs, the individual becomes part of a system transcending his own selfish concerns. Conformity to the prescribed ways of behaving then becomes a way of connecting with the sacred; sacrifices of individual wishes have meaning and are tolerated. Therefore, in a coherent society the beliefs are usually observed.

Traditional ways of living, and the beliefs that support those ways, are challenged by contact with competing sociocultural systems. Sometimes such contact reinforces the unity of the group. For example, the Amish religious group in America settled their own communities, provided their own style of education, and kept out outsiders. However, the more typical "American way" involves conflict among a wide range of ethnic-cultural heritages. Many tales have told how immigrants struggled with their desires to preserve the old familiar ways and still adapt to the new life; a "divided heart" was common. Some immigrants established communities designed to preserve the culture of the old country, but most forged some new version of the old and the new.

The risk is, of course, that the sacred aspects of culture that provided meanings for traditional behaviors may be lost in the transformation; a new sacred system may not evolve, and individuals will lack the central focus that organizes behavior. Behavior then becomes disorganized, unpredictable, and even chaotic. The impact of ethnicity on individual behavior is much tempered by the coherence of the culture; among immigrants, the impact reflects length of time in the new country, the extent and kinds of contacts with other cultures, and the degree of assimilation.

Perhaps it would be more useful to explore the impact of ethnicity using some measures of *ethnic identity:* the extent to which an individual uses ethnicity as an important characteristic in defining himself, finding meaning in the behavioral constraints shaped by the traditional cultural heritage.

It is clear that individuals vary greatly in this respect, though not randomly. In any society, members of outcast minority groups may be more sensitive to their ethnic status—in part because they suffer as a result of it. Some members of the "majority" social classes may have strong ethnic identity, expressed through neighborhood ethnic organizations, churches, and the like, but others think of themselves as simply *American.* The upper middle class is least likely

Some individuals define themselves in terms of their ethnicity. In addition, ethnic status affects life chances.

to have a sense of ethnic identity since their lifestyle is tied largely to occupational status. Moreover, generations differ in ethnic identity: The first native-born generation is most likely to reject any ethnic identity or culture in favor of the land of assimilation; they are often ashamed by their parents' ignorance of the language and culture of the new land. However, later generations may return to discover their ethnic roots and use ethnicity as a way of distinguishing themselves from others.

Beyond these general issues we know little about the effect of ethnicity on personality or other individual characteristics.

Stereotypes and Discrimination

Like sex, ethnicity is one component in allocation of roles and rewards in the social system. At least in America, life chances are affected by visible racial-ethnic characteristics.

Stereotypes exist for all identified ethnic groups, along with "ethnic tags" (such as wop, nigger, squarehead, kike). The stereotypes include both positive- and negative-valued characteristics, though the overall stereotype may be dominantly one way or the other. Stereotypes change, often with socioeconomic mobility of each group. In America the most recent immigrant group starts near the bottom of the status hierarchy and—almost automatically—acquires some of the negative stereotypes associated with the lower class. Some ethnic stereotypes persist (the silent Swede, the hard-drinking Irish, the suspicious Pole, the emotional Italian, and so on).

Like other stereotypes, ethnic stereotypes are important insofar as the individual or others accept them as real—and they then become real in their consequences. There is ample evidence that this does occur: *Racism* is the term given to the systematic exclusion from certain opportunities solely on the basis of race or ethnicity. Evidence about the economic and psychological costs of racism to individuals has led to various attempts to change the racial-ethnic status system. A classic example is the *Brown* versus *Board of Education* school desegregation case in the United States. The Supreme Court accepted psychological evidence that black children in segregated schools suffered even if the all-black schools were supposed to be equal to white schools. The Court ruled that "separate is never equal" and ordered desegregation.

Consequences

We can examine some of the consequences of the current American ethnic stratification system in any statistics on life chances. The ethnic groupings used are approximate; however, it is clear that (1) life expectancy at birth is lower for nonwhites (65.2 years) than for whites (71.9 years); (2) for those who survive to midlife there is little difference in life expectancy at age 50 and somewhat higher life expectancy for nonwhites who survive to 70; (3) nonwhites, especially the elderly, are more likely to have poor health; and (4) nonwhites are disadvantaged in all indices of access to social rewards—education, income, and occupational status (Bengtson, Kasschau, & Ragan, 1977). Perhaps partly as a consequence of such facts, subjective assessments of aging vary by ethnicity, with less favorable attitudes expressed by blacks and Mexican-Americans than by Anglos (Bengtson, Kasschau, & Ragan, 1977). Generally, ethnic minority members feel "old" at a younger chronological age than do Anglos.

Social Policies

Throughout the world today proponents of each ideological perspective fight for policies to implement their viewpoint. Pluralists argue for maintaining the cultural heritage of minority (often immigrant) groups. This policy may be reflected in bilingual instruction programs, in observing religious holidays of various ethnic groups, or in providing ethnically traditional meals at federally funded senior citizens' centers. This ideology has had recent popularity in the United States, as reflected in such slogans as "Black Pride" and "Polish Power."

More traditionally, an assimilationist ideology assumes that the challenge is to help minority members or newcomers to become as much like the ruling group as possible. Native foreign language study (and even speech) is discouraged. Proficiency in standard English is mandated, and ethnic identification is considered backward. Rewards such as better jobs and more money are available to those who assimilate the most. People who immigrated under such a social climate may, in their later years, regret their repressed ethnic heritage, particularly if that heritage provided a more honorable old age than what they now experience.

A third alternative involves some new blend of ethnic heritages, to become Mexican-American, Indian-English, and the like. The blend is distinctive from either of the two original cultures. Such blends are easiest to see in language and food. Sometimes ritual celebrations are modified, or new values emerge. One example is the inclusion of a decorated evergreen tree as part of the Jewish Hannukah celebration in areas that are largely Christian. The Christmas tree is not acceptable as long as it is associated with the Christian holiday, but it has become part of a modified Jewish celebration in some families. Individuals usually make the modifications and blends that help them feel most comfortable in both cultures. Such compromises are not always successful, but the more successful ones are likely to endure and even be passed on from generation to generation.

Social policy recommendations are very difficult within a hybrid perspective, because they inevitably involve judgments about what blends and combinations will be adaptive and tolerated or encouraged. The issue may arise with immigration from one culture to a distinctly different one, such as the movement of Pakistanis to Norway. Some of the cultural groups in Pakistan define family as including a husband, several wives, their children, the spouses' parents, and the spouses' siblings. The unit considered desirable for family functioning is much larger than that recognized in American and European cultures. Pakistanis began immigrating to Norway and then attempted to have their extended families join them. The Norwegians wished to limit immigration but have strong policies about not separating families. The immigration agencies had to establish new policies, which represented a compromise between the Norwegian and Pakistani cultural understandings of family. The Norwegian encouragement of hybridism is also evident in other social policies. By law, every individual is entitled to retain his or her cultural heritage, and immigrant children must be provided with instruction in their native language and history as well as in Norwegian language and customs.

AGE AS A STATUS CHARACTERISTIC

Age is another personal characteristic that influences social status. In part this is simply because the biological organism changes over time, and the biological changes often result in behavior changes. In addition, age is used as a social indicator, to place individuals in the social system. Like sex, ethnicity, and social class, age can be evaluated as a means of influencing individual behavior, through the social system (Riley, Johnson, & Foner, 1972).

However, age has some very distinct characteristics. Chronological age is, first, a continuum—a time line marked at regular, universal units. Second, individuals have guaranteed personal mobility along this continuum: They grow up and grow older, and thus "status mobility" is built into the system. A continuum should be partitioned only if we can show that the divisions reflect socially significant aspects of people and roles. Thus we need to understand how that continuum is divided in socially significant ways to influence individual behavior. This is difficult, in part, because (as we discussed in Chapter 1) chronological age is only a rough index of an individual's position on physical and psychological dimensions.

Meanings of age are subjective; that is, age has meaning only in relation to something or someone else. We are older or younger than someone, nearer to or farther from death. These meanings make age an important variable. In addition, the meanings of age, or any particular age, vary from culture to culture and with the location of an individual in a social system (Bengtson et al., 1977).

Life Periods

Research with adults and children indicates that age becomes a psychological reality as the life span is divided into socially relevant units. The individual makes a "mental map" of the life course and internalizes a "social clock" (Neugarten & Hagestad, 1977). Some life periods—childhood, adulthood, and old age—are recognized in all cultures. It is interesting to ask individuals to name periods on the life line. Some people identify a few periods during the early years, make little differentiation in adulthood, and then identify old age. On the other hand, professionals working with human behavior often make very fine distinctions about meaningful periods in the life course. For example, in the United States we have increasingly differentiated age periods: childhood (infancy, preschool years, early school years, middle-school years, preadolescence, early adolescence, late adolescence); youth; early middle age, late middle age; and, recently, the "young-old" have been differentiated from the "old-old" (Neugarten, 1974).

The fact that people identify and name periods in life also implies that each period is associated with characteristic patterns of behavior. Indeed, in various studies in the United States individuals have distinguished each period in terms of health and vigor, career line, family cycle, psychological attributes, and social responsibilities (Neugarten & Peterson, 1957). To some extent these images of each age period are stereotypes, reflecting some consensus within the culture.

Societies differ in the extent to which there is agreement on the chronological ages that mark periods in life. Some societies have carefully identified periods that one enters and leaves on the basis of chronological age. The contemporary American age system is looser; that is, people are identified as "youth" if they are preparing for a career, are in higher education, or have not yet made final commitments about the life they intend to lead. The difference between young-old and old-old is largely a matter of health status and activity level rather than chronological age.

Social Class and
Sex Differences with Age

The characteristics and chronological ages identified for various life periods differ for members of different socioeconomic classes, according to a study by Neugarten and Peterson (1957). Generally, working-class people see the life course as moving more quickly than do upper-middle-class people. They see young adulthood as the time of settling down and being productive, middle age as stability and stagnation, and a relatively long old age of decline and loss. Upper-middle-class respondents described the life course differently. Young adulthood is seen as a period of exploration, trying things out, and finally making commitments; the middle years, a time of peak power and influence and life satisfaction, last until age 70 or so; old age is a relatively short period of resting on one's accomplishments and enjoying the fruits of one's labor.

In addition, the behaviors of each life period are different for men and for women; it seems almost as if men and women have different life lines. In Neugarten and Peterson's (1957) study, for example, women divided their life line into two parts at approximately age 40: life with children and the life they would have after their children had left home. Men thought their life line was a much more continuous process, with important divisions marked by their work life. It is not clear how these visions of the life line may have changed as more women have become career-oriented.

Age Norms and Behavior

The fact that there is some consensus about the characteristics of each life period means that individuals use these images as models for their own behavior. The expectations act as a system of age norms—guidelines for individual behavior in relation to age. Age norms are attached to a wide variety of behaviors, from the trivial (the age at which a woman should or should not wear a bikini to the beach) to the very important (the age after which a man should not think about changing his career).

Age norms are most focused for events in young adulthood (Neugarten & Peterson, 1957; Kedar & Shanan, 1975). Some individuals experience moving into the later years as an anxious time because they don't know "what to do." This may be a reflection of the looser and poorly defined expectations about behavior in later age periods. On the other hand, many men and women regard the flexibility of age norms as "freedom to become." In general, middle-aged and older people perceive greater age constraints than do the young, who tend to deny that age is important in deciding what behavior is appropriate (Neugarten, Moore, & Lowe, 1965). There seems to be greater consensus on age-appropriate behavior for women than for men, although these expectations may be responsive to social changes.

Age norms act as a system of social control, presumably as other norms (such as those for sex and social class) do. Individuals are aware of their own timing in terms of the predictable life course. Events that are experienced as "off time" seem to be more disruptive than events that are anticipated for that period in life (Neugarten & Hagestad, 1976). For example, women widowed earlier than most of their friends have more disruptions in social relationships and more illness. Marriages contracted in adolescence are more likely to end in divorce. Army officers, whose careers are closely age-graded, evaluated themselves and their careers on the basis of whether their career progress was "late" or "on time" (Huyck, 1969). And, one study found that middle-class women who married "too young" or "too old," in their own eyes, were more dissatisfied with their lives than women who married at what they considered the right time—between 20 and 30. However, sometimes being "early" or "late" has beneficial consequences. Being the youngest executive in the firm can boost morale; and one study indicated that men who become fathers at a relatively ripe age had a much easier and more enjoyable time with their fathering (Nydegger, 1973).

Consequences of Age Stratification

As Riley (1976) has pointed out, the age stratification system has implications for linking between individuals. On the one hand, individuals are likely to feel an affinity with those in their same age group. On the other hand, there is the possibility of segregation and conflict between strata, although this potential is reduced by the inevitability of aging, so that all share in different age strata. In addition, there are obvious ties across age boundaries, both within families and outside of families. However, we know relatively little about such ties, especially outside the family.

Streib (1976) analyzed the impact of age on the various socioeconomic dimensions that measure access to social resources and found that the impact of age is difficult to evaluate. In general, age has mixed results, and probably a less negative impact than is usually assumed. Most adults carry their class status with them into old age, even though they may have reduced income. The "new poor," those whose income is substantially reduced in old age, are perhaps the worst off and may experience the most downward mobility in old age. There seems to be continuity in lifestyles, even though modified in later years. While political leadership increases with age, there is little evidence that older politicians use their power to advance the interests of their age group. The matter of power within the family is complex. Elders have traditionally maintained control through property, though some also maintain control through emotional relationships. We know even less about the ways age may modify the sex status system. Some have charged that women decline in status and power in old age, but others point out that, at least cross-culturally, women increase in power in later years, even though their power may be evaluated harshly by the community (Gutmann, 1977; Safilios-Rothschild, 1977).

The importance of age for role assignment varies by culture, by social conditions, and by cohort. For example, if many men are at war, the young and the old are encouraged to work; if a cohort is small, then younger and older individuals are recruited to fill positions; if the society wants to have low fertility, women are urged to marry late and to enter the work force earlier; and if the culture wishes to increase the birth rate, early marriages and nonemployment for women are encouraged (Riley, 1976). Why are social roles allocated by age? Some roles have a reasonable biological basis that is related to age; mother and combat soldier are obvious cases. However, most social roles are flexible and could be filled by individuals of a wide age range, yet many of those roles are, in fact, somewhat age-graded.

The age grading of social role allocation is breaking down in our society. We have adults enrolled in school throughout their adult and older years; middle-aged adults may divorce, remarry, and begin a new family; and women are starting career development during middle age. It is unclear just how the age stratification system will evolve in the future. As Neugarten and Hagestad (1976) have pointed out, our system seems to be going in somewhat contradictory directions. On the one hand, chronological age is being increasingly used as an index for certain benefits or privileges, such as voting, Social Security, or Medicare. This bureaucratic trend is counterbalanced by the emphasis on doing away with age discrimination (agism), and the notion that age itself should make a difference in how rewards, privileges, and social roles are allocated in adulthood.

Social Policy Perspectives

Pluralism in regard to age acknowledges and celebrates "a time for all things." Each season of life has—and should have—its sorrows, challenges, and joys. No group would be penalized because of age, although one might be censored for being too impatient to move ahead or for lingering behind in arrested development. The assimilationist stance on age seems more popular. Adages such as "You're as young as you look," and "Be as youthful as you feel" support hair dyes, face lifts, cosmetics, and clothing designed to stave off middle age and, later, to make middle age persist to the end. In this view, to admit to being old is to admit to defeat.

The hybrid strategy is to create new forms of aging. The emphasis may be on retaining physical fitness and vigor without covering grey hair or wrinkles. At work, mentoring—the sponsorship of younger colleagues—may be seen as the appropriate form of productivity. Sexual interest does not disappear, but different forms of erotic gratification become important. In a sense, the identification of the young-old as a distinct phase in life represents a hybrid, where accumulated experiences, good health, and freedom from child-rearing responsibilities give possibilities not available if one is either bound by age norms or trying to deny aging.

GROUP PATTERNS
AND INDIVIDUAL BEHAVIOR

We have considered some of the major individual attributes used as a basis for stratifying and locating individuals in the social system. Insofar as stratification systems influence access to social resources and allocation into social roles, the experiences of aging are affected by these characteristics. When strata are highly structured, it is easier to predict individual behavior on the basis of membership in that stratification system. However, individuals belong to multiple status systems—at least the four we have identified—and these systems interact in complex ways to affect individuals.

The statuses we have reviewed provide only general guidelines for individual behavior. As the external structure of a situation decreases, the impact of internal factors—personality and internalized social values and standards—increases (Sherif & Sherif, 1969). We must always remember that individuals respond selectively to the social realities—stratification systems—they have erected, giving their own meaning to these characteristics. Some individuals are more conscious of status characteristics than others; age awareness or sex-role sensitivity are probably tied to personality. We must not regard the social system as simply an external force operating upon helpless individuals. Individuals respond to such systems in terms of their own priorities and needs.

To explore these individual differences, we need to focus on individual predispositions to respond, in terms of biological capacities, actively level, and so on. We need to understand the cognitive processing of external and internal events. We will study personal styles of harmonizing conflicts and adapting the individual–society relationship. In addition, by looking at lifelong patterns of interaction with others and with the environment, we will be better equipped to evaluate and understand individual differences in behavior.

In the rest of the book we will emphasize capacities, potentials, urges, decisions, actions, and dreams. We will look for continuities, transformations, and evolutions over the course of life. And we will expect complexity.

SUMMARY

1   Differences in behavior among adults living in the United States are often related to four characteristics: sex, ethnicity, socioeconomic status, and age. Each of these characteristics is a basis for social status.

2   *Status* refers to the different positions an individual may hold within a social system. Stratification systems, the ways individuals are distributed into various statuses, determine how rewards and responsibilities are allocated. Stratification systems differ in the degree of perceived difference between strata, the stereotypes associated with each status, the extent of discrimination, and the opportunities for mobility, or changing status.

3 *Sex* is an important status characteristic in every culture. To understand the impact of sex on adult behavior it is necessary to differentiate biological sex, gender identity, and social sex role. *Biological sex* is coded genetically into every body cell; the impact of such biological differences during adulthood are seen, for example, in the reproductive roles of men and women. *Gender identity* is the individual's acceptance of belonging to one social category or another—male or female. *Social sex role* describes the sex-linked expectations about how men and women relate to each other and what characteristics distinguish men and women in behavior, personality, preferences, and abilities.

4 There are several consequences of sex differentiation. Power and privileges are distributed largely on the basis of sex, and emotional well-being seems to differ between the sexes. Several explanations for observed patterns of sex differences have been offered, including biological, sociocultural, functionalist, and feminist. Membership in one category and not another has probably been the single most important factor regulating individuals' lives, although the effects change over the life span. It is thus impossible to understand adult development without comprehending the ways in which sex affects behavior.

5 *Socioeconomic status* reflects an individual's place in the social class system. Members of different social classes have unequal opportunities to obtain whatever goods the society has to offer. The social classes also differ in the typical patterns of daily life reflected in occupation, housing, clothing, use of leisure time, values, and morals. Experiences during adulthood are affected by social class and by changes in social status over the life span.

6 *Ethnicity* can be an important characteristic in understanding adult behavior, particularly in a multiethnic setting. The relevance of ethnicity for adult development lies primarily in the sociocultural heritage of typical values and ways of meeting human needs. In addition, being of one ethnic group or another may substantially affect an individual's life chances.

7 *Age* is also used to place individuals within a social system. Age is important when individuals divide their lifetime into socially and personally meaningful units. The adult life course is divided differently by men and women and by individuals in different social classes. Expectations about the age at which events normally occur act as a system of social control on individual behavior.

8 Social policy in response to any of these statuses is generally based on one of three ideological perspectives. *Pluralism* stresses open acknowledgment that people should differ on the basis of sex, social class, ethnicity, or age. Another approach emphasizes *assimilation,* blurring distinctions by helping individuals with the less valued status become more like members of the dominant group. The *hybrid* strategy is to work for distinctive combinations of statuses. The extent to which one or another of these approaches is reflected in public policy and popular sentiment can substantially influence the course of development over the adult years.

PART TWO

FOUNDATIONS

CHAPTER THREE

PSYCHOBIOLOGY

Development is the joint product of biological factors and the experiences of
the changing individual. This chapter presents a picture of the biological processes that change with aging. Interest in the biology of aging can be traced to
the ancient Egyptians, who sought immortality through biological and spiritual
rejuvenation. The search for "fountains of youth" goes on even today. What
happens at biological and physiological levels as we grow older? What interventions are possible not only to lengthen the life span but also to improve the
quality of health throughout life?

A distinction can be made among biological, social, and psychological aging
(Birren & Renner, 1977). As we saw in the first two chapters, social age and
psychological age are relative measures of an individual's position in and adaptation to an age-ordered social system. Similarly, *biological age*—the individual's "present position with respect to his potential life span," to recall Birren
and Renner's definition (1977, p. 4)—can indicate a person's status relative to
others of the same chronological age.

Often people are described along a biological or physical age dimension; for
example, "She looks younger than her age," or "He looks so much older now."
In our society most adolescents want to look like or be young adults as soon as

possible so that they are entitled to the privileges of adulthood. After the age of 21 or so, however, aspirations to accelerate the aging process seem to diminish. Americans place a negative value on growing older mainly because physical or biological development in adulthood is erroneously equated with disease and death.

Although the incidence of various diseases, such as heart disease or cancer, increases with age, it is important to point out that most diseases can occur at any age. Nevertheless, we are increasingly vulnerable to disease, and the effects of disease on our biological status are generally more harmful, as we grow older. Furthermore, chances of death increase throughout the life span for all species. As early as 1832 the British mathematician Gompertz (1779-1865) observed from actuarial data that our chances of death doubled every seven years after the age of 30. This means that the chances of dying are over 100 times greater for a 75-year-old than for a 30-year-old. Sooner or later, most of us encounter disease, and all of us face death. Although the likelihood of disease and death increases as we grow older, we should not equate these events with the processes of biological aging.

SENESCENCE

What Is Senescence?

Normal aging refers to time-related changes that occur in genetically representative organisms living under normal environmental conditions. The term *senescence* describes that point in the life span when degenerative processes that lead to the breakdown of the organism overtake regenerative biological processes (Rockstein & Sussman, 1979). Thus senescence is a subprocess of normal aging that leads to a "decreased power of survival and adjustment" (Comfort, 1956, p. 190). Four characteristics help to distinguish senescence from other normal aging as well as disease processes (Strehler, 1962).

First, senescence is *a universal process,* observable in all members of the species. Since not all people acquire heart disease, for example, this and other diseases do not represent normal aging. By contrast, age-related decline in the effectiveness of the immune system with advancing age is an example of senescence. Our immune system is responsible for protecting us from infection. When viruses or bacteria manage to get through our various barriers—skin tissue, body temperature, pH level, and saline levels—they need to be destroyed by the formation of antibodies that attack and engulf the invading agent(s). Age-related increases in vulnerability to disease, viruses, and infections, as well as lengthened healing time for older people, are due in part to age-related declines in the efficiency of the immune system. Some researchers have extended this general finding into a theory of biological aging. Similar to the immunological explanations of cancer, one currently popular theory of biological aging is that the immunological system goes out of control by destroying "old" or mutated human cells in the same way it destroys bacteria or other foreign substances.

Second, senescence *takes place gradually*. This characteristic helps to distinguish senescence from accident-induced deterioration, such as reduced blood flow to the brain resulting from a stroke, which would generally show a more rapid and specific course.

Third, senescence is mainly the *result of inner-directed changes*. Various extrinsic influences such as stress, disease, and trauma can accelerate the processes of senescence, and these influences are referred to as *secondary aging*. Senescence, or *primary aging*, in contrast, refers to the intrinsic (for example, cellular), irreversible, and probably genetically programmed changes that occur with age (Selye, 1970).

Fourth, senescence takes place at *many levels within the organism*. With advancing age anatomical, biochemical, physiological, and behavioral changes occur. We shall discuss some of these changes more specifically later in the chapter, but for now it is important to recognize that normal biological aging processes operate at a multitude of levels within the organism.

In sum, senescence describes the normal, age-related deteriorative processes that occur gradually within the organism at many levels. Disease processes are distinct from, but may accelerate, the processes of senescence. The processes of senescence, with or without the help of diseases, ultimately lead to the death of the whole organism.

Senescence versus Senile Dementia

Senescence occurs in different ways and at different rates. Some individuals require full-time nursing care at age 45, whereas others are mentally alert and physically active at age 87. We shall discuss some of the reasons for these variations later. First we need to distinguish between senescence and senile dementia.

Senile dementia is a disease. It is characterized by a progressive decline in memory, attention span, intelligence, personality, and physical self-care skills relative to previously attained levels (Hughes, 1978). Behavioral changes accompanying senility will be discussed in more detail in Chapter 13. Physiologically, senility is associated with vascular disease, loss of neurons in the brain, the buildup of lipofuscan pigment in nerve cells, and increased neurofibrillary tangling of neurons (Storandt, 1980), which will be discussed later in this chapter. Although these pathological changes have been implicated as causes of senescence or normal aging, the degree of such changes is far greater for senile dementia than it is for normal aging.

Senile dementia is the primary diagnosis of almost 1 million adults (about 5 percent) over the age of 65 in the United States (Terry & Wisnewski, 1975). Alzheimer's disease, a type of brain impairment caused by the buildup of senile plaques and neurofibrillary tangling, is the most common type of senile dementia; there are about 600,000 older adults suffering from this disease.

Neuropsychological methods and brain X rays (computerized axial tomography) have aided the diagnosis of brain disease and the study of normal aging of the brain. Neuropsychologists study how variations in the state of the brain influence behavior, and such knowledge has contributed greatly to our understanding of the causes of senescence. Neuropsychological test batteries are used to identify brain areas of impaired functioning. For example, poor performance on paper-and-pencil search tasks requiring the subject to alternate letters and numbers (such as A–1–B–2–C–3–D–4) is associated with generally impaired functioning; whereas poor performance on certain other types of tests suggests more specific types and degrees of impairments (Price, Fein, & Feinberg, 1980; Reitan & Davison, 1974).

Combination computer and X-ray technology has also aided the assessment of brain disease. Sophisticated computer-driven X-ray machines, called computerized axial tomography (CAT) scanners, are now capable of providing very precise three-dimensional pictures of the living brain. Tumors, blood clots, and areas of senile deterioration within the brain can be accurately located and identified with this apparatus. CAT scanners have already been helpful in measuring atrophy and the volume of fluid in the brain of older adults (Jernigan, Zatz, Feinberg, & Fein, 1980).

Better diagnostic procedures often lead to better treatment. For example, it can be determined using a CAT scanner whether a stroke was caused by a cerebral hemorrhage or by a blood clot. Although the behavioral symptoms of clot-induced and hemorrhage-induced stroke are very similar, the types of treatment effective with each are different (Cooper, 1976).

SENESCENCE OF THE BRAIN

Much has been learned about senescence through the study of brain pathology. Many of the pathological characteristics of senile dementia represent the extremes of normal aging processes. The distinction between normal and pathological aging often breaks down when we examine the "normal" aging of brain cells and brain tissue. In this section we will consider the following changes as normal aging processes: synaptic loss and neuronal loss, reduced enzyme activity, increased accumulation in lipofuscan, increased buildup of waste products within brain cells, increased cellular atrophy, and decreased brain weight and brain volume.

Neuronal Loss

There are about 10 billion *neurons,* or nerve cells, in the brain at the point of maximum growth. It is well known that we lose a vast number of brain cells each day as we grow older, though the exact number is unknown. The quoted figures vary widely: Some say we lose 20,000 brain cells per day after the age of 30; others say the figure is closer to 100,000 per day. Consuming excessive amounts of alcohol, smoking cigarettes, and living and breathing in polluted environments all accelerate the rate of neuronal loss (and probably also affect the rate of other degenerative processes). Since not many healthy humans will allow researchers to take tissue samples from their brains, most cell counts are done with nonhuman subjects (mice, for example).

The few morphological studies (studies of structure) that have been done together with autopsy observations suggest that neuronal loss involves only some parts of the brain (Brody, 1973). Critchley (1942) reported greater neuronal loss in the human frontal lobe than in the pons, cerebellum, and brain stem areas (see Figure 3-1). Brody (1973) found a reduction in the number of neurons in all cortical layers after the age of 50, with the greatest losses occurring in the frontal lobe. No age-related losses in neuronal numbers have been found in the facial and cochlear nerves of the brain (Bondareff, 1977; Konigsmark & Murphy, 1972) nor in the inferior olivary nucleus (Monagle & Brody, 1974).

Nerve cells are unable to divide or replicate once their development is complete, but it is important *not* to view neuronal loss as the primary characteristic of brain senescence. Since neuron death appears to be a selective process affecting some areas and brain functions more than others, it is possible that neuronal loss is not a totally destructive process. Dawkins (1971) has suggested

Figure 3-1   Side view of the human brain. (After Ranson & Clark, 1959.)

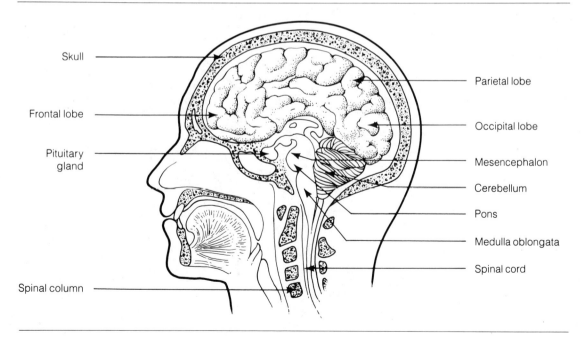

that cell loss may actually reflect the operation of a positive process that selectively eliminates nonessential neurons as we grow older. Furthermore, it is probably beneficial that brain cells do not reproduce as other cells in the body do. The new cells, which would not hold any previously acquired information or experience, would probably mean the loss of memory, personality, identity, and the continuity of consciousness.

A neuron consists of the following parts (see Figure 3-2): a *cell body;* an *axon,* which normally carries information from the cell body to the next neuron; and *dendrites,* which carry entering information from the *synapse* (the junction point of any two neurons) to the cell body. Neurons differ from each other mainly in terms of the number, length, and structure of the dendrites. As

Figure 3-2   Structure of a human neuron. (Adapted from Skoll, 1956.)

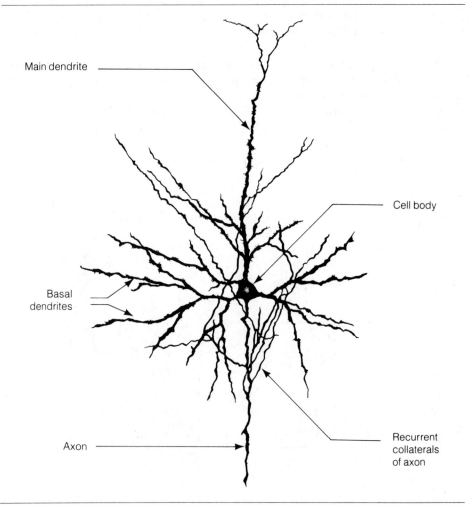

shown in Figure 3-2, human brain cells often have many basal dendrites—secondary dendrites that collect information from many different cells—and many recurrent collaterals branching from the axon that bring inhibitory information back to the cell body.

In addition to age-related reductions in the number of neurons in the brain, there is also an age-related reduction in the number of dendrites attached to some living brain cells (Buell & Coleman, 1979). However, there is also dendritic growth in other nerve cells. Comparing autopsy samples from neurologically normal adults (44–55 years of age), normal elderly adults (68–92 years of age), and elderly adults with senile dementia (70–81 years of age), Buell and Coleman found morphological evidence for *neurological plasticity* in the mature and aged human brain. Dendritic trees were less extensive in the demented brain tissue than in the normal adult brain tissue, and, surprisingly, dendritic trees were more extensive in the nondemented aged than in the adult cases. Buell and Coleman suggested a model of biological aging in which there are both dying neurons with shrinking dendritic trees and surviving neurons with expanding dendritic trees. They proposed that, with advancing age, there is a gradual reduction in the proportion of surviving neurons to dying neurons because of genetic as well as extrinsic (toxicological, infectious) factors.

Brain Size

Humans are very different from all other animals in terms of the relative size of their brain. Some paleontologists think that the size of the human brain has increased by as much as 50 percent in the past half-million years. This amazing rate of growth began about 2 million years ago, and there's no reason to think that the human brain will stop growing at this rate in the next millennium. If each cell were to divide just one more time, the brain would be twice as large as it is now (Rostand, 1973).

We know more about the changes in brain size and weight that take place during the course of an individual life span than we do about the evolutionary trends. Both human and animal studies of brain weight (mass) have consistently demonstrated that there is an age-related size loss from young adulthood to old age (Bondareff, 1977). The average weight of the 20-to-30-year-old human brain is about 1380 grams (3 pounds), compared to an average weight of 1240 grams for an 80-year-old. By the age of 90 years there may be as much as a 20 percent reduction from maximum brain weight (Rockstein & Sussman, 1979). Males and females show similar patterns of brain-weight reduction, with the losses beginning earlier for females than for males (Rockstein & Sussman, 1979). These age-related losses in brain mass can be explained by neuronal loss, atrophy of the neuronal cells, and reduced cerebral blood flow.

Age-related differences in the chemical contents of the human brain might also explain differences in brain weight. For example, there are about 140 grams of protein in the 20-to-30-year-old human brain, compared to about 100 grams in the brain of an 80-year-old. The amounts of water and inorganic salts also decrease with advancing age, while the quantities of potassium and phosphorus increase. Such decreases entail loss of factual information. It is likely that there are cohort as well as age differences in brain weights, which suggest that biological-aging researchers should examine brain-weight differences over time (Brody & Vijayashankar, 1977).

Accumulation of Lipofuscan and Other Matter

With advancing age there is a buildup within the neurons of yellowish pigments collectively called *lipofuscan.* Lipofuscan appears to be a residue or waste product of some sort. Several researchers have shown that lipofuscan buildup can be produced experimentally by a dietary shortage of vitamin E (Omenn, 1977; Zemen, 1974).

The exact chemical composition of neural lipofuscan is still unknown, but it has been shown to contain several amino acids, protein, and lipids (Strehler, 1962). The age-related yellowing of the grey and white matter of the human brain is due to the intraneuronal accumulation of lipofuscan pigments. The age-related increase in lipofuscan begins as early as three months after birth and continues such that, by the age of 35, 84 percent of the neurons have enough lipofuscan to significantly alter the position of the cell nucleus (Brody, 1970; Rockstein & Sussman, 1979).

To date, the effects of lipofuscan buildup on neural functioning are not known. It is possible that lipofuscan has no negative influence on nerve functioning. However, the relatively greater prevalence of lipofuscan in senile dementia patients compared to normals suggests that there might be some connection between lipofuscan buildup and decreased neural functioning.

In addition to the accumulation of lipofuscan there is an age-related buildup of *argyrophilic plaque*—flat, patchlike regions in tissues. The accumulation of such senile plaques at the synapses between neurons reduces the speed of neural conduction and appears to be a cause of Alzheimer's disease. The *cytoplasm,* the viscous component of cells, contains increasing amounts of fatty substances and waste products with advancing age, as well as more *vacuoles,* or fluid cavities, during senescence (Rockstein & Sussman, 1979). As we begin to understand the causes of plaque and lipofuscan buildup, we may be able to develop methods for preventing brain senescence and dementia.

Neurofibrillary Tangling

Some cellular biologists have turned their attention to the study of age-related changes in the structures and mechanism of cell transport. Neurotubules serve as intracellular transport channels and also give shape to the cell (Bondareff,

1977). With aging there is an increased tangling of the neurotubules and neurofilaments, giving the brain a spaghettilike appearance. Electron microscope examinations show these neurotubules to be twisted, abnormal fibers of protein. The dramatic increases in tangling with advancing age may be related to reduced cell metabolism as well as rate of neural conduction. Very little is known about neurofibrillary tangling at this time, although it does seem to be a cause of Alzheimer's disease (Terry & Wisnewski, 1975).

Changes at the Synapse

It is also possible that age-related changes in neural transmitter substances and synaptic morphology affect neural functioning (Bondareff, 1977). The transmission of information from one neuron to another becomes slower with advancing age. In mouse and rat studies it has been found that there are age-associated reductions in the concentration of neural transmitter substances at the synapse. In one postmortem study of humans between the ages of 20 and 50 years, age-related decreases were found in the amount of an enzyme that expedites the synthesis of neurotransmitter substances (McGeer & McGeer, 1976).

Other intracellular substances and intercellular transfer mechanisms may be responsible for age-related changes in neuronal processes. Some of the possible changes are listed in Table 3-1 (see p. 82); readers can find explanations and discussions of them in Finch and Hayflick (1977).

Levels of Senescence

Which analogy is correct?

1 Neurons or nerve cells are like lights on an electric sign; as more and more lights burn out, the message becomes progressively unreadable.

2 Neurons or nerve cells are like flower petals or leaves on a tree; the petals fall from the wilting flower, and the leaves fall from the dying tree.

The first analogy expresses the view that cell loss is the essence of aging. The second analogy expresses the view that cell loss is the outcome of a declining general system. Both views are supported by research, and it would be difficult to reject either in favor of the other. Since senescence takes place on multiple levels within the organism, cell loss can be both an outcome and a cause of aging. Age-related changes at one level interact with changes that occur at other "higher" and "lower" biological levels. In other words, the intracellular and intercellular changes we have discussed interact with changes at the tissue, organ, and whole system biological levels.

Table 3-1 Summary of Senescent Changes at the Intracellular and Intercellular Levels

Accumulation of lipofuscan
Shrinking of the cell nucleus
Enlargement of the nucleolus
Accumulation of vacuoles
Fragmentation of Golgi apparatus
Reduction in the number of mitochondria
Other changes in the mitochondria
Depletion of glycogen in the cell cytoplasm
Increased staining of the cell nucleus
Reduction of vasopressin
Neuronal loss
Increased neurofibrillary tangling
Decreased amount of water and inorganic salts in the cell
Changes in the neurotransmitter substances (serotonin, norepinephrine)
Changes in rate of neural conduction
Decreased amount and distribution of Nissl substance

Some organs (such as the brain) decrease in size, and others (such as the prostate) grow larger, with age (Wallace, 1977). Muscle mass, muscle strength, cardiac output, and breathing capacity also decline with advancing age. Cosmetically, there are changes in the appearance of the skin (wrinkling, sagging, drying out, increased pigmentation, and so on), hair (loss and greying), and facial features (the size of the nose, ears, and eye sockets increases relative to overall face size). There are also age-related postural and motor changes (such as stooped posture, slowed balance, discontinuity of movement). Many of these changes may be caused by cellular aging phenomena. At the same time, such observable physical changes affect other, psychological, aspects of aging, such as feelings of self-worth and attractiveness (Rockstein & Sussman, 1979).

THEORIES OF SENESCENCE

Cellular Theories

Every human begins life as a single cell; by young adulthood there are over 100 trillion cells in the human body. All the cells within an individual do not age and die at the same rate. Because of this fact, one theory of senescence suggests that aging of the whole organism may result from cell loss in critical tissues and organs. Biologists have studied the life span of cells maintained under ideal conditions outside the body (in vitro).

The first significant work on cells raised in vitro was by Alexis Carrel in 1912. Carrel won a Nobel Prize for his work showing that cells derived from chicken heart tissue could live indefinitely, but his finding was later shown to be erroneous. It was Leonard Hayflick's research on cellular aging that helped to clarify that cells cannot live indefinitely. Hayflick (1970, 1974, 1977) has argued that aging can no longer be thought of as resulting from biological changes at the tissue and organ level. Because Hayflick's finding that aging takes place at the cellular level has represented a major breakthrough in the field of biological aging, it is worth looking at the progress of work in this area.

Alexis Carrel was at the Rockefeller Institute when he first put a little sliver of embryonic heart tissue from a chicken into a special culture. This tissue was carefully tended to for the remaining 33 years of Carrel's life and was voluntarily terminated by researchers after 34 years. Carrel's laboratory was well known for its meticulousness—his technicians even wore flowing black gowns with hoods while attending to the heart culture. The "irrefutable" conclusion drawn from the work at Carrel's laboratory was that tissue cells are potentially immortal if raised in vitro as continuously proliferating strains (Harris, 1964).

Other investigators who were unable to establish immortal strains attributed their difficulties to cell contamination or to inadequate laboratory facilities. Hayflick did not specifically set out to challenge Carrel's findings when he and Paul Moorhead began to study human embryonic tissue cultures in the 1950s. However, on the basis of many years of work, Hayflick and his colleagues at the Wistar Institute in Philadelphia and at Stanford University found that cultured normal human embryonic cells underwent a finite number of cell divisions and then died. Cell death was shown to be inherited, fixed, and inevitable after about 50 population doublings (Hayflick, 1970).

Hayflick was not the first to discover that normal cells in vitro have a fixed life span; it was simply that, in the face of the significance of Carrel's work, researchers had been reluctant to believe their own findings (Rosenfeld, 1976). It has since been learned that Carrel's "pure" cultures were inadvertently contaminated by a few stray cells that were continuously adding new cells to the culture. That is, the method of preparing the source of nutrients for the cultures somehow allowed for the introduction of the new cells.

It has now been observed in hundreds of laboratories around the world that there is a finite life span to normal human and animal cells maintained in vitro. Human cells produce 50 plus or minus 10 cell divisions (referred to as *Hayflick's limit*); chicken cells multiply 15 to 35 times (Hayflick, 1970). Nonetheless, the significance of Carrel's early work should not be completely discredited. He was the first to show that cells in vitro can live longer than the whole animal from which they were derived.

The finding that cells or the important components of cells can be replaced only so many times suggests that the basic material of the cell nucleus (that is, the DNA) may be used up as we grow older (Rockstein & Sussman, 1979). This notion is supported by several studies showing an age-related reduction in enzyme activity and production (Wallace, 1977). One popular extension of the "running out of DNA" explanation of aging is that failures in DNA replication lead to the production of malfunctioning RNA and related enzymes. Such malfunctions of replication impair normal growth, as DNA is clearly the "designer gene." Fuller explanations of this theory can be found in Shock (1977b).

Genetic Theories

According to genetic theories, biological aging is controlled by a "prewired" genetic program. Growth in height and weight throughout childhood, pubescent changes during adolescence, greying of hair in middle age, and physical slowing in old age are some examples of inevitable, genetically based development and aging. Menopause in women is an example of a gender-specific type of genetic programming.

Evidence for a genetic theory of aging can also be seen in species other than human beings. Each species has a predictable life span and carries out certain evolutionary functions (mating, length of gestation, parenting, migration, and the like) at relatively fixed times within that allotted life span. Rockstein (1958) has found in species-specific differences in behavior the strongest basis for a genetic theory of aging.

Table 3-2 shows that there are wide variations in longevity among different species. Within-species differences reflect environmental variations as well as genetic divergence within the species. Senescence is rare in natural environments because animals are selectively eliminated by disease and predators before senescent aging becomes evident. As zoo keepers and pet owners know, however, animals can show signs of senescence when they are cared for in "captivity." For example, Dr. Michael Tumbleson has a farm for aging pigs at the University of Missouri. Most farmers do not continue to feed and care for animals after their peak productivity and marketability have been attained, but at Tumbleson's "nursing home," pigs live as long as 22 years (Rosenfeld, 1976).

Studies of the heritability of longevity also suggest that there is a genetic basis to aging. One of the best predictors of the length of your life span is your parents' life span. The most frequently cited studies with humans suggesting

Table 3–2   Typical Life Spans of Some Species

Species	Average length of life (in years)	Exceptions (in years)
Rat	3	5
Guinea pig	3	6
Kangaroo	4–6	23
Rabbit	6–8	15
Pig	10	22
Domestic cat	10–12	26+
Lion	10–15	29
Chimpanzee	15–20	29
Horse	25	50+
Elephant	30–40	71
Human	70–80	130
Eagle	105	115

Adapted from A. K. Lansing, "General Biology of Senescence." In J. E. Birren (ed.), *Handbook of Aging and the Individual.* Chicago: University of Chicago Press, 1959; and the *Information Please Almanac, 1979.* New York: Information Please Publishing, 1979.

that long-lived parents tend to have long-lived children were done in the 1940s and 1950s (see Kallmann & Jarvik, 1959, for a review). However, as Botwinick (1978) pointed out, long-lived parents may generally be healthier, wealthier, and wiser than short-lived parents in ways unrelated to specific genes for longevity. Furthermore, social change and environmental factors such as health, nutrition, and environmental quality can reduce the correlations between parents and offspring. Mothers and daughters and fathers and sons are less likely to experience similar lifestyles today than in the past.

The best evidence for the genetic basis of longevity comes from animal studies (see, for instance, Rockstein, 1958). Recently, geneticists have argued that the key mechanism contributing to longevity is the genetically based ability of cells to repair age-accumulated damage to the DNA molecule (Sacher, 1978; Sacher & Duffy, 1979). Species and organisms within species having relatively efficient "fix-it" genes live relatively longer than their counterparts with less efficient repair systems. Sacher & Duffy (1979), for example, reported that the white-footed mouse fixes DNA damage two-and-a-half times faster than other genetic strains of mice, and its average life expectancy is 8 years, compared to 3.5 years for its cousins. Humans live twice as long as chimpanzees and have a genetic repair rate that is approximately twice as fast.

Sacher (1978) and other gerogeneticists have speculated that longevity is related to genetically controlled reproductive potential. That is, natural selection maintains and extends longevity by improvements made in the genes that repair DNA damage. One problem of the genetic theory of aging is explaining how selective survival can operate after reproduction. Survival of the "fittest" depends on the "fittest" member of the species living long enough to reproduce healthy offspring. Since aging, longevity, and death are postprocreational phenomena, how can genetic theories explain these events (Jarvik, 1975)? There are three possible explanations.

First, from a social evolutionary perspective it is reasonable to argue that stronger parents are better able to protect and provide for their offspring; thus the offspring of "fit" parents are more likely to reach the age of reproduction than the offspring of less fit parents. A second explanation has to do with the pleiotropic effect of genes. *Pleiotropy* is the influence of one gene on two or more characteristics. That is, one gene may influence (1) some characteristic that is important to survival before reproduction and (2) the aging process (Jarvik, 1975). The third possible explanation has to do with the level of genetic control. For example, Dykhuizen (1974) has argued that cell senescence itself, rather than senescence of the organism, is the genetically programmed event selected by evolution. The aging of the total organism depends on what happens to the cells that make up the individual (Hayflick, 1977).

The validity of these three explanations cannot as yet be tested. Nevertheless, most researchers who study aging at a cellular level would agree that to some extent genetic factors control aging, longevity, and death. Many of the manifestations of aging are genetically programmed at the cellular level.

Wear-and-Tear Theories

Gerontologists are just beginning to recognize the potency and pervasiveness of environmental factors on the quality and length of the life span. Many factors, such as comfortable socioeconomic status and satisfying interpersonal relationships, as well as above-average intelligence and a positive self-concept, have been associated with a longer, healthier life span (Pfeiffer, 1977). Although the processes of senescence are biological, environmental events and and contexts can influence them. The most dramatic demonstration, perhaps, is the reports of sudden and unexpected death during periods of environmental stress (Engel, 1971; Rowland, 1977).

In reviewing over 170 cases of stress-induced sudden death, Engel (1971) characterized stress stimuli as "impossible for the victims to ignore and to which their response is overwhelming excitation or giving up, or both." It has been shown that elderly people are especially vulnerable to death following relocation, retirement, or loss of a significant other (Rowland, 1977). There have also been studies showing a "death dip," just before significant holidays; that is, people tend to die after rather than before personally significant events (Baltes, 1977; Rebok & Hoyer, 1979). Further life changes that lead to a feeling of helplessness increase the probability of wear and tear and ultimately death (Rebok & Hoyer, 1979; Seligman, 1975). In Chapter 15 we will consider some of the psychosocial predictors of death.

It has been suggested that the various theories of senescence simply represent different ways of describing "wear and tear" on the organism. Nathan Shock (1977b), for example, observed that the basic notion of the human being "wearing out" has not changed very much since the time of Aristotle; it is mainly the terminology that has changed.

Stress theory is one type of wear-and-tear explanation of aging. According to Selye (1976), stressful events reduce the energy capacities of the aging individual. However, physiological studies of stress with rats have shown that induced stress can actually be beneficial to survival (Fanestil & Barrows, 1965). In human research one critical factor determining whether or not a stressful event will have positive or negative outcomes seems to be whether or not the event can be managed (or controlled) by the individual (Averill, 1973; Rowland, 1977).

Chiriboga and Cutler (1980) have pointed out that any life event that is intense, unexpected, frustrating, fatiguing, or boring can be stress-inducing. Furthermore, individuals differ with regard to what they perceive as stressful. It is becoming increasingly clear that stress involves a combination of external events and the individual's cognitive and physiological response systems (Eisdorfer & Wilkie, 1977; Lowenthal & Chiriboga, 1973). Our coping styles for dealing with stress as well as the stressful events themselves determine our reactions (Lazarus, Averill, & Opton, 1974).

Some geronotologists have made a distinction between primary and secondary aging processes (Selye, 1970). As we saw in the discussion of senescence earlier in this chapter, primary aging refers to changes that are presumed to be genetically programmed (such as brain-cell loss), whereas secondary aging refers to the events and processes that accelerate primary aging. Selye (1970) has pointed out that secondary aging results from the lifelong accumulation of insult to our bodies from stress, emotional tension, physical trauma, and disease. One theory of age-related wear and tear emphasizes the effects of various physical insults on the survival of the organism (Timiras, 1978).

One type of wear-and-tear factor that has been studied in the animal laboratory is cold stress—exposure to cold environments. Some evidence suggests that body temperature is connected with the rate of aging. Fanestil and Barrows (1965) exposed rotifers to water temperatures of 25, 31, and 35 degrees Celsius, and found that the animals in the coldest environment lived *longer*. However, LaBarba, Klein, White, and Lazar (1970) found no effect of early cold stress on the growth of cancers when mice were subjected to a cold treatment of 10 degrees Celsius. These findings bear on the suggestion that there is a link between cancer susceptibility and various environmental and emotional stresses in humans (see Le Shan, 1969).

The research on thermal stress and aging has been guided by hypotheses relating metabolic functions to the total length of life. The idea is that each life is allotted a fixed, predetermined amount of energy. Some organisms and species burn up their allotted energy resources faster than others, owing to both species-specific limitations and individual life history factors.

Recently, S. J. Gould (1978) reviewed the evidence in favor of a fixed-energy hypothesis. He observed that, in general, small animals burn energy more rapidly than do larger animals. Heart rate is faster, pulse is more rapid, respiration is more frequent, and general metabolic rate is faster in smaller animals. This finding is particularly interesting when we consider that smaller animals tend to have shorter life spans than larger animals. Lifetimes may be scaled to different rates of living. In other words, all or most animals may have roughly the same amount of allotted biological time, with some species and individuals using their time faster than others. Humans are the main exception to this size–longevity relationship, because of interventions to prolong the life span. This hypothesis, as well as the specific effects of wear and tear on longevity, represent intriguing areas for future research on aging.

SENESCENCE AND DISEASE

As we saw in Chapter 1, although average life expectancy has increased greatly since 1900, the average *end point* of the human life cycle has not changed much at all since the Middle Ages. People who now reach old age are not living very much longer than people who attained age 60 in the distant past. Nutritional and quality-of-life improvements, as well as medical advances such as new surgical techniques and the control of infectious diseases, have simply enabled more people to reach old age than ever before.

Kohn (1963) showed that, if cancer were eliminated, the average human life span would be extended by only 3 years. If heart disease, cancer, and all other diseases were eliminated, the average length of human life would be increased by only 10 to 15 years. In other words, the elimination of major diseases would enable more people to reach old age, increasing the average life expectancy, but the end point of life would not be dramatically affected. As several writers (for example, Comfort, 1956; Fries, 1980; Hayflick, 1980) have pointed out, the best we can expect is an increasing "rectangularization" of the solid-line curves shown in Figure 3-3. The broken-line curve represents a projection of human survival by age if all diseases were eliminated and people died primarily from senescence.

Heart Disease and Aging

There is still much to be known about various diseases in old age. Heart disease, for example, is the leading cause of death among adults, including those

Figure 3–3   Percentage of survivors (white) by age in the United States in 1900, 1920, and 1940. (Adapted from Hayflick, 1980.)

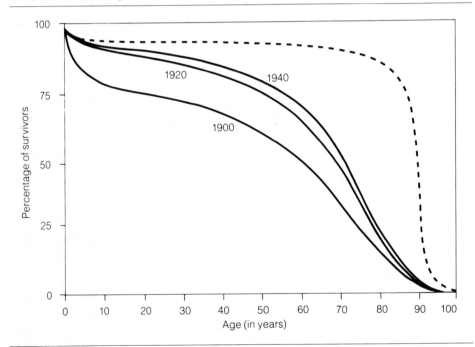

over 65. *Arteriosclerosis* is hardening and thickening of the walls of the arteries, whereas *atherosclerosis* is the buildup of fatty substances on the walls of the arteries. Although arteriosclerosis is generally thought of as a by-product of modern living, it has been around for centuries; evidence of it has been found in ancient Egyptian mummies, for example. Narrowing and hardening of the arteries produce increases in blood pressure, which puts a strain on the heart and on the respiratory and renal systems. The hardening of arteries restricts blood flow by not allowing the arteries to flex as blood is pumped through. Another consequence of arteriosclerotic disease for older persons is a reduction in cerebral blood flow, which affects neural functioning. In the United States about half the deaths for all ages each year can be attributed to arteriosclerosis, including the kind found in coronary heart disease.

Even though heart disease may be found early in life, it is far more common in later adulthood. There are age-related changes in the heart; for example, the left ventricle, the lower compartment of the heart that sends oxygenated blood throughout the body, decreases in size and strength with advancing age. However, the increasing prevalence of heart disease at all ages makes it difficult to determine where normal aging ends and pathological processes begin (Kart, Metress, & Metress, 1978).

Recently, some medical researchers have recommended aspirin as a preventive of heart disease. In one study (see *Newsweek*, October 22, 1979), subjects who took aspirin had fewer strokes and fewer *transient ischemic attacks* (TIAs) than men who did not take aspirin. TIAs, marked by temporary occurrences of slurred speech and blurred vision, are often precursors to a major cerebral vascular accident—stroke. One explanation of how aspirin works to reduce the incidence of heart disease is that it inhibits the production of thromboxane A2, a protein responsible for blood clotting that combines with cholesterol and other substances in the blood to form the senile plaques characteristic of senile dementia and neural senescence.

Several investigators (for reviews see Eisdorfer & Wilkie, 1977; Spieth, 1965) have related cardiovascular pathology to age-associated declines on various types of psychomotor and cognitive tasks. Much of the early research on the distinction between normal aging processes and disease was not informative because of methodological flaws. However, three studies have provided important information.

Wilkie and Eisdorfer (1971), while at Duke University, conducted a longitudinal study of the relationship between intelligence change and blood pressure. Two age groups (60–69 years and 70–79 years at the time of first measurement) were tested, and all participants were free of cardiovascular disease at the first testing. Subjects were divided into three blood pressure groups—normotensive (normal), mildly elevated, and hypertensive. In the 60-to-69-year-old group the three blood pressure groups did not differ from each other in terms of verbal intelligence (as measured by the Wechsler Adult Intelligence Scale). However, there were significant performance changes over the ten-year period. The normotensives showed no decline, the hypertensives showed significant losses, and, surprisingly, the mildly elevated subjects showed a significant improvement in measured intelligence over the ten-year period. In the 70–79 age group none of the hypertensives completed the study, and both the normotensives and the mildly elevated subjects manifested a decline in intellectual performance. This study suggests that, in the absence of cardiovascular pathology, there may be a high degree of stability in intellectual functioning until advanced old age. Another suggestion of the study is that mild increases in blood pressure may serve to maintain intellectual functioning in later life (Eisdorfer & Wilkie, 1971).

Birren, Butler, Greenhouse, Sokoloff, and Yarrow (1963) also found that many of the changes usually attributed to normal aging processes are really a function of cardiovascular pathology. Men between the ages of 71 and 81 and representing a wide range of occupations and lifestyles were selected and grouped on the basis of health status. Healthy older men performed at a much higher level on a variety of psychophysiological measures than their slightly less healthy age peers. Specifically, the healthy older men showed a slightly slower pattern of EEG (electroencephalogram) activity and a reduction in maximum breathing capacity. However, they were not significantly different from younger men in terms of cerebral circulation and metabolism. Healthy older men performed better than their less healthy counterparts on performance measures of intelligence (from the WAIS); further, they were superior to younger men on verbal intelligence (see also Chapter 6). The healthy older men showed increased cerebral blood flow and oxygen uptake and less EEG slowing compared to the less healthy older men. EEG changes in older adults are usually considered to be the result of reduced blood flow to the brain (Marsh & Thompson, 1977). Birren and his associates concluded that both normal aging and disease processes contribute to EEG slowing.

The third study of relevance here also examined the relationships among a variety of intelligence measures (WAIS Digit Symbol and Block Design, Halstead Tactual Performance, and the Trail-making Test [see Reitan, 1955; Reitan & Davison, 1974]) and health status. The subjects were pilots and air-traffic controllers between the ages of 35 and 59, divided into the following four groups: healthy, medicated hypertensives, nonmedicated hypertensives, and nonhypertensives with arteriosclerotic disease. The healthy men performed better than the nonhypertensive men with arteriosclerotic disease, and the nonmedicated hypertensives performed more poorly than the nonhypertensives. On the basis of cross-sectional age comparisons, it was found that healthy older men responded more slowly than healthy young men on psychomotor tasks. In other words, age-related psychomotor slowing occurs even in the absence of cerebral disease factors (Spieth, 1965). It is reasonable to conclude that age-related declines occur even in the absence of pathology, but cardiovascular disease, which becomes increasingly prevalent with advancing age, serves to magnify the normal processes of senescence.

The Ecology of Disease

According to wear-and-tear theories of aging, stressful events are thought to have a cumulative, negative effect on the whole person, which predisposes him or her to disease and, ultimately, death. Older individuals may have several ailments or diseases at once, and the interaction of multiple ailments often complicates treatment efforts. For example, metabolic malfunctions, congestive heart failure, thyroid or vitamin deficiencies, drug toxicities, and liver and kidney failures may occur together; all of these ailments can contribute to brain impairments and senile dementia.

Some diseases exhibit different symptoms at different ages, which can lead to incorrect diagnosis or mistreatment. For example, age-related changes in the removal of substances from the blood by the kidneys can result in little or no sugar in the blood of elderly diabetics, leading to underdiagnosis. Pain sensitivities also affect the reporting of disease. In general, older adults seem less likely to report the symptoms of coronary thrombosis, acute appendicitis, or intestinal obstruction. This may be because the experience of pain is muted by age-related reductions in sensitivity, because older adults have grown accustomed to having many different kinds of aches and pains, or because some older people fear the costs and other consequences of going to a hospital or a doctor's office.

It is also possible that etiologies (the causes of disease) are qualitatively different with aging. For example, anxiety may reduce the cognitive functioning of older adults as much as or more than it does the functioning of younger adults, yet the manifestations of anxiety are different. Younger adults are more likely to exhibit increased heart rate, perspiration, and respiration, whereas the symptoms of anxiety for older adults are more likely to be feelings of confusion and mental stress (Hoyer & Plude, 1980).

Preventive Health Care

One of the current trends in the health sciences is toward making individuals aware that they are responsible for their own health and giving them the knowledge they need to affect it. Many of the infectious diseases that plagued earlier generations have been totally eliminated for all practical purposes, and we are left with diseases such as arteriosclerosis that are related to lifestyle, diet, exercise, nutrition, and environmental quality. These causes are prescriptive risk factors that individuals can control for themselves.

There has been a profound consciousness raising with regard to health—or wellness—in American society. *Wellness* refers to a positive, ongoing approach on the part of the individual to becoming healthier and staying healthy. The treatment of disease and injuries is the concern of professional health-care providers, but the prevention of disease and injury is a personal responsibility.

Not all physicians advocate the wellness movement. Some argue that their patients prefer not to be responsible for their own health. Other critics view wellness as a fad, and they are concerned about the credentials of wellness experts and the economic implications of wellness for the medical profession. Physicians in favor of this movement point out that nearly 50 percent of the people seen on a private outpatient basis do not really need medical treatment. They argue that their time would be better spent if the public were more informed on disease prevention and health-maintenance strategies.

Perhaps wellness should be viewed not as a replacement for but as an adjunct to a physician's treatment. All adults in modern societies should know the symptoms and risk factors associated with major diseases such as cancer and heart disease. Part of the wellness movement involves patient education with regard to both diagnosis and treatment. People of all ages need to know when to go to the doctor or the hospital; but few heart attack victims, for example, even recognize what is happening when they have their first attack. In a more medically educated society the "medicine man" becomes demystified. Physicians no longer talk down to patients when informing them of symptoms to watch for, things to do and not do, and so forth. We have had child-care manuals for a while, but only recently is basic adult health-care information being made available. All the "owner's manuals" that are now beginning to inform us about self-health are indicative of the wellness trend in American society.

Physical Fitness and Aging

Just over 15 years ago Roger Bannister, at the age of 25, became the first human to run the distance of a mile in just under 4 minutes. Since that time over 500 runners have gone under Bannister's record. New athletic records continue to be set and broken in all sports.

At what age is the individual in optimal physical condition? What age-related factors influence the fitness level and potential of adults? The answer to these questions obviously depends on the nature of the activity. However, with the growing emphasis on health and physical fitness in the United States, there has been a general trend for older people to be increasingly active. In the 1950s and 1960s relatively few older people entered athletic competitions. In 1975 there were over 1400 entrants over the age of 40 in the World Masters track and field competition held in Toronto; many of these athletes were over 60 years old.

Dr. Paul E. Spangler was one of the participants in the World Masters competition. Spangler did not formally participate in any athletics while in high school or college; he began jogging in 1966 at the age of 67. At the 1975 Masters competition he set 14 world records in his age category (Webb, Urner, & McDaniels, 1977).

Webb, Urner, and McDaniels measured various physiological characteristics of Paul Spangler while he was involved in his training program. The study revealed a physiological system with characteristics approaching those of younger athletes. Some age-related decrements found for heart rate, maximum oxygen consumption, and maximum pulmonary ventilation were attributed to age-related training considerations as well as to a combination of circulatory, pulmonary, and metabolic factors.

Several other studies have found improved physiological functioning in the aged as a result of moderate exercise (DeVries, 1975). Apparently, it is not age or time alone that causes a decline in physiological capacity. One of the main contributing factors is a sedentary lifestyle. With a well-planned and reasonable physical exercise program even very old individuals can maintain or regain their health.

SEXUALITY AND AGING

Both the nature and the frequency of sexual activity change as people grow older. Part of the change can be attributed to senescent changes that affect sexual capacity and function. We shall first describe the physiology of the human sexual response and then highlight the developmental trends in regard to sexual functioning.

In a classic study Masters and Johnson (1966) observed the physiological responses that occur in men and women during sexual activity. Their study was based on the responses of 382 female and 312 male volunteers. Four phases of sexual activity were identified:

1   *Excitement.* The male and female become sexually aroused. Heart rate, blood pressure, and muscle tension increase. In the male the penis becomes erect due to vasocongestion; in the female there is increased vaginal lubrication and enlargement due to vasocongestion of the clitoris.

2   *Plateau.* In both males and females sexual readiness is accelerated in this stage. Heart rate, blood pressure, muscle tension, and respiration increase. Vasocongestion and vaginal lubrication continue.

3   *Orgasmic.* The female's orgasmic response is characterized by contractions of the orgasmic platform, and the male's response is characterized by ejaculation. An orgasm is generally limited to a few seconds for the male; for the female the contractions of the orgasmic phase may be longer lasting. Also, males exhibit a rest interval (or *refractory period*) between successive ejaculations, in which an erection cannot be achieved; females are less likely to show a refractory period.

4   *Resolution.* During this phase both males and females return to a less aroused state.

Knowledge of sexual changes with aging is informative both in what it reveals and what it does not reveal about changing sexual needs, capacities, and interests of older people. More is said about the sexual interests of different-aged adults in Chapter 10; here we highlight change in sexual physiology with age. Males are affected by aging as follows (Ludeman, 1981; Masters & Johnson, 1970):

1   More time is needed to achieve a penile erection and to reach orgasm.
2   The intensity of orgasm is generally reduced.
3   The quantity of ejaculation is reduced.
4   More time is needed to achieve a second erection and orgasm (in other words, a longer refractory period).

The following changes affect older women (Masters & Johnson, 1970):

1   The vagina is less elastic and less lubricated.
2   Vaginal tissues are more easily irritated.
3   Orgasms may be less pleasurable.
4   Orgasmic length may be shorter.

Although this list seems to support the myth of the sexless aged, there is no evidence that these physiological changes in themselves limit sexual activity or pleasure. For example, Masters and Johnson (1966) reported that women in their 60s who had coitus once or twice a week were able to expand and lubricate the vagina effectively. Katchadowrian and Lundes (1975) and Shearer and Shearer (1977) also reported no physiological limitations to sexual capacity for either women or men with advancing age.

Age-related changes in the biological factors that affect sexual behavior are difficult to assess because of the many psychosocial factors that also play a role in human sexuality.

Kinsey, Pomeroy, Martin, and Gebhard (1953) reported that reductions in the frequency of intercourse in late adulthood are due mainly to sexual waning on the part of men. Christenson and Gagnon made the following observation on age differences in sexuality: "It is probably a general rule that she sets the upper limit on coital activity and that the husband probably sets the lower limit" (1965, p. 355). Support for this observation comes from a study of married couples, in which the wives were younger (age 50), older (age 60), and the same age (age 55) as their husbands (Kinsey et al., 1953). It was found that wives with older husbands had the least sexual activity, and wives with younger husbands had the most sexual activity.

One of the best predictors of sexual activity in later life is the individual's earlier levels of sexual activity. Second, because in middle and late adulthood

It is normal for sexual desire to persist throughout life. Throughout adulthood, people who are more comfortable with sexual feelings and who have a responsive partner are more active sexually.

sexuality is generally viewed as respectable only in the context of marriage, the fact that most older men are married and most older women are widows affects the likelihood of sexual activity in later life. Even more important is the meaning of the sexual experience. On the one hand, an older man or woman might feel less attractive than in the past and might avoid sex because of the risk of rejection or embarrassment. On the other hand, couples often develop an increasingly close relationship with advancing years, and sexuality, albeit less frequent, is one expression of deep intimacy. However, perhaps because of cohort differences in attitudes toward sexual behavior, older people are generally not very open in discussing their sexual patterns.

Because of the difficulties in studying human sexual behavior, many researchers have used animal subjects in their studies of age differences in sexuality (see Elias & Elias, 1977). In laboratory rats and guinea pigs mating behavior increased up until about "mid-life" and then gradually declined in frequency (Antliff & Young, 1957; Jakubczak, 1964). Much of the work with lower animals is concerned with identifying the hormonal factors that control sexual behavior. For example, Jakubczak (1964) reported that age-related reductions in mating behavior occur before the age deficits in androgen, the male sex hormone. In mature humans cases of continued sexual activity following removal of the gonads suggests that sexual behavior is no longer dependent on glandular secretions.

SLEEPING, DREAMING, AND SENESCENCE

Being awake is very different physiologically from being asleep. Why do we sleep and dream? How do our patterns of sleeping and dreaming change as we grow older? The electroencephalogram (EEG) has been a useful tool in answering these questions. The EEG and the different types of brainwaves will be discussed in more detail in the next section.

With the help of the EEG several stages of sleeping and dreaming have been identified. The first stage of sleep is so light that it is probably best considered the last stage of wakefulness. We might "drift off" into minidreams or feel as if we are sinking. In this stage the EEG alpha rhythms disappear and are gradually replaced by low-amplitude, fast, irregular rhythms (see Figure 3-4). In stages 2 and 3 the person begins to sleep more soundly. Sharply pointed waves known as *sleep spindles* appear within 30 to 50 minutes of sleep onset.

Stage 4 is the deepest sleep of all. It is difficult and unpleasant for us to be awakened at this point. The EEG pattern during stage 4 is characterized by high-amplitude, slow waves. Our metabolism drops, heart rate decreases, and muscles relax, yet our bodies perspire because the part of the cerebral cortex that normally inhibits sweating is also at rest. If we are disrupted from stage 4 sleep, we are confused and disoriented. If we are allowed to stay asleep, brain activity becomes vigorous, and there are darting rapid eye movements underneath the eyelids. This stage is known as REM sleep.

There are now numerous published studies showing that dreaming pro-

Figure 3-4   EEG patterns for different stages of sleep and wakefulness. (After Webb, 1968.)

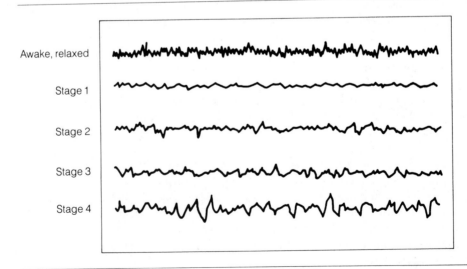

duces changes in EEG brainwave activity and eye movements (Stoyva & Kamiya, 1968). There is even some evidence to suggest that changes in physiological measures are related not only to the level and amount of dreaming, but also to dream content. An unusually high up–down pattern of eye movements was found for one subject who reported dreaming of someone going up a staircase (Dement & Kleitman, 1957).

Figure 3-5 shows the changes over the life span in the average amounts of sleep and REM sleep. It can be seen that the percentage of daily REM sleep declines with age, beginning in early childhood. The small rise in the percentage of REM sleep during adolescence and early adulthood does not reflect an increase in the amount of REM sleep, but rather a decline in total amount of sleep time (Roffwarg, Munzio, & Dement, 1966).

Feinberg and his associates (Feinberg, 1974; Feinberg & Carlson, 1968) have shown that there is a decrease in stage 4, or slow-wave, sleep and a slowing of EEG spindle activity with advancing age. The amplitude and duration of the slow waves also decrease with aging (Agnew, Webb, & Williams, 1967). The consequences of these age-related declines in REM and slow-wave sleep are not fully known, but there is reason to believe that the absence of deep sleep has serious negative effects on cognition and emotionality.

Insomnia, the inability to sleep, is a problem that plagues people of all ages. In New York City and Los Angeles, for example, all-night walking tours are arranged for insomniacs. Biochemists who study sleep are just beginning to know how sleep and wakefulness are regulated in the body. It appears that the enzyme glucose 6 phosphatase in neurons is more active during sleep than during wakefulness. The supply of glycogen in the brain increases rapidly during slow-wave sleep and is then quickly discharged as we wake up. The glucose discharge appears to give us the necessary energy kick to wake up. Perhaps it will someday be possible to synthesize the natural biochemical changes associated with sleep and wakefulness—to eliminate insomnia and other sleep disturbances at all age levels!

REVERSING SENESCENCE

According to Birren and Renner (1977), much of the experimental research on aging began when it was observed that, under a wide variety of laboratory tests, older adults tend not to perform as well as younger adults. How fixed and inevitable are age-related deficits? Can psychological intervention strategies be used to alleviate and prevent age-related losses? One of the most established findings in aging is the tendency toward slowing of physiological and psychological functioning (Botwinick, 1978). Is such slowing physiologically based, and can it be speeded up somehow through intervention? Recently, several investigators have been able to provide evidence on the reversibility of age-related biological decline (Woodruff, 1975).

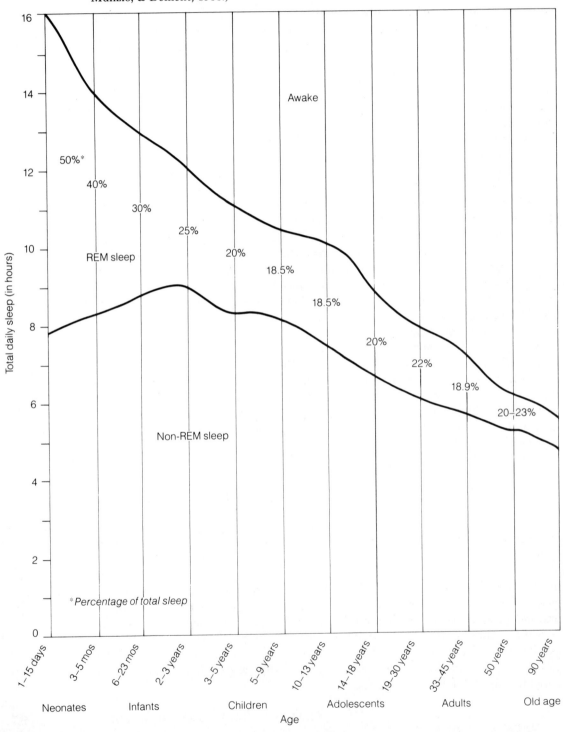

Figure 3-5 Changes in sleep patterns over the life span. (Adapted from Roffwarg, Munzio, & Dement, 1966.)

The electroencephalogram was used as early as 1932 to describe differences in brain activity between young and old individuals (Marsh & Thompson, 1977). An EEG can identify individual differences and changes in brainwave activity along several frequency bands called *alpha, beta, theta,* and *delta,* or a combination of *theta* and *delta* referred to as *slow-wave activity.* The alpha rhythm, in the 8 to 13 Hz range, is generally the most prominent EEG rhythm of humans. Alpha waves are indicative of a relaxed but alert state of mind. Alpha rhythm is recorded from electrodes placed on the sides or back of the head with the subject's eyes closed. Brazier and Finesinger (1944) reported that the mean alpha frequency for young adults ranges from 10.2 to 10.5 Hz. Busse and Obrist (1963) reported a range of 8.0 to 9.7 Hz for adults over 70 years of age. Hospitalized older adults and patients with deteriorated mental abilities show lower alpha frequencies than healthy adults (Obrist & Busse, 1965). Similarly, longitudinal studies with healthy adults in their 60s and 70s show a linear decline in alpha frequency on the average of about .08 Hz per year, but there are individual exceptions (Wang & Busse, 1969).

What causes the age-related decline in alpha frequency? Work by Walter Obrist and his colleagues suggests the role of decreased cerebral blood flow leading to *ischemia*—a localized diminution of arterial blood supply approximating a stroke on a small scale—and *hypoxemia*—a condition of deficient oxygen in the arterial blood supply. Obrist and Bissel (1955), for example, compared age-matched men with and without arteriosclerosis and found lower alpha frequencies in the arteriosclerotic subjects. The vascular insufficiency explanation applies not only to age-related slowing of alpha frequency but also to age-related losses in memory and cognitive functioning due to aphasia, stroke, and heart disease (see Abrahams, 1976; Obrist, 1972; Schultz, Dineen, Elias, Pentz, & Wood, 1979).

The overall tendency toward EEG slowing with advancing age led Surwillo (1963) to propose that the central nervous system is the master timing mechanism for speed of behavior. Woodruff (1972) conducted a biofeedback study with young and elderly adults in order to test the reversibility of alpha frequency slowing. *Biofeedback* is a technique for providing individuals with immediate information about the status of their bodily processes. Polygraphs, or lie detectors, are one type of biofeedback instruments. Immediate changes in heart rate, skin resistance, muscle tension, and brainwave feedback are shown to the subject via continuous changes in a tone, a light, or a digital display. The subject learns to change his or her brainwave activity, for example, simply by concentrating and paying attention to the feedback. Woodruff demonstrated that older adults were just as capable as younger adults of controlling their brainwave activity. However, Woodruff's data did not suggest that brain activity is the master timing mechanism because biofeedback training did not have any effect on the reaction time of the subjects. Biofeedback has been shown to be a useful tool for treating headaches, chronic back pain, hypertension, and high blood pressure, and may prove to be even more widely therapeutic in the next five years (see, for example, Birnbaumer & Kimmel, 1979). There is even the possibility in the near future of cerebellum pacemakers analogous to heart pacemakers, which, when implanted in the brain, would serve to regulate physiological and behavioral functioning (Restak, 1979).

A final issue related to the reversibility of biological senescence is the degree of correspondence between biological aging and psychological aging. In the early 1920s J. R. Kantor suggested that biological senescence precedes but does not cause psychological aging (Delprato, 1980). Kantor's theory of *reactional biography* suggests that, although biological decline is real, and largely irreversible, there is no point at which the psychological growth of the individual necessarily ceases. In other words, psychological development can take place independent of irreversible senescence. The extent of such growth obviously depends on the psychological measures being investigated. Although Kantor greatly underestimated the human capacity to resist senescence, his idea that biological senescence does not restrict psychological growth in old age is an important contribution.

BIOETHICS AND SOCIOBIOLOGY

Less than a decade ago the idea of a heart or brain pacemaker was in the realm of science fiction. Now, not only are heart transplants fairly common, but you can even buy a head transplant if you want it or need it—the price is 1 million dollars (Restak, 1979). We are living in a time of "biological revolution." Mass cloning of humans, test-tube babies, individuals created to genetic specification, behavioral control through chemicals, and the transplantation of new body parts are no longer Orwellian concepts. The technology is increasingly available.

These discoveries often raise ethical issues that we as individuals and as a society have not faced before. For example, is conceiving children a right or a privilege? Do you plan to prolong the length of your life by artificial means? Are you in favor of or opposed to the prolonging of life for others? Should defective fetuses be aborted? What about euthanasia? In the past, many of the decisions were left to fate. *Bioethics* is an emerging discipline that combines biological knowledge with human values. Potter (1971) stated that the goal of this field is to relate our knowledge of the biological world to the formulation of policies designed to promote social good. Potter also noted that codes of bioethics should never be considered finished but should undergo continual reexamination in light of new knowledge.

Many new bioethical issues are raised as human beings gradually achieve control over the processes of senescence and death that have always obsessed them. Many new bioethical issues will be raised as we achieve greater scientific understanding of the processes of senescence and death. As a guide to decision making for ourselves and for others, humans of all ages must recognize their position of interdependence and reciprocity with all other forms of life and with the environment. Kieffer (1979) noted that the principle of reciprocity involves recognition of mutual obligation. What is the good life? What is natural senescence or a natural death as the technology becomes increasingly available to influence these processes? What is really harmful and what is really beneficial? The values that we place on life, as well as our accumulating biological knowledge and technology, serve as the basis for answering these questions and others not yet formulated.

The emerging field of *sociobiology*, representing the synthesis of biological knowledge of evolution with social issues, also provides a way to approach bioethical concerns. E. O. Wilson (1975) has defined sociobiology as "the systematic study of the biological basis of all social behavior" (p. 4). The main concern of sociobiology is social evolution—the social consequences of continuous genetic evolution. Although individuals and populations do not evolve directly by genetic selection processes, populations consisting of individuals have genetic reservoirs (gene pools), and it is the gene pool that evolves through natural selection processes.

Sociobiology's challenge is to understand the consequences of evolving gene pools for the future of humanity. Earlier in this chapter, for example, we mentioned Sacher's (1978) work on the genetic basis of prolonging the life span. Campbell (1975) pointed out that contemporary humanity is the joint product of biological and social evolution; the issues are very complex, and the data currently available are very incomplete. Recent interest in the synthesis of accumulating biological and social knowledge is clearly one of the most significant trends in contemporary science. It is one that is likely to have profound consequences for the development of individuals throughout the life course and for the survival of humanity.

SUMMARY

1   *Normal aging* refers to time-related changes in genetically representative organisms living under normal environmental conditions. A subprocess of normal aging is *senescence,* the stage in the life span in which degenerative processes leading to the breakdown of the organism overtake regenerative biological processes. Changes that are considered part of senescence are universal, gradual, and primarily inner-directed; they take place at several levels within the organism. With advancing age, vulnerability to disease increases. In addition, the probability of death increases as age increases.

2   Normal aging involves several changes in the brain: synaptic and neuronal loss, reduced enzyme activity, increased accumulation of lipofuscan, increased buildup of waste products within brain cells, increased cellular atrophy, and decreased brain weight and brain volume. It is important to distinguish between senescence and *senile dementia,* a disease that leads to a progressive decline in functioning.

3   The rate of aging is different for different organs, tissues, and their constituent cells. Many researchers have observed that there is a finite life span to normal human and animal cells maintained in vitro (outside the body, in ideal laboratory conditions). Such research serves as the basis for a fixed life span *cellular* theory of aging.

4   *Genetic* theories of aging propose that biological aging is controlled by a "prewired" genetic program. Each species has a predictable life span and carries out certain evolutionary functions (such as mating, length of gestation, parenting, and migration) at relatively fixed times within that allotted life span. Support for a genetic theory of aging comes from evidence of species-specific differences and from the heritability of longevity within species. However, a genetic theory of aging has difficulty explaining how selective survival can operate after reproduction.

5   *Wear-and-tear* theories of aging emphasize the effects of various physical insults on the survival of the organism. One variety of a wear-and-tear theory is stress theory, linking environmental events to increased probability of senescence and death. However, it is clear that no simple explanation of aging, such as the "wearing out" of the organism, can explain the biological changes observed.

6   Humans have a finite life span; even if heart disease, cancer, and all other diseases were eliminated, the average life span would be extended by only 10 to 15 years. Diseases commonly occurring in later life often make it difficult to determine what normal aging is like. Heart disease is very common in later life, and serves to magnify "normal aging" deficits in performance. Both preventive health care and physical fitness can help older individuals maintain or regain their health; a sedentary lifestyle contributes to early decline.

7   The nature and frequency of sexual activity change with increasing age. The patterns of slowed responsivity reflect normal physical aging processes. However, sexual activity is related more to social and psychological factors than to biological changes. Generally, sexual interest and sexual activity continue throughout adulthood for those who are moderately healthy, are interested in sex as young adults, and have an acceptable partner available.

8   Patterns of sleeping and dreaming show changes with age. REM sleep is the deepest sleep, a period of vigorous brain activity, lowered metabolism, relaxed muscles, and decreased heart rate. The percentage of daily REM sleep declines with age, beginning in early childhood. The consequences are not clear, but biologists suspect that the absence of deep sleep has negative effects on cognition and emotionality.

9   Physiological declines can be modified, though it is not clear how much or what the consequences are. Some declines can be reversed by providing a replacement for a damaged organ; heart transplants, for example, are no longer experimental. However, the availability of such biological interventions raises complex ethical issues about their use. The field of bioethics struggles to integrate human values with biological knowledge and technology.

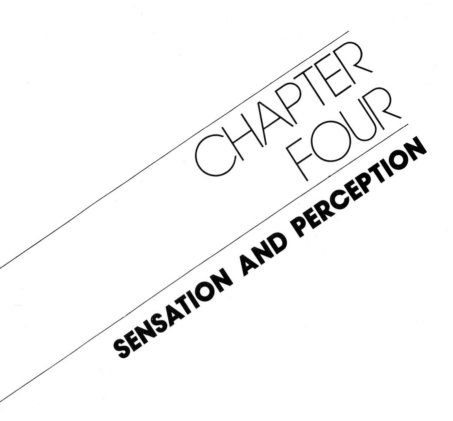

CHAPTER FOUR

SENSATION AND PERCEPTION

The study of sensation and perception is concerned mainly with how we take in, organize, and experience the physical world around us. There are many aspects to this study. One purpose is to explain intraindividual change and interindividual differences in perceptual experience. Why and how do such changes occur? Are the age-related changes genetically programmed or are they experientially produced? Just how subjective or objective are our perceptions of the world around us?

Since the beginning of this century much has been learned about sensory and perceptual structures and how they operate. Less is known about time-ordered and age-ordered changes in perception because it is difficult to study continuous changes in perceptual experiences. Perceiving depends on both previous and present stimulation, and laboratory researchers are just beginning to take into account the background of the perceiver and developmental changes not only in perceptual structures but also in time-related experience. Developmental psychologists are particularly interested in studying changes in the various sensory and perceptual mechanisms that result from maturation and experience; age-related physical and structural changes within the sense organs and the brain go only part of the way toward explaining perceptual functioning in adulthood and old age.

Research in perceptual aging is progressing rapidly along several lines of inquiry. One direction is at the basic sensory level of analysis. A second is the study of the selective aspects of perception: How is it that we direct our attention to some objects, images, or thoughts and not to others? The third direction concerns the interrelationships between cognition (our thoughts, attitudes, beliefs, expectancies) and perceptual and sensory processing. How and to what extent does the individual voluntarily control his or her perceptions? Neisser (1976) has posited that we cannot perceive unless we "expect" to perceive something. What we anticipate actually affects what we see. So, to comedian Flip Wilson's "What you see is what you get," we can add "What you expect is what you see."

In the sections that follow we will discuss some of the recent developmental findings in the areas of sensation and perception. For a thorough understanding of adulthood changes in perception we will look at change throughout the information-processing system, including changes in memory (Chapter 5) and intelligence (Chapter 6).

SENSORY PROCESSES AND AGING

What color is the room where you are now? Can you hear the sounds of any other people? Is it warm or cold where you are? *All that we know about the world comes to us through the senses.* Without the information provided us by the processes we call vision, hearing, touch, taste, and smell, there would be no mental experience, consciousness, or life. As we grow older, our sensory systems change.

One way of knowing how these sensory systems change is to simulate aging processes. Pastalan and his colleagues at the University of Michigan designed eye glasses that *simulated* the aging of the visual world (Pastalan, Mautz, & Merrill, 1973). Wearing these lenses is like seeing through "aged eyes." Two differences in visual experience become apparent with this simulation. First, there is an increased susceptibility to glare, especially from bright illumination reflected from glossy floor and wall surfaces. Second, there is increased blurring, making it difficult to establish perceptual contrasts. For example, when wearing these lenses you would have difficulty finding a room exit if the door and the walls were the same color. Figure 4-1 illustrates the effects of increased glare and blurring on visual experience.

We know the most about the visual system, but it is also possible to simulate changes in hearing, taste, smell, sense of pain, and touch. What would it be like to spend a day with cotton in your ears? How would others respond to your reduced auditory capacity? In general, simulations help us to know about sensory processes and how they change with aging (Sjostrom & Pollack, 1971). However, since sensory declines usually occur gradually over a lifetime, one criticism of simulation procedures is that they exaggerate the experience of gradual sensory decline.

Figure 4-1 A face under normal and blurred conditions. (Courtesy of R. Salzbank.)

The practical value of research on sensory aging is in terms of how it can affect the quality of life. For example, Pastalan's lenses were originally designed for the benefit of interior designers and architects who construct nursing homes and other facilities for the aged. Simulation research strategies can be used in designing optimal environments that take into account the diminished sensory and perceptual capacities of older adults. The next sections of this chapter present the findings of studies on age-related changes in vision, hearing, taste and smell, touch, thermoregulation, and pain. Table 4.1 summarizes the main aspects of these systems.

VISION

By the age of 50 or 55 just about everyone needs corrective lenses of some type—usually reading glasses (Timiras, 1972). Older people simply don't see as clearly as when they were younger. More specifically, we can pinpoint the following effects of aging on visual functioning: reduced visual acuity, reduced accommodation, reduced capacity to adjust to changes in illumination (dark adaptation), shift in color vision, and increased susceptibility to some types of visual illusions.

Some of the aging changes that occur are due to changes in the lens of the eye (see Figure 4-2). The function of the lens is to bring an image into focus at a point on the retinal surface called the *fovea*. With advancing age the lens becomes less flexible (Fozard, Wolf, Bell, McFarland, & Podolsky, 1977). Visual acuity declines as the lens becomes increasingly less plastic and less adjustable.

Visual Acuity

There is a tendency for the point of clearest near vision to move outward after age 40 (Weale, 1963). Near vision is assessed by having the individual read printed letters at distances of 12 inches and less. Distant *visual acuity*, or

Table 4-1   Aspects of Human Sensory Experience

Sense	Physical stimulus	Sense organ and receptors	Types of sensation
Vision	Light waves	Eye: rods and cones of retina	Hue, brightness, saturation
Hearing	Sound waves	Ear: hair cells of organ of Corti	Pitch, loudness, tone, auditory complexity
Smell	Molecules of gaseous substances	Nose: hair cells in the olfactory epithelium	Odors
Taste	Molecules of soluble substances	Tongue: taste cells in taste buds	Salt, sour, sweet, bitter
Skin senses	Mechanical stress or temperature change at the skin	Nerve endings in the skin	Pressure, pain, warmth, cold

Figure 4–2   A side view of the human eye.

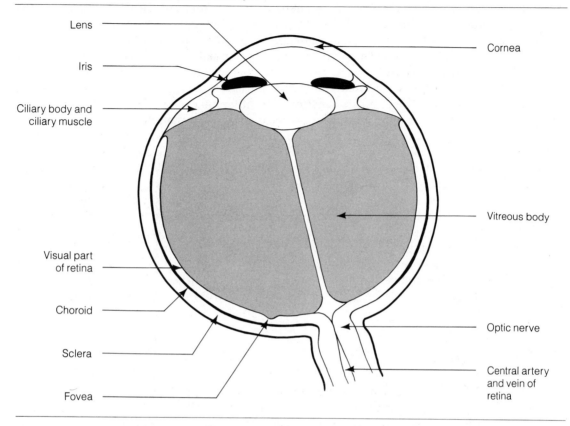

Lens

Iris

Ciliary body and
ciliary muscle

Cornea

Vitreous body

Visual part
of retina

Choroid

Sclera

Fovea

Optic nerve

Central artery
and vein of
retina

sharpness, is usually assessed by having the individual read printed letters of different sizes on a Snellen or Snellen-type eye chart at a distance of 20 feet. If the individual reads letters that are normally seen at 50 feet, visual acuity is recorded as 20/50. Less than 10 percent of 80-year-olds have "normal" 20/20 vision, compared to about 30 percent of 70-year-olds and 40 percent of 60-year-olds. The incidence of poor visual acuity (20/50 or worse) increases from less than 10 percent to more than 30 percent over the 60-to-80-year age range (data from U.S. National Health Survey, 1968).

Accommodation

Accommodation is the process whereby the lens changes its shape in order to bring about a focused image. Like general visual acuity, accommodation is affected by decreased flexibility of the lens.

The ciliary muscles that control the shape of the lens tend to weaken as we grow older. As a result, there is less pressure on the fluid in the eyeball, causing the shape of the eyeball to change slightly from spherical to oval along the horizontal dimension. When the eyeball is rounder, near objects tend to be in focus; as the eyeball changes shape, far objects are more likely to be in focus. This change, known as *presbyopia,* or far-sightedness, becomes increasingly likely with aging.

Another age-related change in the lens is that it undergoes an increased yellowing, which affects sensitivity to different colors (Coren & Girgus, 1972). Light, the stimulus for vision, is measured in wavelengths, and the human eye is sensitive to light at wavelengths between 400 and 700 nanometers (nm). The different colors can be perceived at the indicated wavelengths: violet (450nm), blue (470nm), green (510nm), yellow-green (560nm), yellow (580nm), orange (600nm), and red (650nm). Older people can discern colors at the upper end of the visual spectrum (yellow, orange, and red) more easily than they can colors at the lower end (violet, blue, and green). A rough simulation of the effects of yellowing would be to view the world through yellow sunglasses. Color perception is a very subjective and idiosyncratic phenomenon—for example, is red the same when seen on a sunny day and on a cloudy day, or is your perception of the color orange the same under different conditions of illumination? Consequently, age-related shifts in the color spectrum go largely unnoticed by most individuals.

Cataracts

The most common visual handicap in old age is *cataracts.* A cataract is an opaque lens, but most researchers and writers today use the term to describe a process. The lens of the eye consists of fibers that are being formed throughout life. As new fibers are added to the lens, existing fibers become increasingly compressed, causing reduced transparency. Increased yellowing with advancing age also contributes to the general loss of transparency of the lens. After the age of 20, increasing levels of illumination are needed in order to maximize vision. A cataract operation involves the surgical removal of the lens. In practically all cases it is a relatively simple, safe, and effective treatment for cataracts. Eye glasses or contact lenses serve the focusing function after a cataract operation.

Dark Adaptation

Dark adaptation is the adjustment of the visual system to low light intensities. As we grow older, it takes longer for the eye to adapt to changes in illumination (McFarland & Fisher, 1955). Moreover, visual acuity under low illumination is less clear with advancing age. On the average, 80-year-olds need over 200 times as much light as 20-year-olds to see as well (Domey, McFarland, & Chadwick, 1960).

Age changes in dark adaptation and sensitivity to light can be explained partly in terms of retinal metabolism. A chemical chain of events begins when rhodopsin, a substance found in the receptors responsible for low-light vision (the rods), interacts with light. Changes in the quantity or quality of rhodopsin may be responsible for reduced dark adaptation in older adults (McFarland & Fisher, 1955). Vitamin A deficiencies are related to inadequate production of rhodopsin and consequent "night blindness." Age deficits in dark adaptation and visual acuity have also been explained in terms of the age-related decrease in the diameter of the pupil (Birren, Casperson, & Botwinick, 1950; Weale, 1963). *Senile miosis,* the constriction of the pupillary opening with advancing age, is most evident at low and intermediate levels of illumination (Weale, 1963).

Critical Flicker Frequency

The overall sensitivity of the visual system can be estimated by *critical flicker frequency* (usually abbreviated CFF). If the rate at which a light is flashed is gradually increased, the observer will at some point see a continuous light. CFF is the point at which a flickering light is perceived as a steady light source. Higher CFFs are indicative of more sensitive visual functioning. With advancing age, there is a lowering of CFF (Corso, 1971; Weale, 1965). This decline is due in part to peripheral factors such as lens yellowing, but central nervous system factors that control the rate of visual information processing are also responsible for reductions in visual sensitivity with advancing age.

Illusions

Illusions are simple line drawings in which *perceived* size or shape differs from the *actual* size or shape of some object. Some of the typical visual illusions used in research are illustrated in Figure 4-3. In the Mueller-Lyer illusion the line marked *y* appears longer than the line marked *x*, although both lines are really the same length. In the Titchener Circles illusion the center circle marked *Y* is commonly perceived to be larger than the center circle marked *X*; in fact, both are the same size.

Susceptibility to these and other visual illusions varies with age. Depending on the illusion, experience or age can either decrease or increase one's susceptibility to distortion. Alfred Binet, who is considered to be the principal inventor of the IQ test, was also the first to suggest that there are two types of visual illusions (see Pollack & Zetland, 1965). *Type I illusions* are attributed to innate visual predispositions, and therefore susceptibility to this type of illusion

Figure 4-3   Some typical visual illusions. A: Mueller-Lyer (Type I) illusion; B: Titchener Circles (Type II) illusion.

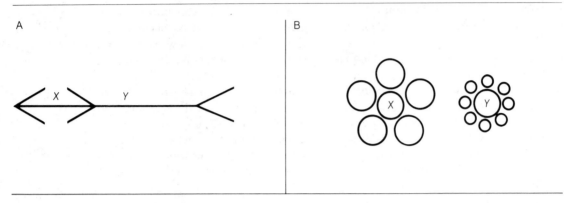

should decrease with experience and age. *Type II illusions,* in contrast, are considered to be acquired through perceptual learning; therefore susceptibility to them should increase with development. Piaget (1969) has provided some evidence to support the distinction between Type I and Type II illusions during childhood development.

Only a few researchers have studied the life-span trends for Type I and Type II illusions (Atkeson, 1978; Eisner & Schaie, 1971; Lorden, Atkeson, & Pollack, 1979). There is a low susceptibility to the Mueller-Lyer illusion (Type I) during childhood, stability during young and middle adulthood, and an increased susceptibility in old age (Comalli, 1970). There is increased susceptibility to the Titchener Circles illusion (Type II) during childhood, stability in middle adulthood, and possibly some decline in susceptibility in late adulthood and old age (Wapner, Werner, & Comalli, 1960).

HEARING

Hearing losses affect about 30 percent of the older population in the United States. About 13 percent of those aged 65 or over require regular professional treatment for their hearing difficulties (Stevens-Long, 1979). The incidence of deafness increases from about 2.8 percent at age 55 to 15 percent at age 75 (Rockstein & Sussman, 1979). People generally begin to notice gradual hearing losses at around age 50 (Bergman, Blumenfeld, Casardo, Dash, Levitt, & Margulies, 1976).

The ear has three main divisions (see Figure 4-4): the visible *outer ear* that funnels sound waves to the eardrum; the *middle ear,* which consists of three little bones, or ossicles (the stapes, incus, and malleus); and the *inner ear,* a fluid-filled cavity that contains the cochlea and the basilar membrane (the skinlike membrane that runs the length of the shell-like cochlea). The receptors for hearing are tiny hair cells located all along the basilar membrane.

Presbycusis is the umbrella term for age-related losses in *audition,* or hearing. As indicated in Table 4-1, the main aspects of audition are pitch and loudness, discrimination, tone sensitivity, and the perception of auditory complexity. Aging affects mainly the discrimination of pitch and the threshold for hearing high-frequency tones (Corso, 1971, 1977). Schuknecht (1974) and Corso (1971) described four specific kinds of age-related hearing loss:

- *Sensory presbycusis.* A relatively abrupt hearing loss caused by atrophy of the basal end of the organ of Corti.
- *Neural presbycusis.* A loss in the ability to discriminate speech because of age-related losses in the number of auditory neurons.
- *Metabolic presbycusis.* A relatively uniform reduction in pure tone sensitivity caused by vascular changes.
- *Mechanical presbycusis.* Age-related hearing loss at high tonal frequencies caused by stiffening of the basilar membrane.

Changes in the inner ear are primarily responsible for presbycusis. An age-related reduction in the number of auditory nerve cells running to the cerebral

Hearing losses are often greater for high frequency tones than for lower frequency tones. In the United States, about 30 percent of the older population is affected by hearing losses.

Figure 4–4 The human ear. The outer ear includes a funnel-like pinna and a canal that enable air pressure changes to reach the eardrum. The vibrations of the eardrum (or tympanic membrane) are transmitted and amplified by three bones, or ossicles, in the middle ear. Amplified vibrations push against the oval window and are transformed into waves of fluid in the cochlea. These fluid waves stimulate hair cells along the organ of Corti on the basilar membrane. (Adapted from Frank H. Netter, M.D. From the CIBA collection of medical illustrations. © CIBA.)

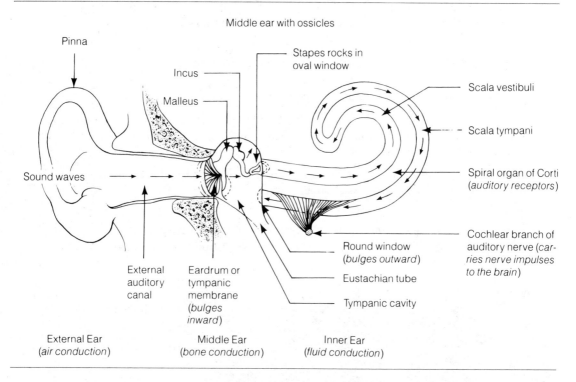

Middle ear with ossicles

Pinna

Stapes rocks in oval window

Incus

Malleus

Scala vestibuli

Scala tympani

Spiral organ of Corti (*auditory receptors*)

Sound waves

Cochlear branch of auditory nerve (*carries nerve impulses to the brain*)

Round window (*bulges outward*)

Eustachian tube

Tympanic cavity

External auditory canal

Eardrum or tympanic membrane (*bulges inward*)

External Ear (*air conduction*)

Middle Ear (*bone conduction*)

Inner Ear (*fluid conduction*)

cortex also causes impaired perception of auditory complexity and speech perception (Weiss, 1959).

Age-related hearing losses are greater for higher-toned pitches. Compared to 25-year-olds, for example, 70-year-olds show an average hearing loss of 10 decibels for a 1000 Hz tone, 25 decibels for a 2000 Hz tone, and 35 decibels for a 3000 Hz tone (Spoor, 1967). The higher the pitch, the louder the sound will need to be for older people to hear it. However, since most speech is in the 500–2000 Hz range, hearing losses above 3000 Hz have relatively little effect on daily living activities.

Age-related difficulties in understanding speech, while they suggest the functional influence of central nervous system decline on audition (Melrose, Welsh, & Luterman, 1963), can also be related to mechanical presbycusis. High-frequency consonants such as *z, s, g, f,* and *t* are quite common in everyday speech (Sataloff & Vassalo, 1966). An older person with reduced sensitivity at high frequencies would hear *ing, ame, on, un,* and *ime* instead of *zing, same, gone, fun,* and *time.*

Another hearing difficulty that accompanies aging is *tinnitus*. The person with this condition experiences a kind of high-pitched "ringing," like a bell or a whistle. The sound is usually more bothersome at night and in quiet surroundings (Corso, 1967). About 11 percent of individuals between the ages of 65 and 74 report this problem, compared to about 9 percent for middle-aged adults and 3 percent for young adults (Rockstein & Sussman, 1979).

Corso (1977) has pointed out that auditory deficits can be considered from what he calls an ecological perspective. Hearing deficits, for example, often significantly alter the individual's social and interpersonal environment. Losses of hearing and speech perception can affect the quality of communication in late life and can lead to reduced life satisfaction and cognitive stimulation.

In a recent study Granick, Kleban, and Weiss (1976) investigated the relationship between hearing loss and cognition in normally hearing aged persons and found that losses in hearing acuity were strongly related to reduced intellectual functioning. The authors interpreted their findings as suggesting the effects of hearing loss on age-related cognitive performance, but it is also reasonable to suggest that hearing and cognition are interdependent systems, each influencing the other.

In the study of adult age differences in learning and other perceptual functions it is important to distinguish the subject's sensory sensitivity from his or her criteria for making a response (response bias). Older adults tend to be more cautious in reporting a target, suggesting that some part of the age-related decline found in studies of perception may be attributable to age differences in response bias.

Signal-detection theory (Green & Swets, 1966) provides a method for separately estimating sensitivity and response bias. Most of the recent investigations of sensation, perception, and aging use signal-detection methods. In one study of auditory signal detection Rees and Botwinick (1971) found that young and older adults did not differ in their ability to detect pure tones in the presence of noise, but older adults were significantly more cautious in their decision criteria. Older people are generally less willing than younger adults to take a guess or make a response if they are uncertain (see Hertzog, 1980).

TASTE AND SMELL

Smell refers to a sensitivity to gaseous substances, and taste refers to a sensitivity to soluble substances. That smells influence taste preferences indicates that these senses are interrelated.

Figure 4-5 shows a side view of the human nose, illustrating the main structures of the sense of smell. Smell receptors are located in the upper nasal passages leading from the nose to the throat. They lie in two small patches just a little off the main breathing passage. Consequently, our sense of smell is relatively inactive under normal breathing conditions; it is activated by a deliberately deep intake of air, such as a sniff.

Figure 4–5 A side view of the human nose, showing the principal structures of the sense of smell. Chemical substances in the air we breathe stimulate the olfactory receptors in the upper part of the nasal cavity. Arrows indicate the flow of air.

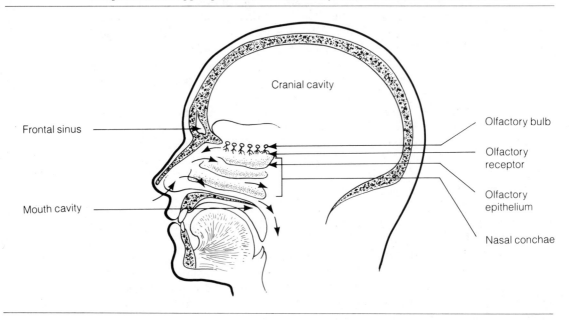

Because of the way we as a species move about our environment, we have come to rely heavily on vision and hearing. Our chemical senses, however, warn us of such basics as bad foodstuffs and clue us in to good food substances. Furthermore, advertisers as well as cosmetic manufacturers are well aware of the significance of smell to 20th-century man and woman.

There is some evidence to suggest that taste and smell senses become less responsive as we grow older. In one recent study, for example, Grzegorczyk, Jones, and Mistretta (1979) measured the salt taste-detection thresholds of adults between 23 and 92 years of age. Consistent with previous findings, they found an age-related decrease in taste acuity. The number of taste buds on the tongue declines after about age 50; people in their 80s have great difficulty distinguishing among the four basic tastes—sweet, sour, salty, and bitter.

Rovee, Cohen, and Shlapack (1975) studied the olfactory acuity of 120 individuals ranging from 6 to 94 years of age. With seven different concentrations of the chemical *n* propanol there was only slight decline in the sense of smell with aging. Because of the importance of the senses of smell and taste to survival, it's likely that these "basic" senses are among the last to decline with advancing age.

The main consequences of age-related losses in the sense of smell and taste are in terms of diet and nutrition. Nutritious foods may not taste as good as they used to to older people, and some older adults actually suffer nutritional deficiencies because of an increased taste for strongly flavored but nonnutritious "junk" foods. Between 30 and 50 percent of the health problems of elderly adults in the United States stem directly from malnutrition (Barrows & Roeder, 1977).

TOUCH

Evidence suggests that there are age-related declines in the skin senses—touch, vibrotactile stimulation (sensitivity to vibration on the surface of the skin), and pressure or pain on the skin. Winkelman (1965) pointed out two changes that occur in the nerve structures of the skin with age. First, there is a period of growth and development of nerve networks, hair follicle networks, and specialized receptor end organs. Much of the development of the skin senses takes place before birth, but Winkelman (1965) and others have found that structural growth of the skin senses continues into early adulthood, although the rate of development of the cutaneous (in the skin) nerve structures seems to slow from infancy to adulthood.

The second change, which begins in early adulthood and continues throughout life, is marked by a gradual and then a more rapid decrease in

Between 30 and 50 percent of the health problems of elderly adults in the United States stem directly from malnutrition, which is related to losses in the sense of smell and taste, as well as to poverty and social isolation.

Figure 4-6   A cross-section of the skin, showing major structures and sense receptors. (After Gardner, 1958.)

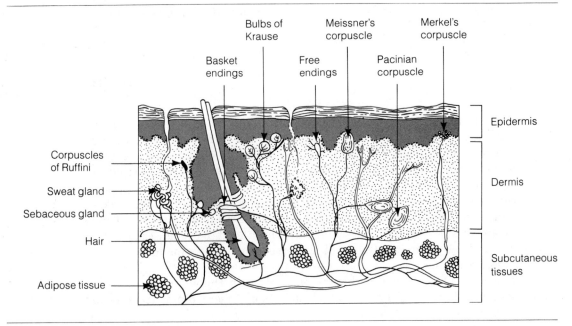

complexity. Several studies have documented an age-related loss in tactile sensitivity with advancing age (Verillo, 1980; Whanger & Wang, 1974). Verillo (1980) tested males and females ranging in age from 8 to 74 years and found a decrease in vibrotactile sensitivity with age at high frequencies and no age differences at low tactile frequencies (25 and 40 Hz). These findings are interesting in light of structural changes that occur in the Pacinian corpuscles over the life span (Cauna, 1965). The *Pacinian corpuscles* are the largest of the specialized nerve endings in the skin (see Figure 4-6). These capsulelike structures start out in infancy relatively small, oval in shape, and with relatively few concentric laminations. With advancing age the corpuscles grow in size and number of laminations but decrease in number (Verillo, 1980).

We can get a pretty good idea of how old people are by the appearance of their skin. As can be seen in Figure 4-6, the skin is composed of three layers: the relatively impermeable *epidermis* or outer layer; the *dermis,* which contains the sensory nerve endings and many blood vessels; and the *subcutaneous tissue,* which is a layer of fat and water that cushions the body from injury and stores energy. Vitamin D and various antibodies are produced at the dermal layer. A network of collagen fibers supports the skin and gives it elasticity and strength. The skin itself shows atrophy in all three layers and in the supporting collagen fibers with advancing age (Rossman, 1976; Timiras, 1972), and also a diminished elasticity. These changes contribute to loss of water storage in the skin.

THERMOREGULATION

The skin responds not only to touch and pressure but also to temperature. *Cold nerve fibers* respond to cooling of the skin with an increased firing rate, and *warm nerve fibers* respond to warming of the skin with an increased firing rate (Hensel, 1968). These cold and warm *thermoreceptors* inform us of absolute external temperature, as well as change in temperatures; this information is crucial because internal body temperature must be maintained or regulated within a very narrow range—around 37°C (98.6°F)—for survival.

Aging is accompanied by reduced efficiency of *thermoregulation*—the homeostatic mechanism that maintains internal body temperature at or near 37°C. (Homeostasis refers to the physiological tendency to maintain an internal bodily state of equilibrium.) Frequently, older people will have lower body temperatures than normal and may be less likely to develop fevers in response to infection (Timiras, 1972). Older people often report an intolerance of extreme temperatures and an inability to maintain a "comfortable" body temperature (McKenzie, 1980). One way they can cope with this is to select clothes that can be easily added or removed so as to compensate for the body's reduced capacity to regulate its own temperature (McKenzie, 1980).

PAIN

Pain is a sensation experienced throughout life. Traditionally, human life begins with a "spank on the bottom." The end of life is marked by the absence of a response to intense, painful stimuli (one of the Harvard criteria of death; see Chapter 15). As pain serves to maintain the homeostasis of many life functions, individuals without a sense of pain will not live.

Several writers (for example, Liebeskind & Paul, 1977; Weisenberg, 1977) have pointed out that pain is a complex response. Cognitive and emotional factors determine how the individual experiences a painful event. People begin to learn how to react to pain in early childhood and continue to adapt physically and psychologically to the experiences of pain throughout the life span. For some, pain is a way of obtaining nurturance and support from significant others. Pain may also be a way of escaping from pressure situations—"I can't take the exam because I have a headache."

Interest in the cognitive and emotional factors that mediate the sensation of pain can be traced to Melzack and Wall's (1965) *gate-control theory*. They proposed the existence of a gatelike control mechanism in the spinal cord that regulates the flow of nerve impulses from the periphery to the central nervous system. When a painful stimulus impinges on the skin, a specialized ascending system of nerve fibers rapidly informs the central nervous system of the painful event. The central nervous system then regulates the opening and closing of the gate through a series of descending nerve fibers.

Although there are critics of Melzack and Wall's framework, the gate-control theory helps to explain many of the factors that influence the experience of pain. For example, it is frequently the case that we can endure painful events longer in some situations than in others. It has also been demonstrated that we are less able to tolerate pain when we are anxious (Sternbach, 1974; Weisenberg, 1977).

The experience of pain is generally more prevalent in the later years; that is, the number of aches and pains seems to increase, independent of the individual's threshold for pain. Brunner and Suddarth (1975) have reported that older people can be free of pain in some acute disorders (such as myocardial infarction, pneumonia, appendicitis, peritonitis) because of reduced sensory sensitivity. Some studies show an age-related decline in the sense of pain (for instance, Schludermann & Zubeck, 1962; Sherman & Robillard, 1960), whereas other studies show older people to be more sensitive than younger adults (Woodrow, Friedman, Siegelaub, & Collen, 1972), and some studies show no reliable age difference in pain threshold (Harkins & Chapman, 1976, 1977). Differences in the type of pain stimulus used in various studies and individual factors such as willingness to tolerate pain (that is, response bias) account for the lack of definitive results in the area of pain sensitivity.

Treatments for reducing or managing pain are discussed later in the book (see Chapter 14). At this point it is important only to consider adult age differences in the experience of pain:

1   The nature and extent of pain are often difficult to assess reliably using medical diagnostic tools. For example, the amount of physical damage evident with torn or sprained muscles, ligaments, and tendons, or hairline fractures may not reflect the amount of *experienced pain*. In other words, there is not a one-to-one relationship of tissue damage to pain intensity.

2   Pain may be felt throughout the body. Pain is not a sense of the skin alone; there are pain receptors (free nerve endings) throughout the body.

3   Physical, sensory, cognitive, and experiential factors complicate the study of pain. For example, anxiety reduction and selective attention strategies, as well as the number and sensitivity of nerve fibers and the thickness of the skin, influence age differences in responsivity to pain.

4   The experience of pain is pervasive and insidious. Poor eyesight and hearing, while affecting many aspects of daily living, can often be corrected; age-related or accident-related losses in mobility can also be compensated for by prosthetic devices. Pain, however, often does not have a direct cure (Sternbach, 1974). Analgesic (pain-killing) medication may reduce the pain, but it does not eliminate the source or the cause of the pain.

It has recently been discovered that there are natural morphinelike substances in the brain which are released under painful conditions. If such substances—endogenous morphines or *endorphins*—can be synthesized, they will aid both in the treatment of pain patients and in our basic understanding of analgesics and the nature of pain.

THE PRACTICAL IMPLICATIONS
OF SENSORY LOSS

As we have seen, all the senses show a decline with advancing age. Age-related sensory impairments contribute to a general reduction in the individual's adaptiveness and responsiveness to external events. Those who have experience with visually impaired or hearing impaired older people know that diminished sensory input can negatively affect a wide range of characteristics including personality, motivation, and mood. The experience of sensory loss contributes to the stereotype of the senseless older person.

Reduced sensory efficiency sometimes leads to social and physical withdrawal. Having a conversation with a hearing impaired older person, for example, can be confusing, effortful, and time consuming for both speaker and listener. Oyer and Oyer (1978) observed increased fatigue, irritability, tension, depression, negativism, and vulnerability as consequences of age-related hearing losses.

A reduced ability to understand speech is a decided limitation. However, there are some means of mitigating it. Sitting close to and directly in front of the hearing impaired person facilitates communication, as do talking slowly, repeating things in a different way, and using low tones. Hearing aids are helpful to some older people and not others. Since hearing aids amplify sound in general, they are most beneficial when auditory functioning is impaired over a wide range of frequencies; they are less beneficial when hearing losses are greater at some frequencies than others. Presbycusis, which most often affects the perception of high frequencies (over 2000 Hz), does not benefit from the overall amplification provided by a hearing aid.

Poor hearing and vision combined with slowed reaction time and unsteady movement are hazardous handicaps when walking or driving in a busy urban environment. Not being able to see traffic signs or hear horns or emergency signals can cause safety problems for the older driver, other drivers, and pedestrians. Panek and his colleagues recently studied the relationship between perceptual information processing and automobile driving (Panek, Barrett, Sterns, & Alexander, 1977) and found selective attention and perceptual motor speed to be important factors in safe driving.

Older adults often have difficulty in visually locating and distinguishing objects under conditions of low illumination. Diffuse lighting creates less glare than does a single light source. Since night vision declines with aging, perhaps older adults should be encouraged to use safe public transportation as an alternative to night driving. The use of bright colors (reds, yellows, and oranges) and contrasting colors for walls, doors, and steps will create a safer and often more appealing environment for the visually impaired adult.

Age-related losses in the senses of touch and pain can have serious consequences because cuts, burns, irritations, and infections may go unnoticed and untreated. Further, as we have seen, reductions in taste and smell can lead to poor nutrition because of reduced appetite for healthful foods. Such sensory losses suggest that, with aging, people need to be more responsible and thoughtful with regard to their own health and safety.

THE PROCESSING OF SENSORY AND PERCEPTUAL INFORMATION

How can we distinguish between *perception* and other processes like *sensation, cognition,* and *memory?* As we mentioned at the beginning of this chapter, we cannot have consciousness without the information that is brought to us through the various senses. Nevertheless, other factors also influence and determine our perceptions; we selectively filter, interpret, and distort incoming sensory information. Before we can address the research on the development of selective perception in adulthood, we must define the basic terms. *Sensation* refers to the first contact between the organism and the environment—that which is directly experienced when sense receptors are activated. Colors, sounds, tastes, and odors are examples of sensation. *Perception,* on the other hand, refers to the interpretation of sensation—our recognition of objects and object relationships. Interpretation of sensory information is influenced by factors such as the perceiver's past experience, motivation, expectancies, values, and so forth.

Ever since Thomas Aquinas (1225–1274) introduced the sensation–perception distinction in the 13th century, it has been a controversial dichotomy for both philosophers and scientists. The first English psychology text, *The Senses and Intellect,* by Alexander Bain (1855), as well as early laboratory work on perception by Wilhelm Wundt (who established the first psychology laboratory at the University of Leipzig in 1879) and others, emphasized the importance of sensation to perception. Since the beginning of the 20th century, psychologists have become increasingly aware of the importance of "higher" processes (cognition, thoughts) to both sensation and perception. Let us look at various theories about the relation of sensation and perception.

Information Processing

Information processing approaches seem to be one way of avoiding the arbitrary distinctions between sensation, perception, thought, cognition, and so forth. The information-processing approach involves the study of the entire sequence from receptor activation to behavioral response. Typically, the sequence is broken down into several component stages.

The earliest stage is *registration* or *sensory memory,* in which information from the senses is stored very briefly (Baddeley, 1976; Craik, 1977). The next stages of the information-processing sequence are *short-term memory, long-term memory,* and *very long-term memory.* Information seems to be organized and stored in different ways in each of these stages, and the stages show different patterns of developmental change. We will look at memory in detail in Chapter 5.

One of the main features of the information-processing approach is that the characteristics attributed to different stages can be tested experimentally. Further, the flow of information is "two-way"—that is, information goes from the senses to the brain and from the brain to the senses. The information-processing approach will be discussed further later in this chapter.

Attention

Attentional processes are responsible for translating and moving information that is in the sensory stores to the stages of short-term and long-term memory. Not all information that bombards our senses can be consciously processed; attentional processes serve to filter information.

The study of attention and attentional limitations has a long history within psychology. In 1898, for example, Edward Titchener used the concept of attention to explain how certain stimuli are selected in consciousness (see Titchener, 1948). He viewed attention as a kind of *sensory clearness.* In contrast, other theorists viewed attention as a preliminary sensory motor adjustment that served to enhance perceptual processing (Marx & Hillix, 1979). In this view attention involves sorting relevant from irrelevant stimulus features (in other words, "what one pays attention to"), but it also involves alertness, visual exploration, consciousness, and access to long-term memory (Posner & Boies, 1971).

Several writers (Layton, 1975; Rabbitt, 1977; Schonfield, 1974) have suggested that older adults experience an "attentional deficit" compared to younger adults. There are now many studies in which age-related declines in attentional performance have been reported (Hoyer, Rebok, & Sved, 1979; Rabbitt, 1964, 1965). In Rabbitt's studies the card-sorting speed of older adults was disproportionately slower as the number of distractors was increased. Hoyer, Rebok, and Sved (1979) also found that increasing amounts of irrelevant information reduced the speed and accuracy of elderly adults (median age, 72.6 years) more than that of young (20.6 years) and middle-aged (52.4 years) adults.

In recent years two models of sensory processing have been useful for guiding research on adult age differences in attention (see Figure 4-7). Broadbent's model (A) is a single-channel, or all-or-none, model of attention. Different

Figure 4-7   The all-or-none and attenuation models of sensory processing. According to an all-or-none model (see, for instance, Broadbent, 1958), only a single input passes through the selector (A). According to an attenuation model (for instance, Treisman, 1960), all inputs pass through, but they are attenuated before reaching short-term memory (B).

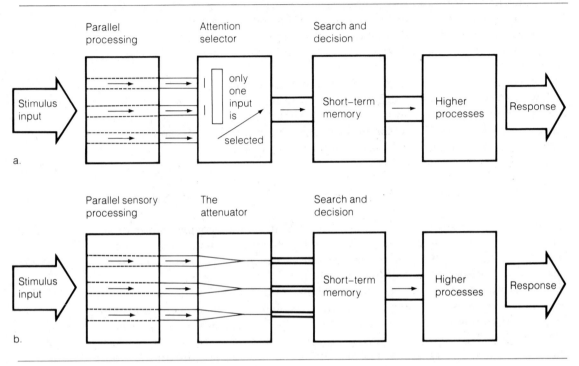

types of sensory information are continuously processed by the eyes, ears, and other sense organs, but, according to Broadbent, only one of these inputs, or channels, at a time can be passed on to short-term memory. This all-or-none model of attention can account for the observed age deficits in psychomotor performance (Welford, 1977).

An alternative model, proposed by Treisman (1960), suggests that multiple channels of information can simultaneously reach short-term memory. However, increases in the number of channels being processed simultaneously reduce or attenuate the intensity of the signals that reach short-term memory. For example, as you study, are you also processing other information (such as music, background conversation)? If you are, is attention being taken away from your reading comprehension? A striking example that supports multi-channel selectivity is the "cocktail conversation effect" demonstrated by Cherry (1953). Assume that you are at a party and attending mainly to one conversation. If your name or other information important to you is mentioned in a conversation across the room, you are likely to hear it even though you were not attending to that conversation.

Modest changes have been made in both Broadbent's and Treisman's models to accommodate recent research findings (Broadbent, 1977; Treisman, 1969). Age-related deficits in attention can be explained by either model. More specific to the research on perceptual aging, however, are the perceptual noise hypothesis and the stimulus persistence hypothesis.

Other Models of Perception

Layton (1975) has defined *perceptual noise* as a reduction in the ability to suppress irrelevant or interfering stimuli while performing a perceptual task. The strongest evidence in support of the perceptual noise hypothesis comes from studies showing selective attention deficits with advancing age (Hoyer, Rebok, & Sved, 1979; Rabbitt, 1965).

The *stimulus persistence* hypothesis states that stimulus information stays longer and travels slower in the nervous systems of older people than of young adults (Botwinick, 1978). The well-documented age-related slowing in the processing of briefly presented information supports the stimulus persistence hypothesis. Kline's sequential integration studies (see Kline & Baffa, 1976; Kline & Orme-Rogers, 1978) showing that older adults are better able than younger adults to integrate brief information presented to one eye with brief information presented to the other eye also support the stimulus persistence hypothesis.

Studying Age-Related Changes in Perception

Since experimental work on vision at the turn of the century there has been an interest in localizing the physiological structures that are involved in various perceptual phenomena. Obviously, the processing of external information involves many structures and mechanisms. Further, the human perceptual system is very complex, with many interconnections occurring at many different levels within the nervous system.

There is and has been much debate as to where and how information is organized and stored and how and where age-related perceptual losses occur. Such controversy centers on the relative emphasis given to "central" versus "peripheral" factors in explaining aging changes in sensation and perception. Are age-related deficits in the processing of complex information caused mainly by losses in the peripheral mechanisms, such as the retina of the eye, or mainly by losses in the brain and central nervous system? Birren (1974) has argued that aging losses in the peripheral mechanisms are minor compared to aging losses in brain and central integrative mechanisms. Studies of adult age differences in visual and auditory masking have clarified the importance of central nervous system factors in information processing.

Masking is one way of studying the amount of interference in and the speed of information processing. When two auditory or visual stimuli are presented in rapid succession, their traces interact (Turvey, 1973). If the first stimulus obscures the second, the phenomenon is called *forward masking;* if the second stimulus obscures the first, it is called *backward masking.* In both forward and backward masking some amount of time is required for the visual system to clear information—like letting water run out of a hose after the faucet has been turned off. If signal processing time is relatively slow, masking effects are more likely to occur.

Older adults are more susceptible to visual masking procedures than younger adults. Kline and Szafran (1975), for example, showed that older adults (mean age 68.2 years) suffered from a visual noise mask (distracting visual information) at significantly longer interstimulus intervals (the time between target presentations) than did younger adults (mean age 23.3 years) (see also Kline & Birren, 1975). In another study Walsh (1976) varied target durations, interstimulus intervals, target intensities, and stimulus onset asynchronies (the amount of time separating the onset of the target stimulus and the masking stimulus; SOA) in a masking investigation with young (mean age 19.5 years) and older (mean age 64.2 years) adults. Walsh argued that SOA is the critical variable in central nervous system processing. Older subjects required 24 percent longer SOAs than younger subjects, indicating an age-related slowing in central perceptual processing.

Some researchers (for example, Till, 1978; Walsh, Till, & Williams, 1978) have found evidence of age-related slowing in peripheral visual processing. One of the challenges in this area of research is to determine where "peripheral" leaves off and "central" begins. It is likely that the neural mechanisms and structures underlying age-related perceptual slowing pervade the entire visual information-processing system (Hoyer & Plude, 1980; Pollack, 1978).

There are relatively few developmental studies of auditory information processing. In one of the few investigations, Inglis (1962) assessed adult age differences in auditory information processing by means of a *dichotic listening paradigm,* in which information is presented simultaneously to both ears of the listener, but the information to each ear is different. Inglis and Caird (1963) and several other investigators (Clark & Knowles, 1973; Elias & Kinsbourne, 1974) have reported age-related deficits using dichotic listening procedures. However, the central versus peripheral locus of the age deficit remains to be clarified.

Another aspect of auditory information processing is the ability to identify where sound is coming from. The localization of sound is most accurate in the left-to-right auditory field in front of the subject. Auditory localization is less accurate behind the person than in front and is least accurate along a vertical plane (Ramsdell, 1970). Time factors and the intensity of sound are the major cues for localizing sound. Herman, Warrren, and Wagener (1977) investigated adult age differences in localizing sound by varying the intensity and time delay of sounds presented in front of the subject. They found an age decline only in the ability to use time cues. When time cues are obscured or confused by background noise, it may be especially difficult for older people to locate sound sources (Herman, Warren, & Wagener, 1977).

Response Persistence

Stimulus persistence and response persistence are different. Before we define response persistence, try to solve the water jar problems in Table 4-2. The task is to obtain the prescribed number of units of water using jars having the capacities shown in columns A, B, and C.

You may have discovered that problems 1–6 are solved by filling the largest container first and then removing some of this liquid by pouring it into the smaller jars. Problems 2–6 are solved by using the formula X (amount needed) = B−1A−2C. Many people continue to use this strategy on the remaining problems, even though there are more efficient solution strategies (for example, X = A−C, or X = A+C). This is the phenomenon of *response persistence.*

Heglin (1956) tested young (14–19), middle-aged (20–44), and older (50–85) adults on Luchins's (1942) water jar task. The older group exhibited most persistence, and the middle-aged group benefited most and the elderly group least from a brief training procedure designed to minimize response persistence. More will be said about response persistence and rigidity in Chapter 6.

Perceptual Rigidity

The ability to recognize a familiar object or to detect recognizable features of an object depends on experience. From birth we are learning to identify objects in our environment using all of our senses. By the time we reach adulthood we are familiar with many of the objects we encounter on a daily basis. Are there adult age differences in our abilities to process new objects and new perceptual information?

Table 4-2   Water Jar Problems

Problem	Size of jars			Quarts of liquid needed
	A	B	C	
1	29	3	—	20
2	21	127	3	100
3	14	163	25	99
4	18	43	10	5
5	9	42	6	21
6	20	59	4	31
7	23	49	3	20
8	15	39	3	18
9	28	76	3	25
10	18	48	4	22
11	14	36	8	6

Figure 4-8

First let's consider the effect of perceptual rigidity on object identification. Suppose that you see a rabbit in Figure 4-8. Do you have any difficulty also seeing the figure as a duck? *Perceptual rigidity* refers to an inability to shift from one type of stimulus to another. Several studies have shown that with advancing age there is an increase in perceptual rigidity (Brinley, 1965; Korchin & Basowitz, 1956; Schaie, 1958).

In one study Korchin and Basowitz (1956) found that elderly adults were less able than young adults to identify ambiguous figures. Thirteen line drawings varying in ambiguity were projected on a screen, and young adults (22–33) and elderly adults (65–85) were asked to identify each drawing as either a cat or a dog. The first drawing clearly resembled a cat, and the succeeding drawings were gradually altered such that the thirteenth drawing clearly resembled a dog. Figure 4-9 shows the first drawing (the unambiguous cat), the seventh drawing (the most ambiguous figure), and the thirteenth drawing (the unambiguous dog). Young adults shifted sooner to the dog response and were generally more consistent in maintaining the dog response to the end. Moreover, the older adults took longer to make ambiguous decisions than the younger subjects. Korchin and Basowitz (1956) interpreted age-related slowness in identifying ambiguous drawings in terms of cautiousness—a reluctance to venture a response because of the risk of being wrong (see Botwinick, 1978).

Perceptual Preference

The effects of perceptual preference on various conceptual tasks such as problem solving and multiple classification has been the focus of several developmental studies (for instance, Odom & Guzman, 1972; Odom & Lemond, 1975).

Odom and Guzman indicated that the dimensions of a task are sequentially processed for solution from most to least salient. Figure 4-10 illustrates how an individual's perceptual preference hierarchy is determined. The subject simply selects which card, A or B, is most like the top card. If the person prefers color to number, then A would be selected, and vice versa. Typically, comparisons are made between color, number, position, and form. The subject's preference

Figure 4-9 Drawings from the cat-dog series. (After Korchin & Basowitz, 1956.)

Figure 4-10 Perceptual preference task. The task is to match either A or B to the top stimulus card. If the subject selects A, he or she is color dominant; if the subject selects B, he or she is number dominant. (After Hoyer, Rebok, & Sved, 1979.)

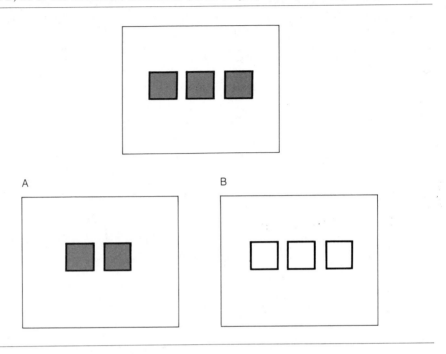

of these dimensions is then used to predict performance on various conceptual tasks.

When a perceptually preferred dimension is relevant rather than irrelevant to the solution of a task, conceptual problems are solved more easily and rapidly. In its extreme form, the perceptual salience view suggests that, with development, perceptual preferences become more sophisticated and dominant. A study by Hoyer, Rebok, and Sved (1979) presented some evidence for adult age differences in perceptual salience. That is, the elderly made most errors when the number, color, and position dimensions (in that order) were relevant to solution, and the young adults and middle-aged made most errors on the number and color dimensions. Mergler (1977) and Rebok (1977) found similar trends in their studies of perceptual salience and problem solving.

PERCEPTION AND COGNITION

Recently, Neisser (1976) has argued that research on perception needs to move beyond the limitations imposed by the prevailing psychophysical and information-processing approaches. Since perception is not simply a sequence of "snap-shots" beginning with sensory input and ending with perceptual image, the study of the components of perception gives us at best an incomplete picture. "If we were restricted to isolated and separated glances at the world," Neisser argued, "we could not consistently disentangle what we see from what we expect to see, nor distinguish objects from hallucinations" (1976, p. 43).

One way of distinguishing perception and cognition is to view the former as going "from the eye inward to the brain" and the latter "from the mind outward to the senses." The point is that, although the pathways might be the same, information flows in two directions.

The study of *top-down* (from the brain to the senses) processing is concerned with how expectancies and motives influence perception. However, we must not overlook the importance of *bottom-up* (from the senses to the brain) processing, in which bits of information are combined to form whole concepts. It is possible that we use both types of processing depending on the type of material to be processed and our familiarity with it (Hoyer & Plude, 1980). For example, when we first learn to read, we begin by detecting letters and then combine letters to form words (see, for example, LaBerge, 1973). However, after we know *how* to read, we are probably more influenced by such top-down influ-

Figure 4-11   Georges Seurat, Side Show (La Parade). 1887–88. Canvas, 39½ x 59¼." The Metropolitan Museum of Art, New York. (Bequest of Stephen C. Clark, 1960)

ences as context and expectancy.

Top-down processing occurs when the whole helps us to recognize the parts. For example, when we look at Georges Seurat's painting "La Parade," (Figure 4-11), recognizing a person's head facilitates our identification of that person's eyes, nose, and ears. Bottom-up processing occurs when component features lead us to the identification of the whole. This would be like watching the construction of a house as it takes shape. *Middle-out* processing takes place in both lower and higher directions (Hoyer & Plude, 1980). It is likely that the individual's past experience with the material to be perceived greatly influences the sequence of information processing (Hoyer, 1980).

One of the most vivid Impressionist painters of the 19th century was Claude Monet (1840–1926). His canvases glowed with reds and yellows even when he was painting gloomy, gray-stone cathedrals. He claimed that he was painting what he saw with his eyes. Was Monet unable to see the world as it actually looks, or did he see colors that were invisible to others? A little biographical digging tells us that Monet was contending with cataracts during much of his life as a painter. At the time he painted the famous water lily panels at the Orangerie in Paris he was very nearly blind (Eliot, 1973). Like the late quartets of the deaf Beethoven, Monet's late masterpieces represent a combination of sensory information with imagination and creativity.

SUMMARY

1   All that we know about the world comes to us through the senses. *Sensation* is the initial contact between the organism and the physical environment. *Perception* is the interpretation of sensory information.

2   All of the senses and some aspects of perception decline with advancing age. With regard to vision there is a reduction in visual acuity and adaptation to changes in light. Age-related losses in hearing affect mainly the discrimination of pitch and the threshold for hearing high frequencies. Taste, smell, touch, thermoregulation, and pain also become less sensitive in later life.

3   Age-related losses in sensory efficiency can negatively affect life satisfaction, motivation, cognitive level, interpersonal involvement and communication, and safety.

4   It is useful to look at sensation and perception from an information-processing perspective. From this perspective distinctions are not made among sensation, perception, memory, attention, and so forth. The processing of information can be bottom-up, top-down, or both. It is possible that there is a developmental shift toward more top-down processing with advancing age.

5   Attention can have several meanings with regard to information processing (for instance, alertness, selectivity, span of attention, access to memory). There is an age-related decrease in the ability to inhibit irrelevant information—that is, a deficit in selective attention with advancing age.

6 Cognition refers to the processes of knowing. Both peripheral and central factors are responsible for developmental changes in perception.

7 Cognitive factors such as rigidity, perceptual preference, and response persistence are related to adult age differences in perception.

8 Two aspects of sensory and perceptual change during adulthood and old age seem particularly promising avenues to further understanding. First, identification of the component processes of sensation and perception that are prone to age-related decline can lead to ways to prevent or at least minimize perceptual losses. Identification of top-down factors that are responsible for individual differences in perception is a second area that deserves further study. Increased knowledge about the influences of personality, attitudes, expectancies, and the like on perception might lead to identification of strategies for developing positive interpretations of perceptual experiences.

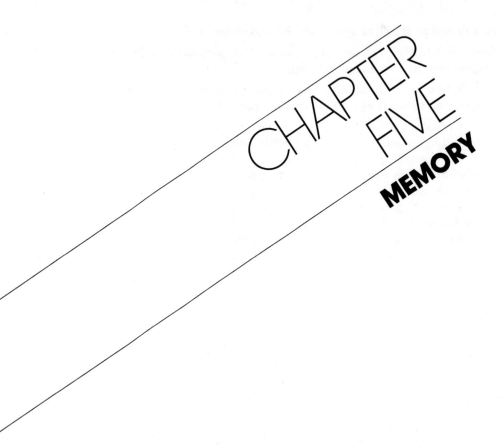

CHAPTER FIVE

MEMORY

Memory involves the storage of learned information. The capacity to store as well as the ability to use learned information are essential human characteristics.

Most people are curious about their own memory and how it will change with aging. They may have some general notion or expectation about what is going to happen to their memory abilities as they grow older, often based on the popular stereotype of the senile older person. Just as there is *some* truth to the myth of the absentminded professor, it is true that some aspects of memory do show an age-related decline. However, memory is a complex attribute, and in order to have a clear understanding of it we need to examine why and how it changes with aging.

There are three aspects to remembering something: First we learn it or encode it, then we store it, and then we must be able to retrieve it as needed. If memory declines as we grow older, is it a problem of encoding, storage, or retrieval? On the basis of what you know about memory, which of the following statements would you judge as correct?

1 Older adults need more time than young adults to learn or to encode new information.

2 Older adults tend to lose stored information faster than young adults.

3 Older adults need more time than young adults to retrieve information from stored memory.

Many studies have addressed this question, with often contradictory results. Adult age differences in these memory functions have been shown to be related to (1) the material to be remembered (that is, meaningfulness); (2) the ability of the individual (memory strategies); and (3) the type of memory and the assessment of memory performance (in other words, short-term memory versus long-term memory).

The study of memory is the investigation of what happens to learned knowledge over time. There are many different approaches to the study of memory and aging; in this chapter we shall emphasize an information-processing view. Even within this framework, however, there are substantial differences of opinion. Some researchers see the individual as an active processor of information, deliberately selecting and reorganizing input from the environment. In contrast, others see the individual as a relatively passive recipient of information; the information more than the individual affects memory development. In other words, some researchers seem to think that we create our memories, whereas others believe it is the information that "finds" or creates us. Different models of memory should not be judged as either correct or incorrect but instead should be evaluated on the basis of their usefulness in explaining memory and how it changes (Reese, 1976). We will begin our discussion with a brief sociohistorical account of the study of memory.

A SOCIOHISTORICAL PERSPECTIVE

In the late 19th century the predominant view of memory and thinking was *associationism*. All mental activity was thought to be made up of two components—*ideas* and *associations*. Associations were simply the connections between ideas, or elements. The doctrines of associationism were first proposed by the Greek philosopher Aristotle (384–322 B.C.), who argued that "ideas" occurring together in time or space become associated, so that thinking one would trigger the other. "Ideas" that were either similar or opposite to each other also tended to be associated in memory. The British philosophers Thomas Hobbes (1588–1679) and John Locke (1632–1704) drew heavily on Aristotle's theories of association.

Alternatives to the early associationistic view did not begin to take hold until the rise of Gestalt psychology in Germany late in the 19th century. The differences between the Gestalt and the associationist approaches are primarily the type of problem each studies and the view each has of mental activity. The Associationists think in terms of stimulus–response connections, strengthened in rote learning tasks, perhaps by repetition. Gestalt psychologists, on the other hand, emphasize the reorganization of elements to produce a novel, insightful mental experience.

Both the Associationists and the Gestaltists relied heavily on introspection as the main source of information about cognition. *Introspectionism* can be defined as the observation of one's own mental activities as they occur. Introspectionists trained other introspectionists in methods of mental self-observation. However, it is difficult if not impossible to be unbiased—to not see what one is looking for—using introspection. What was perhaps an overemphasis may have led to a counteremphasis on *behaviorism* in the 1930s, when psychology was trying very hard to be accepted as a scientific discipline. The Behaviorists argued that, unless mental events such as memory and thinking could somehow be directly observed and recorded, they were not in the domain of science. It was not until the development of cognitive psychology in the 1960s that thinking and other mental events were again acceptable areas of investigation (Neisser, 1976). Unlike the Behaviorists, cognitive psychologists were mainly interested in what goes on inside the mind—the nature of conscious thought (see Chapter 6). Recent books such as *Divided Consciousness* by Ernest Hilgard (1977) and *The Origin of Consciousness in the Breakdown of the Bicameral Mind* by Julian Jaynes (1977) were an indication of the growing scientific and social interest in mental processes. Clearly, what does and does not pass as an acceptable area of scientific inquiry depends on the social, political, and economic climate in which the research is conducted (Mannheim, 1952; Riegel, 1977).

There is still controversy among American researchers about the importance of introspection. For instance, Nisbett and Wilson (1977) took the position that people do not have direct access to their mental processsses. Neisser (1967) and Mandler (1975) also suggested that it is not possible to learn very much about cognition that is objective and scientific by looking inward; indeed, we are likely to be misled by introspective information. However, Smith and Miller (1978) have replied to this argument by recommending that we focus not on *whether* or not we have access to mental processes but on the *conditions* under which we do (or don't) have such access.

With the advent of cognitive psychology in the 1960s and 1970s the study of memory as a process has greatly expanded. In the past decade the predominant representation of memory has been the information-processing metaphor. Developmental psychologists have greatly contributed to our understanding of memory and information processing by pointing out the shortcomings of simple input–output, robotlike models and suggesting the active, constructive nature of memory and thought. We will begin our closer examination of developmental differences in memory by looking at some theories that have been proposed for the structure of memory.

SOME MODELS OF
THE STRUCTURE OF MEMORY

Sensory, Short-term, and Long-term Memory

Ever since the first reported laboratory experiments on memory by Ebbinghaus (1885), researchers have been trying to understand and explain the components and processes of memory. As early as 1890 William James made the distinction between long-term and short-term memory. He referred to the permanent storage of memories as *secondary memory,* and the contents of immediate consciousness as *primary memory.* The information in primary memory—now called short-term memory—stays in awareness or consciousness for only a few moments. It is continuously being replaced by new perceptions, old memories, and the synthesis of new and old information. Research in the 20th century has suggested that there are three types of memory: sensory memory, short-term memory, and long-term memory (see Figure 5-1).

Table 5-1 gives some examples of different types of memory. It can be seen that different situations require of us different types of memory. Manipulating the contents of short-term memory and effortful access to long-term memory are the most difficult for older adults.

Figure 5-1   A multistore model of memory.

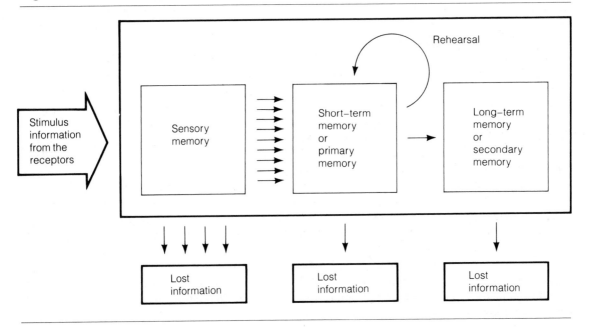

Table 5-1   Examples of Memory Types and Activities

Sensory	Short-term memory span	Manipulation of the contents of short-term memory
Shortest time required to hear a word mentioned in a lecture	The amount of information that can be heard and remembered while you are taking notes in a lecture	Putting a term or definition into your own words while taking notes in a lecture; coming up with your own examples of new terms

Rehearsal of the contents of short-term memory	Access to long-term memory	Autobiographical memory
Repeating to yourself a foreign word or a definition until you "know" it.	Taking an essay test. Some of the information in long-term memory can be readily or automatically accessed (e.g., your name and Social Security number), whereas access to other stored information may require much "mental effort."	Recall of personal events from the distant past

Sensory Memory   Before information from the environment reaches short-term memory, it must be taken in by the senses, translated in some way (that is, transformed from light waves, for example, to neural impulses), and then transmitted to the brain. As we mentioned in Chapter 4, sensory memory is the earliest stage of information processing, in which information from the senses is stored very briefly (Sperling, 1960). Sensory memories are modality-specific—that is, there are different "registers" for visual, or *iconic,* information and for auditory, or *echoic,* information, and perhaps for information from the other senses, too (Craik, 1977).

In order for sensory information to be passed along to short-term or long-term memory, it must be encoded in some way. *Encoding* is the process of transforming sensory information into a code that can be understood in short-term memory. Language or mental imagery is our means of encoding information into verbal symbols, assigning "names" or representations to stimulus information that is about to be deposited in short-term memory. For example, if you were given the letter string BYO, you might encode it as *boy* or as *bring your own.* Depending on the nature of the information and the capacities of the individual doing the processing, information that has never been seen or heard before can be (1) transformed for the first time, (2) encoded in its original form, or (3) not processed. The encoded information that reaches short-term memory is readily available for recall. Age changes in encoding will be discussed later in this chapter.

Sperling (1960) was one of the first researchers to examine sensory memory systematically. He studied iconic memory by presenting young adult subjects with arrays of letters and digits for only 50 milliseconds (1/20 of a second). The subjects' task was to recall specific rows within the array after varying intervals. Recall declined after 300–500 milliseconds.

Sperling was not particularly interested in individual differences in iconic memory. However, other investigators (for example, Kline & Schieber, 1981;

Schonfield & Wegner, 1975; Walsh, 1976) have reported that older adults need more time than younger adults to process briefly presented information. Stimulus persistence and perceptual noise are two explanations that have been proposed for these age-related changes (see Chapter 4).

Short-term Memory   It wasn't until the 1960s that researchers really began to study short-term memory (see Hilgard & Bower, 1975). A test of short-term memory asks subjects to recall information (such as words or number sequences) within a few seconds after it has been presented. Under normal conditions most adults can recall small amounts of nonmeaningful material (for example, a string of six or seven numbers) for 60 seconds or less. There are *no* or *negligible* age differences in short-term memory performance (Botwinick & Storandt, 1974; Taub, 1973). When adult subjects are distracted, however, short-term memory proves to be extremely sensitive. Using college students as subjects, Peterson and Peterson (1959) showed that the recall of nonsense trigrams (such as BYO) decreased markedly (within 16 seconds) when subjects were asked to mentally subtract 3 from a random number during the recall interval.

Sternberg (1969) devised a task for studying short-term memory search. The subject hears several "target" items to be remembered and is then presented with a "probe" item. The subject's job is to decide whether the probe item was or was not in the target set. To do this requires an exhaustive search of short-term memory. Although there are no age differences in short-term memory span, there are age differences in the time it takes to actively search the contents of short-term memory. Older adults are not as fast as young adults in searching the contents of short-term memory (Anders, Fozard, & Lilliquist, 1972).

Short-term memory has a limited capacity; it can hold only a few items of information at any one time. If the information is to be kept in short-term memory, it must be effortfully rehearsed or some other active process must be carried out on it. Although there are no age differences in simple short-term memory performance, older adults are at a disadvantage compared to younger subjects when the contents of short-term memory must be mentally manipulated in some way (Craik, 1977). For example, age deficits are found when a sequence of letters or digits must be repeated to the experimenter in a reversed order (Taub, 1974).

Long-term Memory   According to Atkinson and Schiffrin (1968), each rehearsal cycle transfers some of the information in short-term memory into long-term memory. Long-term memory is a less fragile structure; once information gets there from short-term memory, it is retained relatively permanently. Moreover, in contrast to short-term memory, the capacity of long-term memory is unlimited. Several studies have shown that there is little or no loss in the ability to remember information and events from the distant past (Bahrick, Bahrick, & Wittlinger, 1975; Smith, 1963). It seems that the problem is not one of memory loss over time but rather one of increased difficulty with age in the speed or efficiency of retrieving information in long-term memory (Fozend, 1980).

Semantic Memory and Episodic Memory

The model depicted in Figure 5-1 is basically the three-store model of Atkinson and Schiffrin (1968).

Schiffrin has greatly altered his position on memory stores since 1968. According to Schiffrin (1975), short-term memory is the active, or conscious, processing of information. Information from the sensory register directly activates information in long-term memory; and attention, rather than being a selective filtering system, directs the continuous flow of information from sensory memory all the way to long-term memory. In other words, the notion of short-term memory as a storage bin for briefly presented information is replaced by the notion of *working memory*—an active control process that directs the flow and synthesis of information.

Atkinson, on the other hand, has not changed his theory very much in recent years, with one minor exception: He suggested that long-term store should be divided into a *conceptual* store and an *event-knowledge store*. Atkinson's idea of different memory stores for concepts and events is similar to Tulving's (1972) distinction between *semantic memory* and *episodic memory* as two different types of long-term memory. Tulving (1972) defined semantic memory as a "system for receiving, retaining and transmitting information about meaning of words, concepts and classification of concepts" (pp. 401-402). Semantic memory has to do with knowing the full meaning of sentences and words. Episodic memory refers to memory for personal events and experiences and the relationships among them. Remembering the author or title of a novel would be an example of simple semantic memory; remembering special experiences—a childhood vacation, a nice restaurant, a distant old friend—would be examples of episodic memory.

Baddeley (1976), while acknowledging the importance of semantic factors, has questioned the usefulness of a distinction between semantic and episodic types of long-term memory. Semantic and episodic memories may differ in the degree of abstraction (remembering a mathematical formula is more abstract than remembering a fishing trip, for example) rather than qualitatively. Baddeley cited Byrne's (1976) study in which British housewives were asked to recall meal menus by categories (for instance, an inexpensive lunch). Analysis of their descriptions revealed that semantic memories (a recipe) and episodic memories (personal recollections of specific meals) were inseparably mingled.

The richness and complexity of human memory suggest that a strict distinction between semantic and episodic memory is artificial. To know how to read or to tell time; to recognize people's voices or the sounds of different musicians; to know which way the wind is blowing; and to recognize people you have met—all of these skills require memory, and clearly it is an oversimplification to classify one example as purely semantic and another as purely episodic.

There have been only a few studies of adult age differences in semantic memory, perhaps because little if any age-related decline is found in semantic abilities. Walsh and Baldwin (1977) found no differences between young adults (mean age 18.7 years) and old adults (mean age 67.3 years) in the ability to integrate related content from separate sentences. Furthermore, there were no age differences in the retention of semantic information. Cohen (1979) found that older adults were less able than younger adults to make correct inferences on the basis of reading 60- to 75-word passages, but the difficulty was due to language comprehension, not memory deficiencies. Taub (1979) has also report-ed that some older people are at a disadvantage in comprehending discourse (215-word and 957-word passages). Young and old adults of high intelligence did not differ from each other in discourse comprehension, but there were age differences between adults of average intelligence (Taub, 1979).

Depth of Processing

Postman (1975), in his impressive review of the verbal learning and memory literature, deplored the excessive and increasing proliferation of memory mod-els. Existing theories could no longer adequately account for the research re-sults that were being obtained, but, Postman argued, creating a new model or theory for every new finding was not the way around this dilemma.

Practically all of the existing models of memory in the mid-1970s empha-sized the temporal and sequential aspects of memory; that is, the models ade-quately explained the differences between short-term and long-term memory, and they generally assumed that the flow of information was first to sensory memory, then to short-term memory, and then, under appropriate conditions, to long-term memory. However, little attention was paid to the level, or depth, at which the information was encoded, stored, and processed. A paper by Craik and Lockhart (1972) was a major force in drawing attention to the depth di-mension of memory processing. Craik and Lockhart defined depth of process-ing as "a greater degree of semantic or cognitive analysis" (p. 675).

In studies of depth of processing, subjects first answer some questions or make some decisions about words in a list. The questions, called *orienting* questions, are specifically designed to induce a certain level of processing. After the orienting task the subjects are given an unexpected test of recall or recogni-tion memory for the list of words.

Table 5-2 gives some examples of the type of orienting questions that were used in a study by Craik and Tulving (1975). Questions about the case of the letters (capital versus lowercase) oriented the subject to a more shallow level of processing than questions about category or sentence meaning. Making a cate-gorical decision whether or not a word in the list is a name of an animal, for example, induces semantic processing. The series of experiments reported by

Craik and Tulving (1975) supported the depth-of-processing hypothesis since semantic-orienting questions led to better word memory than orthographic- or rhyming-orienting questions.

If memory is related to depth of processing, one possible reason older people do not remember as well as younger adults is that they do not process information as deeply or as fully. Eysenck (1974) examined this *aging processing deficit hypothesis* in an experiment comparing young (18–30 years) and older (55–65 years) adults under different orienting conditions. The four orienting tasks were:

1 Counting the number of letters in each word
2 Producing a word that rhymed with each word
3 Finding an adjective that appropriately modified each word
4 Forming a visual image of each word

Presumably, the induced processing level deepened from task 1 to task 4, and word recall increased from task 1 to task 4. Older subjects remembered fewer words than the younger subjects, and they did not benefit from the orienting tasks designed to encourage deep processing.

In a more recent study of the aging processing deficit hypothesis Mason (1979) compared young (20–30 years), middle-aged (40–59 years), and older (60–80 years) adults using orthographic-, rhyming-, and category-orienting tasks. Consistent with Eysenck (1974), Mason found that semantic-orienting tasks increased adult age differences in memory performance.

MEMORY AND LEARNING

Botwinick (1978) pointed out that the processes of learning and memory go hand in hand. This interdependence is also evidenced in common usage of the words, where learning is frequently defined in terms of committing to memory.

Earlier in this chapter we said that memory is the faculty of retaining and

Table 5-2 Examples of Orienting Questions and Responses from the Craik and Tulving (1975) Experiment.

Processing level	Question	Response	
		Yes	No
Orthographic	Is the word in capital letters?	TABLE	table
Rhyming	Does the word rhyme with WEIGHT?	crate	MARKET
Category	Is the word a type of fish?	SHARK	heaven
Sentence	Would the word fit in the sentence "He met a _____ in the street."?	friend	CLOUD

recalling learned information. The term *learning* is generally defined by psychologists as a relatively permanent change in behavior due to practice or experience; it includes a broad range of behavior changes from relatively simple forms (perceptual learning) to associative conditioning (classical and operant conditioning) to even more complex forms (complex verbal learning and problem solving). Learning also represents a broad class of environmental inputs or antecedents such as educational and cultural experiences that influence many aspects of human development (Goulet & Baltes, 1970).

How do environmental events influence behavior? The two main ways are:

1   A specific stimulus can either elicit or inhibit a specific response when the stimulus is presented. For example, a college student might have a conditioned emotional response to the professor's statement "Put away your notes; I would like to see how many of you are keeping up with the assigned readings."

2   A specific stimulus can either strengthen (positively reinforce) or weaken (punish) a response that has just occurred. For example, the amount of work that a college student puts into studying might be rewarded by a good grade on a test, praise from others, an inner feeling of success or mastery.

These two well-established procedures for associating stimulus events and responses are referred to as classical conditioning and operant conditioning. *Classical conditioning* occurs when existing responses are attached to new stimuli by pairing a new stimulus with one that already elicits the response. Several studies have shown that, with advancing age, there is a reduction in (1) the magnitude of the classically conditioned response and (2) durability or resistance to extinction of the classically conditioned response (Botwinick & Kornetsky, 1960; Braun & Geiselhart, 1959). In these and other studies, however, it has not been possible to determine how much of the difference in conditioning is due to age modifications in the response system and how much is due to an actual decline in the ability to be and to remain conditioned.

Operant conditioning, in contrast, involves the delivery of reinforcing stimuli contingent on the occurrence of some response. That is, reinforcers serve to strengthen the responses they follow. Although there are relatively few laboratory studies of aging differences in operant conditionability, there have been many reports of the successful application of operant conditioning procedures to the establishment and reestablishment of behaviors in children and adults in clinical and educational settings (for a review of the application with older adults see Hoyer, Mishara, & Riedel, 1975). For all individuals the critical factors in operant conditioning are (1) the schedule of reinforcement (continuous or intermittent) and (2) the potency of the reinforcer to the subject.

The bulk of the research on adult age differences in human learning has involved the study of verbal learning. One of the main concerns of the researchers has been the nature of the relationship between human learning and memory. The length of the "study" interval was found to differentially influence the learning and memory capacities of both younger and older adults. Older people benefit more than young from a slower presentation pace (Arenberg, 1973; Canestrari, 1963). In Canestrari's investigation young and older adults were given the opportunity to extend the duration of either the anticipation interval (the period before the correct response is shown) or the inspection interval (that is, when the stimulus and response items are presented together). He found that older subjects rarely extended the inspection interval, but they did extend the time available to make a response (the anticipation interval).

Canestrari and others (for instance, Eisdorfer, Axelrod, & Wilkie, 1963; Taub, 1967) showed that the elderly tend to make more omission than commission errors. That is, older people will simply not answer rather than guess or take the risk of committing an error. This finding is consistent with other studies (for example, Botwinick, 1978) showing age-related increases in cautiousness and reluctance to venture a response under conditions of high uncertainty.

Different types of learning and memory are more or less important at different points during the human life span. At what age is it easiest, for example, to ski for the first time, or to acquire a foreign language, or to learn to play a musical instrument? At what age is it easiest to use or to apply well-rehearsed skills such as language? The term *preparedness* refers to the organism's readiness to learn a specific skill (Seligman, 1975). During childhood we readily ac-

Different types of learning and memory vary in importance at different points in life. Several researchers have found that older people tend to be more cautious and less willing to take risks in learning situations.

quire many new and essential cognitive, interpersonal, and physical skills. It may be that humans are biologically or maturationally more prepared, or "ready," to learn new and complex skills early in life and relatively more prepared to carry out already learned skills later in development. However, abilities develop and expand as new learning enables further learning. As the developing individual becomes increasingly effective and specialized in his or her interactions with the environment, perhaps the personal utility of the ability to rapidly master complex skills decreases. In other words, rapid mastery may be a more important ability in early life than in later life.

There is some research evidence to support this view. In general, older adults are able to recall present information as well as younger adults, but they do not fare as well under the following conditions: (1) when the contents of active memory must be manipulated or reorganized in some way for efficient processing (Craik, 1977); (2) when the information to be learned is unfamiliar and confusing (Hoyer & Plude, 1980); and (3) when the material to be learned is relatively low in meaningfulness and personal significance (Fozard, 1980).

Schonfield and Stones (1979) noted that the biological utility of immediate recall capacity is vital throughout life since it enables the person to remain alert to change in the immediate surroundings and also provides a basic building block for new learning. A positive interpretation of memory loss in old age is to view it as an adaptive process. That is, the older adult is actually more "prepared" to select well-learned information and to forget the unimportant exceptions to the experience of a lifetime.

AGE CHANGES IN MEMORY

Encoding and Retrieval

Our long-term memory is kind of a filing system. How we *organize* the information to be stored affects how quickly and thoroughly we can retrieve that information. Further, what related bits of information we retrieve from the files, say, in a conversation or when answering an essay test, also depends on our mental organization. There is evidence to suggest a retrieval difficulty as we get older (see Botwinick, 1978; Craik, 1977).

One possible explanation of retrieval decline is that it is attributable to age differences in memory organization. David Hultsch has addressed this question in several interesting studies (1969, 1971, 1974, 1975). In one study Hultsch (1969) gave men from three age groups (16–19 years, 30–39 years, and 45–54 years) a free-recall task under one of three instructional conditions: standard free recall (that is, write down as many of the 22 words as possible in any order); nonspecific organization (that is, try to organize the words in whatever way is best); and alphabetical organization (organize the words alphabetically and then go through the letters of the alphabet one at a time remembering the word that begins with each). His subjects were also classified in terms of high and low verbal facility. The highly verbal subjects showed no age-related decrement in recall under the standard and nonspecific instructional conditions. In other words, age-related organizational deficits may be related to verbal facility.

We can show that we have learned and remembered something in different ways. On a multiple-choice test, for example, we need only *recognize* the correct choice, whereas on an essay test we need to be able to *recall* the information presented. Most studies of adult age differences show greater age-related memory loss on recall than on recognition tests of memory (Drachman & Leavitt, 1972). Recall tasks are more difficult than recognition tasks in general, but Schonfield and Robertson (1966) found that older adults are especially disadvantaged on recall tasks. Schonfield and Robertson did not find age differences in recognition memory.

These findings were interpreted as suggesting a *retrieval deficit* in memory with advancing age. Several other studies have supported this interpretation (Botwinick & Storandt, 1974; Laurence, 1967a). Specifically, Laurence found only a slight age deficit in the recall of words representing a single concept (for instance, animals) but a substantial age deficit in the recall of unrelated words. It was concluded that words representing a single concept can be retrieved or accessed more easily than unrelated words. In a follow-up study Laurence (1967b) found that the age deficit in recall could be eliminated under cued-recall conditions (that is, when category names are given at retrieval). Many other studies have reported that older adults are at a disadvantage compared to younger adults when little retrieval information is given. Similarly, it has been shown that age deficits are less in recognition tasks and in cued-recall tasks where retrieval demands are lower.

Although the evidence supporting an age-related deficit in retrieval is rather clear, many studies suggest that adult age differences in encoding and learning are at least partially responsible for the memory problems of older subjects. Craik and Masani (1969) and Smith (1977), for example, have shown that there are substantial age differences in the encoding of information to be remembered.

In summary, the research on localizing age-related losses in memory suggests either an encoding deficit or a retrieval deficit. Of course, it is possible that both encoding and retrieval processes are responsible for age-related memory loss. Because of the difficulties in distinguishing encoding, retrieval, and other stages of memory, many researchers today prefer to view memory as one aspect of an information-processing continuum.

Encoding Specificity and Cue Overload

Consider the following events:

- The blizzard of 1927
- Valentine's Day, 1975

- John F. Kennedy's assassination
- High school graduation

Such events serve as "markers" for remembering other events in calendar time. It seems that new people, places, and things are best remembered when they are distinctively or specifically encoded, and such markers serve to make encoding more specific. The *encoding specificity hypothesis* of aging suggests that older people do not label incoming information as distinctively as younger adults do (Tulving & Thompson, 1973). The relative lack of encoding specificity in old age may reflect characteristics of the older person's environment or *encoding strategy* differences associated with aging.

Just as environmental and internal markers or cues for recent memories may be less frequent for older adults, older cues may become overworked or overloaded with the passage of time. The *cue-overload hypothesis* suggests that the cues in memory have so many associations that they are no longer distinctive unless they are given extra attention (Schonfield & Stones, 1979). For example, who would be less likely to confuse one semester's experiences with those of a different semester—the professor who has taught for 20 years or the professor who has taught for only four semesters?

With the benefit of encoding specificity and without cue overload, memories might persist indefinitely. Madorah E. Smith (1963) reported an interesting study of one person's recall of the 107 answers to the questions in the *Westminister Shorter Catechism* (see Table 5-3). These answers had been recited perfectly before the child's 13th birthday 60 years earlier. Thus they had been specifically encoded at a time of life when there was no interfering cue overload. While there had been some practice of the earlier portion of the Catechism during adolescence, the latter part of the Catechism had not been practiced at all or tested for 60 years. Although forgetting was more rapid during the last 10 years than during the preceding 30 or 40 years, the degree of recall is remarkable.

All of us have some early memories that are highly resistant to loss. Their existence is evidence to refute a "disuse" notion of long-term memory loss. There are experiences, good and bad, that we seem never to forget even though we don't rehearse or use the information. Perhaps this information remains distinct in long-term memory because we don't rehearse it and so don't subject it to interference from new associations. Motor skills such as bicycling, swim-

Table 5-3   Data from Smith's Study of Catechism Recall after 60 Years

| | Number of answers at time of testing | | |
	1934	1950	1960
Partly forgotten	9	15	34
Prompted once	44	39	32
Remembered	54	53	41

ming, or sailing are also retained during the off-season or for many years without any practice. Clearly, there is more to memory failure than simple passage of time.

Interference

As Botwinick (1977) has noted, it was not very long ago that *interference theory* was the favorite explanation of learning and memory researchers. In numerous studies, with college students especially, it was demonstrated that other information (stimulus interference) or other responses (response interference) negatively affected the organization of ongoing information processing or already existing memories. Interference theory and the study of paired-associative learning clearly reflect the associationistic tradition.

In learning a list of paired associates there are two steps. A stimulus word or item is presented, and the subject must anticipate the response item that is next presented. Thus one step involves learning the responses (*response learning*), and the second step is "hooking together" the stimulus and response items, or *associative learning*. There are two types of associative interference. In the first type preexisting associations (such as table–chair) interfere with the learning and memorization of a new association (table–hair). This is referred to as *proactive interference*.

Retroactive interference is more easily studied experimentally than proactive interference. In a typical study of retroactive interference on memory (see Table 5-4) everyone learns task A. Next only half the subjects (experimental group) learn task B; the rest are the control group. Then all subjects are tested on their memory of task A. If it is shown that the experimental group is *inferior* to the control condition, retroactive interference is said to have taken place. Interference effects on memory must operate on either storage or retrieval processes, not on encoding, since all subjects learn task A to the same degree.

Older people have been shown to be particularly prone to interference in several paired-associate studies (Arenberg, 1973; Wimer & Wigdor, 1958). In Arenberg's study young adults (30–39 years) and older adults (62–77 years) were compared using the classic A–B, A–C interference paradigm. Subjects first learned to associate a stimulus consisting of two consonants with a two-syllable adjective response (for instance, TL with INSANE and SN with COMPLETE). They then learned to associate the same stimulus consonants with different adjectives (TL with ORAL and SN with VULGAR). Gladis and Braun (1958)

Table 5-4   The Basic Retroactive Interference Paradigm

Experimental group	Learn task A	Learn task B	Test memory of task A
Control group	Learn task A	No	Test memory of task A

used the same test materials, allowing subjects 4 seconds between stimulus and response presentation.

Although Gladis and Braun found no age decline in associative learning when individual scores were adjusted for vocabulary and original learning level, Arenberg found an age difference in favor of the younger adults when there was a short (1.9 second) anticipation interval between stimulus and response presentation, but no age difference when a longer (3.7 second) anticipation interval was used. Arenberg thus resolved the discrepancy between the results of the Wimer and Wigdor (1958) and Gladis and Braun (1958) studies: If older adults are given sufficient time for inspecting the stimulus and anticipating the response to it, they perform as well as younger adults. In other words, older learners need more time for inspection than someone younger.

Intuitively, it seems that older people have acquired and stored a vast amount of information because of many years of exposure, and this long-term storage may somehow limit and interfere with the intake of new knowledge. Well-established associations may cause special difficulties with learning new incompatible associations. Or difficulties may arise for the older learner mainly when existing knowledge no longer aids the acquisition of new information (Schonfield & Stones, 1979). Craik (1977), however, has commented that there has not been much empirical support for the interference proneness explanation of age-related memory loss.

Nevertheless, Botwinick (1977) and Schonfield and Stones (1979) have suggested that we shouldn't bury the interference proneness hypothesis just yet. Taub (1968) and Taub and Greiff (1967) showed that older subjects are more vulnerable to interference at the time of processing. Taub's 1968 study demonstrated that the task of actively rehearsing information while simultaneously trying to recall other stored information was considerably more difficult for older adults. As Schonfield and Stones (1979) have pointed out, interference theory needs to be tested using experimental paradigms in addition to the retroactive design.

Reconstructive Memory

Early Gestalt psychologists were particularly interested in the problem of memory distortion with time, and recently there has been a strong, renewed interest in the study of bias in memory. The process is analogous to the game of "gossip," as it might occur in an elementary school classroom. As a message is passed from one child to the next, it undergoes distortion. Irregularities might become exaggerated and other aspects might be normalized. Bartlett (1932) was one of the first to call attention to what is now referred to as *reconstructive memory*.

Often memory involves an active reconstruction of the past. We do not retrieve static, unadulterated memory traces; rather, our memories are reorganizations and reconstructions of past experience. Schachtel (1974) has pointed out that "the organization and reconstruction of past experiences and impressions is in the service of present needs, fears, and interests" (p. 3). In other words, the present influences *how* the past is remembered.

It is relatively easy to explain how a memory might decay with advancing age, but it is less easy to explain how a memory can "grow" or reorganize itself with time. Several types of biasing mechanisms have been proposed to account for the reconstructive nature of memory. From a developmental perspective the notion of schemata is especially relevant. In Bartlett's (1932) classic study he pointed out that memory involves dynamic interaction and reconstruction. Bartlett used the term *schemata* to refer to internal structures that are continuously modified by new information. According to Bartlett, remembering was the process of activating relevant schemata and drawing on them to construct events in memory. The concept of schemata is also central to Piaget's theory of cognitive development (Piaget & Inhelder, 1973). Piaget argued that schemata, defined as internal representations of thought, are continuously enriched through the process of *accommodation* of new input. It could be that, as we get older, we do not take in new information easily unless it can be accommodated within existing, well-established knowledge schemata.

In contrast to contemporary schemata theories of memory reconstruction, some memory theorists take an Associationist stance to the reconstruction problem. Anderson and Bower (1973), for example, have suggested that memory consists of "nodes" of interconnected associations. Memory reconstruction takes place by the development of new associations and new interconnections, not through structural change, according to Anderson (1976).

It's possible that older people can remember as well as younger adults, but what they choose to remember is different from what younger adults remember and different from what is typically measured on memory tests. In other words, at different ages adults construct and reconstruct different aspects of experience.

Older adults are often thought to have excellent recall of events in the distant past and poor recall of recent events. Is it that the past is more salient or more personally important than the present? The idea that an individual constructs and reconstructs events in memory depending on present and past schemata draws researchers away from an overreliance on accuracy of recall as an index of memory toward a concern for the *personal meaning* of events in memory. The result is a more positive picture of the effects of aging on memory. Recall, for example, that age-related declines are typically not found in studies of semantic memory (Fullerton & Smith, 1980; Walsh & Baldwin, 1977).

Reconstructive memory has also been shown to depend on the present and past circumstances surrounding the memory. For example, Loftus and Zanni (1975) have demonstrated the effects of type of questioning on the answers given by witnesses in courtroom testimony. In one experiment witnesses observing the same event responded differently—and as predicted—to the following questions:

- How fast was the car going when it *bumped* against the other car?
- How fast was the car going when it *smashed* against the other car?

In other words, different memories can be evoked or constructed depending on how questions are asked.

Reminiscence

Reminiscence, or life-review, refers to a detailed self-evaluation of personal experiences throughout life. It is an aspect of memory that probably has most significance late in the life span. Studies by LeBlanc (1969) and Fink (1957), for example, have shown that there is an increase after about age 45 or 50 in life-review themes while telling stories. Butler (1963) has pointed out the adaptive function of reminiscence in later life. Reviewing one's life experiences is a constructive process that enables the individual to positively assess his or her contributions and accomplishments. Some important aspects of life-review and reminiscence, both positive and negative, are as follows (Butler & Lewis, 1977; Fallot; 1980):

Reviewing one's life experiences is constructive; it enables people to evaluate their contributions and accomplishments. Such reviews occur throughout adulthood.

1   Self-reflection is not a sign of a motivation to live in the past or a sign of memory loss; rather, it is a normal process of identity consolidation and personality integration.

2   Reevaluating past events and experiences permits the solution of previously unresolved conflicts and leads to a more positive self-concept.

3   Life-review can lead to an honest appraisal of one's self-worth and realistic awareness of present vulnerabilities and mortality. As in self-psychoanalysis, one reviews past behavior and thoughts in order to gain an understanding of present circumstances.

4   Life-review can lead to a sense of bitterness, regret, and despair. Individuals who are unable to accept how they have spent their life may feel depressed. Hopefully, such individuals sooner or later will come to terms, rationally and emotionally, with this information.

5   Life-review may provide a realization of mistakes and a desire to change one's actions and beliefs. For example, the person may want to make friends with past enemies or make right old wrongs.

6   It may be difficult for some people to listen meaningfully to another's life-review. Reminiscence may seem like a preoccupation with the self. To listen is often time consuming, with no apparent benefit to the listener. In some cases, however, sharing a life-review process may be a very insightful and significant experience for a listener.

Reminiscence about the past is likely to affect what will be stored in memory in the future. Meacham and Singer (1977) have offered the distinction between *prospective memory* and *retrospective memory*. Prospective remembering involves the retention of information that has a direct bearing on our future actions, whereas retrospective memories are those that involve the retention of information from the past. For example, remembering if you have already locked the door and remembering to lock the door in the future are distinguishable tasks of memory. If prospective and retrospective in fact represent different types of memory, it is reasonable to expect that there will be adult age differences for these aspects of memory. Little research exists on adult age differences in prospective memory; however, it seems that older adults are less future-oriented than younger adults and less interested in remembering future events than remembering past events.

Metamemory

In a recent study Perlmutter (1978) tested young adults between 20 and 25 years of age and older adults between 60 and 65 years of age on several aspects of memory. She collected information about the subjects' medical, educational, and occupational histories, as is customary in psychogerontological research. What was different about her study was that she also asked her subjects questions about day-to-day memory problems—what was easy and difficult for them to remember and what memory strategies they used. Consistent with previous findings, sizable age-related differences favoring the young adults were found in word recall and recognition. The answers to the questions about memory were not predictive of actual memory performance. However, this was one of the first systematic studies of adult age differences in memory-related phenomena, and it suggests that further research is warranted.

Metamemory, self-knowledge about one's own memory processes and outcomes, has recently caught the interest of developmental psychologists (for instance, Brown, 1975; Flavell & Wellman, 1977). Youssen and Levy (1975) studied the accuracy of predicting one's own recall and found that prediction accuracy increased from the preschool to the college years. However, college students were influenced by "false" norm information about peer performance, suggesting that even adults have uncertainty about their exact capabilities.

Lachman, Lachman, and Thronesbery (1979) studied the "feeling of knowing" phenomenon in adults ranging from 18 to 75 years of age. Subjects either knew the answers to questions of general world knowledge (such as, Which direction does the Statue of Liberty face? What was Mohammed Ali's previous name?) or said, "I don't know." Subjects were probed further on their "I don't know" answers as follows:

- Do you definitely not know?
- Is it that you might not know?
- Could you recognize the correct answer if I told you?
- Could you recall the answer with some hints?

The "I don't know" questions were then readministered in a multiple-choice format, and ratings of the subjects' confidence in the answers were obtained. Compared to the young adults, the older participants were more accurate. That is, the "feeling of knowing" judgments of the older adults more closely predicted their performance on the multiple-choice test.

More recently, Murphy, Sanders, Gabriesheski, and Schmitt (1981) compared the metamemory skills of college-age (mean age 20 years) and older (mean age 69 years) adults and found no age differences in the accuracy of metamemory. However, younger adults were better able to adjust their study time (that is, subjects could study as long as they wanted to) to the difficulty level of the memory task and therefore recalled the material more accurately than the older adults.

Other memory-related phenomena, such as cautiousness, need to be considered in the study of memory. Kvale (1975), Meacham (1972), and Riegel (1977) have stressed the usefulness of involving the subject in the purposes of the research. The dialectical emphasis on breaking down the alienation between subject and object can lead to some significant research on memory in adulthood and old age. We shouldn't forget that older people have been remembering for a long time, and they have much memory and knowledge of memory to share and to understand.

Instead of asking, "How good is your memory?" perhaps we should ask, "What kinds of things do you forget?" Are there developmental differences in what is forgotten as well as what is remembered? Consider the types of forgetting listed in Table 5-5.

Zalenski, Gilewski, and Thompson (1980) asked younger and older adults to rate their frequency of forgetting using categories similar to those in Table 5-5 and found little if any reliable age difference by category of forgetting (see also Cheffin and Herrmann, 1979, as cited in Herrmann, 1979). It is likely that researchers will be expressing more interest in aging and various types of forgetting in the future.

CLINICAL ASPECTS OF MEMORY

Some kinds of memory do show an age-related decline. At the same time, we must recognize that there are large differences among individuals in the rate at which various memory processes decline with advancing age. Some people "lose" their memory "prematurely" in their 40s or 50s, whereas others are unaffected by memory loss until their 70s or 80s. How can we explain these individual differences?

First, biologically programmed factors affect memory and other cognitive and intellectual proficiencies. Neuronal loss, reduced cerebral blood flow, the buildup of plaques and lipofuscans within nerve cells, and neurofibrillary tangling are some of the underlying biological factors that account for general age-related decline and the individual differences therein (see Chapter 3). Inglis (1970), and more recently Erikson and Scott (1977), have reviewed the work on specific types of memory disorders.

Table 5-5   Types of Forgetting

Type	Example
Names	Difficulty in recalling people's names or street names
Stories, movies, conversations, jokes	Difficulty in recalling the punch line of jokes or how a certain movie or TV program ended
Things to do	Forgetting to stop at the store or mail a letter on the way home; forgetting to carry out a planned activity or action
Places	Losing keys, leaving a sweater, or misplacing a wallet or purse
Losing track	Forgetting what one was just talking about because of a distraction or brief interruption
Remote events	Forgetting something that happened many years ago

Reprinted by permission of Douglas Herrmann.

Korsakoff's Syndrome

One of the more identifiable memory disorders is *Korsakoff's syndrome,* which was first described in 1887. The Korsakoff patient is characterized by disorientation and memory impairment. Traditionally, the syndrome is associated with severe and chronic alcoholism; however, it is more precisely brought about by vitamin deficiency secondary to alcoholism. It can also be related to other kinds of brain damage. Sometimes it is difficult to spot the Korsakoff patient because he may be able to keep up a normal conversation about immediate events and situations; it is only when memory is required that the impairment can be easily recognized. Talland (1965) found that Korsakoff patients followed instructions fairly well, but when interrupted they would not remember where they had left off. Korsakoff patients also showed deficits in dividing attention, breaking well-established habits, reproducing story narratives, incidental and intentional learning, and benefiting from corrective feedback and practice.

Baddeley and Warrington (1970), using a variety of tasks, showed that subjects with amnesia (mostly Korsakoff patients) had defective long-term memory and normal short-term memory. In contrast, Cermak (1980) reported that Korsakoff individuals had no difficulty with either verbal or nonverbal information in long-term memory, but they showed rapid forgetting of verbal information in short-term memory (using the Peterson & Peterson [1959] task). In another one of Cermak's studies (Cermak & Butters, 1972) no deficit was found with regard to nonverbal short-term memory, but severe deficits for verbal information (visual and aural) were demonstrated. This pattern of results suggests an encoding problem for Korsakoff patients. Milner's (1970) work at the neurological level supports the various findings for verbal and nonverbal memory loss. When brain damage can be pinpointed as to left or right hemisphere, differential memory loss can be observed (see Cermak, 1977).

Senile Dementia

A common memory disorder in old age is senile dementia, which we described in Chapter 3 as a general decline in cognitive function from a previously attained level (Hughes, 1978). Dementia can occur at any point during the life span, but it is most common in later life. About 40 percent of the population over age 65 are diagnosed as having some degree of senile dementia. Only 4 percent of the elderly living in the community are considered senile, but about 80 percent of the older adults in institutions carry this diagnosis.

The main causes of senile dementia in old age are vascular disease such as arteriosclerosis and Alzheimer-type deterioration. Alzheimer's disease, the most common type of senile dementia in old age, is discussed in Chapter 3. In a recent study by Storandt (1980) memory, personal orientation, problem solving, community functioning, functioning at home, and personal care were studied in normal and demented older persons. Older people with mild Alzheimer-type dementia experienced some memory loss, especially for recent events, and some disorientation and difficulty in problem solving. Severely demented subjects exhibited a very high degree of memory disorder and much difficulty in home and community functioning. The degree of dementia was directly related to the extent of functional debilitation in the six behavior categories that were investigated.

Memory Loss and Depression

The relationship between memory loss and depression is a subject of increasing interest. In fact, it is reasonable to question how much of memory loss is age-induced and how much of it is brought about by age-related increases in such clinical states as depression, dementia, and anxiety. Presenile and senile dementia are clearly associated with memory impairment (Inglis, 1970; Miller & Lewis, 1977). Miller and Lewis attempted to show that elderly depressives and elderly persons with senile dementia perform poorly on memory tasks for different reasons. For example, senile dementia patients exhibit poor memory because of neurological status, whereas a depressed older individual's thoughts may serve to limit attention and short-term processing of new information. An alternative hypothesis is that older depressives are more cautious in their responses and require a greater level of certainty before responding.

One method psychologists use to separate response factors, such as cautiousness, from sensory sensitivity, is *signal-detection analysis* (Hertzog, 1980). Signal-detection analysis has been used widely to study human sensory processes (see Chapter 4); it has also been used to study memory and aging (Harkins, Chapman, & Eisdorfer, 1979; Miller & Lewis, 1977). As can be seen in Table 5-6, there are four possible outcomes whenever an individual makes a decision about the presence or absence of a signal (stimulus). Subjects can be correct either by detecting a signal that is present or by indicating *no* on a trial in which a stimulus was not presented. They can be wrong either by missing a presented signal or by saying *yes* on a trial when no stimulus was given.

Signal-detection analysis is a psychophysical method that takes into account both decision threshold and sensory threshold in measuring behavior. In one study of memory, depression, and aging, Miller and Lewis (1977) used a signal-detection procedure to examine continuous recognition performance in depressed and nondepressed elderly adults. Words were presented one at a

Table 5-6 All Possible Signal-Response Relationships in a Signal-Detection Experiment

	Subject's response	
Signal	Yes	No
Actually present	Hit	Miss
Actually absent	False alarm	Correct negative

time, and the subjects were asked to recognize words that had been presented previously by saying *yes*. By analyzing hits, misses, false alarms (saying *yes* to words not previously given), and correct negatives, Miller and Lewis found that elderly depressives exhibit a poor memory because of a conservative response strategy rather than because of an actual memory impairment.

Intervention

There is more to the clinical study of memory than the diagnostic identification of specific types and causes of memory disorder. Although some memory disorders are caused by irreversible, time-related brain damage, one research goal might be to determine if anything can be ameliorative when an older person exhibits memory problems.

First, we need to be sure that there actually is a problem. Friends, spouses, relatives, and even older people themselves are sometimes too quick to attribute occasional forgetfulness to advanced aging or senility. Memory capacity might be the same, but the person's heightened sensitivity to aging might exaggerate occasional normal absentmindedness. A self-fulfilling prophecy of memory loss can also occur.

When there is a real memory loss, treatment depends on the severity of the deficit. Most age-related memory declines can be easily compensated for by taking notes or relying on some other written or nonwritten mnemonic aids. If one is likely to forget an umbrella on leaving the house in the morning, for example, then it can simply be put by the door the evening before (assuming, of course, that one remembers to do that).

The best way to determine the severity of a memory disorder is through attempts at remediation or amelioration. For a person to have recent memories, new learning and new experiences are necessary. Thus intervention could begin with the provision of meaningful information to remember. We will look further at cognitive interventions in Chapter 14.

SUMMARY

1   Memory is one aspect of a larger cognitive system that includes information pickup, storage, reorganization of acquired information, and knowledge retrieval.

2   Not all types of memory deteriorate at the same time or in the same way with advancing age.

3   The purpose of memory research in relation to adult development is to understand how and why age-associated losses come about. Some important questions that were addressed in this chapter are:

- What are the component processes of human memory and information processing?

- Are some component processes (for instance, encoding, storage, retrieval) more affected by age-related change than other processes? If so, how?

- Are the same processing strategies used for different kinds (such as semantic or episodic) of information?

- When memory losses are observed, where in the processing sequence does the "breakdown" occur?

- What is the role of context in explaining adult age differences in memory?

- Are there adult age differences in reconstructive memory?

- To what extent can clinical and normal age-related memory deficits be ameliorated?

4   Our knowledge of memory has increased tremendously in the past decade, but some caution regarding current trends in memory research is appropriate, as there is a tendency toward overproliferation of models and theories that deal in abstractions and have little or no relevance or application to a real person's memory.

5   The study of memory development in adulthood and old age has been strongly influenced by multistore information-processing models. Information from the receptors first enters sensory memory. Some of this information is then passed to short-term memory (analogous to consciousness or awareness), where it is actively rehearsed. Information in short-term memory is either forgotten or passed along to long-term memory.

6   Short-term memory has a limited capacity, whereas long-term memory is assumed to have an unlimited storage capacity. There are no (or only minimal) age differences in the span or capacity of short-term memory. However, young adults have an advantage compared to older adults when the contents of short-term memory need to be manipulated in some way (for example, repeat backwards your Social Security number).

7   Adult age differences in memory performance are found in long-term memory. A large part of the problem has to do with getting information into long-term memory (that is, the encoding stage), but there is also evidence suggesting age deficits in depth of processing, interference proneness in storage and retrieval, and the organization of long-term memory.

8   The tasks of encoding and retrieving long-term memories should not be confused with the task of describing events and experiences in the distant past. Such descriptions give evidence that there is memory, though they do not tell us much about the processes of memory (that is, how memories develop or how they are forgotten). Most adults can provide seemingly clear descriptions of many past events, but it is difficult to verify the accuracy of these events. Once

memories are acquired, they are often reorganized and modified by the individual (reconstructive memory).

9   What goes on during encoding influences memory performance. Efficient encoding increases the accessibility or retrieval of information in memory. Having the same cues available at encoding and retrieval also enhances memory performance. The aspects of a stimulus that are attended to are the features that will be retained and accessed as needed.

10   As the complexity of memory tasks is increased, adult age differences increase. Cognitive tasks that are difficult for young adults are likely to be even more difficult for older adults.

11   A good understanding of basic memory processes is useful to designing effective interventions for memory disorders. Some explanations of age-related memory loss are as follows:

- Older people can remember as well as younger adults but do not because of lessened motivation or interest.

- Older people can remember as well as younger adults but do not because their environments are typically less structured and differentiated (the encoding specificity hypothesis).

- Older people remember different aspects of experience than young adults; usually the aspects remembered by older persons are not those that are measured in research.

CHAPTER SIX
INTELLIGENCE AND COGNITION

According to Botwinick (1967), no area of aging research has received greater attention than the study of intelligence. Interest in intelligence has a long history that predates the emergence of any social science discipline. Philip H. Du-Bois (1968) has credited the ancient Chinese with the invention of the psychological test. As early as 1200 B.C. the Chinese emperor hired, promoted, and dismissed his officials on the basis of an examination of performance in the six arts: music, archery, horsemanship, writing, arithmetic, and protocol. During the next thousand years tests in the geography of the empire, civil law, military intelligence, agriculture, and accounting were added to the Chinese "civil service" examination.

Intelligence testing was also common in ancient Greece (Doyle, 1974). The Greeks were interested in the practical as well as theoretical aspects of mental testing, and the abilities that they measured represented the characteristics of the ideal Greek citizen, which varied somewhat from one geographic area to the next (Dobson, 1932).

In theory and practice the ancient Greeks were aware of the problems of reliability (consistency) and validity (meaningfulness) in testing intelligence. Both the Greeks and the Chinese "recognized that relatively short performance

under carefully controlled conditions could yield an estimate of the ability to perform under less rigorously controlled conditions and for a longer period of time" (DuBois, 1968, p. 254). Thus, we have the standardized test. Plato, however, was concerned about the arbitrariness of the criteria used to define intelligence.

If the tiny children are to decide, they will no doubt give the award for the man in the puppet show. . . . The bigger boys for the comedian; the cultivated women . . . for the tragedy. . . . Whereas oldsters like ourselves would be likely to get the most pleasure from a reciter who gave a fine rendering of the Iliad, or Odyssey, or a Hesiodic poem. . . . Then, who would be the rightful winner? (Laws, 658)

Standardization, reliability, validity, and predictive criteria are still important considerations in psychological testing, and they are of special concern in attempts to make comparisons among groups who differ with regard to age, sex, and cultural or ethnic background.

Probably the best place to begin our discussion is with the definitional problem: What is intelligence? Then we will look at the various factors that influence age differences and age changes in intellectual performance and conclude with an examination of recent research trends and conceptualizations of intelligence.

DEFINING AND MEASURING INTELLIGENCE

What Is Intelligence?

Intelligence is a characteristic of people and their actions. For example, the label *intelligent* is often used to describe people who stand out from others in the breadth or depth of their knowledge. People who can accomplish things or solve problems that others cannot or do not do and people who carry out complex tasks quickly, better, or more efficiently than others also are called intelligent.

Because there are many ways to be intelligent, and because intellectual abilities change and develop as we grow older, no definition of intelligence has remained satisfactory to many people for very long. Many themes can be found in ordinary dictionary definitions of intelligence. For example:

- The ability to deal effectively with symbols or abstractions
- The ability to acquire and understand knowledge
- The ability to adapt successfully to new situations

- The ability to appreciate and/or create significant art or ideas
- The ability to fully enjoy each day and to experience happiness through life

Such ordinary definitions of intelligence are not the same as *operational* definitions. Intelligence can be operationally defined as the score an individual manifests on a standardized intelligence test. Operational definitions change as tests evolve; thus the specification of intelligence is a never-ending process involving observation, validation, reliable assessment, and experimentation (Kaplan, 1964; Matarazzo, 1972).

It is important to distinguish between practitioners and theorists in the study of intelligence. Alfred Binet, Louis Terman, David Wechsler, and Nancy Bayley, among others, represent the intelligence practitioner model because of their pragmatic concerns with test construction and human assessment. Charles Spearman, L. L. Thurstone, J. P. Guilford, and R. B. Cattell represent intelligence theorists, who seek to understand the structure and composition of human intelligence. All of these practitioners and theorists are in the *psychometric* tradition; that is, they are interested in the measurement of intelligence by means of tests. Others, such as Piaget, are much more concerned with thought processes than outcomes and place far less emphasis on tests; they represent the cognitive approach to intelligence.

One major research question has been whether intelligence has a structure. The term *structure* has been used to describe the organization of the various mental abilities that make up intelligence (Sternberg, 1979). Adult developmental psychologists are interested not only in improvements and decline in intellectual performance (quantitative change) but also in qualitative or structural changes in intelligence with age—that is, the changing nature of intelligence. During the 20th century, largely with the help of computer technology, great strides have been made toward understanding both the quantitative and the qualitative aspects of adult intellectual development. One approach that has many adherents is factor analysis.

Factor analysis is a statistical tool for determining the degree of relationship and independence among variables and clusters of variables. Variables that cluster together form a *factor*. For example, consider the following types of intelligence test items:

Fill in the blanks below with vowels to make real words:
P __ NC __ L
H __ M __ N
V __ RB __ L

Unscramble the letters below to form real words:
OBOK   _____
MNAIAL   _____
RDWOS   _____

Complete the sentences below by giving as many different explanations as possible for each simile:

A baby is like tomorrow because . . .
A book is like a box because . . .

List two things that are wrong with the picture below:

Do all of these sample items measure the same intellectual ability or different abilities? If performance on one type of problem was predictive of performance on the other types, it would be said that the items *cluster on one factor.*

The first type of test item, called *disemvowelled words,* and the second type, called *scrambled words* or *anagrams,* represent a cognition factor involving symbolic content and units (see Guilford, 1966, 1967). Guilford found that the third type of problem represents a different factor because it involves cognition of semantic content at a relational level. Recognizing familiar words as letter structures depends on quite different intellectual abilities from knowing the meaning of words. The fourth type of problem represents yet another factor of intelligence—*evaluation* of a system to discover internal inconsistencies.

Guilford's Structure of Intellect Model

J.P. Guilford's *structure of intellect* model (Guilford, 1966, 1967) represents one of the most ambitious attempts to organize the factors of intelligence. Guilford classified the factors of intelligence along three dimensions: *contents* (type of information), *operations* (what an individual is required to do with the information), and *products* (the form of the information). This structure of intellect model is represented by a cube (Figure 6-1). The dimensions are further divided into four different types of content (figures or numbers, symbols or letters, words, and behaviors); five different operations (evaluation, concurrent thinking, divergent thinking, memorization, and cognition) the individual uses to solve test items; and six products, which represent the form in which the information is conceptualized by the examinee (units, classes, relations, systems, transformations, and implications). The various operations are defined specifically: *Cognition* is the recognition of old information and the discovery of new information; *evaluation* is judgments of the veracity, accuracy, or suitability of the information; *convergent thinking* is the deduction of single correct conclusions; *divergent thinking* is inducing multiple answers or solutions; and *memory* is the retention of the outcomes of cognition. The resulting cube has 4 × 5 × 6, or 120, different cells, each representing a separate mental ability. For example, for Guilford verbal comprehension consists of *cognition* of *units* with *words*.

Guilford, like other psychometricians, was interested primarily in describing the organization of human intelligence. When Guilford proposed the tridimensional model in 1961, about 40 separate abilities had been labeled. As of 1973 researchers had identified almost 100 different intellectual abilities. Guil-

Figure 6-1   Guilford's structure of intellect model (1967). (After Guilford, 1967.)

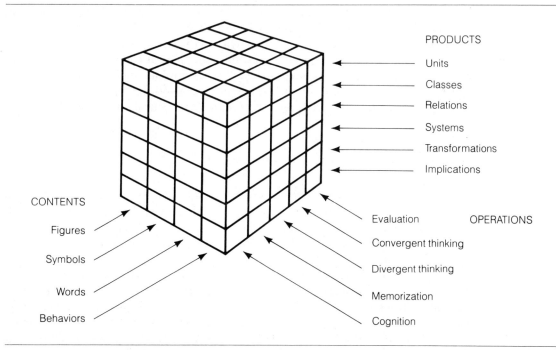

ford and his colleagues are still trying to provide empirical evidence to support the structure of intellect model.

The General Factor Theory

In contrast to Guilford's approach Charles Spearman was struck more by the consistency than the differences among various measures of intelligence. Spearman's (1927) *general factor theory* represents one of the earliest applications of factor analysis to the area of intelligence. He proposed that g, or general ability, was involved in all intellectual tasks that we perform, and s, or specific ability, was involved in some tasks and not others. Someone with a low level of g would be expected to perform generally at a poor level on all cognitive tasks. Variations from task to task would be explained by s factors—abilities that are situation-specific and unique for that individual.

For some psychometricians the general ability factor that supposedly permeates all that we do provides a definition of intelligence. However, it is important to point out that no single test yields a perfect or complete measure of general ability, and therefore g must be viewed as an approximation or estimate of true mental ability.

If there is a true g, what determines it? How does it develop and change as we grow older? When Spearman (1927, Ch. 9) conceived of g, he thought of it as some kind of electrochemical energy in the central nervous system. Some problem-solving situations required more of this energy than other situations or tests, and some individuals possessed more of it than other persons. Similarly, Thorndike, Bragman, Cobb, and Woodyard (1927) suggested that intelligence reflected plasticity, or the number of modifiable neural connections in the individual's central nervous system. Again, some problem-solving situations required the activation of more of these neural connections than other situations, and individuals differed with regard to number of neural connections.

The Primary Mental Abilities Model

Even though some factor theorists seem to agree with Spearman that there is a biological basis to intelligence, many rejected the notion of g. Their factor analysis research suggested instead the existence of several independent intellectual abilities, each indicated by different combinations of intelligence tests. The *primary mental abilities* model of Thurstone and Thurstone (1941) represents one of the important theories. They postulated that intelligence was not one ability but actually several independent abilities. On the 1941 version of the primary mental abilities (PMA) test the following abilities were tested: number, word fluency, verbal meaning, memory, reasoning, space, and perceptual speed. On a current version of the PMA five primary mental abilities are represented: number, word fluency, verbal meaning, reasoning, and space (Thurstone, 1958). These abilities were shown to be relatively independent of each other. At the same time, there was also some evidence to suggest the pervasiveness of a *g* factor embedded within these different primary mental abilities. Schaie and his collaborators have used the PMA test in their carefully planned longitudinal and sequential studies of adult intelligence and have shown that the different primary mental abilities exhibit different age trends (Schaie, 1979; Schaie & Labouvie-Vief, 1974; Schaie & Parham, 1977).

Current Factor Analytic Models

In an excellent review of the history of the study of intelligence Matarazzo (1972) observed that different views of the nature of intelligence were determined by (1) the particular tests and measures used, (2) the particular types of statistical analysis used, and (3) the characteristics of the population or sample of people studied. It is reasonable to expect that the factor composition of intelligence would vary depending on the age of the individuals studied. Spearman, Guilford, and Thurstone all studied the nature of intelligence through factor analysis of the scores of young adults (college students or Army enlistees). Recently several factor analytic models of adult intellectual development have emerged (Baltes & Nesselroade, 1973; Horn, 1970; Horn & Cattell, 1966; Reinert, 1970).

The Integration-Differentiation-Dedifferentiation Model   Reinert (1970) was interested in the instability of intelligence factors across adulthood. Although there is considerable uniformity (or reliability) of intelligence factors from one adult age group to another, Reinert suggested that the structure of intelligence varies with age during adulthood. From a life-span perspective it can be argued that the individual begins life with something akin to a *g* factor that is largely genetically based and that reveals itself in all mental activities. The individual's repertoire of knowledge or capability expands with age due to the operation of both prewired genetic programming and experience (that is, environmental influences).

As people continue to develop intellectually, experience begins to play a relatively greater role in determining their intellectual activities, and the *integrated g*-type factor structure yields to a *differentiated* factor composition. That is, on the basis of what the individual does and does not experience different individuals develop some types of abilities and not other types. Abilities that are fairly interrelated in childhood become independent in young and middle adulthood.

As the individual grows older, a *dedifferentiation* of abilities occurs. This return to a uniform intelligence construct can be explained in part by genetically based biological aging and in part by an age-related disengagement from environmental stimulation that previously fostered intellectual diversity. Because of the difficulties in conducting the kind of research that would be needed to confirm the integration-differentiation-dedifferentiation hypothesis, relatively little empirical attention has been given to Reinert's (1970) formulation (however, see Cunningham, 1980).

Crystallized and Fluid Intelligence   Horn's (1970) distinction between fluid intelligence and crystallized intelligence generated a considerable amount of attention and some controversy in the field of intellectual aging (see also Horn & Cattell, 1966). *Fluid intelligence* refers to the individual's general mental ability independent of acquired knowledge, experience, and learning. Fluid intelligence is reflected in tests of inductive reasoning, Raven's Progressive Matrices, and memory span. *Crystallized intelligence,* in contrast, refers to knowledge acquired through experience. Vocabulary tests and untimed tests of general information and verbal comprehension are indices of crystallized intelligence.

Crystallized intelligence continues to improve or increase during the adult years, whereas fluid intelligence exhibits an age-related decline (see Figure 6-2). *Omnibus* tests combine the scores on many different subtests of intelligence; the fact that different abilities show different developmental trends is obscured when intelligence is represented by a single omnibus score.

The distinction between crystallized and fluid intelligence has been important to the study of adulthood and aging in two ways. First, it is now accepted that different aspects of intelligence show different developmental trends. Second, researchers are increasingly interested in the interrelation among abilities and the factors responsible for their development through the adult life cycle.

The Simulation Approach   Researchers are very interested in knowing how developmental changes in the structure of intelligence come about. They usually approach this question by conducting either a cross-sectional or a longitudinal study, using a variety of intelligence tests or subtests, and then analyzing the results in terms of qualitative and quantitative changes in factor structure (see Cunningham, 1980). However, in addition to the practical (time, cost) and methodological problems in any type of developmental research, the findings of developmental studies are limited because many of the variables that affect development are not under the direct control of the investigator. When systems and processes cannot be directly investigated using experimental methods, *simulation strategies* provide an alternative. With the assistance of a computer, researchers can construct settings and conditions that are assumed to parallel selected aspects of reality.

Baltes and Nesselroade (1973) demonstrated the usefulness of the simulation approach to the study of adult intelligence by mimicking the short-term and long-term effects of different environmental conditions on the structure of intelligence. They were thus able to simulate Reinert's (1970) model of intellectual integration, differentiation, and dedifferentiation. They observed changes in the dependent variables of intelligence as a function of the *expected* effects of various independent variables: The independent variables operated as hypothesized. The usefulness of simulation strategies depends on the degree to which the hypotheses represent "real" developmental change (however, see Baltes, Cornelius, Nesselroade, & Willis, 1980; Cunningham, 1980).

Figure 6-2   Intelligence performance as a function of age. (Adapted from Horn, 1970, p. 463.)

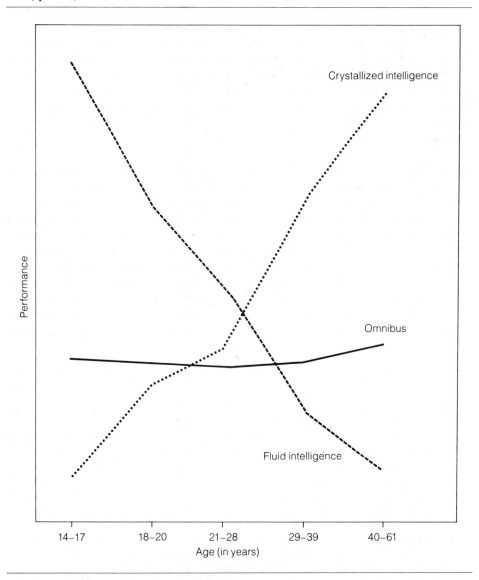

Reliability and Validity

The worth of the various psychometric models of intelligence and intellectual aging depends on two distinct features of the psychometric instruments used to measure intellectual performance—reliability and validity.

Reliability   As we saw in Chapter 1, reliability refers to the consistency of a test, the degree to which people obtain the same or similar scores each time they take the test. If a measure is not reliable, it is of no research value.

We can assess reliability by determining the extent to which the test correlates with itself. Self-correlation can be obtained by giving different forms of the same test at different times (test-retest reliability) or by asking the same information in two different ways at the same testing occasion (the split-half method). There are special difficulties in establishing test reliability in developmental investigations: Differences between test and retest scores may reflect not only the reliability of the test instrument but also developmental change for the tested subjects.

Validity   In contrast to self-correlation, *validity* refers to the correlation between the test and some criterion. For example, if the criterion is a trait, we want to know whether the test measures the trait it is designed to measure.

There are several different kinds of validity (see Table 6-1). One important type in the area of intelligence research is *construct validity*. An intelligence test has construct validity if strong relationships exist between scores obtained on the test and on other measures (tests or other criteria) of the intelligence construct. It is important to note that the intelligence construct may be different for different-aged individuals, and age-appropriate criteria should be used for validation purposes. *Content validity* refers to evidence that the items or subtests that make up the test adequately and fully represent the construct,

Table 6–1   Descriptors for Aspects of Test Validity

Content validity	Content relevance
Predictive validity	Predictive utility
Concurrent validity	Diagnostic utility
Construct validity	Substitutability of tasks
Convergent validity	Interpretive meaningfulness
Discriminant validity	Coherence of intelligence components
Trait validity	Distinctiveness
External validity	Trait correspondence
Ecological validity	External relatedness
Task validity	Ecological generalizability
Temporal validity	Task generalizability
	Generalizability across historical periods; continuity across developmental levels

After Messick, S. Test validity and the ethics of assessment. *American Psychologist,* 1980, *35,* 1012–1027.

trait, or skill being tested. In other words, we add and subtract items from a test to improve its content validity—the extent to which it maximally represents the criterion it is supposed to predict.

Two other types of validity, concurrent validity and predictive validity, differ mainly in terms of when the criterion measures are obtained. *Concurrent validity* refers to the relationship between a test and its criteria at a given time. *Predictive validity* means that the criterion measures were obtained some time after the test was administered. For example, if we wish to know whether individuals who showed superior intellectual performance on a test at age 20 or 30 maintained the same level into their 70s or 80s, we are concerned with the test's predictive validity. If we are developing a new and better test for 60-year-olds, we are primarily concerned with concurrent validity. One familiar example of predictive validity is the use of college entrance exams to predict aptitude for college work. How well an aptitude test correlates with the actual academic performance of college students is a concurrent validity question. Obviously, many factors (personality, coping strategies, motivation) in addition to intellectual capacity determine college success. Some examples of the predictive validity of various psychometric tests of intelligence are given in Table 6-2.

Table 6–2 Predictive Validity of Intelligence Tests

Test	What was being predicted	Degree of prediction or correlation	Subject group	Reference
Scholastic Aptitude Test, Verbal (SAT-V)*	High school class rank	.56	Black college students	Cleary, 1968
Scholastic Aptitude Test, Verbal (SAT-V)*	College grade-point average	.47	White college students	Cleary, 1968
Armed Forces Qualification Test (AFQT)	Occupational status	.50	Adults	Jencks, 1972
Beta IQ Test	Academic performance	.25	18–25-year-old delinquents	Levine & Megargee, 1975
Otis Quick-Scoring Intelligence Test	Guilford's Expressiveness Scale	.43	Grade 11 students	Jacobs & Shin, 1975
Mental Ability Test	Fluency test			
Black Intelligence Test	Shipley Institute of Living Scale	.01	College students	Boone & Adesso, 1974
WAIS	Slosson Intelligence Test	.84	Adults	Watson & Klett, 1975
Army General Classification Test (AGCT)	Offense severity	−.13	Male prisoners	Holland & Holt, 1975
WAIS	Bender-Gestalt Memory Test	.44	Adults	Armentrout, 1976
WAIS	Peabody Picture Vocabulary Test	.92	Adolescents	Covin & Covin, 1976

*Note: Actual SAT-V scores have declined in recent years, presumably because of "grade inflation" and various cohort factors, but degree of predictability has not changed.

One of the most important features in assessing adult intellectual development is *external validity*. Schaie (1977, 1978) has discussed the need for externally valid assessments of adult intelligence. Few if any psychometric instruments validate, concurrently or predictively, how well elderly people cope with situations of daily living. The research of Scheidt and Schaie (1978) illustrates one way of developing externally valid tests of intelligence. They began their research by talking with elderly persons in natural settings such as public parks, shopping centers, and senior centers, asking about their daily problems and situations.

The intelligence testing movement, since its inception, has been oriented toward formal schooling, with the main purpose being to predict educational attainment from a global IQ score. Traditional psychometric tests may simply be irrelevant to the abilities and interests of older people, and therefore these instruments may not meaningfully reflect "real" levels of intellectual functioning. Tests designed for younger adults probably should not be used with older people because both the predictive validity and the external validity of the findings may be inaccurate (Windley & Scheidt, 1980). The subject of ecologically valid age comparisons will be discussed further later in this chapter.

MODIFIERS OF INTELLIGENCE

Investigators have become sensitive to a wide variety of social and biological factors that influence patterns of intellectual growth and decline in adulthood. While declines in some types of intellectual abilities are a reality of aging, recent research has shown that some declines begin later than was once supposed (Botwinick, 1977). Furthermore, the number of declining intellectual functions, as well as the rate of age-related decline, are less than originally thought (Labouvie-Vief, 1977).

The correlation between age and intelligence is about −.40 to −.50. This means that age accounts for only between 16 and 25 percent of the variance in intelligence scores. The variance remaining (75–84 percent) must be explained by various social and biological factors that affect the age–intelligence relationship. Some of these factors are cohort, educational level, life history and experience, anxiety and stress, health status, motivation, and demand characteristics of the testing situation. Let us now look at these modifiers of intelligence.

Intelligence and Cohort

In studies of adult intelligence wide age comparisons (for instance, 30–39 versus 50–59) are often made without regard to various cohort-specific variables (Abrahams, Hoyer, Elias, & Bradigan, 1975). In Chapter 1 we mentioned Schaie's (1965) general developmental model, in which age, cohort, and time of measurement are treated as distinguishable sources of variance. Schaie and his colleagues have reported several applications of the general developmental model to the study of adult intelligence (see, for example, Nesselroade, Schaie, & Baltes, 1972; Schaie, 1970; Schaie & Labouvie-Vief, 1974; Schaie, Labouvie, & Barrett, 1973; Schaie, Labouvie, & Buech, 1973). The main finding has been that cohort-related factors often account for more of the developmental variance in adult intelligence than do age and time of measurement factors. Younger cohorts outperform older ones on crystallized intelligence, cognitive flexibility, visual–motor flexibility, and visualization.

Botwinick (1977) reanalyzed Schaie's data to see if the longitudinal age sequences showed greater or lesser decline than the cross-sectional sequences at each age level. Botwinick found that both the longitudinal and the cross-sectional functions showed little or no age-related decline up to the mid-40s. For the oldest age range, 67–81 years, both cross-sectional and longitudinal data indicated substantial age declines. However, the cross-sectional method showed greater age decline than the longitudinal method for people who were between 46 and 67 years of age. The largest difference between the two methods was obtained for the 53-to-67-year-olds, with the cross-sectional sequences showing much more decline than the longitudinal sequences. Researchers are now beginning to look at the generational factors that are responsible for cohort differences in intelligence.

Intelligence and Educational Level

Matarazzo (1972) has discussed many of the problems involved in standardizing adult intelligence tests. Economic, educational, and occupational factors are not evenly distributed by age or cohort in contemporary society. For example, consider the relationship between intellectual performance and level of scholastic attainment. Levels of education tend to vary for different age, ethnic, gender, and geographic segments of the population.

Kuhlen (1940) was one of the first writers to point out that most inferences based on cross-sectional research results are deficient—perhaps equivocal—because investigators did not adequately take account of educational level as an age-associated concomitant of intellectual performance. More recently, Granick and Friedman (1967, 1973) and Green (1969) investigated the role of educational level in adult intellectual decline. Granick and Friedman (1967) proposed that, when the negative correlation of education with age is statistically controlled, the widely reported decline in intellectual functioning with advanced age is reduced.

Some support for their hypothesis was obtained. The number of significant negative correlations of test scores with age was reduced by 30 percent when the education factor was partialed out from each of the correlations. In Green's (1969) study of intellectual development between ages 16 and 64, WAIS standardization groups were altered so as to be nearly identical with regard to educational level distribution. When this was done, full-scale score means increased to age 40 and then remained stable, scaled verbal means rose to age 50 and then stabilized, and total performance showed only a small decline after 40. Decline was found mainly on the digit symbol substitution task. Additional analyses of the unaltered standardization groups taking into account educational level confirmed the finding of intellectual stability in late adulthood. Green noted that educational level serves as a rough measure of a variety of sociocultural factors in addition to being a concomitant index of scholastic aptitude or potential.

Intelligence and Occupation

The nature and rate of intellectual decline is influenced by the individual's life history and present functional status (that is, occupation). For example, cognitive flexibility (the ability to modify established behaviors in response to environmental demands) generally declines more rapidly with advancing age than do such crystallized abilities as language usage and vocabulary (Schultz, Kaye, & Hoyer, 1980). However, individuals who continue to *use* their cognitive abilities in late adulthood and old age are likely to not show a decline in intelligence.

The effects of individualized life history factors on intelligence can also be

Individuals who continue to use their cognitive abilities, like this ballet master, are less likely to show a decline in intelligence in later life than are those who do not exercise their mind.

seen in studies or situations where older people are already very familiar with the stimulus materials or where, as part of the experiment, they are given practice to bring about familiarity (Labouvie-Vief & Gonda, 1976; Plude & Hoyer, 1981; Poon & Fozard, 1978). Even choice reaction time, a traditional index of age decline, can be improved with extensive practice by older subjects (Murrell, 1970).

Based on an unusually large sample of 18,782 men, two military psychologists, Thomas Harrell and Margaret Harrell, examined the relationship between an enlisted man's score on the Army's test of intelligence (AGCT) and his preservice occupation. Some of the results of this study are reported in Table 6-3. Although these results are fairly old (they were obtained during World War II), they suggest that there is a relationship between occupational status and measured intelligence. Also, the careers (for instance, law) that required the most formal schooling seem to be the ones having the highest average intelligence scores. It is interesting to speculate that jobs select or reject individuals rather than individuals choosing jobs. These data are based on young white males in the 1940s; currently researchers are investigating the degree of relationship that now exists between intelligence level and occupation for men and women, for many ethnicities, and for different-aged adults.

Intelligence and Anxiety

Sigmund Freud can be credited with introducing the term *anxiety* to the psychological lexicon. Although Freud never fully described the characteristics of anxiety, the construct was definitely an important one in his psychosexual developmental theory (Sarbin, 1968).

Today different researchers and theorists use the term to refer to various characteristics. For example, Cattell and Scheier (1961) observed that at least 120 specific procedures or tests were used to assess anxiety. The term is applied sometimes to transient emotional conditions (He is anxious before the meeting)

Table 6-3 Median Intelligence Scores for White Army Enlistees by Their Civilian Occupations

Civilian job	Median intelligence score*	Range of scores*
Accountant	128	94–157
Lawyer	128	96–157
Engineer	127	100–151
Teacher	123	76–155
Photographer	118	66–147
Musician	111	56–147
Mechanic	108	60–155
Lumberjack	96	46–137

*Scores rounded to the nearest whole number.

Adapted from Harrell, T. W. and Harrell, M. S. Army General Classification Test scores for civilian occupations. *Educational and Psychological Measurement,* 1945, 5, 231–239.

and other times to relatively enduring characteristics (He is usually anxious). Spielberger's (1972) state–trait anxiety inventory recognizes that anxiety is sometimes transient (that is, a state variable) and sometimes enduring (a trait variable).

Ross (1968) examined the effects of supportive, neutral, and challenging instructions on paired-associate learning in young (18–26 years) and older (65–75 years) adults. The older individuals exhibited a greater performance decrement on more difficult paired-associate task. The older subjects did least well under challenging (in other words, threatening) instructions and best with supportive instructions. Age-related differences in such variables as subject's self-confidence, susceptibility to negative feedback, and anxiousness may account for some of the reported age-related declines in intelligence and learning (Bellucci & Hoyer, 1975).

Being too anxious or stressed can have a negative effect on measured intelligence. Carl Eisdorfer and his colleagues (see, for example, Eisdorfer, Nowlin, & Wilkie, 1970) have reported several studies of the relationship between stress and intellectual functioning in older people. Wilkie and Eisdorfer (1971) reported that subjects in their 60s with heightened blood pressure (over 105 mm Hg.) showed greater intellectual loss as measured by the WAIS over a ten-year period than did 60-year-olds with either normal or borderline elevated blood pressure levels. Schultz and his colleagues (1979) further studied the relationships between hypertension and intellectual performance and found that good health is an important factor in maintaining a high level of intellectual functioning in later life.

Intelligence and Plasticity

Baltes and Willis (1980) defined intellectual plasticity as the range of intellectual performance displayed by an individual under different environmental conditions. Recently, Baltes and Willis have conducted several studies of intellectual plasticity as part of the Adult Development and Enrichment Project (ADEPT) at Pennsylvania State University (see also Willis & Baltes, 1980). Using a variety of crystallized and fluid measures of intelligence and a variety of training procedures designed to enrich intellectual functioning, Baltes and Willis and their colleagues have been able to demonstrate a relatively high level of intellectual plasticity in old age. Their findings are consistent with the results of other training studies (those designed to improve performance experimentally) of adult intelligence (for instance, Labouvie-Vief, 1976; Zaks & Labouvie-Vief, 1980) and with Schaie's (1979) sequential research showing that cohort or generational factors play an important role in explaining changes in adult intelligence.

Research aimed at demonstrating the plasticity of adult intelligence has been in reaction to the biologically based decrement models of aging (Baltes & Schaie, 1976; Sanders, Sanders, Mayes, & Selski, 1976; Schultz & Hoyer, 1976).

Only recently have researchers begun to abandon the assumption of universal, biologically based decrement in favor of interactive contextual and cognitive models of intellectual aging.

Intelligence and Terminal Drop

In longitudinal studies some of the participants drop out during the course of the study for one reason or another. Several longitudinal studies of intelligence (Baltes, Schaie, & Nardi, 1971; Riegel & Riegel, 1972) have shown that such dropout or attrition is selective rather than a random process.

Selective attrition means that the participants who leave the study are different in some way from those who remain in the investigation. In what ways are the "dropouts" and "survivors" different? Health status, mobility, motivation, and willingness to participate are some of the factors that have been related to selective attrition (Botwinick, 1977; Siegler, 1975). Those who enjoy the experience of taking part in the project are likely to be those individuals who are doing well on the tests. People who perceive their performance as poor are more likely to leave the study than those who are performing at a superior or even average level. Figure 6-3 illustrates how selective attrition can lead to

Figure 6-3 Hypothetical data showing the effects of selective attrition on the distribution of intelligence text scores in longitudinal research. Even if survivors and dropouts show the same rate of decline from one time of testing to the next, a curve showing no age-related decline is obtained when the scores of the dropouts are removed.

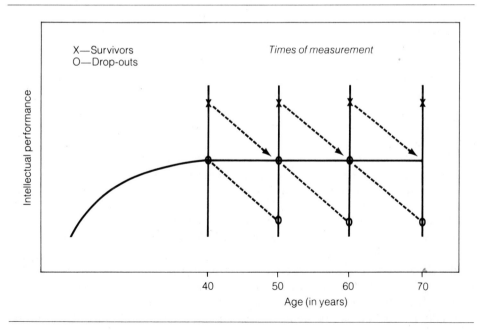

positively biased results in longitudinal research. If the poor performers drop out at each time of testing, the average performance of the total sample does not reflect a "true" developmental trend.

Riegel and Riegel (1972) and Kleemeier (1961, 1962) have suggested that there actually may be little or no decline in intelligence until just about five years before death. The *terminal drop hypothesis* states that time prior to death, more than time since birth, predicts intellectual decline. Kleemeier measured the intelligence of 13 men over a period of 12 years and found that a rapid decline in cognitive abilities was predictive of death. In their longitudinal study of senescent twins Jarvik and Falek (1963) found that more of the poor performers than good performers died prior to retesting. That a decline in intelligence can reliably predict death is an intriguing hypothesis, but one that needs further verification.

Some Conclusions

When we review all the various modifiers of intelligence discussed in this section, it appears that three general types of factors act and interact to produce adult age differences in intelligence (Baltes, Reese, & Lipsitt, 1980). These are age-ordered influences, cohort-specific influences, and nonordered influences.

According to Baltes, Reese, and Lipsitt, *age-ordered* or *age-graded* influences refer to biological and environmental determinants that are strongly related to chronological age. Age-ordered influences are normative or universal in that they affect all individuals in a similar way—for example, neuronal loss. Changes in the family life sequence (singlehood, married life, parenthood, empty nest, grandparenthood) or age-graded career development opportunities are also examples of normative, age-ordered environmental influences.

Cohort-specific influences refer to biological and environmental determinants associated with being born and developing at a given historical time (Baltes, Reese, & Lipsitt, 1980; Neugarten & Datan, 1973). The Great Depression of the 1930s, major wars, and epidemics are examples of cohort-specific influences that interact with chronological age-ordered influences to determine development.

Nonnormative or unpredictable life events significantly affect an individual's development, but they are not necessarily experienced at the same age or at the same point in time by other people—for instance, accidents, divorce, or death.

Baltes, Reese, and Lipsitt (1980), in reviewing research and theory in life-span developmental psychology up to 1980, have proposed that the relative strength or impact of age-ordered, cohort-specific, and nonnormative events might show different developmental patterns during the life span. Figure 6-4 shows a possible pattern of developmental influences with regard to adult intelligence. It is suggested that the strength of nonnormative influences increases gradually during the adult life span, but cohort-specific and age-ordered influences are expected to exhibit a U-shaped function. A U-shaped pattern is suggested for cohort-specific influences because cohort identification is generally of greatest significance in adolescence and old age (Elder, 1979). There is some evidence to suggest that chronological age is a good predictor of intelligence early and late in the life span but not necessarily in the middle years (Flavell, 1970).

DEVELOPMENT OF COGNITION IN ADULTHOOD

The study of cognitive development has as its goal the understanding of changes in thinking, memory, perception, and attention. We have considered some of these topics separately in Chapters 4 and 5, with a focus on perception and memory. However, in general the cognitive perspective emphasizes the study of all mental activities, often without the arbitrary divisions of sensation,

Figure 6-4   A theoretical pattern of developmental influences on adult intelligence. (After Baltes, Reese, & Nesselroade, 1980.)

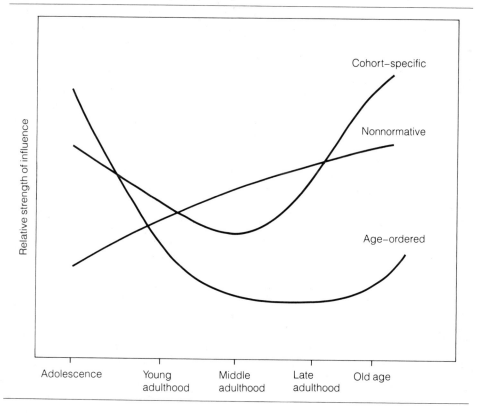

perception, attention, memory, problem solving, thinking, and so forth. For cognitive psychologists *cognition* refers to all the processes and functions of the human mind (Flavell, 1977).

The Stages of Cognitive Development

Piaget   The study of cognitive development from birth through adolescence has been strongly influenced by the ideas of Jean Piaget (1896–1980). He identified four qualitatively different stages of cognitive development: sensorimotor (birth to about 2 years), preoperational thought (2 to about 7 years of age), concrete operations (7 to about 11 years), and formal operations (11 years and beyond). Piaget's stage theory of cognitive development can be understood by picturing how children at different stages might play a game of Monopoly (Table 6–4). It has only been in the past decade that some theorists have attempted to extend Piaget's view of cognitive development to the adult portions of the life span (Arlin, 1975; Hooper, Fitzgerald, & Papalia, 1971; Labouvie-Vief, 1980; Papalia & Bielby, 1974).

A main criticism of psychometric studies of adult intelligence is that age comparisons are made using standardized tests designed for young adults or children. Sinnott (1975) pointed out that many investigators using Piagetian tasks have fallen into the same error by asking mature adults to mold clay into spheres and cylinders and to carry out other childlike tasks. Piagetian researchers have generally assumed that the content used to assess a subject's cognition has relatively little impact on the obtained findings, but recent studies have shown that adults exhibit higher levels of cognitive performance when tested on familiar, everyday materials (Hornblum & Overton, 1976; Labouvie-Vief & Chandler, 1978). At this point, the cognitive approach appears to have contributed more to the conceptualization of adult intelligence than to its measurement.

Piaget considered formal operations to be the main stage of adult cognition, even though not all adults reach this step. Formal operational thinking can be distinguished from earlier stages of cognitive development by the presence of scientific, systematic, and deductive reasoning. In 1972 Piaget himself ad-

Table 6–4   Piaget's Stages of Development Illustrated by a Game of Monopoly

Stage	Behavior
Sensorimotor (0–2 years)	The child puts houses, hotels, and dice in mouth; crumples the Community Chest cards.
Preoperational (2–7 years)	The child plays the game but does not fully understand the instructions.
Concrete operational (7–11 years)	The child plays by the rules but does so egocentrically. For example, he or she does not transact mortgages, rents, and trades effectively.
Formal operational (11 or over)	The child plays the game effectively, correctly negotiating complex and hypothetical transactions.

Adapted from Fehr, 1976.

dressed the question of intellectual evolution in early adulthood, making the point that the stage of formal operations can be reached at different times by adults depending on their aptitudes and experiences. However, Piaget regarded adult development as *nonqualitative;* that is, he saw no evidence to suggest further evolution of cognitive growth.

Riegel   According to Riegel (1973), Piaget's theory was incapable of interpreting mature thinking, which is more than being able to solve scientific problems. He argued that Piaget's theory describes a kind of cognitive development that is logical but not artistic or creative.

Riegel (1973) postulated a fifth developmental stage, called *dialectic operations,* and Arlin (1976) also proposed a fifth stage, which she called *problem finding.* Riegel's idea is based on the recognition of the importance of contradiction throughout development. Riegel (1973) suggested that there is conflict within the individual's thinking at different levels. That is, depending on the task before us, we might be functioning at a concrete level or at a formal level of reasoning. Furthermore, there are inner-biological and outer-cultural and historical levels of cognition that are sometimes in conflict for each person.

From a dialectical perspective, conflict serves as an incentive for intellectual growth (see Chapter 1). The developing individual is continuously striving to resolve contradictions, and each superordinate resolution or solution leads to a new contradiction and then to a new synthesis, and so forth (Riegel, 1977). The dialectical view of cognition in adulthood has received much theoretical attention in recent years and has led to a broader, more comprehensive understanding of adult intelligence. Researchers and theorists now have an appreciation of the myriad factors that influence the structure and expression of intelligence.

Some Aspects of Adult Cognitive Development

Cognitive Regression   There is some evidence to suggest a "regression," or a reversal, of the Piagetian cognitive stages with advancing age (Papalia & Bielby, 1974). Several studies (for example, Clayton & Overton, 1976; Papalia, 1972) have compared the performance of different-aged adults on concrete operations and formal operations measures. Subjects of all ages performed less well on the formal operations tasks than on the tasks of concrete operations. Generally, younger adults performed better than older adults. However, one problem with studies using the standard Piagetian tasks to assess adult age differences is that age-related performance differences do not necessarily reflect developmental differences in cognitive operations.

Wisdom   Clayton and Birren's (1980) recent work on wisdom provides an interesting framework for understanding some of the positive aspects of cognitive development in later life. The term *wisdom* is used to describe positively the cognitive level of some older people. Think of the characteristics of people you consider as having wisdom. In American society, as in most present and past cultures, the people considered wise have a combination of *reflective* characteristics, such as introspection and intuition, and *affective* characteristics, such as empathy, gentleness, peacefulness, and understanding. Clayton and Birren see wisdom as an age-related integration of personal knowledge.

Humor Comprehension   Schaier and Cicirelli (1976) conducted a study of adult age differences in humor comprehension and interpreted their findings in terms of Piagetian cognitive development. Humor appreciation is assumed to be greatest when a joke provides the greatest amount of cognitive stimulation or challenge but is still understandable. Schaier and Cicirelli hypothesized that age-related declines in logical thinking would lead to less humor comprehension but greater humor appreciation. Their findings were consistent with their expectations: For both men and women, 60-to-69-year-olds showed greater humor comprehension than 70-to-80-year-olds.

Self-Knowledge   Perhaps in adulthood our most difficult intellectual achievement is to discover and to continue discovering a personal identity. Therapists have written about the continuity of this search as a process not of being but of constantly becoming. An understanding of self is not suddenly obtained at age 18, 21, 30, or any predesignated chronological age. "Becoming" is a gradual process that begins irrationally at birth and continues (perhaps irrationally) throughout life. At first, the parent must have the confidence that the child will become a significant person. The parent, and hopefully others in society, transmit this sense of identity to the child, and in time the identity of the developing individual emerges. In this view a sense of self is part of the concept of intelligence, though very little research looks at intelligence or cognition in this way. Perhaps in the future cognitive theories will take into account the interplay between self-knowledge and the development of adult intelligence.

INTELLIGENCE IN CONTEXT

For the most part, the study of intelligence has been psychometric in that it has been viewed as a measurable characteristic of individuals. Tests have been designed for distinguishing between and classifying individuals (for example, the WAIS) and for analyzing the structure of intelligence (Guilford's test of the structure of intellect, for instance). Intelligence can be viewed as *adaption* to the tasks of daily living. Relatively little research has been done, however, on intelligent behavior as it occurs in everyday life and on how environmental conditions differentially influence the expression of intelligence as we grow older (Labouvie-Vief, 1977). A contextual approach to the study of intelligence would include:

- Observing and recording everyday intelligent behavior and the specific situations in which it occurs for people of different ages
- Observing age-related changes in intelligent behavior as a function of the environment

Environmental Taxonomies

A taxonomy is a way of classifying things, whether they be plants, books, people, insects, or environments (Fredricksen, 1972). Usually there's more than one way to classify phenomena, and sometimes a theoretical orientation can be helpful as a guide to categorizing human environments and the behaviors that occur in them. Several writers have discussed the usefulness of constructing *environmental taxonomies* for assessing the competence of older adults (Baltes & Labouvie, 1973; Lawton, 1975; Schaie, 1978), but few researchers have actually constructed such taxonomies (for an example, see Scheidt & Schaie, 1978).

Recently, Scheidt and Schaie (1978) asked persons aged 60 and older to report events or situations occurring in their lives within the past year. Questionnaires, unstructured interviews at senior centers or on park benches, and situational diaries were used. Some "situations" that were listed included doing the weekly shopping, listening to a friend complain about health, filing income tax forms, and daydreaming. Elderly raters then evaluated and classified the situations as to whether they were common or uncommon, supportive or depriving, solitary or social, and whether they required a passive or an active role on the part of the person. Schaie (1978) has pointed out that the next step in this research program is to examine age and cohort differences in environmental taxonomies. Although relatively little work has been done from this perspective, everyday environmental factors do play a significant role in accounting for individual differences in intelligence (Labouvie-Vief, Hoyer, Baltes, & Baltes, 1974; Schaie, 1978).

One of the most important trends in psychology is the plea for ecologically valid inquiry. Not only in the study of intelligence, but also in the fields of perception, memory, and personality, a greater sensitivity to the contextual continuities and potentialities of adult behavior is developing (Gibbs, 1979). The contextual and ecological approaches to intelligence (whether based in the laboratory or in the "real world") reflect the active interplay between the behaviors of the developing individual and the contexts (or situations) in which such behaviors occur. For example, older adults who return to the college classroom behave differently than 20-year-old students, but in both cases the interaction between the environmental context and the individual is important.

The Competence–
Performance Distinction

The *competence–performance distinction* is important for many aspects of developmental psychology, but it is especially significant when we talk about the valid measurement of the development of adult intelligence. Older adults may perform less well on intelligence tests because they are less motivated to achieve on a test that has no real meaning or consequence for them. In addition, age-related ability-extraneous factors (that is, those not related to the ability being tested) such as difficulty in seeing or hearing directions, slowed writing of answers, unfamiliarity with test pressure, unfamiliarity with standardized answer sheets, and fatigue may keep performance from being indicative of actual intelligence (see Figure 6-5).

Several studies have shown that older adults are especially vulnerable to the demands of ability-extraneous variables (see Birkhill & Schaie, 1975; Furry & Baltes, 1973; Hoyer, Labouvie, & Baltes, 1973; Labouvie-Vief & Gonda, 1976; Schultz & Hoyer, 1976). In the Furry and Baltes study, for example, a test battery consisting of boring and repetitive tasks interspersed among the various subtests of the Primary Mental Abilities test was administered to adolescents (11-to-14-year-olds), middle-aged adults (30-to-50-year-olds), and older adults (51-to-80-year-olds). Subjects in the oldest age group were most negatively affected by inclusion of the fatigue-inducing materials.

Some evidence also suggests that the content of standardized intelligence

Figure 6–5 Theoretical curves showing an increase in the gap between competence and performance with advancing age.

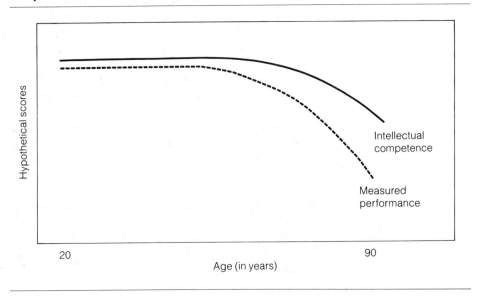

tests favors young adults. To make this point, both Lorge (1956) and Demming and Pressey (1957) constructed intelligence tests that included items that were familiar and nonthreatening to older test takers. Older adults performed better on these tests than younger adults.

The most thorough study of the problem of age appropriateness of test materials is Gardner and Monge's (1977) investigation of adult age differences using a wide range of age-appropriate tests of basic learning, intelligence, and information. In Phase I of this project participants in the 20–80 age range were asked to describe in detail a problem requiring thought that they had experienced recently. These descriptions were then used as background content for the construction of age-appropriate intelligence tests. Gardner and Monge developed the following tests: word familiarity; knowledge of new and old modes of transportation; knowledge of death and diseases; knowledge of new and old slang words; knowledge about financial matters; and 14 measures of interests, experience, and ability to follow directions. In Phase II these tests were administered to large samples of men and women between the ages of 20 and 79 years. The findings of the Gardner and Monge study showed that age differences in intelligence are related to individual differences in interest level and test-relevant experience. The youngest age group obtaining the best score was the 30-to-39-year-olds on the knowledge of transportation subtest, and the oldest age group obtaining the best score was the 60-to-69-year-olds in the knowledge of death and diseases subtest.

A developmental-ecological approach goes beyond test construction and conceptual–definitional issues by its emphasis on the interplay of changing individuals in changing contexts. In the future, researchers will be examining real-world expressions of competence that may be age-specific, situation-specific, cohort-specific, gender-specific, and so on.

PROBLEM SOLVING AND CONCEPT LEARNING

Problem solving is a pervasive everyday experience. Much of our conscious mental activity involves solving problems of one sort or another. Does problem-solving efficiency change with aging?

Because many different types of tasks are called problem solving, research findings are sometimes inconsistent from one study to the next. In Giambra and Arenberg's (1980) recent review of problem solving and aging they made a distinction between concept learning and other problem-solving tasks. *Concept learning* is a type of problem solving that involves establishing some rule (a concept) for sorting objects or events and then identifying which objects or events are examples of the rule. Because Giambra and Arenberg used a precise definition of concept learning in organizing and classifying the research on problem solving, they were able to draw some conclusions from a diverse and confusing research literature. They reported a clear age-related decline in the ability to sort and identify concepts (Hayslip & Sterns, 1979; Hoyer, Rebok, & Sved, 1979; Mack & Carlson, 1978; Offenbach, 1974; Rogers, Keyes, & Fuller, 1976). Deficits in concept learning were associated with age-related declines in memory, selective attention (the ability to separate relevant from irrelevant information), and the ability to shift from one dimension or aspect of a problem to another.

Testing Problem-Solving Ability

Since problem solving involves several component processes, Rabbitt (1977) has pointed out that researchers need to examine where in the problem-solving sequence age differences occur. For example, age deficits could occur in one or more of the following steps of problem solving:

1 Recognizing the problem
2 Identifying and limiting the number of solutions
3 Weighing costs and benefits of the various alternatives
4 Distinguishing relevant from irrelevant information
5 Manipulating the contents of memory
6 Decision making
7 Evaluating outcome
8 Relating outcome to future problems and solutions

Different processes and strategies operate at different points in the problem-solving sequence. Brainstorming, for example, would be helpful for problem recognition and identifying solutions, but it would interfere with selective attention and evaluation of outcome.

Arenberg's (1974) study is one of the few longitudinal investigations of problem-solving performance. At the beginning of this study the subjects were between 24 and 87 years of age; the mean interval between the first and second testing of subjects was 6.7 years. As expected, the cross-sectional results favored the younger subjects. Longitudinally, however, age declines in problem solving were found only for participants who were in their 70s or older at the beginning of the study. Arenberg emphasized the role of selective attrition in explaining the positive longitudinal results.

Problem-solving performance is often assessed using various psychometric ability subtests. In Guilford's structure of intellect model his "cognition of figural relations" test is basically a problem-solving task. Similarly, Raven's progressive matrices test, which is one of the most widely accepted and highly regarded tests of general ability, can be seen as a multidimensional classification task, which means that the individual must combine information from one aspect of the task with information from another aspect(s) that is simultaneously available. Raven (1938) has described the test as "a test of a person's present capacity to form comparisons, reason by analogy, and develop a logical method of thinking regardless of previously acquired information" (p. 12).

Evidence of Age-Related Deficits

Age-related deficits are consistently reported on Raven's test, which is generally considered to be a measure of fluid intelligence (Horn, 1970; Storck, Looft, & Hooper, 1972). In one of the few studies of adult age differences in problem solving, concept learning, and intelligence, Hayslip and Sterns (1979) found age deficits in fluid intelligence and concept learning though no age differences in crystallized intelligence and anagram problem solving.

In recent years several important studies of adult age differences in multiple classification and concept identification have been supported by Denney and her colleagues (Denney, 1974, 1979; Denney & Cornelius, 1975; Denney and Denney, 1973, 1974; Denney & Lennon, 1972). Denney and Cornelius found that middle-aged adults (mean age 34.5 years) were superior to community-dwelling elderly adults (mean age 73.2 years) and nursing home residents (mean age 76.2 years) on multiple-classification and class-inclusion tasks. Furthermore, the healthy elderly subjects drawn from the community performed better than the nursing home residents.

In a study of adult age differences in the ways people ask questions Denney and Denney (1973) tested middle-aged (mean age 38.3 years) and elderly (82.5 years) women on the "twenty questions" game. In trying to guess the target object by asking as few yes-or-no questions as possible, subjects can use either *constraint-seeking* questions, which eliminate many possibilities at once (for example, "Is it larger than a breadbox?"), or *hypothesis-seeking* questions, which eliminate only one object per question (for example, "Is it a breadbox?"). Elderly adults used the less efficient hypothesis-seeking questioning strategy more than the middle-aged subjects.

However, in a follow-up study Denney and Denney (1974) showed that the elderly can easily be trained to use more efficient strategies by exposing them to constraint-seeking models. This finding suggested that use of efficient interrogative strategies is more a matter of experience than irreversible age-related decline. Similar positive training effects have been obtained for free classification. Compared to middle-age (25–55 years) subjects, the elderly (67–95 years) grouped objects more on the basis of perceptual features than function (Denney & Lennon, 1972). However, training showed that age differences represent classification preference rather than a classification deficit. Both Denney (1979) and Giambra and Arenberg (1980) acknowledge the importance of training as an intervention technique in problem solving and as a method for demonstrating that age-related problem-solving "deficits" are not biologically based and immutable. Experiential factors seem to play a major role in accounting for problem-solving ability.

It is also possible that older adults are just less motivated to solve problems than young adults. According to Arlin (1975, 1976), problem finding—that is, knowing the relevant issues—may be a more salient concern of older adults than problem solving. Adults at the fourth stage of Piaget's theory of cognitive development are focused on problem solving, whereas adults at Arlin's fifth stage are focused on problem finding. Formal operational thought is logical, scientific, systematic, and deductive. Problem finding, in contrast, is less logical; it corresponds to the ability to think divergently. Arlin's theory is intriguing, but it is new and there is little sound evidence to support it so far.

CREATIVITY, FLEXIBILITY, AND CURIOSITY

Creativity

According to Wallach and Kogan (1965), *creativity* is the ability to generate relevant and unique associations. Torrance (1966), in contrast, viewed creativity as a kind of problem solving. First we become sensitive to gaps in knowledge or other problems; next the difficulty is identified, solutions are sought, and hypotheses are tested and retested; finally, the outcome is achieved and communicated.

Creativity—the ability to generate distinctive, relevant associations—is often maintained throughout adulthood, especially in fields where experience is important.

There have been two approaches to the study of creativity in old age. One approach has been to examine the age of maximum creative output by individuals in a diversity of fields (Dennis, 1966; Lehman, 1953). In Lehman's study it was found that, for most professional fields, the quality of productivity was highest in the 30s, with 80 percent of the individual's superior work completed by the age of 50. Dennis found, however, that the individual's peak level of creative productivity varied according to professional field. In the humanities 70-year-olds can be just as productive as 40-year-olds, whereas in the sciences 40-year-olds are more productive than those in their 70s. New studies of creativity using this approach are needed to determine if these patterns have persisted over time.

It is possible that the "knowledge explosion" of some fields has made it difficult for an older professional to stay current compared to someone who has just completed formal training. However, in vocations where direct experience is the main source of knowledge, the person who has worked the longest may have the advantage. Probably the productivity formula for most business and scientific careers is to be able to combine direct experience with current knowledge. In the arts and humanities current knowledge may be a less important factor than the creativity derived and expressed through experience. Many visual artists (for instance, Pablo Picasso, Georgia O'Keeffe, Joan Miró), musicians (Leonard Bernstein, Arthur Fiedler, Artur Rubinstein), and literary or theatrical artists have developed or maintained their creativity throughout their lives. An attitude that encourages individuals to move to different occupations that match their experiences, creative capabilities, and interests as they grow older appears to be emerging in contemporary American society.

A second approach to the study of creativity centers on the relationship between creativity and intelligence. In Guilford's structure of intellect model, for example, creativity is associated with divergent-thinking abilities. In an early study of creativity and intelligence in adults from 17 to 82 years of age Bromley (1956) reported that the quality of intellectual output and creativity declines with advancing age. More recently, Alpaugh and Birren (1977) studied the relationship between creativity and intelligence in adults aged 20 to 83 years using two subtests of the WAIS (information and similarities), six divergent-thinking tests from Guilford (1967), and the Barron-Welsh art scale. Alpaugh and Birren concluded that declines in creativity in later adulthood are a function of decreased divergent-thinking ability as opposed to a decline in intelligence.

Flexibility

Related to creativity is the concept of *spontaneous flexibility,* which has been defined as the ability to generate new and unique ideas relevant to situational demands (Chown, 1961). Spontaneous flexibility is not the same as intelligence (Schultz, Kaye, & Hoyer, 1980). Spontaneous flexibility can be viewed as one end of a continuum, with the other end being rigidity, the tendency to adhere to previously established behavior patterns in situations where responsive change would be adaptive (Botwinick, 1978). Traditionally, rigidity has been viewed as a *trait*—that is, a relatively stable ability or personality characteristic. However, research has shown that rigidity comprises several different dimensions, such as cognitive, perceptual, behavioral, and attitudinal (see Schultz, 1977). Flexibility is probably best viewed as a cognitive style that fosters intellectual growth. It may be a cognitive characteristic that is especially important to adaptation in later life.

Curiosity

Curiosity, like many other cognitive constructs, is not a unitary human characteristic. Berlyne (1954), for instance, proposed that there are at least two types of curiosity—perceptual and epistemic. *Perceptual* curiosity refers to an uncer-

Georgia O'Keeffe is an artist who has maintained her creativity throughout her lifetime.

tainty stimulated by events in the real world, whereas *epistemic* curiosity refers to an uncertainty fostered by symbols and abstractions. Later Berlyne (1960) distinguished between *specific* curiosity, which refers to a state of arousal brought about by ambiguity, complexity, incongruity, or novelty; and *diversive* curiosity, which is induced by boredom or monotony.

While much more needs to be known about the nature of curiosity and how it changes as we grow older, it is reasonable to assume that individuals choose to keep active and involved in a changing world because of curiosity. It has been suggested by Fitzgerald (1980) that curiosity in the form of uncertainty is a motive for learning and cognitive development throughout life. Compared to younger adults, older adults may need to make work harder or think harder to maintain curiosity. Perhaps age-related increases in rigidity and decreases in creativity can be avoided through such efforts.

SUMMARY

1   The study of intelligence is concerned with describing the organization and structures of human abilities and assessing individual differences in mental performance. Psychometric, cognitive, and contextual approaches represent three currently important and distinct ways of looking at adult age differences in intelligence and cognition.

2   The *psychometric* approach emphasizes the quantitative measurement of specific abilities using standardized tests. Psychometricians often use factor analysis methods to determine the organization of measured intelligence. *Reliability* (consistency) and *validity* (meaningfulness) are two important characteristics of intelligence tests.

3   Several psychometric theories of intelligence were discussed in this chapter. Guilford's *structure of intellect* model represented intelligence along three dimensions: contents (type of information), operations (use of information), and products (form of information). Spearman's *general factor theory* represented intelligence as a combination of *g*, or general ability, and *s*, or specific abilities appropriate to the task at hand. Thurstone's *primary mental abilities* model postulated that intelligence consisted of five independent mental abilities. Reinert proposed the integration-differentiation-dedifferentiation model to describe the developmental changes in the structure of intelligence. Finally, Horn has distinguished between fluid and crystallized mental abilities. Crystallized abilities, based on learning and experience, show no age-related decline and often improve with aging. In contrast, fluid abilities, which are neurophysiologically based, show an irreversible age-related decline beginning in the mid-40s.

4   The *cognitive* approach gives emphasis to the conceptualization of the processes and functions of the human mind and to the understanding of qualitative differences and changes that occur during the course of cognitive development. Piaget identified four qualitatively different stages of cognitive development: sensorimotor (birth–2 years), preoperational thought (2–7 years), concrete operations (7–11 years), and formal operations (over 11 years). According to Piaget, mature thinking is represented by the stage of formal operations. Formal operational thinking, which is scientific, systematic, and deductive, is distinguished from the previous stage, concrete operations, in that the individual can logically extend reasoning to situations and tasks not previously seen. There is some evidence to suggest "regression" or reversal of the Piagetian cognitive developmental stages with advancing age, but the measures used in these studies may reflect age-related performance differences more than cognitive competency differences.

5   With the *contextual* approach intelligence is studied as it occurs in the natural everyday life of different-aged individuals. This approach has become increasingly popular in recent years because it takes account of what abilities are needed and used by adults of different ages.

6   Recent work has shown that age-associated decrements in intellectual functioning are to some extent experientially based and reversible. Only recently have researchers begun to abandon the assumption of universal biologically induced age decline in favor of models that give emphasis to the positive and desirable aspects of aging, such as wisdom.

7   Cross-sectional studies and longitudinal studies of adult intelligence often yield discrepant findings. Longitudinal studies, which measure age change for one cohort, typically show less age-related decline than cross-sectional studies, which measure age differences. Longitudinal studies are positively biased because of selective attrition of participants and terminal drop.

8   Sequential studies suggest that developmental differences in adult intelligence are related more to cohort than to chronological age. Other modifiers of adult intelligence are educational level, occupation, anxiety, health, and plasticity. Compared to younger adults, the aged are more sensitive to ability-extraneous factors such as fatigue and time pressure.

9   Performance on *problem-solving* and *concept-learning* tasks generally declines with advancing age. Adult age differences in problem solving depend on the task-relevant experiences of the individuals solving the problems and the components of the problem to be solved. Young adults may be better problem solvers than older adults, and older adults may be better problem finders than young adults.

10   Age differences in *creativity* depend on professional field. Psychometric studies of *flexibility* and *rigidity* suggest that rigidity—as expressed through thoughts, perceptions, attitudes, and behaviors—increases with advancing age. *Curiosity,* which may be a response to either novelty or monotony, is a motive for learning and cognitive development through life. Compared to younger adults, older adults may need to make extra efforts to maintain and strengthen creativity and curiosity in order to avoid rigidity of thought and action.

CHAPTER SEVEN

MODELS OF ADULT PSYCHOSOCIAL DEVELOPMENT

In explaining or predicting human behavior, some scientists emphasize the importance of individual dispositions, or personality. Others stress the ways environmental situations or circumstances shape behavior. Most explore the intricate interactions between the changing individual and his or her changing world. In this book we are endorsing a perspective of *interactionism,* according to which, aspects of the personality mediate between the objective environmental circumstances and actual behavior. Behavior is not simply responsive to circumstances; we cannot predict behavior simply by knowing the situation. Responses to circumstances are filtered through the cognitions and feelings we identify as personality.

As we saw in Chapter 1, a researcher's perspective influences the questions asked, the kinds of information accepted as evidence, and the conclusions drawn from observations of behavior. In this chapter we will summarize several models of behavioral continuity and change over adulthood. As you read, be alert to the kinds of behaviors considered, to the relative importance each model gives to personality and environmental determinants, and to the visions of change during the adult years.

The models we discuss were selected because they offer provocative views

of the life cycle. David Gutmann offers the broadest perspective, studying changes in the context of *species* dimensions of the life cycle. Erik Erikson emphasizes the *psychosocial* dimensions of the life cycle, exploring the ways culture shapes development. Robert Havighurst describes the *age-grading* of the life cycle in contemporary Western culture. Finally, the *dialectic-interactionist* model of inevitable change is illustrated primarily by the work of Daniel Levinson. Remember that our review is very selective; it is intended to give you a basis for evaluating various theories as they emerge in your reading.

DAVID GUTMANN: PARENTING AS A KEY TO THE SPECIES LIFE CYCLE

Concepts

David Gutmann assumes that an individual's life proceeds simultaneously along three distinct axes: (1) the idiosyncratic life cycle, having to do with individual circumstances; (2) the socially shared life cycle, reflecting cultural circumstances; and (3) the species life cycle, relating to human genetics (Gutmann, 1973). Most contemporary psychology deals only with the individual life cycle, leading to an emphasis on assessing happiness, morale, or self-actualization at various stages. Gutmann, however, is most interested in understanding the *species life cycle*. This involves identifying and explaining universal patterns of change over the life cycle, patterns that are evident in most cultures and in most historical periods. The model is not intended to account for the ways cultures differ, nor does it attempt to explain why individuals within a culture differ from each other. Rather, the emphasis is on finding patterns across cultures and over historical periods that presumably reflect some basic realities of the human condition. Cultural and individual variability is assumed to occur within the limits of such species-wide patterns.

Gutmann has been most impressed with the ways men and women differ over the course of adulthood. He began his work by documenting changes in "masculine" and "feminine" styles of behavior from middle to later years. He then suggested that a major explanation for the observed changes is involvement in parenting.

Gutmann, a psychoanalytically trained clinical psychologist, developed his theory largely on the basis of cross-cultural anthropological field work and on clinical interviewing and practice with adults. His work began with the Kansas City Studies of Adult Life (Gutmann, 1964; Neugarten & associates, 1964). These analyses were followed by field work in widely different cultural settings: the highland and lowland Mayan Indians of Mexico (Gutmann, 1966, 1967), the Navajo Indians in Arizona (Gutmann, 1971a, 1971b, 1972), and the Galilean and Syrian Druze (Gutmann, 1974; Gutmann & Kassem, 1975). These diverse settings were selected in order to assess the presence and strength of common themes; presumably, such commonalities reflect inner developmental realities ("nature") rather than sociocultural constraints ("nurture"). More recently, Gutmann and his colleagues have been interviewing men and women admitted for the first time as psychiatric patients at age 50 or older (Gutmann, Grunes, & Griffin, 1980).

In all his investigations Gutmann uses research methods that assess basic personality: dreams, responses to thematic apperception tests, and clinical analysis of unstructured interviews. The results are examined in terms of the relation of underlying personality factors to ways of choosing and dealing with psychosocial environments. His focus is on finding aspects of experience that are important in understanding why individuals respond as they do to various options. One of these aspects is what Gutmann terms *ego mastery style,* the general, basic ways individuals relate to themselves and their world. It is assessed in terms of the rationale underlying the behavior, not the particular manifested behavior itself. Gutmann sees ego mastery style as shifting in predictable ways for men and women over the life course. Gutmann has identified three major ego mastery styles, which he calls active, passive-accommodative, and magical mastery.

(1) *Active mastery* is characterized by strivings toward autonomy, competence, and control, and mistrust of any dependent wishes that might lead one to trade compliance for security. The individual acting in an active mastery mode tries to change outer reality in accordance with his or her wishes. Aggressive motives are openly expressed, and aggressive energy is used to change external circumstances.

(2) The *passive-accommodative style* is also used to gain some control over sources of pleasure and security. However, the individual with this style sees others as having exclusive control over valued resources; the route to security involves accommodating to the wishes of the powerful other person. The emphasis in passive-accommodative mastery is on changing oneself. Overt gentleness, avoidance of strife, and humility are characteristic; aggressive impulses are constrained. (The passive-accommodative style was called simply passive mastery in Gutmann's early writings; he has since come to believe, as we do, that accommodation is a more accurate term to convey the style.)

(3) An individual using the *magical mastery* style does not attempt to change either external reality or the self. Rather, one deals with trouble by saying it doesn't exist. This style involves rather marked distortions of reality; unfortunately, the distortions make it difficult to act effectively on either the self or the outer world. Gutmann found this style among only a few elderly respondents.

Active and accommodative mastery styles represent different ways of defining and meeting needs. Both may be effective strategies, though to different degrees in different circumstances. An individual may use both active and accommodative styles to some extent; however, Gutmann believes that one ego style is typically dominant and compelling during a particular phase in life. Furthermore, the dominant style is fairly predictable on the basis of age and sex.

Human Development

Male and Female Patterns   Drawing on his cross-cultural research, Gutmann (1977) proposes that, across cultures, men move from active to accommodative mastery modes, and sometimes into magical mastery in late life; women move from accommodative mastery into active mastery, and sometimes into magical mastery. The critical transition period during the middle years contributes to the "mid-life crisis" (Gutmann, 1976).

The description of shifts in "masculine" and "feminine" modalities is not novel. For example, the psychologist Carl Jung identified masculine (similar to active mastery) and feminine (accommodative) components coexisting within each personality (Jung, 1933). One aspect was always predominant—usually, and ideally, the aspect congruent with biological sex. Jung postulated that by middle age the major mode is fully developed and even "used up"; each individual then develops the minor mode. In addition, anthropological accounts describe the open assertiveness of older women; typically, they do not hold elective or formal power but exercise increased power in the family or are recognized as the power behind the scenes (Gutmann, 1977).

The challenge is to explain the shifts observed across cultures and over time; any such explanation must reflect some reality common to those diverse groups of people. Gutmann has proposed that one of the standard experiences of our species may be responsible for the observed shifts. This standard species experience is involvement in parenting.

Gender Shifts and the Parental Imperative   Gutmann argues that parenting may account for the observed shifts on the basis of several observations. First, each species, and each subgroup within the species, must evolve patterns of behavior that ensure that children are conceived and cared for until they can survive on their own and become parental. This species requirement is one aspect of what Gutmann calls the *parental imperative*. Another aspect is experienced by individuals when they accept the responsibility for a dependent child. The parenting adults experience the child's vulnerability and neediness as an imperative to change their own behavior in ways that will guarantee the child's well-being. Because of the continual series of unanticipated crises in the normal course of rearing children Gutmann refers to parenting as involving the "chronic sense of parental emergency" (Gutmann, 1975).

Gutmann argues that the behaviors distinctive to younger men and women have evolved in response to the universal needs of children for two kinds of security—emotional and physical. Particularly for the very young child, emotional security requires continuous caretaking that is attuned to the individual

According to Gutmann, fathers provide distinctive forms of nurturance. Typically, fathers repress their own feelings of dependency and emotionality and stress effectiveness in the world outside the home. This father is helping his child learn about the world through books.

needs and schedules of the child. In virtually all cultures the provision of daily emotional security to the young is the responsibility of the mother (or female surrogate). Women, particularly when they become mothers, develop or emphasize those personal qualities that will best ensure the provision of protection and sustenance for themselves and their children. This involves the careful management of aggressive and competitive impulses that could alienate a male provider or damage a vulnerable and needful child. A mother who is intent upon imposing her own order on the world—that is, exercising active mastery— may damage the child when he or she does not fit into that order.

Conversely, fathers are traditionally responsible for providing the physical and material security needed by the child and the mother. Such provision generally requires movement outside the home, to bring home resources (such as money) and to fend off intruders. When resources are scarce, as they are in most societies for most people, one must compete with others to obtain desired resources. Individuals who are too tender and too accommodating may be unable to compete effectively or to protect their family (or their nation) against intruders; they will fail to be good providers for their families. In order to provide physical and material security, men must repress many of their own inclinations to be dependent and deny their own feelings of vulnerability. According to Gutmann, mothers of young children support this repression of male dependency because they can be better mothers when the fathers are able and willing to be responsible for their economic security.

Gutmann emphasizes the consequences of these sexually distinct patterns for the species rather than for the individual. From an individualistic perspective it is clear that mothers of small children often feel trapped and overwhelmed; that fathers often feel they have traded adventure for domesticity; and that rearing children involves sacrifices of energy, money, and self-indulgence for both parents. Renouncing or repressing aspects of the self is not the most rewarding, interesting, or enjoyable path of action for individual men and women. However, Gutmann argues that such renunciations are necessary for the survival and well-being of the social system as a whole and for the species. The cultural forms that have evolved are based on social requirements that the vulnerable young must be protected and socialized to carry on the species. The social arrangements that validate, honor, and support parenting and the necessary personal sacrifices meet the needs for species and cultural survival; individuals who are well parented will be willing and able to parent the next generation. In Gutmann's theory the sexual division of labor between parents of dependent children must be understood within this broader perspective.

Postparental Transformations   On the basis of his own research and data from other investigators Gutmann describes a normal, gradual shift in personality organization, with the phasing out of the parental emergency (Gutmann, 1975, 1977). As children take over the responsibility for their own security, both parents can afford to shift from the strategies exercised in behalf of the children. Each parent reclaims those aspects of the self repressed in the service of parenting. Men get in touch with the more sensual, nurturing aspects of themselves; they become more interested in love than in power and may be less troubled by their own dependency needs. Men are more apt to use passive-accommodative mastery modes in later life than they are when they are young, particularly in the domestic sphere of the household. Many older men view women, especially their wives, as powerful controllers of the valued resources of comfort, companionship, and pleasure. Women, on the other hand, become more interested in power and less guilty about their own competitive urges. Older women are more apt to use active mastery styles than they were as mothers of young children.

Critique of the Theory

Gutmann's model provides a provocative hypothesis about the ways individual lives emerge in congruence with social and biological realities. Unlike most models, his proposes a dynamic explanation of *why* particular patterns of change are observed over adulthood. Individuals develop during childhood and emerge into adulthood with particular personality dispositions. These dispositions in part determine whether an individual is willing and able to become parental. Those who do become parental enter into a developmental process linked to the requirements of parenting. The distinctions between mothers and fathers during the period of active parenting, and the blurring of those distinctions in the postparental period, are seen as embedded in social and species survival.

Not all psychologists agree there is evidence for common, universal shifts of the sort Gutmann describes. Rather, they emphasize the variability within any group and argue that the differences among men in mastery styles are as great as the differences between men and women.

In particular, it is not clear how applicable Gutmann's model is for modern Western life. The model is derived from analysis of cultures in which parenting is often carried out under conditions of physical danger, hardship, deprivation, and scarce resources. The characteristics required of adults may be substantially different from those needed to survive and thrive in a modern, industrialized country. Some critics argue that children can be reared best when both parents share equally in providing emotional and material security.

Responding to these points requires at least two kinds of evidence. First, we must identify the consequences for the child at different ages of having parents who differ on the dimensions of mastery style, such as active mastery mothers and accommodative fathers or two active mastery parents. Good research with varied populations designed to answer this question is not available at the present time.

Secondly, we must find out whether other social institutions will allow or tolerate equal-sharing parenting. That is, even though the traditional division of labor may not be necessary for the child, it may be the only feasible arrangement in a particular society. From this perspective the division of labor still seems both widespread and useful. Conditions of scarcity still prevail for much of the U.S. population. One must compete for education, for employment, and for promotions. Economic rewards often go to individuals displaying qualities of active mastery; thus such persons are best able to provide economic security. The parent who provides economic security usually has to meet the schedules and requirements of the employer, and those work schedules are seldom compatible with being available to respond to the various emergencies of child care. The employer usually assumes that the energies of the worker are available for work; if the employee is distracted or absent because of family emergencies, the worker may be denied promotions or even fired. Relatively few jobs allow the flexibility and control over one's own time necessary to combine working with providing emotional security for children.

In addition, reliable parent substitutes are not easy to find and maintain. Many mothers and fathers rearing children without a coparent have discovered the practical dilemmas of arranging both employment and child care. Moreover, many mothers find they do not wish to turn over substantial portions of child care to others, particularly to strangers; they prefer to give mothering priority and reduce their own employment to fit the needs of the child (Daniels

& Weingarten, 1979). Some fathers raising a child alone make a similar decision. In any case, it remains very difficult to be the sole provider of economic and emotional security for the child; most social systems recognize that fact and build in a division of responsibility. Gutmann's model thus seems relevant in understanding the impact of parenting even among contemporary families.

Another challenge for Gutmann's model concerns its emphasis on parenting for ego development. He selected parenting as an explanatory variable because it is a universally standard adult experience that has at least the potential for redirecting lifestyles and inner life. Moreover, parenting has regular phases and so could possibly explain phases in psychological development. However, there are a number of other common adult experiences that also may be tied to changes in mastery style and self-concern—biological and hormonal changes and work experiences outside the home, for example. More research is needed to assess the extent to which observed changes are, in fact, linked to parenting.

Gutmann's model of aging is limited because it does not consider what happens to adults who do not become parental. We must remember that being a biological parent does not necessarily make one *parental* in Gutmann's sense. The developmental shifts described, and the consequences of not becoming parental, are presumably tied to the investment of self in a child. Nonparents are not considered because the model aims at the species life cycle more than individual life cycles. As Gutmann points out, until very recently parenting has been a part of the average expectable life cycle—a standard life experience. In some cultures barren women are still considered outcasts, unfit to be wives and a disgrace to their families. A portion of every population is unable to bear living children, and many people have chosen to limit the number of children born. However, childlessness, and especially voluntary childlessness, has been (and still is) culturally deviant. Recently, Gutmann and his colleagues have been extending the model to include the consequences of childlessness in later life (Gutmann, Grunes, & Griffin, 1980). This is an important addition if we are to understand the ways parenting or other life experiences contribute to adult development.

Gutmann's theory deals explicitly with the species life cycle, looking for universal patterns. We will now look at the theories of Erik Erikson, who also proposes a universal pattern of transformations in the ego, though he emphasizes the ways a particular sociocultural setting shapes development.

ERIK ERIKSON:
THE PSYCHOSOCIAL LIFE CYCLE

Erik Erikson is one of the leading figures in the field of psychoanalysis and human development. He has studied the process of growing up in a variety of cultural and social settings and has had a clinical practice treating children. Erikson began, as did Sigmund Freud, with the study of patients—that is, people with identified psychological problems. However, Erikson moved to the study of cultures and an emphasis on normal and outstanding rather than inadequate personality development. His book *Childhood and Society,* first published in 1950 and later revised, is a classic (Erikson, 1963). In two studies of historical figures (Martin Luther and Gandhi) Erikson (1958, 1969) explored the subtle interactions between the social and psychological dimensions of development.

Concepts

Erikson uses many of the concepts developed in the traditional psychoanalytic theory of Sigmund Freud.

Unconscious Motivation   One of the important concepts of both Erikson and Freud is the unconscious motivation of behavior. ("Forgetting" your home phone number when you have to call in to report very bad news is one example; selecting a marriage partner because he or she unconsciously evokes in you the same sense of warmth and security you enjoyed as an infant is another.) By now this principle is so widely accepted that our common speech contains references to such things as "Freudian slips." Accepting this concept means that we cannot assume individuals can accurately report on the "real" motivations for their behavior; they can, and will, report the more conscious aspects, but they will not have access to less conscious motivations. Nevertheless, their unconscious motivations can be at least as powerful in shaping behavior, and perhaps more so, because they are not subject to conscious awareness and, thereby, control.

Three-Part Structure of Personality   Freud suggested a *three-part structure of personality* and used a new metaphorical terminology to represent the intrapsychic processes (Freud, 1933). The *id* is conceptualized as the repository of primitive infantile strivings for comfort, power, and union—that is, for gratification of the instincts. Gratification is inevitably thwarted in the course of normal life; restraints necessarily exist in all cultures and social systems because all humans have impulses that could disrupt family ties and community collaboration.

Community standards, transmitted primarily by parents to child, are internalized as the *superego,* sometimes called the policeman of the personality. The small child constructing the superego usually creates an internal force that is far more restrictive and punitive than most parents (or parent-figures) are in reality. The superego is so restrictive partly because the child realizes the force of his rageful, demanding id impulses. Wishing to protect against the loss of parental love, the individual turns his rage at having gratification thwarted against the self.

The negotiation between id demands and superego restraints is the task of the *ego*. The ego must develop the capacity to appraise reality and decide how best to manage impulses. The ego is strong insofar as the individual does not feel as if he or she is overwhelmed by needs or terribly repressed by constraints.

Freud emphasized the importance of wishes and needs originating in the id. In contrast, Erikson, most impressed with the ego capacities for rational appraisal and decision making, developed a model that describes the ways ego development occurs throughout life.

The Individual and Society   Perhaps Erikson's most significant departure from Freudian thinking is in the relation of the individual to society. Freud assumed that individual needs originating in the id were invariably in conflict with social needs. Erikson, on the other hand, assumes a basic compatibility between individual and social needs. Erikson developed his model on the basis of work in several cultures, and he was very sensitive to social-cultural variables in development. According to his perspective, each society sponsors development by providing the kinds of experiences the person needs to grow at various stages of life. He assumes that

1. the human personality develops in steps predetermined in the growing person's readiness to be driven toward, to be aware of, and to interact with, a widening social radius; and 2. society, in principle, tends to be constituted so as to meet and invite this succession of potentialities for interaction and attempts to safeguard and to encourage the proper rate and the proper sequence of their unfolding. (Erikson 1963, p. 270)

This quotation makes clear the basic premises of Erikson's model: Each individual will naturally seek out certain kinds of experiences as he or she develops, and each society is naturally organized to make those opportunities available at the appropriate time. Erikson does not assume the perfect environment; rather, the patterns of growth he describes are based on the individual having a "good enough" environment. Environments are not always good enough, of course, and in this model difficulties in development can be attributed partly to environmental resources being inadequate at the time they are needed. The individual may also be unable to deal with the challenges of any developmental stage. These are aspects of the *mutuality* between the individual and society that Erikson emphasizes.

The concept of compatible mutuality is reflected in differing views of the nature of instincts and their management. Freud regarded instincts as typically impulsive: ready to erupt, demanding gratification, and requiring strict controls from within and without. He developed this view from his work with patients—individuals who were, indeed, having substantial difficulty with instinct gratification. Normal paths of gratification were unavailable, and in consequence the instincts were expressed as impulses. In particular, the Victorian society of most of Freud's patients produced individuals who were troubled by the constraints placed on sexual expression. Consequently, Freud assumed (incorrectly) that sexual instincts were usually dangerous.

Erikson, on the other hand, studied normal, "average" adults relating to each other in relatively stable cultural circumstances; thus he presents a different view of human instincts. Erikson still sees behavior as motivated by gratification of instinctual drives, but he suggests that normal, coherent social structures and human relationships are, indeed, admirably suited to the age-appropriate expression and gratification of instincts. The instincts do not become impulsive and destructive, except when the relationship between the individual and others is disturbed.

For example, Erikson recognizes sexual instincts as powerful motives for behavior. In the normal course of infancy the needs for tactile stimulation, cuddling, excitement, and union are met as the mother cares for the baby. The sensual–sexual pleasures the mother receives from nursing and fondling the infant and the infant's pleasures with such contact are mutual—natural, and in the service of strengthening the tie between the mother and child in ways that will safeguard the child's future well-being. Similarly, the mature sexuality of adults is, in a well-ordered cultural system, mutual and in the service of bonding the partners in pleasure. Neither partner controls sexual gratification. Rather, the process is one of reciprocal excitement, response in one inspiring response in the other. Mature sexuality, for Erikson, is understandable not in terms of an individual's autonomously felt drive for gratification, but as the capacity to respond to the sexuality of one different from the self in a distinctive, mutual relationship.

The mutality of regulation emphasized by Erikson relates to the survival of societies as well as individuals. Presumably, societies are most likely to survive when individual pleasure and gratification and social need coincide. For example, when parents derive a great deal of sexual pleasure with each other, this usually strengthens the family bond; a strong family bond is in the interests of society because children are most likely to be cherished and adequately socialized within the family. In addition, if individuals can derive pleasure and self-esteem from regulating their behavior for some collective welfare, the society is more likely to survive. It must be noted that this line of analysis is contrary to much contemporary American psychology, which stresses the well-being of the individual and largely ignores the survival or welfare of the larger social system.

Human Development:
The Eight Ego Challenges

Erikson's theory of human development identifies eight sequential challenges for the ego (Table 7-1). These challenges are described in terms of conflicts between two possible extremes of outcome. Most individuals resolve the struggle with a mixture of the two extremes; "good" development means emerging from the stage with the balance weighted on the side of the more positive out-

Table 7-1 Erikson's Psychosocial Model of Development

Challenge to the ego	Focal social sphere	Favorable outcome ("basic virtues")
I. Overcoming basic mistrust and establishing a sense of basic trust	Mother	Drive and hope
II. Overcoming shame and doubt and establishing a sense of autonomy	Parents	Self-control and willpower
III. Overcoming guilt and establishing a sense of initiative	Family	Direction and purpose
IV. Overcoming inferiority and establishing a sense of industry	Community, school	Method and competence
V. Overcoming role confusion and establishing a sense of ego identity	Nation	Devotion and fidelity
VI. Overcoming isolation and establishing a sense of intimacy	Community, nation	Affiliation and love
VII. Overcoming stagnation and establishing a sense of generativity	World, nation, community	Production and care
VIII. Overcoming despair and establishing a sense of ego integrity	Universe, nation, community	Renunciation and wisdom

Adapted from Erikson, E. *Childhood and Society.* N.Y.: Norton, 1963, Revised edition, especially pp. 247–274. Reprinted by permission.

come. The conflicts are not necessarily crises for each individual, though the individual may experience a crisis in attempting to deal with the issues. Generally, it is assumed in Erikson's model that the ego develops its executive capacities best under conditions of challenge; from conflict and even crisis growth can occur.

The ego challenges link the individual to an ever-widening social sphere. The theory is distinctly psychosocial: The challenges occur because of the emergence of capacities within the individual *and* because the social world makes different demands upon the individual as he or she matures. Relationships with others are crucial to the ways the challenges are posed and resolved.

The eight challenges of Erikson's theory have become so embedded in current popular psychological applications in education, therapy, and so on that it is important to understand each as fully as possible. This understanding involves an appreciation of the context of each challenge. Four challenges are identified for childhood and four for the adolescent and adult years. The resolution of each challenge affects the way successive challenges are met. The childhood ego challenges are important for understanding adult development because the outcomes of each challenge are carried throughout life. In addition, every parent meets these challenges again in the process of parenting, though from a different perspective.

Basic Trust versus Mistrust   The first ego challenge occurs during the first year of life, within the context of the relationship with the primary caregiver. (Erikson identifies this person as mother; although it usually is, it need not be the biological mother. For ease of discussion, we will refer to the caregiver as *she*.) The challenge is to establish a sense of *basic trust* in the world and in oneself. This sense develops when the caregiver accommodates herself to the needs of the infant. The infant learns that the mother is separate from the self, but can be counted on to reappear even if she leaves temporarily. If she reappears in response to the infant's communications of distress or need (crying, cooing, moaning), the baby gains a sense that both are trustworthy; that is, mother and child can be counted on not to offend or alienate the other. They can regulate each other's behavior for their mutual benefit.

The sense of trust is at the base of toleration of separation: One cannot tolerate separation if there is no assurance that the needed comforting person will reappear. One's own needs may become intolerable if they seem to drive away the crucial sources of comfort. To the extent that the caregiver is unreliable and mutual regulation does not occur, a sense of *basic mistrust* may develop. The adult residues of basic mistrust may show up in extreme denial of needing anyone else or an inability to tolerate separation from those one depends on.

The favorable outcome of this challenge is the development of drive and hope.

Autonomy versus Doubt and Shame   The second challenge emerges from the increasing capacities for cognitive discrimination and for self-control, which appear, for instance, in the abilities to time elimination (be "toilet trained"), feed oneself, and learn some speech. This challenge is confronted during the second and third years of life. The young child relates importantly with both parents and can differentiate them from each other and from himself. The ego challenge is to establish a firm sense of *autonomy,* of self as a distinct person capable of internal self-regulation and not ruled only by external forces. The positive outcome is most likely when the child has opportunities to regulate his or her own behavior in ways that are acceptable within the family. The risk is that the child will be incapable of self-regulation or will be given too little opportunity for self-regulation; in this case a sense of *doubt* about the self and *shame* in one's impulses may overwhelm one's sense of autonomy. Adult manifestations of the sense of doubt and shame include an excessive preoccupation with issues of control—either keeping too tight control over oneself or yielding too much control and direction to others. Establishing the right balance between autonomy and doubt results in the development of self-control and willpower.

Initiative versus Guilt   The third challenge is to establish a sense of *initiative* and overcome excessive *guilt*. These issues are most crucial between the ages of three and five or six, and they link the child in mutual regulation to the wider family unit. The child is capable of initiating action directed at using the environment to meet personal needs and has the physical and language skills necessary to rearrange things. Children of this age can be very inventive—and untidy—in their early efforts. The challenge of the ego is to direct behavior so that the needs of the child are met without violating too many of the family rules.

Parental responses should provide an arena for the child to exercise initiative without the risk of getting into situations he or she clearly cannot handle. Unfortunately, sometimes the child's attempts to take initiative, to compete with parents (and siblings), are met with ridicule, rejection, or indifference. The child may then come to feel a sense of guilt about desires and efforts to act on those desires.

A special challenge involves the competition between the child and the same-sex parent for the attention and affection of the opposite-sex parent; this is traditionally referred to as the *Oedipal situation,* or the *family romance.* A positive outcome of the Oedipal situation for the boy is more likely if the mother can admit, admire, and enjoy her son's attempts at demonstrating "manhood," at the same time telling him that, while she is allied with Daddy, he will have his own wife when he grows up. The father also needs to acknowledge his son's challenges and assure him that he will not be ridiculed or rejected for being assertive and competitive. Many adult men have lingering problems stemming from this period. They may feel guilty about acting on their own sexual and competitive desires, and they may be unable to accept successful achievement. They may still be seeking assurances from a father (or any person they regard as like a father) that competing—and winning—will not alienate or destroy the father. Men who have not adequately resolved these issues may be very threatened when their own sons start challenging them and pressing for competition; this will, of course, affect their ability to deal with their children's developmental issues.

Girls also have the challenge of dealing with their early and immature sexual and competitive desires. These are played out first in the family. As Erikson points out, the daughter needs to feel that she can take initiative without alienating or destroying the mother. If the girl child shows her (still immature) sexuality by being seductively affectionate with her father and gaining his admiration, will she alienate the mother? If alienating the mother is the "cost" of taking the initiative, then it may be too risky. Of course, competition with the mother extends into many areas in addition to sexual attractiveness. It may involve any of the mother's activities, though in this model the most crucial ones would be those that gain the father's admiration.

The favorable outcome of this period is to become capable of direction and purpose.

Industry versus Inferiority   The fourth ego challenge links the child to the wider world of peers and adults outside the family. This phase usually begins with entrance into formal education at age six or seven and ends with puberty. In previous stages desires and capacities are tested largely within the realm of the family in which, ideally, the child is loved, idealized, and protected as a unique and special individual. However, the child must learn to function outside such a nurturing environment; the self must be tested against the more impartial standards of peers and outside adults. The child learns about "the rules of the game." In conforming to these rules, the child enters into mutual regulation with a wider social order. For example, bargaining over the "proper" way to play marbles or baseball is one way the child learns that individual behavior must conform to some rules that transcend the individual and the situation—but also that individuals may collaborate to make new rules that are acceptable to those who will be governed by them.

The challenge is to establish a sense of *industry*—the sense that one is a worker who can develop whatever skills and competencies are needed to be productive and admired in that particular culture. The risk is that the child will not acquire the necessary skills to relate effectively outside the family and will develop a sense of *inferiority*. Some adults have a lingering sense of incompetence; they fear they cannot achieve anything well enough to be evaluated by an impartial judge. They may have great difficulties in work settings that are not "familial"—that is, warm, accepting, and appreciative of whatever efforts are made, regardless of objective merit. They may be unable to regulate their own behavior sufficiently to master the skills required to function adequately as an adult.

The child who has been fortunate in his or her development will arrive at adolescence with a fairly good sense of trust (in self and others), experiencing himself or herself as a separate and autonomous person capable of initiating action and with the skills and competencies needed to be a productive worker in the particular culture.

Ego Identity versus Role Diffusion   The adolescent challenge is to develop *ego identity,* a sure sense of what the individual stands for. The challenge emerges during adolescence in part because of maturing sexual and aggressive desires and capacities; these energies must be directed in ways that meet the needs both of the individual and of the social order. Moreover, the adolescent has the cognitive capacities to comprehend complexity, to anticipate the future, and to do hypothetical thinking—characteristics of the stage Piaget termed formal operational thought (see page 182).

These cognitive abilities are used in establishing a secure sense of ego identity. The process includes reevaluating aspects of the self-concept developed in earlier years, determining which are most centrally important and characteristic of the self, perceiving equivalence and differences between the self and groups of others, finding an ideology one can be faithful to, and anticipating consequences of actions.

Not all aspects of the self-concept are equally important in forging a sense of identity. For example, one may recognize a flair for artistic design and yet not accept being an artist as part of one's identity. When one accepts "artist" as part of identity, then one also accepts an identity or equivalence with others who are artists; one "fits" into the social world as an artist. An identity as artist means that the individual must accept the tasks and qualities of an artist as compatible with the self. It also means that other people must experience the individual as an artist. Most importantly, before an identity as artist can be secure, the individual must successfully meet the unexpected challenges set by other artists. It is not enough to feel like an artist, dress like an artist, and be accepted by one's mother as an artist; other artists must also take the individual seriously as an artist.

Ego identity involves boundaries. Only by rejecting what is "not me" is it clear what is distinctively and reliably "me." If one accepts an identity as an artist, one cannot then be indifferent or hostile to questions of form and communication. If one accepts as a core component of identity being American, one cannot then side with those who would destroy whatever is distinctively American.

The mature sense of ego identity is forged primarily from aspects of the self-concept that have some degree of choice and are thus achievements of the individual. For example, one may acknowledge one's biological sex as female; it is part of the self-concept. However, more is needed to build a sense of identity as "feminine." Each woman chooses which aspects of the biological potentials and social sex role she will incorporate as her identity. One woman may emphasize the reproductive, nurturing aspects and include in her identity the "nurturing woman." As she does this, she rejects as alien to her identity styles and actions that seem to destroy nurturance. Another woman may ignore the biological-reproductive potentials but accept as "feminine" any behavior that facilitates things by bringing people together to work cooperatively.

A mature resolution of ego-identity struggles links the individual to the wider social order: With an identity one understands one's place in a complex social world. One is unique in some aspects but also linked with other people and with ideals. Ideals are an important component of ego identity. An ideology—for instance, a set of religious beliefs—is especially important in establishing mutual regulation between the self and something transcendent. In addition, it provides a basis for making choices. Every time one chooses between two desired alternatives, some potential pleasure is renounced. The secure sense of ego identity helps the individual, even while sacrificing some pleasures, to gain a sense of self-esteem from making choices that are "true" to one's identity. If one can do this, one is also reliable, to one's self and to others; one can make commitments and honor them. As Shakespeare said, "To thine own self be true. . . . Thou cannot then be false to any man."

Forms of identity development. Children typically have immature forms of identity. That is, they have a sense of self but lack the cognitive maturity and life experience to forge a sense of a unique self linked predictably to a complex social system. Adolescence is a crucial time for selecting the aspects of the self that are most central and working them into a coherent whole. Even when the ego is established, however, an *identity crisis* may occur whenever enduring beliefs about the self and one's place in the world are seriously challenged to the extent the individual no longer knows what he or she stands for. The challenge may spring from internal or external sources, or both.

Before crystallizing a sense of identity, an individual may be in *moratorium*—that is, have some tentative sense of identity but not yet be ready to act fully on the commitments it entails. College-bound young adults may be in a stage of moratorium, working out identity formation or seriously preparing for the life their identity dictates. When this period extends beyond the 20s, it is usually the sign of troubled development. However, an adult may resume a period of moratorium in the process of major identity changes later in life.

The opposite extreme of achieving a sense of ego identity is developing *ego diffusion* or *confusion*. When an individual is unable to make choices about what he or she stands for, there is no internal, coherent sense of self to direct behavior. Behavior for the diffuse person is regulated externally, by situational factors. The diffuse individual is unpredictable from time to time and from situation to situation, and unreliable both to others and to the self.

Sex and identity. Erikson sees gender identity as a crucial component of ego identity. In his model one risks ego diffusion by refusing to accept some boundaries and limits in sexual identity. One cannot be both male and female. One may be neither, but the result is identity diffusion or confusion in this important aspect, and ego development cannot be considered healthy. Erikson's views on the importance of sexual differentiation for healthy adult functioning are not universally accepted as valid; his observations on the ways sex differences are established and maintained in the sense of ego identity have been controversial.

According to Erikson's formulations, patterns of identity formation are based on the facts of biological-reproductive potential. He emphasizes the stark fact that women bear children and men impregnate. Those *potentials* are experienced by individuals as part of the "ground plan of the human body" (Erikson, 1974, p. 301). Erikson's emphasis is on potential and predisposition, not mandate: Men and women do not necessarily use their biological potentials to reproduce, nor is either sex unable or necessarily unwilling to do whatever the other sex usually does. Rather, given open options, men will "naturally" exhibit certain characteristics and women others. Erikson (1974) defines the essential differences in terms of body.

Clinical observation suggests that in female experience "inner space" is at the center of despair even as it is at the very center of potential fulfillment. Emptiness is the female form of perdition—known at times to men of the inner life, but standard experience for all women. (p. 305)

According to Erikson's perceptions, not only are women uniquely able to bear children, they typically—and naturally—wish to rear the children they bear. This potential is best actualized if the mother and children are assured protection and provision of their needs, the appropriate male/father responsibilities. Masculine identity formation is central to a man's capacity to work productively and responsibly in behalf of the mate and children who received his commitment. The young man must, therefore, establish a sense of identity that will direct a choice of occupation and mate capable of sustaining his commitment and overcome his own tendencies toward diffusion, confusion, and lack of commitment.

A woman, on the other hand, must attract and nurture the commitment of the man who can be husband and father. Her identity should remain sufficiently flexible to accommodate to that of her mate. Her *primary* sense of identity, then, is bound to her most crucial need to assure adequate (or the best possible) provision for herself and her children. She may, and frequently does, undertake a career, engage in meaningful, productive work, and have a positive sense of self. However, the yielding necessary to establish and maintain an intimate relationship is regarded as primarily a feminine capacity and need, and this affects the course of her ego development.

As Erikson notes, this view is not popular today, in an era of intense reevaluation of sex differences and of any theories positing limitations on human potential. In fact, Erikson's view of "inner space" and femininity has drawn some extremely vigorous, outraged responses (see for example, Strouse, 1974; Weisstein, 1971). In reply, Erikson (1974) observed:

It is the idea of being unconsciously possessed by one's own body, rather than owning it by choice and using it with deliberation, which causes much of the

According to Erikson, a woman's primary sense of identity is bound to her need to assure adequate provision for her children. The ability to be yielding and accommodating helps to maintain an intimate relationship with a husband and father. Erikson does not see these qualities as conflicting with career success or positive self-esteem.

most pervasive anger. . . . A corollary to the attempt to raise consciousness is the determination to repress the awareness of unconscious motivation, especially where it contributes to the adaptation to what suddenly appear to be physical "stigmata" of sex, age, or race. (p. 323)

If a sense of identity is achieved, the individual becomes capable of devotion and fidelity.

Intimacy versus Isolation   The sense of identity is the prerequisite for establishing a sense of *intimacy;* this is, roughly, a challenge of young adulthood. Only after one has accepted the finiteness, the boundaries, and the uniqueness of the self can one really tolerate or appreciate a unique other. The other is not then expected to be a mirror-extension of the admired self. The danger is that the individual will develop a sense of *isolation* when the other exists as real only in terms of meeting the individual's needs, or the qualities of a partner are distorted to fit a desired image. Isolation is overcome to the extent one can experience and appreciate others in their actuality and in turn be responded to as one really is, with all the ambivalence and complexities of human life. A sense of intimacy enables one to experience affiliation and love.

Generativity versus Stagnation   The next challenge for the mature ego is to establish a sense of *generativity* and overcome *stagnation,* a challenge often associated with middle age. Generativity involves a deep concern for the welfare of future generations and a willingness to work with the younger adults who will inherit leadership. This concern is based on the appreciation of the uniqueness and rights of others. Generativity may be related to parenting, but parents are not necessarily or always capable of generativity, and nonparents may develop this aspect of their personality. Those who cannot develop this sense may experience a sense of stagnation—of withering away, of dying. Those who do will be capable of production and care.

Ego Integrity versus Despair   In Erikson's developmental model the final challenge, in old age, is to develop a sense of *ego integrity,* that one's life had meaning. This is an overall sense that, given the accidents of fortune, one did the best one could and that the struggles were not unimportant. One's life has meaning, then, from a perspective transcending culture and historical time. The ego must overcome the sense of *despair* that may accompany the end of life if the person feels bitter about opportunities lost or energies wasted. A sense of integrity allows one to develop wisdom.

Erikson's model is not, strictly speaking, a *stage theory,* one that sees the personality going through definite stages of development. The eight ego challenges he identifies are presumed to become predictably salient during particular periods in the life course, but the ego deals with these challenges (or conflicts) throughout life. A ten-year-old has some sense of identity, but it is not the mature version that may emerge with fuller cognitive development and wider, more responsible participation in the world. Nor does the struggle for ego identity end at adolescence; it is quite likely, and fully acceptable within Erikson's framework, to find major reassessments of ego identity at later periods in life. The "mid-life" identity crisis and the "retirement identity crisis" identified in the popular media are using an Eriksonian concept. However, the reevaluation, or disintegration-reintegration, of an established sense of identity is not the same as the initial challenge in adolescence. Recognizing this, Erikson emphasizes what he sees as the *major* important conflict for the ego at different life periods.

The "developmental energy"—that is, what compels movement along the particular sequence of ego challenges—is not entirely clear in Erikson's theory. Psychoanalytic theory ties such movements in earlier life to the development of biological-instinctual capacities. For example, the emergence of neural control adequate to control bowel movements means that the pleasures, punishment, and power attendant on that act can become a source of pride or problems for the individual and others. Similarly, the emergence of sexual maturity during adolescence in some sense compels the individual and others to deal with those new capacities and urges. Erikson accepts the shifting basis of instinctual pleasures as one organizing force, but he also links development to the average expectable life cycle, which includes work, love, marriage, parenting, and death. The theory assumes that the ego challenges are universal, intrinsic aspects of the human life cycle; the timing and the specific nature of the challenges reflect cultural constraints and opportunities.

Critique of the Theory

Erikson's model of life-span psychosocial development is one of the more imaginative and comprehensive theories available. The scope and vivid imagery that contribute to the strength and appeal of the theory are also sources of its major liabilities. As in psychoanalytic theory, the terms used are not always clear; concepts are seldom (if ever) defined precisely, and each researcher must decide on an operational definition. It has proven difficult to translate the theory into research terms acceptable to most rigorously scientific investigators. Partly because of the difficulty of measuring the concepts, it is hard to determine which issues an individual is really "working on"—and thus to assess the developmental stage properties of the theory. On the other hand, personality theorists who accept the basic premises of internal, often unconscious psychodynamics of behavior and Erikson's metaphorical language may find this conceptualization of development compelling.

Erikson's view of sex differences is provocative but unproven. The extent to which sexual differentiation is necessarily in the service of individual or cultural welfare is, of course, a central issue in both Erikson's and Gutmann's theories of adult development. Erikson's view of sex differences as rooted in biological predispositions has been challenged by those emphasizing more social grounds for sexual differentiation.

Erikson's theory has had widespread popular appeal. Consequently, as frequently happens, the theory has been applied loosely and often distorted by oversimplifications. The ego challenges posed by Erikson become identified as a kind of achievement ladder, with individuals (especially children) to be coached and evaluated in terms of their progress toward the "good" end of the challenges. However, it is not clear just where on the continuum the optimum balance for mental health rests. Erikson no doubt would see it depending on culture, individual, and specific setting; it certainly would not be the same balance for all people at all times.

Some researchers have suggested substages within the major periods identified by Erikson; such a concept is well within the Eriksonian model of change. For example, Peck (1968) divided the second half of life into two periods, each with challenges for adaptation. Peck identified specific challenges during the middle years (roughly corresponding to Erikson's ego challenge to achieve a sense of generativity) as (1) learning to value wisdom (judgment) over physical power; (2) learning to socialize as well as (and perhaps more than) sexualize human relationships; (3) developing cathectic flexibility, that is, the capacity to shift emotional investments from one person to another and from one activity to another; and (4) maintaining mental flexibility rather than developing mental rigidity. Peck identified the challenges in old age as (1) developing a sense of identity apart from work-role preoccupation; (2) developing body transcendence and avoiding body preoccupation; and (3) developing a sense of ego transcendence and overcoming ego preoccupation.

Other researchers have listed even more specific challenges for the life span. Robert Havighurst (1972), for example, has applied Erikson's framework to contemporary Western societies to describe what he calls developmental tasks. We will turn now to an examination of Havighurst's ideas.

ROBERT HAVIGHURST: THE AGE-GRADED LIFE CYCLE

Concepts

Robert Havighurst, a contemporary and colleague of Erikson, shares the concern for identifying the patterns of interaction between the individual and society. He was impressed by the fact that societies seem to have a timetable for the accomplishment of various life tasks. When most people in a society expect particular life events to occur around specific ages, we speak of an *age-graded* system. Havighurst used Erikson's conceptualizations and identified specific *developmental tasks* confronting individuals in Western society. His belief that educational systems should help prepare individuals to deal with these developmental tasks is summarized in his book *Developmental Tasks and Education;* this book has been translated into many languages and has formed the basis for education and intervention programs (Havighurst, 1972).

According to Havighurst, a developmental task arises at a certain period in the life of an individual because of the combined influences of physical maturation and cultural pressure. Successful achievement of the task at the appropriate time leads to happiness and to success with later tasks; failure leads to unhappiness for the individual, disapproval by the society, and difficulty with later tasks. The ability of an individual to meet a developmental task successfully is influenced by his or her personality, which has emerged from prior interactions between the individual and the environment.

Some developmental tasks are universal (for example, women adjusting to menarche and to menopause); others are highly variable from culture to culture (for example, the extent and timing of withdrawal from the work force). Some tasks are nonrecurrent (such as learning to control one's body in walking, toileting, and the like), but, most important, some are recurrent. For example, learning to get along with age mates, learning a masculine or feminine social role, and learning to participate responsibly as a citizen are challenges that reemerge in the forms appropriate for each phase of life. Thus the particular behaviors that demonstrate socially appropriate masculine and feminine social roles may be age-graded.

Tasks in Human Development

Havighurst identifies six to ten tasks for each period in life, noting some of the causes and variabilities for each. Tasks are not listed in the order in which they are expected to occur but rather are grouped according to the life period in which they emerge.* Havighurst describes the major developmental tasks for adulthood as including:

For early adulthood (roughly ages 18–30)
1   Getting started in an occupation
2   Selecting a mate
3   Learning to live with a marriage partner
4   Starting a family
5   Rearing children
6   Managing a home
7   Taking on civic responsibilities
8   Finding a congenial social group

*From *Developmental Tasks and Education,* Third Edition, by Robert J. Havighurst. Copyright © 1972 by Longman, Inc. Reprinted by permission of Longman, Inc., New York.

For the middle years (roughly 30–60)

1   Assisting teenage children to become responsible and happy adults
2   Achieving adult social and civic responsibility
3   Reaching and maintaining satisfactory performance in one's occupational career
4   Developing adult leisure-time activities
5   Relating to one's spouse as a person
6   Accepting and adjusting to the physiological changes of middle age
7   Adjusting to aging parents

For later maturity (roughly 60–end of life)

1   Adjusting to decreasing physical strength and health
2   Adjusting to retirement and reduced income
3   Adjusting to death of one's spouse
4   Establishing an explicit affiliation with one's age group
5   Adopting and adapting social roles in a flexible way (such as expansion in family, community, or hobbies, or a slowdown in all activities)
6   Establishing satisfactory physical living arrangements

Critique of the Theory

Havighurst's model is an interesting description of the kinds of challenges many people face, and many educators have found it a useful framework for developing programs. However, two major criticisms can be raised, one dealing with the accuracy and limits of the tasks as described and the other with the basic concept of age-graded developmental tasks.

Havighurst developed his model largely on the basis of work with contemporary Western, middle-class groups. The tasks thus describe a version of common adulthood. The model does not deal with people who do not marry or do not have children, and historical, subcultural, or ethnic variations are not explored systematically. On the other hand, other investigators can use this model to identify developmental tasks relevant to specific groups in any social system; once such regularities are found, a list can be made as a guide to education and intervention.

Some investigators reject the whole concept of developmental tasks, which implies a desirable ordering and timing of events and predicts negative consequences when the timing is not observed. One can argue that in contemporary society life is not so neatly ordered, that events do not and need not proceed in sequence, and that consequences of being "out of phase" may be beneficial rather than harmful. For example, it is not so unusual for a man in middle age to divorce, remarry a younger woman, and begin a second family; or for some individuals to delay first parenthood until their mid- or late 30s. Neugarten

(1979) has argued that ours is becoming an age-irrelevant society, where chronological age is not and should not be used as a criterion for expecting particular kinds of behavior. To the extent that this view is accurate the notion of developmental tasks would have to be revised to remove the developmental or age-linked aspects. We could speak of tasks associated with occupational life, with starting a first family, with divorce, or with remarriage, but we would not expect these to arise at particular phases in life.

In our opinion the concept of developmental tasks remains a useful and important one. Most of the tasks described are meaningful in terms of underlying biological and social realities. For example, the timing of parenting should not be regarded as only a matter of individual choice or preference. While it is biologically possible for a woman to bear a child for many years (roughly 13 to 45), there is substantial evidence that babies born to women in their 20s have the least risk of birth defects. In addition to biological readiness, potential parents should be emotionally mature and skilled enough to care for a child but young enough to complete child rearing and launch the child into adulthood before they become feeble or die. For these reasons it makes good sense for the welfare of the social system as a whole to encourage people to become parents at the optimum time; this becomes a developmental task of young adulthood.

The chronological ages regarded as appropriate for various developmental tasks shift somewhat as biological and social realities change. For example, improved health and advances in medical technology may be making it less risky for older parents to conceive a child and thus more acceptable to defer childbearing until the 30s. If older adults maintain health and vigor, and if workers are needed in the labor force, adjusting to retirement from work may become a developmental task for the 70s rather than the 60s as it is now. Regardless of such changes, however, the concept of a fairly predictable series of challenges to be mastered over the course of life stands as a useful guide.

DIALECTICAL PERSPECTIVES ON CHANGE

The models we have reviewed so far all describe predictable sequences of psychosocial changes during adulthood. The sequences are predictable, and universal, insofar as they are tied to biologically based realities that are expressed in social arrangements. In other words, parenting "belongs" in the first half of adulthood because that is when women (and, to a lesser extent, men) are fertile. Psychosocial changes have a predictable sequence across cultures because fertility potentials are also regular across cultures. Similarly, male aggression is most troubling in late adolescence and early adulthood; this biologically based reality is reflected in social institutions that encourage young men to deploy their energies in competitive, productive enterprises, leaving contemplation for less driven older men.

There is, however, another perspective on change. A *dialectical* theory, in its most simple form, assumes that change is inevitable simply because every action has a reaction. The action may be trivial. For instance, you peel and eat a banana, discarding the skin in the grass. The reactions may be minimal: You experience the taste and texture of the banana, you digest it and the elements are absorbed into your body, and you evaluate the goodness of the banana. You are changed subtly by the encounter, the banana is definitely changed, and the skin will decompose and alter the earth and insect hosts.

A dialectical perspective on human development focuses interactions between the changing individual and the changing world. Every action made by an individual changes not only that person but the immediate environment; the response from the environment (another person or the physical environment) fosters change in the individual.

Klaus Riegel was the chief proponent of applying dialectical principles to adult development. He built on earlier formulations of dialectics by Rubenstein (1963) and Wozniak (1975). According to Riegel, dialectical theory should focus on the gradual modifications or sudden shifts in biological makeup that force individuals to change their individual operations and, thereby, the social conditions under which they live. In addition, the dialectical perspective focuses on both gradual modifications and sudden shifts in the sociocultural conditions that force change in the individual's psychological operations, in turn creating change in the inner biological state. Development is thus seen as mutually determined by inner biological and sociocultural shifts (Riegel, 1977).

The dialectical orientation assumes that growth comes out of conflicts that occur when individual-biological and sociocultural needs do not mesh. Such conflicts are seen not as undesirable interruptions in the course of development but as the very crux of development.

DANIEL LEVINSON:
THE SEASONS OF A MAN'S LIFE

Concepts

Although he has not identified himself as a dialectical theorist, Daniel Levinson (1978) has described a model of adult male development that is, in fact, more dialectical than developmental. The distinction is based primarily on the explanations offered for change. Where the developmental theory of Gutmann ties change to a universal, intrinsic, unfolding sequence, dialectical theory assumes change is inevitable but cannot really predict sequences or explain why observed patterns occur.

Levinson and his colleagues have based their model on published autobiographies and biographies and on intensive analyses of working- and middle-class American men (Levinson, Darrow, Klein, Levinson, & McKee, 1974; Levinson,

1978). Comparable research on the lives of women is lacking, although Gail Sheehy included some of her own interviews with women in her popularized summary of Levinson's work, *Passages* (Sheehy, 1976). Until further research is completed, the life phases described by Levinson must be regarded as reflecting men's lives. Levinson and his colleagues have, as it were, described the details of the developmental tasks identified by Havighurst as they were experienced and reported by a small group of men. The ways of conceptualizing and studying changes over the life course may be equally appropriate for women, but the content and timing of the issues will undoubtedly be different for women than for men.

The key construct used by Levinson and his colleagues is *life structure,* the "underlying pattern or design of a person's life at a given time" (Levinson, 1978, p. 41). The life structure is considered in terms of three perspectives: (1) the individual's *sociocultural world* (including social class, religion, ethnicity, family, occupation); (2) aspects of the *self* (regarded as a complex patterning of wishes, conflicts, anxieties and ways of resolving or controlling them, fantasies, talents and skills, moral values, and modes of feeling, thought, and action); and (3) the individual's *participation in the world* (or how he selectively uses and is used by his world). Life structure is revealed primarily through the *choices* a person makes; the researcher must come to understand the meanings and functions of each choice within the life structure. The choices made reveal the central components of the life structure. Levinson found that the most common central components were selected from the realms of occupation, marriage-family, friendship, ethnicity, and religion; usually one or two of these were central at any given phase in life.

Levinson and his colleagues described developmental periods in terms of changes in life structure. They identified five *eras* in the human life cycle, each lasting approximately twenty years. Within the eras are *phases* (lasting approximately seven years) and transition periods (of three to six years each). Each era, phase, and transition period is qualitatively different from the others. The difference is established in terms of the *meanings* that actions and events have for the individual rather than changes in visible behavior.

Human Development: Eras and Transitions

On the basis of their research Levinson and his colleagues described the changes in life structure that occur in each of the major eras and transition periods.

Early Adulthood   This era (ages 17–40) is the period of greatest energy and strongest impulses; it is also the time of greatest contradictions and stress. Considerable change is evident within the era. The young man forms an initial identity, usually centered on an occupation, and forges a *dream* or vision of what he hopes to accomplish in life. He determines a path for his future and sets out to establish strategies to accomplish his intentions. After he marries, he is most concerned with his role as provider; his major energies are focused outside the family. He begins the era trying to gain acceptance as an equal from his own parents, and by 40 he is regarded as a potential provider for his parents.

Mid-life Transition   This phase (roughly 39–45) involves recognizing and integrating the changes within the self and in the relationship of the self to the world. By the end of the early adult era the life structure established to pursue the dream is no longer serviceable. Most men do not accomplish what they set out to do at the beginning of the young adult era, and by the end of the era this fact becomes increasingly clear. A major challenge then becomes reevaluation of the youthful dream and the commitments made in behalf of that dream. Many of the men Levinson interviewed experienced a sense of dismay and even crisis when they confronted the disparity between what they were and what they had dreamed of becoming.

A few men had surpassed their dream, at least objectively; they then had to face the reality that even outstanding occupational success or public acclaim could not entirely protect them from feelings of vulnerability and impotence. In addition, most men reported an increased sense of physical vulnerability as they became aware of physical aging; aging or frail parents often made them aware that, when their parents died, they were "next in line." This awareness of becoming the oldest surviving generation made their own death a personal reality. As personal death became psychologically real, they began to measure time in terms of how much time they had left to accomplish their unmet goals. With a finite sense of time they increased their reassessment of prior commitments, trying to sort out which ones were still worth pursuing and honoring and which should be discarded as irrelevant, unpleasurable, or even demeaning. Men became intent on proving themselves—BOOM, or Becoming One's Own Man and loosening ties to paternal figures or mentors became a major issue. Most men had begun the BOOM process by the end of the young adult era; however, most found that even that did not protect them against the reevaluations of the transition period. A new life structure had to be evolved, often out of a sense of struggle and chaos, that would fit the plans of the next era.

Middle Adulthood.   Appropriately, this is an era (roughly 40–65) in which the qualities of wisdom, judiciousness, magnanimity, unsentimental compassion, breadth of perspective, and tragedy can develop. Levinson noted that this was the era of most effective contributions in politics, diplomacy, organizational leadership, philosophy, and the human services professions. Among the men interviewed the emphasis shifted from sheer technical skill or quanitity of output to achieving more long-range goals and facilitating the growth of others. Men who reported good relationships with older mentors during earlier years were often able to become mentors themselves after the mid-life transition;

they took pride in the productivity and increasing competence of younger men rather than feeling threatened and competitive. Many men reported shifting their focus from work to the family, seeking the nurturance and comforts that they had denied needing during young adulthood. Most of the men reconciled themselves to the fact that they were both masculine and feminine, both destructive and constructive, both young and old.

Late Adult Transition   This period (roughly 59–65) involved a new reality and experience of bodily decline in oneself and one's age mates. Not all of Levinson's respondents had experienced this transition yet, but the men who were in this period and those who anticipated it reported anxiety about passing into the culturally defined status of old age. They feared that the youthfulness in them was dying. Most recognized they had less authority and power and had to redirect their energies into new forms of work and play. The transition period dealt with forging a life structure appropriate to these new realities.

Critique of the Theory

Levinson insists that he has discovered a universal model of development, a regular sequence that will reveal itself in all individuals provided one focuses on underlying meanings rather than on overt behavior. However, there are two critical issues in evaluating Levinson's model: the generalizability of the transformations described and the conception of change over adulthood.

Levinson has described, in vivid detail, the lives of relatively few contemporary American men, all living in the eastern part of this country. Claims for universality cannot be made without cross-cultural work. To some extent, it may be more accurate to view Levinson's work as an account of how some middle-class men have responded to the opportunities and pressures they faced. Men in other sections of the country, in other social classes, in other countries, or coming to adulthood in other historical periods may report different experiences. On the other hand, the general themes he describes are compatible with those identified by researchers such as Gutmann, Erikson, and Havighurst. All portray young men as intent on mastering their own strong sexual and aggressive impulses, on making their mark in the world of work, on experiencing themselves as somewhat distant providers of economic sustenance for wives and children, and on struggling to be seen as independent and autonomous. Middle-aged men are described as more settled, more secure, and more comfortable in the family setting.

There is, of course, little evidence that these concerns are the same for women. Women's lives seem to be ordered by motherhood and the realities of providing direct child care more than by the needs to manage aggression or make their place in the world of employment. Any description of adult transitions for women must account for variability in combining motherhood and employment. Preliminary research indicates that there are quite distinct patterns of change over adulthood for women who opt not to bear children, who bear children early or late, or who combine mothering with employment part-time or full-time (Daniels & Weingarten, 1979; Sheehy, 1976).

Even the approximate ages suggested by Levinson tie change too closely to chronological age to be acceptable to most developmental theorists. Such age specification ignores the research on social class differences in the timing of the life cycle. It also ignores the fact that there is nothing intrinsic about chronological age that explains behavioral changes; there must be some explanatory principle beyond the mere passage of time.

Levinson's explanation for observed change is essentially circular: Life structures change because change is inevitable. Life structures evolve to meet needs, but they become outmoded as circumstances change; each life structure created contains, as it were, the seeds of its own destruction. This vision of a continuous process of construction-stability-destruction-construction is a dialectical one; in this model the least likely characteristic of adulthood is long periods of stability. However, although the model predicts change, it cannot predict direction of change. Thus one may well conclude that the common themes observed among Levinson's respondents reflect the fact that they grew up in a fairly common culture, not that the changes described would be found in individuals in all cultures.

The research done by Levinson and his colleagues is provocative and provides a model for other researchers to explore changes in life structure among many different kinds of individuals. On the basis of further research the accuracy of the theory can be assessed.

SUMMARY

1 This chapter has presented various models of adult psychosocial development. All emphasize the interactions between a changing individual and his or her changing world. Responses to circumstances are seen as mediated by personality.

2 David Gutmann has presented a model of the species dimensions of the life cycle aimed at identifying and explaining universal patterns of change. Gutmann documents shifts in ego mastery style, the general, basic ways the individual relates to him- or herself and the world. Mastery style is assessed in terms of the rationale underlying behavior rather than particular behavior. Gutmann identifies three mastery styles: active, passive-accommodative, and magical. In younger adult years males are more apt to use active mastery modes and females to use passive-accommodative styles to master themselves and their world. However, these patterns change over the life course. Although the shifts may vary across cultures, basically, men move into a more passive-accommodative style during the second half of life, and women become more openly active and assertive. Gutmann regards the shifts in mastery style as normal responses to standard life events.

3   Gutmann proposes that the most important standard life experience that accounts for shifts in ego mastery style is *parenting*. Normally, both sexes renounce considerable self-concern and idealize their child when they become parents. As the child grows up, parents are free to reclaim a portion of that self-concern. Gutmann also suggests that sexual differentiation is generally a useful response to the needs of the vulnerable child for physical and emotional security. Consequently, sexual differentiation is greatest among parents of small children and decreases during the second half of life as active parenting phases out. Gutmann's model is distinctive in suggesting an explanation for the direction of changes observed during adulthood; the model is provocative but not yet systematically tested.

4   Erik Erikson's model focuses on the psychosocial dimensions of the life cycle. Although he is in the psychoanalytic tradition, Erikson substantially revised psychoanalytic principles. Erikson focuses on ego capacities, the more rational, decision-making aspects of the individual, and stresses the importance of sociocultural forces. Much of his model is based on cross-cultural work. He assumes there is a basic compatibility between individual and social needs.

5   In Erikson's model normal ego development continues throughout life. Each individual deals with a series of eight predictable and unavoidable ego challenges: (1) trust versus mistrust, (2) autonomy versus shame and doubt, (3) initiative versus guilt, (4) industry versus inferiority, (5) ego identity versus role confusion, (6) intimacy versus isolation, (7) generativity versus stagnation, and (8) ego integrity versus despair. Erikson describes human development in terms of these conflicts and the ways the individual deals with them.

6   Robert Havighurst identifies age-graded *developmental tasks* that are, in effect, specific examples of the challenges discussed by Erikson. Havighurst's model is based on Erikson's assumptions about the basic compatibility of the individual and the social system. Developmental tasks reflect the combined influence of physical maturation and cultural pressure; accomplishment of developmental tasks is mediated by personality.

7   The *dialectical* approach to psychosocial development assumes that change is inevitable because an individual's every action changes not only that person but the immediate environment. The response from the environment in turn fosters change in the individual. This orientation also assumes that growth occurs as a result of conflicts between individual-biological and sociocultural needs.

8   Daniel Levinson describes changes in the *life structure* of American men and presents a model of inevitable change. Levinson proposes that change occurs in a predictable sequence, with periods of stability alternating with periods of transition. The model was developed with men; timing and issues may be quite different for women. Levinson's model is essentially dialectical, assuming that change is inevitable, but it has no basis for explaining or predicting the kinds of changes that occur.

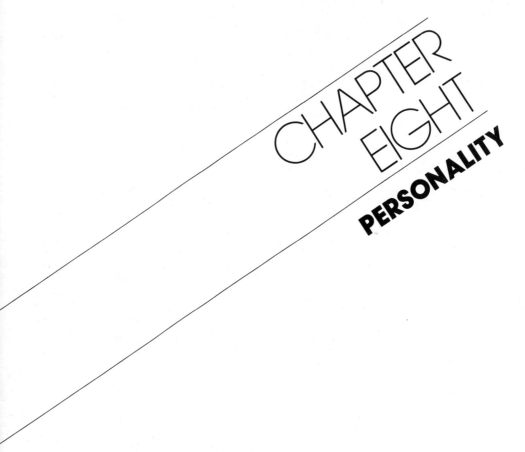

CHAPTER
EIGHT

PERSONALITY

CHALLENGES IN
THE STUDY OF PERSONALITY

Personality is an individual's distinctive pattern of organizing perceptions, beliefs, and ways of acting and reacting (Britton & Britton, 1972). We perceive ourselves as objects, we experience ourselves as agents acting upon our world, and we have feelings about ourselves (White, 1975). We may logically ask, How do aspects of personality and self-concept change over adulthood? What factors account for continuity, change, and variability?

The models of development we reviewed all imply that changes are normal, patterned, and predictable—that is, developmental in a narrow sense of the word. Each model, or theory, has been based on some information about some adults; the continuing challenge is to evaluate the usefulness and correctness of these models.

The following general conclusions can be offered about personality changes during adulthood: (1) There is impressive variability among adults at any age on personality measures. (2) There is substantial individual stability in most aspects of personality during adulthood. (3) Social age is more important than

chronological age in transformations of personality. (4) There is a consistent shift toward greater "interiority" in later adulthood. (5) There is a shift toward less sex-role-stereotypic personality during the second half of life. The next three chapters will consider these conclusions by reviewing the empirical evidence on personality, involvements in personal relationships and loving, and involvements in work and leisure.

The kind of research used to study personality can affect whether we see continuity or change over adulthood. There are two major ways of assessing changes in personality with age. The first is to pick a personality trait (or measure) and compare test results in samples of individuals of different ages. The second approach is to examine the relationship between traits over the course of adulthood—that is, to assess the structure and organization of personality over time. The latter approach was followed by Freud, Erikson, and Gutmann, among others. When the relationship among variables changes, we speak of change in the *structure* or *constellation* of personality. When the relationship among variables is the same at different points in time, we speak of *structural invariance*. The structure of personality is another way of assessing stability and change.

The question of continuity over time is complex. For example, researchers in an ongoing, large-scale study of some 2000 adult men (Costa & McCrae, 1977) have accumulated many standard objective personality measures from the respondents. In analyzing the data by age, they found stability—or consistency—in degree of extroversion (how much the individual "reaches out" toward others). Younger men who were high on extroversion were also high on political and power values, indicating that they were particularly interested in dominating others. Older men who were high on extroversion, however, were more likely to be high on social and humanitarian values; they emphasized the healing, affiliative side of relating to others. Thus there was stability in one measure—extroversion—at the same time that the relationship with other measures, and thus the meaning, of the variable changed.

Another example can be found in the research on time orientation (Knox, 1977). Young adults who were the most future-oriented were also less competent and lower on self-rated health than were present- or past-oriented young adults; this suggests they may be looking to the future to escape from present problems. Future-oriented older adults, on the other hand, were among the most competent and the healthiest; their time orientation reflected engagement in life and good physical and psychological adjustment. Once again, a consistent measure—future orientation—had a different meaning at different ages.

The research on personality changes summarized in this chapter is drawn from studies that have used cross-sectional or longitudinal and, occasionally, cross-sequential research designs (following cross-sectional samples over time). Some of the evidence comes from objective, self-report measures and some from intensive, probing, clinical investigations. We will pay more attention to longitudinal studies and cross-cultural research for evidence about genuinely developmental transformations, though consistent results from cross-sectional studies can be good evidence of age-linked change and stability.

PERSONALITY VARIABLES THAT
SHOW NO RELATIONSHIP TO AGE

Personality characteristics may be independent of age in two ways: (1) The characteristic may be stable over time, or (2) changes may occur but not in any pattern related to chronological age. Investigators have documented substantial stability or continuity in personality over time, though the extent of stability and change varies with the methods used and the personality variables considered. We will examine some of the most significant recent studies.

The Normative Aging Study
and the Baltimore Study of Aging

Among the strongest advocates of stability in personality traits are Paul Costa and Robert McCrae. Their conclusions are drawn from reviews of research on adult personality change and on their own research (Costa & McCrae, 1980; Costa, McCrae, & Arenberg, 1980). Their own research has used data collected as part of two longitudinal studies: the Normative Aging Study, a Veterans Administration project based in Boston, and the Baltimore Longitudinal Study of Aging, a branch of the National Institute on Aging. Both studies involve samples of over 1000 male volunteers tested in the mid-1960s and retested over the next decade. Compared to the male population as a whole, subjects in both studies are better educated and of higher socioeconomic status.

Dimensions of Personality   Costa and McCrae (1980) point out that empirical research on adult personality repeatedly suggests two basic dimensions of personality: extroversion and neuroticism. On the basis of their own research, they include a third broad domain of personality, openness to experience. They have used a variety of measures to assess these personality traits and are confident that they are able to measure these three domains. In order to make their conclusions about stability more understandable, we will first describe the three personality domains.

Costa and McCrae distinguished six facets of *extroversion.* Three are measures of sociability: (1) *attachment* (a warm, friendly style of personal relations); (2) *gregariousness* (a desire to be surrounded by people); and (3) *assertiveness* (a preference for forceful social interaction). Three aspects of extroversion are temperamental: (4) *activity;* (5) *excitement seeking* (or sensation seeking); and (6) *positive emotions* (propensity to experience joy, happiness, laughter, and excitement).

Neuroticism is also composed of six facets in Costa and McCrae's model of adult personality. Four of the characteristics describe *affects* (feelings): (1) *anxiety* (the tendency to experience fear, panic, worry, and nervousness); (2) *hostility* (irritability, hot temper, quickness to take offense); (3) *depression* (dispirited disposition, tendency to experience excessive guilt, low self-esteem); and (4) *self-consciousness* (shame, excessive shyness, feelings of social inferiority). Two describe behaviors: (5) *impulsiveness* (the tendency to give in to temptations or to feel overwhelmed by internal desires and drives); and (6) *vulnerability* (inability to cope with external pressures and difficulties).

Openness to experience is conceptualized by Costa and McCrae (1978) as including openness to fantasy, aesthetics, feelings, actions, ideas, and values. In each of these areas the open individual has broad interests; a need for variety; and toleration for, if not active pursuit of, the unfamiliar.

Costa and McCrae argued that these three domains are useful because one can predict and explain a number of important attitudes, behaviors, and feelings on the basis of scores on these measures. They point out that traits are weak in predicting specific behaviors in specific situations, but they are useful in predicting the general pattern of behavior across many situations and are related to a wide variety of phenomena.

For example, individuals who score high in neuroticism complain more about their health, even though there is no evidence that they are actually physically sicker, than those who score low; are more likely to smoke and less likely to quit and are heavier smokers and report more reasons for smoking; drink more alcohol and are more likely to have drinking problems. They report more difficulties in sexual adjustment and financial troubles, and are more likely to be separated or divorced. They perform less well on measures of intellectual functioning; Costa and McCrae suggest this may be because they are less able to cope with the stress of the testing situation. Neurotic individuals are also likely to be unhappy, dissatisfied with life, and have a low sense of well-being. However, neuroticism did not influence the values and occupational interests of the men in this sample.

Extroversion, on the other hand, was related to occupational interests and values. Extroverts in the Normative Aging sample were attracted to social work, business administration, advertising, and law. By contrast, introverts preferred such occupations as architect, physicist, or carpenter, jobs in which accomplishing a task is more central than dealing with people (Costa & McCrae, 1980). When extroverts drink, it is likely to be in company or with members of the opposite sex. Extroverts seem to value power and humanitarian goals somewhat more than introverts do (Costa & McCrae, 1977); they are also happier and report more positive feelings and general well-being.

Openness to experience shows considerable relationship with occupational choice in the Normative Aging sample (Costa & McCrae, 1977, 1978). Compared to men who score low on openness to experience, men who score high are more likely to prefer the occupations of psychologist, psychiatrist, or minister to the jobs of banker, veterinarian, and mortician. In addition, open men are more likely to quit a job, be demoted, or begin an entirely new line of work. Interestingly enough, open men are higher on both positive and negative affect scales; their lives seem to be more eventful, and they seem to experience both the good and the bad more forcefully.

Evidence for Stability and Change   After demonstrating the importance of these three personality domains, Costa and McCrae examined evidence for stability and change over time in objective self-report measures of the domains. They found no consistent evidence of age changes in any of these domains but considerable evidence of stability in all three.

Men in different age groups did not differ in average neuroticism scores, and the scores of individual men retested after intervals of up to 12 years were very stable. In addition, studies by other researchers, using various methodologies, have found no age-linked changes in the neuroticism domain (see Douglas & Arenberg, 1978; Siegler, George, & Okun, 1979).

Results were similar but not as unanimous in the extroversion domain. Moss and Susman (1980) reviewed stability and change throughout adulthood and reported marked stability in certain socially desirable traits that Costa, McCrae, and Arenberg (1980) interpreted as falling into the broad domain of extroversion. An analysis of data from the Baltimore Longitudinal Study of Aging (Douglas & Arenberg, 1978) found no maturational change in sociability and only slight declines in general activity, in both cross-sectional and longitudinal data.

Costa and McCrae point out that, although the full domain of openness to experience has not been tested in longitudinal studies, evidence thus far suggests stability in openness (Costa & McCrae, 1980; Siegler et al., 1979).

In addition to the consistency on each dimension, Costa and McCrae argue that stability is demonstrated because the relations between the variables making up the dimensions of neuroticism, extroversion, and openness did not differ in three age groups. They interpret their results as showing structural invariance, another clue to stability of personality characteristics.

On the basis of their analyses Costa and McCrae (1980) argue strongly for the importance of enduring personality characteristics. While they found unmistakable age changes in the specific behaviors that express enduring traits, the researchers do not believe that all those changes amount to changes in personality. They do admit, however, that personality changes may be found in variables not included in the domains they studied; in some individuals; as responses to changes in major life events or intelligence; or in unconscious, intrapsychic variables.

The Berkeley Guidance Study and the Oakland Growth Studies: From Adolescence to Middle Age

One hundred and forty-six persons from two studies have been followed from childhood through middle age by investigators at the Institute of Human Development in Berkeley, California (see Block, 1971, 1981; Livson, 1976a, 1976b, 1981). The adult samples were obtained by combining two earlier studies of children and following them over time. In 1929 Jean Macfarlane started the

Berkeley Guidance Study with a random sample of babies born that year in Berkeley; that sample was intensively studied through high school. In 1932 Harold and Mary Jones began the Oakland Growth Studies of children who had been born in the early 1920s; these children were also studied through high school. In the late 1950s subjects from both studies were reevaluated at the Institute of Human Development. The sample at that time included 84 men and 87 women, then aged 31 (from Macfarlane's study) and 38 (from the Jones study). In the late 1960s the Institute again studied 70 of the men and 76 of the women from these samples. The analyses of the adult time periods have emphasized comparisons with early and late adolescence.

These studies are impressive for their duration and for the extensive data available for each person studied. The files for each individual include interest and attitude check lists; intelligence test records; teacher ratings; Rorschach (projective test) responses; ratings of home and mother; photographs; interview protocols from subject, parents, teachers, and spouse; and news clippings involving the subjects; as well as X rays, tracings of psychophysiological reactions, muscular coordination indices, and so on. As Block (1981) describes it, the task of regularizing and transforming the accumulated materials into usable data was a formidable one.

The researchers opted for personality *ratings* as a way of organizing the vast amount of material. The ratings, made after a psychologist read all the materials available on an individual, reflected the psychologist's judgment about what personality variables were characteristic of the individual compared to the other individuals in the group being rated.

In order to assess continuity and change after the last evaluations, several precautions were taken in rating the data. First, four files were prepared for each subject, one for each age period: junior high (ages 13 and 14), senior high (ages 15 through 17), the 30s, and the 40s. Every effort was made to ensure that files did not contain information about any age period other than the one being rated so that the personality ratings for each age period could be considered independent of each other. Secondly, the researchers brought in psychologists who were unfamiliar with the subjects to be rated; this was necessary because many of the researchers had worked with the subjects for so long that their ratings at the last age would be colored by their earlier experiences with the person. Three psychologists rated each file, and the ratings were averaged to give a consensual personality description. The ratings for each of 90 personality variables at four different age periods were then compared to assess the degree of stability or change.

One measure of stability is the correlation between personality variables. Over half of the 90 personality variables were significantly correlated over the 30- to 35-year period between junior high school and the mid-40s (Block, 1981). This indicates that for some personality variables one can predict the ratings in middle age from knowing the rating in early adolescence. For example, among males there were relatively high correlations for the variables "genuinely values intellectual and cognitive matters," "is self-defeating," "has a high aspiration level," and "has fluctuating moods." In the female sample relatively high correlations were found for variables such as "pushes and tries to stretch limits to see what she can get away with," "is an interesting, arresting person," and "is cheerful." These data describe considerable consistency in the ordering of individuals over time; the most self-defeating adolescent boys were likely to become the most self-defeating adult men, and the most cheerful adolescent girls became the most cheerful adult women.

As we pointed out in the discussion of Costa and McCrae's research, another measure of stability is to evaluate the relationship of variables to each other within one individual at different periods of time; this is the assessment of personality structure or constellations. Analyses of the patterns in early adolescence and in the mid-40s revealed that some individuals were very stable or predictable, and some were very different at the two periods. In discussing these results, Block suggested that the proper questions should now be: "What kinds of people are consistent and what kinds are not? Is consistency a sign of positive change or a failure to grow?" (Block, 1981, p. 36). The questions of individual variability and growth will be considered further when we review findings on sex differences in personality change later in this chapter.

Growing Old in a Community

For nine years Britton and Britton (1972) studied 17 men and 29 women in a rural community, assessing the same individuals in 1956, 1962, and 1965. The subjects were aged 65 to 85 when the study began and 73 to 84 at the last assessment. The Brittons were interested in evaluating the extent of continuity in personality and adjustment; their personality measures reflected social adjustment more than basic personality characteristics. The measures assessed participation in everyday activities, satisfaction in ordinary affairs and activities of life, feelings of happiness and usefulness, personal relations and sociability, conformity to opinions of the community, perceptions of older people, and personal adjustment. In addition, interviewers evaluated the subjects and the extent to which they could communicate and interact with the investigator.

Longitudinal trend scores (LTS) were developed to show the direction and degree of changes for each individual. Table 8-1 shows the mean (average) longitudinal trend scores on all measures for men and women. Scores over +.50 indicate marked positive change (improvement); −.49 to +.49 indicate no real change (maintenance); and −.50 and above indicate rather marked negative change (decline) over the nine-year period. No person showed marked improvement. Seventy-eight percent of the men and 62 percent of the women showed stability; 21 percent of the men and 37 percent of the women showed decline in functioning.

More impressive than the average changes was the marked variability with-

Table 8-1   Mean Longitudinal Trend Scores (Percent)

Mean LTS, statistics		Men	Women
Mean LTS*			
+.25 to +.49 ⎫		21%	7%
+.00 to +.24 ⎪ Maintenance		—	11
−.01 to −.24 ⎪		14	22
−.25 to −.49 ⎭		43	22
−.50 to −.74 ⎫ Decline		21	33
−.75 to −.99 ⎭		—	4
(Number in sample)*		(14)	(27)
Range		−.72 to +.44	−.76 to +.37
Mean		−.20	−.25
Average deviation		.31	.27

Adapted from J. Britton and J. Britton, *Personality Changes in Aging: A Longitudinal Study of Community Residents*, p. 79. Copyright © 1972 by Springer Publishing Company, Inc., New York. Used by permission.
*Scores were calculated only for respondents having four or more out of the seven measures available.

in the sample. On nearly every measure some improved, some declined, and some were stable in functioning.

The factors associated with change were unclear. For example, good physical health was associated with both decline and improvement, but so was poor health. Economic security, educational background, or religious affiliation were not always related to improvement or maintenance. Britton and Britton (1972) concluded by proposing that,

among adults at least, with their capacity to evaluate, remember, sum up, hypothesize, and integrate experience, highly specific events and influences are less potent uni-directional influences. The older person becomes less of a passive responder and more of an active perceiver and mediator than he was formerly. (p. 94)

Actual and Remembered Continuity

People may think they have changed more than they really have. Woodruff and Birren (1972) found no statistically significant age changes in the ways 85 respondents completed a standard test of personal and social adjustment in 1944 (average age 19.5) and 1969 (average age 44.5). In 1969 the respondents were asked to complete the personality test as they thought they had answered in 1944. They remembered themselves as much lower in personal and social adjustment than they actually were; thus they perceived much more change than was shown in actual scores. This study is particularly significant in evaluating retrospective accounts of individual change: Current statements about how things were in the past are not necessarily accurate accounts.

PERSONALITY CHARACTERISTICS
SHOWING CHANGES WITH AGE

Varied kinds of research have revealed two personality shifts with age. Both reflect intrapsychic *processes* of personality more than the content or "socio-adaptational" aspects discussed in most of the research summarized above.

The first shift is toward increased interiority, or turning inward to the self. Older people seem to have less psychological (and physical) energy, and it is used to deal more with individual problems and less with external, social problems (Chown, 1968; Neugarten, 1973; Leon, Gillum, Gillum, & Gouze, 1979). The second general shift is toward less sexually stereotypical personality styles.

Decreased Sex-Typed Qualities

By sex-typed characteristics here we are concerned primarily with the psychological meanings of sex roles: those characteristics that distinguish men and women in behavior, personality, preferences, abilities, and so on (Angrist, 1969).

Masculinity/Femininity   The personality components of sex role can be summarized in two dimensions. One dimension, labeled *agency* (Bakan, 1966), is comparable to the style Gutmann (see Chapter 7) calls active mastery. This cluster of qualities, often described as *instrumental-competence,* includes descriptions of the self as ambitious, concerned with achievement, dominant, assertive, competitive, rational, independent, practical, direct, adventurous, never crying, intellectual, comfortable with aggression, separating feelings from ideas, active, and having little need for security. The other major personality cluster, *communion* or sensitivity (Bakan, 1966), relates to *warmth-expressiveness.* It is analogous to Gutmann's passive-accommodative mastery style. This dimension includes such characteristics of the self as idealistic, tactful, able to devote self to others, submissive, helpful, gentle, kind, careful, religious, aware of the feelings of others, understanding of others, comfortable with expression of emotions, sociable, affectionate, warm in relation to others, and needing emotional support from others.

These have been shown to be two separate personality dimensions, though an individual can have characteristics of both in varying degrees (Spence & Helmreich, 1978). There is substantial evidence, however, that younger adult men are more often characterized, both by themselves and by others, as instrumental-agentic than are younger women; younger women are characterized as more expressive and sensitive than younger men (Carlson, 1971; Douvan & Adelson, 1966; Hoyenga & Hoyenga, 1979; Rosenkrantz, Vogel, Bee, Broverman, & Broverman, 1968; Spence & Helmreich, 1978). These two dimensions are the core elements of what we identify as masculinity and femininity.

Masculinity and femininity are global aspects of self-concept. Individuals with clear gender identification have an organized belief system about the psychosocial meaning of being "a man" or "a woman." Although the behavior that is considered masculine or feminine varies from culture to culture, two dimensions seem consistent (Spence & Helmreich, 1978).

Recently, researchers have constructed separate measures for masculinity (M) and femininity (F) and have assessed individuals on both dimensions. Individuals who score high on M and low on F are "traditional male"; those with high F and low M are "traditional female." High M and high F combinations are sometimes termed *androgynous* (Bem, 1974), indicating that strength in both personality dimensions is evident. Individuals low on both M and F, termed *undifferentiated* (Spence & Helmreich, 1978), seem to lack the strength of either dimension.

Using instruments designed to assess these dimensions, Spence and Helmreich (1978) and their associates have tested various groups of high school students, young adults, and middle-aged parents of college students. Their results indicate that males, indeed, scored higher on the M dimension and females scored higher on F. Women are not necessarily dependent, but they are somewhat less independent than men; men are not usually insensitive, but they are typically less sensitive than women. Even individuals who are high on both dimensions (in other words, "androgynous") are typically higher on the sex-appropriate dimension than the other.

The pattern of sex difference in interests and inclinations shows up even among children reared in countries where there have been ostensible efforts to remove sex-role stereotyping. For example, a comprehensive review of studies from East Germany and Poland indicated that boys were interested in "man as an individual active in every way and battling against the odds," whereas girls were primarily interested in man as a "sensitive participant in the human community" (Fogarty, Rapoport, & Rapoport, 1971, p. 66). The researchers also noted that girls were described in school as well-behaved, orderly, fearful of punishment, shy, and emotional; boys were described as determined, bold, self-possessed, strong, and taking the initiative. The reviewers saw considerable continuity between childhood interests and qualities and the occupational choices made during young adulthood. Similar patterns of sex differences have been reported among children and young adults reared on a kibbutz to be non-sex-typed (Spiro, 1979).

Generally speaking, as we saw in Chapter 7, men become more expressive and women more instrumental during the second half of life. Those who take young adult personality patterns as the standard for comparison describe older men as becoming less "masculine" and older women as becoming less "feminine." One survey of midwestern adults found that middle-aged and young men were perceived as most masculine and old men as least so; middle-aged and young women were seen as most feminine and old women as least feminine (Cameron, 1976).

Male Patterns   Several longitudinal, qualitative studies describe the consolidation of instrumental-competence qualities during young manhood. Young men, particularly well-educated ones, are described as "moving toward qualities appropriate to achievement in the outside world" (White, 1975, p. 335); more self-confident and assured, controlled and dependable, goal-oriented, satisfied with themselves, and detached; also compulsive and less relaxed, responsive, and sensitive (Block, 1971; Livson, 1981; Vaillant, 1977; White, 1975).

As we noted in Chapter 7, Gutmann's cross-cultural research indicates that younger men are more likely than older men to stress themes of active mastery, sometimes to the point of being troubled by their own inner sexual and aggressive impulses. For example, a study of daydreaming among 1200 well-educated men and women aged 17–92 found that males 17–29 had mostly sexual daydreams; others in the study reported problem-solving daydreams most often (Giambra, 1977). However, young men are also concerned with controlling their own responses and dominating the world around them. The world described by the younger men in Gutmann's cross-cultural research was typically full of conflicts and challenges—which they intended to meet.

By later life (age 50–60 in American culture) men seem to become more expressive and sensitive. At least some older men score lower on activity, need

Across cultures, many older men become more expressive, sensitive, and interested in foods. As a leisure activity, cooking is more common among older men than it is among younger men in the United States.

for achievement, energy level, and impulsivity (Fozard & Thomas, 1975). As a middle-aged policeman explained, "Your life becomes more simplified and your strains lessen. You become more compatible. You do things automatically. The struggle is over—you have no real drive; there's no pressure or tension. Your kids are raised and you are sitting pretty good" (Spence et al., 1972).

Young men are likely to be troubled by desires to be more "competent," or more "masculine"—that is, more aggressive, less emotional, and more dominant (Komarovsky, 1976; Levinson, 1977; Steinman & Fox, 1974); older men do not seem as much troubled by such desires (Foley & Murphy, 1977).

Participation in typically "masculine" activities—such as those involving physical skill, daring, danger (Strong, 1943, 1951), and guns and spectator sports as leisure activities (Gordon, Gaitz, & Scott, 1976)—declines with age. Cooking as a leisure activity is substantially more common among older American men than younger men (Gordon et al., 1977), a finding that supports Gutmann's (1971b) observations on the increased interest in food and oral pleasures among older men in various cultures.

Female Patterns   Young women score higher than young men on personality measures of sensitivity-expressivity. Young women who emerged into adulthood several decades ago were described as warm, giving, nurturant, understanding in human relations, and finding security and comfort in interpersonal relations; also worried and guilty (Block, 1971). Worry and guilt are apparently related to sensitivity to the feelings and responses of others (Hoyenga & Hoyenga, 1979) and to concerns about transgressing sex-role boundaries.

The concerns about transgressing sex-role boundaries may be greater for women with higher occupational aspirations and/or more autonomous personality characteristics. One recent study of high school senior women assessed the self, ideal self, and perceptions of "man's ideal woman" (Hansen & Putnam, 1978). The students who were not intending to go on to college described themselves and their ideal woman as quite traditionally other-oriented. The women who planned to continue their education described an ideal woman in similar terms. However, they described themselves as equally balanced between self- and other-orientation—in other words, "androgynous" but not as feminine as they thought ideal.

Furthermore, all the students thought that men wanted a woman to be very feminine. Other research has also shown that women think that men prefer a woman who is very family-oriented and subordinate and not interested in self-achievement (Steinmann, 1963; Steinmann & Fox, 1966; Steinmann, Fox, & Levi, 1964). Interestingly, the "male ideal woman" was seen as much more other-oriented by college-bound women than others (Hansen & Putnam, 1978), suggesting that androgynous women may be under more stress than traditionally feminine women in their relationships with men.

Older women seem to be more accepting of their own desires and capacities for competition and direct mastery. They express more pleasure in and less guilt about being in control (Gutmann, 1977; Lowenthal, Thurnher, Chiriboga,

Older women are most likely to take on and to value agentic qualities.

& associates, 1975; Neugarten, 1973). After age 40 achievement-oriented day-dreams were more important for women than for men (Giambra, 1977). Older women do not necessarily become less sensitive or expressive, but they are likely to take on—and value highly—more agentic qualities (Foley & Murphy, 1977).

Individual and Group Variability   The evidence is quite persuasive that, with age, both men and women become less differentiated in some aspects of personality. The data show two measured changes. One is in group averages. For example, a group of young adult men will have higher average scores on competence/agency measures than a comparable sample of women or older men. The other shift is for a particular individual over time. The data imply that a man will be most agentic and least "feminine" during his young adult to early middle years and more evenly balanced, including expressive-sensitive aspects, during his later years. The longitudinal evidence is considerably more limited than the cross-sectional data, however, so the conclusions about change over time are not clear.

There is substantial variability within each age–sex group. For example, Spence and Helmreich (1978) reported masculinity and femininity scores for several populations. Among their samples of high school and college students the greatest percentage of each sex was conventionally sex-typed, the next large percentage was androgynous, and the least were cross-sex-typed. So far there are no really comparable data for older adults, although parents of college students tended to be somewhat more androgynous than the students themselves.

Among the populations Spence and Helmreich tested were male and female homosexuals, who differed from the college students on all measures. Male homosexuals scored lower on the masculinity scales and higher on femininity than college males. Lesbian women scored higher on masculinity than did gay men, reversing the usual sex differences. Another group studied were female varsity athletes; they were least likely to be traditionally feminine and most likely to be androgynous or masculine.

Finally, Spence and Helmreich report data on male and female scientists. Male scientists scored higher on masculinity than did college student males; however, the scientists were no higher than the fathers of the students. These results suggest an age shift into more pronounced masculinity—at least from college to middle age. Female scientists had higher M scores than college women or mothers of college women but lower scores than male scientists.

Further Questions

So far we do not have adequate evidence to answer definitively the questions about personality stability and change during adulthood. Most of the samples used in the longitudinal studies cited are small, predominantly middle class, white, well educated, and generally blessed with supportive environments. Californians and respondents born in the 1920s are overrepresented. The major exceptions are the cross-cultural data cited by Gutmann (1977), though little of that is comparable to the long-term longitudinal American studies.

It is not clear to what extent cohort effects have influenced age differences in personality. For example, the data reported by Spence and Helmreich on male scientists (1978) summarized above could be interpreted in terms of cohort effects. The fact that the college-age male students scored lower than older male scientists could reflect the changing standards and expectations about what constitutes appropriate behavior for educated males. Further research is necessary to sort out the relative effects of developmental events (such as parenting) and cohort.

Furthermore, there is little evidence about the factors associated with variability *within* age–sex groups. All studies report considerable variation in personality measures even among those who are the same sex and age; this variability may be especially important when considering age–sex shifts. Some of the differences reflect social class; for instance, working-class adults seem to begin the postparental shift at younger ages than do middle-class adults (Gutmann, 1977).

There are undoubtedly ethnic and cultural differences. For example, expectations among blacks for young black men in the United States include considerably more warmth and expressiveness than whites expect for white males (Turner & Turner, 1974). Black men may still show developmental shifts in later life; however, research on this question is lacking. Another interesting set of comparisons is available in Gutmann's own research among several different cultures. While he found similar shifts across cultures from young adulthood to later adulthood, he also found differences between the cultures in the extent to which men showed active or passive-accommodative modes at any age. Men in Kansas City were more passive than Mayan Indians, and urbanized Mexican Indians were more passive than rural Indians (Gutmann, 1977).

In addition, the impact of particular life experiences on personality shifts needs to be explored further. For example, there is some evidence that parental involvement is related to personality shifts. Such patterns are reported in a study of parents at the "launching" and "preretirement" phases of life (Lowenthal et al., 1975). Some of the women in the preretirement stage (whose husbands were facing retirement) had children still at home. These women resembled the younger launching-stage women who had children at home in focusing on family relationships in response to the "Who Am I?" questionnaire. By contrast, women whose children had left home referred more to personal characteristics and values.

Sex-linked personality styles may also be related to work experience outside the home. Perhaps the most fascinating data are in the biographies of high-achieving business women, each interviewed in middle age after achieving a position of substantial success in a largely male arena (Hennig & Jardim, 1977). Most of these women told similar stories of adult development, including renunciation of feminine expressive-sensitive qualities during young adult years of career building. At mid-life they experienced a period of personal reassessment, following which most of them began "reclaiming" the more expressive-tender aspects of themselves. At that point a number of them married; a few had children then or acquired stepchildren. Much like highly successful men, the outstandingly successful women managed to integrate both personality dimensions in later life. In this instance the work that apparently "sponsored" the pattern of personality development was not parenting but career achievement.

It is not yet clear how experiences of equally shared daily parenting or equally serious career building by both man and woman may affect personality development. A minority of individuals are apparently androgynous as college students or young adults; it is not clear whether they will become more or even less sex-typed as they get older. Nor are the consequences of lessened sexual differentiation on various people (including children) at various points in life clear; we will address this question further in both this chapter and later chapters.

EGO FUNCTIONING

Adaptiveness

Over the course of adulthood individual ego functioning becomes more stable and reliable, and there is substantial consistency in the adaptiveness associated with ego functions (Neugarten & associates, 1980). The ego's "executive" capacities are much involved in exercising judgment and choosing actions that are appropriate for the situation and for the individual. In part, the changes reflect increased independence from the impact of daily experiences. For example, Robert White (1975) describes the changes in one of the men he studied over time. At 19 the young man said, "I can't make a decision on my own and back it up; it's always guided by some factor outside my own intellect," whereas at 29 he commented, "It dawned on me after a while that I was knowing what I wanted. I was able to make up my mind" (p. 337).

The improved functioning of the ego is reflected partly in the decrease of impulsiveness (Fozard & Thomas, 1975). Also, there is often a decrease in the use of immature defense mechanisms (such as projection, masochism, and hypochondriasis) and an increase in the use of more mature defense mechanisms (such as repression, sublimation, and altruism). (For a description and examples of these defense mechanisms see Table 12-2, Chapter 12.) These changes have been observed from late adolescence through middle age (Haan & Day, 1974; Vaillant, 1977). However, longitudinal studies of the kind needed to assess changes in these aspects of functioning are limited, and there is less evidence about changes in later life than during the first part of adulthood.

Improved ego functioning seems strongly related to general effects of living or maturation. In addition, being advantaged in social class and intelligence during young adulthood seems to aid individuals in developing the ability to cope with life problems.

Maladaptiveness

It is not clear how stable maladaptive characteristics are over adulthood. On the one hand, an unusually long-term study comparing individuals in young adulthood, when they were parents of young children, and 40 years later found that, of the variables studied over this long period, the most consistent was ego disorganization—an inner life marked by tension, fearfulness, and constriction (Maas & Kuypers, 1974). Individals who showed these maladaptive characteristics in old age had similar problems much earlier in life. Looking at the early lives of these individuals for clues to their maladaptation in late life, the researchers found that seriously disturbed marriage relationships predicted later life problems for women, and economic and educational disadvantages predicted later life problems for men.

Similar evidence about the stability of personality difficulties is reported for groups of individuals facing important life transitions (Costa & McCrae, 1978; Lowenthal & Chiriboga, 1972; Neugarten, 1973). Individuals who reported substantial difficulty dealing with menopause, middle age, or retirement were usually those who had a history of being unable to deal with earlier events.

Moss and Susman (1980) offered several conclusions on the basis of their review of research on consistency and change in personality over the life span: (1) Severe psychological disturbances tend to be long-standing, whereas isolated symptoms and mild reactions tend to be transitory. (2) Consistency is most obvious for personality characteristics that are socially valued, such as high achievement motivation and culturally prescribed appropriate sex-role behaviors. Attitudes, which are susceptible to changing cultural values, were one of the least stable personality characteristics. (3) The younger the individual is at the time of assessment, the higher the probability of inconstancy and change.

Our earlier cautions about interpreting consistency and change also apply to ego functions. For example, men may remain high on mastery; that is, they seek to control their sources of pleasure, and they may well continue to do so over adulthood. However, the experiences defined as pleasurable and the strategies used to obtain pleasure may shift. Gutmann (1977) found younger men valuing dominance, imposing their definition of order on the world, and using direct power in order to achieve their goals. Older men valued harmony and more passive sensual pleasures—eating, drinking, relaxation, pleasant company—and, in order to assure these gratifications, were willing to be more accommodative. In other words, both continuity (in level of mastery) and change (in the form and meaning of mastery) may exist in the same individual.

Maladaptive behavior will be discussed in detail in Chapter 13.

MORAL DEVELOPMENT

The requirements of living together in society have traditionally been referred to as *moral* (White, 1975). The way an individual perceives those requirements and responds to them is described as *moral behavior,* and the patterns of changes in moral behavior with age are studied as *moral development.* Most current theories of moral development imply that moral behaviors can be characterized from least to most mature.

Moral Behavior

Moral behavior reflects the persons and ideas that an individual values; such values are an important component of identity. Three major factors contribute to moral behavior. (1) The *parental standards* for living together are the first and most enduring standards acquired by the child. As we saw in Chapter 7, they are incorporated as part of the child's superego and continue to influence moral behavior throughout adult life. (2) *Cognitive* aspects influence the way the individual perceives and interprets reality. According to Piaget, the ways that children see and evaluate reality undergo regular transformations; these cognitive developments are linked to moral development. Piaget, for example, found that the ways that children explained "the rules of the game" reflected their level of cognitive maturity (Ginsberg & Oppler, 1979). (3) *Motivation* to reevaluate one's moral standards and to conform personal behavior to moral ideals is crucial. One's experiences are conducive to developing a more mature, more humane morality.

The more mature, higher levels of moral behavior are characterized by the expansion of caring to an increasingly wide range of people. Caring involves genuine concern for the welfare of other persons and human interests; "it refers only to the things one really has at heart" (White, 1975, p. 358). One index of caring is how naturally and spontaneously an individual does the things required to promote the well-being of another; universal ethical principles extend this sense of caring beyond one's personal family to the "human family."

Kohlberg's Stages of Moral Development

Lawrence Kohlberg is one of the psychologists most interested in moral development. He and his colleagues have studied moral behavior primarily by asking children and adults to respond to hypothetical situations. One problem situation involves a husband who breaks into a drugstore and steals medications necessary for his sick wife because he cannot afford to pay for them and the druggist has refused to give him the medicines free. The answers are evaluated in terms of what rules of social behavior the respondent uses to justify the consequences recommended.

Kohlberg (1969) proposes that moral development can be characterized in six or seven stages. The early stages reflect largely biological and cognitive development. The first stage emphasizes obedience to authority; punishment should follow disobedience, regardless of intention or consequences of the disobedience. The second stage involves more instrumental reciprocity; that is, if one individual does something beneficial to another, that act should be repaid. These first two stages are most characteristic of young children, although some adults continue to function at these levels. The third stage emphasizes the mutuality involved in interpersonal relations and the morality of meeting expectations of others; young adult women often give responses reflecting this kind of morality. The fourth stage of morality stresses the maintenance of the social order through fixed rules and clear lines of authority; young adult males often give responses classified in this level.

Apparently relatively few adults reach higher levels of moral behavior (Kohlberg, 1969). By the mid-20s, some individuals give responses reflecting the fifth stage, which includes the concept of a social contract, a democratic emphasis on the ways people construct laws to serve the needs of social order. Later, in the late 20s or 30s, some individuals reflect the sixth level of moral development, applying universal ethical principles in their moral behavior; Kohlberg sees Gandhi, Martin Luther King, Jr., and Jesus as exemplifying this style.

Kohlberg and his associates suggest (Kohlberg, 1973, 1974) that the last two stages (five and six) of principled morality emerge only in adulthood, if at all, because their development requires several experiences available only during adulthood. Caring for small children, honoring marriage commitments, supporting an ailing parent, or being responsible in one's job may be experiences that foster moral development. First, the experience of having the sustained responsibility for the welfare of others may lead to an appreciation of the importance of arranging personal priorities to include others. Furthermore, as White (1975) pointed out in his intensive analysis of young men maturing into adulthood, genuine caring is fostered by experiences where the individual has opportunities to give the kinds of nurturance that are truly beneficial to another.

For Kohlberg the capacity to develop and follow a coherent ethical policy is tied to personal identity. Moral development requires some degree of personal choice; an individual must be able to feel responsible for moral behavior, and this is not likely in situations where there are no choices. Values are often clarified in the process of confronting conflicting values. Adults have many opportunities to be confronted with values not in agreement with their own. However, their responses do not always result in more principled moral behavior. Caring about and for others may be blocked by anxiety and defensiveness, desires to be cared for, preoccupation with self-interests, envious rivalry, and wishes for personal triumph. Principled moral behavior may also be unlikely in individuals who have very limited intellectual capacity or very restricted social experiences.

Fortunately, many individuals develop the capacity to care for others. The mutual caring that characterizes especially the third and fourth levels of Kohlberg's model provides the basis for the stable human relationships required for well-being throughout life. The concerns reflected in principled morality probably affect relationships with those beyond our personal contact more than our treatment of family and friends. Actions reflecting democratic or universalistic notions of morality may have substantial impact on the community, society, nation, or world as a whole.

SELF-CONCEPT AND AGE

Age Identification

The labels *young, middle-aged,* and *old* all carry meanings beyond chronological age. We hear this all the time in popular speech: "When I finally picked up the tab for a family dinner out, I really felt grown up." "Suddenly I'm feeling middle-aged, and I want a makeup lesson." "I've aged ten years since the accident last fall." "She looks so young for her age!" "I feel old since my mother died." Calling someone "97 years young" stresses the contrast between chronological age and the "complimentary" age. One's felt age is a component of self-concept.

As we saw in Chapter 2, felt age seems to be related to social class. Working-class individuals move along the life line "faster" than middle-class individuals; that is, they feel "adult," "in the prime of life," "middle-aged," and "old" at earlier chronological ages than people in the middle class (Neugarten, 1973). In part, these perceptions reflect the usual timing of important life events: Working-class people leave school, marry, and start a family younger.

The personal clues of moving into middle age have been described poignantly by novelists and explored systematically by some researchers. Physical appearance is an important criterion, especially for middle-aged women. For example, a 45-year-old feminist "confessed":

A few weeks after my 45th birthday, I looked in the mirror and said to myself, "Joan, you look old!" The skin under my chin and neck suddenly sagged and wrinkled. . . . I tried pulling the skin to one side and agreed that this made me look better (younger). . . . There I was face to face with me. I did not like what I saw, but I was finding it hard to admit this. I had never felt like this before. I had always been happy with me: with my body, my face, my skin . . . [Israel, 1977, p. 66].

The middle-aged women in a study of 120 middle-class women aged 18 to 70 had difficulty distinguishing between attractiveness and youthfulness: If a woman was judged to look youthful, she was also regarded as attractive. Interestingly, young women, older women, and men at any age did not equate youthfulness and attractiveness (Nowak, 1977).

The transition into defining oneself as middle-aged is sometimes described as traumatic, and numerous research studies and popular books present case studies of people who have difficulty accepting this change (see, for example, Gould, 1972, 1978; Levinson, 1978; Sheehy, 1976; Vaillant, 1977). This is not always the case, however; one's self-perceptions may shift gradually and include physical changes in appearance and functioning as well as shifting interests and concerns. Changes in relationships with others are noted, especially an increased distance from the young. There is often some sense of urgency, of measuring time in terms of "time left" to accomplish desired goals. Many individuals speak of a greater sense of self-understanding and an increased sense of competence and mastery (Neugarten, 1968).

Identifying onself as "old" rather than middle-aged seems to represent a major change in self-concept, and one that is resisted by many people. According to Turner (1979), nearly half of those over 65 identify themselves as middle-aged; these tend to be people with better adjustment and higher morale than those who identify themselves as old. Those who say they are still middle-aged also tend to say they have better than average health, are currently more active and involved, are employed (at least part-time), and have not suffered major age-related deprivations such as widowhood or major illness. In contrast, those over chronological age 65 who say they are "old" or "elderly" are more likely than those who say they are middle-aged to be in poorer health, less active, unemployed, and widowed.

A more refined vocabulary for periods in later life might help people deal with gradual changes in functioning and interests. For example, Neugarten has suggested that there is, in fact, a "new" stage in later life, which she describes as the *young-old:* no longer middle-aged but not yet ready for the implied deterioration of *old* (Neugarten, 1974). The term *young-old* has become increasingly popular among gerontologists, and it will undoubtedly find its way into the popular vocabulary. Even old age may be differentiated further, into the *old* who are beginning to experience some notable declines in functioning, and the *old-old,* who are near death.

Women are typically seen as being old at younger ages than men; this is part of what has been called "the double standard of aging" (Sontag, 1972). However, there is wide individual variability; some women over 65 have a younger age identity than men of the same chronological age (Turner, 1979). Sex alone is not an adequate predictor of age identification.

Research on age identification suggests that how old an individual *feels* may be a better predictor of behavior than chronological age. Even more important, however, is discovering why an individual feels he or she is in a particular age group.

Self-esteem

Self-esteem is the evaluation an individual has of him- or herself, the answer to the question, "How worthy a person am I?" Self-esteem is usually assessed on a continuum, from high/positive to low/negative. The sense of positive self-esteem can come from varied sources, including good relationships with others, love from others, success in work, sexual gratification, and feeling in command of one's own aggressiveness. Self-esteem also comes from an optimal relationship with the superego and the ego ideal; such an inner harmony helps make one relatively independent of occasions of praise and scorn from outside and able to assert oneself in a manner appropriate for the occasion (Kuiper, 1972).

This inner sense of self-regulation is also sometimes described as an internal *locus of control* (Rotter, 1966). How one perceives the source of control over one's actions correlates closely with self-esteem. Generally, individuals who feel that they are "in charge" of what happens to them and can exert some influence in their lives have higher self-esteem than those who feel that their lives are ruled primarily by forces external to them and beyond their control.

Age Differences in Self-esteem   Generally, self-esteem seems to increase from young adulthood to middle age and then stabilize or gradually decrease, especially from age 50 to 80 (Kogan & Wallach, 1961; Lehrer & Gunderson, 1953; Lowenthal & Chiriboga, 1972; Veroff, Feld, & Gurin, 1962). Increases in self-esteem seem related to self-limitation and reducing one's aspirations on the basis of a realistic appraisal of options and limits rather than on the basis of irrational or neurotic anxiety (Knox, 1977). Decreases in self-esteem seem to be influenced by disruptive life experiences such as loss of job or spouse or having a lower standard of living than anticipated (Kaplan & Pokorny, 1970).

Self-esteem is a composite of many aspects. Compared to younger adults, older adults are more likely to feel they have positive moral values, somewhat more likely to feel adequate as a spouse and parent, equally likely to feel adequate in job performance, almost as likely to think themselves as intelligent as others, less likely to feel they are in good health, less concerned about their weight, and less likely to admit their shortcomings (Riley & Foner, 1968).

Sex Differences in Self-esteem　　There is little agreement on the extent of sex differences in self-esteem. Some reviewers state that, regardless of age, females have lower self-esteem than males (Turner, 1981). Others claim that there are no reliable consistent sex differences in self-esteem (Spence & Helmreich, 1978). One observer (Helmreich, 1977) suggested that the reason there are so few systematic differences in self-esteem associated with sex, race, or social class is that individuals use others of the same sex and social milieu (or "social situation") to evaluate their own social competence. In other words, if an older woman compares herself with other older women, she may feel she is doing "pretty well"; at the same time, she might feel less positive if she compared herself with her daughter or with herself at early middle age.

Aspects of both "masculine" and "feminine" personality styles are associated with self-esteem. Generally, masculine or agentic qualities are strongly correlated with positive self-esteem; the crucial components seem to be the sense of control over oneself and one's fate. At the same time, Spence and Helmreich (1978) concluded that concern with interpersonal relationships, a component of feminine styles, also tends to result in higher self-esteem and social competence. However, a low degree of aggression and dominance combined with emotional vulnerability (and stronger empathic reactions to the emotionality of others) is associated with lower self-regard.

The value of masculine agentic qualities for positive self-esteem is quite clear for men throughout life. Younger men who are low on the masculine dimension and high on the feminine, or low on both dimensions, are also likely to be low on self-esteem (Spence & Helmreich, 1978). The challenge during the middle years seems to be to add or strengthen the more "feminine," communal qualities; men who turn to passive dependency are likely to suffer from low self-esteem as well (Breytspaak, 1974; Livson, 1981). The old men Gutmann studied in other cultures had higher self-esteem when they maintained some areas of life where they exercised control.

Women show a more complex picture with regard to the value of agentic or masculine dimensions. Recent studies with college students indicate that more androgynous women show higher self-esteem than more traditionally sex-typed women students. In some studies women who were high in masculinity and lower in femininity showed high self-esteem (Orlofsky, 1977). However, the picture changes somewhat after the college years. A number of studies (Birnbaum, 1975; Rossi, 1965) report that young women who have not married but are pursuing careers have lower self-esteem and more self-doubts than more traditionally occupied women, presumably because the career-oriented women were violating their own and others' expectations about finding a mate and settling down to motherhood and homemaking. The achievements of the traditional woman are tangible during young adulthood—marriage and motherhood represent "mature" femininity. However, careers take a long time to develop, and success is not apparent until middle age.

The self-esteem of the most traditionally feminine women, those who are more passive-accommodative and other-oriented, seems to decrease over adulthood. During middle age the women with higher self-esteem are those who have agentic, self-directing qualities as well as nurturing empathic feminine qualities (Lowenthal et al., 1975; Bart, 1972; Spence & Helmreich, 1978; Livson, 1981). This is particularly apt to be true now, when increasing emphasis is placed on self-determination for women.

Several studies suggest that the bases for self-esteem vary for men and women over the life course. The measures of self-esteem for women seem to be less consistent and more influenced by current life circumstances than those for men (Maas & Kuypers, 1974; Turner, 1981). Other researchers have found that in later life men's self-esteem is linked more to indications of their past status achievements (such as educational level and income) than to current life situations (Turner, 1981).

In a national survey of adult Americans (Campbell, Converse, & Rogers, 1976), in addition to obtaining responses to questions about happiness and sense of control, the interviewers recorded the physical height of each respondent and rated each respondent on physical attractiveness. Attractiveness ratings were related to sense of control for women under 35 and over 65; that is, younger and older women who were regarded as physically more attractive were also more likely to report they felt in control of their own lives than were less attractive women. Sense of control was not related to attractiveness ratings among the middle-aged women (35 to 65). Among men the sense of control over one's life was not related to physical attractiveness ratings but was related to physical height; tall men (often seen as more powerful) felt more in control than did short men.

In old age positive self-esteem for both men and women is related to maintaining a consistent lifestyle from middle age, having relatively good health and adequate income, and being still married (Turner, 1981). There is wisdom in the toasts that wish us "Health, wealth, love—and time to enjoy them!"

Maintaining a positive sense of self is a challenge throughout life. Every age holds its own potential threats to a sense of adequacy. We will review some of the processes by which individuals maintain or restore self-esteem in Chapter

12 when we discuss adapting to change. Positive self-esteem is one clue that things are going all right; it is a sign of good mental health. People with positive self-esteem are not insulated from hurt; painful experiences are a natural, almost inevitable part of development for everyone. However, self-esteem helps provide the strength to continue taking the risks essential to growth in spite of the pain. A generally positive self-image allows us to integrate negative experiences and put them into perspective.

CRISIS OR CONTINUITY? THE CASE AT MID-LIFE

Dozens of books have been written on how to survive the "mid-life crisis," promising solace and guidance through a period sure to be filled with anxiety, self-doubt, and reassessment of one's life. Difficulties are typically presented in terms of loss—of youthful vigor and attractiveness, of sexual drive, of career opportunities, of marital zest, of parents, and of personal dreams. Death is personalized; we realize that death comes not just to others but to ourselves, and there is limited time left. The realization of losses already experienced and others to be anticipated is presumed to produce distress and erratic behavior among those facing the second half of life.

However, there is considerable disagreement among psychologists about the universality, the severity, and the outcomes of such transitions at the mid-life period. Some see evidence for universal, troubling changes during the mid-life period; others see no evidence of more or different kinds of psychological problems during mid-life than at other times; and still others find patterns of people who experience difficulty and those who do not.

The Crisis-for-All Position

Daniel Levinson is one of the more articulate spokesmen for the view that nearly everyone undergoes a major reorientation during mid-life (see Chapter 7 for a brief review of his theory). From autobiographies and biographies of historical figures and intensive studies of 40 working- and middle-class middle-aged men Levinson concluded that there is a regular, predictable pattern of transformations of the life structure, including the inner sense of self and the self in social interaction (Levinson, 1978). One of the transformations is the mid-life review, which occurs between the ages of about 40 and 45 (some men began at 37, but none began after 43).

Reassessing the Dream   The major challenge of the mid-life crisis is to set up an alternative to what Levinson calls "The Dream." According to Levinson, every young man establishes some vision of what he hopes to be and to become as an adult; this dream includes accomplishments in work, in love, and in friendship. Most crucially, the dream includes an assumption—often unacknowledged—about what will happen if the aspirations are accomplished. For instance, a man may believe that if he becomes a corporate vice-president or manages his own gas station, then (and only then) will he be immune to feelings of self-doubt or inadequacy. His parents will love and applaud him, and his enemies will fear and respect him. Such a dream is usually a fantasy; most men do not achieve their dream goals, in work or in love. And even if they surpass them, they are still not completely protected against feelings of hurt, self-doubt, or boredom. The mid-life crisis hits as the awareness of these realities emerges.

Reevaluating the Polarities   Levinson describes the challenges of mid-life as involving the most intensive reevaluation of some basic polarities of human existence. Human life is characterized by continuing tension between opposites, and the ways one resolves the conflict color one's life for that period. The polarities include one's sense of young and old—redefining what it means to be "young" and taking steps to ensure a kind of immortality through a legacy for the next generation. Another dichotomy that must be resolved involves destruction and creation. On the one hand, the sense of one's own mortality intensifies the wish for creation. At the same time, one acknowledges that one holds rage against others for damage done to the self and that, in spite of good intentions, some of one's actions have brought harm to others. The guilt engendered by this awareness can bring a crisis of self-esteem, according to Levinson. Another polarity that must be renegotiated in mid-life is that between attachment and separateness: how much to merge with others in an effort to guarantee comfort and how much to stand apart and keep one's own counsel.

Finally, a major task is to reassess the polarities of masculinity and femininity, to incorporate the strength of each into a new, more creative, more genuinely loving whole. The men in Levinson's study considered "masculine" creativity as making something to one's own design. The challenge was to incorporate the "feminine" style of creativity—enabling others to be productive and innovative. Men to whom femininity represented weakness, defeat, and vulnerability experienced severe stress when they became aware of their own "feminine" feelings and responses; they could barely tolerate the recognition of those feared potentials in themselves.

Transformations of Childhood Illusions   A similarly universal view of the mid-life crisis is presented by Roger Gould (1975). Gould began his research with people who had come to psychiatric clinics because they were troubled, charting the kinds of problems identified by each age group. Gould and his associates then developed a questionnaire and gave it to 524 people aged 16 to 50 who were not patients. They found that "patients and non-patients of the same age shared the same general concerns about living" (Gould, 1978, p. 14). Gould identifies a series of transformations of childhood illusions of safety, with each transformation presenting some degree of crisis. The final crisis identified by Gould occurred between the ages of 37 and 43.

Both Levinson and Gould believe that inner reworkings of private fantasies, dreams, and illusions combined with the usual social role changes in work and family virtually guarantee a mid-life crisis. In effect, too much happens for there not to be an identifiable crisis period at this time of life.

Results and Resolution of the Crisis The signs of disturbance may be varied. Levinson, Gutmann, and other psychologists working in the analytic tradition stress the meaning of changes for the individual rather than the symptoms. A sense of inner changes may not be identified as an emotional or psychological problem at all, either by the individual or by others. On the other hand, disturbance may show up in a variety of physical symptoms—heart attacks, colitis, sleeping disturbances, or in increased drinking, erratic behavior, and the like. The individual may vigorously deny—for a while at least—that anything is troubling him. However, these psychologists assume that skillful consideration of the person's psychological functioning will often reveal emotional aspects of disturbances, and that the disturbances will be patterned in predictable ways.

Levinson was able to give quite complete assessments of how each of the 40 men in his sample defined and responded to the mid-life transition—in other words, the outcome of the period of renegotiation. Most (22 of the 40) were described as advancing within a stable life structure. These men regarded their "culminating event"—what should have been a peak of achievement—to be somehow flawed, regardless of how others perceived it. Their sense of crisis was highly personal and often very private; an outsider would not necessarily suspect any difficulties.

Seven of the 40 men experienced serious failure or decline within a stable life structure. Even if they had had a promising start, by mid-life it was evident that they were not going to achieve their aspirations and would fall far short of accomplishing what they had intended as young men. A few men left their old life structure behind and tried for a new life, with a new career, a new wife, or even more drastic changes. Such men—and similar women—are favorite features of mass media presentations on mid-life crises. Although they offer dramatic testimony to pain and desires to escape through change, such cases are relatively unusual.

A few men in Levinson's study made some advancement at the end of the mid-life transition period that produced a new life structure; for instance, a job promotion combined with a move to a new community. And a few men (three) ended the transition with no stable life structure. Thus, although Levinson concluded that every man experienced a major upheaval at about the same age, individual styles and outcomes varied considerably.

The Continuity Position

Many psychologists object to the idea of a universal mid-life crisis. Costa and McCrae (1978) constructed a scale to assess the concerns and symptoms associated with mid-life. Men were asked to respond to statements taken from a review of the literature (including research by Gould and Levinson) such as: "I feel the years I have spent at my job were meaningless and unfulfilling." "My life now is boring, tedious, and unchanging." "I find myself becoming more emotional than I used to be" (Costa & McCrae, 1978, p. 136). The questionnaire was given to 315 men, aged 33 to 79, involved in a large-scale, ongoing research project (the Normative Aging Study; see Chapter 12).

The researchers found little evidence of age differences in total mid-life crisis scores. That is, men aged 40 to 45 (the usual age for mid-life crises) were not significantly more likely to report symptoms of crisis than were men under 40 or over 45. Men who reported they experienced the concerns and symptoms of the mid-life crisis also were likely to have a high score on a standard test of neuroticism, a measure of general anxiety usually regarded as an indication of poorer mental health. On the basis of this evidence Costa and McCrae (1978) argue that "most men do not go through a mid-life crisis at all; those who do, do so at no particular age; and the crisis itself may be nothing more than a manifestation of long-standing instability or neuroticism" (p. 137).

Critics of these conclusions feel that the kinds of self-report statements used by Costa and McCrae are inadequate to understanding the phenomena of mid-life crisis. Those men who may be least able to admit—even on a paper-and-pencil test—that they have such concerns may still be troubled by them, and their behavior may reflect those concerns.

However, other psychologists also suggest that some people have difficulty at mid-life and others do not. Bernice Neugarten (1973) reviewed a series of studies on adult life done at the University of Chicago over several decades and concluded that there is little evidence of a unique, pervasive, mid-life crisis. Rather, she found general patterns of decreased power and vigor and increased interiority, which show up in many different kinds of changes from the 30s to the late 50s. The "success" of these changes largely reflects ego strength, the individual's capacity to deal with internal and external changes. Similar conclusions were reached by researchers who intensively studied men and women whose children were making the transition into young adulthood (Lowenthal & Chiriboga, 1972). Problems reported during this period seemed to be continuations of past difficulties rather than new problems of middle age.

The Differential Position

If some people have more difficulty than others in meeting challenges of middle age, why is this the case? Various efforts have been made to identify factors that lead to strength or difficulty. As we saw above, the personality variables of ego strength and neuroticism have been suggested as explanations of why some people have difficulty and others do not; these personality characteristics are presumed to be quite stable over the adult years. Another set of explanations focuses on the "fit" between personality and the social environment.

The research reported by Florine Livson (1976a, 1976b, 1981) is based on longitudinal data offering insights into transitions from adolescence through middle age. Livson used data from extensions of the Oakland Growth Studies, described earlier in this chapter. Data were available for white, middle-class men and women who were studied as high school students (ages 12 to 18) and again around ages 40 and 50. She compared the more and less psychologically healthy men and women at age 50 and traced patterns of development for each of these groups. The psychologically healthy adults were those who scored above the group mean on an index of psychological health with qualities such as warm, giving, responsible, productive, insightful, and relatively free of neurotic signs.

Healthy Women   Livson found two groups of healthy women at age 50—seventeen whose psychological health had improved from ages 40 to 50 and seven whose health had remained high and stable since age 40. All but one were married and had children.

The stable group turned out to be traditionally feminine women: nurturant, gregarious, pleased with their appearance, conventional, and placing high value on closeness to others. They handled conflicts by repressing rather than turning inward. Their personality qualities seemed well suited to the social roles of wife and mother. The traditional women had displayed their personality traits in early adolescence, though at that point their social skills were not as well developed as they became later. They became popular, sociable young women with little sign of anxiety and by 40 had matured into close, trusting, giving relationships with others; they seemed well into Erikson's (1963) stage of intimacy and showed little sign of crisis. By 50 the traditional women were into Erikson's stage of generativity, and they continued their home-centered, nurturing lifestyles.

The women whose health improved showed a different developmental pattern. From early adolescence these were independent women, valuing intellectuality. As teens they were described as introspective, achievement-oriented, and unconventional. By late adolescence they appeared brighter than the traditional women (though there were no tested differences in intelligence). By 40, however, the independent women were depressed, irritable, conflicted, and given to daydreaming and fantasy; they scored relatively low on psychological health. By 50, they had improved. At that point they were seen as ambitious, skeptical, unconventional, and intellectual; they were more autonomous and more in touch with their inner life than were the traditional women. Their main satisfactions came from developing their "self" rather than attachment to others. The independent women revived the identities they had been developing in adolescence and by 50 were able to be warm, giving, and genuinely intimate with others.

Livson (1976a) explained the differences between these two groups of women in terms of the fit between a woman's lifestyle and her personality. Traditional women were able to live out valued aspects of themselves in conventional feminine roles; they continued finding satisfaction in relationships with others even when their children left home. Independent women did not find it as easy to meet conventional definitions of femininity, although they recalled their young adult years with pleasure and took pride in their mothering and home-making skills. Their suppressed intellectual competence reemerged as child caring phased out, and they faced a crisis in finding new ways of integrating the concerns that had been evident even in early adolescence.

Healthy Men Livson (1981) also identified 21 psychologically healthy men for whom data were available during adolescence and at ages 40 and 50. Seven of these men had remained healthy at 40 and 50, and fourteen had improved from 40 to 50. All were highly successful in their careers, and all but one were husbands and fathers.

The stable men were traditionally masculine from adolescence on; they valued thinking rather than feeling and were self-controlled and not very spontaneous. Their ambitions and personalities remained consistent from early adolescence to age 50, although by age 40 their masculinity became tempered by softer, more affiliative qualities. While their personalities became more balanced during middle age, they continued to value intellectual competence, rationality, self-control, and achievement; there was a good fit for traditionally masculine role expectations.

The men who improved were less traditionally masculine, even in adolescence. In youth their emotionality was impulsive and dramatic; they did not seem to make a choice between the expressive and assertive sides of themselves. By age 40 the nontraditional men had suppressed emotionality in favor of active, instrumental behavior. However, their masculinity was power-oriented and exploitive, and they seemed hostile, generally anxious, and concerned about body functions. By age 50 these men had given up their defensive hyper-masculinity and had become more openly nurturant and sensual. They were less angry and anxious than they had been at 40. They integrated their feminine aspects with their ambition, and their psychological health improved.

Livson's research indicated that by age 50 the psychologically healthy men and the healthy nontraditional women had reclaimed aspects of cross-sex qualities repressed during young adulthood. Overall, the psychologically healthy men and women were less different from each other at age 50 than they had been at age 18 (Livson, 1976b). The men had added the qualities of nurturance, and the nontraditional women had reclaimed their intellectuality. These data support psychologists such as Jung (1933), Bakan (1966), and Gutmann (1977), who regard this as a crucial developmental issue. These three groups illustrate how the psychological shifts can lead to "new capacities for enjoyment, to new sensitivities, and to the maturation of new executive capacities" (Gutmann, 1979). The shift was not as noticeable in the group of traditional/stable women.

Livson suggests that the dislocations experienced by the men and women whose health improved were tied to the degree to which their life structure did not support their preferred gender identity. She thus offers one explanation for differential experiences with mid-life shifts: Those who improved managed to overcome their difficulties. It is clear that some individuals experience substantial difficulties with mid-life transitions and are not able to resolve them well; we need further research to understand more fully how those who are successful manage the transition.

Unhealthy Men and Women   Several kinds of data suggest that "casualties" of mid-life may be rooted in earlier experience. Individuals who are unable to negotiate the potentials of middle age successfully seem to be people with long-standing personality problems, even though these may not be obvious in behavior problems during earlier years. For example, we can recall the evidence of Costa and McCrae (1978) that men who seemed to be having the most difficulty during mid-life were those who also scored highest in neuroticism.

Livson (1976b) also assessed the developmental patterns of people who were psychologically unhealthy at age 50. Although healthy men and women became more like each other than they had been in late adolescence, unhealthy men and women remained set in stereotyped sex-role personality patterns. Furthermore, unhealthy men and women failed to develop as many socially desirable aspects of the male and female roles as healthy persons did.

As teens the unhealthy men were ambitious but lacked self-discipline. They tended to be self-defeating and self-concerned. At 40 these men were productive and proud of their objectivity; however, they were also condescending and tended to blame and punish others when things went wrong. Less expressive than before, they were also more anxious and irritable. By 50 they cast off their defensive masculinity and became more openly dependent and expressive of feelings. Thus healthy men became more androgynous by developing their nurturance; unhealthy men moved into androgyny by becoming more dependent.

As teenagers the unhealthy women were dependent, unassertive, conforming, and sensitive to slights. They sought attention and reassurance through talkativeness and self-dramatizing behavior. By age 40 these women had become less outgoing and more openly dependent, fearful, self-defeating, and submissive. Unlike the healthy women, they did not widen their interests by age 40. By age 50 they were more talkative and dramatizing (as they had been in adolescence) but still fearful and dependent. Unhealthy women were the least likely to develop opposite-sex characteristics by age 50; they were also the most anxious at 50.

Livson's data suggest that the unhealthy men and women were vulnerable even in adolescence. However, they did manage adult responsibilities and did not necessarily seek help with their trouble. Although the data are provocative, they do not tell us very much about the ways in which such vulnerability might develop.

The intensive analysis of middle-aged and older psychiatric patients provides further suggestions about the ways mid-life developmental potentials may interact with long-standing personality problems to produce symptoms of emotional distress. Gutmann and his colleagues and students at Northwestern University have been conducting close clinical studies of individuals who have sought inpatient or outpatient psychiatric treatment for the first time in their later years. A summary of some types of "developmental casualties" Gutmann has identified so far will illustrate his approach (see Gutmann, Grunes, & Griffin, 1980). (We will discuss developmental perspectives on psychopathology further in Chapter 13.)

The men regarded as developmental casualties ranged in age from the mid-40s to the late 50s. They usually came to the hospital in a state of agitated depression: anxious, unable to sleep, without appetite for food or sex, and unable to concentrate on work despite a prior history of steady employment or even high achievement. They complained about trouble on the job and problems with a newly assertive, newly achieving, sometimes unsupportive wife. They viewed the wife's move toward independence and self-direction as a kind of dismissal of their own importance in the household.

Not only did the men share common symptoms and complaints, they had similar histories. Typically, they were the youngest sons of aging parents; brothers or sisters were at least seven years older. The father was almost always absent or seen as weak, while the mother was seen as strong and competent. The adult sons often indicated they believed (and feared) that the mother effectively stripped the father of his strength and power. The sons lacked a strong sense of masculine strength within themselves. However, they used work to provide direction, control, and self-esteem; work activities and identifications with men at work served as a substitute for this inner sense of masculinity. They married women who were nurturant and nonassertive, and who recreated the important bond to the mother. These arrangements stabilized them during the earlier adult years.

The dislocations of mid-life can provide serious problems to such men. Work often becomes less compelling and less challenging and can no longer support grandiose fantasies; when this occurs, there is less motivation for controlling one's behavior to gain the support of superiors at work. Furthermore, if work and self-definition become more important for the wife, and she refuses to be the docile woman, he can no longer project his own femininity onto her; he must confront his *own* closeted maternal self. For such men the sense of their own emerging emotional, "maternalistic" self is very threatening. They feel a sense of panic that they, too, will be "emasculated" (by the wife), and that they—like their fathers—will prove too weak to defend themselves.

Livson describes the unhealthy men in her sample as using "defensive masculinity"—a kind of hypermasculine stance that is exaggerated because it covers up the lack of a firm inner sense of masculinity—to ward off a sense of femininity. Some of the men Gutmann interviewed can be described in similar terms. They came to the hospital when their defenses no longer worked, or when defensive behaviors (such as drinking or recklessness) became problems.

The crucial factor seems to be that these men never really achieved adequate separation from maternal figures; they failed to establish a secure sense of masculinity. Livson's findings suggest that such men may make the transition into androgyny by becoming openly dependent. The men seen by Gutmann's group have been unable to make even that shift.

Women in their late 40s and 50s, most admitted with a diagnosis of depression, are also being clinically studied by Gutmann's group (Gutmann, Grunes, & Griffin, 1980). Such mid-life depressions are usually explained in terms of losses suffered: menopause, the empty nest, the husband's disinterest, or widowhood. Such losses may indeed lead to pain, sadness, and some depression. However, intensive interviewing and analysis of projective fantasy material revealed another kind of loss, not so much the loss of some external object as the loss of self-esteem.

For example, consider the case of a woman, hospitalized for depression, who is diagnosed as suffering from a kind of pre-emptive mourning for a terminally ill husband. The patient had been going to school, and was soon to begin a post-graduate career. However, these plans were aborted by the patient's decision to stay home and nurse her dying husband. The couple had been close, and the diagnostic formulation presented the patient as suffering and depressed in anticipation of the husband's oncoming death. However, the projective test data were full of images of imprisonment, claustrophobia, and rage. Clearly, the patient was bitter over her imprisonment in a nursing role, at a time when she was looking forward to an expanded and self-expressive life. Again, the patient was not chiefly suffering the pain of loss, but the pain of guilt and self-reproach: she could not forgive herself for desiring the quick death—the death that would free her to an expanded life—of a beloved husband. Clearly, in such cases the therapist should not concentrate on the irreversible loss (which is no news to the patient), but on the guilt which is both unconscious and reversible. (Gutmann, Grunes, & Griffin, 1980, p. 127)

Women who cannot accept their emerging masculinity seem to be frightened of their own aggression, perhaps fearing it will make them less feminine, less desirable, or terribly destructive. (Depending on their partner, these fears may be partially justified.) In their early years they may live out their assertiveness vicariously through their husband. If he becomes milder, or ill—or if he dies—the woman can no longer use him in this way. Some such women become chronically ill, possibly as a way of "helping" the threatened husband remain the stronger partner.

Common factors in early development have not been identified for women who experience clinical depression in mid-life, although the data from Livson's sample suggest severe problems with normal assertiveness even as adolescents; those data seem compatible with Gutmann's clinical observations. The recognition that unacceptable, rageful parts of the self exist and are pressing for direct expression provokes a sense of shame and a loss of self-esteem. Further research is needed to identify the early precursors of such vulnerability.

Social changes emphasizing the desirability of masculine and feminine characteristics for both sexes throughout adulthood may make mid-life transitions easier to deal with. However, the acceptance of these dual characteristics will have to be translated into the intimate spheres of earlier childhood in order to influence the kinds of personality structures that seem to make some individuals vulnerable to changes in the life course.

Some Conclusions

The controversy about transitions from one life period to another will probably continue for some time. In part, the extent of disruption that is seen seems to reflect the kind of analysis used. Close, intensive analysis of the process of change through the middle years suggests more private troubles and varied symptoms than show up in more limited, objective self-report measures. Troubles at mid-life seem related to uncertainty: Some capacities and options are lost, while new ones that may emerge are not yet clear.

The data suggest that most adults deal with transitions adequately, and with minimal signs of anything like a "normal," predictable crisis. However, some individuals do experience substantial difficulty with life transitions. The ability to cope with changes from within and without seems linked to personality characteristics of the individual and to how well personality style fits current situational and life-stage expectations.

We reviewed a few provocative suggestions about the sources of problems in dealing with mid-life transitions: that some (neurotic) individuals simply have more difficulty in life generally (Costa & McCrae, 1978); that the "match" may be poor for some men and women at particular social periods (Livson); or that particular childhood deficiencies may make one vulnerable at some (but not all) transition points (Gutmann). Each of these hypotheses recognizes the importance of personality in mediating interactions between the individual and the environment. In the next three chapters we will see how personality affects behaviors in two important areas of life: relating to others through love and friendship, and meeting competence needs through work involvements.

SUMMARY

1   This chapter reviewed research on aspects of personality and morality during the adult years. *Personality* is an individual's distinctive pattern of organizing perceptions and beliefs and way of acting and reacting. At every age there is marked individual diversity in personality.

2   Assessments of individual developmental changes from young adulthood to later life reveal about as much stability as change. The extent of continuity varies with the methods used to assess personality and with the personality variables considered.

3   Longitudinal studies with adult men suggest that personality character- istics of *extroversion, neuroticism,* and *openness to experience* show little change over adulthood.

4   One of the consistent personality shifts with age is toward increased *in- teriority.* Older people seem to have less psychological energy, and what they have is used to deal more with individual problems and less with external, so- cial problems.

5   Another major personality change over adulthood involves sex-typed qualities. Sex differences in personality characteristics are most evident during young adulthood; men and women become less stereotypically masculine or feminine in later life. Changes in masculinity/femininity, the reasons for them, and the differing reactions of individuals have been extensively studied by many researchers.

6   Individual ego functioning becomes more stable and reliable over adult- hood. There is substantial consistency in the *adaptive* capacities associated with ego functions; in general, those who manage stress well at one life phase do so at other phases. However, not much is known about the stability of *mal- adaptive* characteristics.

7   *Moral development* refers to changes in the ways individuals perceive and respond to the requirements of living together in society. According to Kohlberg, the higher stages of moral behavior emerge only in adulthood—if at all—because their development requires experiences of sustained responsibility for the welfare of others. Furthermore, the capacity to develop and follow a coherent ethical policy is tied to personal identity.

8   One's felt age is a component of self-concept. One's sense of age seems related both to social class and to sex. Identifying oneself as "old" rather than "middle-aged" represents a major change in self-concept that is resisted by many people.

9   *Self-esteem* describes one's evaluation of oneself. Overall, self-esteem in- creases from young adulthood to middle age and then stabilizes or gradually decreases in later life. Older people with positive self-esteem are likely to have maintained their middle-aged lifestyle, to have relatively good health and ade- quate income, and to be married. Women seem more influenced by current life circumstances, and measures of their self-esteem show less consistency than those of men. The self-esteen of men seems more tied to their own status achievements, even in later life. Many, but not all, studies indicate women have lower self-esteem than men.

10   Researchers take different positions on the *mid-life crisis.* Some see in- evitable, profound changes for all individuals, whereas others see continuity and gradual change over adulthood. The mid-life transition seems to center on a reevaluation and transformation of one's early illusions and expectations for the self. How an individual reacts to and responds to such changes varies great- ly, depending on early psychological health as well as integration of masculine and feminine patterns.

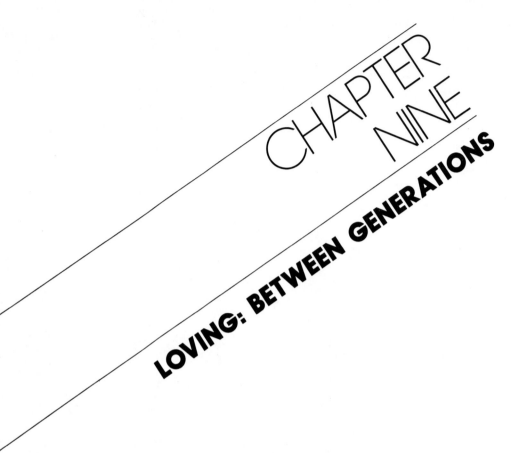

WHAT IS THIS THING CALLED LOVE?

"No man is an island."

"The reliable presence of people who love us facilitates our perception and toleration of painful reality and enriches our lives." (Vaillant, 1977, p. 28)

"Love is the response to the source of pleasure." (Rado, 1969, p. 99)

Humans are uniquely and intensely social creatures. Other animals are also sociable; they gather together, form dominance hierarchies, mate, rear their young, cooperate in protecting insiders from strangers, and communicate with each other more than with outsiders (Wilson, 1980). However, humans have additional capacities of intellect, memory, and language, which allow elaborate, self-reflective patterns of interpersonal relations to evolve.

The next two chapters will consider some of the varieties of human interpersonal relationships. In this chapter we will review research on parent–child relationships at different periods of adulthood; in the following chapter we will focus on how adults in contemporary Western society relate to each other as friends and lovers. Our focus is on the *affective,* or feeling, aspects of close

relationships, although it is also important to understand the activities people engage in together.

Affective relationships have typically been analyzed in two ways: (1) as reflections of intrapersonal sentiments, needs, dispositions, or personality characteristics; and/or (2) in terms of the institutional or quasi-institutional social forms recognized to meet individual and societal needs. After summarizing some of the evidence about love as a personality characteristic, we will look at the family as a social institution.

Most psychologists postulate a universal drive, motive, or need for emotional relationships with other humans. Individuals are often assumed or shown to vary in the strength of various manifestations of this general characteristic. Thus Murray's (1938) theory of personality was based on identifying the relative strength of various needs, including *affiliation,* or the need to be in friendly association with others, to love, to cooperate; and *succorance,* or the need to receive aid, protection, love, consolation, and guidance from another. The relative strength of such needs is presumed to motivate an individual toward or away from various patterns of action. An individual with strong needs for affiliation, for example, will seek out occasions to be in close collaboration with others; this may involve putting more energy into a love relationship than into education, or preferring to work on a team rather than alone.

Several forms of love or affiliation are recognized in Western tradition. Because different meanings of the term *love* are often not distinguished, it is best to use caution in interpreting results from different studies. Rollo May (1969) differentiates four major forms of love: (1) sexual or lusting love; (2) love aimed at creating (Eros); (3) friendship (Philia); and (4) love devoted to the welfare of others (Agape). May sees a blending of all four aspects in what he terms "authentic" human love. Furthermore, May says, love is connected with will in that both involve the process of reaching out to influence others and the openness to being influenced. Thus commitment to interpersonal relations involves the willingness to direct our behavior toward the needs and wishes of another and to accept that the other will act similarly toward us.

Intimacy is a dimension of love that describes the relationship rather than the sentiments expressed by either individual. Researchers use different definitions of intimacy, though most include the degree of close and confidential communication between people. No specific behavior is inherently intimate; for example, the fact that two people are living together, dine together weekly, or have sexual relations does not necessarily mean they experience intimacy in that relationship. The degree of intimacy must be assessed separately from the number and kinds of contacts.

The Capacity to Love

The capacity to love develops over time. The most crucial experiences occur in the family; for most people the first model of affection and love is within the family that receives us in infancy. Our earliest experiences of love are particularly powerful ones, perhaps because we do not fully or consciously remember them, and they may consciously as well as unconsciously influence our later emotional responses to people. However, we also have later opportunities to revise our expectations of love and to experience different forms of relating to others. The friendships of childhood, for example, are important in aiding separation from parents. They are even more important in developing the sensitivity to what matters to another person that is crucial in adult relationships. The exchange of confidences in friendship, in an atmosphere of trust and mutuality, overcomes our feelings of isolation (White, 1975). Early relationships can be facilitating to later life functioning, or they can be destructive if the relationships are unsympathetic, exploitive, and unreliable. The capacity to trust in oneself or in another can be damaged to the point where adult commitments to others are tenuous and guarded.

The capacity for intimacy and effectiveness in personal relationships seems to grow with experience, and sometimes in the face of crisis, though the ability to learn new responses may be limited by the individual's defense mechanisms. Defensive behavior is one way to deal with anxiety, but often it also works to make the individual more rigid and less open to new learning. People at any age who respond impulsively and defensively to others have difficulty developing and maintaining close, supportive relationships (Vaillant, 1977; White, 1972).

The capacity for intimacy and loving, then, comes with maturing sufficiently to accept both oneself and another as unique beings. It has something to do with developing the more "mature" defense mechanisms (see Table 12-2, Chapter 12). In a sample of men studied over some 30 years Vaillant (1977) found that those who were comfortable with their own aggression responded more lovingly to the world in general and to those closest to them.

Developmental Changes in Affiliation

Interest in affiliation varies not only with personality but with shifts over the life cycle in opportunities for different kinds of social relationships. Experiences in which family and neighborhood provide many satisfying opportunities for interpersonal activity can result in persons who have a strong commitment to affiliation. On the other hand, it is also possible that being deprived of social interaction or having an inadequate sense of autonomy and identity can lead to a strong need for affiliation. Low commitment to affiliation may characterize an individual with a strong sense of identity in a setting with only moderate opportunities for interacting. Low self-esteem and feelings of mistrust and inferiority may also serve to block moves toward affiliation with fears of rejection.

Research indicates that, in general, commitment to interpersonal relationships shifts over the life course (Knox, 1977). However, there is a great deal of variation among individuals at any point in life. Such interindividual variability reflects both early childhood antecedents and current influences. Concern with affiliation seems to be relatively great in late adolescence and young adulthood, as individuals search for identity, intimacy, and a career. In later life the concern may be somewhat different. People who develop and maintain close friendships or have confidants in old age report higher levels of life satisfaction, involvement, and functioning than those who are less affiliative (Lowenthal & Haven, 1968), but the affiliation may be guided more by the need for companionship than the need for intimacy. Further, adult age differences in energy level and the increased energy required for personal functioning probably affect the nature and extent of interpersonal behavior. Further study of the varying intensity of emotions in personal relationships over time is needed.

To make the question even more complex, there are sex differences in the manifestations of commitment to interpersonal relations over time. The question does not seem to be who needs whom the most; men and women need each other and acknowledge that commitment in various ways at various times. However, there appear to be differences in what men and women *think* they want and in how they establish and maintain various kinds of relationships over the life course.

We will now review some of the evidence about commitments in various kinds of relationships as they evolve over the course of adulthood. Because the family is the most important arena for interpersonal commitments, we will look first at the family and discuss how relations between generations change over time.

FAMILIES: MYTHS AND REALITIES

It may seem to some readers of the popular press that the family is an obsolete institution, with "free love," divorce, temporary alliances, and "child-free" lifestyles replacing the traditional family unit consisting of mother, father, children, and grandparents. However, there is little real evidence that the family, as a social institution or as a reality for individuals, is either dead or obsolete—though it is indeed changing.

Family Functions

A *social institution,* as we saw in Chapter 2, is an organized group of individuals who have functions, relationships with each other, and behaviors recognized by others in the society. The expected patterns of behavior are often formalized by laws. Social institutions develop to serve the survival needs of the society. Although aspects of a particular institution may be uncomfortable for a given individual, overall those institutional forms survive that enable the society as a whole to be preserved.

Families are one of the major social institutions in every culture. For example, every society must replace its members, and families are usually responsible for rearing the young. By locating this responsibility within the family, the society generally ensures the best care for the helpless infant; parents are usually most able and willing to provide the consistent, warm, concerned care needed to assist the development of the infant into a responsible adult.

Maintenance   The family provides *maintenance* for both children and adults. Individuals need to eat, sleep, wash, launder clothing, and obtain care during minor illnesses; these needs are met by the family in most societies. In addition, many societies expect that the individual's needs for love, psychological security, sexuality, and passing on some legacy to future generations will be met within the family context.

Societies differ in the extent to which the family is expected to meet individual needs. In some societies, the individual is expected to meet nearly all needs within the family; an individual without a family will have difficulty surviving, though this is more likely to be true for women than for men. In more communal systems, such as the original kibbutz of Israel, the community more than the biological family is the basic unit (Spiro, 1979).

Some critics charge that our society has removed the meaning of the family by providing alternative ways of meeting individual needs. Restaurants will feed us, laundries will clean our clothing, maids will vanquish our bathtub rings, hospitals will nurse our illnesses, and friends will warm our bed—all for a price less than a familial commitment. However, such a critique overlooks the importance of emotional maintenance, for adults as well as for children. There is ample evidence that humans need to be needed, recognized, and valued as special individuals fully as much as they need fresh vegetables, clean underwear, and back massages. Physical maintenance can be purchased, but emotional maintenance remains almost exclusively a function of the family.

Socialization   Another traditional, and continuing, function of the family is *socialization,* the process of learning whatever is necessary to adequately survive in a particular culture and to participate in its social institutions. Clearly, if the society is to survive, the young must learn the culture and eventually take over management of the society from the elders. Children must learn the skills and attitudes necessary to become functioning adults; adults must learn how to fulfill various new roles as they become older. Within the family system the roles of lover, bride/groom, newlywed, spouse, parent, grandparent, widow or widower, and divorcee are all learned. Although this learning is supplemented in peer groups and through the mass media, the family is still the primary source of this information.

Social Control   A third function of families is *social control.* Every society must have ways of keeping individual actions within the bounds it considers tolerable. Though all social institutions share in this function, the basic arena for social control is the family. The legal system is formally designated as the institution in charge of behavior control; however, no society could have enough enforcement officers to adequately supervise individual behavior, and no legal system has yet devised a completely effective means of enforcement. Fines, imprisonment, and even death are relatively ineffective compared to the informal ways the family shapes and controls the behavior of its members: withdrawal of approval, esteem, and affection.

Humans will modify selfish—sometimes even antisocial—behavior primarily when rewards or positive reinforcers are provided for change or when considerable punishments are the consequences of transgression. All infants need, want, and respond to human warmth, approval, and nurturance; normal children and adults continue to need and respond to these if they have previously found them gratifying. Only when individuals have experienced the warmth and satisfaction of love and approval is the possible loss of these rewards threatening. Because the family is ideally set up for nurturant, warm, loving relationships, the family also becomes endowed with a unique power to shape individual behavior. By rewarding socially desirable behavior with approval and love, and punishing undesirable behavior with emotional coldness, scorn, or censure, families are a powerful source of social control.

Obviously, the family serves this function well for the society as a whole only when the family reinforces the behaviors desired by the society. And this is more likely if there is some consensus or agreement about what those desirable behaviors should be. One of the difficulties confronting families in contemporary American society is the lack of clear ideals and norms to transmit to the children.

Social Placement   One acquires a place in most social systems on the basis of one's family. One aspect of place is social class, as we discussed in Chapter 2. In most societies it is considered legitimate and desirable to accumulate wealth in the family and to use whatever resources one can gain to help family members achieve and maintain the highest possible social class status. American parents, particularly those in the middle and upper classes, want their adult children also to be middle-class (or higher). Parents try to provide the kinds of education and other experiences they hope will lead to middle-class jobs; after their children marry, parents who can do so frequently provide gifts, services, and job-placement assistance that help the young adults establish a middle-class lifestyle (Hill, Foote, Aldous, Carlson, & MacDonald, 1970). Inheritance laws reflect the belief that families should be entitled to pass along resources to the next generation. The cumulative effect of the desire to ensure the success of one's own family members and social opportunities to do so is that all children do not begin life with equal opportunities to succeed. The likelihood that an individual will have the experience and resources that can lead to success is strongly linked to family connections.

In societies where there is relatively little geographical mobility and people know one another personally, one's place in the social system may be influenced by the family's reputation as well as economic class. For example, one poor family may be regarded as hardworking, honest, and thrifty, and family members will find it relatively easy to find employment, while a person from an impoverished family of shiftless repute may find it difficult to obtain work. Family reputation is less powerful in urban societies or among groups of geographically mobile individuals.

Some societies have a deliberate political policy of reducing the importance of the family in social placement. Societies can forbid or limit inheritance from one generation to another, provide equal public access to educational opportunities, and make jobs available on the basis of open competition. The goal of such policies is to allow individuals to achieve their place in the social system on the basis of demonstrated competence rather than family connections.

Legitimacy   Perhaps because families are given substantial responsibility for such socially important functions as emotional maintenance, basic socialization of the young, social control, and social placement of the child and adult members, most societies have formalized marital arrangements and emphasized legitimacy as a means of assuring continuance of the family. In fact, although more unmarried couples now live together openly than in previous times, approximately 90 percent of the adults in the United States still marry, and most have children. Among adults 60 or over, 80 percent of those who have ever married have at least one living child (Harris & Associates, 1975; Murray, 1976; Shanas, 1973). Voluntary childlessness and rearing children outside a recognized family are increasing for the generations now young in American society, but it is probable that these alternatives will remain minority positions.

The notion of legitimacy is intrinsically linked to the larger social structure, particularly the economic and sex-role systems. The concepts of legitimacy and illegitimacy acknowledge the importance the society places on the family as an identifiable social institution. The implicit assumption is that, although mothers can certainly bear children of uncertain paternity, no currently viable alternatives to the family can fulfill the society's needs for socializing the young. In societies that define the family as a husband, a wife, and their children, children are *legitimate* if born within such a legally recognized union; an *illegitimate* birth is essentially one that occurs outside the boundaries defined as appropriate by the society.

These perspectives are important when we consider the kinds of social and individual pressures adults feel as they seek to meet their needs for interpersonal commitments within existing socially recognized arrangements (such as monogamous heterosexual marriage) or try to create and sustain alternatives (such as homosexual marriages or sexually open marriages). Currently, some of the ideals about family stability and solidarity seem to be challenged. However, divorced and "reblended" families, for instance, are altering, rather than rejecting, the family as an important way to meet personal needs. Let us now consider how various arrangements serve individual adult needs for emotional sustenance and the consequences of such arrangements for the larger social system.

Family Structure

One of the ways families vary is in *family structure*—that is, who is included in the family, and how they relate to each other. The "family" includes different people in different cultures. Virtually every culture recognizes the basic *nuclear* unit as mother, father, and their offspring. Some cultures include other adults (grandparents, uncles, aunts, cousins) who live with or very near the nuclear unit as part of the family. Such family members may share economic resources and serve as a mutual support system. For example, in some traditional African societies and some urban Polish groups the family includes a large network of kin; any member of the family who is employed or who has access to resources (such as a vegetable garden, soap, cut-rate clothing, or carpentry skills) is expected to share them with all family members. Such a system operates in effect as a welfare system, where those temporarily or permanently without funds are provided for by others in the family.

The family form most common in the United States today is the *modified extended family,* with ongoing interactions between family members beyond the nuclear unit of parents and children. There is much variability in who lives together and counts as family. At one extreme a study of black urban families found 79 identifiably different kinds of family structures (Kellam, Ensminger, & Turner, 1977). The most common was, indeed, mother/father/child, but mother/grandmother/child and mother/child families were also quite common; other combinations included mother/stepfather/child, mother/boyfriend/child, mother/sister/child, and grandmother/child. Single-parent families headed by fathers are becoming increasingly common for both blacks and whites in the United States as divorce rates increase.

Family structure is important because it greatly influences the ways family functions are carried out. The models available for socialization and learning about adult roles are obviously more limited in a mother/child household than in one with child, mother, father, grandmother, grandfather, and unmarried aunt. The burdens of parenting and the support available from other adults are different in different family structures; the isolated mother/child family seems to be the least satisfactory for the mother and the one that places the child at the most risk for developing learning and behavior problems (Kellam et al., 1977). A tight network of mutual obligations among many extended kin may be more effective in controlling the behavior of family members than the alliance of two adults isolated emotionally and physically from their kin. Partly for these reasons, societies tend to encourage family structures that mesh well with the needs of individuals and the society.

The Family Life Cycle

It is a myth that there is *a* family life cycle. That is, no single, normative, predictable pattern shapes and times the events within the family life cycle

(Nock, 1979; Spanier, Sauer, & Larzelere, 1979). It is true that the history of a family is influenced by births, marriages, and deaths and the patterns of husband–wife and parent–child relationships those events create. Furthermore, there is an "ideal" sequence of events: Courtship is followed by marriage, then pregnancy; the first-born child leaves home to marry, followed by the remaining children in sequence; and the spouses die after the children are reared, thus ending that particular family cycle. However, the *sequences* and *means* of family events often do not follow the "ideal" pattern.

For example, Bill Bytheway (1977) examined the family data for 597 families of the British nobility. Although these families certainly were not "typical," they were selected for study because data on the dates of various changes in the family composition were quite complete. Bytheway found that only 65 percent of the marriages both produced children and avoided divorce; the remainder failed in even this elemental way to conform to the idealized family life cycle. Furthermore, only 22 percent of the families had an empty nest period, with both parents alive, at home, and still married, but with no children living at home. Within the 597 families, Bytheway found 214 different sequences of events involving pregnancy, marriage, and death, the entrances and exits of the family cycle. On the basis of this analysis he suggested that it would be productive to give up the notion of a normative, *normal* family cycle and look instead at the different kinds of family patterns and their consequences for different phases of the life cycle.

Bytheway's point about the "normal" life cycle of the family is particularly important in contemporary Western society. Rising divorce rates are now contributing to the variability in family structures and family patterns. It is quite possible to have more than one "family," or to be in different phases in different families at the same time—for example, launching young adult children from a first marriage and starting again with small children in a second marriage.

Contact among Family Members

One of the common myths about families is that, because of the geographic mobility in the United States, most family members—particularly old people— live a great distance from each other. In fact, several surveys in the 1960s showed that 75 percent of the old people with children live within one-half hour of at least one child; 52 percent lived within ten minutes of at least one child. In 1968, 18 percent of the older Americans with children lived in the same household with a child; this decline from 36 percent in 1957 reflects the mutual desires of both generations to live separately but nearby (Troll, Miller, & Atchley, 1979).

There may be a period when children are establishing their own households and careers and parents are middle-aged when they live more geographically distant. Most studies have found that young adults, especially after they have children, want to live near but not in the same household with parents and grandparents (Troll & Bengtson, 1979). In general, working-class families are more likely to live near each other than middle-class families; this fact seems related to the greater opportunities and willingness of middle-class families to move geographically in order to pursue career success.

However, even geographic distance does not mean that family members do not see each other. Some young adults see their parents frequently; contacts are most likely between daughters and mothers, particularly those daughters who are interested in becoming parents themselves (Ryder, 1968; Ryder & Goodrich, 1966). In one study of 100 three-generation families in Minneapolis, 70 percent of the married young adults saw their parents weekly (Aldous & Hill, 1965; Hill et al., 1970). Most older parents and middle-aged children generally see each other often. Shanas (1979) reported that 53 percent of older people interviewed in a national survey had seen one of their children the day they were interviewed or the day before that; other surveys indicate that from 78 to 90 percent had seen a child within the previous week (Troll et al., 1979), and only 10 percent had not seen at least one child for a month or more. These contacts may be brief and ritualistic or lengthy and individualized; by and large the data do not speak to the quality of contacts. But the data appear to indicate that parents and adult children maintain contact with each other; this is one index of commitment to the relationship.

Affection and the "Generational Stake"

Another index of commitment to the relationship is how adult children and parents feel about each other. There is, however, less research on such qualitative aspects of family relationships and on factors contributing to changes over time.

In general, family members report positive sentiments toward other generations. In fact, as a review of this research points out, "it is the amazing lifelong persistence of some parent–child bonds in the face of geographic separation, socioeconomic differences, and even value conflict which we must explain" (Troll & Bengtson, 1979, p. 150).

However, there seem to be some systematic distortions in reports of family solidarity. Studies of parents and adult children from the same families suggest that older parents consistently overestimate the degree of attachment, understanding, and communication between the generations in their family (Bengtson & Troll, 1978). In other words, parents report more closeness than their adult children do. Bengtson and Kuypers (1971) suggest that these patterns reflect the different "stake" each generation has in the relationship. According to the *generational stake* hypothesis, parents are concerned about the young living up to normative expectations and continuing the values and lifestyles established by the parent. Thus the parents overemphasize the agreement and closeness with children (and, potentially, grandchildren) and overlook or minimize disagreements and differences. Children, on the other hand, are concerned with differentiating themselves from the older generations and thus emphasize the ways they are different from their parents. Clearly, we cannot take the report of any one member of a family as the "truth" about what goes on in that family. Each family member reports what goes on from the perspective of his or her own position in the family, and this position, of course, shifts over time.

Cultural Variability

Interactions in a family context follow culturally defined expectations. People of different ethnic backgrounds perceive family boundaries, responsibilities, and expectations differently; these perceptions in turn affect the patterns of help and social-emotional support across generations and between kin (Woehrer, 1978). For example, many of the indices of family interaction cited above vary by ethnic identification. A 1967 national survey of Americans (summarized in Woehrer, 1978) showed that weekly visits to parents were reported by 79 percent of the Italian-Americans, 65 percent of the Polish-Americans, 61 percent of the French-Americans, and 39 percent of the English- and Scandinavian-Americans.

Interactions of the family with the wider society also differ between cultural groups, according to a review by Woehrer (1978). The Polish and Italians seem to value kin over friends and belong to few organizations outside the family. The Irish value kin primarily as friends, for enjoyment and mutual equalitarian relationships. Blacks often have relatively fluid family boundaries, with friends "going for" kin and a stress on mutual help. The Scandinavian-Americans, like Scandinavians in their native countries, seem to have the lowest reliance on kin; they have the highest rates of organizational membership and the greatest belief in collective responsibility. Though these statements are generalizations and overlook the variability within any group, they suggest that cultural values guide individuals to learn to depend on different social resources. The family seems to be most important as a social resource for Italian, Mexican, Polish, Jewish, and French people; friends are relatively more important to the Irish and blacks; and formal organizations are important resources for Scandinavians.

In addition, variability in interaction patterns and reliance on family is linked to social class differences and rural-urban differences. Social changes are important, particularly as they affect expectations and opportunities for interaction.

The Family as Caregivers

Perhaps the biggest myth of all about the family is that, because of the availability of human-service bureaucracies and other alternative sources of care, the family is no longer important as a source of care for its members. In fact, no institution satisfies the needs of children, adults, and older people as well as the family. No other form of care has proven as effective as the family for child development; and although the welfare of children is not our central concern here, we cannot ignore those experiences that form the next generation of adults.

In any case, it seems clear that all generations both give and receive care through the family, though the kinds of aid desired and exchanged vary. The period of peak giving seems to be middle age, with more receiving than giving in childhood and late old age (Hill et al., 1970; Shanas, Townsend, Wedderburn, Friis, Milhoj, & Stenhouwer, 1968). The amount of aid exchanged is not closely related to residential nearness or frequency of visiting.

The kinds of aid exchanged vary with stage in life. The youngest adults often want (and receive) money and child care. The middle-aged seem to prize emotional gratification and the benefits of "patron" status that come to the generation in the middle; these benefits are, of course, more possible for those who have financial and emotional resources to share. On the whole, the aged seem to place a higher value on affectional support from their children than on material or financial assistance, though they do expect help in dealing with illness and in household management if necessary (Kutner, 1956; Shanas, 1960; Streib & Thompson, 1960; Tobin, 1978).

Factors Strengthening and Weakening the Family

Families have, as we have seen, great potential for satisfying the most important of human needs. They can provide continuing care, affirmation, and identity that cannot be obtained elsewhere. However, many families do not function well, and individuals find themselves unable to count on their family for the caring they want. (Families may not function well because individual members are dysfunctional. The relationships between individuals and the larger family system are complex.)

Several factors seem to weaken family ties and inhibit intergenerational contacts. Reviews of research on the relationships between adult family members by Boyd (1969) and Hess and Waring (1978a) identified the following as family-weakening factors: (1) spatial and social mobility and distance; (2) differing beliefs and ideologies; (3) preoccupation with activities and affairs outside the family to the exclusion of family members; (4) infrequent family get-togethers; (5) pride in independence when associated with decreased opportunities for helping each other; (6) family members undergoing difficult transitions at the same time; (7) illness or debility; and (8) residues of earlier conflicts.

Difficulties arising from these factors can contribute to the inability of the family unit to respond well in a crisis situation. A fairly typical crisis for the older family involves making decisions about when to act and what to do with an increasingly debilitated older parent. Kuypers and Trute (1978) pointed out that one of the barriers to effective mobilization of the family during such times is the image of "usual" changes in the family, an image typically shared by both generations and supported by social mythology. One of the images is that the intensity of family involvement will and should decrease as children grow up and establish themselves as adults. Because a family crisis involving the older parent threatens to intensify involvement again, it may be resisted as "unnatural" and undesirable. Moreover, authority, caregiving, and responsibility are defined as flowing primarily from parent to child, and under "normal" circumstances this direction of aid is in fact characteristic. However, a crisis with the parent, when adult children are asked to provide help and sometimes direction, challenges images of parental competence.

A further weakening factor is that the family may have difficulty working together as a unit, partly because of the general expectations that adult children and their parents no longer constitute a "family," and partly because of the myth that problems of older persons are simply problems of old age and cannot be linked to family relationship issues. Professionals who work with older people and their families can frequently see the problems of older people as symptoms of problems within the family system, but middle-aged children are often reluctant to accept this definition. There is little incentive to work on long-term difficulties between adult child and older parent and more incentive to work on an immediate specific problem (such as where will mother live now that she has broken her hip). And, of course, each family has a long history of unresolved tensions by the time its members reach the later years; these can interfere substantially in the ability to provide care for any family member when needed.

Given these potential, and actual, difficulties in maintaining the supportive capacities of families, it is important also to identify some of the sources of family strength. These include, not surprisingly: (1) propinquity (or nearness in terms of time and effort required to get together); (2) personal attention, gifts, and services exchanged; (3) shared group activities; (4) desirable personal qualities of the people involved (such as pleasant disposition or attractiveness); (5) socialization processes, which include the transmission of values, role modeling, and moral and religious upbringing; (6) norms of filial piety ("honoring thy father and thy mother"); and (7) the new functions for adult children of negotiating with the bureacracy on behalf of elders and supervising the terminal phases of life (Boyd, 1969; Hess & Waring, 1978; Shanas & Sussman, 1977).

One of the challenges of our era is to find ways to strengthen families of various forms and at all periods of life. We can do that better by understanding more about the special relationships in the family as they are transformed by time and circumstances. We will look next at transformations in child–parent relationships.

DEVELOPMENTAL ISSUES
IN PARENT–CHILD RELATIONS

For most people the relationship with parents remains central throughout life, enduring in the face of desertion, divorce, and even death. When Lillian Troll (1972) asked adults of all ages to describe any person, they spontaneously referred to their parents more often than to any other person. Even the oldest respondents, in their 70s and 80s, were still using their parents as a point of reference in thinking about people. Troll's research results are supported by clinical work. Psychotherapists find that older adults may still be troubled by unresolved competition with parents, rage over feeling abandoned or unloved, or guilt about being unloving toward the parent or "unworthy" of the parent's love and devotion. Children, like parents, become and remain important to adults; there is little evidence that spouses, lovers, friends, or colleagues can replace the specially important relationship with even an adult child. We will next look at some of the common psychological and subjective themes in parent–child relationships.

Phase I:
Immature Child and Responsible Adult

For each individual the parent–child relationship begins with an *immature child and a responsible adult.* The characteristics of life in this earliest period may have long-lasting consequences for adult functioning. As Dorothy Dinnerstein (1977) points out, the child, born helpless, apparently goes through an early, preverbal "fusion," or symbiosis, with the primary caregiver. There is also an early, basic ambivalence, as one learns that the caregiver (usually the mother) is separate and can grant or withhold comfort, security, and union.

Male–Female Differences   Given that caring for infants and small children has been almost exclusively in the hands of women, differences between boys and girls emerge as a consequence of child-care patterns. Girls find separation from the mother difficult because of that earliest fusion and because they learn that they are also female, and like the mother. One frequent adult consequence is that the daughter never feels as competent as her infantile memories of her mother. On the other hand, she is apt to learn the nurturing, accommodative skills and styles that accompany mothering.

Boys learn fairly early that they are separate from the mother, and not like her. This message is communicated both subtly and directly by the mother and by others. According to Dinnerstein's analysis, boys and men long forever for the ultimate security and fusion of that earliest period in life. However, men also fear the powerlessness and dependency that relationship implies. This ambivalence—yearning for and fearing closeness with women—is, according to Dinnerstein, carried through life. Boys do not have the same kind of relation with the father (and other men) because the boy identifies with the father after verbal and rational capacities are better developed and the boy can thus more easily see himself and his father as distinct individuals. Boys often compete with the father, but they compete as individuals; boys suffer far less often from the sense of fusion that is part of the relationship with the earliest, most intimate caregiver.

The Consequences of Childhood Experience   There are many different outcomes of childhood for adults. Dinnerstein asserts that adult relationships between men and women are always tinged with men's lingering ambivalence toward women. Other evidence also suggests that the individual's basic sense of self and the world is derived in part from the ways parents respond to the child; those expectations seem to linger on, although they may be subconscious (Chodorow, 1978; Erikson, 1963; Rollins & Thomas, 1975). Expectations about family responsibilities, trust, values, and so on are established within the family of origin (the family into which one is born) both by lecture and—more pervasively and importantly—by example. One learns how to behave as a parent largely from being a child. Relationships with each parent (including stepparents, if any) are established primarily during childhood; the usual feelings about the relationships carried into adulthood seem to be a mixture of affirmation, disappointments, pride, and repressed rage. Bonding and attachment are colored by the inequities of power and the limits of the child's understanding. And the "truths" constructed by the child's powers of understanding, however irrational, endure—at least in the subconscious—and influence the ways in which the adult parents his or her own children. This is why we pay attention to facts of childhood even when our primary concern is with adults.

Becoming Parental   The survival and welfare of children is dependent on the availability of an adult who will act as a responsible parent. This person need not be the biological parent, of course, but it must be an adult who is able to become parental. Not all adults who can begin life can honor it. Throughout history we have known that some fathers ignored or denied paternity, and some mothers abandoned, neglected, maimed, or murdered their young. Most parents, however, manage to deal with the difficulties of parenting. It is important to understand what enables adults to become good parents.

There are a variety of motivations for wanting to become parents, some reflecting social expectations and some based on personal needs, some recognized by the individual and some not. Sometimes unconscious motivations may be operating in "accidental parenthood," since many babies are conceived and borne by girls and women who are in reality unprepared to become responsible, caring, and committed parents.

Hoffman and Hoffman (1973) identified nine basic values of having children in a review of research on motivations for parenting. (1) Becoming a parent validates adult status and social identity. (2) By having a child, one achieves a measure of immortality, assuming that the child survives the parent.

(3) Parenting is a way to achieve moral values in cultures emphasizing altruism, giving to the group, and the control of impulsivity required for good parenting. (4) Children enlarge the family group beyond the couple and provide more sources of affection and love. (5) Babies are enjoyable, novel, and fun. (6) Having a baby is a creative experience, and caring for it contributes to feelings of competence and achievement. (7) An infant baby is more under the parent's control than any other person ever has been or ever again will be. (8) A parent who can feel he or she has the cleanest, healthiest, best-behaved baby around the neighborhood can derive competitive satisfaction. (9) A baby may represent a new helper when the baby becomes a child or teenager or when the parent is old.

Adequate research is not yet available to identify how these different meanings of parenting characterize men and women in different subcultures and how these different values may relate to child-bearing and child-rearing practices.

Feelings about Parenting   Pregnancy and childbirth are important psychological events. Myra Leifer (1977) studied 25 first-time mothers from the time they learned of their pregnancy until seven months after birth. Leifer identified a series of stresses during pregnancy and early motherhood. Anxiety during pregnancy about the fetus, the self, or both was a common experience, and Leifer suggests that it is a normal, healthy part of the process of bonding between the mother and child.

The women in Leifer's sample all reported some negative feelings about the pregnancy, although those who viewed motherhood as a chance for personal growth were less dissatisfied than those who valued the pregnancy as a measure of security and status. During the last trimester of pregnancy increased emotional vulnerability, marked mood swings, tension, and irritability were common, as were intensified feelings of well-being. A sense of elation and satisfaction at the birth process was often followed by feelings of depression and anxiety. The postpartum period was very negative for more than two-thirds of the sample.

For most of the women in Leifer's group postpartum depression and anxiety gave way after two months to a sense of boredom with child-care routines. Even after seven months of motherhood most women reported moderate to high degrees of stress over general changes in their lifestyle, restrictions on personal freedom, and changes in the marital relationship. On the other hand, some indicated an increased sense of completeness as a person.

Similar results have been reported by other researchers. For example, two husband and wife teams (Cowan, Cowan, Coie, & Coie, 1978) studied 14 expectant couples from mid-pregnancy to a period of approximately half a year following birth. The couples were all from San Francisco, ranged in age from 21 to 40, and represented a cross-section of racial, educational, and financial backgrounds. The couples reported an emotional "high" following birth, which they attributed to the sense of fulfilling their biological roles and working together to fill the baby's needs. However, the women found, without exception, that they had underestimated the difficulties and delays in recovering from pregnancy. The fathers, too, found themselves conflicted about establishing some new acceptable balance between home and employment commitments.

Handling the Tasks of Parenting In support of much other research evidence (for instance, Brown & Harris, 1978; Fogarty et al., 1971; Lowenthal et al., 1975) the couples in the Cowan et al. study reported that, regardless of their initial style of dividing up work roles, they had shifted to more "traditional" division of household tasks after becoming parents. This was a source of conflict for these couples, who presumably were interested in working out role-sharing arrangements that ignored usual sexual distinctions. This particular strain is not experienced in families that accept sex-role division of labor from the beginning of the household.

All the couples in the San Francisco study modified their attitudes about what they would do as parents once the child was actually part of the family. Those who had resolved not to surrender their own needs tended to give more importance to the infant's needs and demands than they had planned, and those who had thought before the baby was born that experiencing some frustration and anger would be good for their infant seemed less convinced that this was a good strategy after the baby was born.

It is possible to interpret these findings as reflecting a move toward a more realistic assessment of the kinds of household and family arrangements suited for the care of small children. There are alternatives to a traditionally sex-linked division of labor within the household; some couples spend equal time on child care, for example, or have the father assume primary care of the child while the mother supports the family. These alternatives are more unusual than including more adults in the household to share in child-care and housekeeping responsibilities. The latter solution is not available to many people now because of labor costs, but it was a fairly common practice in earlier periods to bring in cleaning women, cooks, nannies, and the like to assume some of the work load. Our era may be unusual in assuming that couples are able to provide for parenting even if both parents are fully involved in career building. We will return to the question of integrating work and parenting in adult life since this is one of the crucial issues for our time (see Rapoport, Rapoport, & Streilitz, 1977).

Factors Contributing to Parenting Abilities The ability of an individual or a couple to become parental, to accommodate the needs of the child, and to benefit from the experience, seems to depend on several important factors. Probably the most important variable is the extent to which the individual was nurtured adequately as a child. There is considerable evidence for the "inheritance" of both adequate parenting and child abusing from generation to generation (see Cohler & Grunebaum, 1981; Gelles, 1973; Steele & Pollock, 1974). This is not difficult to understand since we learn what we will do to others primarily through what is done to us.

The ability to be parental also relies on sociocultural supports, which are unevenly available. One form of social support is shared norms that honor the kinds of sacrifices made by adults in the interests of children. Such norms emphasize the dependency of the child and grant esteem to adults who provide good care for the next generation. Current cultural norms in our society do not give much support for such a "parental imperative." For example, about half the adults surveyed in America (Yankelovich, Skelly, & White, 1977) endorsed "equal rights" of parents and children, with the assumption that parenting should not involve much renunciation of personal interests. In addition, the stress on personal fulfillment and on equal, substantial career advancement for men and women carries with it the implicit—sometimes explicit—demand that no sacrifices should be necessary for child bearing and child rearing. Such cultural beliefs make it difficult to gain a sense of esteem from placing the interests of a child over personal development.

Sociocultural supports for parenting may take the form of sharing some of the burdens and responsibilities for child care. Emphasis on the similarity of maternal and paternal capacities and responsibilities; released time from employment for both mother and father during the delivery and postpartum period; flexible, reduced-time work involvement for parents of small children; cash bonuses to parents; and high-quality collective child care to enable both parents to work outside the home are forms of aid to parents already available in some American communities and some other countries. They are all ways of potentially reducing the stresses currently associated with parenting (Rapoport et al., 1977). However, each of these options carries with it consequences for personal, family, and social life, many of which will not become clear for several decades.

Consequences of Parenting   What are the consequences of parenting, aside from inconvenience and expense? In a sense, it is strange to even raise the question; parenthood has been one of the most standard, and least optional, adult experiences in history. Perhaps the question of consequences only becomes relevant when parenthood becomes optional; at that point one searches for evidence regarding probable outcomes of choosing one or the other option. Certainly, there is considerable emphasis now on parenthood as a choice, to be evaluated against competing possibilities for adults' time, energy, and enjoyment. There is virtually no research documenting conclusively the consequences of parenting on adult lives, particularly over a long span of time (Lerner & Spanier, 1978). It does seem clear, however, that parenting can be a stressful experience: The demands are considerable, and some parents feel overwhelmed by the complexity, the mundanity, the unpredictability, and the relentlessness of the "parental emergency" (Gutmann, 1975).

On the other hand, in spite of the difficulties, most parents prefer parenthood to not having children. In one national survey of 1230 households where a child under 13 resided, 90 percent of the parents said that, if they had to do it over again, they would still have children (Yankelovich et al., 1977). Fewer of the working mothers (83 percent), single parents (72 percent), and minority parents (72 percent) were so sure. Among the satisfactions mentioned by the parents were pride, maturity, self-fulfillment, fun, and joy.

Psychologists as well as parents often identify the possibilities for personal growth as an important consequence of parenting. The capacity to renounce narrow self-interest and preoccupation is regarded as an indication of maturity. In addition, parents are often provoked into reexperiencing their own development vicariously through their children. This entails the risks of confronting buried memories of the past but also offers potentials to "rework" earlier developmental problems more adequately as an adult and to gain a sense of mastery by helping the child deal with the developmental issue.

Research illustrating these potentials is found in the work of Heath (1972) on the impact of fatherhood on the maturing of young professional men. His sample included 68 men in their early 30s, all of whom had been studied earlier as college freshmen and upperclassmen. Of the 60 married men 48 were fathers. Many of the fathers did not acknowledge fatherhood as influential on their development. However, when the investigators compared responses of the fathers and the nonfathers as college students and as young men, they found that the fathers had become more mature, psychologically and physically healthy, and competent in marital, parental, interpersonal, and vocational adaptation than the nonfathers.

Parenthood apparently provoked maturing in some areas more than in others. The fathers reported increased self-awareness and a clarification of personal values, particularly as these were challenged by their children. They learned how to relate to children and how their own interpersonal style affected others. Empathic concern increased in response to feeling responsible for the welfare of children. Fatherhood also enhanced the sense of personal integration, primarily by helping the men relate to their own underdeveloped childlike, emotional side. On the other hand, parenthood had little apparent effect on the maturing of cognitive skills or nonfamilial relationships.

Phase II: Adult Child and Adult Parent

The next major transformation in the relationship occurs as the *child matures, and the parent moves into middle age* (Lewis, 1978). As the child moves into adulthood and establishes him- or herself as adult, the parents phase out of the parental emergency. This transition offers the potential for adult–adult mutuality and enhanced appreciation of the perspective and strengths of the other.

From the perspective of the child's development this period is commonly characterized as involving the process of individuation, forging that sense of self that is unique, different from the parents, and yet linked in special ways to the family and the larger community. The challenge becomes to establish autonomy from the parents without sacrificing relatedness with them (Murphy, Silber, Coehlo, Hamburg, & Greenberg, 1963). Moves away from the parents are presumed to be in the interest of establishing one's own sense of identity, forming compelling bonds with an age peer, and being able to assume the responsibilities of the parental imperative. The stereotype usually assumes a pull away by the young and an identifiable "generation gap" between beliefs and behaviors of younger and older members in a family.

Intergenerational Similarities and Differences   However, the evidence suggests a more complex story. Troll and Bengtson (1978), for example, reviewed the research on similarity of values between generations and found, overall, substantial but selective intergenerational continuity within any family. In fact, the differences between families were likely to be greater than differences between members of various generations within a family. They found the most similarity in religious and political affiliations and the least similarity in sex roles and personality. Such similarity is moderated by historical and current social forces, of course, so we find more similarity where it is encouraged and less where it is discouraged.

The evidence also suggests the ambivalence of the young in separating from parents (Cohler & Grunebaum, 1981; Stierlin, 1974). After all, the young adult can feel substantial admiration for and dependency toward parents. For example, an 18-year-old black girl whose parents were divorced when she was 12 and whose mother worked on an assembly line described her feelings about her mother:

Most of my years have been centered around my mother and she has played an important role in my life. She has made me the person that I am and without her I do not think I could have made it this far in life. I admire my mom a lot and I hope that I can be as strong as she has been when the going gets tough. Outside of everything else her love has been the single most important factor in my development (personal files of author).

While feeling such a sense of connectedness and reliance, young adults may proclaim more autonomy than they really feel, particularly since contemporary norms encourage the young to go off on their own. They may still, however, regard home—and their parents—as a place to return to. As one disenchanted young woman said, explaining why she was moving back home after a period of living alone and with roommates, "They love me, my clothes are still in my closet, and where else could I have that kind of comfort and security?"

Launching Adult Children   The stereotype of parents at this phase centers on dread and anxiety of the "emptying nest," as if they suddenly stopped parenting and life became bereft of its central meaning. Such a view assumes that parents resist the individuation of children and long for continued dependency. Such is not usually the case in actuality.

The evidence is strong that launching adult children is a process, defined differently by mothers and fathers and in various subgroups (Barber, 1979). Transformations take time. When did you "know" that you had "moved out," or "grown up" (if you have)? If you have, will you ever return to your parents' home? Was the transition marked by physical distance (getting another place to sleep), financial independence, being treated as a guest by parents, or finding your clothes moved out of the bedroom closet and into the storage area? While most research uses some fairly arbitrary measure of "launching" (such as graduation from high school, or marriage), it seems clear that different sorts of questions are applicable for parents and for children.

Parents, like children, report mixed emotions about launching: relief, anticipation, pleasure, anxiety, and loss (Glenn, 1975; Glenn & Weaver, 1979; Harkins, 1978; Lowenthal & Chiriboga, 1972; Neugarten, 1968). Most parents anticipate the launching period and are not greatly upset when the changes occur as anticipated. Parents express concern about young people who are later than expected in moving into adulthood and taking on adult roles of work and marriage (Pearlin & Radabaugh, 1979). Some parents do feel bereft when children leave home. This response seems more likely among women who have invested the major part of their identity and energy in mothering and who have few other resources for feelings of self-worth (Bart, 1971). Most parents derive a sense of satisfaction and pride from feeling that their children are doing adult tasks, particularly if they are on an "appropriate" timetable. There is often shame, anger, and self-doubt when the children do not leave "on time," or when they return (as after a broken live-in or marriage relationship) to "clutter up the nest," or when they are very "late" in assuming adult responsibilities.

Parents may also feel anxiety about the right thing to do with adult children who do not meet parental (or grandparental) expectations of timing and activities. When things do not go as expected, doubts about one's competency as a parent are raised. As one middle-aged mother said,

One thing frustrating for a parent is that the idea of a parent has always been to help raise a child into the world where he is going. But I don't understand it—my children understand that world better than I do. And I feel a little mad sometimes inside. I do. Everything I always felt was right has gone haywire, and I can't help but feel a little mad. . . . (Higgins, 1976)

And other parents facing the same situation are not always present to provide support for parents of young adult children.

Part of the problem is not having someone to share it with, going through the same thing. We were all such comforts to each other when our babies were little. Is he supposed to be doing that, or is that something I should worry about? But if you're the only one of your friends who has a 23-year-old living at home, that is lonely. You don't have anyone to talk it over with. . . . Every night we have a discussion, my husband and I, should we kick him out or not. He's not capable of living by himself. But this is tearing us apart. There's so much stress. . . . Where did we go wrong? (Higgins, 1976)

As children leave, parents do face the issue of what to do with the energy formerly focused on the children. As parents redirect their energies into social activity, the spouse, or the self, they may feel envious of their children for the freedom, resources, and self-confidence the children display. They may suspect—sometimes correctly—that the child obtained such strengths at the expense of the parent. They may be especially resentful if the adult children then refuse to make similar accommodations to the demands of parenting—to the continuity of the family and the culture—and demand a continuation of the self-indulgent state of childhood or late adolescence.

Parents generally accommodate to the lifestyles of children even when they differ substantially from what they had envisioned. Many parents even alter their own lifestyles and values under the influence of their adult children. As one mother put it,

I've had to change, because of my children. I really think I've turned that corner. There are a lot of things we've had to accept, there's no question about it. . . . I accept the way they do things, or else we don't have a relationship. . . . They don't have the guilt feelings I would have because they just don't feel the same way. (Higgins, 1976)

However, even when parents do not change, and children do, the relationship is usually maintained, as the qualitative aspects of the relationship are not much tied to parent–child similarity (Troll, Miller, & Atchley, 1979). The mutuality of attachment and bonding transcends most lifestyle and value differences.

Becoming Grandparents   One way the parent–child relationship changes is for the child to marry and become a parent. When an adult child becomes a parent, the parent becomes a grandparent and thus takes on a new role. Nowadays grandparenting is a middle-aged rather than an old-age phenomenon, and younger grandparents are likely to have living parents themselves, and sometimes even grandparents. Several important questions about these transformations arise: What is the nature of the relationship between the adult parent and grandparent? How do grandparents respond to this unchosen role? What do we know about relationships between grandparents and their grandchildren?

There are perhaps a dozen studies on grandparenting, but few consistent findings have emerged yet (Troll, 1980). Only a few studies relate directly to the questions posed above, and many important questions have not yet been explored.

Mothers and Grandmothers   In a fascinating study of personality and child care across three generations Bert Cohler and Henry Grunebaum (1981) selected four multigeneration, working-class Italian-American families. They chose to focus on the adult women because so much research shows that families tend to be linked through females, with middle-aged women playing the most substantial role (Gutmann, 1977; Troll, Miller, & Atchley, 1979). Furthermore, the mother–daughter bond seems to be the most intense and potentially conflictual one. Mothers and grandmothers were interviewed over a number of weeks and given paper-and-pencil and projective tests in order to assess more and less conscious aspects of personality. In several families grandfathers and fathers were also interviewed, and parents and children were observed together. This study, therefore, represents fairly complete and naturalistic research on intergenerational relations.

In each of the four families studied the mothers and grandmothers were in frequent contact and exchanged assistance and support. The contact and exchange seemed to be facilitated by the urban situation, where it is easier for families to live close together, help each other find employment, and provide services to each other.

It was clear that all four adult daughters depended on their mothers for information and emotional support, in spite of the American myth that young adult children establish independent and autonomous relationships with parents. Cohler and Grunebaum suggest that this continuing dependency on the mother is rooted in several aspects of preadult and adult socialization. First, women are taught to be dependent from early childhood across the first half of the life span. Second, as the daughter acquires a household and becomes a mother, her life is increasingly similar to that of her own mother, and her mother becomes an ideal role model. Third, mothers of small children typically need help from others. For all these reasons, daughters are likely to turn to their mothers for emotional sustenance as well as for help in knowing what to do in particular situations and assistance in doing it.

In these four families intimacy between husband and wife was of less significance to a woman than a continuing close tie with her own mother. The husbands did not object; rather, they seemed to enjoy the support from an extended family. The pattern of pragmatic dependence on the mother more than the husband is more characteristic of working-class adult daughters than middle-class women, who seem to feel more ambivalent about their dependency. In addition, some middle-class husbands resent the strong mother–daughter bond.

Although the adult daughters were comfortable with their increased dependency on their mothers, the grandmothers often felt frustrated and annoyed that their daughters demanded so much intimacy at that time. Cohler and Grunebaum see the responses of these late-middle-aged grandmothers as partly developmental. The women were experiencing increased interiority (see Chapter 8), expressed as greater egocentrism and aggression. They were less interested in meeting the needs of others and thus less tolerant of the demands for continued nurturing.

In attempting to generalize from these findings, it is important to remember that the responses reflect the particular ethnic heritage, historical times, and personality of the individuals studied.

Patterns of Grandparenting   The Cohler-Grunebaum study revealed complex patterns of interdependency. Other studies are less complete but are useful in showing the variability in importance, meaning, and activities associated with grandparenting.

One of the early studies of grandparenting included analyses of interviews with 70 grandmothers and 70 grandfathers, all in middle-class, urban families (Neugarten & Weinstein, 1964). A second study included 125 grandmothers and 132 grandfathers, all living in a working-class area of Madison, Wisconsin (Robertson, 1977; Wood & Robertson, 1976). Positive meanings of grandparenting mentioned included biological renewal, emotional self-fulfillment, being a resource person, and pride in the accomplishments of grandchildren. In both studies approximately one-third of the respondents were remote, uninvolved, or unconcerned with the grandparent role. Such remoteness may be linked to personality style (Wood & Robertson, 1976).

A majority of the grandparents in both studies indicated they felt comfortable and easy with the role. The one-third who felt discomfort complained primarily about being asked to assume responsibility for child care.

Grandparenting does not seem to be a particularly important role for most people. For instance, among the Wisconsin grandparents the levels of involvement in grandparenting were not related to life satisfaction (Wood & Robertson, 1976). Even persons living in a home for the aged, with few opportunities to establish new relationships, did not derive much basic satisfaction from their grandparenthood (Kahana & Coe, 1969).

Grandparents and Grandchildren   The relationship between grandparents and grandchildren seems to vary with age of the grandchild. Kahana and Kahana (1970) found that children under age 10 felt closer to their grandparents than did older children; grandparents also liked younger grandchildren more than older ones. Four- and 5-year-olds valued indulgence in grandparents; 8- and 9-year-olds wanted them to share in their fun. By 11 or 12, the children began to withdraw from their grandparents. During adolescence some children become alienated from their grandparents. However, many adolescents and young adults seem to turn to grandparents as a special family resource (Gilford & Black, 1972; Hagestad, 1978; Robertson, 1976).

The grandparent–grandchild relationship also varies with sex. Grandmothers are more likely to have warm relations with their grandchildren, and most of the relationships are along the maternal line (Hagestad, 1978).

Furthermore, relations with grandchildren reflect grandparental style. Grandparents who raised children emphasizing the child's needs, such as

Being a grandparent can be a challenging, sensitive position. Individual responses to grandparenthood reflect a variety of personal and situational factors.

autonomy and dependence, were less intrusive and authoritarian with grandchildren (Sussman, 1965).

The valued grandparents in contemporary society seem to be those who realize differences between their generation and those of their children and grandchildren, and who wait to be asked rather than imposing their own needs on other generations (Boyd, 1969). It can be a challenging, delicate position.

The responses to grandparenthood seem to reflect a variety of personal and situational factors, most of which are not yet understood. It will be interesting to see how the styles and meanings of grandparenting change in future cohorts, as four- and five-generation families become common and most families include divorced and recombined families.

Phase III:
Older Adult Child and Elderly Parent

The third major transformation is likely to occur as the *middle-aged child relates to aging parents*. This phase can sometimes be characterized as "becoming your parents' parents." The stereotype is that parents demand care, which is refused by the middle-aged child in the throes of his or her own mid-life development. This is sometimes the case; often it is not.

Families take care of the needs of the individual. Here an adult helps his older father.

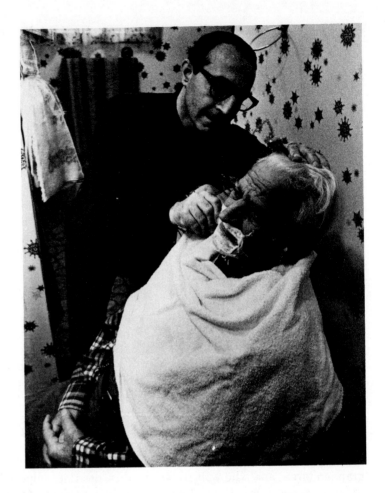

Filial Maturity   Middle age does seem to bring with it reassessments of one's position in the life cycle and one's relationship to others. In part, this involves what Blenkner (1965) termed *filial maturity*—a stage in personal development when one realizes that one's parents are neither omnipotent nor immortal and that one may play a "parent-caring" role with them. This assumes the ability to care without demeaning and without fears for one's own aging. The acceptance of filial responsibility is widespread (Seelbach, 1978; Tobin, 1978). The responsibility seems to be defined largely in terms of financial support for sons, and of emotional support, "worrying," monitoring, being available, and coordinating services for daughters.

Models of the Future Parents often act as models for our own aging, a glimpse into the future. Adults ask themselves, "Is this what I will become?" The recognition of similarity to a parent may come as a shock after the illusions of young adult autonomy. It can bring a sense of pride and hope for those with parents who demonstrate a spirit and/or lifestyle admired by the children; it may also bring a sense of shame and dismay. In our response to our aging parents we may also have the sense of modeling for our own children: As we do, so shall it be done to us. Responses to this phase of the relationship reflect, of course, both what has gone before in the relationship and current stresses and resources.

Coming to Terms with Death The death of a parent is profoundly significant for most people, at any age. The death may be anticipated, and even welcomed, as a release from pain and burdens. However, death also means that any unresolved rage, disappointment, guilt, and love will remain unresolved. One's last chance for an idealized, longed-for parenting relationship with that person—whatever that may be, and however unconscious that wish may remain—is gone. Such feelings enter into the mourning process. Finally, particularly when our last parent dies, we must accept our own aging as inevitable: we are the next generation to go. Parents stand between us and mortality; as long as a parent is alive—and functioning as a parent—we can remain, in some senses, a child. Even a 78-year-old son can hurry home from a meeting to assure his 98-year-old mother that he is all right. When that parental barrier is removed, we must struggle alone with adulthood.

The Changing Parent–Child Relationship The aging parent must also adapt to changes in the relationship with adult (and aging) children. There is a general norm of independence, particularly economic. Most elderly people prefer to have their own households and their own friends, and most *do* retain independence, sometimes much more than their children (or grandchildren) expect and often more than they themselves thought possible. Young-old parents and grandparents (or great-grandparents) are apt to be self-reliant; not much engaged in active grandparenting; and involved in a variety of recreational, friendly, and daily-round activities. Such patterns of healthy activity are likely to increase for the cohorts of adults now moving into later life.

However, at some point many old parents need help. Changes from reciprocal aid to more aid flowing from the adult child to the older parent seem to reflect deterioration in the health and/or financial situation of the parent. Generally, old parents seem to expect help to the extent that they are very poor, ill, living alone, or very old, and children seem to grant aid on the basis of such needs.

For example, about 8 percent of elderly Americans are bedfast or housebound, twice the percentage who are in institutions. Approximately 80 percent of their care comes from family members, who provide meals, housework, personal aid, and the like, with limited assistance from outside paid professionals (Shanas et al., 1968; Wilder, 1972). When possible, the spouse provides such care. However, children, particularly daughters, supplement that care and are the ones most likely to provide care in the absence of a capable spouse (Tobin, 1978).

In cases of extreme need the older parent and adult child may move to be in the same household. One study (Sussman, 1976) found that 19 percent of the 356 respondents, aged 18–64, were unwilling to care for an elderly relative in their own home under any circumstances, regardless of cash and service incentives offered. The others indicated a willingness to do so. Such a move is often regarded as preferable to institutionalization, even though institutionalization may ultimately be necessary.

The ways in which children select—and are selected—to aid parents are interesting and complex. Aid somewhat follows availability: Unmarried children are more likely to move in with an elderly parent than are married children with their own children at home. In part, aid also seems to follow sex lines: Daughters provide direct, personal care and emotional support, and sons provide financial aid. Widowed mothers are more likely to move in with a daughter than with a son (Bernard, 1975; Kosa & Schommer, 1960; Sussman, 1965).

Aid may also reflect long-standing emotional relationships, with outcomes that are neither obvious nor straightforward. A study of elderly people and their responsible others (mostly children) indicated that the elderly with more than one child often identified one child as providing instrumental help (such as taking the parent shopping) and another as providing affection (such as telephoning or visiting on holidays). The child providing the most aid was not necessarily the most loved (Tobin & Kulys, 1980).

The greatly or extremely impaired elderly who live with a spouse or with children are not as likely to be institutionalized as those who live alone. Direct care and help in dealing with bureaucracies providing aid for older persons are important services families give elders (Shanas & Sussman, 1977). The truth is that it is difficult—perhaps impossible—to purchase the kind of commitment and care that is characteristic of even reasonably well functioning families.

The quality of care, and the impact of particular arrangements, are little investigated so far. Long-standing conflicts do not necessarily mean that aid will be withheld—or refused. However, the aid arrangements are sometimes stressful for all involved (Horowitz, 1978; Silverstone & Hymen, 1976).

The challenges for elderly parents are considerable. It is not easy to become dependent in a relationship after so many years of being dependable. Often it is necessary to renegotiate relationships of interdependence with adult children. The fortunate parents are those who can take pleasure in being cared for, even as they took pleasure in caring in earlier life.

It is a challenge to transmit the culture and values of the family without seeming to impose them on resistant younger family members. Too much accommodation to the "current way" can lead to loss of the sense of family culture and continuity, but too little accommodation to changing realities and values can result in the elder being isolated and the family fragmented. Old parents need all their resourcefulness to continue working on troubling relationships with children. If they can do so, they can leave a valuable legacy of peace and well-being with their children; perhaps they will then be more likely to die in peace themselves.

SUMMARY

1 The *capacity to love* develops during childhood, largely within the family. Early experiences and current opportunities combine to determine the widely varying kinds of love individuals desire at different ages and their ability to form intimate relationships.

2 The family remains important as a *social institution*, with many consequences for individual development. The family has the general responsibility for (1) the physical and emotional maintenance of children and of adults; (2) socialization for family roles; (3) social control; and (4) social placement of children and adult members.

3 *Family structure* is the term used to describe who is included in the family and how family members relate to each other. The nuclear family includes father, mother, and their children. An extended family structure may include a wide range of other relatives, especially grandparents. Family structure influences the ways family functions are carried out.

4 The most common family structure in America today is the modified extended family. Several generations of family members remain actively involved with each other over the life course. Generally, each generation accepts some responsibility for the welfare of other generations. The amount and kinds of help exchanged depend partly on the norms of the ethnic and social class group and partly on more personal factors.

5 Factors that *weaken* family ties and inhibit contact between generations include: (1) spatial distance; (2) differing beliefs and ideologies; (3) preoccupation with activities and affairs outside the family to the exclusion of family members; (4) infrequent family get-togethers; (5) pride in independence, when associated with decreased opportunities for helping each other; (6) family members undergoing difficult transitions at the same time; (7) serious or prolonged illness; and (8) residues of earlier conflicts.

6 Factors that *strengthen* family ties include: (1) propinquity, or geographic closeness; (2) the exchange of personal attention, gifts, and services; (3) shared group activities; (4) desirable personal qualities of the people involved; (5) socialization processes involving the transmission of values and religious beliefs; (6) norms of filial piety, or respect for parents; and (7) the new functions for adult children of helping elderly parents deal with bureaucracies.

7 Parent–child relations evolve as the participants change over time. The first phase includes an immature child and an adult who is able and willing to become a responsible parent. Each person learns about being a parent from being a child; as children mature and become parents, their own early experiences influence the ways in which they parent. Becoming a parent has varied meanings for people. Pregnancy and childbirth are important psychological events for both parents, though more research has been done with mothers. Parents of small children often experience strains in trying to establish satisfactory balances between employment, child care, and home management. Parenting provides opportunities for personal growth; satisfactions from parenting include maturity, pride, self-fulfillment, fun, and joy.

8 During the second phase young adult children and their parents renegotiate the relationship. Both generations are challenged to establish autonomy or separateness without sacrificing relatedness with the other generation. Parents and young adult children report mixed emotions about the launching process: relief, anticipation, pleasure, anxiety, and loss. Parents are more concerned about young people who are delayed in moving into adulthood and taking on adult roles of work and marriage than they are about the normal expected transitions that occur as anticipated.

Young adult children and their parents remain in contact with each other, even when they do not live close together. Mother–daughter contacts are the most frequent, particularly after the daughter has children. Research suggests that there is substantial but selective similarity of values between parents and their young adult children, with more similarity in religious and political affiliation and least in sex-role behavior. More research is needed on the quality of contacts between the generations, particularly in the period when the young adult is in the late 20s and 30s.

9 The third phase involves middle-aged children and their aging parents. Most elderly parents prefer, and in fact have, their own income, household, and friends; both generations prefer to live near each other but not in the same household. Old parents provide a model for aging. Most middle-aged children accept filial responsibility; they expect to and do provide substantial care for parents when parents become poor, ill, or very old. Unmarried children are more likely to move in with an elderly parent than are married children with their own children at home. Daughters are more likely than sons to provide direct care and emotional support, and sons are more likely to provide financial aid. Adult children provide services that postpone institutionalization of frail parents.

10 Grandparenthood is now more likely to come during middle age than in old age, and many people live to become great-grandparents. In addition, many experience the divorces and remarriages of younger members in the family. The fact that today there are more living generations and more complex systems may affect the relations between generations in ways that are not yet clear. The research so far indicates that parents respond to becoming grandparents in varied ways. For most it seems to be a pleasant but not very important part of their lives. About one-third of grandparents seem to be remote, uninvolved, or unconcerned with the grandparent role. Some grandparents play an active parenting role with grandchildren.

CHAPTER
TEN

LOVING: MARRIAGE AND FRIENDSHIP

SOME PERSPECTIVES ON MARRIAGE

The religious and legal regulations concerning marriage tell us something about the characteristics of the marriage relationship and the society's expectations for it. These expectations are sometimes not apparent until the reciprocal obligations involved are violated. For example, the fact that a spouse's unwillingness to be a sexual partner constitutes legal (and sometimes religious) grounds for divorce, and that one spouse can be legally awarded "damage" payments for loss of sexual partnership if the husband or wife is killed or injured tells us that sexual partnership is considered a crucial aspect of the marriage relationship in our culture.

However, marriage is in fact a very personal matter, with a reality quite distinct from legal and religious expectations. It is a relationship composed of two individuals who have agreed to honor such a commitment, although that relationship is, of course, embedded in other systems. As Jessie Bernard (1973), a wise scholar of marriage and other relationships between men and women, pointed out, we must remember there are at least three marriages to consider: his, hers, and theirs.

Strain in Marriage

According to Bernard, *strain* is often a characteristic of marriage for both partners. In part, the strain reflects the reality that human beings want, simultaneously, apparently incompatible and conflicting things: continuity and change, safety and excitement, security and adventure, stability and variety, dependence and independence, intimacy and individuality. Such conflicting needs become evident in any enduring human relationship. Whenever we expect to meet all these needs within one relationship, there are inevitable conflicts and difficulties, as can be seen from the marriage–divorce ratios shown in Figure 10-1, later in this chapter.

In addition to the strains experienced by both partners in marriage, there are some sex differences in the kinds of burdens and gratifications experienced. To some extent these shift over time; we will review some of the burdens and gratifications as we discuss marriage in different phases of adulthood. In general, though, the expectations for ensuring economic stability seem to be a considerable challenge and a strain for men. Men who can do this successfully usually find the experience of marriage gratifying; those who cannot often feel distressed and burdened. In general, women who restrict themselves or are restricted to the most isolated style of traditional housewife role are most likely to experience psychological distress. The stress is particularly acute for women who see themselves as dependent but who feel their husbands are, in fact, undependable (Bernard, 1973). Efforts to redefine the marriage relationship to include greater equality between partners and to protect against the vulnerabilities imposed by some of the traditional restrictions may be having some impact on the ways women and men experience marriage.

Marriage as Process

Marriage is a process, not a static state. Contrary to the fairy tales of our youth, we do not marry and live happily ever after. While we may indeed have moments and periods of happiness, the circumstances associated with that happiness are usually changing. The capacities, interests, and skills needed to enter and sustain a marriage develop gradually, beginning in the cradle and often continuing to develop throughout adulthood.

The process of marriage reflects each partner's personal development; this is one reason it is important to understand as much as possible about varieties of adult development. We will summarize some of the research on marriage in broad periods of the standard life course, recognizing that chronological age is not a very good predictor of what issues will be pressing for any given individual. Obviously, the woman who establishes a career, dates fairly casually, marries at 32, and has her first child at 34 will be dealing with different kinds of family-related problems at age 40 than her cousin who married her high school sweetheart at 18 and had four children by the age of 26.

The process of marriage also reflects social-historical factors. For example, the fact that more people now survive to become old means that the pledge to honor a marriage commitment "till death do us part" has a considerably different import than when the pledge was originally instituted. Survival rates affect chances for marriage and for remarriage after death or divorce breaks a relationship. In the past (and in some other cultures) men were likely to outlive several wives because of deaths in childbirth. Women now give birth less often and usually survive. In times of war many young men may be lost from a group of potential marriage partners forever, thus affecting women's chances of marrying. Other social facts may also affect chances of marriage. For example, in 1970 there were a million more black women than black men in America. The fact that there were about 83 black men for every 100 black women aged 25–44 is one reason there are more black women than white women heading households and rearing children alone (Jackson, 1971). The higher death rates of older men than of older women make it likely that women will end life unmarried.

Social-historical factors also have a profound influence on the expectations for the marriage relationship and the accepted ways of meeting those expectations. While some degree of friendliness and attraction between partners has long been desired and honored, the importance placed on passionate or romantic love or on similarity of social-familial background and mutual interests as bases for marriage varies considerably over time and across cultures. Some norms for marriage emphasize the "friendly alliance" notion, with marked sex segregation and separate spheres of influence and activity. Such relationships are probably more characteristic among older and more "traditional" social groups. Performance within the marriage is evaluated largely on how well each partner performs the role obligations of the relationship (such as economic provider, housekeeper, kin-keeper [the one who maintains contacts with kin], mother, father, and so on).

The expectations of young people now emphasize personal, psychological characteristics. Marriage is seen in terms of companionship, intimacy, and friendship and is evaluated in terms of its ability to promote individual growth at the same time as providing the security and love of stable partnership. Such expectations require different qualities in partners from those expected in a task-oriented marriage; in particular, interpersonal skills are extremely important for both partners in a companionate marriage.

In addition, many couples now insist on equality within the marriage relationship. This represents a shift from traditional forms of marriage, in which the husband is assumed to be the dominant partner; family residence is determined by his job location, and household schedules are expected to revolve around his schedule. In such marriages women today often feel put down, humiliated, and powerless. However, such relationships are more stable than more equalitarian relationships, if we count as stability lack of overt conflict or divorce. When a marriage includes equality between partners, the possibilities of conflict increase considerably. It is in such situations that the arts of negotiating disagreements may be most useful and necessary.

DEVELOPMENTAL ISSUES
IN MARRIAGE

We can expect changes in marital relationships over time. The changes will reflect individual developmental histories, accidental social-historical circumstances, and the history each couple creates. Experts on marriage see such changes both as opportunities for growth and as risks of crisis. Roger Gould (1978) has studied adults and the ways they define important areas of their lives. It is clear from his research with both individuals who have sought psychotherapeutic help with personal problems and those who have not that marriage is an important and troubling area for many people.

The central issue in marriage, according to Gould and other psychologists, is how to tolerate change and growth. Gould describes a desirable condition where change is not only tolerated but welcomed:

Ideally, in a really happy, really adult marriage, change in one partner is met gladly by the other partner, who is not afraid of the growth, but welcomes it— intellectually, at least—as an interesting improvement in the relationship and also sees it as the beginning of his or her next induced-growth step. . . . In a growth marriage, we are married and divorced many times in the sense that we are continually divorced from old arrangements and married to new ones. . . . (pp. 323–324)

The likelihood of such a marriage is not very great. Alvin Toffler (1970) has argued that it is utterly unlikely that marriage as a long-term commitment can last; he finds serial marriage, with a pattern of marriage-divorce-remarriage-divorce-remarriage, best suited for what he sees as an era that does not value permanence in anything.

Lillian Troll (1975), however, has offered some possibilities that partners in a marriage can remain compatible over the course of years. She describes the outcomes that are likely on the basis of the personality growth and development of the partners. If neither partner becomes more complex, the match can remain good. The match can also remain compatible if both partners become less complex (as sometimes occurs in late life), or if both partners become more complex and move in compatible directions. The prospect of increasing, compatible complexity is a currently popular ideal among young adults. It is also the one that seems to be most difficult to sustain. If one partner grows toward greater complexity and the other does not, or if one becomes less complex and the other remains stable, it is easy to see how the possibilities for uneven growth and mismatching can be acute.

Young Adulthood

The period of young adulthood launches individuals from their family of origin and establishes them in adult life. Making commitments to intimate relationships outside the family of origin is one of the most important challenges of this life period.

Young adults are often preoccupied with love, both compelled and terrified by the strong emotions aroused. Passionate love, especially, is frightening. As Rollo May (1969) pointed out,

To love means to open ourselves to the negative as well as the positive, to grief, sorrow, and disappointment as well as to joy, fulfillment, and an intensity of consciousness we did not know possible before. . . . Death is always in the shadow of the delight of love. . . . Will this new relationship destroy us? When we love, we give up the center of ourselves. (p. 99)

Once we accept the uniqueness of another person, and the importance of that person to us, we are vulnerable to loss. This vulnerability emphasizes the ultimate separateness of male and female, even at the times of most ecstatic union.

Nevertheless, most young adults confront the question of love. Each young adult must decide how compelling his or her social and intimacy needs are and how to meet them; this usually includes decisions about how to deal with sexuality, if and when to marry, and whether and when to become a parent. Sociocultural changes over the past few decades are evident in the ways these decisions are being made (Bell, 1978). Women are more likely than before to approve of and engage in premarital sexual intercourse. In the United States people are waiting somewhat longer to marry; the median age at first marriage in 1977 was 21 years for women and 23 years for men (Glick, 1980). And fewer people are choosing to marry; in 1975, 87 percent of women were married by age 30, compared with 92 percent in 1960 (Bell, 1978).

Mate Selection   Young adults choose to marry for varied reasons, some conscious, others less so. Overall, people marry those who are similar to themselves in various ways; this pattern of similarity is termed *homogamy*. Most partners are similar in race, educational level, socioeconomic background, residential location, previous marital status, and age; there is some evidence that partners are also similar in sex drive and sex interest and physical attractiveness (Murstein, 1980). (When partners marry because of premarital pregnancy, they are less likely to be similar on these characteristics.) This pattern is reasonable since individuals with such similarities are more likely to be available for the processes of friendship and courtship. These characteristics seem to act as a form of "skeleton" for the relationship: Marriage is more likely to occur, and to endure, when the individuals are thus similar.

However, these characteristics are not necessarily the ones identified when individuals are asked what attracted them to their spouse. For example, a recent survey of 3880 adults, all married, included questions about reasons for marrying (Pietropinto & Simenauer, 1979). The researchers found a break with old ideals of romanticism, and a sense of "affection and respect" among even the recently married couples.

Spouses select each other on the basis of individuality rather than on the promise of meeting traditional role expectations for husbands, wives, and parents. Personality has become the most important factor in mate selection. Men still rely on sexual attractiveness and physical beauty to a greater degree than women in choosing a partner, but those attributes are secondary to personality. . . . While marriage between people who are alike predominate over matches between opposites, the similarities seem to lie more in the sharing of common goals and ideals, rather than similar backgrounds. (p. xxiii)

Identifying a person who has the "right" social and personality characteristics for a spouse may be a matter of timing as much as anything else. There are widely shared expectations in each social group about the "best age" to marry, and these social norms may exert pressure on a young adult to find a partner. In addition, each individual has an inner developmental course, and one may come to feel at a certain point that one is ready—and eager—to make and appreciate an intimate commitment like marriage. Given either or both of these incentives, a person may decide it is time to look over the available candidates for marriage and select the most promising one. In other words, some sense of timing may influence the perceptions of who is "right."

We cannot predict much about the quality of a marriage relationship from knowing how socially similar a couple is. The personal experiences of each partner are partly irrational passions that are beyond the scope of even sophisticated computerized matchmakers. Passionate erotic attraction to another person includes subconsciously recognizing someone who recreates the sense of our earliest intimate and passionate relationships, usually those with our parents. Interactions may be tinged with the conscious and unconscious anticipations from early interactions.

In choosing a mate, we try to select a partner we can live with now and in the future. This partnership may be based on a model from early experiences. However, we also try to use marriage in young adulthood to emancipate ourselves from the sense of being a child and responding as we did then—which may be quite difficult to do.

Building a Partnership   Many couples experience strains as they build a marriage relationship. Part of the strain involves efforts to separate from parents enough to feel confident about establishing one's own family, which may differ from the parental home. For example, a study of working- and lower-middle-class young married couples found that they spent a great deal of time discussing their parents' ideas and values (Lowenthal et al., 1975). Such discussions help the young persons to clarify their own values and negotiate the kind of marriage they wish to create.

Each couple must find ways to negotiate differences around household routines, relations with other family members, allocation of family resources (especially time and money), work, and parenting. Most couples evolve a style of interacting, a typical way of resolving conflicts. Marriage interaction styles have often been characterized on the dimension of power, the relative influence of the husband or wife in the relationship. At least three styles have been identified: husband as head and wife as complement; husband as senior partner and wife as junior partner; and husband and wife as equal partners (Scanzoni & Scanzoni, 1976). Among young adults classification of the marriage by wife as equal, junior partner, or complementary was associated with predictable differences on variables such as household task performance, fertility control, and sex-role preference (Scanzoni, 1980).

Variations of such patterns were evident in the problem-solving behavior of more than 1000 couples studied for the first few years of marriage by Miller and Olson (1980). Miller and Olson found that the style of the marriage was usually set within the first year of marriage and remained unchanged (at least for the five years of the study) unless the couple sought therapy. Although 80 percent of the couples interviewed claimed to have "shared leadership cooperation" marriages, the researchers rated only 12 percent as having such an equalitarian relationship. According to the researchers' ratings, the most common marital patterns were what they called *husband-led disengaged* (characterized by rare fights, not particularly strong love, and husband as boss) and *husband-led cooperative* (characterized by cooperation between spouses but where the husband's views carried more weight). About 20 percent of the sample of 1000 couples showed each of these two types of marriage. Ten percent of the sample were in *wife-led disengaged* marriages (with minimal conflict but also minimal expression of love), and 10 percent were in *wife-led congenial* relationships (characterized by compatibility and average emotional involvement for the sample). The rest of the sample were in four other marriage types. Obviously, these typologies capture only some of the complexity in marriage relationships; one can expect considerable variability among couples characterized as being in a husband-led cooperative marriage. Nevertheless, such typologies do reveal the common themes in relationships.

Sexuality   In healthy individuals some form of sexual appetite is present throughout life (Kaplan, 1979). The intensity of sexual appetite changes with age, and sexuality develops differently in males and females.

Freud (1917) made the important observation that the earliest nongenital infantile sexual feelings have a great deal in common with later emotional experiences of sexuality. Our early sensual pleasures include the cuddling, sucking, smelling, gazing, and stroking that are part of normal parent–child interaction.

The fact that sensuality develops in a relatively dependent, helpless child who obtains the earliest gratifications from powerful adults means it is unlikely that sexuality is ever completely free of connotations of submission and dominance (Person, 1980). Adults may yearn for the diffuse sensual pleasures experienced in infancy and early childhood and yet be terrified by the passive submission that such an experience subconsciously recreates. The challenge for adults is to be able to give in to their own passionate feelings, to lose control knowing that they can regain it.

Sexuality becomes associated with other motives early in life. Throughout life the same behaviors may have different meanings particular to the sex, developmental stage, or personality of the individual. It is more important to know what a particular activity means to a person than to know how many sexual partners he or she has had, what positions are used in sexual intercourse, or how often a married couple has intercourse. One may have intercourse to show dominance, compliance, passion, compassion, or spite, as well as to gain the pleasures of ecstasy, relief from sexual tension, or union with a beloved person.

Person (1980) suggests that every individual develops a "sex print," as distinctive as a fingerprint, which includes those stimuli that elicit erotic desire and those specific erotic techniques that gratify desire for that person. This sex print is experienced subjectively as *preference,* a deeply rooted part of the private self. Preference is revealed in what is a sexual "turn-on"—sexual feelings may be triggered by opposite-sex or same-sex partners, by feeling helpless and cared for, by a sense of danger, by floral scents or dark beards. Person regards the sex print as an important aspect of identity; as such, it is very resistant to change in adulthood.

Person also suggests that one of the crucial differences between males and females is the importance of genital sexual activity (masturbation or intercourse) in identity. Genital sexual activity is a very important feature of masculine gender identity. Little boys very early discover the pleasures involved in manipulating their penis and become aware that the presence of a penis is a distinctly male attribute. By adolescence the ability to achieve erections and (later) to complete intercourse seems crucial to maintaining a secure sense of masculinity. For example, adolescent males who never masturbate usually have a seriously disturbed sense of masculinity and sexuality (Gadpaille, 1975). In contrast, feminine identity seems not so closely tied to genital sexuality. Girls are slower to discover that rubbing their clitoris brings pleasure, and sexual pleasure remains more diffuse and tied to an intimate relationship. The most distinctive biological feature of women, the womb, is not a sexual organ. (Breasts may have emotional significance to women comparable to the penis for men, but breasts are not sources of the same intense erotic pleasure.) Women may not like abstaining from intercourse, but they are less likely than men to feel neutered by it.

The sex differences in identity suggested by Person contribute to sexual adjustments typical in young adulthood (and later). Each partner brings to a relationship his or her distinctive sex print and the conscious and unconscious expectations, fantasies, and fears developed during earlier years. Most children and adolescents repress most of their sexual feelings, especially since many of these feelings are directed toward family members. When sexual activity becomes permitted and encouraged during young adulthood, it may be difficult to drop the repressions sufficiently to feel sexually responsive. In addition, the partners may assume that their own early experiences will be replicated, that what turns them on also excites their partner, and that they can expect an intimate relationship similar to that of their parents. This, of course, seldom happens. Ideally, each partner comes to understand and appreciate the perspective of the other. As they do so, both can enjoy their sexual responses.

Four phases of the sexual response cycle have been identified: desire, excitement, orgasm, and resolution. Each phase has a distinct physiology and age-related changes, a distinctive pattern of associated problems, and special therapeutic requirements (Kaplan, 1979). The phases of excitement, orgasm, and resolution were described by Masters and Johnson (1966) on the basis of research with humans in their sexual research institute. Kaplan (1979) identified desire as a separate phase on the basis of her clinical work with many patients seeking treatment for sexual dysfunction.

Sexual *desire* is experienced as specific sensations that move the individual to seek out or receive sexual experiences. The sensations are produced by the physical activation of a specific neural system in the brain, although the exact nature of the neural activity is not yet well understood (Kaplan, 1979). The presence of some testosterone hormone is required for sexual desire in both males and females; however, there is little evidence that additional quantities of testosterone above the necessary minimum will increase sexual desire. Humans seem to learn what, when, and whom to desire; the learning is part of acquiring the sex print. No matter how strong it is, sexual desire can be inhibited by fear or pain.

Most studies of sexual desire indicate that young adult men and women experience stronger sexual desire than middle-aged and older adults (Kinsey, Pomeroy, & Martin, 1948; Kinsey, Pomeroy, Martin, & Gebhard, 1953; Masters & Johnson, 1966). There is considerable variability between groups of young adults, with some reporting very strong sexual desires (and, often, frequent sexual activity) and others reporting mild sexual desire. In general, more young men than young women report strong sexual desire. Such reported sex differences may reflect the lingering double standard of sexuality, where all men are assumed to be easily interested and arousable and "nice" women are assumed to be sexual only within a committed love relationship. This stereotype is not accurate for either sex, since most men and women experience desire most readily in the context of a warm, loving relationship.

The phase of sexual *excitement* is signaled in both sexes by the reflex (automatic) dilation of the genital blood vessels. The penis becomes hard and enlarged to penetrate the vagina, and the vagina balloons and becomes wet to accommodate the penis. In young adulthood these changes occur rapidly.

Young men become erect within seconds, sometimes in response to touching of the penis but often in response to sexual thoughts or being near an attractive partner; young women begin vaginal lubrication within minutes of becoming sexually aroused through kissing, caressing, stimulating the clitoris, or erotically exciting mental images. Women who are fearful, guilty, or resentful about being sexually aroused take longer to lubricate than those who are relaxed and able to enjoy their own arousal.

The excitement phase is followed by the *orgasm* phase, with rhythmic contractions of genital muscles. Male orgasms are accompanied by the ejaculation of seminal fluid and highly pleasurable sensations. While research does not document different patterns of orgasm for men (Masters & Johnson, 1966), individual men report considerable variation in the intensity, duration, and subjective pleasure in orgasm. Women may experience a number of orgasmic response patterns: several mild, brief contractions; contractions increasing in intensity to a peak and then decreasing in intensity; or several intense contractions (Masters & Johnson, 1966; Kaplan, 1974). The contractions may be so mild that they do not provide relief from the muscular constriction built up during the excitement phase, in which case the woman may feel she has not had an orgasm.

Resolution is the final phase of the sexual response cycle. During this phase the body returns to its normal nonaroused state. In men there is a *refractory period* after orgasm during which further sexual stimulation will not result in erection, regardless of desire or techniques used. In young men the refractory period may be very brief (10–20 minutes) or longer (several hours), depending on the man's health, number of previous orgasms, strength of desire, and so forth. Women have no refractory period; they can be sexually rearoused at any time during resolution and can experience multiple orgasms.

Sexual problems may be experienced within any of the first three phases. Kaplan (1979) notes that sexual problems of the orgasmic phase are the easiest to treat since they are often rooted in ignorance of the sexual response cycle. Many young women experience some difficulty becoming orgasmic, or experiencing the full release of sexual tensions. Sometimes women and their partners do not understand that the clitoris, and not the vagina, is the sensual counterpart of the penis (because the clitoris comes from the same embryologic tissues as the penis). Few women are orgasmic without appropriate stimulation of the clitoris. In addition, women must feel self-confident enough to be able to lose control during orgasm, without fearing that they will be rejected by their partner or that they will not be able to regain control over themselves. Men's difficulties during the orgasm phase are largely those of "premature" ejaculation— that is, coming to orgasm before the man or his partner is ready. (The quotation marks around *premature* are to indicate that the decision of what constitutes prematurity is a judgment to be made by the participants; there is no rule about how long one should be aroused before coming to orgasm.) The problem of prematurity usually reflects anxiety. In young men it may also be a bad habit acquired during adolescent years of hurried, secretive masturbation or intercourse; if it is continued into a regular relationship, it can be distressing not to be able to prolong the pleasures of intercourse. Fairly simple techniques can be learned to control the timing of ejaculation (Kaplan, 1974).

Sexual problems during the excitement phase are more complex in origin and more difficult to treat therapeutically than orgasmic-phase problems. Most young men experience occasional impotence, when their penis does not become erect; such incidents are usually normal consequences of fatigue, excessive alcohol consumption, medications taken for treatment of an acute disease, or feeling pressured to have intercourse. Young women have arousal difficulties for similar reasons. When young men or women have chronic difficulty in becoming sexually aroused when they feel desire for an appropriate and available partner, it usually means that sexually related anxiety is blocking normal sexual responses. Such problems can often be successfully treated in brief therapy (14–20 sessions) (Kaplan, 1979).

Disorders of sexual desire are the most complex in origin and the most difficult to treat. Kaplan (1979) indicates that the prolonged (over six weeks) absence of sexual desire or interest for an appropriate, available partner is a sign that a problem exists. (It is not a disorder to repress sexual desire for a parent, supervisor at work, or child, or not to feel sexual desire for a spouse who is slovenly or abusive.) According to Kaplan, many young adults seen in sexual therapy complain that their lack of sexual desire creates problems in self-esteem and in marriage relationships. The individual with a desire problem may maintain sexual functioning (that is, men may have erections and orgasms) but without much pleasure. The lack of desire is usually interpreted by the partner as a personal rejection, even though this may be a distorted perception. More typically, the individual is inhibited in experiencing sexual desire by powerful feelings of anxiety, anger, or depression (Kaplan, 1979).

Many individuals are able to enjoy their sexuality within a loving, committed marriage. Couples with good sexual relationships manage to modify childhood fears and prohibitions by adult knowledge and experience. They learn to communicate, and sex becomes part of their communication pattern. For example, several studies indicate that satisfaction with marital sex is closely related to feeling free to confide in one's spouse (Bell, 1979). Perhaps most of all, they learn to accept the normal rise and fall of sexual desire and the variable ways of responding to desire; they learn that no single sexual experience is as important as the larger pattern of the relationship (Levin & Levin, 1975).

Homosexual Coupling   Some adults choose to have a primary sexual relationship with a partner of the same sex. Many individuals try heterosexual relationships before affirming they are more comfortable in a same-sex partnership. Our focus here is on those who make a commitment for partnership with someone of the same biological sex. In keeping with current terminology, we will speak of gay men and women or lesbians (women).

One of the marked changes in our society in recent decades has been the increased openness about admitting that homosexual partnerships exist, and pressure for changes in the law and social opinion that would give such couples some of the same protection and support available to heterosexual couples. Homosexual couples are likely to have the same range of adjustment and living-together problems as heterosexual couples, plus additional ones accompanying any lifestyle that is regarded as deviant or undesirable in the larger culture.

Gay males and lesbians establish a variety of lifestyles. Bell and Weinberg (1978) interviewed 979 gay people and 477 heterosexuals who were similar to the homosexuals in age, education, and religion. The study was conducted in San Francisco in 1969; at the time that city had less repressive attitudes toward homosexuals than many other places. Thus the diversity found in the study suggests how homosexuals might respond to more liberalized attitudes about homosexuality.

Bell and Weinberg found about three-fourths of the homosexuals were included in five basic gay lifestyles: (1) The *close-coupled* style included those who had partners to whom they were committed emotionally and sexually. They preferred to spend time at home with the partner and seemed to have little trouble communicating with the partner. They had little regret about being homosexual and differed little from the heterosexual sample in psychological adjustment. (2) The *open-coupled* style describes the life of homosexuals who often looked for social and sexual satisfaction outside the primary relationship. The lesbians in open relationships had lower self-esteem than other gay women; however, gay men in open styles were about average among all the gay men in adjustment. (3) The *functional* style included people who were not coupled but were sexually active. They were more interested in sex and friendship than in long-term partnership. (4) The *dysfunctionals* regretted being homosexual; found little gratification in life; and were generally lonely, depressed, tense, and unhappy. Contrary to stereotypes, only 12 percent of the men and 5 percent of the women in the sample were considered dysfunctional. (5) The *asexuals* were generally isolated, relatively secretive about their homosexuality, and lowest in any kind of sexual activity.

The Bell and Weinberg research reported fewer differences between homosexual and heterosexual lifestyles than might be expected from stereotypes. Qualitative aspects of love relationships were studied in another sample of 127 lesbian women aged 18–59, mostly well-educated, middle-class whites (Peplau, Cochran, Rook, & Padesky, 1978). The investigators were particularly interested in the dimensions of autonomy and attachment. Most of the women in this sample reported a high degree of closeness and satisfaction in their current relationship; this is not so different from studies of younger heterosexual marriages. Although virtually all the women (97 percent) believed in equal partnerships, only 64 percent said their current relationship was "exactly equal." The struggles toward such equality are often common themes in heterosexual relationships as well.

A strong emphasis on autonomy was associated with spending less time with the partner, being less willing to maintain the relationship at the expense of work or education, being more likely to have a sexually open relationship, and worrying more about having an overly dependent partner. Women who valued attachment over autonomy spent more time with the current partner, reported greater closeness and satisfaction with the relationship, expressed greater confidence that the relationship would continue in the future, and worried less that personal independence would create difficulties for the relationship. The researchers propose that the values of autonomy and attachment are also likely to be important for gay men and heterosexuals.

Perhaps the most important lesson to be learned from available research on lesbians and gay men is that they are diverse, in love relationships and in other aspects of their lives. Sexual preference is only one aspect of commitment to others.

Fractured Unions: Divorce and Re-pairing   Many unions do not survive, ending in desertion, separation, annulment, or divorce. Every social system has some way of ending a relationship; the forms and consequences reflect the values and options of the time and place.

An American couple marrying today can statistically expect about 35 years of marriage before the relationship ends through either divorce or the death of one spouse (Bell, 1978). Divorce is an important reality in the lives of many people—and more all the time. Current estimates are that nearly half the couples marrying now will get divorced. In the United States the proportion of the population who had ever been divorced increased from 2.5 per 1000 in 1965 to 5.3 per 1000 people in 1979 (Price-Bonham & Balswick, 1980).

Increased divorce rates seem to reflect increased options for women outside of marriage, lower fertility, and greater general prosperity. In spite of an overall increase in the percentage of marriages ending in divorce, the timing has not been changed substantially; the likelihood of divorce is greatest during the first seven years of marriage (Troll, Miller, & Atchley, 1979). The percentage of people by age, sex, and race, who are divorced or separated is shown in Figure 10-1.

Several factors are associated with the probability of being divorced (Price-Bonham & Balswick, 1980). Couples who marry because the woman is pregnant are very likely to get divorced. Individuals who marry early (in their teens) are more likely to divorce, partly because they are more likely to be pregnant at marriage. Lower-income families experience more divorce, but it is not clear whether the low income causes divorce or divorce causes low income. As seen in Figure 10-1, blacks have higher rates of divorce than do whites; this difference is attributable largely to the fact that a greater percentage of blacks than whites have low incomes, and low income is associated with higher divorce rates. Black–white and Jewish–gentile marriages are more likely to end in divorce than same-race or Jewish–Jewish marriages. Women with very low (less than eighth-grade) or high (beyond college graduation) education are more likely to divorce than are women with high school or college educations.

Divorce, or the termination of any marriagelike union, is a painful experience. It may or may not be, ultimately, a "growth experience"; nevertheless, it is a painful one. The disintegration of an important relationship is a process; there is no universal point at which divorce is an inevitable outcome. People

Figure 10–1 Percentage of each group separated or divorced, by age. (From U.S. Bureau of the Census Subject Report: Marital Status, PC(2)-4C, 1972.)

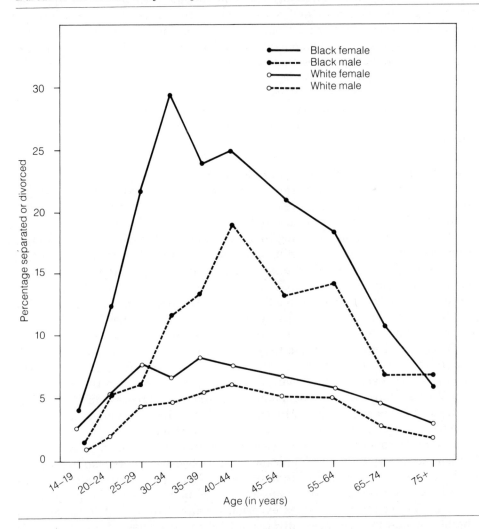

can tolerate much maladjustment without divorce or choose divorce under conditions that seem quite satisfactory to others.

The reactions of individuals to divorce are greatly determined by existing cultural values (Bell, 1978) as well as by personality factors. There is often a sense of liberation and freedom, combined with a sense of failure and guilt. Loneliness is a common consequence. Divorce often upsets relations with friends and family (Miller, 1968). Divorced people often suffer a reduction in social status, self-esteem, and standard of living. The changes in life circumstances affecting psychological well-being may be more upsetting than the divorce itself (Pearlin & Johnson, 1977).

Many terminated relationships involve children, and concerns about the welfare of the children and one's adequacy as a parent become important. There is no clear evidence about the impact of divorce on children since it depends upon many factors. While it is undoubtedly best to grow up with loving, adequate parents committed to the family unit, it may be preferable to contend with separate households, stepparents, and stepsiblings than to deal daily with resigned or active hostility.

Most adults who divorce remarry—about three-fourths of the women, and five-sixths of the men; others may make fairly long-term commitments that do not show up in remarriage statistics. Over half of those divorced remarry within three years; remarriage is faster for men than women, for younger than older people, for those who sought the divorce, and for those with more substantial incomes (Hunt, 1966). New alliances are subject to the usual relationship problems plus residues of the former relationship. Second marriages seem about as happy as first marriages, though partners are more willing to end an unhappy marriage through divorce (Hunt, 1966).

Some individuals seem to be divorce-prone, that is, more likely than most to divorce at least once. A longitudinal sample of 80 men and 85 women indicated that prediction for divorce could be made for the women but not for the men (Peskin, 1975). Women who were divorced by early middle age were described as nonconforming and self-centered in adolescence; unlike women who remained married, they did not transfer this energy from self-development to the marriage unit. The same study found that men were differentiated mainly in likelihood of marrying: Those who were high in attachment and affiliation needs in adolescence married, while those low in such needs were less likely to marry at all. Presumably, some women who felt pressured into reluctant marriage in previous decades would now be more likely to remain unmarried (thus avoiding divorce) or negotiate a more equalitarian marriage that did not require total investment in the couple.

Middle Adulthood

What we call the middle years begin around 35 for working-class men and women and five to ten years later for middle- and upper-class men and women. Cues for middle age are varied (Neugarten, 1968): (1) biological changes, particularly the menopause for women; (2) family developments, such as having late-adolescent children or having a parent die; (3) changes at work—knowing how far one will really go in a job, being treated like a mentor or senior advisor; (4) socially, receiving subtly deferential or derogatory treatment by younger adults; and (5) psychological changes, such as distancing from younger generations, an understanding of death as inevitable, increased interiority, and some blurring of sex roles.

The period may usefully be divided into two phases: early middle age, roughly 35 or 40 to 50 or 55, when children are being launched and work productivity is high; and late middle age (the *young-old* in Neugarten's [1974] terminology), roughly 55 to 70, when parental responsibilities are minimal, health is fairly good, employment responsibilities are phasing out, and leisure/ recreational activities assume greater importance. Commitments to intimacy are carried out within the framework of these shifts in other domains.

The Quality of Relationships during the Middle Years   Both cross-sectional and longitudinal studies report the lowest marital satisfaction in early middle age, often associated with the mid-life crisis (Spanier & Lewis, 1980). However, only 8 percent of the variation in marital satisfaction is related to "stage in the family cycle" (Troll & Turner, 1976); thus we must look to explanations other than simply age or stage of life. In any event, the data on marital satisfaction over time are difficult to interpret. Most of the data are cross-sectional and thus cannot inform us about changes over time in particular marriages. Marriages that have terminated because of dissatisfaction do not appear in the research. On the other hand, because of few perceived alternatives or because the person is so attached to the situation that it is impossible to actually leave, resignation may be recorded as "satisfaction."

Compared to the marital relationship during young adulthood, satisfactory relationships in middle age are often described as having "mellowed." By middle age many couples have worked out acceptable styles of dealing with each other and accomplishing daily life tasks (Cuber & Harroff, 1965). However, there is likely to be some ambivalence about the shift from the active negotiating involved in young adult marriage, as can be seen from a discussion about marriage among some middle-aged, middle-class women (Higgins, 1977):

I don't think mellowing is sad at all. It's not as exciting as with all that tension, but who the hell wants all that excitement all the time? It gets awfully tiring!... Maybe this mellowness and acceptance is really happiness....

You let go of an awful lot of stuff that isn't very useful any more—old expectations, old judgments, old dreams (nervous laughter)... old wives (very nervous laughter).

For some men the marriage relationship appears to become more central in middle age than other life arenas. As Sears (1977) observed after studying a group of intellectually gifted men from childhood to mid-life, "In spite of their autonomy and great average success in their occupations, these men placed greater importance on achieving satisfaction in their family life than in their work...."

An intensive study of lower-middle-class men and women in four adult transitions (Lowenthal et al., 1975) explored the quality of marriage relationships. Those persons in the launching stage were the most negative about marriage. Women were especially critical, giving twice as many negative as positive descriptions of spouses; while confident about their own role performance as wives and mothers, they were unhappy about their husbands' limited interpersonal skills. They saw themselves as placating and giving in to husbands to avoid arguments, though they felt that such placating was not a substitute for the communication and companionship they longed for. Husbands described their wives positively, although admitting they had a very limited relationship with them. They evaluated themselves positively, primarily in terms of their ability to be a "good provider," "reliable," "steady," and "faithful." On the other hand, some men recognized they were not meeting their wives' needs for companionship or emotional closeness, nor did they feel very optimistic about their abilities to do so. Arguments revolved primarily around children, and they expected the relationship to improve as the last child left.

There were clues that this, indeed, occurs. At least, the couples in the preretirement stage were more positive about their spouses and the relationship than the launching-stage couples. Many enjoyed greater companionship. The women had greater power in the relationship, a shift that was disturbing to some and gratifying to other men and women.

Love and marriage remain important to women, but increasingly they seem to want—and need—to exert more direct control in their lives. Although this seems to be a general shift occurring cross-culturally (Gutmann, 1977), it has no doubt been heightened by recent moves for women in general to seek more equality with men. Such a shift may be expressed in many arenas, including the marriage; a fairly common complaint of middle-aged men is that their wives are too bossy, while middle-aged and older women are more apt to complain of overdependent husbands (Lowenthal et al., 1975; Turner, 1981). Both complaints reflect a shift in personality adaptive style described by Jung (1933), Gutmann (1964), Levinson (1978), and others. The marriage relationship may be troubled by such shifts if either partner is guilty, enraged, or defensive about the changes and unable to alter behavior (Livson, 1977). The relationship can be strengthened and enhanced by the "new" flexibility.

Sexuality   Although, in general, sexual factors seem to play a secondary role in marital adjustment in later years (Troll, Miller, & Atchley, 1979), infidelity may be an important strain on the relationship, and preserved or "rediscovered" sensual pleasure may be a source of comfort and strength. Variability in sexual interests and activities is great, probably greater than in earlier and later periods of life; thus figures listing "average" sexual activity or interest may be misleading for understanding either current or future individual behavior patterns.

Sexual emergence is possible for many years, in the sense of becoming aware of the sensual pleasures one can receive and give. Some women become orgasmic for the first time in later life, and some men experience a depth of passion unknown in earlier years (Huyck, 1977). However, the most impressive findings suggest continuity, particularly for men. Men who showed moderately strong interest in sex and were still active in their sixth to eighth decades (some even increased from their 50s and 60s) were those who reported strong interest and frequent activity as young men; men who had ceased sexual activity in later life had only mild to moderate interest in it as young men (Pfeiffer, Verwoerdt, & Wang, 1968). The sexual activity of older men is not much tied to marital status, and their interest is typically stronger than their activity (Verwoerdt, Pfeiffer, & Wang, 1969).

Most studies of older women show that they report less interest in sex than men do and that their sexual activities are tied to the availability of a regular, socially sanctioned partner, usually a husband. Sexual involvements reflect the woman's general health, her emotional state, her relationship with her husband, and/or the availability of other functional sexual partners. Thus even though women retain their capacity for sexual responsivity until death, they may have no one they can accept as a desirable—or even tolerable—partner.

In one interview study of 50 women over 65 (Hoyt, 1980) most of the women reported high life satisfaction and low sexual interest or activity. The oldest women especially were very critical of men, enjoyed the companionship of other women, and expressed no desire or intention to make the accommodations they regarded as necessary to sustain a heterosexual relationship. (Nor were they interested in a homosexual relationship.) It seems likely that the low levels of sexual desire expressed by many currently older women partly reflect cohort effects, the fact that these women grew up in a social system that repressed rather than enhanced female sexuality. In addition, there are cross-cultural reports of older women who relish the freedom of movement and sense of independence that accompanies movement out of the role of sexual partner (or sexual object, in some cultures) (Safilios-Rothschild, 1977). Ideally, of course, women in our culture would rather not choose between autonomy and sexuality; they want both, at all ages, but they may feel that this is a difficult if not impossible combination. We do not know whether these patterns may change as current cohorts of younger women grow old.

Female sexuality in later years is affected somewhat by normal biological changes. The process of menopause, with the decrease of estrogen production, involves some periods of physical discomfort ("hot flashes" and "cold sweats") for most women; they may not feel very sexy at such times. As those discomforts phase out, the postmenopausal woman may be troubled by physiological changes: slower, decreased vaginal lubrication, thinned vaginal walls, lessened vaginal elasticity, and increased susceptibility to vaginal infections (Stewart, Guest, Stewart, & Hatcher, 1979). However, exercises, proper nutrition, topical creams, and regular, effective sexual stimulation seem to reduce or eliminate such potential problems.

Male sexual patterns change during the middle years. Most studies report a decreased frequency of sexual activity, within and outside the marriage (Kinsey et al., 1948; Masters & Johnson, 1966; Martin, 1977). The quality of sexual pleasure begins to shift, from the intense, genital sensations of youth to a more diffuse, prolonged sensuality (Kaplan, 1974). There are several normal physiological changes: It often takes more time for the penis to become erect (several seconds to a few minutes following stimulation), and the erections may not be as full or at as high an angle. The refractory period, the time after ejaculation and before another erection can develop, often lengthens; some men in late middle age report they do not develop another erection for 12–24 hours (Masters & Johnson, 1966). The ejaculation experience may be less intense, and the amount of fluid ejaculated less than when the man was young.

These changes can be threatening to some men and their partners if they fear it means they are "too old" for sex. Many old people hope they are never too old for the caressing, pleasure, affirmation, and good feelings that accompany mutual sexual sharing. Many men and women find they enjoy the more relaxed, diffuse sensuality of later life, but most still want foreplay to culminate in intercourse (Adams & Turner, 1981).

Some men and women complain about lack of sexual pleasure or interest. In men the signs are visible: impotence, when the penis does not become erect enough to insert in the vagina. The lack of responsivity may be a side effect of medications, alcohol, or some physical illness; more often it is caused by fear, rage, boredom, fatigue, or some other emotional problem. Medical aspects should, of course, be checked out. For adults who are unhappy with the sexual aspects of their relationship, couple-based therapies can be very useful (Hartman & Fithian, 1972; Kaplan, 1974, 1979; Masters & Johnson, 1970). For both men and women the most powerful sexual stimulant is a compassionate, enthusiastic, responsive partner. Varied techniques are helpful (see Comfort, 1972), but not as crucial as enjoying the sexual potentials of the partnership.

Broken Relationships   Though divorce is less common in the middle years than in young adulthood, the incidence is increasing substantially. And along with divorce come problems of readjustment, particularly for women who have not been employed outside the home and who married with an expectation that their involvements as wife, mother, and homemaker would be part of a lifelong mutual commitment. Little is known about such "displaced homemakers," though it is clear that they endure economic hardships and loss of self-esteem (Troll, Miller, & Atchley, 1979). It may be very difficult for homemakers to gain the training and employment necessary to support themselves. Women who have established themselves in work may use their self-confidence and economic independence to push for changes in the marriage; if those fail, divorce may result.

The feelings of men and women about divorce during middle age may be very mixed: relief at being out of a daily painful relationship, mourning for the loss of a dream and the presence of another human being, pride in autonomy and independence, and shame that they could not, after all, make the marriage "succeed" (Hunt, 1966). Both men and women typically experience a decreased standard of living, particularly when children must be supported. Both partners may find relationships with adult children and other kin disturbed by a middle-age divorce. The consequences in later life for being able to call on children for care when needed are not clear.

Marriages are most likely to terminate during middle and old age by death. The consequences of widowhood differ by sex, social class, and ethnicity.

The average age at which women become widows is in their middle 50s (Bell, 1979). Women who are widowed after young adulthood are unlikely to remarry; only 5 percent who become widowed after 55 do so (Cleveland & Gianturco, 1976). Most widowers remarry, however, especially if they are under 70. Because more women survive to old age, and because men are apt to marry somewhat younger women, many more men than women have a spouse in late middle age and old age.

Overall, "no aspect of widowhood appears demonstrably more difficult for older widowers than for older widows, but widows are clearly worse off than widowers in terms of finances and prospects of remarriage" (Troll, Miller, & Atchley, 1979, p. 79).

Responses to widowhood in part reflect personality. Grieving may begin before the actual death and continue for a short or long time afterward. Lopata (1973), who has studied widows in different cultures, found that 48 percent of the widows said they were over their husband's death in a year; 20 percent said they had never really recovered and didn't expect to. Depression is a common component of the bereavement response to the death of a spouse, reflecting the sense of loss; women often feel deserted and abandoned, and men are apt to feel they have lost a part of themselves (Glick, Weiss, & Parkes, 1974). The loss is real, and irremediable.

However, as Gutmann (1979) has shown on the basis of clinical practice with older adults, part of the depression may reflect guilt about real or imagined neglects of the dead person, or shame for the feelings of rage toward the deceased or relief about the death. Some of these feelings are tied to the sense of emergent power and competitiveness older women feel; an ill spouse may pull them back to the home when they most want to be exploring new arenas of achievement. In any case, most intimate relationships are tinged with ambivalence; it is quite possible to love the spouse and mourn the loss of the relationship—and at the same time be relieved that the annoyances or the period of ill health, nursing care, financial drain, or whatever preceded the illness, is ended. Of course, some relationships are genuinely hostile; the partners may endure for many years and find death a respite. Such feelings about the dead are not considered "nice" and usually are not admitted to others or even to the self. Individuals may suffer a loss of self-esteem, or depression, as a consequence of such feelings.

Reactions against such depressive feelings may help explain another of Lopata's (1973) findings: Widows were likely to sanctify the memory of the dead spouse, forgetting the negative characteristics and exaggerating the good qualities; this was true even for women who hated their husbands. This reconstruction may help the survivor by giving meaning to the sacrifices made in the relationship, as a reflected honor for having such a magnificent spouse, and as a form of penance for unacceptable feelings following the death. Though Lopata did not study widowers, men may also sanctify a spouse. For both men and women sanctification may be one way of dealing with the complex feelings of loss, rage, guilt, and relief following the death of a spouse. We will review the factors affecting the process of adjustment to widowhood further in Chapter 12.

Remarriage   The likelihood of remarriage after a relationship has ended by divorce or widowhood is greatest for younger adults. Although 60 percent of men over 45 had remarried within five years, only 11 percent of the women had (Bell, 1979).

Those who do not remarry include several psychological types (Bell, 1979): (1) the *bitter,* who assume another spouse would be as unsatisfactory as the last one; (2) the *frightened,* who are not willing to risk another personal failure; (3) the *overdemanding,* who may be searching for the "perfect partner" to guarantee success the next time around after an unpleasant divorce or to match the "saintly" qualities of a deceased spouse; (4) the *rejected,* who would like to remarry but do not find a partner; (5) and the *adjusted,* who have accepted being a single person and reject remarriage. It is interesting to note here that, compared to less educated women, highly educated women are more likely to be divorced and least likely to remarry (Safilios-Rothschild, 1977).

Those who do consider remarriage during the middle years face some similar issues as in younger adulthood and some different ones. They must deal with the feelings and associations remaining from the past relationship. In earlier adulthood such ties are likely to involve dependent children and the challenges of negotiating child care, as well as residual remnants of past love (Hunt, 1966). In the middle years it may be more necessary to deal with sanctifications or idealizations of the departed spouse and the sense of persistent attachment that comes from long relationships. A widow or widower may have feelings of disloyalty to the dead spouse; the new spouse may feel jealous of the past relationship. New family ties may be resisted by adult children or extended kin or accepted with a mixture of tolerance and welcome.

These hazards were identified by a widow who wrote the letter below to a personal relations columnist to advise "all the widows in the world who are longing to remarry."

When my husband died, I was sure my life was finished. We had a beautiful marriage, and I was certain I could never look at another man. Several months later the loneliness set in. I began to accept invitations from interesting bachelors and widowers. One day a very attractive man asked me to marry him. I said yes.

Here are the questions I wish I had asked myself:
1. Does the man have children?
2. How do they feel about his remarrying?
3. Do the children get along with one another or are they still fighting over their mother's estate?
4. What about your children? Does the gentleman want to include them in his family circle?
5. When decisions are made will he consult you or does he go to his children?

6. Does the man really want you or is he looking for someone to take care of him?

Had I asked myself these questions, I would not have put myself through three years of hell. I'm out of that marriage now, thank God, regaining my health and enjoying "widowhood"—something I never thought possible. Signed: Learned the Hard Way. (Reprinted by permission of Ann Landers and Field Newspaper Syndicate.)

Not all remarriages are unsuccessful, of course. A study of 100 remarriages where the bride and groom were past age 60 and had been remarried at least five years gives some clues about remarriages (McKain, 1972). Successfully remarried couples were more likely (1) to have known each other well before their marriage; (2) to have the approval of friends and relatives; (3) to have adjusted well to the changes of aging; and (4) to have sufficient income to sustain the new relationship.

Relationships of Older Gay People   Relatively little is known about the impact of homosexuality on aging. A few recent studies have challenged the assumptions that older homosexuals face the problems of aging without the traditional supports of family, church, and community that are available to heterosexuals. Three researchers have studied older gay men: Friend (1980) interviewed 43 gays aged 32 to 76, Kimmel (1979) interviewed 14 gays over 55, and Kelly (1977) interviewed 30 gays over 65. Raphael and Robinson (1980) interviewed 20 lesbian women over 50. Although the research is far from conclusive, several themes emerge from these studies so far: First, older gay people are diverse, in lifestyle and in psychological well-being. Second, the stereotypes of lonely, depressed, sexually frustrated aging homosexuals are not valid for the majority of the respondents studied (Kimmel, 1978; Raphael & Robinson, 1980). Third, the experience of growing older as a homosexual has become less stressful since the gay rights movement began in 1969. Finally, aging homosexuals do report some distinct problems and compensations associated with the homosexual lifestyle.

Some of the homosexual men and women "came out," or revealed their homosexual preference, in middle age. Responses of family members and straight (heterosexual) friends to learning about the homosexuality were varied, although some of the respondents who came out during the gay rights movement felt they experienced less rejection and more support than they had anticipated (Friend, 1980; Raphael & Robinson, 1980). Both men and women reported that homosexual friends acted as surrogate family (Bell & Weinberg, 1978).

Some of the men and some of the women were in long-term relationships; the lesbians were more likely than the gay men to be in sexually monogamous relationships. If one of the partners became ill, or died, many of the gays reported special problems: visiting regulations in hospitals that allowed only "family" in intensive-care units, family members who might forbid gay friends to visit in a nursing home, and legal problems with inheritance and property ownership. The general lack of openness about the relationships with the two families, medical personnel, and funeral directors often meant that the bereaved partner had little opportunity to mourn openly and receive the support normally extended to survivors of an important relationship.

Sexuality was important to many of the gays and lesbians studied. Some of the lesbians reported feeling much more interested in sexuality than they were during their menopause, some said that their interest and activity had lessened from their earlier years, and several indicated that they were enthusiastic about sex whenever they were in a good love relationship (Raphael & Robinson, 1980). In contrast to the findings that older unmarried heterosexual women report little or no sexual activity (for example, Verwoerdt, Pfeiffer, & Wang, 1969), even the older lesbian women who were not currently in a relationship anticipated little difficulty in establishing a sexual relationship when they wanted one.

Kimmel (1978) suggests that one reason that the homosexuals studied so far are coping well with aging may be that the experience of coming out tested and strengthened their abilities to adapt to change. Most of the individuals reported making substantial changes in lifestyle when they came out; usually they became much more involved with homosexual friends and activities rather than family or work associates. Those who managed the changes well are probably more likely to volunteer for studies such as the ones summarized here than those who have never come out or who are unable or unwilling to discuss their homosexuality. The adaptive capacities required in dealing with such changes are undoubtedly useful for coping with age-related changes as well as lifestyle changes.

Old-Age Partnerships

One of the more outstanding characteristics of people who survive to old age is their diversity. Most have dealt with loss, of significant others and of at least some aspects of valued social roles, and they have survived changes in physical health and personal relationships. The survival bias is particularly notable in research on marital relationships in old age: We are studying not only those who survive, but those who have a living spouse and who are willing to be studied. For example, some recent studies have examined couples who celebrated a golden wedding anniversary, marking 50 years of legal marriage; such couples are certainly a statistical minority, though their numbers are increasing.

The available evidence suggests several themes in old-age marriages. First, it is fairly clear that spouses are a relatively good welfare system. They are the first line of care during the illnesses of old age, and they ward off loneliness. These facts are reflected in the fact that the married are likely to be advantaged in longevity, health, morale, and financial comfort in old age. Marital interactions seem to be characterized by decreased passion, increased conventionality, and concern with health (Troll, Miller, & Atchley, 1979). Although both spouses are likely to rate the marriage positively (Roberts & Roberts, 1975), men are more satisfied with marriage than women are (Sporakowski & Hughston, 1978; Stinnett, Collins, & Montgomery, 1970).

Old men are reported as less satisfied with the amount of respect received in the relationship (Stinnett et al., 1970), and many of those who are in poor health feel dependent on their wives and not happy about the fact (Vinick, 1978). A study of remarriage among people aged 65 or over indicated that the men had experienced more difficulty being single than the women, and the men had taken the initiative for the new relationship; they were looking especially for companionship and care (Vinick, 1978).

Older women (like younger ones) seem least satisfied with communication in the marriage (Stinnett et al., 1970); they evaluate the relationship more positively if they have the support of friends, a good income, and good housing (Vinick, 1978). Older married women may recognize that they are a minority among women and respond to it in varying ways (Maas & Kuypers, 1974). Some devote themselves to "mothering" the spouse, a relationship that can be exaggerated with ill health. Some husbands and wives have a nearly symbiotic relationship, spending virtually all their time together and acting as a unit. Some develop a companionate camaraderie, enjoying the special gratifications that come only with a long shared past. Others end life in a devitalized relationship, drained by years of antagonism but unable to extricate themselves from the relationship. However, even a bitter, quarrelsome tie may be sustaining.

A matter of particular agony in old age is the disintegration of a spouse with a terminal illness. Some die rapidly, without much failing in physical or cognitive functioning. However, the transformation of a familiar, beloved person into a vestige or his or her former self can be a special pain of old-age marriage and close friendship. The burdens and gratifications of care are accepted largely by the spouse; this can represent a challenge for love and honor, or a bitterly resented chore. Such an experience probably contributes to the reluctance of many elders to remarry. Since women live longer than men, and usually marry men older than themselves, women are more likely than men to consider the possibilities of providing nursing care when they think of remarrying in later life.

Marriage occurs in old age, but less frequently than in any other age group (Treas & Van Hilst, 1976). First marriages constitute 6 percent of all marriages for older brides and grooms. The divorced are more likely to remarry than the widowed.

Remarriage in old age may be discouraged not only by the greater number of women than men but also by beliefs that elders "don't need" marriage and certainly could have no interest in love and sex; fears (of adult children) that estates would be dissipated or reallocated; beliefs that a past union is best honored by celibacy; and the sense that old age is a time of assessment of past accomplishments rather than new ventures. Furthermore, courtship activities require health, mobility, and money, which some elders lack (Treas & Van Hilst, 1976). The fact that old people do, in fact, enter into new marriages reemphasizes the diversity among individuals. Many elders know very well that they enjoy the companionship of another person in the room, an affectionate body in bed, and the vitality of discovery. They may find a special kind of intimacy in late life, when life is not as constrained by learning how to be adult, caring for small children, and involvement in careers. Particularly for those in reasonably good health, marriage can be very satisfying.

OTHER RELATIONSHIPS AND LIFESTYLES

The Never-Married

Less than 5 percent of the current population of older Americans have never married. Though the proportion of adults under 35 who had never married increased between 1960 and 1976 (Bell, 1979), longer-term marriage rates are not yet clear. The experiences of adults who never marry are not as well documented as those who marry at least once.

Overall, the women who end up never marrying tend to be better educated, more successful in careers, and more upwardly mobile than most married women. For example, female scientists and engineers are six times as likely as their male counterparts to be single (Davis, 1973). In addition, never-married women are likely to have grown up in families where both parents shared power and where children were encouraged to think for themselves (Spreitzer & Riley, 1974), which may have contributed to their sense of options besides marriage. For women now old the choice seemed clear: marriage or career, with great pressure to marry in order to be considered an acceptably adult woman.

Apparently some women rarely consider marriage, even when they are young. Motivations for "opting out" of the courtship process are varied, but they could include homosexuality, fear of rejection, fear of motherhood, hostility to men or marriage, strong attachment to family of origin (often linked to a caregiver role in the family), or intense career interests. More women probably emerge into singleness; that is, they assume they will marry "some day," but an idealized romance does not develop into marriage, new family emergencies command their attention, they have the care of illegitimate children, or they are preoccupied with work or education during young adulthood. Some high-achieving older women describe how they didn't take their work very seriously until they were in their early 30s. When they realized they probably would not marry, they began to plan career advancement seriously. As one woman in her 60s said, "When I talk to other spinsters about retirement I always point out that we *wanted* it this way. We all had opportunities to marry, and we all found reasons not to. Some women aren't even willing to admit that they made that choice. We did other things."

Men seem to have different motivations for refusing marriage. They are likely to be lifelong isolates, who do not seek out company and do not report special loneliness in old age (Gubrium, 1975). They are more likely than women to seek escape from familial involvements like those they experienced in childhood (Troll, Miller, & Atchley, 1979). Some are homosexual or so strongly attached to their mothers that they cannot marry. Never-married men are likely to be among the least successful men occupationally, although this is less true for homosexuals than for heterosexuals.

Research indicates that most never-married people report moderately high life satisfaction in later years; this could be expected insofar as they have constructed a lifestyle that is compatible with their personality. By the second half of life many are successfully autonomous and self-reliant (Clark & Anderson, 1967). Bachelors are more likely than married men to be unhappy and more likely than divorced or widowed men to be depressed. Single women, however, are less likely than widowed or divorced women to be depressed. These findings suggest that marriage may be more beneficial for men than for women, at least on the dimensions of happiness and depression.

One "advantage" of the never-married is that they presumably do not suffer the loss of a spouse. While that is technically true, some of the never-married have been in relationships of long duration and great intimacy; the loss of such partners is just as grievous as widowhood. Thus, in looking at relationships in old age, we should focus on commitments to intimacy over adulthood rather than on legal ties.

Not only the never-married but married adults use options for attachment outside of marriage and outside the parent–child bond. Unfortunately, at this point we know relatively little about these other resources, such as siblings, friends, and lovers. In the following section we will look briefly at these other types of relationships.

Brothers and Sisters

Approximately 80 percent of older Americans have at least one living sibling (Harris & Associates, 1975). As family size decreases, the likelihood of having a brother or sister through the life cycle also decreases—and the likelihood of having a compatible sibling may decrease even further. The evidence is conflicting about how much contact there is between siblings at different ages or what meaning such attachments have with or without physical contact. Generally, there seems to be an upsurge of interest in siblings during old age, especially among the never-married (Shanas et al., 1968). Sister–sister ties are the strongest and brother–brother ties weakest, in agreement with other evidence about the importance of women as kin-keepers (Adams, 1968; Cumming & Schneider, 1961; Irish, 1964).

Love, caring, significance, and support may all be experienced in relationships outside the family. Friends can be a buffer against stress; this is especially true of a confidant, someone who understands us and in whom we can confide. Even one confidant, particularly one outside the family, is a powerful antidote against loneliness and illness in old age (Blau, 1973; Lowenthal & Haven, 1968).

Relatively little is known about friendships over adulthood. Deeply felt same-sex friendships were apparently accepted as normal in 19th-century America (Smith-Rosenberg, 1975); only later did such relationships become suspect. It was assumed that women especially should find sufficient friendship within the family and that rivalries and jealousy would weaken most alliances with friends outside the family. Particularly for men, one of the barriers to close same-sex friendship has been fear of the sexual feelings that may be roused in any close emotional relationship. And, insofar as emotionality and "loving skills" have been defined as feminine, men who have intimate friendships may be regarded as strange, effeminate, or homosexual.

Interestingly enough, the ideal standard for friendship now seems to be a feminine one, at least to judge by current research and writings on friendship. Many studies find that female friendships are likely to involve mutual trust

Even one confidant, particularly one outside the family, is a powerful antidote against loneliness and illness throughout adulthood.

and shared feelings, thoughts, and vulnerabilities. Males do not show the same friendship style. Men are most likely to direct such intimate self-disclosure toward the wife (or another woman) but rarely to male friends (Bell, 1979; Booth, 1972; Bultena, 1974; Clark & Anderson, 1967; Pastorello, 1974; Powers & Bultena, 1976; Weiss & Lowenthal, 1975). Male friendships seem to be based more on doing things together, particularly activities that require mutual co-operation, such as team sports, combat, or work. Nevertheless, men may derive considerable support from such relationships, even though they are not characterized by the same open sharing of personal feelings that women engage in.

Very little research on friendship explores the potential positive or negative effects of male and female patterns of friendship. The fact that women are more interested and skilled in intimate communication than men are may help account for the attractiveness of marriage for men and the dissatisfactions with marital communication among women. Many men depend on women, particularly their wives, as their primary or sole confidant. Men's dependency on women for emotional expressivity and support balances the dependency of many women on men for occupational achievement and status for the family unit. As Tresmer and Pleck (1976) point out, this form of male dependency is often overlooked and only women's dependency acknowledged.

Cross-sex friendships seem governed both by opportunity and by current norms (Booth & Hess, 1974). The pattern in America has been to allow considerable, but not complete, access of men and women to each other, at all ages.

One opportunity factor is less than full sexual integration of the workplace. Since many adults meet friends through work, this limits the likelihood of making cross-sex friendships. As work becomes integrated, such friendships are becoming more common. New norms emerge to meet the changing circumstances, and constraints against cross-sex friendships may be changing (Bell, 1979).

There is often an assumption (implicit or explicit) that adult cross-sex friendships will or may become sexualized. Therefore, cross-sex friendships among married adults are often discouraged or regarded with suspicion, though they are encouraged among unmarried people. Sexual attraction is a possibility in any relationship; whether or not it is inevitable in a heterosexual friendship is a matter of debate. The complexity and possibilities are evident in data reported by Bell (1979) that most of the high-achieving, self-confident women who had varied cross-sex relationships acknowledged and enjoyed the sexual tensions involved in the friendships. However, not all the friendships included explicitly sexual activity; friends did not necessarily become lovers. And even if friends did become lovers for a time, they sometimes stopped being lovers but maintained the friendship.

The view of cross-sex friendship and the potentials for danger and growth vary over the life cycle, though in largely unknown ways. The distinctions between friends and lovers may be quite clear in late adolescence and young adulthood, the usual period of mate selection; it may be most blurred during old age (Hess, 1972). It is not yet clear how current changes in sex roles and age norms may affect the availability of same- and cross-sex friendships across adulthood.

Friends may become lovers, lovers may become friends, or lovers may not be friends. A *lover* is a sexual partner in a union unsanctioned by church or state. There has always been sex outside of marriage, expressed in a wide variety of relationships—from one-time chance encounters to long-term committed intimacy. Unfortunately, many discussions of "affairs" do not distinguish between the kinds of intimacy and commitment involved.

Cohabitation, or living together, is one way of meeting intimacy and sexual needs without legal marriage. It may serve different needs at various stages in the life cycle, and the needs served are mediated by personality. Among young adults, particularly those still in school, cohabitation may be linked to learning about the other sex but not necessarily with the expectation that this partnership will lead to marriage (Bell, 1979). Divorced adults may live together if they have legal or personal reasons not to establish another formal relationship. Old people may cohabit because they cannot afford to marry and deal with the financial penalties attached to some pension systems.

Affairs, where sexual partners do not live together, are fairly common, especially among unmarried persons. Among those who are currently married, approximately half of the husbands and perhaps one-fourth of the wives have had sexual experience outside of marriage (Hunt, 1974; Kinsey et al., 1948, 1953; Masters & Johnson, 1966; Pietropinto & Simenauer, 1979). Many of these experiences involved only one other partner, and relatively few were of long duration. The incidence of women's extramarital affairs has increased more rapidly than men's, probably reflecting greater opportunity and the relaxation of the double standard of sexual behavior. On the other hand, more women than men say they are "above temptation" (Pietropinto & Simenauer, 1979).

Marital fidelity remains an ideal for most people, and affairs are typically threatening, but not necessarily fatal, to marriage (Glenn & Weaver, 1979). Very few (less than 5 percent) affairs are with the mutual consent of both spouses (Pietropinto & Simenauer, 1979); this pattern is known as a sexually open marriage. After a popular book was published in 1972 extolling the benefits of a marriage where each partner was free to develop independent interests and intimate relationships (O'Neill & O'Neill, 1972), many more people discussed and tried this option than had been true in previous decades. A decade of experience and research with this marriage style reveals several themes. "Open" marriages are more acceptable to younger, better educated, less religious couples with few or no children (Wachowski & Bragg, 1980). Extramarital intimate friendships, sometimes including sex, are experienced as exciting, pleasurable, and growth enhancing; they are also tied to feelings of guilt and difficulties in maintaining multiple intimate relationships (Bunk, 1980; Ramey, 1975, 1976). Couples who openly maintain nonmarital sexual relationships usually evolve special rules to minimize the threat to the marriage; common strategies are to keep the marriage primary by (1) limiting the intensity of other relationships, and (2) being open about the extent and nature of the involvement (Bunk, 1980; Macklin, 1980). Research indicates that relatively few couples will opt for a marital style acknowledging sexual relationships outside the marriage.

Does loving change over time? Relatively few researchers have taken such questions seriously, leaving them to poets and historians. Neiswander and Birren (1973) have pointed out a good many relevant questions about love in later life. Are there any characteristics peculiar to early-life relationships? Are the same mechanisms involved in initiating and developing sequentially occurring relationships? Do old people "fall in love"? Do they fall in love in the same way as younger people? To what extent is falling in love, or being in love, critical to beginning a love relationship? To a more permanent bond? To continuing a relationship over time? Most of these questions are not yet answered, but a few clues are emerging.

For example, Reedy (1977) located 12 married and 12 unmarried couples from four age groups (adolescence/young adulthood/middle age/older) who had "healthy love relationships" and rated them on their experiences and attitudes. They found (1) that being older did not mean giving up sex or romantic notions of love; (2) that experiences and beliefs were not consistent since all believed in romantic true love but assessed their own relationship quite realistically; and (3) that the unmarried males and the married women were more romantic than the others. The greatest difference between the middle-aged and older adults in the importance ascribed to various components of the love experience was in terms of physical love: This was rated as most important by the adolescents, young adults, and middle-aged, but as fourth in importance by the older adults. Although idealization of the mate was not regarded as very important by any of the respondents, it was more important for adolescents and older adults than for the others.

In this chapter we have reviewed some of the varied ways individuals meet needs for companionship, intimacy, and ecstasy through marital and friendly relationships over adulthood. One of the important influences on the arrangements made to accommodate love is work, just as work is affected by love relationships. In the next chapter we will discuss work over the course of adult life.

SUMMARY

1 Marriage is a common arrangement for meeting a variety of personal and social needs. The process of marriage reflects the social and economic conditions of the times as well as the developmental history of the individuals involved. As social and individual circumstances change, marriages also change; one of the central issues in marriage is how to accommodate change and growth.

2 Most people marry as young adults; the average age for first marriages is now approximately 21 years for women and 23 years for men. People tend to homogamy (similarity) in initial mate selection. Though there are diverse marital styles, a common ideal among younger couples is companionate sharing with substantial sexual equality. Increased sexual differentiation is common after the birth of the first child.

3   In later life married persons are advantaged in longevity, health, morale, and financial comfort. Marital interactions among older people seem to be characterized by decreased passion, increased conventionality, and concern with health. Although both spouses are likely to rate the marriage positively, men are more satisfied with marriage than women are.

4   Sexuality is an important aspect of close relationships throughout life. Patterns of sexual response show age changes that reflect other biological and psychological changes; in general, responses become slowed and less specifically genital. Among heterosexuals and homosexuals there are wide individual variations in sexual interest and activity at all ages.

5   Divorce is more common now than in previous times. The increase in divorce rates seems to reflect increased options for women outside of marriage, lower fertility, and greater general prosperity. The likelihood of divorce is greatest in the first seven years of marriage. Those most likely to divorce are those who married early (before age 20), who were pregnant before marriage, whose parents were divorced, or who are childless. Divorce is less common in the middle and later years than in young adulthood, though the rate is increasing substantially. Economic deprivation is a common consequence of divorce for older women.

6   Most younger divorced persons remarry. Men are more likely to remarry, and more rapidly, than women. Middle-aged and older women are substantially less likely to remarry than are younger women or men. Remarriages have about the same chances for success as do first-time marriages.

7   Marriages are most likely to terminate during middle and old age by death. There is a wide range of responses to widowhood, including lifelong mourning, relief, rage, and loneliness. Responses are tempered by financial resources, previous lifestyles, and ethnicity. Widowed women are unlikely to remarry; widowed men under 70 typically remarry within a few years after being widowed. Men are more likely to end life married; whereas women are most likely to end life as widows.

8   Homosexuals establish a variety of relationships to meet needs for sociability and sex. Homosexual couples are likely to have the usual range of adjustment and living-together problems as do heterosexual couples, but they have additional special problems that relate to living a devalued lifestyle. Older gays may have particular problems dealing with separations, illness, or the death of a lover, since the support of families, medical professionals, and the legal system are often not as available as they are to heterosexuals.

9   Approximately 5 percent of the older American population have never married; the percentage of each cohort varies with opportunity and social

norms. Among currently older cohorts, never-married older women tend to be better educated, more successful in careers, and more upwardly mobile than married women. Never-married men seem to be lifelong isolates; they are less successful occupationally and less happy than married men. Some never-married people have long-term homosexual or heterosexual relationships, and some have close ties to parents and siblings.

10 Relatively little is known about friendship patterns throughout adulthood. Men and women seem to have different styles of friendship. Women use friends to share feelings, thoughts, and vulnerabilities; men are more likely to engage in mutually enjoyed activities with male friends and to disclose feelings to women. Same-sex friendships are more common than opposite-sex friendships, particularly after marriage. A substantial minority of married persons seek not only friendship but sexual relationships outside of marriage. The duration, meaning, and consequences of such relationships are varied.

CHAPTER
ELEVEN
WORKING AND RELAXING

The busy bee has no time for sorrow.

William Blake, 1757–1827

In order that people may be happy in their work, these three things are need-ed: they must be for it; they must not do too much of it; and they must have a sense of success in it.

John Ruskin, 1819–1900

Work affects virtually every adult in some way, and consequently people have very strong—often quite individual—ideas about it. Though it would be hard to find one definition of work that everyone thought adequate, we can consider work an activity that produces something of value for other people. This may involve organizing human or material resources to achieve, create, or produce a wide variety of socially valued services (Barnett & Baruch, 1978). *Relaxation* and *leisure* activities are more personal and more discretionary; the activity is undertaken for personal pleasure rather than social value. In addition, there may be a sense of playfulness about leisure pursuits that is often missing in work.

Working and relaxing are important aspects of adult experience. In this chapter we will look at motivations for working, the worlds of work, work involvements throughout adulthood, and leisure involvements throughout adulthood.

MOTIVATIONS FOR WORKING

Meanings of Work

Work is closely tied to feelings of identity, worth, and self-esteem, reflecting, in part, an inner sense of mastery of the external environment. Psychologists have identified intrinsic urges for independence and mastery, a basic human need to be competent and to interact effectively with the environment (White, 1959). This need has also been described in terms of a personality characteristic, *achievement motivation,* the need "to master, manipulate and organize physical objects, human beings, or ideas . . . to overcome obstacles and attain a high standard . . . to excel one's self . . . to rival and surpass others" (Murray, 1938).

Although all individuals desire to be competent, the need for achievement varies between individuals and within individuals at different times. The strength of achievement needs affects the ways an individual directs and interprets working and nonworking experiences. Men and women with strong achievement needs are more apt to end up in positions of power and influence than are those who have stronger interests in smooth, rewarding personal relationships.

On the other hand, work behavior cannot be predicted directly or exclusively from the strength of needs to achieve. Other personality characteristics—for example, the "motivation to avoid success"—can modify achievement behaviors. If the outcomes of work achievement include social or personal rejection (a frequent fear of women), the individual may be very ambivalent about striving for occupational achievement. Or if it is likely that they will not succeed at some activity, individuals are less likely to work diligently.

The self-esteem derived from achievement efforts depends partly on how one interprets the experience. Self-esteem and sense of competence are most likely when success is attributed to internal, stable factors, and failure to external, unstable ones (Weiner, Frieze, Kukla, Reed, Rest, & Rosenbaum, 1971). Women are more likely to attribute their success to luck or the ease of the task; men credit their own superior abilities. When confronted with failure, women are likely to conclude they lack ability, whereas men say they made insufficient efforts (Frieze, 1975). Thus women may derive less self-esteem and sense of competence than men from the same kinds of achievement (Barnett & Baruch, 1978).

Work has the same general meanings for the poor and welfare recipients as for the middle-class and employed (*Work in America,* 1973). The poor and the unemployed, however, derive more negative feelings about themselves from their work status.

Work has social as well as individual importance. It is a source of social esteem. By providing something of value to others, we obtain approval and rewards from them. And, since work is generally done by adults, becoming recognized as a worker is an important part of growing up. Work also provides an important basis for social participation. Many kinds of work provide opportunities for valued social interaction. And even outside the work setting, we may relate to others in terms of the work we do.

When work is performed for money, working permits economic self-sufficiency and can allow one to provide for others, such as a family.

Finally, work is one way to occupy and structure time. This meaning of work is very obvious to people who find themselves with too little work to do and too much "time on their hands."

In addition to all these general meanings, working or particular kinds of work may have special meanings to a particular individual. The meanings of work form one basis for the satisfactions and burdens people experience in working.

Satisfactions and Burdens in Working

The experience of work can be understood partly by knowing *what* a person does, or what cognitive skills the work requires. We must also look at the people, events, and relationships that are part of the experience even though they may be far from the physical arena of work (Sarason, 1977). One way to assess the work experience is to find out what people like and dislike about it, over time.

Job satisfaction is somewhat difficult to assess since most people do not want to admit, either to themselves or to others, that they have a bad job. One possible indication is whether people would choose similar work if they were to start over again. Some responses to this question from different occupational groups are shown in Table 11-1.

The rankings of job satisfaction in Table 11-1 are nearly identical with general social prestige rankings of these jobs, which implies that there is general agreement on how "good" the jobs are (*Work in America*, 1973).

Research with workers in many different jobs has identified several factors contributing to job satisfaction: autonomy, participation, challenge, security, pay, mobility, comfort, and opportunity to interact with co-workers (*Work in America*, 1973). As one 84-year-old said, in reflecting on his working life:

The job I enjoyed the most was being a stone cutter, because it was an outside job. I liked it because I was very good at it—better than most of them. My job was to prepare the stone for monuments. My work had to be perfect. It was more distinctive work than being a block cutter. You had to watch it and get the right grain on the stone. I was born to it. When I was a boy, I would examine every rock I would pick up from the quarry. Later I would play around in the quarry and help the guys cut that stone. I loved it. That's how I would get my experience. When you are young, you are anxious and you pick everything up fast. That is the best job I had in my working days. When I was young, strong, healthy, and I enjoyed the outdoors.

Different requirements for satisfaction were mentioned by some of the hairdressers interviewed for a study of "pink-collar" workers (Howe, 1977): coworkers being friendly and cooperative, enough work to go around but not so much that they could not have some flexibility in the hours they worked, ability to choose the kind of background music played in the shop, and challenging tasks to perform.

Often, however, these satisfaction factors are missing, and people experience their work as burdensome. For instance, professors, in general quite satisfied with their jobs (see Table 11-1), may work in departments where the department head requires close accounting of time spent or where unpleasant rivalries and daily bickering make the work experience very stressful. Unhappiness with work is associated more with working conditions than with age, sex, social class, or race (*Work in America*, 1973). Most of the negative conditions relate to self-respect; workers need a chance to perform well in their work, to gain a sense of personal achievement and growth in competence, and to contribute something personal and unique. When these needs are not met, people may become alienated from their work and feel that it is not an important part of themselves. Work alienation is most common among workers who (1) are in

Table 11-1 Percentages in Occupational Groups Who Would Choose Similar Work Again

Professional and lower white-collar occupations	%	Working-class occupations	%
Urban university professors	93	Skilled printers	52
Mathematicians	91	Paper workers	42
Physicists	89	Skilled autoworkers	41
Biologists	89	Skilled steelworkers	41
Chemists	86	Textile workers	31
Firm lawyers	85	Unskilled steelworkers	21
Lawyers	83	Unskilled autoworkers	16
Journalists (Washington correspondents)	82	*Blue-collar workers, cross-section**	*24*
Church university professors	77		
Solo lawyers	75		
*White-collar workers, cross-section**	*43*		

*The cross-sections are a randomly selected group of workers in each of the occupations in the white-collar or blue-collar groups.

Source: *Work in America: Report of a Special Task Force to the Secretary of Health, Education, and Welfare.* Cambridge, Mass: MIT Press, 1973, p. 16. Reprinted by permission.

work situations and hierarchical organizations providing little discretion in pacing and scheduling of work; (2) have a career that has been blocked or chaotic, with earlier jobs not leading to more responsible, higher-paying ones; and/or (3) are in a stage of the life cycle that puts pressure on the worker (such as money required for many dependent children) (Seligman, 1965).

Satisfaction with work is an important part of satisfaction with life. In fact, in one 15-year longitudinal study work satisfaction was the strongest predictor of longevity—better than physical examinations, tobacco use, or genetic inheritance; those who lived the longest were also those who were the most satisfied with their work (Palmore, 1971). Conversely, job dissatisfaction has been related to a number of physical and mental health problems (*Work in America,* 1973).

THE WORLDS OF WORK

Work situations vary partly in terms of extrinsic, visible aspects—the amount of formal training required, the pay range, social status, clothing or uniform required, the range of promotions or upward mobility possible, availability of jobs in the field, and so forth. Even people in the same kind of job may have quite different work experiences because of the specific tasks they do or the work setting. In order to understand the relationships between work and other factors in adult life, let us look at the ways work is socially structured.

Social Stratification of the Work Force

As we point out in Chapter 2, individual development occurs in structured social settings. The social stratification system in America is based in large part on the kind of work one does. Not all work is considered equally "valuable" to society. The value our society places on intellectual competence and entrepreneurial skills is reflected in the occupational status system.

We can distinguish at least four broad strata in the work force: marginal workers, blue-collar workers, white-collar workers, and upper-level managers and professionals. One's place in this hierarchy at any point influences one's lifestyle, social rewards, and sense of self. We will consider paid workers here, since unpaid workers are usually not included in studies of occupational stratification. Most unpaid workers are women who work as housewives; their social status is derived from their husbands' employment status.

Marginal Workers   These people are employed occasionally, but they do not have a stable relationship with any particular employer or use any set of skills consistently. They may be marginally employed for a variety of reasons. Some are immigrants lacking necessary language skills and facing discrimination; some have criminal records; and many are physically or mentally ill in ways that make them unable to fit into the regular work force. Such individuals are often socially "invisible." Their inability to work certainly influences the ways in which they develop in other areas of life.

Blue-collar Workers   Blue-collar work includes jobs that do not require formal education beyond high school and that presumably require manual skills more than intellectual skills. The range within this broad classification is considerable, from unskilled labor that can be performed by any able-bodied person after little instruction to the complex skills and learning required of master electricians. Although workers are likely to move from one job to another in search of work, better pay, better job security, or variety, there is relatively little mobility into progressively more interesting, challenging work.

Interviews with contemporary blue-collar workers reveal considerable dissatisfaction with work conditions (*Work in America,* 1973)—in particular, the few options for mobility and the fact that education is no longer regarded as offering a way up or a way out into white-collar work. Technology has had the unfortunate impact of lowering status and satisfaction since mechanization has replaced craft in many jobs. The blue-collar work force is largely composed of second- and third-generation Americans, better educated than their immigrant parents and grandparents, who did the jobs dreaming that their children and grandchildren would become educated and surpass them. Many blue-collar workers feel denigrated by upper-middle-class professionals, and they resent the kinds of privileges available to white-collar workers (for instance, going to the toilet when you want to instead of when the supervisor tells you).

The lifestyles of the blue-collar workers have been described in a number of interesting books illustrating the diversity among blue-collar workers and their families (see Howell, 1973; Rubin, 1976; Shostak & Gomberg, 1964).

White-collar Workers   White-collar work occurs in office settings rather than outdoors or in factories. The skills presumably required are more intellectual and social in nature. Pay may be no better, or worse, than upper-level blue-collar jobs, but the jobs have somewhat higher social status. Post–high school formal education is required for many (but not all) white-collar jobs, even though there is little evidence that such advanced training is directly related to job performance. Mobility opportunities vary greatly; they tend to be much greater for men than for women.

Job dissatisfactions of white-collar workers primarily reflect the fact that the demand for higher academic credentials has not been matched by increased status, prestige, pay, or job challenges (*Work in America,* 1973). Secretaries complain that they are expected to have some college education but are not allowed to exercise independent judgment and are regarded as an extension of the typewriter; middle-level managers complain that they must implement policies they do not create or influence.

Managers and Professionals   Work in this category has the highest social status. Business owners and managers usually have formal education beyond high school, and they must have social and entrepreneurial skills. Professional work requires advanced, specialized education beyond college; the knowledge and skills acquired during education are applied first under close supervision, and the individual is then certified or licensed to practice independently. The concept of a *career* is often used in discussing professional work to signify a series of related jobs, each of higher responsibility, status, and pay. Comparisons are made between professionals in *how far* (to company president, district or head nurse) and how *fast* they progress in the career line.

Professionals are in the best position to obtain the kinds of gratifications desired by many workers. However, most professionals now work in bureaucratized settings, which reduce the sense (and the reality) of independent practice. As this happens, professionals have complaints similar to those of white-collar workers—that they have much pressure to perform but little opportunity to act on their education and accumulated wisdom (Sarason, 1977).

Advancement   Who gets ahead in the work force? This question has challenged Americans for many years, particularly since we still have an ideology of equal opportunity. Christopher Jencks and his colleagues (1979) have summarized the evidence from dozens of studies on career success. They defined occupational success in financial terms: who earns the most money. (This is, of course, only one of several ways to define success; it was selected in part because it is easy to compare individuals on the measure objectively.) Among men 25–64 the best-paid fifth earn approximately six times as much as the worst-paid fifth. Economic success is related to four major factors, none of them surprising. (1) Family and racial/ethnic background accounts for an estimated 15–35 percent of the total variance. Sons of professional-level fathers earn the most and blue-collar sons the least; whites earn more than blacks at comparable occupational levels. (2) Intelligence, as measured on standard tests, accounts for some 10–15 percent of the variance. (3) Formal education (the number of years completed and degrees received) accounts for about 20 percent of the variance. (4) Personality traits, while more difficult to assess, also contribute to adult career success. For example, teacher ratings of "executive ability" made on tenth-grade boys and self-rated leadership ability in high school were very good predictors of adult financial success.

Such research indicates that no one factor determines the outcome of work experience; rather, a complex interaction of factors—including luck—is important. In addition, the researchers found a good deal of change over the period of adulthood; highest earners at one time were not necessarily the highest earners at another time. The social structure of the workplace and the job market are important in understanding how men and women act on their needs to be competent and to do good work.

Sexual Division of Labor

Even a brief examination of the ways work is done makes it clear that most work in our society is different for men and women. Sex differences are evident in two major areas: pay for working and kind of work performed.

Table 11-2 shows the employment status of males and females in 1979. Seventy-two percent of males over 16 years old and 47 percent of females over 16 were employed either full- or part-time. Nearly half of the females compared to one-fifth of the males were counted as not in the labor force; this group includes students, housewives, retired persons, and disabled persons who are not actively seeking employment. As Table 11-2 indicates, black and other racial minority people are less likely to be employed than whites; black women are somewhat more likely than white women to be in the labor force. Women who are employed are more likely than employed men to be working part-time, a discrepancy that did not change between 1970 and 1978 (see Table 11-3).

Table 11-2 Employment Status by Sex and Race, 1979

	Employed[1]	Not in Labor Force[2]
All males[3]	72.3	21.3
(Black and other nonwhite males)	(61.6)	(26.8)
All females[3]	47.2	49.2
(Black and other nonwhite females)	(46.4)	(46.7)

[1] Persons 16 years and over employed part-time or full-time

[2] All persons 16 years and over who are neither employed nor unemployed

[3] Includes blacks and other nonwhites

Source: Adapted from U.S. Bureau of the Census, *Statistical Abstract of the United States: 1979* (100th edition). Washington, D.C., 1979, p. 394.

Table 11-3 Full-time and Part-time Status of Labor Force, 1970 and 1978 (percentage of all persons employed)

	1970		1978	
	% Full-time	% Part-time[1]	% Full-time	% Part-time[1]
Males 20 years and over	95.3	4.7	95.1	4.9
Unemployment rate	4.5	7.6	5.5	9.0
Females 20 years and over	78.5	21.5	79.0	21.0
Unemployment rate	4.8	4.5	6.0	5.8

[1] Part-time includes persons working less than 35 hours per week on a volunteer basis

Source: Adapted from U.S. Bureau of the Census, *Statistical Abstract of the United States: 1979* (100th edition). Washington, D.C., 1979, p. 397.

In addition, most paid jobs are sex-typed. Most employed women work in a relatively narrow range of jobs; in 1970, 70 percent of the female paid work force was in four fields: nursing, teaching, secretarial work, and social work (Tangri, 1972). Another way of assessing sex-typing of work is to look at the percentage of each sex in each job. Table 11-4 indicates the percentage of people employed in various jobs who were female, for 1972 and 1978 and the change between the two years. In the total listing from which this table is taken most of the jobs have either many or few women; relatively few of the jobs have between 40 and 60 percent female employees, which would indicate a nearly even proportion of men and women.

Men and women tend to work in different settings; even within similar or identical work settings, however, they are likely to have different jobs. For example, 96.9 percent of receptionists are female, whereas 22.8 percent of shipping and receiving clerks are female.

Table 11-4 Percentage of Women Employed in Selected Occupations, 1972 and 1978

Occupation	% of Total Employed Who Are Female		
	1972	1978	Difference
Secretary	99.1	99.2	+ .1
Child-care worker	98.0	98.1	+ .1
Registered nurse	97.6	96.7	+ .9
Private household worker	97.6	97.7	+ .1
Dressmaker and seamstress	97.0	97.4	+ .4
Receptionist	97.0	96.9	+ .1
Prekindergarten and kindergarten teacher	96.8	96.5	− .3
Telephone operator	96.7	94.2	− 2.5
Bank teller	87.5	91.5	+ 4.0
Elementary school teacher	85.1	84.0	− .9
Librarian, archivist, curator	81.6	80.7	− .9
Nursing aide, orderly, attendant	83.4	87.0	+ 3.6
Textile operative	55.2	59.9	+ 4.7
Social and recreation worker	55.1	61.0	+ 5.9
Vocational and educational counselor	50.0	52.6	+ 2.6
Secondary school teacher	49.6	51.6	+ 2.0
Factory checker and examiner	48.5	48.8	+ .3
Health administrator	46.6	46.2	+ .4
Manager and superintendent, building	42.6	50.3	+ 7.7
Real estate agent	36.7	45.0	+ 8.3
Bus driver	34.1	45.1	+10.0
University and college teacher	28.0	33.8	+ 5.8
Computer specialist	21.7	30.1	+ 8.4
Bank officer and financial manager	17.6	23.4	+ 5.8
Shipping and receiving clerk	14.9	22.8	+ 7.9
Physician, medical and osteopathic	10.1	11.3	+ 1.2
Engineering and science technician	9.1	13.4	+ 4.3
Taxicab driver and chauffeur	9.0	9.9	+ .9
Mail carrier, post office	6.7	11.7	+ 4.0
Lawyer and judge	3.8	9.4	+ 5.6
Police and detective	2.6	5.9	+ 3.3
Dentist	1.9	1.7	− .2
Telephone installer and repairer	1.9	6.7	+ 4.8
Engineer	.8	2.8	+ 2.0
Other construction craftworker	.6	1.5	+ .9
Carpenter	.5	1.0	+ .5
Truck driver	.6	1.9	+ 1.3
Automobile mechanic	.5	.6	+ .1

Source: Adapted from U.S. Bureau of the Census, *Statistical Abstract of the United States: 1979* (100th edition). Washington, D.C., 1979, pp. 416–418.

Women who enter traditionally "male" jobs or men in "female" jobs often find themselves highly visible. Like any visibly different minority entering an occupation as an equal, the pioneers often experience additional job stress. (See Kanter, 1977, for an analysis of women in high-level corporate positions and the ways sexual or racial minority status affect career experiences.)

The least sex-typed jobs are sometimes the newest ones. In the United States, at least, new jobs and new careers emerge regularly in pace with technological demands. For example, computer science did not exist as a career field a few decades ago. As the skills required to market, operate, design, and repair this new technology were not clearly masculine or feminine, women were recruited into the field from the beginning. The percentage of female computer specialists increased from 21.7 in 1972 to 30.1 in 1978. The example of computer science, in fact, leads us to the influence of historical circumstances on work experiences.

Historical and Cohort Differences

In addition to sex, social class, and particular work setting, work experiences are influenced by the particular cohort of workers and the socioeconomic realities of the time.

The Structure of the Work Force   The first way of looking at paid work over adulthood is to examine the structure of the labor market: Who is considered available for employment and which people are actually employed? Since ways of calculating the labor market and unemployment vary from time to time and between countries, it is important to know how the figures are calculated. The definition used by U.S. economists of who is "in the labor market" is fairly broad. The U.S. Department of Labor gathers information from a representative sample of households in the United States by asking about the work status of everyone in the household during the week of the survey. People are counted as in the labor market whether they are employed or unemployed. *Employed* people worked for pay or profit for at least one hour during the week the report was made, worked 15 or more hours as unpaid workers in a family enterprise, or were not working that week but had jobs or businesses from which they were temporarily absent (for vacation, illness, strikes, or the like). *Unemployed* persons are those who had no employment during the week data were collected, who had made specific efforts to find a job within the previous four weeks, and who were available for work during that week; and persons on layoff from a job or waiting to report to a new job within 30 days. All other persons 16 years of age and over are regarded as not in the labor market (U.S. Bureau of the Census, 1979, p. 390).

The nonlabor force includes individuals who do not choose to work for pay, who are not interested in employment at that time, or who are unable to be employed. However, it also includes a number of individuals who may prefer to work but who do not see any realistic options for doing so or who have given up hope of finding employment. This group is the largest pool of workers who could be recruited into the labor force if the social and economic conditions warranted. Several conditions affect the likelihood of such people's being employed.

One of the relevant conditions is the age and sex distribution of the population at a particular time. As we saw in Chapter 1, population distribution varies over time. For example, during World War II many younger men, traditionally the most desired employees for many kinds of work, particularly physical labor, worked in the military service and were not available for civilian employment. As a result, alternate workers were hired, especially women and older people. One reason so many women have been employed in Eastern Europe is that these countries suffered heavy war losses of males and at the same time had periods of great economic advancement; under these circumstances an ideology of equal male and female employment fit the needs of the larger socioeconomic system (Fogarty et al., 1971).

Another relevant condition is, thus, the economic condition in the society as a whole. Sometimes there is a great demand for labor, sometimes less. The total demand for workers is a crucial factor in the likelihood of "less desirable" workers' being able to find employment. Economic expansion maximizes the chances that older people, members of minority groups, and very young people will be employed (*Work in America*, 1973). When workers are needed in the labor force, employers offer whatever incentives are needed to attract the desired workers, such as part-time work, child-care facilities, flexible scheduling, or promotional opportunities.

A third relevant condition is the prevailing social and political opinion on making employment available regardless of sex, race, or age. The past decade or two has been marked by intensive efforts to lessen sex and race discrimination in employment; the results are partly evident in the increased proportion of women in the work force and in "male" jobs (see Table 11-4). In the absence of an expanding economy it is unlikely that marginal workers will be employed unless there are special regulations encouraging or mandating the employment of workers without regard to sex, race, or age.

Fourth, employment patterns are affected by family behavior, including the timing of marriage, the number of children born, and the prevalence of divorce.

The conditions that affect labor-force participation are complex. We can see some of the consequences of these factors by examining some additional data about employment rates. Table 11-5 indicates the percentage employed by race, sex, and age for the years 1960, 1970, and 1978. Several patterns are evident. (1) Regardless of race or age, males are more likely than females to be employed. The difference is greatest between ages 25 and 64. Nearly all males aged 25 to 54 are employed. (2) Black males are less likely to be employed than white males; black females are more likely to be employed than white females. (3) The most notable change since 1960 is the increased percentage of employed women in every age group under 65. (4) The proportion of people over

65 who are employed has decreased from 1960 to 1978, more sharply for men than for women. The dramatic reduction in employment among older male workers may level off. According to some analysts of employment trends, the cohorts of workers who are now middle-aged will reach normal retirement age at a time when there are relatively fewer younger workers to replace them in the labor market because of lowered birth rates, and therefore these cohorts of older workers may be encouraged to remain actively employed (Sheppard & Rix, 1977).

Table 11-5 Labor-Force Participation Rates by Race, Sex, and Age, 1960 to 1978 (percentage in the labor force who were employed)

Group	1960	1970	1978
TOTAL U.S. POPULATION	59.2	60.3	62.7
Race/sex			
White male	82.6	79.7	78.0
White female	36.0	42.0	48.8
Black and other nonwhite male	80.1	74.7	70.8
Black and other nonwhite female	47.2	48.9	52.8
Age/sex			
Males			
18–19 years	73.1	68.8	74.0
20–24	88.9	85.1	85.6
25–34	96.4	95.0	94.3
35–44	96.4	95.7	94.6
45–54	94.3	92.9	90.4
55–64	85.2	81.5	72.5
65 and over	32.2	25.8	19.7
Females			
18–19 years	51.0	53.4	62.2
20–24	46.1	57.5	68.2
25–34	35.8	44.8	62.0
35–44	43.1	50.9	61.3
45–54	49.3	54.0	56.8
55–64	36.7	42.5	41.1
65 and over	10.5	9.2	7.8

Source: U.S. Bureau of the Census, *Statistical Abstract of the United States: 1979* (100th edition). Washington, D.C., 1979, p. 392.

Moreover, the cohorts of older workers in future decades will be different from past and current cohorts of older workers in America. People in their 50s and 60s are likely to be in better health, and each cohort has somewhat more formal education. These factors influence the kinds of work people desire, what they can reasonably do, and their options for retirement.

Personal Expectations of Work   The varying meanings of work over historical periods influence individual experiences of working. For example, in the past century the "Protestant work ethic" was strongly endorsed by many people in the Western world. According to this belief, in its purest form, all men work to glorify God. Profits from work should not be used to purchase material comforts but should be reinvested to make more wealth or to further the Kingdom of God on earth. Individuals were expected to select a vocation (or *calling*) and pursue it religiously; success (that is, wealth) would be proof that one's work efforts were pleasing to God (Zaccaria, 1970).

Work was thus considered a form of salvation on earth, and serious, diligent work was worthwhile in itself. Although literal interpretation of the Protestant work ethic was tempered over time, the idea that work was inherently worthwhile (yet would be rewarded materially) continued to be a strong influence in our culture.

Many of the people who are now old grew up with such a work ethic. At the same time, many of those who are now old were immigrants or born to immigrant parents; they had poor language skills in their new country and started at the bottom of the work hierarchy. Many early immigrants were thankful to have any steady work, and they worked long hours at tedious, often dangerous work in order to survive and provide better opportunities for their children. Both situations contributed to the attitude that one should sacrifice immediate personal desires to hard work, in the hope for a better future.

The general attitude toward work has changed during this century. In his analysis of these changes as they affect American workers Sarason (1977) sees World War II as an important turning point for work expectations. That war involved many men and women in career changes, and after the war the G.I. Bill made university-level education available to many who would not otherwise have gone to or beyond high school. The values of the better educated have become accepted on a wide scale: autonomy, authenticity ("being your real self"), having new experiences, and expecting personal growth.

Work has not changed fast enough to keep up with the rapid and wide-scale changes in worker attitudes, aspirations, and values. A general increase in their educational and economic status has placed many American workers in a position where having an interesting job is now as important as having a job which pays well [Work in America, 1973, p. xvi].

The extent to which opportunities for personal growth are valued affects the ways individuals select work, allocate time and energy to work and other activities, and view retirement from employment. We will explore these issues as we consider how involvements in work shift over the course of adulthood.

WORK INVOLVEMENTS THROUGHOUT ADULTHOOD

Individuals make a series of occupational and occupationally related choices at different points in life, and there are a number of theories that attempt to explain them. (Joseph Zaccaria [1970] has presented a useful summary of these theories, and we will draw heavily on his work.)

Sociological perspectives have stressed *occupational inheritance,* which may work in one of two ways. One may learn an occupation more or less directly from one's parent; for instance, a cabinetmaker's son being "apprenticed" to his father. Or one's socioeconomic status may limit occupational choices (Caplow, 1954; Gross, 1964). Sociologists also point out the ways chance and uncontrollable fluctuations in the labor market influence occupational decisions. For example, because of the low birth rate over the past decade, there are fewer positions in education; many teachers are leaving the field, and many people who would have selected teaching are making other choices. During times of war, many jobs become available in defense industries.

Psychologists, on the other hand, have emphasized personality characteristics. *Trait* theorists assume that each occupation requires a fairly unique set of characteristics; the individual matches his or her set of psychological traits with those required in the job in order to get the best possible fit.

Donald Super (1957) proposed the most useful theory for exploring vocational development beyond the initial choice of work. According to Super, each individual develops and implements a self-concept in the world of work; the "vocational self-concept" is part of a global self-concept. Both global and vocational self-concepts guide the individual into and through his or her career experience. Super drew together the work of previous researchers to propose a series of stages through which the individual passes in developing a career. These stages are summarized in Table 11-6.

Table 11-6   Stages of Vocational Development in Super's (1957) Theory

1. *Growth Stage* (birth to 14 years):	A period of general physical and mental growth.
a. Prevocational substage (to 3):	No interest or concern with vocations.
b. Fantasy substage (4–10):	Fantasy is basis for vocational thinking.
c. Interest substage (11–12):	Vocational thought is based on individual's likes and dislikes.
d. Capacity substage (13–14):	Ability becomes the basis for vocational thought.
2. *Exploration Stage* (15 to 24 years):	General exploration of work.
a. Tentative substage (15–17):	Needs, interests, capacities, values, and opportunities become bases for tentative occupational decisions.
b. Transition substage (18–21):	Reality increasingly becomes a basis for vocational thought and action.
c. Trial substage (22–24):	First trial job is entered after the individual has made an initial vocational commitment.
3. *Establishment Stage* (25 to 44 years):	The individual seeks to enter a permanent occupation.
a. Trial (25–30):	A period of some occupational change due to unsatisfactory choices.
b. Stabilization (31–44):	A period of stable work in a given occupational field.
4. *Maintenance Stage* (45 to 65 years):	Continuation in one's chosen occupation.
5. *Decline Stage* (65 years to death):	
a. Deceleration (65–70):	Period of declining vocational activity.
b. Retirement (71 on)	A cessation of vocational activity.

Cited in Zaccaria, J. *Theories of Occupational Choice and Vocational Development.* New Hampshire: Time Share Corporation, 1970, pp. 51–52. Reprinted by permission.

Within this general framework Super has tried to analyze different *career patterns,* which describe the types, sequences, and duration of various work and work-related activities. For example, research on actual career patterns has identified four male and seven female career patterns:

Male Career Patterns

1   *Stable career pattern:* School is followed by a stable job for the remainder of the individual's working life.

2   *Conventional career pattern:* School is followed by one or more trial jobs and then stable employment.

3   *Unstable career pattern:* School is followed by alternating sequence of trial and stable jobs, with no permanent job or occupation.

4   *Multiple trial career patterns:* School is followed by a series of trial jobs without any kind of work sufficiently prolonged or dominant to establish a career.

Female Career Patterns

1   *Stable homemaking career pattern:* School is followed by marriage, with no significant work experience outside the home.

2   *Conventional career pattern:* School is followed by relatively brief work experience before marriage.

3   *Stable working career pattern:* School is followed by a stable job for the remainder of work life.

4   *Double-track career pattern:* School is followed by work; after marriage both homemaking and outside work careers are followed.

5   *Interrupted career pattern:* School is followed by some work experience. Withdrawal from labor force during heavy involvements in marriage and child rearing is followed by return to employment.

6   *Unstable career pattern:* School is followed by any sequence of work, marriage, work, child rearing, work, and so on, usually resulting from economic pressure; no stable work or homemaking experience.

7   *Multiple trial career pattern:* School is followed by a series of unrelated trial jobs resulting in no genuine vocation.*

Super's theory is probably the broadest and most widely accepted of the contemporary theories of vocational development. It has evolved slowly, revised after research and reanalysis. Like most theories of vocational development, it seems more adequate to explain the work behavior of men than of women.

*Adapted from Zaccaria, 1970, p. 53. Reprinted by permission.

MEN AND WORK

Early Socialization for Work

The capacities and sense of self that enable an individual to work consistently, productively, and "happily" develop from childhood. Erik Erikson identified some of the early psychological components of this capacity in his theory of ego development (see Chapter 7): achieving a sense that one can reasonably take the initiative, and gaining a sense that one is industrious, capable of mastering whatever general skills are required to survive in one's particular culture. These capacities underlie the more systematic review of where to direct one's talents and energies that accompanies the adolescent process of identity formation.

In addition, the social skills of getting along with peers, superiors, and inferiors are learned largely before one enters the job market. Boys learn these important skills through the games they play. They learn to compete by rules, not to take defeat too personally, to respond to the directions of a team captain, and to work their way up to a leadership position by demonstrating competence in whatever is valued by the others.

Boys learn very early that men are known by their work outside the home, and they typically receive a great deal of encouragement for visualizing their future in terms of work ambitions. Vocational achievement is considered a core element of masculinity; those men who manage to rise (or remain) high in occupational status and/or salary feel more "potent," and those who do not often feel threatened in their masculinity.

Vocational Development

Sex typing of work choice starts very young (Barnett & Baruch, 1978). Boys list a wide range of occupational possibilities even at an early age. As they grow from childhood through adolescence, their occupational aspirations change from romantic, highly visible jobs (cowboy, detective); to visible blue-collar jobs (policeman, fireman, garage mechanic); to less visible, higher-status jobs (manager, engineer, lawyer). Aspirations during high school tend to be unrealistically high; not all will become professionals, and many will not finish or even attend college.

A greater proportion of male high school graduates than female graduates do continue on to college, and more male college students than female complete college and continue into further professional training. In fact, one study found that college senior men who had C+ averages believed they were perfectly capable of earning Ph.D.s, whereas women with B+ averages did not believe they could do so (Baird, 1973). A year later, women who had A grades were no more likely to be attending graduate or professional schools than were men with B grades (Barnett & Baruch, 1978). These realities reflect, in part, the cumulative impact of rearing men to prepare themselves seriously for work achievements outside the home.

Blue-collar Workers   Blue-collar workers enter the labor market relatively early. The exploration stage of Super's theory of vocational development may be quite short for them. Young men who find academic work difficult or school life intolerable, or who must work to support themselves and often other family members, may not have much opportunity to assess their interests in relation to the job market. They take the employment that is available, though often with the dream or hope that they can work their way toward a better job. The "better" job may be defined in terms of safety, pay, stable hours, desirable shifts, or having less boring and tedious work or shorter travel time.

The mid-life reassessment identified by some psychologists may come in the mid-30s for blue-collar working men. They have been in the work force for long enough by then to realize that many of their ambitions and dreams will probably not be realized. A classic study by Eli Chinoy (1955) of automobile factory workers demonstrated the ways men dealt with their disappointments at work. As younger men, they talked and fantasized about leaving the factory and opening up their own gas stations; few did so, and some who tried failed and returned to the factory. Gradually, the men lowered their aspirations so that a "better job" was simply one off the assembly line. Such workers now seem to be expressing their disenchantment and boredom through absenteeism and excessive use of drugs and alcohol (*Work in America,* 1973).

Blue-collar workers are more likely to experience disruptions in working than those in higher-level jobs. They are apt to find themselves laid off, fired, unable to find work, or expected to work fewer or longer hours than usual if necessary. Though unions provide some measure of job security and protection, not all workers are unionized, and not all unions are effective. Disruptions in work experiences—the unstable career patterns identified in Super's theory— have consequences for the individual and for his family. Men who cannot work and provide economically for their families are considered, by themselves and by others, as having failed in an essential challenge of adulthood.

White-collar Workers   Compared with blue-collar workers, men working in white-collar jobs are less likely to experience the disruptions of seasonal lay- offs, strikes, and such. They also have greater possibilities for career mobility. The possibilities for advancement are regarded as challenging and exciting to young men of talent and ambition, but they may be frightening to those who are uncertain about their competence or their commitment to the work.

The process of selecting the "right" career may require considerable trial and error of the kind identified in Super's model. A man may try several jobs in his 20s, some at the same time as he is completing his education. If he is ambi- tious, he will try to find a position where not only is the work reasonably inter- esting but the prospects for advancement are good.

Many white-collar jobs are in business, which demands a kind of loyalty from employees unusual in most blue-collar jobs. Regardless of the job, the worker is expected to appear ambitious, to be productive for the company, to work whatever hours are necessary to exceed his competitors, and to be able and willing to travel as needed for the job.

Mid-life career reassessment seems to be very common among white-collar workers, coming usually during the 40s. The reevaluation of "the dream," to use Levinson's (1977) term, involves the realization that the hopes and aspirations of young manhood are not likely to be accomplished. Even if the man achieves considerable occupational success, it may not bring the desired sense of security. Many men are bored with their work by this time of life and wish to redirect their energies. Often the desired new directions are away from a highly competitive, productive orientation to a more nurturing, humanistic, or comfortable position.

On the other hand, many men feel at their most competent and productive during their middle years (Neugarten, 1968). They feel a great sense of mastery, autonomy, and efficiency in their work. Some are able to become genuinely generative in their working relationships, appreciating the competitive energy of young men and helping them develop their emerging careers. Men who can move into managerial or supervisory jobs where this type of generativity is important may have an easier time with their working experiences in the second half of life.

Professionals   Men in the professions have the longest preparation period for their work and also the longest working life. Career selection may begin very early—for instance, a boy deciding in childhood to become a physician or an engineer. Serious planning must be part of the man's college-level education, in order for him to qualify for competitive specialized professional training. Professional training is directed at developing the skills required to practice without direct supervision, setting and maintaining standards with professional peers. It also means revising the sense of self as a professional identity, and a strong commitment to the values and goals of the profession must become central in his life. The loyalty of a professional is presumed to be to the profession and to his colleagues in that profession, not to the particular job or a particular employer.

These expectations may present conflicts to the individual if he feels that the standards of professional practice must be compromised because the employer refuses to pay for high-quality service. Such conflicts are one of the work risks for many professionals who work in settings where they do not really control the kind of services they can provide. Psychologists may be expected to provide competent career counseling on the basis of one half-hour interview, physicians may be unable to get welfare payments for early-intervention health care, and engineers may be instructed to use a grade of concrete in a highway they know will crack in two years.

Reassessment of career goals is likely to occur later for professional men than for white-collar or blue-collar men. Working experiences during the second half of life depend partly on the field. Some of the old, established professions, such as law, may provide relatively good opportunities for men to shift into a more generative, "statesman" role. However, this is possible only in fields where age, maturity, and experience contribute to increased competence and wisdom in the field and where such perspective is acknowledged and valued by younger workers. Career fields that acknowledge the competitive, productive energy of younger men as the only standard of excellence are likely to be less satisfactory for older men; sales and marketing are such jobs in business.

Working experiences also reflect personality. Some men are very comfortable shifting into different styles of professional competence; others are threatened by their own inclinations toward nurturance and by the competitive challenges from younger men and—even more—women.

Retiring from Employment

Retirement is a *process* that involves withdrawing from a job and taking on the social role of a retired person (Atchley, 1977). Definitions of who is retired vary, but we will accept the one used by Robert Atchley in his research on retirement. (We will draw heavily on his discussions of this process.)

An individual is retired if he or she is employed at a paying job less than full-time, year-round (whatever that may mean in a particular job) and if his or her income comes at least in part from a retirement pension earned through prior years of employment. Both of these conditions must be met for an individual to be retired. (p. 139)

The process of retirement begins whenever the individual starts thinking about life without employment; this is done less seriously during the early middle years than during later middle age. Generally, most people anticipate retirement with pleasure, and most retired people express positive attitudes about retirement. As Table 11-7 indicates, the majority of individuals (61 percent) retire by choice. The data in this table are from a national survey of persons 65 and over interviewed in 1974, 63 percent of whom were retired at the time

Table 11–7 Retirement by Sex, Income, Race, and Education (percentage of persons over 65 who said they retired by choice or were forced to retire)

Total	% Retired by choice	% Forced to retire	% Not sure
	61	37	2
Men	58	41	1
Women	66	32	2
Under $3000	53	46	1
$3000–$6999	62	36	2
$7000–$14,999	68	30	2
$15,000 and over	65	35	—
White	63	36	1
Black	43	50	7
Some high school or less	58	41	1
High school graduate, some college	67	30	3
College graduate	70	30	—

Reprinted from *The Myth and Reality of Aging in America*, a study prepared by Louis Harris and Associates, Inc., for The National Council on the Aging, Inc., Washington, D.C., © 1975, p. 87. Used by permission.

(Harris & Associates, 1975). Fifty percent of black men and women, 46 percent of retired people with incomes under $3000, and 41 percent of retired men said they were forced to retire.

Money   Attitudes toward retirement seem to reflect several factors. The most crucial factor is money. The higher an individual's expected retirement income, the more favorable are the attitudes toward retirement. Those with adequate retirement incomes (at least half their preretirement income) are more likely to favor early retirement. Men at lower occupational levels favor retirement but dread poverty. Men at higher occupational levels generally have favorable attitudes toward retirement, but they also are more likely to regard their jobs as interesting and to retire later (Atchley, 1980b).

Preparation for Retirement   The decision to retire, or when to retire, is influenced not only by one's expectations of the retirement period. The kinds of planning and preparations for retirement are also important. Such preparations may include launching adult children, remodeling an old home or moving to a smaller or more convenient one, building a savings account to a certain level, and so on. Less often, people think about retirement in terms of the psychological adjustments that may be required.

The hiring and retirement policies of employers are also important when assessing retirement. Relatively few people are any longer forced to retire by a mandatory retirement age. Some employers allow a worker to retire on full pension after a specified length of employment (20 or 30 years); others penalize workers for early retirement. Many people "retire" because they cannot find employment. Older workers who quit, are fired, or are displaced often find it impossible to find regular paid work. Unemployment figures do not reflect the number of older people who would prefer employment but who have given up and phased into retirement.

Norms and Attitudes   The informal norms of the work situation influence norms about retirement. For example, older workers in a Norwegian manufacturing company were asked if they would like the option of changing to a less physically demanding job. Most said they would rather retire than change to a "soft" job—if they couldn't do the work required, they should leave. In addition, there was a shared belief that jobs should be made available to young men who were getting established and supporting growing families.

The attitudes of family and friends are also important in the retirement decision. The first person to retire in a circle of friends may feel rather awkward about his new status and feel left out of daily routines built around work. Conversely, the last person in the group to retire may be impatient to do so and eager to join the new round of activities available to retired people.

Health   Finally, health is often a very important factor in deciding about retirement. Poor health is a common reason for seeking early retirement. Contrary to popular misconceptions, there is no evidence that health deteriorates after retirement; in fact, unskilled workers showed a slight improvement in health (Streib & Schneider, 1971). They are able to remain active without the strain of employment.

Phases of Retirement   On the basis of his research with retiring and retired persons Atchley has described a series of phases in the retirement process (1977). Near retirement the individual begins to separate from the job and have more fantasies about what retirement will be like. Immediately following the retirement transition there is a "honeymoon" period, in which people often try to do all the things they have fantasized and left undone before. However, a good honeymoon requires a positive outlook and money.

Many people settle into their desired routine quite smoothly, especially if their lives off the job were satisfying and full before retirement. Others become disenchanted and realize that they can't tolerate, afford, or actualize their fantasies but must restructure life on more realistic terms. After a period of reorientation, most develop ways of living within the retirement role. They are self-sufficient and have a stable life, often very full and rewarding. This is particularly true of people who have friends and varied organizational activities.

Termination of the retirement role occurs with death or when illness or

During the "honeymoon" period of retirement, people often try to do everything they have fantasized about and left undone before. Most people then settle into their desired routines smoothly.

disability makes health the primary factor in organizing the individual's reality. The "sick and disabled" role is distinct from the "retired" role.

Adjustment   Retirement inevitably brings changes. Nearly all people experience a drop in income, and most accept a reduced standard of living as a predictable part of the life cycle. Few people move; only 2 percent move across state lines, for instance. Those who do move are likely to be widowed, disabled, well-educated, or living in households not their own (Atchley, 1977).

Family interaction patterns also may change. Some research indicates that, among working-class couples where men have not been very involved in the household throughout adulthood, an increased involvement after retirement is seen as undesirable by both spouses. Middle-class wives seem more willing to welcome greater involvements in shared household affairs (Kerchkoff, 1966). Family interaction is affected, of course, by prior patterns and expectations. Greater role sharing during the middle years may make the retirement transition smoother for both men and women.

Retirement itself does not necessarily produce problems in social or emotional adjustment. Poor health, low social activity, and unsatisfactory living arrangements are, indeed, associated with poorer mental health, but the relationships do not seem necessarily tied to retirement. In a national longitudinal study of over 4000 men and women in a variety of jobs (Streib & Schneider, 1971) 70 percent said they "never" had felt useless during retirement. Twelve percent of the sample said they felt useless before retirement and 27 percent of the sample said they felt useless afterward. Those who feel useless may be a source of concern to themselves and to others, but there is little evidence of general decreased self-esteem after retirement (Cottrell & Atchley, 1969).

Most men, then, adjust to retirement quite well. Several studies indicate that about one-third have substantial difficulty in making that adjustment (Cottrell & Atchley, 1969; Harris & Associates, 1975; Streib & Schneider, 1971). A national survey of older persons sponsored by the National Council on the Aging (Harris & Associates, 1975) found that adjustment problems were related primarily to income inadequacy (40 percent). Some 22 percent miss their jobs and some individuals are too inflexible to change. The death of a spouse, ill health, or other changes that make it impossible to carry through retirement plans are also sources of adjustment problems.

Good adjustment in retirement is enhanced by sufficient income, good health, the ability to give up the job gracefully and turn to other interests, and having few changes in other aspects of life to deal with at the same time (Atchley, 1980).

Research on the ways retirement experiences may differ for men and women is still scarce. Most of the basic work on retirement has been done with men on the assumption that work was a primary role for men but only a secondary concern for women. We will look at retirement issues for women after we discuss women's involvement in work throughout adulthood.

Men work from sun 'til sun;
Women's work is never done.
                    (Folk saying)

Women's experiences of working have traditionally been shaped primarily by their potential to be mothers. This is true from early childhood, and it remains true even for many women who never rear children. This biological fact is reflected in different socialization for boys and girls, different opportunities, and different experiences in working. Some of these distinctions are undoubtedly harmful and unnecessary; other differences seem understandable and reasonable consequences of society's concern for the continuation of life (Brown, 1970).

Early Socialization

Girls primarily learn skills and attitudes that help them establish and maintain a family. Interpersonal skills and an accommodative style are useful in becoming competent as a wife, mother, and homemaker, which, until very recently, were the jobs girls were expected to be preparing for. Girls have been socialized to view themselves as part of a future partnership, with the husband working outside the home and providing economic support for the family and the wife running the household and providing child care and emotional support. A wife might work outside the home when it was economically necessary and when it did not disrupt her primary responsibilities to the family. Given such an emphasis, girls grew up with the idea that a successful woman married a good provider; for a woman to have to support herself or her family was a sign of failure.

Until the women's movement of the past 10–15 years employment possibilities outside the home were not a serious concern for most girls, and job choices during childhood and adolescence were largely limited to a few "helping" or accommodative fields (Fogarty et al., 1971). Regardless of social class or race, one-third to one-half of school-age girls aspired to be teachers, nurses, or secretaries, and they did not alter their aspirations significantly later. The scope of women's aspirations is changing as commercials, toys, children's books, and real life change to present women working in varied occupations. However, nearly all the women who are now adults grew up in a social system where career achievement for women was uncommon and where women who place primary emphasis on career development were unusual. Young adult women have had more exposure as teens to media stories about women employed in many occupations; many of these women expect to combine employment and parenting.

Black parents seem less likely to distinguish between sons and daughters in encouraging their children to work achievements (Turner & Turner, 1971). Black women are reared to expect to provide economic support as well as be responsible for homemaking.

Vocational Development

Women's work experiences fall into a variety of patterns. As we saw, Super identified seven, based on when the women were employed. The likelihood of a woman's entering the labor force depends in part on her marital status and age, and the ages of her children, if she has any. Table 11-8 makes it clear that at all ages single women are most likely to be employed; divorced, widowed, or separated women the next most likely; and married women living with their husbands the least likely to be employed. There has been a substantial increase in labor-force participation rates of married women from 1960 to 1978.

Table 11-8   Female Labor-Force Participation Rates[1] by Marital Status and Age, 1960 to 1978

Age/marital status	1960 %	1970 %	1978 %
20–24 years			
Married, spouse present	31.7	47.9	60.4
Single	77.2	73.0	75.3
Other[2]	58.0	60.3	69.9
25–44 years			
Married, spouse present	33.1	42.7	56.5
Single	83.2	80.5	80.7
Other[2]	67.2	67.2	74.9
45–64 years			
Married, spouse present	36.0	44.0	45.4
Single	79.8	73.0	65.8
Other[2]	60.0	61.9	59.6
65 and over			
Married, spouse present	6.7	7.3	7.1
Single	24.3	19.7	14.1
Other[2]	11.4	10.0	8.5

[1] Percentage of the civilian labor force who are employed part-time or full-time or counted as unemployed
[2] Other = widowed, divorced, and married (spouse absent)
Source: Adapted from U.S. Bureau of the Census, *Statistical Abstract of the United States: 1979* (100th edition). Washington, D.C., 1979, p. 399.

Table 11-9 shows that marital status and age of children also affect women's employment patterns. Women whose children are aged 6 to 17 are more likely than mothers of younger children to be in the labor force. Divorced women are the most likely to be employed and to be working full-time regardless of the age of their children. Married women living with their husbands are least likely to be in the labor force and most likely to be employed part-time if they are in the labor force. The table makes it clear, however, that many women are combining full-time employment with child rearing; as we shall see, that is a combination associated with both high stresses and distinctive satisfactions.

Table 11–9   Employment Status of Women by Marital Status and Age of Children, 1978

Marital status/age of children	% in labor force[1]	% employed full-time[2]
Married, husband present		
No children under 18 years old	44.7	76.9
Children 6–17 years old only	57.2	67.3
Children under 6 years old	41.6	65.7
Separated		
No children under 18 years old	54.7	83.9
Children 6–17 years old only	61.8	82.6
Children under 6 years old	54.9	78.6
Divorced		
No children under 18 years old	71.2	87.5
Children 6–17 years old only	81.4	89.5
Children under 6 years old	67.0	85.5

[1] Women 16 years old and over who were employed part-time or full-time or counted as unemployed
[2] Of the women in the labor force those who are employed 35 hours a week or more
Source: Adapted from U.S. Bureau of the Census, *Statistical Abstract of the United States: 1979* (100th edition). Washington, D.C., 1979, p. 400.

For many women being counted as unemployed means having only one job: homemaker. Since work in the home is not officially counted as work, only women who are paid for their labor are in the work force according to official labor and economic calculations. Women who work in the home and are also employed outside are essentially pursuing two career lines, with two separate sets of expectations, rewards, and time pressures.

The Job of Housewife   A *housewife* is a woman responsible for running her home, whether she is married or not and whether she performs the tasks herself or hires other to do them (Lopata, 1971a). The work typically is divided into two parts: housekeeping and mothering (if she has children). In earlier times housekeeping was time consuming, economically valuable, and honorable work. For many, complex reasons these aspects of the work have been devalued, especially in the middle class, and more emphasis is now placed on the work involved in mothering. Such devaluation of housekeeping means that women do not get a sense of pride and self-esteem from performing the work competently, and if women do not have children or when the demands of mothering phase out, the housewife role may seem indefensible.

Helena Lopata (1971a) studied urban and suburban housewives in the late 1950s; these women are now older and mothers of emerging groups of housewives. Their experiences as housewives help us understand this most common work of women.

The housewife job has certain distinctive characteristics compared to other

jobs. There are no clearly defined, widely understood standards for performance in the job. This means that there is great freedom and flexibility in the
way the work can be carried out, but it is also more difficult to get a sense of
satisfaction from having done a good job. The work is never finished, and much
of it shows only if it is not done. The work is done at home, so there is none of
the usual separation of working life and home life. And, although the work is
valued, there is no pay. Housewives without other occupations are not economically self-sufficient, and their ability to continue their work depends on the
willingness of someone else to provide economic support. Housewives, of course,
contribute labor and services for the husband and the children, but they receive
no direct acknowledgment of their contributions in being able to claim a portion of the husband's salary for their services. Nor can housewives claim any
public retirement benefits (such as Social Security) for the contributions they
make by rearing children, nursing family members, or providing support services for employed family members. The power and self-esteem issues involved
in such situations are complex.

Lopata found great variations in the ways women approached the occupation of housewife. As girls and teens, most did not have a vocational orientation
toward their future role as housewife; that is, they did not think about getting
the kinds of training useful for performing the work or selecting a husband on
the basis of the kind of work setting he could help them establish. Entrance
into the housewife role is usually through another, more romantic role: wife.
Wives are neither selected for their competence as homemakers nor trained
systematically for it.

Most of the women Lopata interviewed assumed they would become and
remain full-time housewives. Some women, like those Lopata interviewed in the
1950s and 1960s, became dismayed—and outraged—to find they had been
"fired" from their job because of divorce, desertion, or widowhood. They cannot
continue in their work without financial support, and they are often unprepared for employment. In recent years many special programs have been established to help such "displaced homemakers" enter paid employment.

Lopata described several sequential periods in the housewife role. The first,
becoming a housewife, often involves alterations in other areas of life as well;
some of these were discussed in Chapter 10. Many women continue outside
employment or school during this phase, and work within the household is apt
to be shared between husband and wife more equally than at any other period.

The greatest changes occur during the *expanding circle* phase, which lasts
from the birth of the first child to the addition of the last child. In the case of
divorced and recombined families this process can be very complex. Women
report many pleasures in their work during this phase: making important decisions affecting their lives and others, not having to meet a clock or calendar in
the same way as in an office or factory, rewarding interpersonal relations, an
increasing sense of competence in role-related duties, and anticipating the future with their children (Goodman, 1979; Howe, 1977; Lopata, 1971a).

Some women consider the increased sense of responsibility one of the frustrations of their work. The lack of the time controls of an outside job also bothers some, especially those who lack the initiative or managerial skills to organize their own time and energy effectively. Women are likely to feel—and be—overworked during this period and have little or no time for self-expression. More educated and career-oriented wives talk about the need to justify their work as mothers and housewives, to others and to themselves. Some also fear that the enforced economic dependency strains the marriage partnership they had established before this phase (Goodman, 1979). They are in conflict because they want to be with their small children and they enjoy many of the pleasures in homemaking; however, they also want to be regarded as an equal partner, an interesting person, and a socially esteemed individual. The devaluation of homemaking as worthy work contributes to the sense of conflict felt by many women during this phase.

The *full-house plateau* is that period when no new family members are added but before children move away completely. Many women experience this as the peak of the housewife career, as they function competently in a complex system. If they have several children, women may continue this period right into grandmothering and other family-oriented activities; this was a common pattern for many women in the past but is less common now among better-educated or divorced women. During this phase women are likely to return to paid employment or for further education, moves that are incompatible with the previous phase.

The last phase, the *shrinking circle,* involves an automatic drop in social status connected with the work. Child launching and widowhood are part of this phase. Full-time housewives with no other work history who find they must work or wish to work may find opportunities in the labor market restricted. Women who wait until this phase to seek employment have often discovered they could not find jobs; they were considered too old, or not worth the investment, for training. They have also encountered age bias in hiring even for jobs requiring no training. They may be considered too near retirement age, and companies are reluctant to take on someone who may not work long enough to justify retirement benefits. In the past women worked as volunteers in a wide variety of jobs. More recently volunteer work has also been devalued, thus limiting the self-esteem available from such activity. In addition, women who need to be economically self-sufficient cannot volunteer their work and still survive.

Lopata was impressed with the diversity of ways women managed their responsibilities as housewives and mothers. Some, primarily uneducated, lower-class women, are very restricted in their roles; they often feel inadequate in the work and place most emphasis on the physical demands of the job. At the other end of a continuum are educated women with higher family incomes, who extend homemaking into the community through their volunteer work and who are very involved in helping the husband in his career advancement.

Women are often very involved in helping ensure their husband's work success, and they may gain a vicarious, shared achievement in his work. Some jobs are really a "two-person career" where the husband's success depends in part upon the wife's ability and willingness to perform certain tasks (Papaneck, 1973). For example, wives of ministers, diplomats, and business executives have traditionally been expected to perform unpaid work as part of their husband's job. The husband has the official job and the official status; his wife has "reflected glory." This works well as long as the husband acknowledges her contributions, she is pleased to have this shared job, and she does not feel the need to establish a separate domain of work achievement.

Even when women do not have specific duties associated with their husband's work (such as entertaining, organizing charity work, and so forth), many women provide the support services that enable the husband to function most effectively in his work. A wife has been expected to organize and run the household, mother the children, arrange social life, relate to the extended family, and, of course, provide comfort and companionship for her husband when his work schedule allows him to be around and when work pressures make him need such comfort most. All activities of the household are arranged around the time schedules of the husband's work, allowing him to give full attention to his work and still have a functioning family life.

The Shifting Balance   Many women are now resisting such expectations and are pursuing their own employment or achievements. Even if they are not employed, some housewives feel that they should have time off for activities that could provide an independent source of esteem and pleasure. Such time is most available if the husband can assume greater responsibility in running the household. Many husbands are resentful when they feel their wives are withdrawing support of their work. As one man emphatically said:

From my point of view, what I see has happened with all this stuff about women's equality is that I've gotten the shaft. A decade or two ago, a man like me who was filling his side of the bargain would have gotten some service in return. He would have had a wife who took care of him, who bolstered his ego, who was proud of him, who appreciated the fact that he worked to support her and the kids at a job that didn't really thrill him. Now . . . I'm supposed to feel guilty for keeping her at home and unfulfilled. Not only am I supporting her, but I personally am not supposed to ask for a thing in return [Goodman, 1979, p. 131].

Housewives are often ambivalent about moving into the outside work force. Most regard employment as an imposition and a burden during the expansion phase of homemaking. This is usually a period when men are most involved in establishing themselves in work and are not happy to share household work. As the work at home lessens and women mature, many look toward developing another career.

Psychiatrist Roger Gould (1978) has identified some of the conflicts expressed by women wishing to develop careers outside the home in mid-life. As women talked about their motivations for employment, it became clear to Gould that, in part, they were disillusioned with the man's caretaking ability. Many women enter marriage with a strong sense that it is impossible to live without a protector. They feel that, if they select a husband with some care, he will, in fact, protect them and provide for them, and they will thus find fulfillment, happiness, and security. This does not always happen (some argue that it almost never happens). In any event, women who think about entering the job market may be confronting their own competitive urges and desires for power and status that they have denied for a long time. As we saw in Chapter 7, these are the issues that Gutmann and others have identified as fairly normal mid-life conflicts. For some women, returning to school or to the work force after working as a full-time housewife includes these psychological considerations.

Recent changes in what is considered normal and desirable competitiveness and independence for women may be making these less problematic issues at mid-life. However, there is certainly evidence that many women who are moving from the home into the competitive labor force find it very difficult to deal with their feelings of disappointment, rage, fear, hope, and pride that may be involved in the transition.

Women Employed   What happens to women working outside the home? The experiences are varied, and they are quite different for career-oriented business and professional women and other employed women.

Most employed women work in jobs where most of the other workers are also women (see Table 11-4). The pay is usually low, unionization is absent or weak, and equal-pay-for-equal-work laws have little meaning because women usually compete only with other women (Howe, 1977). Women employed in traditionally male jobs receive much attention, but they are not typical; they have special problems in being one of few women in the job and may be subject to distinct harassment on the job. However, they may also derive special satisfaction from being distinctive.

Seven out of eight women in the labor force today do not have college degrees (Howe, 1977). This fact largely restricts them to jobs that have limited possibilities for advancement and do not require continued involvement and commitment. One can drop in and out of such jobs (for example, store clerk or nurse's aide) relatively easily.

Most women are reared not to value career advancement as much as making a balanced life between family and employment. However, employment provides rewards not found in the family, such as independence, accomplishment, and friendship. A recent study found that working wives found their paid employment more satisfactory than their housework; full-time housewives were more bored with their work than employed women were with theirs (Newberry, 1979). Among older women, retired workers have higher morale than women who have never been employed (Jaslow, 1976).

Employment over adulthood varies with "push" factors and "pull" factors.

Economic need is the most compelling push to work, particularly for women who are not married. Personal desires for independence and social status also motivate women. Women can be pulled into the labor force by offers of good pay for work near home with flexible hours. Many women would prefer part-time employment that would allow them to do both home work and outside work well. Unfortunately, such work is most likely to be available only for the highest-level professionals or in lower-paid jobs with little or no job security or fringe benefits.

Careerists: Business and Professional Women We know more about the challenges facing women pursuing higher-status occupations than we know about women in pink-collar (similar in status to men's blue-collar jobs) and white-collar jobs. Women in high-status occupations are unusual: They are usually working in a man's world. Many of their experiences are shaped by the pressures that come with trying to "think like a man, act like a lady, and work like a dog."

Developing a professional career demands commitments to that work being central in one's life. Particularly in the younger years, one is expected to be willing to put in long hours of serious work in order to compete effectively and to master the required skills. The expectations about how fast and how far one should rise are based on what has been true for most men: A wife will take care of the "personal" side of life, while the husband tends to the career building. When a woman enters such a career, she lacks this important ingredient for success—most husbands will not play a comparable role; career women are more likely than other women to be unmarried; and many women feel uncomfortable living with a man who would, in fact, provide the services of a "good wife."

The strain imposed by trying to develop and maintain what are essentially two careers—inside and outside the home—is substantial. We are developing a new mythology of the "superwoman": she deftly cuddles her baby, keeps the romance alive in her marriage, whips up a gourmet dinner for eight, and manages an expanding investment portfolio on her way to becoming a bank executive. This image is perhaps unfortunate for it denies the tremendous efforts required to manage home or professional career developments in the early years of adulthood. In spite of the successes it is clear that there are no easy answers for combining professional and personal life in ways that make them both satisfying.

The women who aspire to demanding careers and survive the screening processes to function in these positions are a select group. Girls seem to "specifically and intentionally avoid high-prestige occupations" (Barnett & Baruch, 1978, p. 133). Among those women who enter high-status occupations very few reach the top. Fogarty, Rapoport, and Rapoport (1971) analyzed data on career women in Eastern European socialist countries and in Western democratic societies. They concluded that women were not kept out of top positions because of lack of ability, reluctance to enter nontraditional fields, or lack of commitment to work. Rather, the major reason so few women reach the top in any country is work overload: They are unable to manage both home and career demands. Support services such as child care and shopping are expensive and inadequate.

In addition, patriarchal ideas about the family persist, although less strongly than in the past. A survey of a representative nationwide sample of 3000 women and 1000 men 18 years and older interviewed in late 1979 revealed some shifts in opinions from earlier polls (Roper Organization, 1980). In 1970, 40 percent of women and 44 percent of men favored most of the efforts to strengthen and change the status of women in society; by 1980, 64 percent of both men and women approved such changes. Endorsement of change is most evident among younger, single or divorced, college-educated, and black women—73 to 77 percent of these groups endorse the changes. The increase in approval of change is most marked among older, less well-educated women; for example, of women 50 years and over, 35 percent in 1970 and 55 percent in 1980 favored changes in the status of women.

By 1980, women tended to admire the same qualities in men and women: intelligence, sensitivity, a sense of humor, and gentleness. Men, in contrast, differentiate sharply the qualities admired in each sex. Men value gentleness and sensitivity in women but not in men.

Marriage is the favored way to live. In 1974, 50 percent of the women and 48 percent of men said they personally would prefer a traditional marriage with husband as provider and wife as housewife-mother. By 1980, 42 percent of men and women endorsed this option; 52 percent of women and 49 percent of men said they preferred a marriage where both husband and wife work and share homemaking and child-raising responsibilities. Preference for either type of marriage is related to age, with younger women preferring more equalitarian relationships and older women preferring traditional arrangements.

In 1980, 46 percent of the women interviewed preferred to have a job outside the home rather than stay home and take care of a house and family, an increase from 35 percent in 1974. However, despite the emphasis that women give to jobs, 77 percent of women and 68 percent of men said a woman should quit her job and relocate with her husband if he were offered a very good job in another city. Since the question specified that the couple had no children, these responses reflect the endorsement of the traditional view of the importance of the male breadwinner. Only 10 percent of the women and 18 percent of the men said the husband should turn down the job offer and stay where they were so the wife could continue with her job. And only 4 percent of men and women favored living apart and seeing each other whenever they could.

Despite increasing numbers of women pursuing careers, employers so far have not developed recruitment, training, and promotion practices adapted to the typical life cycle of married women. Until they do so, women are essentially forced to choose between a total emphasis on career development and maintaining a less intense career involvement combined with home and family.

Increasingly, men are confronting similar choices between heavy career involvement and balancing career and family. More men may be choosing to increase family involvement and place less emphasis on career striving. As we saw earlier, such a choice may result from a man's mid-life reassessment, although many younger men are now also making such choices.

Overall, ambitious, educated women probably have more support, career success, and self-esteem in a *dual-career marriage,* where both partners are committed to developing careers outside the home, than they would have in a more traditional marriage; men probably experience less support and career success than they would in a more traditional arrangement. However, there is little adequate research to assess the long-term consequences of such arrangements. There are special strains in these relationships, particularly during the child-rearing years (Rapoport & Rapoport, 1976). For instance, career progress may be blocked if one partner cannot travel or move when requested by the employer or to take advantage of better opportunities. The decision not to become parents may ease career pressures, but of course it has other consequences for each partner. Couples who can survive the period when careers and parenting are being established are in an excellent position to enjoy the rest of their adult years together. They are likely to be closer together at mid-life than most traditional couples and closer to their children.

Women who become successful in careers outside the home are much studied (Barnett & Baruch, 1978; Bernard, 1964; Hennig & Jardim, 1977; Mednick, Tangri, & Hoffman, 1975). Their adult career behavior reflects the combined influences of values, future aspirations, sex-role ideology, present life situation, and early socialization (Friedman, 1975). Career-successful women are likely to have one or more of the following characteristics in their background: being foreign born, having immigrant parents, coming from an affluent family, having one or both parents with high occupational and/or educational status, being the eldest or only child, having no brothers (Barnett & Baruch, 1978). Parents seemed to offer them warm encouragement to meet high standards for achievement and to set high goals. In addition, within the family and, often, in education they seem to have been less exposed to restricting sex-role stereotyping.

Among 1500 women achievers in *Who's Who,* significantly more attended all-women's colleges than coeducational colleges. Coeducational colleges typically have a great majority of male faculty and a majority of male students. Women achievers were more likely to come from coeducational colleges with a high proportion of female faculty members and a relatively low proportion of men as faculty and as students in the college environment than from colleges with few women faculty or students (Tidball, 1973). This suggests that women have more chances to develop vocationally in settings where women are not in the minority. In part, this reflects opportunity: If there are no men around, women will move into leadership positions with less ambivalence. It also reflects the presence of women as peers and role models for achievement and career-oriented behavior.

Male Responses to Women Achievers

There are many anecdotes and considerable evidence suggesting that men simply cannot tolerate women competing with them at work—and it is even less tolerable if the women succeed. The reluctance, or inability, of men to accept women as able and entitled to compete successfully with men is one explanation offered for the segregation of jobs by sex and the fact that few women succeed in "male" jobs.

However, many men are at least ambivalent about women's achievements, and some men seem very comfortable with them. One of the most interesting analyses of how men respond to a woman who achieves success in a traditionally male career was done by Judith Bakshy (1977). As part of a larger study on factors related to the career aspirations of women (Huyck, 1975) Bakshy used responses from 199 men, aged 18–45; most were white, urban, Christian, middle-class, and single. Bakshy was especially interested in how the men handled achievement and affiliation issues: Did they see the women as able to both work and love, or did they think one aspect would be dominant? Respondents were asked to write a story to the cue: "After the first-term finals, Anne finds herself at the top of her medical school class." They were also asked to write stories to other cues that did not have such a clear career achievement theme. (The cues were those used originally by Matina Horner [1972] when she found evidence of ambivalence, or motivation to avoid success, among college women and men.) The respondents in Bakshy's study also responded to objective measures of sex-role ideology, demographic, and socialization experiences. The responses to story cues reflected four kinds of themes, which correlated well with the objective measure of sex-role ideology.

The *accepting* group (17 percent of the sample) told stories where Anne successfully integrated both work and love. They saw her as successfully practicing as a physician and also as enjoying boyfriends, dating, married, feminine, kind, and/or warm. Most mentioned some conflicts for Anne but saw her as able to resolve them. The men in this group had the most liberal beliefs about sex roles, came from higher socioeconomic status families, were younger, and said they resembled both parents intellectually. They seemed to be the most role-flexible men and (based on other analysis of the study data) were the most secure in ego and gender identity.

The *instrumental* group (20 percent of the sample) wrote stories in which the woman's desire for and success in work was accepted, but there was no reference to love. These men did not mention the sex of the person when describing her behavior. Only task-related behaviors were included as relevant. These men were of similar social class to the accepting group, but, unlike the accepting group, they tended to identify intellectually with the father rather than with both parents.

The *stereotypical* group (35 percent of the sample) wrote stories in which Anne's achievements were devalued, rejected, or denied. They portrayed great conflict between love and work. These men had the most traditional sex-role ideology, emphasizing sexual division of labor. They came from lower socioeconomic status families, were in later stages of their own life cycle (that is, were already married and fathers), and identified with fathers whom they perceived as very critical. Bakshy deduced that these men seemed to have relatively immature ego identities, with self-esteem linked to maintaining a masculine stance and not accepting females into masculine worlds.

The *instrumental-stereotypical* group (12 percent of the sample) wrote stories acknowledging and accepting woman's work achievement only in the Anne story, where it was most clearly stated; the other stories resembled those of the stereotypical group. That is, only outstanding and obvious achievement by a woman was acknowledged; otherwise, she was seen in very traditionally female ways. These men were similar to the stereotypical group in social class, but they were younger and more confident about their academic achievements. These patterns again suggest that confidence about their own achievement, as well as age and life-cycle stage, influence men's reactions.

Men in the *hostile* group (16 percent of the sample) told stories with very negative comments about women in all areas. Anne was portrayed as a source of grave unhappiness to herself and to others because of her academic success. Themes of overt and covert retaliation against her were developed. These men resembled the accepting men in social class and relative confidence about their achievements. They differed largely by identifying intellectually with the mother rather than with both parents. Moreover, they were more likely to experience both parents as critical. The results suggested that these men lacked a clear sense of gender identity themselves; their confusion over their own masculinity may have made it impossible for them to deal reasonably with women.

The implications of Bakshy's research are that some men are able to accept and enjoy women's independent career achievements without feeling them as a threat to their own self-esteem and identity, but this capacity is not common. Such acceptance seems to depend on a man's developing a secure sense of his own identity first. Bakshy suggests that those concerned with career equality between men and women may have to help boys and men establish and maintain a strong and flexible sense of self. Further research is needed to evaluate other components of these various responses and to assess how the attitudes revealed in these kinds of tests are translated into actual behavior at work and at home.

Retiring from Employment

Relatively little is known about how women respond to the process of retirement. It used to be assumed that, since women were not very involved in work, retirement would be easy: They simply returned home where they "belonged." However, recent research makes it clear that some women experience considerable difficulty withdrawing from employment. A national study of older workers found that women with higher incomes, better education, and higher-status occupations wanted and continued work longer than women in less advantaged jobs (Streib & Schneider, 1971). Women who began working after child rearing may be at the peak of their careers when their spouses retire or they are expected to retire. Single women may be very attached to their employment, and even married women may shift many of their social relationships into work when they become employed; women do express more concern over social relationships after retirement than men do (Fox, 1977).

Women are likely to experience the same phases of retirement that men do. The practical issues raised during retirement are similar for both sexes. However, some things are distinctive: Women are far more likely than men to face a long period of retirement because they live longer, to face retirement alone because they are widowed, and to be poor because they have little or no pension. One issue for both men and women throughout adulthood is how to achieve a personally satisfying balance in the arenas of work and leisure.

RELAXATION AND LEISURE

The rhythm of working is established partly by periods of nonwork. The study of how people spend time, why they spend it in the ways they do, and how they feel about it over adulthood is a relatively recent interest. One concern is how best to distribute working, loving, and playing over the life course.

Leisure activity is often described as that which is done voluntarily, without any particular outside pressure (Kaplan, 1961); where the rewards and gratifications are intrinsic to the activity itself. Actually, there is little agreement in our society about what specific activities should be considered as *leisure* or *relaxation,* for two main reasons. First, and most important, the same activity can have various meanings. One may garden as a productive enterprise, to use the vegetables; as a relaxing change from work routines; or as a shared family activity. Secondly, for many people "work" and "play" are mingled and not neatly separated. For instance, some scholars enjoy reading and writing more than they enjoy anything else. Havighurst (1972) pointed out that many leisure activities have potentially the same meanings for individuals as jobs. Leisure pursuits can provide a sense of individual worth, social participation, status and prestige, new experiences, opportunities to be of service, and ways to make the time pass.

Theories of Leisure Behavior

People generally develop their lives in three areas—work, family, and leisure. Although we can think about these spheres as distinct, individuals combine them to form whole-life patterns. What happens in one sphere definitely influences the others. Thus our discussion of leisure over adulthood will necessarily relate back to our earlier discussions of family and work involvements.

Rhona Rapoport and Robert Rapoport (1975) used intensive studies of whole-life patterns to develop a model of how leisure changes over adult life. The model combines psychodynamic and sociocultural perspectives on human behavior. They remind us that observable lifestyle patterns reflect underlying motivations; it is necessary to understand these motivations in order to understand people's life requirements.

At the most fundamental level of motivation are *preoccupations,* defined by the Rapoports as "mental absorptions," less and more conscious; these are the underlying needs that serve to direct behavior toward some activities and not others. Preoccupations may be translated into *interests.* "Interests arise in people's awareness as ideas and feelings about what they want or would like to have or do, about which they are curious, to which they are drawn, through which they feel they might derive satisfaction" (p. 23). Any given interest may be channeled into various *activities,* such as driving, dancing, participating in or watching sports, visiting, and so on.

Thus any particular activity has different meanings for different people in

A sense of excitement and stimulation my be expressed in different ways for different people.

terms of the interests pursued. And a given preoccupation (for example, a sense of excitement and stimulation) may be expressed in different ways for different people.

The lifestyles—including leisure—of individuals have underlying patterns. There are some variations in preoccupations and interests by sex, social class, and education. However, the Rapoports suggest that leisure is well understood in terms of the *family life cycle,* which includes sex and age variables and also changing role and value orientations. They suggest that preoccupations change as the individual matures. Patterns of leisure interests and activities can be understood in terms of these regularly changing major preoccupations.

Leisure Involvements over Adulthood

On the basis of their own and others' research Rapoport and Rapoport (1975) identified central preoccupations and interests from adolescence to old age. The Rapoports' research involved intensive qualitative studies of families in England, but it is equally appropriate for the United States (see Gordon, Gaitz, & Scott, 1976). Their model is summarized in Table 11-10.

Adolescence In the Rapoport and Rapoport model, adolescence is a period characterized by varied preoccupations. Gordon et al. would describe the preoccupations for this period listed in Table 11-10 as attempting to balance intimacy and autonomy. Adolescents need opportunities for excitement and new activities. Some need to be shown how to have these within acceptable social and personal limits, and some need to be helped to enjoy appropriate leisure involvements.

Young Adulthood In young adulthood interests narrow and reflect a major preoccupation with how to identify with social institutions (such as the family and job). Expression of these core concerns affects all life areas. Heavy involvement in career development, for example, may close off leisure and family spheres, or intense interest in developing a family may cut off work and leisure. The Rapoports see one major challenge of this period as keeping alive other interests during courtship and early marriage. Failure to do so seems to have consequences for the individual and for the couple relationship at later periods. In addition, a particular group "at risk" are those who are involuntarily unemployed; leisure activities can provide some of the compensations for a job, but such individuals may withdraw from leisure as well as work.

The Establishment Period The establishment phase (roughly 25–55) in the Rapoports' model is divided into subperiods on the basis of stage in family rearing; such a model will be less relevant for those without children. The focal preoccupations move from productivity to performance, and finally to evaluation of commitments made during the period.

The Rapoports found that the ways preoccupations were expressed during the early part of this period depended very much on the type of family involved. In conventional families, where the husband was employed and the wife a homemaker, interests and activities reflected this split. Men were interested

Table 11–10   Preoccupations and Interests in Life Phases*

Phase	Preoccupations	Interests
Later adolescence	Autonomy Stimulation-boredom Work Sociability Physical maturation Mental development Environmental experiences Moral sensitivity Balance	Variety "Doing one's own thing" Rapidly changing activities and situations Brightness and noise Work prospects Body: sex play, fashion Acquiring knowledge Exploring, feeling, seeing life Religions, politics, etc. Novelty
Young adulthood	Identification with social institutions	Occupational development Developing more permanent heterosexual relationships Successful reintegration of relationships with family Friendships

Early establishment (preschool-age children)	Productivity: choices and plans	Depends on family type:
		Conventional families
		    Husband—work-centered interests
		    Wife—home-centered interests
		New-conventional families
		    Husband—work-centered interests
		    Wife—home-centered, but returns to work mid-establishment
		Dual-worker families
		    Wife—keeping up with dual work roles

Mid-establishment (children in school)	Performance: effectiveness; competence at what is chosen	Family-centered activities Sensory gratifications: sexual, taste sensations Competitive events enjoyed vicariously Do-it-yourself projects
Late establishment (children out of school)	Evaluation: meaningfulness of commitments (psychological "payoff")	
Preretirement	Anticipation of occupational retirement	Forging a sense of integration in life Finding new meanings in life
Retirement	Realignment of commitments	
Old age (75+)	Life before death	

*Note: There is no one-to-one relationship between preoccupations and interests. Expression of interests may be facilitated through specific activities.

Derived from Rhona Rapoport and Robert Rapoport, *Leisure and the Family Life Cycle.* Boston: Routledge and Kegan Paul Ltd., 1975. Reprinted by permission.

primarily in activities that contributed to their work or provided relief from work pressures; women had a variety of home-centered interests and activities. The new-conventional families were those where the wife withdrew from the labor force for a period of child rearing but intended to resume employment; her "leisure" often involved activities that helped maintain this interest (such as reading, going to school, visiting with friends from work). In families where both partners were employed the time demands of work and family were typically so substantial that little leisure time was available. In fact, Rapoport and Rapoport suggested that "free time" does not exist for most people in the establishment life stage. (The Rapoports identified two special challenges for professionals involved in planning leisure. Nonworking mothers tend to be bored but are often scared of developing leisure interests that could relieve their work tensions. And dual-employment families need ways of *sharing* leisure together.)

During the later establishment period, concerns focus on evaluating what one has done. Leisure pursuits can bring warm responses from others, provide structure at a period when there is more free time, and help stave off personal despair if other areas of life are not going particularly well (Gordon et al., 1977).

Later Years   In later years preoccupations are with achieving social and personal integration and a sense of personal meaning and harmony. Older retired people in four large Western communities reported they had between 18 and 26 hours of free time per week (Peterson, 1973). Many of the older people indicated they were not using their free time wisely and would like to develop new leisure activities. Twenty-seven percent said they would like to return to school, 21 percent said they would like to participate in exercise classes, 20 percent wanted to be with others, 13 percent wanted to travel, and 4 percent said they would like to do volunteer work. The respondents indicated they were not involved in such activities at the time because of lack of opportunity, poor health, or financial limitation. Other researchers have also found that involvement in leisure activities reflects education, income, and health (Gordon et al., 1976; Rapoport & Rapoport, 1975; Schmitz-Scherzer, 1976; Videbeck & Knox, 1965). Individuals who are advantaged in these areas are also more likely to show high rates of leisure activity, to take advantage of whatever opportunities exist, or to create the opportunities desired. This implies, of course, that, as people move into old age with higher levels of education, better health, and adequate incomes, they will be more involved in leisure activities than are current cohorts of older people.

Age Changes in Leisure

Information about age differences in leisure activities in the United States is available from two major studies. The National Council on the Aging included questions on leisure activities in their national survey of adults 18 and over in 1974 (Harris & Associates, 1975). Gordon, Gaitz, and Scott (1976) used a structured interview with 1441 persons aged 20–94 living in Houston, Texas, in 1969–1970. Their respondents answered questions about present involvement in 17 categories of leisure activities. The questions asked are comparable in the two studies but are more detailed in the Houston study.

Data from the Houston Study of Leisure and Mental Health (Gordon et al., 1976) show that, overall, leisure activity declines regularly with age. The total group of 1441 respondents was divided into two groups: Those above the mean (average) leisure activity score were termed high, and those below the mean were low. Eighty percent of the 20–29 year olds and 24 percent of those over 75 scored high in leisure activity.

Not all the leisure activities show the same relationship to age. Data from the NCOA/Harris study are summarized in Table 11-11, showing the percentage in different age groups who said they spend "a lot of time" in various activities. In both the NCOA and the Houston study, older people were less likely than younger people to participate in sports or physical exercise or read; in the Houston sample the older adults were less likely than younger adults to go out dancing and drinking, use guns for hunting or target shooting, or be involved with cultural productions. Older people were more likely than younger ones to engage in solitary activities (especially sitting and doing nothing) and gardening; in the Houston study leisure cooking increased among older men and decreased in frequency among older women. In the NCOA study television viewing was more common for older than younger respondents; there were no

Table 11-11 Involvement in Activities by Age (percentages of people who said they personally spent "a lot of time" doing various activities)

	% 18–64	% 65 and over	Net difference
Socializing with friends	55	47	− 8
Caring for younger or older members of the family	53	27	−26
Working part-time or full-time	51	10	−41
Reading	38	36	− 2
Sitting and thinking	37	31	− 6
Gardening or raising plants	34	39	+ 5
Participating in recreational activities and hobbies	34	26	− 8
Watching television	23	36	+13
Going for walks	22	25	+ 3
Participating in sports, such as golf, tennis, or swimming	22	3	−19
Sleeping	15	16	+ 1
Participating in fraternal or community organizations or clubs	13	17	+ 4
Just doing nothing	9	15	+ 6
Doing volunteer work	8	8	—
Participating in political activities	5	6	+ 1

Reprinted from *The Myth and Reality of Aging in America,* a study prepared by Louis Harris and Associates, Inc., for The National Council on the Aging, Inc., Washington, D.C., © 1975, p. 57. Used by permission.

age differences for this activity in the Houston study. In the Houston study there were minimal age differences in participation in conversation, spectator sports, attending cultural events, entertaining, participating in clubs and organizations, and home embellishment.

Overall, older people are markedly more likely than younger people to engage in solitary relaxations such as thinking, daydreaming, planning, or doing nothing. However, older people are also likely to socialize with friends, garden, or watch television (see Table 11-11).

It is not clear just how satisfied people are with the leisure component of their lives at various stages. In one study of 502 people aged 46–71, 80 to 90 percent said they were either satisfied with the amount of free time they had or wished they had more (Pfeiffer & Davis, 1971); of course, these people are in the young-old stage, when they are most likely to have the health to appreciate their leisure.

Atchley (1977) claims that retirement does not present a crisis of "excess leisure" for most people; they accept the leisure as a legitimate, earned right and devise ways of using their leisure time that reflect their interests. The Houston study data, on the other hand, indicate reduced pleasure with leisure among older groups. Their measure of "pleasure" included self-rated importance and enjoyment as well as frequency of participation. They found four patterns over the course of adulthood. (1) Less pleasure in older groups was reported for dancing, drinking, movies, sports participation, outdoor activities, travel, cultural consumption, and reading; (2) pleasure was greatest in middle age for spectator sports, discussion of important issues, organizational participation, and home embellishments; (3) pleasures were comparable across age groups for visiting with friends, cooking, and watching television; (4) and the pleasures derived from relaxation and solitude increased over the life span.

THE CHALLENGE: BALANCING THE WHOLE LIFE

Love, work, and leisure are the three major aspects of a whole life. People construct varying lifestyles placing more and less emphasis on these components. For most of us it is a continuing challenge to keep some sense of balance among them. The balance at one time is likely to change as we grow older.

The challenge of forging and maintaining the kind of lifestyle we need and want is partly an individual matter. Each person makes critical choices about what activities will express interests and preoccupations, and the choices made shape his or her life. However, finding ways to facilitate personal development is also a social challenge. We have seen, for example, how the structure of work can restrict the options for developing family and leisure components of life and how heavy involvements in family responsibilities can limit activities in work and leisure.

For some time we have had experts who try to find ways to help people with the love/family and work areas of their lives. Now there is an evolving occupational field dealing with leisure over the life span. Leisure specialists evaluate the needs for leisure and study how best to provide opportunities to develop the leisure component of life.

We have reviewed a great many concepts we think are valuable in understanding how humans develop throughout adulthood. And we have tried to summarize some of the patterns of change and stability in different aspects of adult functioning. In the next section of the book we turn to more specific applications of what we have learned thus far. We will consider how adults adapt to change and maintain mental health, and what happens when their efforts to adapt fail and result in psychopathology. Intervention involves maintaining or restoring functioning, and we will review some of the ways used to facilitate adult development. These perspectives will help us analyze one of the important, inevitable changes: loss through death. Death is a part of life, and we will see how people deal with the dying of loved ones and how individuals confront their own demise. Finally, we will look ahead to our own future and think about the kinds of personal and social actions we wish to take in order to ensure living a whole life to the end.

SUMMARY

1 Work is an activity which produces something of value for other people. Relaxation and leisure activities are more personal and discretionary: the activity is undertaken for personal pleasure rather than social value and may include a sense of playfulness that is often missing in work.

2 Work is closely tied to feelings of identity, worth, and self-esteem. The strength of needs for achievement varies between individuals and within individuals at different points in time. Many women derive less sense of self-esteem and competence than do men from the same kinds of achievement because women are more likely to attribute their own success to luck or ease of the task; successful men credit their own superior abilities.

3 Job satisfaction is related to autonomy, participation, challenge, security, pay, mobility, comfort, and opportunity to interact with co-workers. Unhappiness with work is associated with work conditions more than with age, sex, social class, or race.

4 The social stratification system in America is based largely on the kind of work one does. There are at least four strata of paid workers: marginal, blue-collar, white-collar, and upper-level managers and professionals. Success in work is related to family background, intelligence, formal education, personality traits, and luck.

5 Most work is sex-typed. Within each stratum, men's work generally receives more status and higher pay than women's work. Most women retain the unpaid job of homemaker throughout life; the work demands of that job vary with stage in the family cycle. Because of the structure of the work force and the division of labor within households, men and women have quite different experiences with work over adulthood.

6   Cohort differences in work experiences are also evident. The availability of work and the flexibility in working conditions are related to the deficit or surplus of workers in the labor force at a particular time. Changes in educational level and level of affluence are reflected in the qualities desired in work. Better-educated and more economically secure workers value an interesting job as much as a well-paying one. Many jobs have not changed enough to meet revised expectations, and job dissatisfaction and alienation is one outcome.

7   Donald Super has proposed a series of stages in vocational development, from childhood through retirement. Within that framework Super identified four male career patterns: stable, conventional, unstable, and multiple; and seven female career patterns: stable homemaking, conventional, stable working, double-track, interrupted, unstable, and multiple. The greater diversity of female patterns reflects the ways women integrate work and child rearing.

8   Most males aged 20 to 64 are employed full-time. Employment rates for older men have decreased steadily during this century; in 1978 one-fifth of men over 65 were employed part-time or full-time. Boys are socialized from early childhood to know that they should be able to support themselves and a family and that the work they do will influence their lifestyle. Work experiences differ by social class, personality, and work setting.

9   Women's experiences of working have traditionally been shaped primarily by their potential to be mothers and the likelihood that they will work as unpaid mothers and homemakers. At all ages women are less likely than men to be employed and more likely than men to be employed part-time if they are in the labor force. Single women are more likely than married women to be employed. The percentage of women employed has increased since 1960, particularly among married women. Divorced mothers with small children are more likely to be employed than are mothers living with spouses. Work experiences are also affected by social class, early socialization for work, and personality variables.

10   Retirement is a process that involves withdrawing from employment and taking up the social role of a retired person. Most retired people express positive attitudes about retirement; the exceptions are those who would rather be employed. Financial security is the most important factor in favoring or enjoying retirement. Retirement itself does not necessarily produce problems in social or emotional adjustment. Women are more likely than men to face a long period of retirement, to be unmarried during retirement, and to be poor.

11   Many leisure activities have potentially similar meanings to work. Leisure patterns change as individuals develop and proceed through various phases of the family life cycle. Focal preoccupations of each adult phase have been identified by researchers. Overall, leisure activity declines regularly with age. Older people are more likely than younger ones to engage in solitary activities, and pleasures derived from relaxation and solitude increase over the life span.

PART THREE

APPLICATIONS

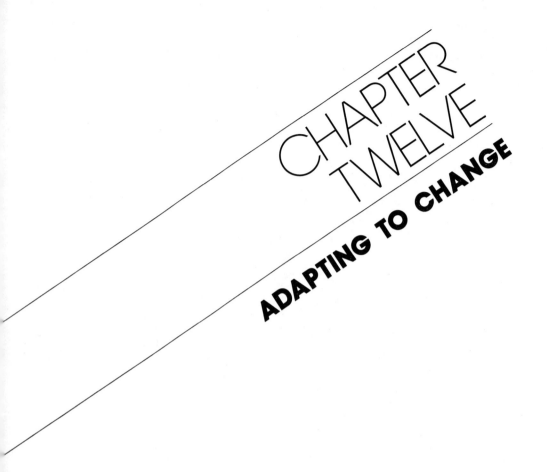

CHAPTER TWELVE

ADAPTING TO CHANGE

Adaptation is the ability to meet biological, social, and psychological needs under changing circumstances without substantial pain to the self or to others. Adaptation is usually required when individuals or circumstances change so that former ways of meeting needs are no longer effective. The point at which one realizes that the usual ways are no longer adequate and new, revised strategies are still emerging is a transition period. Changes initiate transitions.

In this chapter we will review research on how adults experience and respond to change. Our emphasis is on understanding the process of adaptation and the factors that influence the process. We believe the processes are similar throughout adulthood, even though the content of the changes varies. We have used examples from all phases of adulthood, but our analysis is not organized chronologically. Many of the more troubling changes are not causally tied to age. Rather, age becomes one of the variables influencing adaptation—for example, age affects the younger and older women who experience mastectomy and widowhood differently. In discussing the nature of changes in adulthood, we will use Pearlin's (1975) division of changes into two general kinds: normative and nonnormative.

DEFINING AND ASSESSING
ADAPTATION TO CHANGE

The Nature of Changes in Adulthood

Normative Changes   Many changes during adulthood are normal and expectable because they are bound to usual life-cycle changes and the role transitions that accompany them. Some of these *normative* changes have been discussed in earlier chapters: becoming parents, having children leave home, and retiring from full-time employment. In this chapter we will consider adaptation to another normative change, menopause.

The transitions associated with normative life events are not usually experienced as very stressful (Pearlin & Lieberman, 1979). This is probably because such changes are anticipated and "rehearsed" considerably before the actual change occurs. Moreover, other people have experienced similar transitions and can provide models, explicit advice, and support during the transition. However, a minority of adults find normative life transitions highly stressful. It is important to understand why this is so and what can be done to ease the transition.

Nonnormative Changes   Some changes are unexpected, either because of the nature of the event itself (such as the death of a child or being fired from a job) or because of the timing (such as "early" widowhood). *Nonnormative* events are often very stressful. In the Pearlin and Lieberman (1979) survey of life strains among adults 18–59 the most stressful circumstances included being fired, giving up employment for homemaking, moving into a new job, entry into occupational life, work overload, loss of spouse, and illness and/or death of a child. In this chapter we will discuss mastectomy and widowhood as examples of nonnormative events.

Defining "Successful" Transitions

It is not easy to decide when a transition has been successful and when an individual is not developing revised ways of meeting needs and could use some help. We must decide what *level* of functioning is required for adaptation to be successful. Sometimes mastery and competence are expected following changed circumstances; for example, adapting after a job promotion involves functioning at a higher level than before the promotion. In other circumstances adaptation is good if there is no evidence of breakdown, and the individual manages to function at approximately the same level as before the stress (Lieberman, 1975), as, for example, after the death of one's parent or spouse. Individuals who were not functioning very well before the change are not expected to do any better after the change; they should not, however, do much worse.

Another criterion is the time interval involved. As adaptation is a process, it is sometimes difficult to decide when the transition period ends and adaptation has occurred. Measurements at several times make it easier to evaluate the pattern of change to see when a more stable set of responses emerges.

It is also necessary to decide which behaviors to evaluate. The wide variety of measures that have been used can be grouped into biological, sociopsychological, social adjustment, and emotional functioning; we will describe each type of measure before discussing adaptation to some particular life changes.

Biological Measures of Adaptation   One index of how well an organism responds to stress is the extent to which biological needs are met. One measure is survival: Obviously, those who are still alive following a stressful event have adapted more adequately than those who died. For example, survivors and non-survivors of major surgery, imprisonment in concentration camps, and relocation from one geriatric mental hospital to another have been compared to see what characteristics differentiated the groups.

However, death is an extreme response to stress, and psychologists are usually more interested in the range of well-being among survivors. Physical health status, determined either by physical examination or by self-reported health ratings, can be used as a measure of adaptation.

Sociopsychological Adaptation   Psychologists often want some measure of adequacy in meeting needs without causing pain to self or to others. The phrase *mature, fully functioning individual* used by various personality theorists implies standards of mental health that involve social role performance and emotional functioning. Included are such characteristics as flexibility, self-reliance, creativity, realistic orientation, acceptance of self and others, ability to sustain intimate relationships, and competence in life. (See Maddi, 1976, for a review of such definitions.)

Social Adjustment   Perhaps the most common notions of good functioning concern social behavior. Every social system has norms of appropriate behavior; the well-adjusted individual is, by definition, one who conforms to the generally accepted norms for his or her age, sex, and social group. Those who violate the norms of social behavior extensively are termed deviants, sociopaths, or even criminals. For example, endorsement of attitudes prevalent in the community was one index of adjustment for older adults used by Britton and Britton (1972, summarized in Chapter 8).

The usefulness of social adjustment as a measure of adaptation depends on being able to establish reasonable criteria for rating conformity to social norms. Often someone other than the person being judged—researcher, therapist, or teacher—defines the desirable and expected behavior, and adaptation is assessed in terms of those expectations. However, this approach overlooks the meaning of the social behavior to the individual. In addition, there are often conflicting standards for social behavior within subcultures, particularly in times of social change.

Emotional Functioning   Emotional health may be seen as an indication of adaptation. Individuals who experience many symptoms associated with emotional problems—such as difficulty sleeping, cold hands, trouble concentrating, crying, or thoughts of death—are often seen as less well adapted than those who report few such symptoms. Seeking therapeutic treatment is only a rough index of mental health. Those who are able and willing to use such services may actually be healthier, or simply better informed or nearer to services than those who do not use them.

Probably the most widely used adaptation measures are those assessing the subjective, or personal, sense of well-being called *happiness, life satisfaction,* or *morale.* Changes in morale in response to stress can be evaluated for a particular individual by someone who is familiar with that person's typical behavior (Rosow, 1976). The indicators may be highly personal—for example, the widower who, as he recovers from grief, starts shaving again, puts on a clean shirt, switches from dark, sombre ties to more colorful ones, and begins to greet people when he goes out to shop. Though such clues may be very helpful for understanding an individual, they are not very useful for comparing responses of many different people to stress.

Most large-scale research generally uses self-reports of morale or life satisfaction, assessing them according to various standard measures (Larson, 1978; Knapp, 1976). Some of the measures are very simple, such as the question, "In general, how happy are you these days?" Others assess the balance between positive and negative feelings (Bradburn, 1969); respondents may be asked to answer several questions, such as "I would not change my past life even if I could," "I've gotten pretty much what I expected out of life," "Most of the things I do are boring and monotonous," and "My life could be happier than it is now" (Harris & Associates, 1975, p. 157). Researchers may also rate interviews on several dimensions of life satisfaction (see, for example, Neugarten, Havighurst, & Tobin, 1961).

Examples of Changes Requiring Adaptation

In previous chapters we have discussed how men and women deal with a variety of changes, such as marriage, parenthood, divorce, retirement, and aging. In this chapter examples were selected to illustrate three kinds of changes encountered in adulthood: (1) a totally normal, predictable change—menopause; (2) a common loss of a major personal and social role—widowhood; and (3) a possibly life-threatening illness resulting in loss of a valued body part—mastectomy (breast removal). Two of these changes, menopause and mastectomy, happen to women, but they also affect men. Widowhood happens to both men and women, and, as might be expected, the process of adaptation is affected by sex as well as by age.

Responses to each of these potentially stressful changes show both common themes and individual differences. We will see clearly how responses to the stressful circumstances change over time; it is even possible that adaptation proceeds in fairly regular sequences. The importance of various mediating factors may also shift over time.

MENOPAUSE

Menopause is a universal change for middle-aged women. *Menopause* itself is the cessation of the monthly bleeding of menstruation; the broader physiological and psychological changes associated with it are called the *climacteric*. For most women menopause occurs naturally. However, for some menopause is brought on artifically by *hysterectomy*, removal of the uterus and/or ovaries for medical reasons.

Menopause is the subject of much popular mythology as well as scientific research, and attitudes toward it vary greatly. Some regard the period when menstruation ceases as the "pause that depresses"; others emphasize "PMZ"—Post-Menopausal Zest. We will review the research on the climacteric and the personal and situational factors that help explain how women adapt to the changes involved.

Understanding the Changes

Menopause is the end of the recurring physiological cycle that began with *menarche*, the onset of menstruation. Three major physical changes are involved in menopause: (1) The body decreases production of the hormones estrogen and progestin; (2) the monthly bleeding associated with the menstrual cycle ceases; and (3) the ovaries stop producing eggs. These changes mean that the woman can no longer become pregnant and must adjust to the changes that accompany lowered estrogen production.

Estrogen is thought to have important functions in protecting against heart attack, keeping bones from breaking, preventing hair from growing on the face, and keeping vaginal tissues from thinning. Perhaps more important psychologically, estrogen is popularly regarded as the "feminine" hormone, the ingredient that ensures sexiness, youthfulness, and attractiveness. To the extent that women and men believe these myths, menopause is feared as signaling the end of highly valued qualities.

Menopause is a change of the middle years. By age 40 only 1 percent of women have undergone a natural menopause; by age 45—10 percent; by age 48—31 percent; by age 52—76 percent; by age 54—92 percent; by age 56—97 percent; and by age 58 100 percent (Lake, 1979). The age when menopause occurs is not affected by the age menstruation started, marital status, body build, or whether a woman is a mother or not. It does seem to depend on heredity, constitution, and environmental factors (Clay, 1977).

There are many patterns of stopping menstruation. Some women stop suddenly; they have a menstrual period and then have no more. Such a pattern seems to be frequently associated with some major upset such as bereavement, moving, or serious illness (VanKeep & Freebody, 1972). More typically, the menstrual period tapers off in amount and duration of flow, and periods may become irregular, closer or more widely spaced. The process usually takes two to three years.

The climacteric, then, is not a completely standard experience for all women even when we consider only the biological changes.

Menopause occurs when other changes may also be present: Children are getting launched into adulthood, some women will be facing widowhood, work may be reassessed. Some women have small children at home when they undergo menopause, some are grandmothers, and some have no children. Thus even this universal natural change is somewhat different for each woman. And women deal with the change in many different ways.

Outcomes: From Symptoms to Zest

The medical literature identifies a great many symptoms that are presumed to accompany menopause; that is, women undergoing menopause have described these symptoms in addition to stopping menstruation. The Blatt Menopause Index (Kupperman, Wetchler, & Blatt, 1959) is used to assess climacteric women in terms of the following symptoms: vasomotor disturbances (the infamous hot flashes and cold sweats that come on suddenly, last for a few seconds to a minute, and cause mild to severe discomfort), abnormal skin sensations such as itching, sleeplessness, nervousness, melancholia (extreme saddness), dizziness, weakness and fatigue, inflammation of the joints, muscular pain, headache, and palpitations of the heart. Other symptoms sometimes regarded as outcomes of menopause include thinned vaginal walls, weight gain, depression, emotional instability, irritability, restlessness, confusion, inability to concentrate, hypersensitivity, intolerance, and hypochondria (excessive and unreasonable concern with one's health).

All the symptoms listed above have been associated with menopausal women and are sometimes regarded as constituting a "menopausal syndrome." However, this view is incorrect and misleading. It is clear from current research that very few of the symptoms listed above are reliably linked to hormonal changes of the climacteric. In fact, only two emerge repeatedly as hormonally linked: vasomotor disturbances and thinning of vaginal walls with slowed lubrication during sexual arousal. However, the vaginal changes are not well studied, and it is unclear what effect continued sexual activity has on such changes (Clay, 1977). The rest of the symptoms are, therefore, linked to other problems experienced by women during this life period. Women's experience of menopause can be ranged along a continuum. At one end are women who report many of the symptoms in the "menopausal syndrome," and at the other end are women who report few symptoms and renewed energy and enthusiasm for life after menopause. What explains this variation in outcome?

Figure 12-1 Percentage of women suffering symptoms associated with the menopause, by biological/menopausal age. (Data collected by Jaszmann on over 6000 women aged 40–60. Figure adapted from Vidal Clay, *Women: Menopause and Middle Age.* Pittsburgh, Penn.: KNOW, Inc., 1977, p. 65. Used by permission.)

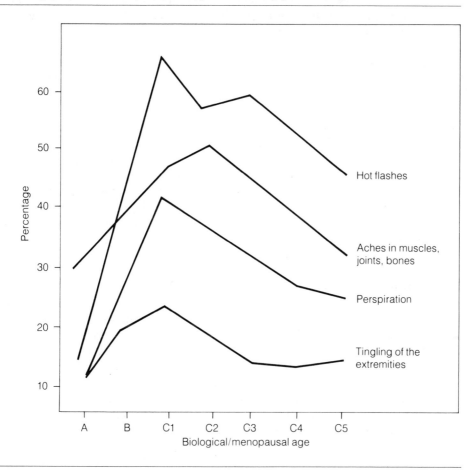

Factors Explaining
Variable Symptom Reports

Biological Age   A study of symptoms and complaints of the climacteric was done with some 6000 women aged 40–60 in the Netherlands. These data (by Jaszmann, summarized in Clay, 1977) provide good clues about the relation of symptoms to stage in menopause. Some of the data are summarized in Figure 12-1. The women were grouped according to menstrual age: those with their normal menstrual patterns (A); those whose cycle had become more irregular but who still had had at least one menstruation in the previous 12 months (B);

and those who were in the postmenopause for one to two (C1), three to four (C2), five to six (C3), seven to ten (C4), and ten or more (C5) years.

These data make clear that hot flashes were the most common complaint—reported by 65 percent of the women in the first year or two after the end of menstruation. Even then, approximately half of the women reported none of the common symptoms.

Previous Problems   Women who report many symptoms during the climacteric may be those who had similar problems before menopause. During the climacteric these problems may be relabeled as "menopausal," but that does not mean they are, in fact, related to the menopause. For example, a study of 110 patients referred for "menopausal symptoms" revealed that 95 percent of these women had similar problems prior to the climacteric (Hallstrøm, 1973). The same researcher did a study of nearly 1000 women in Sweden and found that previous mental illness increased the risk of a recurrent mental illness at the climacteric. Such findings are in line with what we have stressed before: Poor coping ability may show up throughout life, taking different forms at different life stages. During the middle years women who have difficulty coping may be more irritable or depressed, but this does not mean that these symptoms are caused by hormone deficiencies.

Social and Psychological Conditions   Interestingly enough, the "menopausal syndrome" does not appear in all cultures. There are some cultures where women report many symptoms and cultures where few women seem troubled by menopause (Bart, 1967; Hallstrøm, 1973; Maoz, 1973; Maoz, Dowty, Antonovsky, & Wijsenbeck, 1970; Neugarten, Wood, Kraines, & Loomis, 1963). Anthropologists have identified characteristics of cultures where women are likely to report many menopausal symptoms (Holte, 1978). Such cross-cultural perspectives are crucial in evaluating the behaviors we observe in any one particular culture. If there is wide cultural variability in menopausal symptoms, then hormonal shifts alone do not explain the symptoms reported in the American medical and popular literature.

"High-symptom" cultures usually have patriarchal social organization, with social power concentrated in men and few social roles available for older (postmenopausal) women (Bart, 1967). In addition, in cultures where women report many symptoms, older women and women who cannot bear children have low social status. Emotional problems are often regarded as "natural" consequences of being older or infertile (Bart, 1967; Maoz, 1973). Also in such cultures a woman is more tied to her husband than to her parents or siblings and moves away from her family when she marries; the nuclear family is recognized as the primary unit; sex is regarded as an end in itself (rather than primarily in the service of reproduction); the maternal bond is less strong than the paternal; the grandmother role is not regarded as important; the mother-in-law does not train her daughter-in-law; there are minimal menstrual taboos; and youth is valued over age (Bart, 1967). Of course, each culture where women report many menopausal symptoms will not have all these characteristics, but

these are the ways in which high-symptom cultures are distinct from low-symptom cultures.

In *"low-symptom" cultures* older (postclimacteric) women have higher status than younger women, and climacteric complaints are rare or unknown. Women in such cultures maintain strong ties to their parental extended family. Reproduction is important, and a strong mother–child tie is maintained throughout life. The grandmother and mother-in-law roles are valued, with formally recognized responsibilities and privileges. There are extensive restrictions placed on any menstruating woman; the postmenopausal woman is freed from such restrictions. Age is likely to be valued over youth (Bart, 1967).

In many ways contemporary American society has characteristics associated with high-symptom cultures. Although a strong mother–child tie is maintained, there are few formal roles associated with grandmothering or being a mother-in-law. It is unclear to what extent nonfamilial roles may take the place of such traditional roles in the future; some women do move with zest into the labor market, as we saw in Chapter 11. Certainly, sexuality is valued more as an expressive or recreational activity than for reproduction, and a premium is placed on youthful beauty and "sexiness"—Playboy Bunnies and Cosmopolitan cover girls are not postmenopausal.

Personal Circumstances Within a particular culture some women report far more menopausal symptoms than others. Women from industrialized Western cultures who report many complaints during the climacteric are apt to be from a low social class, have low family income, and have little formal education (less than high school) (Hallstrøm, 1973; Jaszmann, Van Lith, & Zaat, 1969). Complaints are more frequent among full-time housewives who have an overinvolved, overprotective relation to their own children (Bart, 1967; Klemsche, 1968; Prill, 1964; Van Keep et al., undated manuscript cited in Holte, 1978). Further, the high-problem women seem to have few contacts outside their own family circle and feel they have few kin they can turn to in time of trouble (Bart, 1967).

Men's Responses to Menopause

Men are influenced by myths about menopause and by experiences with women who are suffering estrogen-deficiency symptoms. Their responses influence the ways women deal with the climacteric. To some extent men's responses to menopause reflect the sense of secrecy and embarrassment that traditionally accompanies menstruation, an experience that men cannot really share. In many cultures menstruating women are believed to be harmful to men. In our culture only recently have sanitary products for menstruation been advertised on television along with toothpaste, deodorants, shaving supplies, and toilet paper. One result of treating menstruation as a taboo topic is that men often feel removed from all processes of menstruation, including menopause.

Some men ascribe too much to the menopause. Some believe that if middle-aged women are irritable, critical, depressed, tired, or moody, the most likely explanation is that they are menopausal. Ascribing all difficulties experienced during the middle years to menopause is a way of implying that (1) the problems are "natural," (2) the problems will have a "natural" end, (3) there is nothing the man is doing to contribute to the problems, and (4) there is nothing he should do to help resolve the problems. Such men may simply not understand the biology of the menopause, or they may feel unable or unwilling to help the woman deal seriously and constructively with her problems. It is easier, in the short run, to ascribe complaints to menopausal instability than to understand why a woman may want changes in her marriage or in her work situation. Such reluctance to confront the realistic and common problems of middle-aged life may make it much more difficult for women to deal with the climacteric period.

Other men do not understand the real nature of menopausal symptoms and do not take any reports of menopausal problems seriously. As we saw, some women experience substantial distress with hot flashes and cold sweats, and they appreciate the sympathetic acceptance of these periods by husbands and co-workers. Women whose estrogen levels have dropped substantially may experience pain during sexual intercourse; if a woman keeps silent about the reason for the pain and instead avoids intercourse, her partner may well feel personally rejected. If a woman explains her discomfort but finds her partner insensitive and reluctant to use additional lubricants or refrain from intercourse, the relationship will suffer. The relationship will also suffer if he is unable to respond to her sexually once the normal postmenopausal body changes become evident.

Some men are upset by the discomforts experienced by their wives or lovers during the climacteric and would like to help them deal with the physiological and psychosocial issues. The relationship will be strengthened if the couple can find ways to involve both partners in deciding how to deal with the discomfort and how to redirect energies and activities in the later years.

Facilitating Adaptation to Menopause

It is obvious that women vary greatly in how they adapt to the changes of the climacteric—and to whatever the physical changes signal in terms of other life changes. In part, the individual's experience is biological, reflected in the timing of the menopause and (possibly) the extent and severity of vasomotor disturbances. Some physicians have recommended a biological "cure" for menopause: taking estrogenic hormones. This has proven to be a very controversial intervention, however; while such administrations reduce some symptoms (such as hot flashes and cold sweats), they increase the risk of other problems (such as cancer) (Clay, 1977; Rosenwaks, 1981). In addition, some women object to treating menopause as a "disease" that must be treated to keep a woman youthful (Boston Women's Health Book Collective, 1976).

Of course, biological treatments do little to deal with those many symptoms of the "menopausal syndrome" that are related to sociocultural, situational, and personality factors. Sometimes menopausal women are advised to "get a job" to cure their sense of anxiety about becoming older. However, if women take mothering and only mothering seriously, then employment outside the home may only serve to emphasize the loss. Many women are ready to focus more on work outside the home; if reasonable opportunities are available, they experience movement into employment as affirming their options, personal power, and optimism (Holte, 1978).

How a woman feels about mothering and about options for the second half of her life reflects her culture, her personal history, her intimate relationships, and her core sense of self. They all interact to influence the ways she adapts to the life change of the menopause.

The Male Climacteric

There is considerable debate about whether men also experience a climacteric (Henker, 1981; Lear, 1974). *Climacteric* is a term derived from a word for ladder, with the connotation of having reached the top with no way to go but down; thus, as one physician noted, it is equally appropriate for either men or women (Henker, 1981). One can argue, however, that the term is equally inappropriate in presenting a vision of the life course peaking at mid-life and running inevitably downhill after that. As we have seen throughout this book, other models stress the distinctive strengths and potentials that emerge at different phases of the life course.

The description of a male climacteric first appeared in the medical literature in the 1930s, at which time it was considered to be a hormone deficiency and testosterone replacement was offered for treatment. Although early reports of testosterone treatment were very positive, later results were not. Systematic measures showed that natural testosterone levels remain fairly constant, with gradual declines, at least through the 80s. Current medical opinion is that, while the very gradual decline in hormone production might contribute to the symptoms described as climacteric among middle-aged men, the decreased hormone production could not be the total cause (Henker, 1981).

According to a physician reviewing the research on male climacteric (Henker, 1981), a man becomes diagnosed as climacteric if he has previously been healthy and productive, is between 45 and 60, and has suffered an onset of disability within a period of days to weeks. Obviously, making this diagnosis is considerably more difficult than evaluating the cessation of menstruation. Symptoms of male climacteric fall into three categories: emotional, physical, and sexual. All are not present in all male patients diagnosed as climacteric, but most symptoms are present to some degree. Symptoms include depression, variable anxiety, and occasional hostility; weakness and fatigue; and partial or total loss of sexual desire and potency.

Henker points out that the data on incidence of male climacteric are not exact; men in that age group probably fall on a continuum from those who experience few symptoms to those who are grossly impaired. Henker estimates that "about 5 percent of the middle-aged male population manifest some degree of troublesome climacteric symptoms, with less than 1 percent becoming severely disabled. The incidence would be higher if it were not for our cultural belief that men must be strong and not complain, other than about life-threatening disturbances" (1981, p. 307).

According to Henker, one of the following incidents often triggers the disabling processes of the climacteric: (1) death, severe illness, or menopause of the wife, because the loss of security produces feelings of weakness and vulnerability in the husband; (2) business reversals; (3) retirement, when it represents an end to usefulness; (4) children leaving home, when the father feels less needed and older; (5) serious illness; or (6) death of parents, because it means he is the eldest generation.

Treatments of male climacteric symptoms are similar to those advocated for women. Hormone replacement is recommended for men with abnormally low levels of testosterone (as such replacement is recommended for younger men with such a condition). However, since sex hormone treatments do not relieve anxiety or depression, very cautious use of mood-altering medications or, preferably, psychotherapy are recommended. Therapy is directed at helping the individual realistically assess his options, monitor his physical illnesses without becoming preoccupied by them, and reassuring or reeducating him about sexual performance potentials.

Because men experience nothing as marked as the cessation of menstruation, it has been difficult to conceptualize or research the male climacteric. It is not clear what the concept adds to our understanding about middle age. It is, perhaps, another way of describing the fact that men may experience difficulty with some of the normal and unanticipated changes during these years.

WIDOWHOOD

Men and women are widowed at all ages, but the likelihood increases with age. Before age 45 less than 3 percent of men and women are listed with the marital status of widow in the U. S. Census reports; Table 12-1 shows the percentage of men and women over 45 who were widowed in 1978. These figures underestimate the proportion of the population who have experienced widowhood because they do not include individuals who have remarried after being widowed.

Table 12-1 Percentage Widowed, by Sex and Age, 1978

Age	Males	Females
45–54	1.6	7.2
55–64	3.2	18.4
65–74	9.7	41.2
75 and over	23.0	69.3

Source: U.S. Bureau of the Census, *Statistical Abstract of the United States: 1979.* (100th edition.) Washington, D.C., 1979, p. 42.

Older women are more likely than men to live as widows: Among those 75 years and over, 69 percent of the women and 23 percent of the men are widows.

We can look at widowhood as a common, though not usual, event that challenges the individual to readjustments in many areas of life. The processes of mourning are reviewed in Chapter 15; here we will focus on the larger questions of adapting to a major life change.

Understanding the Changes

Widowhood may be stressful for many reasons—the loss of a significant person, a trusted companion, a primary source of economic support, and a socially acceptable sexual partner. The extent to which each of these is felt to be a substantial, or irreplaceable, loss varies between individuals.

Helena Lopata (1979) supervised extensive interviews with 1169 widows in the metropolitan Chicago area in 1970; the results of that study, and others, provide important information about the varied experiences of widowed women. Lopata found that the stressfulness of the event was affected partly by the circumstances surrounding the death. Many widows in Lopata's study had been nursing their husbands during a long terminal illness; the actual death was often regarded as a relief for both spouses. Sudden, violent deaths hit women the hardest, and the widows of suicides had the most traumatic after-effects.

The "event" is defined not only by the nature of the death and the previous marital relationship but by the total context of the survivor's life. Lopata described this context in terms of resources used by the widows to adapt to changed circumstances.

Resources for Widows

Lopata classified resources listed by the Chicago-area widows into three areas: (1) possessions, (2) people, and (3) the self.

Possessions   The most important possessions in widowhood are money and housing. Many widows are poor; Lopata found 40 percent living at or below the poverty level as defined by the U. S. Social Security Administration. Older widowed women, particularly, are likely to have inadequate economic security as most of them were not employed consistently and have no pension. Obviously, poverty limits the potential to maintain good health by proper eating and medical care, and to maintain social contacts.

Lopata found that over half the women in the sample were living in the same housing unit as before the husband's fatal illness or accident, and many found it difficult to maintain the home.

People   Lopata was interested in identifying the various social supports available to and used by widows. Such supports may come from all people and groups with whom one has an established relationship.

The expectations about what other people can and should provide the widow vary greatly from culture to culture. Lopata (1979) has summarized the anthropological evidence about varied options for widows. Some tribes have expected the widow to remain with her late husband's family, sometimes with remarriage to a male relative (usually a brother) of her deceased husband. Or she may remain with her late husband's family and have her son take over as head of the household. Either of these two options provides considerable continuity in her life. At the same time, she may have greater freedom of movement in the society, especially after menopause, when she can no longer be impregnated by the "wrong" man.

Some other cultures expect the widow to return to the home of her family and start again, either hoping to remarry or resuming her previous daughterly role.

Contemporary American society does not provide such special family roles for widows, but many social roles outside the family are open to women. In contrast to more traditional societies, American women are less tied to the male family line. They have more freedom—but also less continuity and structured belonging; widows must typically negotiate their own altered social roles. However, some of the more traditional ethnic communities in America (such as Mexicans, Puerto Ricans, black and white Appalachian migrants to Chicago) provide supports that do not require the widow to seek out new ties on her own.

The most important personal support identified by the Chicago widows was the *husband,* both during the terminal illness and even after his death. The memory of a supportive husband seemed to be a source of continuing strength for many widows. In fact, Lopata constructed a "sanctification scale" to assess the extent to which a widow idealized her dead husband. His idealization seemed to help maintain morale during difficult periods: The survivor gained comfort—and perhaps status—from having been married to such a perfect person. The process of sanctification may also occur with men in memory of a dead wife.

Not all women sanctified their spouses; black women, especially those less well educated, were less likely to sanctify dead husbands than were white women (Lopata, 1979). Some women reviled their dead husband and did not count him as part of their past or current support system.

The next most important supports for widows are *children,* particularly daughters. Most of the Chicago women in Lopata's study were mothers (91.4 percent), and they valued the role of mother and wife above other roles. Typically, the widow was most involved with one adult child, usually a daughter, who provided very important emotional and social supports.

Parents were important resources mostly for the youngest widows. Other *relatives,* such as siblings, nieces, and nephews, were not often mentioned as providing economic, social, emotional, or service supports to the widow.

Friends were important for social contact but did not seem to replace the spouse or a child. Only 22 percent of the Chicago widows had a "close male friendship" since becoming widowed; only 6 percent had remarried. Those who had such relationships were usually relatively young and well educated, had been married before to a well-educated man earning relatively good money, had dependent children, and were employed. Those who remarried were also less likely to sanctify the late husband.

Lopata found that surprisingly few widows emphasized friends as important. At the extreme were the "friendless widows" (one-sixth of the Chicago sample), who claimed to have no friends before or since becoming widowed, and the "casually interactive widows," who identified informal friends but did not regard them as emotionally supportive. The "polite companionship" widows meet socially with their friends and may list them as people they most enjoy being with and who make them feel accepted. However, only the widows with "multifaceted friendships" had confidants who contributed to comfort and positive self-feelings. Generally, the widows agreed that friendships changed after the spouse died; in particular, married couples often "dropped" the widow (but did not drop the widowers) from the social round.

Social contacts are more likely to be maintained if the widow remains in the same neighborhood. As a sensitive observer of older women (Matthews, 1979) points out, the long-term resident has a biography, a reputation in his or her community; the "newcomer" is seen first as *old* and is assumed to be no longer independent. Good friends made after widowhood are usually women—often other widows.

More formal support possibilities were not usually used by the Chicago-area widows. Very few mentioned ministers, psychologists, social workers, or social-service agencies as providing support. Lopata concluded that the skills required to locate and use such services were beyond the experiences of most of the current groups of older widows. Only the better-educated, middle-class, urbanized women recognized that such services might be available and useful.

The Self   By far the most important resource a person has for coping with major change is the self. Lopata found that older widows, more than younger widows, were likely to derive positive feelings about themselves from themselves. Women responded to the changes in widowhood with different feelings about themselves. Many felt more independent and self-reliant after widowhood; surviving the grief work helped release them from the dependency they felt in marriage. Other women experienced little change in themselves after widowhood, either because they had never felt dependent while married or because, even after widowhood, they still lacked a sense of self-sufficiency. Some women lost whatever positive feelings about themselves they had had as wives. The ways personality characteristics help widows maintain or reconstruct a positive sense of self and the world are important areas for further research.

Other Factors Affecting the Impact of Widowhood

Age and Time   Age at widowhood affects what other areas of life may be disrupted and what options exist for restructuring life (Lopata, 1979). For example, young childless widows may slide back into the single life, though they may also have a sense of "unfinished business" with the husband (Blauner, 1966), if they had married expecting to bear children with that man, or had not worked out a satisfactory marital relationship. Such women often find it difficult to become emotionally involved with a new man. The mother (or father) of dependent children is the hardest hit, since widowhood comes off the usual time in the life cycle, and she (or he) must deal with the children's grief as well. Arranging for economic support and child care can be very difficult. During the postparental phase, or later middle age, widowhood is more "normal," statistically speaking, for women; however, chances of remarriage are slim. Unemployed women are likely to become destitute. Older women or men who have no involvements outside the home may become very isolated when widowed.

The experience of widowhood also reflects the time in which one lives. For example, changing attitudes toward sex roles may make it easier for men and women to adjust to widowhood than in earlier times. In a national survey of adults 18 and over in the United States a majority (53 percent) of men and women said they thought women were looked on with more respect as individual human beings in 1980 than they were in 1970; the remaining respondents said women had less (21 percent) or the same (23 percent) respect now as ten years ago (Roper Organization, 1980). Over half the men in the study were willing to help out with areas of housework traditionally assigned to women;

Social life may be difficult for widows because they are no longer included in couple activities. It is especially important for single individuals to find activities that welcome people regardless of marital status.

college-educated men were far more likely to help out in this way than were men with less education. Although only a third of the men said they assumed frequent responsibility for cooking, cleaning, shopping, or laundry, most of the men presumably have the skills to run a household should they need to do so. More young women are preparing for economic independence; in 1980, 83 percent of women said that by the year 2000 almost all women who can will be working. The percentage of women with savings and checking accounts or credit cards in their own name has risen since 1972. Though less than a third of married women have such financial independence, it is likely that even women with joint accounts with husbands may be taking more responsibility for the management of money now than they were previously And, though nearly all the respondents said they preferred to be married, the majority endorsed remaining single for longer and divorce as preferable to a bad marriage.

The attitudes reflected in this survey indicate a shift toward greater acceptance of singleness and less sexually stereotyped behaviors. These shifts in public opinion, if they continue, may make it easier for men and women to adjust to widowhood. On the other hand, attitudes have not changed equally in all segments of the population. Women in lower income groups and lower educational levels resist the idea of a man taking care of the home, and men in these groups are less likely to help out with household chores.

Sex Differences   Is widowhood "worse" for men or for women? This is probably not the most useful way to question sex differences in the experience. We must ask, rather, in what ways men and women are especially vulnerable in widowhood.

The worst effects of widowhood for women seem most related to serious economic problems. Widows are more likely than widowers to have inadequate incomes. Widows with low incomes have lower social participation and greater loneliness than widows with high incomes (Atchley, 1975; Harvey & Bahr, 1974; Lopata, 1971b).

The evidence is mixed concerning social participation of widows and widowers. Widowers are far more likely than widows to remarry, and to remarry more quickly after the death of a spouse. Several studies report that women are more likely than men to be dropped from couple activities after the spouse's death. A widower is usually included and invited to bring a companion or serve as an escort for a woman invited by the hostess, whereas it is more difficult to find a partner for a single woman and less acceptable to have an "extra" woman at social gatherings with both men and women (Lopata, 1973, 1979). Middle-class women whose social lives are more organized around couple activities experience greater disruption with widowhood than women living in a more sex-segregated world (Lopata, 1973). Some studies find that widowers participate more frequently in clubs and organizations and have more friends than widows do; part of the difference may be explained by the fact that older men are more likely than older women to drive (Crandall, 1980) and to have higher incomes, both of which are associated with higher participation in clubs. However, other studies of older people have found that widowed men have less interaction than women with friends and neighbors (Arens, 1979; Kunkel, 1979).

Several studies report that widowed men show more severe symptoms of disorganization than widowed women. Widowers have relatively higher rates of suicide, physical illness, mental illness requiring treatment, alcoholism, and automobile and work-related accidents (Berardo, 1968; Bernard, 1973; Bock & Webber, 1972, 1979), and widowed men report overall lower morale than widowed women (Arens, 1979; Barrett, 1977). These data may indicate greater vulnerability of men living alone. However, they may also reflect the fact that the more socially adept, healthy men have remarried.

Overall, the research suggests that sex interacts with social class and personality to affect patterns of response to widowhood.

Race   The experience of widowhood is also influenced by race. In the United States as a whole more nonwhites than whites are widowed, and widowed earlier; the average age at widowhood is 67 for whites and 58 for non-whites. Black women are educationally disadvantaged and have even less economic security than white widows. Lopata (1979) found that black widows were less likely to recall their dead husbands as providing basic emotional support and less likely to sanctify the dead husband; they were more likely to have current husbands or boyfriends. Moreover, black widows were more likely to gain feelings of independence and self-sufficiency from children and to depend more on siblings, parents, and friends for care during illness. These racial differences reflect broader sociocultural patterns of opportunity and lifestyle and point again to the diversity of experience with a common stressful event.

Outcomes of Widowhood

The process of adapting to a major change such as widowhood can have many different outcomes. Perhaps the most negative outcome is death; some widows and widowers, unable to adapt, lose the "will to live."

Lopata asked the Chicago-area widows whether they had a "new life"; nearly half the older widows reported no change in themselves or in their social life. Of those who reported changes 25 percent said it took them two to eleven months, 20 percent said one year, 23 percent said one to two years, and 16 percent said it took more than two years or that they would "never" develop a new life (Lopata, 1979).

Loneliness and lingering depression seem common. A longitudinal study of life transitions found that being widowed was the only family transition that increased depression over time (Pearlin, 1979). Younger widows reported more loneliness than older ones (Dooghe & Vanderleyden, 1977; Glick, Weiss, & Parkes, 1974; Lopata, 1973). Loneliness among younger wives may come in part from their being so involved in the family system that they have little time and energy to develop supports beyond the husband. Loneliness among older women is linked to being alone, having poor health, and having few or no hobbies

Loneliness and depression are common experiences of widowed men and women. Older women are more likely than men to be widowed and are less likely than men to remarry.

(Dooghe & Vanderleyden, 1977). Interestingly, while loneliness was identified as a major problem by widows in Lopata's (1973) first studies of widowhood, relatively few of the widows in the second major study (Lopata, 1979) described themselves as lonely: 35 percent said they were "never" or "rarely" lonely. Lopata suggested that such women may have been used to greater isolation, or they may have had sufficient and satisfactory social relations.

Being alone is not the same as being lonely. As Helen Hayes described her change from the hectic life of a married actress to one of a retired widow, "Solitude—doing things alone—is the most blessed thing in the world. The mind relaxes and thoughts begin to flow and I think I am beginning to find myself a little bit" (Koval, 1973).

On the other hand, Lopata suggested that some women deny feelings of loneliness. The women who claimed not to be lonely also claimed never to have been angry at anyone, either before the husband's fatal illness or accident or afterward. Such women may be out of touch with their more negative feelings. Such denial may be adaptive if it maintains morale.

Most people do adapt to widowhood. They can keep their morale high and restructure their lives to accommodate changed realities. Poverty, lack of education, and inflexible personal responses limit the likelihood of successful adaptation.

Lopata listed four common problems described by the Chicago-area widows. First, the widows felt they did not have enough opportunity to grieve. They needed to talk about the dead and about their grief, but, because such talk tends to make others uncomfortable, the widows felt they could not be open about their grief. They did not want to be burdened with other people's problems at the time of their own mourning but often found they were. Second, the widows expressed a desire to return to traditional rituals or develop some new rituals for death. Such rituals provide comfort by allowing everyone involved to express grief and caring in appropriate ways. In the absence of ritualized ways of handling death, people are often unsure of what to do; being unsure, they do nothing. Third, many of the widows needed more emotional support after the short official mourning period, often well into the second year. Neighbors and relatives brought casseroles during the period right after the death, but phone calls and visits disappeared with the casseroles, leaving the widow with her solitude and unresolved grief. Finally, the widows complained about the lack of daily help or contacts extending beyond the funeral. They appreciated rides to the grocery store, calls, visits, or invitations even more when they were out of the deepest grief, yet such contacts were sparse.

After the initial period of bereavement, the needs of the recently widowed seem to be similar to those of women who had been widowed longer (Barrett & Schnewies, 1976). It is a challenge for all to consider what can be done to ease the adaptation to this major life change.

COPING WITH TRANSIENT LIFE CRISIS: MASTECTOMY

Sometimes we are faced with situations that threaten our very survival. For example, each year many women discover an unfamiliar lump in a breast. Most are terrified by such a discovery as it is a warning sign of cancer.

A woman who suspects she may have cancer faces two adjustment challenges. First, she must deal with the actual threat of death. Secondly, she must confront the possible loss of a highly valued, specifically feminine body part. In our breast-idealizing culture, *mastectomy,* or removal of one or both breasts, is very threatening.

Several scientists have studied women undergoing diagnosis, surgery, and recovery from breast cancer. Most agree that women go through several stages in the process of adjusting to this life crisis.

Phases of Adjustment

Anticipation   The anticipatory phase begins when the woman begins to suspect she may have a cancerous tumor. This is a period of considerable anxiety. Most women seek medical advice, though some may deny their own suspicions and put off having any tests. Such denial may provide short-term relief from anxiety but at the possible expense of survival. Some women who go for medical check-ups, however, may refuse to acknowledge that it could lead to mastectomy (Polivy, 1977). Other women accept from the beginning that they may have cancer, particularly if they have a close relative who has had it.

The Operative Phase   If a woman is found to have a lump that may be cancerous, she must usually prepare for diagnostic surgery, in which tissue from the growth is removed and examined for evidence of cancer. One very interesting study involved 30 women who underwent such surgery (Katz, Herbert, Gallagher, & Hellman, 1977). Women used different ways of coping with their distress during the period immediately before, during, and after surgery. The women who reported the least psychological and physiological disruption (such as depression, sleeplessness, constipation, and so on) were those who took a stoic-fatalistic stance ("What will be, will be"), who used prayer and faith, or who denied the possible severity of their problem because they were "so strong" or "too healthy" to have cancer. On the other hand, such stoic denial may help the women delay seeking help. Thus short-term adaptation or ease of mind may be at the expense of longer-range adaptation.

The Reparation Phase   After surgery, women face reality. Some learn that the growth was not cancerous, and they can resume their preoperative life. Others are confronted with a diagnosis of malignancy and must decide on a course of treatment.

Several options are available to women who have some degree of malignancy in one or both breasts: chemotherapy (taking drugs designed to kill cancer cells); radiation therapy (to kill cancer cells); lumpectomy (the removal of only the site of most obvious cancerous growth); partial mastectomy (removal of breast tissue only); or radical mastectomy (removal of breast tissue plus lymph nodes and tissues adjacent to the breast). Each of these treatments has different probabilities of success and undesirable side effects. Because the cancer cells that proliferate in breast tissue are likely to have spread throughout the body by the time a lump is discovered and diagnosed, physicians often recommend a combination of mastectomy (to remove the obvious sites of cancerous growth) and chemotherapy (to kill yet-undetected cancer cells) for maximum effectiveness (Kushner, 1981). The mastectomy is a major surgical procedure involving permanent alteration of appearance. Chemotherapy often has side effects of nausea and increased vulnerability to other diseases (because cells other than cancer cells are destroyed). The necessary continued vigilance over dosages, side effects, and recurrence of cancer means one can no longer take one's health for granted.

Most women who confront the possibility of actual loss of a breast or of life experience depression followed by rage and resentment (Bard & Sutherland, 1965; McDonough, 1979; Polivy, 1977). Most women ask "Why me?" and seem to need to assign some meaning or cause for the illness. In one study of women who had undergone mastectomy (McDonough, 1979), most women reinterpreted the event to have some positive outcome: They felt that it showed them the value of life, or demonstrated how much a husband loved them, or gave them an opportunity to help others with similar problems. Women who said the cancer was caused by uncontrollable sources (such as "accident" or "fate") showed relatively poor social adjustment. And a few women felt that their own guilt (over some wrongdoing) "caused" the cancer; not surprisingly, such women were least likely to show good adjustment after the mastectomy.

Recovery from mastectomy is complex, apparently entailing several levels of adaptation. Following a period of physical recuperation from the surgical procedures, most women seem to resume participation in the normal activities of daily living. However, they face new dilemmas: deciding whether they want and can use plastic surgery to construct a new breast and nipple; whether they want a "substitute" removable breast and finding an acceptable one (or two); selecting clothing that fits; dealing with undressing and mirrors. They must decide how and when to let the husband see the scar, or touch it, or what to tell boyfriends or prospective lovers. (See Rollin, 1976, for a personal account of the real problems faced.) Most women are self-conscious about their appearance and anxious about revealing themselves to a man.

In our culture breasts symbolize sexuality and femininity to many men and women. Girls whose breasts mature earlier than those of their age peers are regarded as psychologically more mature and more interested in sex, and large-breasted women are popularly considered sexier than small-breasted women. One consequence is that women may feel de-sexed or neutered when a breast is removed; they may feel less sexually responsive or less entitled to sexual pleasure. Women may also assume that their partners will find them nonsexual or even repulsive. Even though they may desperately want reassurance of their attractiveness, and want to continue the sensual pleasures they enjoyed before the mastectomy, women may avoid sexual situations or become inhibited in responding sexually to their partners.

Men are also confronted with conflicting feelings about mastectomy. Most importantly, they must confront the possible loss of a partner and deal with the sense of rage and injustice that this loss arouses. In addition, men must deal with their feelings about sexuality and body integrity. Men who were sexually attracted to a woman partly because of her breasts may find it difficult to respond to her sexually with the same feelings as before. Some men are deeply frightened at what they regard as sexual mutilation and at an unconscious level feel that they must avoid contact with such a woman in order to ward off becoming de-sexed themselves. Such a response reveals a man's marked insecurity about his own sexuality, and his withdrawal will make his partner's adjustment more difficult. Some men fear hurting the mastectomy scar and may avoid contact or be more tentative than the woman prefers in sexual play. However, men who have been in a sexual relationship with a woman for a period of time are usually more sensitive to her responsivity to his sexual overtures than to her physical appearance; he may withdraw if she is reticent about responding, or he will respond with passion if she is comfortable in enjoying his sexual interest and her own sexual feelings. Adjustments in these intimate encounters are easier for men and women who are confident about their own sexual responsivity and about their ability to arouse sexual responses in their partner.

Both men and women must deal with the anxiety during the posttreatment period (five years or more) before the cancer is considered "cured." Perhaps because of the association of breasts and sexuality, people have been secretive about breast cancers. Only recently have women in public life (such as Betty Ford, the wife of the former U. S. president) spoken openly about their experiences with breast cancer. Acknowledging the problems openly may help both women and men deal with the traumatic changes involved.

The impact of mastectomy may be long-lasting. In a study of women who had undergone surgery four years earlier, 67 percent said it had not changed their lives, and one-third said it had (Woods & Earp, 1978). Women who reported a low to moderate number of physical complaints connected with the mastectomy but who felt they had strong social supports were unlikely to be depressed. However, women who had many physical complaints were likely to be depressed even if they had good social supports. This is another illustration of the importance of physical health and the complexity of the potential mediators in our model of the adaptive process.

Coping with Other Transient Life Crises

What can we say about coping with transient life crises such as mastectomy? Two psychologists who reviewed this research point out that "success or failure in coping is a fairly stable property of persons" (Monat & Lazarus, 1977, p. 213). Poor adjustment to a wide variety of transient life crises was evident in such reactions as severe depression and violent behavior. Such responses occurred mostly among patients who had difficulty with life prior to the event.

The illustrations presented in this section make one point very clear: For any particular change, the responses will be varied. In the next section, we will discuss some of the major factors related to variability in adaptation: cognitive processes, personality, coping strategies, and social resources.

FACTORS AFFECTING ADAPTATION TO CHANGE

Cognitive Processes and Adaptation

Cognitive processes—thinking, perceiving, and conceptualizing—affect the ways people adapt to change. One of the most consistent themes in research on how people respond to potentially stressful circumstances is that "emotional experiences, and to some extent physiological and performance measures, are partly a function of the perceptions, expectations, or cognitive appraisals which the individual makes of the situation" (McGrath, 1977, p. 67). Three aspects of cognitive processes are particularly important: the individual's cognitive style, implicit personal constructs, and level of functioning.

Cognitive Style   The characteristic ways an individual conceptually organizes the environment are that person's *cognitive style* (Goldstein & Blackman, 1978). Dogmatism, intolerance of ambiguity, rigidity, and authoritarianism are examples of cognitive styles. In addition, some individuals are "sharpeners," emphasizing the distinctness of sensations and experiences; others are "levelers," blurring differences and emphasizing similarities between stimuli. Some people are very concrete in their thinking, tied to the particular experience; others operate more abstractly, drawing inferences about how a particular experience represents a broader kind of experience. Cognitive style seems to be one of the most stable individual characteristics (Mischel, 1968). Differences in cognitive style affect adaptation by influencing the perception of circumstances as threatening or requiring changes in the usual ways of meeting needs.

Implicit Constructs   Individuals construct models or theories about the world. Kelly (1955) described this activity in terms of general *personal constructs;* Bruner & Taguiri (1954) described beliefs about people as *implicit personality theory.*

Wegner and Vallacher (1977) summarized research on how individuals select, organize, and use information about others and concluded that interpersonal relations are based largely on implicit personality theory, or inferences about others. As they say,

People fall in love, they beat one another over the head, they live happily ever after, they lob grenades at one another, they erect monuments to each other, and in general carry on life as we know it—all on the basis of inferences. . . . Inferences, although they are only educated guesses and can be utterly wrong, are a focal point of social interaction. (p. 108)

The inferences people make about others are important to adaptation because other people are such an important potential resource.

Level of Cognitive Functioning   Individuals who have substantial intellectual impairment do not adapt well to marked change. Studies of elderly persons who have been relocated from one institutional setting to another indicate that a minimal level of intellectual functioning is necessary before the person is able to comprehend the change well enough to adapt to it (Lieberman, 1975). It may be especially difficult for a person who has had normal intelligence to continue adapting adequately if his or her intellectual functioning deteriorates markedly, as sometimes happens with diseases of old age. This subject will be discussed further in the next chapter.

Above the minimal level of intelligence, however, it is not clear how much intelligence contributes to adaptation. Very bright individuals seem to show about the same range of adaptation to normal life events as those of normal intelligence (Sears, 1977). The importance of specific kinds of abilities (such as mathematical, verbal, or artistic) probably depends on the nature of the adaptive challenge.

Personality and Adaptation: Type A and Type B Personalities

As we have seen, general personality style is very important in responding to potentially stressful circumstances. Friedman and his colleagues have described what they call *Type A* and *Type B* individuals (Friedman & Rosenman, 1974). Type A people struggle aggressively and chronically to achieve more and more in less and less time. Environmental challenges serve as a fuse for explosive forces. They usually feel stressed, and are especially prone to heart attacks. Type B individuals may be as intelligent and ambitious as Type A individuals, but they are rarely driven by such intense desire for achievement. Table 12-2 illustrates how personality style affects experiences of stress (Ferguson, 1978). Although Joe and Roscoe are exposed to many of the same pressures—such as getting stuck behind a slow driver—they respond very differently.

Similar findings have been described by Suzanne Kobasa (1979). She found many male business executives who were experiencing high degrees of stress. Some became ill, but some did not. The men who did not respond to stress with illness had what she termed "hardy" personalities. They believed they could control or influence their experiences. They were able to feel deeply involved in or committed to the activities of their lives and to their sense of self. And they anticipated changes as exciting challenges to further development. Kobasa's research and the research on the Type A and Type B personalities make it clear that challenge alone is not hazardous to one's health; rather, it is the response to changes and challenges that counts.

Personality and Aging: The Kansas City Studies

A series of investigations carried out at the University of Chicago have explored personality and adaptation. Over 2000 individuals, middle-aged and older, have been involved in studies of normal adult development during the past few decades. One of the investigators in those studies concluded that "personality organization or personality type is the pivotal factor in predicting which individuals will age successfully and . . . adaptation is the key concept" (Neugarten, 1972, p. 12).

We will summarize one of the investigations because it is a classic and important study and because it illustrates so well the complexities of understanding personality as an influence in adjusting to aging.

The Kansas City Studies of Adult Life involved community residents aged 40 to over 70 in the late 1950s (Neugarten & associates, 1980). It was a pioneering study of normal, noninstitutionalized adults, using a wide variety of data on social behavior and personality. The investigators collected several personality measures for each respondent and used data analytic techniques to see which personality characteristics clustered together.

Table 12-2   Dealing with Potential Stress: A Day in the Life of Joe and Roscoe

Potential stress	Joe (chronic stress pattern)	Roscoe (healthy stress pattern)
Oversleeps—awakes at 7:30 instead of 6:30	Action: Gulps coffee, skips breakfast, cuts himself shaving, tears button off shirt getting dressed.	Action: Phones office to let them know he will be late. Eats a good breakfast.
	Thoughts: I can't be late again! The boss will be furious! I just know this is going to ruin my whole day.	Thoughts: No problem. I must have needed the extra sleep.
	Result: Leaves home anxious, worried, and hungry.	Result: Leaves home calm and relaxed.
Stuck behind slow driver	Action: Flashes lights, honks, grits teeth, curses, bangs on dashboard with fist. Finally passes on blind curve and nearly collides with oncoming car.	Action: Uses time to do relaxation exercises and to listen to his favorite radio station.
	Thought: What an idiot! Slow drivers should be put in jail! No consideration of others!	Thought: Here's a gift of time—how can I use it?
Staff meeting	Action: Sits in back, ignores speakers, and surreptitiously tries to work on monthly report.	Action: Listens carefully, and participates actively.
	Thoughts: What a waste of time. Who *cares* what's going on in all those other departments? I have more than I can handle keeping up with my own work.	Thoughts: It's really good to hear my co-workers' points of view. I can do my work a lot more effectively if I understand the big picture of what we're all trying to do.
	Results: Misses important input relating to his department. Is later reprimanded by superior.	Results: His supervisor compliments him on his suggestions.
Noon—behind on desk-work	Action: Skips lunch. Has coffee at desk. Spills coffee over important papers.	Action: Eats light lunch and goes for short walk in park.
	Thoughts: That's the last straw! Now I'll have to have this whole report typed over. I'll have to stay and work late.	Thoughts: I'll be in better shape for a good afternoon with a little exercise and some time out of the office.
Evening	Action: Arrives home 9 p.m. Family resentful. Ends up sleeping on couch. Does not fall asleep until long into the morning.	Action: Arrives home at usual time. Quiet evening with family. To bed by 11 p.m., falls asleep easily.
	Thoughts: What a life! If only I could run away and start over! It's just not worth it. I'll never amount to anything.	Thoughts: A good day! I felt really effective at work, and it was nice reading to the kids tonight.
	Results: Wakes up late again, feeling awful. Decides to call in sick.	Results: Wakes up early, feeling good.

With grateful acknowledgment to John Farquhar, who used a similar approach in his chart, "One Day in the Life of Mr. A and Mr. B," which appeared with his article, "Stress and How to Cope with It," *The Stanford Magazine*, Fall/Winter 1977, pp. 50–55 and 71–75. Both chart and article will appear in his upcoming book, *The American Way of Life Need Not Be Hazardous to Your Health*.

Source: Tom Ferguson, M.D., in *Medical Self-Care*, No. 5, 1978, p. 11. Reprinted by permission.

Personality Types   Four personality types were identified with these procedures; each type was labeled with a term descriptive of the various traits that distinguished that type. Individuals showing the *integrated* pattern of personality were well-functioning persons with a complex inner life, intact cognitive abilities, and competent egos. They maintained a comfortable degree of control over their impulses and were flexible, mellow, and mature. The *armored-defended* personality types were striving, ambitious, and achievement-oriented, with high defenses against anxiety and tight controls over impulses. The *passive-dependent* types had strong dependency needs, sought responsiveness from others, and were often apathetic. The last pattern was termed *unintegrated* because, although such individuals lived in the community, they had gross deficits in psychological functions, loss of control over emotions, and deteriorated thought processes.

These four types are not definitive and did not include all the individuals in the Kansas City studies. Other researchers using similar research strategies come up with different numbers and varieties of types, depending on the measures used and respondents assessed.

Disengagement Theory   The Kansas City studies were undertaken when the dominant model of successful aging was the *activity theory*—a belief that the people who age best are those who remain involved in social roles and personal relationships. This theory is still very prevalent today, at least in popular opinion.

Initial analysis of the Kansas City data suggested an alternative perspective, which Cumming and Henry (1961) called *disengagement theory*. They suggested that the withdrawal of older people from active participation in social roles was, in fact, a mutually desired change. Clearly, social participation declined with age, with the loss of occupational and, often, spouse roles. It was usually assumed that the society withdrew from the elderly, rejecting them and providing little opportunity to continue active involvement. Disengagement theory proposed that society's withdrawal from the elderly was a way of easing the transition that would come with death. The older person should not be so involved that his or her departure would be difficult for the social system to accommodate. Moreover, disengagement theory proposed that the individual, voluntarily and wisely, withdrew from active involvement in response to diminished psychic and physical energy. In this view high morale and life satisfaction should be the outcome when mutual withdrawal is accomplished at a pace acceptable to both the individual and the social system. The disengagement should be considered natural, inevitable, and mutual.

Further analyses of the Kansas City data led to a revision of this theory. Disengagement was often observed, but it was not necessarily mutual. Only a minority of the individuals studied had both low activity involvement and moderately high life satisfaction, thus meeting the criteria of disengagement theory. Most of those with high life satisfaction in fact also had high involvement in activity.

Other criticisms of disengagement theory came from researchers who suggested that individuals who appear disengaged in later life have been relatively uninvolved throughout adulthood; their pattern represents continuity rather than a change with aging (Maddox, 1968). Furthermore, cross-cultural researchers have pointed out that what was identified as disengagement represents withdrawal from the normal social role involvements of *middle age*. Our culture may provide few alternative roles, but in some cultures the old reengage in the social roles particular to that state of life. For example, old Druze men withdraw from active production but become equally involved in spiritual life (Gutmann, 1974). In such a view disengagement might describe the transition period between middle and old age but would not represent good adaptation to the changes accompanying later life.

Although disengagement theory was very provocative, it has not proven an adequate description of normal, universal aging, as the authors intended. It is, rather, a description of one of many possible patterns of aging.

Personality, Social Role Activity, and Life Satisfaction   The analysis of the Kansas City data took a new turn when personality was introduced into the relationship between extent of social role activity and degree of life satisfaction (Neugarten, Havighurst, & Tobin, 1968). For this analysis, the investigators used only the 59 respondents aged 70–79 who remained in the sample over the six years of the study; this was a relatively advantaged group in terms of health, cooperativeness, and general well-being. Thus the specific patterns of relationships may not hold for other groups, even though the power of personality to account for variance would.

Individuals in each of the four personality types described above were assessed for current social-role activity (high/medium/low) and for life satisfaction (high/medium/low).

Integrated personality types had high life satisfaction, even though some had high, some medium, and some low role activity. Among the armored-defended personalities high life satisfaction was reported for both high and medium role activity; these were people who were holding on to their middle-aged lifestyles. Only two persons showed high life satisfaction among the passive-dependent and unintegrated personalities, regardless of role activity level.

Since the Kansas City studies dozens of research projects have explored the relationships between longevity, morale, or life satisfaction and various personal and situational aspects of aging. The studies are in basic agreement that successful aging relies on both personality and situational factors.

COPING WITH CHANGE

Coping Strategies

Individuals develop ways of responding to stressful situations in order to prevent, avoid, or control emotional distress. These ways of responding to potentially stressful circumstances are termed *coping strategies*. The characteristic pattern of coping strategies used by any individual is called his or her *adaptive style*. Some individuals use the same strategies in most situations; others have a flexible approach and use different strategies in different situations (Pearlin & Schooler, 1978).

Some individuals deny or distort the threat, and others confront the situation directly. Some turn to other people for help, and some withdraw and try to work it out for themselves. Some focus their efforts on changing the situation that troubles them, and others try to change themselves to adapt to the situation. There are a wide variety of coping strategies, many representing conscious, logical, learned ways of confronting and resolving problematic situations. When those tactics fail, the individual may resort to unconscious strategies. These are known as *ego defense mechanisms*.

Ego Defense Mechanisms Freud identified the defense mechanisms as mental operations that reduce the inner sense of conflict and anxiety by making a compromise among conflicting impulses or by reducing the individual's awareness of the frustrating circumstances. Ego defense mechanisms are presumed to operate unconsciously. They may protect the person from his or her own threatening impulses, or they may help the individual substitute attainable goals for an unattainable goal. The classic folk tale of the fox and the sour grapes is a good example of such strategies at work; a goal that is unattainable (the luscious purple grapes hanging far overhead) is devalued (as sour). As an alternative, the fox could have continued to pine for the grapes and become depressed over his inability to obtain them, or he could have devised some method of reaching them, perhaps with the aid of friends.

There is little consensus on how many defense mechanisms there are. (We cannot discuss all the possibilities here; see Anna Freud, 1967, for a classic statement.) On the basis of his intensive longitudinal studies of American men George Vaillant (1977) suggested that common defense mechanisms could be arranged in a hierarchy, from those that are immature and maladaptive to the most mature and adaptive. The more common mechanisms from this model are presented in Table 12-3.

The "psychotic" level I defense mechanisms alter the sense of reality of the person using the defense mechanism and appear "crazy" to those who behold them. Individuals who use them are not necessarily psychotic. They are common in healthy individuals before age 5 and in adult dreams and fantasy. The level II immature mechanisms are common in healthy individuals age 3 to 15, in adults in psychotherapy, and in some kinds of psychopathology. The mechanisms seem to reduce anxiety related to interpersonal intimacy or its loss. Others usually regard those mechanisms as socially undesirable. The level III "neurotic" defenses are, according to Vaillant, common in healthy individuals aged 3 to 90, in attempts to master acute adult stress, and in neurotic disorders (which we will discuss further in the next chapter). These are apt to be regarded as individual quirks or neurotic "hang-ups," although the individuals are not necessarily seen as having any neurotic disorder. The private feelings of the user are altered by these mechanisms. At the most mature and adaptive level are the level IV mechanisms, common in healthy individuals aged 12 to 90. These defense mechanisms integrate reality, interpersonal relationships, and private feelings. They appear to others as convenient virtues.

Table 12-3   A Hierarchy of Common Ego Defense Mechanisms

Level I. "Psychotic" Mechanisms

Delusional projection—Frank delusions about external reality, usually believing one is being persecuted. One may feel that other people or their feelings are literally inside oneself, as with the patient who claims "the devil is devouring my heart."

Denial—Rejecting or distorting those aspects of reality that are consciously unacceptable. One may maintain that a loved one did not die or use fantasy to create a "new him" in one's own mind.

Distortion—Grossly reshaping external reality to suit inner needs. There may be a pleasant merging or fusion with another person.

Level II. Immature Mechanisms

Projection—Attributing unacceptable ideas or impulses to others rather than acknowledging them as one's own. For example, a person with unconscious destructive impulses may declare that someone else is trying to harm him; the person then becomes troubled by the aggressive behavior of other people and not by his or her own desires.

Hypochondriasis—The transformation of reproach toward others arising from bereavement, loneliness, or unacceptable aggressive impulses first into self-reproach and then into complaints of pain, physical illness, and fatigue.

Passive-aggressive behavior—Aggression toward others expressed indirectly and ineffectively through passivity, or directed against the self. It includes failures, delaying, or illness that affects others more than the self. It also includes silly or provocative behavior in order to receive attention and clowning in order to avoid a competitive role.

Acting out—Direct expression of an unconscious wish in order to avoid being conscious of the feelings that accompany it. For example, one may use drugs chronically or give in to "temper" to avoid the tension that would result from postponing expression of an impulse.

Level III. "Neurotic" Defenses

Intellectualization—Thinking about instinctual wishes in formal, bland terms and *not* acting on them. The feeling is missing from the conscious idea. For example, one may pay undue attention to things (machines, numbers, theories) to avoid intimacy with people.

Repression—Excluding unacceptable impulses, ideas, or feelings from consciousness. For example, feelings of lust or hatred toward one's child are blocked from awareness.

Displacement—Shifting impulses and feelings about one person or object toward a safer or less dangerous person or object. For example, aggressive feelings toward one's husband may be inhibited but expressed toward children, pets, or fellow workers.

Reaction formation—Behaving in a fashion diametrically opposed to a dangerous or painful urge, even though the original urge persists unconsciously. The transformed urges may be felt or expressed in exaggerated ways. For example, an elderly mother may overtly worry about her daughter when she really wants her daughter to worry about her.

Level IV. Mature Mechanisms

Altruism—Vicarious but constructive and instinctually gratifying service to others. Philanthropy and service to others are examples. It provides real, not imaginary, benefits to others.

Humor—Overt expression of ideas and feelings without individual discomfort and without unpleasant effect on others.

Suppression—The conscious or semiconscious decision to postpone paying attention to a conscious impulse or conflict. This includes looking for "silver linings," keeping a "stiff upper lip," and deliberate postponing but not avoiding. For example, one says, "I will think about it tomorrow," and the next day thinks about it.

Anticipation—Realistic anticipation of or planning for future inner discomforts. This includes goal-directed but overly careful planning or worrying, premature but realistic anticipation of death, surgery, or separation.

Sublimation—Modifying unacceptable impulses into socially acceptable activities. For example, sexual impulses may be channeled into painting or sculpting nudes, or aggressive impulses into competition for job promotions.

Adapted from *Adaptation to Life* by George Vaillant. Copyright © 1977 by George Vaillant. Reprinted by permission of Little, Brown & Company. Some of the descriptions of ego defenses are adapted from Richard S. Lazarus and Alan Monat, *Personality*, 3rd ed., © 1979, p. 163. Reprinted by permission of Prentice-Hall, Inc., Englewood Cliffs, N.J.

The Utility of Coping Strategies   An interesting question concerning adaptation to change is which adaptive styles or coping strategies are best suited for different kinds of stresses and how strategies may vary at different periods of life. Vaillant's model implies both developmental and effectiveness criteria: One moves, usually, from level I ego defense mechanisms to level IV defenses, which are presumed to be more effective.

Pearlin and his associates have explored the kinds of strategies people use in coping with everyday problems (Pearlin & Schooler, 1978). In general, Pearlin and his colleagues found that individuals who had many varied coping strategies were better able to adapt to stresses. Also, they found somewhat different coping strategies to be useful in the family and occupational areas of life. For stresses associated with marriage and parenting it seemed important to remain committed to the relationship and use nonhostile ways of persistently exploring the problems. In dealing with stress in occupational or financial areas, however, withdrawing psychological investment, devaluing the importance of money and/or intrinsic work satisfaction seemed to be more effective in reducing the psychological distress.

Pearlin and Schooler suggested, as have others, that active coping strategies aimed at changing conditions over which one has little direct control may be maladaptive; such changes must come from collective efforts. In such situations individual adaptation resides in those personality characteristics that help one make the best of a bad situation or define the situation as not too threatening.

Stressful circumstances were not evenly distributed among the group of Chicago-area respondents in the Pearlin study, nor were effective coping mechanisms. Women were more likely than men to have psychological attitudes or use responses that either contribute to stressful outcomes or are of limited coping value; they thus were exposed to more stress and dealt with it less effectively. Full-time housewives in particular are more likely to have low self-esteem and feel controlled by others, compared to men and employed women. These attitudes make it difficult to cope effectively with many stresses. Better-educated and better-paid respondents had more effective psychological resources, such as a sense of mastery and positive self-esteem; they were more able to maintain an optimistic outlook and to cope better with stress.

Among the Chicago-area respondents coping efficiency did not vary with age, although the younger and middle-aged respondents tended to use different coping strategies. For example, younger adults faced with marital problems tended to seek advice or express their feelings openly and directly; the middle-aged were more likely to selectively ignore their marital problems. These results support Lieberman's (1975) suggestion that particular coping techniques may be more useful at some ages than others. He found that denial and an aggressive stance are generally maladaptive in younger adulthood; however, such a coping style is found among the better-adapted survivors in institutions for the elderly.

Adaptive style can change as a result of experience and/or deliberate efforts to change. One of the explicit goals in therapy and personal growth experiences is often the development of more effective ways of responding to stress.

Social Resources and Adaptation

The ease with which a person adapts to change also depends on the availability of outside resources. We have already discussed some of the factors that affect an individual's ability to take advantage of such resources. In this section we will identify some of the social resources that facilitate adaptation.

Community Characteristics   One social resource is the characteristics of the community in which a person lives—opportunities for good employment, appropriate housing, freedom from crime, good transportation, recreational facilities, medical care, and so forth. In addition, the extent to which there are opportunities to maintain various social roles or to replace those that are lost is important. For example, a community where older women greatly outnumber older men offers few options for women to remarry. And even if there are single men and women, the prevailing attitudes may discourage courtship and remarriage. Generally speaking, a social setting that has strict norms for behavior based on age, sex, or race will limit the possibilities for adapting to changed circumstances. Adaptation is easier in a system that provides clearly defined new social roles when circumstances change.

Support System   *Support system* describes the consistently available relationships that help an individual maintain psychological and physical integrity (Caplan, 1974). The support may be long-term or occasional and may come from informal ties (family and friends) or formal organizations.

There is currently a great deal of interest in identifying the kinds of support systems desired and actually used to facilitate adaptation. We will review some of the research further when we discuss intervention in Chapter 14. Here we will stress a few of the central issues and findings.

Relatives, especially spouse and children, are usually seen as the most appropriate support givers, followed by friends. Formal organizations are regarded as appropriate only when the level of technical skill or time involvement is beyond the resources of the informal support system (Gurian & Cantor, 1978). As we saw in Chapter 9, family members continue to support each other in spite of changes in family structure.

The importance of family and extended kinship networks may vary at different life stages. For example, mothers of young children were less able to deal with stress when they felt isolated from kinship networks (Pearlin, 1975). Middle-aged women, however, seemed to adapt better when they were not extensively involved in large family networks (Lieberman, 1978). In other words, involvement that is supportive at one period may be oppressive at another.

Probably the most research on support systems has been done for elderly persons. The research indicates that various support systems are regarded as appropriate for particular tasks:

The kinship system is seen as most appropriately carrying the traditional tasks involving long-term history and intimacy. Given the geographic dispersion of many children, however, only those tasks not requiring proximity or immediacy may be appropriate for kin. Neighbors can be expected to assist with tasks requiring speed of response, knowledge of and presence in the territorial unit. Friends are uniquely able to deal with problems involving peer group status and similarity of experience and history. (Gurian & Cantor, 1978, p. 189)

Undoubtedly, the welfare of individuals at all ages is best served when strong informal and formal support systems complement each other.

SUMMARY

1   *Adaptation* is the ability to meet biological, social, and psychological needs under changing circumstances without substantial pain to the self or to others. The ability to adapt is linked to mental and physical health.

2   Normative life changes are built into the standard sequences of social roles tied to the family cycle. Normative life changes produce minimal strain for most people. On the other hand, nonnormative events and chronic problems are often very stressful and frequently entail problems of adaptation.

3   Successful adaptation can be assessed in several ways, including (a) physical health, (b) personal maturity, (c) social role adjustment, and (d) self-defined emotional functioning or morale. Measures may be made during the process of transition following changed circumstances or at some particular point to see whether equilibrium has been reestablished. Individuals who perform as well as or better than before the change are usually judged to be adapting well.

4   Menopause is an example of a universal normative life change for women. Cross-cultural research on responses to menopause suggests that hormonal changes alone cannot account for the experiencing of "menopausal symptoms." Many, though not all, of the symptoms commonly associated with the menopause seem to be linked to sociocultural and personality factors.

5   Widowhood is a common event, particularly in later life; after age 75, 69 percent of women and 23 percent of men are widowed. The consequences of widowhood depend on age at widowhood, social class, race, the time in which one lives, personality, and sex. Many older widows are poor. Widowed men show more severe symptoms of disorganization and lower morale than do widowed women. Lopata found that the best predictor of adjustment to widowhood is the widow's ability to reconstruct or maintain positive feelings about herself. Loneliness and lingering depression are common but not inevitable outcomes.

6   Cancer of the breast is a life-threatening illness that may result in mastectomy, the removal of a highly valued, specifically feminine body part. Women go through several phases in the process of adjusting to the crisis of breast removal: anticipation, operative, and reparation. The ability of women to deal with mastectomy is related to the severity of physical complaints, the acceptance and support received from husbands, lovers, and friends; and the women's personality. Stoic fatalism or denial was associated with fewer problems before surgery; after surgery women who reinterpreted the event to have some positive outcome showed better social adjustment. A minority of women (about one-third) experience long-term or permanent changes in their lives as a result of mastectomy, but most women adjust to the change.

7   Adaptation is affected by cognitive processes, including cognitive style, implicit personal constructs, and level of functioning. These are fairly stable personality characteristics that help determine the ways individuals understand and respond to people and situations.

8   General personality style has important influences on adaptation to stress. Some personality types generate more stress and respond to it less adequately than others. The Kansas City Studies of Adult Life suggest that patterns of aging are probably best predicted by personality organization, which the studies grouped into four types: integrated, armored-defended, passive-dependent, and unintegrated. Adaptation reflects the best fit between an individual and his or her circumstances.

9   Adaptive style or coping strategies also influence the outcome of change or potential stress. Individuals use a variety of coping strategies; evidence suggests that those who use several strategies do better than those who use only a few. Defense mechanisms are unconscious coping strategies that include "psychotic" mechanisms, immature mechanisms, "neurotic defenses," and mature mechanisms. Different strategies are useful in coping with family or work stresses. In addition, the effectiveness of various coping strategies may vary by age.

10   Community characteristics may contribute to the alleviation of stress or create additional problems that require adaptation.

11   Most support systems are informal, with family and friends preferred as support providers and actually providing most support. Formal organizations provide specialized services or replace missing informal support network members.

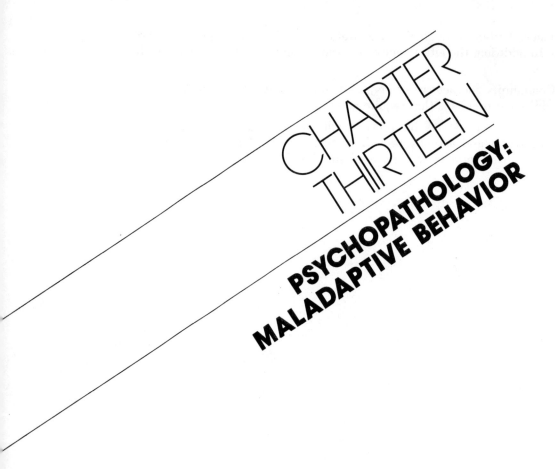

CHAPTER
THIRTEEN

PSYCHOPATHOLOGY:
MALADAPTIVE BEHAVIOR

SOME DEFINITIONS AND EXAMPLES

In Chapter 12 we looked at adaptive behavior—the various ways individuals meet biological, psychological, and social needs under changing circumstances. In this chapter we will focus on maladaptive behavior—behavior that meets these needs but only at the expense of causing substantial pain to the self or to others. *Maladaptive behavior* is the broadest term used to describe any behavior that has undesirable consequences for the individual or the group. Other terms are used to emphasize various aspects of maladaptive behavior, such as the presumed cause or the severity of the symptoms. The terminology of maladaptive behavior should be clearly defined, as many terms are often used loosely or interchangeably in inappropriate circumstances. The resulting misunderstanding can have serious consequences for diagnosis or interventions. (Definitions in this chapter are from Coleman, Butcher, & Carson, 1980, p. 17.)

Psychopathology, abnormal behavior, and *mental disorder* all refer to inner personality or outer behavior patterns that deviate from commonly accepted standards of healthy, adaptive behavior. Symptoms may be mild to severe,

specific to pervasive, or short- to long-term. These terms will be used interchangeably in this chapter. We will discuss later how we arrive at such judgments of behavior.

Several other terms describe variants of abnormal behavior. *Behavior disorders* are maladaptive patterns that are assumed to reflect faulty learning, either because the individual failed to acquire the needed competencies or because maladaptive coping patterns were learned. *Mental illness* is used for abnormal behaviors that are assumed or known to arise from pathology of the brain; typically, symptoms are severe. *Insanity* is a term not much used by mental-health professionals; it is, however, an important legal term. The legal term implies a serious mental disorder in which the individual is judged incompetent to manage his or her own affairs or to foresee the consequences of actions. The judgment of insanity may be made for a mental illness or a serious behavior disorder.

Mental health and *normality* are used to describe various degrees of positive well-being (Offer & Sabshin, 1968). The terms may mean merely the absence of any diagnosed mental disorder. However, *positive mental health* sometimes describes the condition of substantial psychological well-being—that is, not merely the absence of pathology but the presence of good health.

Any transition that requires substantial changes in daily routines may be accompanied by periods of maladaptive behavior. Because loss and change are common experiences in normal life, most people experience at some time some of the behaviors described as psychopathological—for example, anxiety, depression, or confusion—or are unable to apprehend situations realistically or respond to them appropriately. Most people recover spontaneously, in the course of time and without professional treatment, although some find brief therapies helpful in managing these normal but disruptive periods. In other words, maladaptive behavior may be a brief episode on the continuum of adult development. In this chapter we will review the range of maladaptive behaviors. For example, consider the following portraits, which we will refer to in the course of our discussion.

Mr. A, 26, was an assistant sales manager in a sporting goods store. After his last promotion he and his wife purchased a home. Mr. A wanted his wife to stay home and care for the house and their small daughter. She agreed, pleased that they could now afford for her to stop working outside the home. About a month after they moved, his supervisor noticed that Mr. A's work was becoming more and more erratic and that sometimes he did not show up for work at all. At home Mr. A was irritable and short-tempered; he began staying away from home at night. Soon he requested a divorce. On the urging of his supervisor and his wife Mr. A came to a psychiatric clinic. They found him suicidal, and he was hospitalized for observation and treatment.

At 42 Mrs. B suffered almost daily sieges of painful migraine headaches for several months; often she experienced nausea and backaches as well. She was busy with her final month's work in law school and with interviewing for positions after graduation. Her two teen-age children and her husband took over even more of the household routines, but her headaches continued. After three months, Mrs. B mentioned her headaches to her family physician.

Mrs. C, Mrs. B's mother, retired at 64 from teaching elementary school. She had taught for 18 years, found the work challenging but totally exhausting, and had threatened for 10 years to retire early. About a month after her retirement Mrs. C had an argument with her husband about the proper way to hang up the wash. She went upstairs, took a large quantity of sleeping pills, and went to bed. Her husband assumed she was resting as usual; when he came to wake her for dinner, he could not rouse her. Mrs. C was rushed to the hospital, where she regained consciousness. She was placed on the psychiatric ward for observation.

Mr. D lived with his wife of many years and their unmarried daughter; their married son and his family lived nearby. At 76 Mr. D spent his time puttering around his large yard. He stopped driving after he twice became confused and did not know where he was. At home he was no longer mild-mannered but irritable and often insulting to his wife and visitors. He frequently forgot where he had placed things. More troubling, he began having toileting "accidents" and didn't recognize his grandson. Mr. D's grandson took him to the family physician after a year of these changes.

Each of these individuals exhibited maladaptive behavior—difficulties in meeting their own needs or doing so at the expense of pain to themselves or others. The purpose of this chapter is to help you understand different explanations of abnormal behavior and the processes involved in maladaptation, to identify some of the common forms of psychopathology, and to appreciate the special expertise involved in diagnosing and treating these problems throughout adult life.

DEVELOPMENTAL PERSPECTIVES ON PSYCHOPATHOLOGY

Stress is experienced when circumstances require responses that are outside of the usual familiar range of the individual. Stresses may be external, arbitrary, and *imposed*—for instance, natural disasters, disease, or the loss of a loved partner. The stress may be *provoked* by an individual who puts him- or herself in a stressful situation (such as mountain climbing). Stresses may also be developmental or *maturational;* the organism develops new potentials, functions, or structures that can be tested and exercised only by moving into new situations. For example, as an adolescent becomes sexually mature, sexual feelings and behaviors are integrated into the self by gradually establishing relationships that acknowledge sexuality and allow the adolescent to try out new modes of behavior. Because the situations are unfamiliar, they are stressful.

Individuals who develop normally are at risk for maladaptive behavior for a brief period when they are moving into unfamiliar territory and establishing ways of mastering novel situations. Most parents expect young adolescents to show some signs of distress and alternating mature and less mature behaviors as they begin dating and dealing with sexual feelings. Leifer's (1980) research on the transition into first-time motherhood (summarized in Chapter 9) also found high stress and some maladaptive behavior. In the course of normal development the novel becomes familiar and is no longer stressful.

As this happens, the individual achieves new strengths and derives pleasure from the mastery of previously stressful situations.

However, development may get "derailed"; that is, rather than showing mature, adaptive behavior, the individual may show a pathological caricature of the failed development. The problem may arise either because the individual lacks the necessary past experiences, represented in inner structures or resources to deal with the challenge of new potentials, or because the society does not provide situations in which potentials can develop into successful capacities.

A developmental perspective emphasizes the ways psychopathological behavior may reflect the patterns of strength and vulnerability specific to various life periods. As an individual encounters each developmental imperative (such as the ability to walk or sexual maturity, both of which impel the person into new situations), he or she may encounter situations that are so novel they cannot be normalized and mastered. Instead, the stress is experienced as overwhelming, and the person retreats to earlier, familiar modes of behavior and avoids dealing with the new demands. The person not only may avoid the external, social demands (for example, dating and, eventually, petting and intercourse) but also may avoid inner awareness of the stressful challenge by repressing the feelings and desires aroused.

Individuals who avoid dealing with a developmental challenge do not master it, and they remain vulnerable to the stresses invoked by anything that reminds them of the situations avoided. Because a normal potential has not been developed, further developmental challenges will be blocked. For example, people who avoid feelings and situations that arouse sexual desires will have difficulty establishing an intimate relationship in young adulthood; even if they marry and have children, they may find the emergence of their children's sexual maturity very threatening.

The developmental approach is a fairly common perspective on psychopathologies of early life. Mental-health programs geared to those in the first half of life often consider the individual's difficulty in incorporating newly emerging strengths and capacities. For example, 26-year-old Mr. A's maladaptive behavior became evident when he had moved clearly into adult "success"—marriage, parenthood, job promotions, and a family home. His therapist might want to consider events in his life up to that point that led him to feel unable to enjoy and preserve the things he had fought for. Individuals may help bring about their own painful circumstances, or the ways they interpret the circumstances and respond to them may make them more rather than less painful. When younger adults experience loss or pain, the therapist usually assumes that they are partly responsible for the painful experiences they complain about and focuses on helping them understand how they are contributing to the experienced pain. And when losses are sustained, younger people are expected to restructure their life and, as far as possible, replace what is lost.

Unfortunately, psychopathology in later life is often not viewed from a developmental perspective. We know a good deal about the imposed stresses associated with the losses of middle and later life. From middle age on, change is typically seen as a process of depletion, with loss of health, fertility, loved ones, and social status as the predictable consequences of aging. Most discussions of psychopathology in older adults focus only on the losses, which are regarded as inevitable and irremediable. Therapies are often suggested as ways to dull the pain (especially through medication), to reconcile the individual to the losses, and, at best, to help the older person adapt to a life with less of what both the therapist and the older patient value. When a group of patients are defined as helpless victims of circumstance, a therapist has little incentive to work with them; indeed, many therapists avoid working with older people precisely because they feel nothing can be done about the losses of aging.

However, David Gutmann and his colleagues make strong appeals for a genuinely developmental psychology of later life (Gutmann, 1980; Gutmann, Grunes, & Griffin, 1980). They assert that much psychopathology in middle and late life is based on masked emergent growth potentials. As we saw in Chapter 8, some men are troubled by the internal changes toward increased sensitivity and emotionality experienced in mid-life, characteristics that are viewed as feminine. Middle-aged women are often troubled by the emergence of more agentic potentials, which they fear will render them less feminine. Middle-aged men and women may respond to their emerging feelings and desires with depression, physical illness, alcoholism, or even suicide attempts. In the developmental model the therapist's task is to help the person understand his or her own fears, normalize the emergent desires, and turn the potentials into new strengths.

It is useful to view even the oldest patients from a developmental perspective, as some strengths and capacities to deal with loss and illness seem to be age-linked. The elderly are often unafraid of death, and they have seen too many others die to feel that death cannot happen to them or that they have been singled out by bad fortune when they or a loved one die. Many have learned the paradox that loss also implies a gain—a freedom from others' claims on energies, possibilities, and affections (Gutmann, 1980). Furthermore, elderly patients who are pained or anxious seem to improve their level of adaptive behavior with very minimal psychotherapeutic contact; their ability to benefit from brief encounters with a therapist makes it efficient for the therapist to work with them as patients (Goldfarb, 1964).

On the other hand, the normal physical problems of later life, as well as approaching death, terrify some elderly people, and their fears may be related to earlier failed development. For example, many women who seek psychiatric help in late life have never been mothers. Gutmann, Grunes, and Griffin (1980) have suggested that, by avoiding motherhood, some of these women have never loosened the tie to their own mothers; they have never fully entered into the life cycle and thus have difficulty facing their own aging and inevitable death (Johnson, 1981).

Unfortunately, a developmental perspective on psychopathology is not the dominant view at the current time. In the next sections we will review the kinds of explanations of abnormal behavior now being proposed and the predominant ways of classifying psychopathological behaviors.

EXPLANATIONS OF ABNORMAL BEHAVIOR

Consider Mrs. B and Mr. D, introduced in the brief case histories. We can call their behavior abnormal because Mrs. B's headaches, backaches, and nausea and Mr. D's forgetfulness and irritability interfere with their own functioning and decrease the well-being of those around them. How can we understand these behaviors?

Erratic, unpredictable, or unusual behavior has been regarded in different ways at different historical periods and in various cultures—as normal, as evidence of spiritual possession, as willfully spiteful or self-indulgent, as a clue to brain damage, or as a reasonable response to a repressive social situation. Our observation and explanation reflect our view of the relationship between the individual and his or her social and personal world. Treatment recommendations also vary, depending on the viewpoint of the individual, the family, and the professionals involved.

There are two broad kinds of explanations offered for abnormal behavior: biological and psychosocial. Abnormal behaviors that have an identifiable biological cause are often called *organic;* the term *mental illness* is also used. Those psychopathologies where no organic factors are identified and behaviors reflect psychosocial factors have been broadly termed *functional* or *behavior disorders.* The term *functional* is not as widely used as it used to be, but distinctions are still made between organic or biosocial causes for abnormal behaviors. On the other hand, there is increasing recognition of the ways biological and psychosocial factors are related and influence each other. We will emphasize this interrelation as we look at several various explanations for abnormal behavior and the major classifications of psychopathology.

Biological Explanations

A variety of biological, or organic, factors have been implicated in abnormal behaviors. Some biological factors are congenital, present at birth even though they may not be detected until months or years later. For example, the brain may be inadequately devcloped because of genetic defects, inadequate maternal nutrition during pregnancy, or drugs taken by the mother during pregnancy, leading to mental retardation. Other biological factors may be the result of postnatal environmental conditions. For instance, mental impairment may result from a blow on the head or breathing toxic fumes. Genetic and environmental contributions may combine in organic conditions that induce abnormal behavior.

Chemical imbalances in the central nervous system have long been recognized as potential contributions to mental disturbance (Mears & Gatchel, 1979). It is unclear exactly how biochemistry is related to psychopathological behaviors, but biochemical treatments have been remarkably successful in altering some maladaptive behaviors. Later in this chapter we review the research on biochemical treatments of severe depression.

Destruction or damage of the brain or central nervous system may cause abnormal behaviors. However, as we will see when we discuss organic pathologies, it is impossible to predict maladaptive behavior simply from knowing how much brain damage has occurred. Abnormal behaviors have also been related to genetic defects, viruses, bacteria, and malnutrition.

We will discuss some organically based disorders later in this chapter.

Psychosocial Explanations

Psychosocial explanations see abnormal behavior as a result of individual responses to special conditions, such as childhood traumas; parental deprivation; pathogenic parent–child relationships; pathogenic family structures; or special frustrations, conflicts, and pressures (Coleman et al., 1980). These factors are not independent of each other. In addition, they always interact with genetic and constitutional factors. An individual may have a genetic vulnerability to certain kinds of stress. What follows after such a stress depends on the setting and on prior learning. The processes of learning are extremely important in the development of abnormal behaviors. According to Coleman and his colleagues (1980),

In the operation of psychosocial influences, learning is of paramount importance. This is true not only of simple learning processes like conditioning, but also of more complex varieties of learning in which cognitive elements are central. It is abundantly clear that life experiences leave a more or less permanent record in the individual's nervous system, which both limits and helps channel the individual's reactions to subsequent events. (p. 141)

A number of the psychosocial factors that lead to maladaptive behavior may occur during the earlier years of life, though the symptoms or disturbing behavior may not show up until later childhood or the adult years. It is crucial for students of adult development to understand how early events can contribute to later vulnerabilities.

Traumas A psychological trauma is any experience that inflicts serious psychological damage on the individual. Traumatic experiences temporarily shatter feelings of security and worth. They are likely to leave lasting wounds; later stress that reactivates such wounds is apt to be particularly difficult to handle. Generally, early traumas seem to have more far-reaching consequences than later ones, in part because children have not yet developed sophisticated defense mechanisms and cognitive understandings that help protect them. Nevertheless, traumatic experiences during adulthood can also have long-lasting impacts.

Parental Deprivation The lack of emotional warmth and stimulation normally provided by parents may occur because the child is institutionalized or, more often, because the child receives inadequate care at home. The short-term and long-term consequences of such deprivation are usually substantial, with impaired development and functioning. It is not clear when, how, and under what conditions it is possible to compensate for parental deprivation.

Clinical evidence suggests that parental deprivation may be an important factor predisposing an individual to problems in adult life, such as being an adequate parent. Grossly abnormal parenting seems to run in families; lack of love has been referred to as a "communicable disease" (Coleman et al., 1980, p. 146).

Pathogenic Parent–Child Relationships A relationship that produces maladaptive behavior in one or more of the participants is termed *pathogenic*. Pathogenic parent–child relationships are associated with abnormal behaviors during childhood and in later years. For example, many adults who were rejected by their parents in childhood have serious difficulties in giving and receiving affection (Pringle, 1965). Parents may be overprotective and restrictive, making it difficult for children to develop the competence and responsibility necessary to function in adulthood. Conversely, the children of overpermissive and indulgent parents may readily enter into close adult relationships but exploit others for their own purposes. Parents may have very unrealistic expectations about what the child can accomplish, leaving lingering self-doubts and/or continued pathological efforts to please even in adulthood.

Maladaptive behavior may also result from inadequate or irrational communication between family members. Parents may contradict, undermine, or ignore the child's statements, conclusions, or experience in the world, so the child is left confused, devalued, and disconfirmed as a person (Coleman et al., 1980).

Children may learn undesirable behaviors from parents who are emotionally disturbed, are addicted to drugs or alcohol, or have serious difficulty in coping with their own problems. However, a pathological parent does not necessarily produce a pathological child who carries that pathology into adulthood. The child may use the inadequate parent as a negative model, or the parental inadequacies may be compensated for by other persons.

A child may continue to use the parent as a model well into adulthood. Middle-aged adults often speak of how they are like (or unlike) their parents in approaching aging and how they fear they will age like their parents. Although we usually think of parental influences on the young child, such influences may continue until both are dead.

Whenever we consider the ways that disturbed early parent–child relationships lead to adult psychopathologies, we must remember the child's contributions. Some children are difficult to love "from birth on." For example, *autistic* children are withdrawn and unresponsive, often from birth; they do not offer the same enthusiastic responses to warm attention that normal babies do. In the past this was described as the result of parents who were cold, emotionally reserved, and rejecting. However, many now believe that the infant autistic response is related to a congenital neurological deficit, and the parental response is one way of coping with such an unresponsive child (Schopler, 1978). In such cases it would be wrong to see the responses of the parent as pathological or as causing the child's pathology.

Pathogenic Family Structures   Family structure may contribute to individual abnormal behavior, although it is difficult to clearly differentiate "healthy" and "maladaptive" families. When certain families or family patterns regularly produce problems in individual family members, they are termed pathogenic. However, pathogenic families may have healthy members, and "healthy" families may have pathogenic members.

One common pathogenic form is the disrupted family—families that are incomplete as a result of death, divorce, separation, or other circumstances. Dissolution of a marriage can produce both mental and physical disorder in children and in adults. One reviewer of the research on marital disruption concluded that such disruption is a major cause of psychopathology, physical illness and death, suicide, and homicide (Bloom, Asher, & White, 1978). On the other hand, the long-range effects of dissolution may be favorable compared to life in a brutalizing or conflictual "intact" family. It remains to be seen how increased divorce rates will affect children as they develop into parents and grandparents.

Other family forms may predispose individuals to problems at various points in the life course, such as the "developmental casualties" studied by Gutmann and his colleagues (see Chapter 8).

Severe Stress   Stress during adulthood, such as strains at work and in the family (see Chapter 12), is often linked with maladaptive behavior, even when it may be difficult to sort out what "causes" what. Frustrations that produce self-devaluation, such as repeated failure, loss of valued individual resources, guilt, and loneliness, can be so severe that they lead to mental suffering and maladaptive behavior (Coleman et al., 1980). Value conflicts may lead to serious inner turmoil.

Stresses, and the abnormal behaviors associated with them, are, as we pointed out in the last chapter, unevenly distributed in the population. *Epidemiology,* the study of where pathology is found in a social system, indicates that psychopathology is more common among low socioeconomic groups, those subject to group prejudice and discrimination, old people, and widowed and divorced people. The reasons for these patterns are complex and probably involve the interaction of biological and psychosocial factors. A supportive environment can help marginal individuals continue functioning adaptively. And even quite competent individuals may develop pathological behaviors if overwhelmed by highly stressful, nonsupportive circumstances.

The presumed causes of abnormal behavior are important clues in classifying such behavior. Before summarizing some of the major forms of adult psychopathology, we will consider the classification of abnormal behavior.

ASSESSING BEHAVIOR: DOES THE DIAGNOSIS DESCRIBE THE POPULATION?

Reasons for Assessing Mental Health

We assess mental health for several reasons. Sometimes we are curious about how people are managing their lives; evaluating kinds of stresses and maladaptive responses may be part of that research. There are standard "short-form" questionnaires designed for such purposes.

More often, assessments are made in response to some problem. When an individual, or others, appeals for help, assessments are necessary to diagnose mental disorder, possibly in order to determine the person's ability to handle his or her own affairs. This may be an issue at any age, but it is a very common problem with the elderly. At what point, for example, should Mr. D be allowed to alter his will?

We may also wish to evaluate psychological functioning in order to gather baseline information before beginning an intervention program. Progress in any psychotherapy is usually assessed in terms of changes toward more adaptive behavior, and this assessment depends on accurately understanding the individual's condition at the start of the treatment.

Psychologists also evaluate the mental and emotional functioning of individuals who anticipate or have already made changes in life roles. For example, during Mrs. B's final year of law school, she and a therapist together could have reviewed her feelings about working as a lawyer in order to assess the anxieties and compensations she would encounter. Preretirement counselors may evaluate the ability of an individual to remain on the job or predict what special stresses might be experienced after retirement.

Classifying Abnormal Behavior

Classification, or *diagnosis*, of patterned behaviors generally involves describing the symptoms and the causes (*etiology*) of the disorder. Such description can facilitate understanding and treatment. However, a diagnostic category must include consistent, coherent descriptions. For example, in identifying a particular variety of polio virus, a physician has a reasonable expectation about what caused the disease and how it will respond to various treatments.

The diagnosis of abnormal behavior in many modern societies follows guidelines established by the World Health Organization and the American Psychiatric Association. These organizations developed criteria for making standard diagnoses of mental disorders in 1968; these criteria are listed in the *Diagnostic and Statistical Manual,* known as DSM II (American Psychiatric Association, 1968). The DSM II was helpful in comparing data across cultures and across years. The manual was revised in 1980, and the DSM III (American Psychiatric Association, 1980) suggests that individuals be assessed on the following five dimensions:

1 The psychiatric syndrome present, with clear descriptions of the major symptoms associated with the disorder

2 The personality and developmental disorders in the patient's history, to identify long-standing problems

3 The assessment of any medical or physical disorders

4 The severity of psychosocial factors that may have been placing the individual under stress, rated on a seven-point scale from "none" to "catastrophic"

5 A rating of the highest level of adaptive functioning in the past year, from "superior" to "grossly impaired"

Diagnosis is based on assessments of these dimensions. A composite picture is formed, including the kinds and severity of present symptoms, how long these symptoms have been present, and what past and present factors might explain the symptoms. For instance, assessment of the highest level of adaptive functioning in the past year can indicate how severe the current impairment is, and it may provide a goal for how well the individual could function after appropriate therapy. Despite the detail of this system of classification, arriving at a useful diagnosis still relies on the skilled clinical judgment of the person making the assessment.

MAJOR FORMS OF ABNORMAL
BEHAVIOR DURING ADULTHOOD

An outline of the DSM III is shown in Table 13-1. We will discuss only some of the forms of psychopathology found among adults, particularly older adults; more complete discussions of these and the other disorders can be found in texts on abnormal psychology such as Coleman et al. (1980) and Mears and Gatchel (1979).

Neurosis

The chief characteristic of neurosis is a maladaptive lifestyle marked by defensive behaviors designed to avoid or lessen anxiety. *Healthy anxiety* is a perfectly normal experience for everyone; the anxiety has an obvious, immediate cause, and the individual prepares to meet the threat. The heart beats faster, sweat breaks out, and one is ready to fight or flee. *Neurotic anxiety* involves a persistent generalized sense of dread when no danger is present, or a much exaggerated response to real trouble. The neurotically anxious person may be restless, fidgety, and unable to relax.

The DSM III eliminated the general category of neurosis and includes instead various forms of neurotic disorders within affective, anxiety, somatoform, disassociative, and psychosexual disorders. We will discuss some of these forms.

Anxiety Disorders

In anxiety disorders either the anxiety itself or the individual's attempts to deal with the anxiety results in pathological behavior.

Some people live in an almost continuous state of *generalized anxiety,* marked by tension, worry, and vague uneasiness. Generally anxious individuals may also experience acute *anxiety attacks* (called *panic disorders* in DSM III), which last from a few seconds to an hour or more. The attacks come on suddenly, become very intense, and subside, all in the absence of any obvious cause. Physiological symptoms may include shortness of breath, coldness, urge to urinate, gastric sensations, sweating, and a terrifying feeling of imminent death.

Generalized anxiety disorders may arise because individuals are unable to handle impulses toward dangerous or socially disapproved forms of action. Efforts to repress the feelings are unsuccessful, and diffuse anxiety results. Furthermore, anxiety may increase when an individual has to make a decision involving moral values or possible loss of security and status. A particular situation may elicit anxiety if it strongly reminds an insecure person of an earlier trauma. Anxious behavioral styles also may be learned from parents or other models.

Table 13-1 DSM-III Classification: Axes I and II Categories and Codes

NEUROTIC DISORDERS

These are included in Affective, Anxiety, Somatoform, Dissociative, and Psychosexual Disorders. In order to facilitate the identification of the categories that in DSM-II were grouped together in the class of Neuroses, the DSM-II terms are included separately in parentheses after the corresponding categories.

ANXIETY DISORDERS

Phobic disorders (or Phobic neuroses)

300.21	Agoraphobia with panic attacks
300.22	Agoraphobia without panic attacks
300.23	Social phobia
300.29	Simple phobia

Anxiety states (or Anxiety neuroses)

300.01	Panic disorder
300.02	Generalized anxiety disorder
300.30	Obsessive compulsive disorder (or Obsessive compulsive neurosis)

Post-traumatic stress disorder

308.30	acute
309.81	chronic or delayed
300.00	Atypical anxiety disorder

AFFECTIVE DISORDERS

Major affective disorders

Code major depressive episode in fifth digit: 6 = in remission, 4 = with psychotic features (the unofficial non-ICD-9-CM fifth digit 7 may be used instead to indicate that the psychotic features are mood-incongruent), 3 = with melancholia, 2 = without melancholia, 0 = unspecified.

Code manic episode in fifth digit: 6 = in remission, 4 = with psychotic features (the unofficial non-ICD-9-CM fifth digit 7 may be used instead to

indicate that the psychotic features are mood-incongruent), 2 = without psychotic features, 0 = unspecified.

Bipolar disorder,

296.6x	mixed, _____
296.4x	manic, _____
296.5x	depressed, _____

Major depression,

296.2x	single episode, _____
296.3x	recurrent, _____

Other specific affective disorders

301.13	Cyclothymic disorder
300.40	Dysthymic disorder (or Depressive neurosis)

Atypical affective disorders

296.70	Atypical bipolar disorder
296.82	Atypical depression

SOMATOFORM DISORDERS

300.81	Somatization disorder
300.11	Conversion disorder (or Hysterical neurosis, conversion type)
307.80	Psychogenic pain disorder
300.70	Hypochondriasis (or Hypochondriacal neurosis)
300.70	Atypical somatoform disorder (300.71)

DISSOCIATIVE DISORDERS (OR HYSTERICAL NEUROSES, DISSOCIATIVE TYPE)

300.12	Psychogenic amnesia
300.13	Psychogenic fugue
300.14	Multiple personality
300.60	Depersonalization disorder (or Depersonalization neurosis)
300.15	Atypical dissociative disorder

PSYCHOSEXUAL DISORDERS

Gender identity disorders

Indicate sexual history in the fifth

digit of Transsexualism code: 1 = asexual, 2 = homosexual, 3 = heterosexual, 0 = unspecified.

302.5x Transsexualism, _____

302.60 Gender identity disorder of childhood

302.85 Atypical gender identity disorder

Paraphilias

302.81 Fetishism

302.30 Transvestism

302.10 Zoophilia

302.20 Pedophilia

302.40 Exhibitionism

302.82 Voyeurism

302.83 Sexual masochism

302.84 Sexual sadism

302.90 Atypical paraphilia

Psychosexual dysfunctions

302.71 Inhibited sexual desire

302.72 Inhibited sexual excitement

302.73 Inhibited female orgasm

302.74 Inhibited male orgasm

302.75 Premature ejaculation

302.76 Functional dyspareunia

306.51 Functional vaginismus

302.70 Atypical psychosexual dysfunction

Other psychosexual disorders

302.00 Ego-dystonic homosexuality

302.89 Psychosexual disorder not elsewhere classified

FACTITIOUS DISORDERS

300.16 Factitious disorder with psychological symptoms

301.51 Chronic factitious disorder with physical symptoms

300.19 Atypical factitious disorder with physical symptoms

DISORDERS OF IMPULSE CONTROL NOT ELSEWHERE CLASSIFIED

312.31 Pathological gambling

312.32 Kleptomania

312.33 Pyromania

312.34 Intermittent explosive disorder

312.35 Isolated explosive disorder

312.39 Atypical impulse control disorder

SUBSTANCE USE DISORDERS

Code in fifth digit: 1 = continuous, 2 = episodic, 3 = in remission, 0 = unspecified.

305.0x Alcohol abuse, _____

303.9x Alcohol dependence (Alcoholism), _____

305.4x Barbiturate or similarly acting sedative or hypnotic abuse, _____

304.1x Barbiturate or similarly acting sedative or hypnotic dependence, _____

305.5x Opioid abuse, _____

304.0x Opioid dependence, _____

305.6x Cocaine abuse, _____

305.7x Amphetamine or similarly acting sympathomimetic abuse, _____

304.4x Amphetamine or similarly acting sympathomimetic dependence, _____

305.9x Phencyclidine (PCP) or similarly acting arylcyclohexylamine abuse, _____ (328.4x)

305.3x Hallucinogen abuse, _____

305.2x Cannabis abuse, _____

304.3x Cannabis dependence, _____

305.1x Tobacco dependence, _____

305.9x Other, mixed or unspecified substance abuse, _____

304.6x Other specified substance dependence, _____

304.9x Unspecified substance dependence, _____

304.7x Dependence on combination of opioid and other nonalcoholic substance, _____

304.8x Dependence on combination of substances, excluding opioids and alcohol, _____

SCHIZOPHRENIC DISORDERS

Code in fifth digit: 1 = subchronic, 2 = chronic, 3 = subchronic with acute exacerbation, 4 = chronic with acute exacerbation, 5 = in remission, 0 = unspecified.

Schizophrenia,
295.1x disorganized, _____
295.2x catatonic, _____
295.3x paranoid, _____
295.9x undifferentiated, _____
295.6x residual, _____

PARANOID DISORDERS

297.10 Paranoia
297.30 Shared paranoid disorder
298.30 Acute paranoid disorder
297.90 Atypical paranoid disorder

ORGANIC MENTAL DISORDERS

Section 1. Organic mental disorders whose etiology or pathophysiological process is listed below (taken from the mental disorders section of ICD-9-CM).

Dementias arising in the senium and presenium

Primary degenerative dementia, senile onset,
290.30 with delirium
290.20 with delusions
290.21 with depression
290.00 uncomplicated

Code in fifth digit: 1 = with delirium, 2 = with delusions, 3 = with depression, 0 = uncomplicated.

290.1x Primary degenerative dementia, presenile onset, _____

290.4x Multi-infarct dementia, _____

Substance-induced

Alcohol
303.00 intoxication
291.40 idiosyncratic intoxication
291.80 withdrawal
291.00 withdrawal delirium
291.30 hallucinosis
291.10 amnestic disorder

Code severity of dementia in fifth digit: 1 = mild, 2 = moderate, 3 = severe, 0 = unspecified.
291.2x Dementia associated with alcoholism, _____

Barbiturate or similarly acting sedative or hypnotic
305.40 intoxication (327.00)
292.00 withdrawal (327.01)
292.00 withdrawal delirium (327.02)
292.83 amnestic disorder (327.04)

Opioid
305.50 intoxication (327.10)
292.00 withdrawal (327.11)

Cocaine
305.60 intoxication (327.20)

Amphetamine or similarly acting sympathomimetic
305.70 intoxication (327.30)
292.81 delirium (327.32)
292.11 delusional disorder (327.35)
292.00 withdrawal (327.31)

Phencyclidine (PCP) or similarly acting arylcyclohexylamine
305.90 intoxication (327.40)
292.81 delirium (327.42)
292.90 mixed organic mental disorder (327.49)

Hallucinogen
305.30 hallucinosis (327.56)
292.11 delusional disorder (327.55)
292.84 affective disorder (327.57)

Cannabis
305.20 intoxication (327.60)
292.11 delusional disorder (327.65)

Tobacco
292.00 withdrawal (327.71)

Caffeine
305.90 intoxication (327.80)

Other or unspecified substance
305.90 intoxication (327.90)
292.00 withdrawal (327.91)

292.81	delirium (327.92)
292.82	dementia (327.93)
292.83	amnestic disorder (327.94)
292.11	delusional disorder (327.95)
292.12	hallucinosis (327.96)
292.84	affective disorder (327.97)
292.89	personality disorder (327.98)
292.90	atypical or mixed organic mental disorder (327.99)

Section 2. Organic brain syndromes whose etiology or pathophysiological process is either noted as an additional diagnosis from outside the mental disorders section of ICD-9-CM or is unknown.

293.00	Delirium
294.10	Dementia
294.00	Amnestic syndrome
293.81	Organic delusional syndrome
293.82	Organic hallucinosis
293.83	Organic affective syndrome
310.10	Organic personality syndrome
294.80	Atypical or mixed organic brain syndrome

ADJUSTMENT DISORDER

309.00	with depressed mood
309.24	with anxious mood
309.28	with mixed emotional features
309.30	with disturbance of conduct
309.40	with mixed disturbance of emotions and conduct
309.23	with work (or academic) inhibition
309.83	with withdrawal
309.90	with atypical features

PSYCHOLOGICAL FACTORS AFFECTING PHYSICAL CONDITION

Specify physical condition on Axis III.

| 316.00 | Psychological factors affecting physical condition |

PERSONALITY DISORDERS

Note: These are coded on Axis II.

301.00	Paranoid
301.20	Schizoid
301.22	Schizotypal
301.50	Histrionic
301.81	Narcissistic
301.70	Antisocial
301.83	Borderline
301.82	Avoidant
301.60	Dependent
301.40	Compulsive
301.84	Passive-Aggressive
301.89	Atypical, mixed or other personality disorder

DISORDERS USUALLY FIRST EVIDENT IN INFANCY, CHILDHOOD OR ADOLESCENCE

Mental retardation

(Code in fifth digit: 1 = with other behavioral symptoms [requiring attention or treatment and that are not part of another disorder], 0 = without other behavioral symptoms.)

317.0(x)	Mild mental retardation, _____
318.0(x)	Moderate mental retardation, _____
318.1(x)	Severe mental retardation, _____
318.2(x)	Profound mental retardation, _____
319.0(x)	Unspecified mental retardation, _____

Attention deficit disorder

314.01	with hyperactivity
314.00	without hyperactivity
314.80	residual type

Conduct disorder

312.00	undersocialized, aggressive
312.10	undersocialized, nonaggressive
312.23	socialized, aggressive
312.21	socialized, nonaggressive
312.90	atypical

Anxiety disorders of childhood or adolescence

309.21 Separation anxiety disorder
313.21 Avoidant disorder of childhood or adolescence
313.00 Overanxious disorder

Other disorders of infancy, childhood or adolescence

313.89 Reactive attachment disorder of infancy
313.22 Schizoid disorder of childhood or adolescence
313.23 Elective mutism
313.81 Oppositional disorder
313.82 Identity disorder

Eating disorders

307.10 Anorexia nervosa
307.51 Bulimia
307.52 Pica
307.53 Rumination disorder of infancy
307.50 Atypical eating disorder

Stereotyped movement disorders

307.21 Transient tic disorder
307.22 Chronic motor tic disorder
307.23 Tourette's disorder
307.20 Atypical tic disorder
307.30 Atypical stereotyped movement disorder

Other disorders with physical manifestations

307.00 Stuttering
307.60 Functional enuresis
307.70 Functional encopresis
307.46 Sleepwalking disorder
307.46 Sleep terror disorder (307.49)

Pervasive developmental disorders

Code in fifth digit: 0 = full syndrome present, 1 = residual state.
299.0x Infantile autism, _____

299.9x Childhood onset pervasive developmental disorder,
_____
299.8x Atypical, _____

Specific developmental disorders

Note: These are coded on Axis II.
315.00 Developmental reading disorder
315.10 Developmental arithmetic disorder
315.31 Developmental language disorder
315.39 Developmental articulation disorder
315.50 Mixed specific developmental disorder
315.90 Atypical specific developmental disorder

V CODES FOR CONDITIONS NOT ATTRIBUTABLE TO A MENTAL DISORDER THAT ARE A FOCUS OF ATTENTION OR TREATMENT

V65.20 Malingering
V62.89 Borderline intellectual functioning (V62.88)
V71.01 Adult antisocial behavior
V71.02 Childhood or adolescent antisocial behavior
V62.30 Academic problem
V62.20 Occupational problem
V62.82 Uncomplicated bereavement
V15.81 Noncompliance with medical treatment
V62.89 Phase of life problem or other life circumstance problem
V61.10 Marital problem
V61.20 Parent-child problem
V61.80 Other specified family circumstances
V62.81 Other interpersonal problem

Adapted from the *Diagnostic and Statistical Manual of Mental Disorders* (Third Edition). Washington, D.C.: American Psychiatric Association, 1980, pp. 15–19. Reprinted by permission of the publisher.

Anxiety may be focused on obsessions or compulsions. An *obsession* is a recurrent, unwanted, irrational, and persistent thought. A *compulsion* is a repeated action, based on an obsession, that must be performed in order to get some feeling of reduced tension. Obsessive-compulsive behavior is maladaptive because it reduces flexibility and the capacity for self-direction.

Obsessive-compulsive behaviors may be substitutes for more troubling, anxiety-producing thoughts or behaviors. For example, compulsive housecleaning or report writing may be a way of avoiding thoughts about a painful marriage or confronting the issues with one's spouse. Obsessive-compulsive behaviors also may be an effort to deal with guilt. Lady Macbeth, trying endlessly to wash the blood of King Duncan's murder off her hands, is the classic example.

A neurotic compulsive individual may try to maintain some sense of control and order in a threatening world by having a rigid pattern of behavior. For instance, people who have tight, never-changing schedules for themselves (and, often, for others close to them) may be using these ways to control their own level of anxiety.

Anxiety may also be revealed through *phobia,* a persistent fear of some object or situation that presents no actual danger to the person or in which the danger is magnified out of all proportion to its actual seriousness. Phobic disorders are more common among adolescents and young adults than among older people (Coleman et al., 1980).

Phobias may be a defense against threatening sexual or aggressive impulses. For instance, a mother may develop a phobia about being near open windows because of recurring fantasies of pushing her unwanted child out the window. Phobias may also represent a displacement of anxiety from the original threatening situation. The reduction in anxiety experienced by avoiding the feared situation helps maintain the phobia.

Psychosexual Disorders

The DSM III includes four classes of psychosexual disorders. *Gender identity disorders* are characterized by the individual's feelings of discomfort and inappropriateness about his or her anatomic sex and by persistent behaviors generally associated with the other sex. The *paraphilias* are marked by sexual arousal in response to objects or situations that are not typically part of sexual activity; such preferences may interfere with the capacity for reciprocal affectionate sexual activity. *Psychosexual dysfunctions* are inhibitions in sexual desire or responsivity.

Homosexuality is classified as a disorder when the individual has a persistent wish to be heterosexual. Homosexuals who are comfortable with their same-sex arousal pattern are not considered to have a psychosexual disorder.

Affective Disorders and Suicide

In *mood disturbances,* or *affective disorders,* a single mood—either extreme depression or elation—is characteristic. The mood disturbance accounts for whatever loss of control exists; the loss may be mild to total.

Depression   We have all felt sad, inhibited, and apathetic at times. Depression is a normal emotion in response to loss and disappointment; the feelings are an important part of normal mourning for loss, in order to carry on living without something we have valued. Depression is considered pathological when it is more intense and/or more prolonged than the stressful situation warrants.

Depression is a common psychiatric problem from adolescence on. At all ages depressions are often crippling, and sometimes fatal. However, they can be treated successfully.

The manifestations of depression vary considerably. The basic depressive symptoms include abject and painful sadness; generalized withdrawal of interests and inhibition of activity; and a pervasive pessimism, manifesting itself as severely diminished self-esteem and a gloomy evaluation of one's future as well as one's present situation. Biological functioning is also affected: Sleeplessness, loss of appetite, weight loss, fatigue (especially in the morning), and constipation are common. Depressed people often experience guilt over minor actual or major fantasied wrongdoings. They may feel severe anxiety. Some maintain a belief that everything would be all right if only some one factor in the situation were changed.

Causes of Depression   Professionals do not agree on the causes of depression. Some depressions seem to be induced by physical stresses, such as infections or drugs. There is evidence for some inherited vulnerability, especially for serious forms of the disorder: There is a family history of depressive illness in 80 percent of those becoming severely depressed before age 50, and in 44 percent of those developing the disorder after 65 (Pitt, 1974).

Recently, investigators have established links between clinical depression and the social environment. George Brown and Tiril Harris (1978) studied several groups of women being treated for depression and a random sample of untreated women in the same district of London. Their imaginative and important research offers some reasons working-class women are much more likely to be depressed than middle-class women. Brown and Harris's model included three factors to explain the varieties of depression: *provoking agents* influence when the depression occurs, *vulnerability factors* influence whether these agents have an effect, and *symptom formation* factors influence the severity and form of the depressive disorder. The model tells us that the factors are causally related to the disorder, though it does not really tell us why.

The depressions Brown and Harris studied were usually provoked by events that resulted in the sense of loss or disappointment, defined broadly to include

threat of or actual separation from a key figure, an unpleasant revelation about someone close, a life-threatening illness to a close relative, a major material loss or general disappointment or threat of them, and miscellaneous crises such as being made redundant after a long period of steady employment. In more general terms the loss or disappointment could concern a person or object, a role, or an idea. (p. 275)

In general, the presence, type, and frequency of provoking agents did not relate to the form or severity of depression. Events lead to depression primarily because of the *meanings* attached to them. For example, a relatively minor event could lead to depression if it forced a reassessment of the meaning and purpose of life. This supports our position in Chapter 12.

However, vulnerability factors were important. In Brown and Harris's sample a woman who did not have someone she could trust and confide in, particularly a husband or a boyfriend, was much more likely to break down in the presence of a severe stress or major difficulty. Women who had lost their mother (but not father) before age 11 were more at risk, as were women with three or more children under age 14 at home. The fourth vulnerability factor was absence of employment. Working-class women with children were more likely to be depressed because they were more likely to be at risk on these four factors.

The four factors identified by Brown and Harris seem to make women more vulnerable to depression because they lower the ongoing sense of self-esteem. The women are then more likely to feel hopeless when confronted with a provoking event. Women with higher self-esteem are able to confine their responses to more adaptive grief, sadness, or distress.

Social factors have also been identified in depressions of later life. Losses in late life are less likely to be compensated. The common physical illnesses of later life also are often associated with depression.

Suicide   One danger with depression is suicide, the ultimate expression of despair or aggression toward others or toward the self. Ruminations about suicide are common in severe depressions and must be taken seriously. One warning sign is an apparent sudden recovery from depression; the person may be gathering enough energy to carry out a suicide. Some people threaten suicide frequently but never carry through, or make only dramatic attempts. Annoying though these are, such actions are serious cries for help in dealing with despair.

The frequency of suicide is measured by death certificates indicating that death was self-inflicted. The official statistics on suicide may be misleading because of (1) varying definitions of suicide, (2) varying criteria for classifying deaths as suicide, or (3) varying prevalence of attempts to hide suicide. Atchley

Figure 13-1 Mean suicide rate by age and sex for 20 countries, 1963–1966. (Source: Robert Atchley, Aging and suicide. In U.S. Department of Health and Human Services, *Epidemiology of Aging,* NIH Publication No. 80–969, 1980, p. 146.)

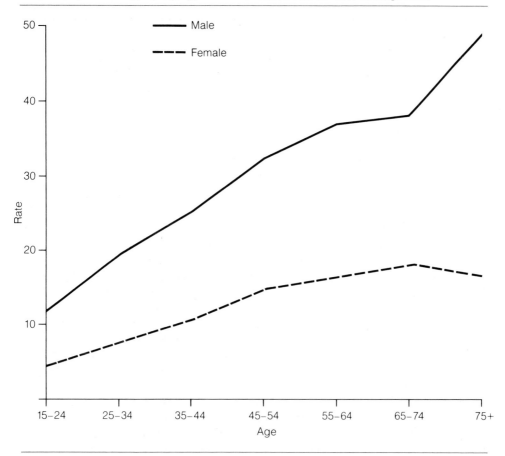

(1980a) reviewed patterns of suicide from data covering 25 countries (including the United States) from 1955 to 1966 and two sets of data from the United States covering 1920 to 1968. Figure 13-1 shows the mean suicide rate by age and sex for 20 selected countries.

Male suicide rates are higher than female suicide rates at all ages in all countries for which there are adequate data, though male suicide rates are higher in some countries than in others. In addition, for males there is a strong correlation between age and suicide rates; a pattern of steady increases with age is found across cultures and within different cohorts in the United States. For females the relationship between age and suicide varies by culture; in the United States, suicide rates are lower among young and old women and higher among middle-aged women (see Table 13-2).

Table 13-2 Suicide Rates by Age and Sex: United States, 1955–1968

	Male		Female	
	1955	1968	1955	1968
All ages	16.0	15.8	4.6	5.9
15–24 years	6.1	10.9	2.0	3.4
25–34	12.4	17.1	4.6	7.2
35–44	18.8	22.0	6.1	10.7
45–54	29.7	22.2	9.5	12.4
55–64	40.6	34.0	9.8	10.8
65–74	44.5	34.5	9.2	7.7
75 and over	53.1	43.1	7.8	6.0

Source: Robert Atchley, Aging and suicide. In U.S. Department of Health and Human Services, *Epidemiology of Aging*. NIH publication No. 80–969, 1980, p. 153.

In the United States, suicide rates for both men and women have risen in the younger age categories and declined in the older age categories. The suicide rate for nonwhites is generally lower than the rate for whites (U.S. Bureau of the Census, 1980). The reasons for these patterns are not clear.

Suicide figures undoubtedly underestimate the importance of suicidal behaviors, since they count only suicides that resulted in deaths labeled as self-inflicted rather than accidental. In addition, an undetermined number of individuals attempt suicide but do not complete it. Since the turn of the century reported suicide attempts have been three times as common among women as among men. Young people are more likely than old people to attempt suicide as a means of calling for help (Miller, 1979). Old people are less likely than young people to warn others of their intentions and are likely to use methods that surely result in death. Some suicides in late life are related to depression and could be prevented by treating the depressive illness. Some old people kill themselves as a way of exercising control over their own death and over their survivors. Some lovers may make sacrificial, romantic suicide pacts. And some make a rational or philosophical decision to kill themselves rather than suffer pain or bankruptcy, or be burdensome to loved ones (Butler & Lewis, 1977).

Treatment of Depression   According to one psychiatrist, there is a natural tendency for depressive illness to get better, spontaneously, after a few months or a year or two, "provided the person does not succumb to malnutrition, suicide, or institutionalization" (Pitt, 1974). Depressive illnesses are likely to recur, and the pattern closely follows the first episode. Treatment can cut short the course of the illness, aid more complete recovery, and lengthen the time between relapses. Current therapeutic techniques include the use of anti-depressive drugs, electroshock treatments, brain surgery (for extreme and otherwise untreatable cases), and a range of individual and group psychotherapies.

Clinical psychologists tend to favor minimal drug use for depressions, though it may be necessary in cases of suicidal threats. The emphasis is on identifying the underlying causes for depressive reactions and dealing with the anger that covers deeper problems such as needs for intimacy or a sense of deprivation. Psychiatrists who believe there is a substantial biochemical basis for depression emphasize chemical (drug) therapies.

Mania   Mania is an affective disorder with symptoms that are the mirror image of depression. The individual feels extremely elated and optimistic and is often hyperactive. There may also be general irritability, outbursts of anger, or paranoid (suspicious) thinking. Periods of weeping or depression may occur between the general euphoria. The individual may respond well to chemical therapies.

Somatoform Disorders

According to DSM III, the symptoms of somatoform disorders suggest a physical illness. However, the cause of the symptoms is emotional rather than organic. The symptoms are not under conscious control.

Formerly called hysteria, *conversion disorders* involve a neurotic pattern in which symptoms of some physical malfunction or loss of control appear without any underlying organic pathology. Conversion disorders are rather rare in a period when people are given more freedom to express sexual and aggressive feelings.

The physical symptoms are defensive; that is, they enable the individual to escape or avoid a stressful situation. For example, soldiers in combat frequently develop symptoms, such as paralysis in the legs, that get them out of battle without being called a coward. The loss of function is usually limited and selective; typically, the "target" organ has some relation to the stress being avoided.

The symptoms often resemble actual, organically based pathology very closely, and expert diagnosis is needed to distinguish conversion reactions from organic disorders. Four criteria are used to make such differential diagnoses (adapted from Coleman et al., 1980, p. 232):

1   The patient has *la belle indifference* ("beautiful indifference")—that is, describing what is wrong with little of the anxiety and fear usually experienced by people with the symptoms.

2   Often the dysfunction does not conform clearly to the symptoms of any known disease or disorder.

3   The dysfunction is selective, so that "paralyzed" muscles can be used for some activities but not others.

4   Under hypnosis or narcosis the symptoms can usually be removed, shifted, or reinduced (brought back after removal) by therapeutic suggestion.

Psychosomatic disorders are physical disorders in which psychological factors play a major causative role. Health and illness illustrate the fundamental unity of mind and body. The recognition that many—perhaps all—disorders have some psychological factors is part of psychosomatic or behavioral medicine. In this approach it is "more important to know what kind of patient has the disease than what kind of disease the patient has" (Dunbar, 1943, p. 23).

The psychological processes producing psychosomatic disorders are similar to those in neuroses. The person usually has acquired unrealistic fears or anxieties that severely limit effective coping behaviors, and thus needs often are not gratified. Defensive and self-defeating strategies are useful in controlling the amount of anxiety experienced but lead to frustration and continued high arousal; one must always be vigilant to protect against the feelings that provoke anxiety. In some persons the resulting stress acts on a vulnerable part of the body and produces real physical changes. There must be, then, some predisposition for the illness in order for the stress to be manifest in that way. The term *psychosomatic* reflects the joint contribution of the *psyche* (mind) and the vulnerable *soma* (body).

Headaches, peptic ulcers, skin rashes, essential hypertension, and asthma are among the ailments that are now regarded as having some psychosomatic basis. However, these same diseases can occur without any significant psychological components.

Family therapy has been useful in treating some psychosomatic disorders. The most promising treatments seem to be in behavior therapy and biofeedback. Therapies emphasizing understanding problems and learning more effective coping techniques have been less effective (Coleman et al., 1980).

Hypochondriacs are preoccupied with their supposed physical ailments. However, their complaints are usually not limited to any logical symptom pattern. Although convinced they are seriously ill, they are often in good health. They tend to show an excessive preoccupation with bodily functions, perhaps as a result of overemphasis on such functions in early life.

Because hypochondriasis is more common in later life than earlier, it may reflect disappointment in life. The hypochondriac's pattern may be rewarding, allowing the individual to avoid unpleasant situations while getting sympathy and attention. By stressing their symptoms, hypochondriacs may get others to be more attentive and considerate and take over chores usually performed by the sick person.

Hypochondriac patients are very difficult to deal with. Pointing out the emotional bases of their symptoms may work with younger adults and older adults who seem reasonably competent and intact. However, some individuals find such suggestions threatening. They may intensify their symptoms and go from doctor to doctor in order to find someone who will give them serious attention.

Eric Pfeiffer and Ewald Busse, two psychiatrists who have done a good deal of work with older hypochondriacs, suggest several specific techniques for dealing with such people and their relatives. They advise against explaining the medical condition by confronting the patient with the emotional origins of the complaints, explaining the emotional problems to the patient's family, or treating the presented symptoms with assurances of a speedy recovery. Rather, the patient's psychological defenses must be maintained. Health-care professionals and family should remember that the person is indeed sick and needs to be cared for. Medication for a specific complaint or a placebo may be helpful (Pfeiffer & Busse, 1973).

Other researchers recommend changes in the social sphere. Such suggestions reflect another reality of mental health: Social factors and mental illness are closely related.

Substance Use Disorders: Alcoholism and Drug Abuse

When a person shows excessive reliance, either psychological or physiological, on a drug, that individual has an addictive disorder.

Alcoholism   Alcohol is a common coping device. In itself the use of alcohol can hardly be regarded as evidence of psychopathology. However, when alcohol reduces or destroys the capacity to carry out normal daily life, then it is part of a pathological syndrome. Alcoholism is a serious and common disorder; in fact, it is the third major health problem in the United States. Cirrhosis of the liver causes many alcoholics' deaths because the alcohol destroys liver cells. In addition, many home and highway accidents are due to drinking.

Alcoholism results from excessive intake of alcohol or unusual intolerance for alcohol. There are gradations of alcohol abuse. According to current terminology, a *problem drinker* drinks enough to cause problems for him- or herself and society. *Acute alcoholism* is a state of intoxication with temporary and reversible mental and body effects. *Dipsomania* refers to periodic or "spree" drinking. *Chronic alcoholism* is the fact and consequence of habitual abuse.

Alcoholism may develop at any period in life, though admission to psychiatric hospitals and outpatient clinics is highest for the 35-to-50-year age group. Alcoholism may be more prevalent during those years, or people of that age may be more likely to be treated because their excessive drinking causes more problems at work and in the family than it does for younger and older people. Although the incidence of alcoholism seems to decline with age, a significant number of older people are alcoholics. Studies of older people report from 17 percent alcoholism among persons over 60 coming to a community mental-health center to 56 percent of male hospital patients over 70 (Simon, 1980). Old alcoholics may have had serious drinking problems for a long time; they are likely to be in poor health and have a lower life expectancy than moderate drinkers. Alcoholism that emerges for the first time in late life is often a reaction to age-related stress, especially physical illness and depression (Simon, 1980).

Males are far more likely than females to be diagnosed as alcoholic; however, women are more likely than men to drink at home and have their habits undiscovered or concealed by others.

There is little agreement about the causes of alcoholism. Some view it as a disease, caused by a biological defect that makes the individual unusually susceptible to alcohol. They regard "will" as being no more relevant to alcoholism than it is to tuberculosis. Others regard alcohol abuse as a learned adaptation to psychological stress or evidence of inability to tolerate stress. The "culture of alcohol" is blamed for encouraging this drug dependency among some sectors of the population. In addition, the miseries of poverty and old age are often seen as legitimate reasons for escaping into alcoholism.

Drug Abuse   Some individuals abuse drugs and become addicted to them as ways of dealing with what seems to be an unpleasant, boring, or intolerable reality. Alcohol is the most commonly abused substance. However, virtually any substance that chemically alters mood or perceptual processes can be used to excess. Most abused drugs are from the family medicine cabinet, particularly if it is well supplied with prescription tranquilizers and mood elevators. Active experimentation with drugs and combinations of drugs is most common among the young. Middle-aged drug abuse evolves more from reliance on mood-altering substances to cope with even normal pressures of daily life. Misuse of drugs is common in old age. Most people have one or more chronic ailments for which they are likely to take drugs, and drug tolerance changes in old age. Some elderly become confused about multiple drug prescriptions; drug interactions may produce further confusion and conditions that closely resemble psychotic thought disorders. We will discuss appropriate and hazardous uses of drugs further in the next chapter

Psychotic Disorders

Schizophrenias   The schizophrenias are a group of psychotic disorders marked by gross distortions of thinking and withdrawal from social reality. Perception, thought, and feeling are disorganized and fragmented. Hallucinations, delusions, and poor ability to objectively evaluate the external world are characteristic. These disorders are usually severely disabling, and many schizophrenic individuals require prolonged or repeated hospitalization.

The etiology of schizophrenic disorders is unclear. It seems most likely that three sets of factors are all involved: (1) biological factors, including heredity and various biochemical and neurophysiological processes; (2) psychosocial factors, including faulty learning, pathogenic interpersonal and family patterns, and severe stress; and (3) sociocultural factors, which influence the types and incidence of schizophrenic reactions (Coleman et al., 1980).

No adequate treatments for schizophrenia have been developed, though some of the symptoms are modified by chemical therapy. Public mental hospitals have many older patients who are admitted as schizophrenic young adults, and who have grown old in the institution. More fortunate are those who receive treatment during periods when they are most disturbed and then return to relatively protected environments, where they can function reasonably well.

Paranoid Disorders   Paranoia involves attributing to other people motivations that do not, in fact, exist. A *delusion* is a strongly held belief with little or no basis in reality; paranoid persons often have one or more delusions that distort their mood, behavior, and thinking. The delusions may involve personal grandiosity ("I am God" or "I can cause illness in another person by my very thoughts") or the conviction that others are plotting against one.

Paranoid disorders may be mild or severe, and they may be the central problem or a minor part of another disorder. For example, paranoid delusions may be part of a schizophrenic disorder (paranoid schizophrenia), or a central delusion may so seriously distort orientation to reality that the paranoia is the primary problem. Short-term paranoid delusions tend to occur under adverse conditions, such as imprisonment, drunkenness, isolation, or blindness. Long-term paranoid delusions also exist; they may be either very limited (for instance, a belief that the neighbor upstairs is sending lethal rays out of one's telephone) or extensive (the conviction that a master plot, organized by the neighbor, is in effect to bring one bad weather, tasteless food, short change, backaches, and evil thoughts).

In earlier adulthood, paranoia is usually a sign of serious emotional disturbance, and it may make normal developmental challenges insurmountable. However, in later life some forms of paranoia may be adaptive. For instance, acknowledging illness, death, or internal disintegration might be too demoralizing, and the individual cannot struggle against them. A heightened general sense of suspiciousness and vigilance against potential dangers may energize an old person to fight. Some researchers have found that, when old people are in harsh, nonsupportive environments (for example, some nursing homes), the grouchy, suspicious, "paranoid" individuals have better chances for survival (Turner, Tobin, & Lieberman, 1972).

Paranoia frequently develops with severe sensory impairments, such as deafness, in individuals who are already prone to suspiciousness (Corso, 1977); the delusions may be an effort to "fill in the blank spaces" of the individual's cognitive environment (Pfeiffer, 1977).

Paranoid people may become increasingly isolated in later years. They may withdraw from those they believe are trying to do them harm, or former friends and allies—particularly if accused—may reject their company. For example, one elderly woman became convinced that her landlord was coming into her apartment and scattering dust around. In order to track him, she spread a thick layer of flour around her door and on the path leading to the landlord's entrance. After several such episodes, the landlord took action to have her placed in the state mental hospital.

Treatment is more effective in the early stages of paranoia than later. Once a delusional system is well established, it is often impossible to communicate rationally with the person about the problem. Hospitalization removes their offending presence from the public, but paranoids are not likely to cooperate in treatment and are apt to remain difficult for all who deal with them.

Organic Mental Disorders: General Characteristics

Organic brain syndrome (OBS) is the general term used to describe behavior related to changes in the brain ranging from barely perceptible to profound. Two factors are considered: the actual damage to the brain, and the syndrome, or pattern of behaviors found in individuals with brain damage.

The clinical manifestations of organic brain damage (that is, those visible to the observer or revealed in various psychological tests) depend partly on the extent and location of brain impairment. Damage may be localized, as with a small cerebral vascular accident (stroke); the behaviors affected then depend in part on the controls that are located in the damaged area. Damage also may be diffuse throughout the cortex, resulting in a general overall lowering of functioning or substantial loss of function (to the point of death).

The pattern of onset also is important in determining observed behavior. Sometimes there is slow, progressive deterioration over a period of years; the individual adapts his or her functioning to "cover" the losses, and only an autopsy may reveal the extent of brain damage. Sudden changes, particularly if they are substantial, can lead to much more disorganized behavior than if the same damage occurred gradually.

In addition, the personality resources and psychopathologies of the individual affect the ways brain damage may be expressed. Individuals with adequate coping styles are used to adapting to changes and can employ a variety of defense mechanisms to avoid consciously recognizing and admitting memory deficits, confusions, and the like. Personality resources are also crucial in the possible outcome of various therapeutic interventions.

Finally, the manifestations of organic damage are influenced by the characteristics of the surrounding environment, including the conditions at the time of testing if behavior is being evaluated in a testing situation.

Some environments allow an individual to function quite well even with brain damage. A simple, very familiar setting calls forth habits and routines. The same person might do badly if moved to a different place where it was necessary to learn new locations, controls, and routines. Even a familiar setting can affect level of optimal functioning, however. For example, one older man who had suffered a series of minor cerebral strokes continued to live in his own apartment. If the lights were bright and the radio or television turned on, he could not focus his attention sufficiently to carry on a conversation or dial the telephone; if these distractors were eliminated he could concentrate enough to behave quite "normally."

In constructing a patient profile, the dimensions described above are used to assess the likely course of the pathology. In addition, it is crucial to assess whether the damage is progressive or stable. Some brain impairment is a consequence of disease processes in which continued deterioration can be expected unless the disease process is stopped. Brain damage resulting from a single episode—a blow on the head or a cerebral stroke, for example—will remain stable after the incident.

Dementias: Nonreversible Brain Syndromes

Dementia is probably the most serious psychiatric disorder of old age. Because brain tissues cannot regenerate when they are damaged, brain damage results in intellectual deterioration and personality disintegration. Reports on the incidence of cognitive disorders in persons over 65 range from 10 to 18 percent (Kay, 1977). The term *cognitive disease* is used to distinguish cognitive problems resulting from a disease process from those resulting from congenital abnormalities (such as mental retardation) or neurotic anxiety. The fact that incidence of cognitive disease increases sharply with advancing age is a cause for concern as more people are surviving into advanced old age.

Dementias with fairly gradual onset generally begin with various emotional and behavioral changes, such as depression, fatigue, irritability, social withdrawal, emotional outbursts, irregular attendance at work or regular activities, and changes in standards of behavior (such as grooming or manners). These changes mask underlying losses of higher-level intellectual abilities. Disorientation of time and place and recent-memory losses are followed by losses of distant memories. Garbled speech and impaired motor control are evidence of advanced brain deterioration. The final stage is reached when the person can no longer remember his or her own name; death usually follows (Pfeiffer, 1977).

Dementias are described in terms of syndromes and presumed causes. There is a great deal of research currently under way on the varieties and causes of dementias. In Chapter 3 we looked at the neurological components of these conditions; in this chapter we will describe the symptoms and presumed causes.

Primary Neuronal Degeneration: Senile Dementia of the Alzheimer's Type   Also called Alzheimer's disease, senile dementia is characterized by loss of memory and orientation; interest may dwindle into apathy. The onset may be very gradual, with minimal changes in cognitive functioning barely noticed by family members. In later stages patients may show restlessness, perserveration (the pathological repetition of a word or phrase or activity even when inappropriate), marked aphasia (loss of the ability to use language), and rapidly changing emotions. Eventually, the person may not remember who he or she is or recognize family members. Bladder and bowel control may also be lost (Eisdorfer & Cohen, 1978).

The symptoms are presumed to reflect neuronal degeneration, a rapid increase in the rate of brain-cell death. However, in two studies about 8 percent of the individuals who had died with marked signs of cognitive disturbance did not show the expected structural changes in the brain on autopsy (Terry & Wisniewski, 1973, 1977). The causes of neuronal degeneration are unclear. There may be some inheritance of the disorder, especially when the onset is in late life. One line of evidence for the heritability of the disorder comes from the studies of twins. Among nonidentical twins, if one develops senile dementia, the risk of the other twin getting it is 8 percent; among identical twins the risk increases to 43 percent (Kallmann, Feingold, & Bondy, 1951). Furthermore, individuals who have a close relative with senile dementia show a statistical risk of the disorder four times as great as that of the general population (Larsson, Sjögren, & Jacobson, 1963).

Cerebrovascular Variants of Dementia   These variants involve localized death of brain tissue, which is presumed to result from damage to cerebral blood vessels that makes it difficult for adequate oxygen and nutrients to reach the brain cells. Often a series of "little strokes" occurs—episodes of confusion, slurred speech, or weakness on one side of the body or in one limb. After each little stroke there may be marked improvement, until the next episode. A succession of such strokes leads to less and less complete recovery.

The brains of persons who died with clear diagnoses of arteriosclerotic dementia have been found to show profound softening, involving relatively large amounts of tissue. Brains of persons with a diagnosis of "probable" cerebrovascular dementia showed softening in several areas, involving less tissue (Tomlinson, Blessed, & Roth, 1970). Such careful pathologic analyses are essential to assess the relationships between observed behavioral changes and the kind and extent of actual brain damage.

At the present time it is very difficult to distinguish between primary neuronal degeneration and cerebrovascular disease in living patients. It is virtually impossible to make such a differential diagnosis on the basis of one-time behavioral observations (Eisdorfer & Cohen, 1978); the judgment must be based on detailed physical examination and medical history to find evidence of possible vascular lesions and to rule out other causes for cognitive impairments (Hall, 1976).

Subcortical Variants of Dementia   Mental impairments are also linked to degenerative changes in areas of the brain below the cerebral cortex. Some researchers posit that degeneration of the cortex (the outer layer of the brain) usually results in deficits in language and perceptual-motor functioning. Subcortical degeneration, in contrast, is associated with (1) memory deficits; (2) slowed cognitive performance; (3) affective changes such as apathy or rapidly changing moods; and (4) impaired learning, especially of abstractions (Albert, Feldman, & Willis, 1974). One hypothesis is that the "common mechanisms underlying the subcortical dementias are those of impaired timing and activation" (Albert et al., 1974, p. 129). If this hypothesis is correct, drugs that affect those parts of the brain responsible for timing and activation may be useful intervention strategies (Eisdorfer & Cohen, 1978).

Pick's Disease   This is a rare cognitive disorder. Symptoms are similar to those of Alzheimer's disease; however, initial personality changes may be more severe than memory loss. After death the brains of persons with Pick's disease are distinguishable from those with Alzheimer's disease.

Jakob-Crutzfeld Disease   This very rare disease has symptoms similar to Pick's and Alzheimer's diseases. Jakob-Crutzfeld appears to be caused by a slow-acting virus. The disease has been experimentally transmitted between animals and from humans to animals; it may also be transmitted between humans (Eisdorfer & Cohen, 1978). The severity of dementia depends on the amount and rapidity of brain-cell loss, the individual's intellectual and personality resources, and the complexity and friendliness of the environment (Pfeiffer, 1977).

Cognitive disorders may also accompany other diseases, such as the severe nutritional deficiencies sometimes associated with alcoholism, Huntington's chorea, and Parkinson's disease.

Treatment of Chronic Brain Syndromes   Treatment of chronic organic brain disorders is, at present, very difficult, though several strategies may be used to maximize functioning. Agitation may be treated with minor tranquilizers, but they should be carefully monitored and withdrawn as soon as possible. More important is adjusting the environment to provide a simple, orderly setting with moderate stimulation. Care should be balanced with continued efforts to have the person care for him- or herself. Individual and group therapies may be useful for the afflicted person and, even more, the family and others who are sharing the care (Burnside, 1978; Herr & Weakland, 1979).

A moving documentary of the course of arteriosclerotic dementia is presented in *Gramps* (Jury & Jury, 1976). After the death of Gramps—Frank Tugend—his grandsons assembled family photos and showed how the family responded to the illness of a beloved husband, father, and grandfather.

Gramps started to fail at the age of 77. The first year was marked by changes, each of which was minor—Gramps stopped hanging out at the garage where he had gone for 15 years; he turned from a shy, overly polite man into an "outspoken lion"; he began having toileting accidents. He became increasingly dependent on others (mostly his two grandsons) to shave him and to be with him. When he went to the family physician, he couldn't identify the correct day, person he was with, or where he was. By 79 he was into his private world of red rabbits and "whatchacalls," dressing "creatively" in whatever clothing he found, accusing people of stealing tools (which he had placed upstairs), and searching for his mother (long dead) at the neighborhood carnival. Even at this time, however, he had moments of clear awareness, winking at a visitor "like he knew what was going on." A year later he washed his hands in the toilet bowl,

Caring for a person with a serious chronic organic brain disorder is very difficult. This elderly grandfather, Gramps, was cared for at home by his family. Many others requiring intensive care end life in a nursing home.

passed his false teeth to be buttered, and forgot where his room was. He became very destructive, moving things, tearing all the sheets off his bed, and dismantling lamps. By the time he was 81 and had lost complete bowel control, the family found his behavior "an awful ordeal."

Gramps received major care from his wife and two grandsons, as well as other family members. He continued to live at home with his wife; family members washed and shaved him, fed him, frequently changed bedding and clothing when he became incontinent, cleaned up bowel movements from the floor and furniture, replaced the many items Gramps moved, and had their sleep disturbed when he began wandering about the house all night. Because he was at home, Gramps was involved in the daily activities of the family and participated in the celebrations of holidays, birthdays, and picnics. He undoubtedly received more stimulation and attention than he would have had in a nursing home, benefits that probably helped slow his rate of deterioration. He could continue taking care of himself using long-standing habits for longer in his familiar environment than if he were moved to a new place. However, he could not be left alone as his disease progressed, and the family members arranged their schedules so that one person could always be with him.

One day Gramps took his false teeth out and said, "Here, you take these. I won't be using them anymore." During the next month he stayed in his room, refusing to eat. He dozed quietly, went into a coma, and died. Gramps died at home, cared for by the family whom he had nourished and loved for so many years. Few elderly are so fortunate to have a family who can bear the prolonged strains of such care. It is a challenge of our times to find ways to ease the final passage of those who will go like Gramps.

"Acute"/Reversible Brain Syndromes

Perhaps 10 to 20 percent of organic brain syndrome disorders are reversible (Pfeiffer, 1977). Such damage usually occurs during a relatively brief period (from hours to days) of intense dysfunction; hence the term *acute*. Symptoms that suggest a possible acute brain syndrome include overwhelming anxiety, vivid delusions or hallucinations, and cognitive dysfunctions. A geriatric psychiatrist describes one variety:

The onset is fairly sudden, leading from normality to gross disturbance in the course of a day or two. Confusion, the cardinal sign of organic mental illness, is always present, but the severity fluctuates. There is impairment of memory, especially for very recent events, and disorientation, as the patient may not know where he is, the time of day, or those about him. Typically, confusion is most marked in the evening, when the light is starting to fail and the surroundings are less readily perceived. The confusion is associated with clouding of consciousness, a state . . . of reduced wakefulness. This varies greatly in the course of the day or even within a few minutes, from a state approaching lucidity to one of babbling incoherence. Concentration is exceedingly limited; attention is hard to gain, and harder to keep because of the patient's marked distractability. . . . The mood is labile, a dreamy state changing with disconcerting suddenness to one of fear, danger, excitement, suspicion, or perplexity. . . . People are misidentified, and their actions misunderstood, which can form the basis of delusions. Illusions [false perceptions] occur, usually visual and promoted by poor lighting and strong sound. For example, the pattern of wallpaper may be seen as a swarm of cockroaches on the ceiling above, the fluff on a blanket may look like the waving fronds on a fungus, or the low voice of a nurse giving a night-report might be heard as a plotting or a threat. . . . (Pitt, 1974, pp. 24–25)

Delirium is a symptom in acute OBS indicating the presence of a very harmful or poisonous process affecting the whole body and interfering with the brain's activity in various ways. Several causes of acute brain syndrome have been identified so far (Butler & Lewis, 1977; Eisdorfer & Cohen, 1978):

1   *Structural causes,* such as brain tumors, produce mental changes in about half the patients (Eisdorfer & Cohen, 1978).

2   *Drug intoxication,* including alcohol, is a special hazard for older adults, who metabolize drugs more slowly and in a different way than younger adults. In addition, misuse of prescription drugs among the aged is common (Hemminki & Heikkila, 1975), including use of multiple prescriptions, use of drugs "inherited" from neighbors, use of outdated drugs, or substitution of one medication for another.

3   *Hypoglycemia,* a condition of diabetes, may set off an acute brain syndrome if the diabetic has inadequate caloric intake for the amount of insulin taken or cannot adequately process the food because liver or excretory functioning is impaired.

4   *Congestive heart failure,* particularly in individuals who already have marginal or deteriorated cognitive functioning, may set off an acute confusional state.

5   *Infections,* either acute or long-standing, may result in cognitive impairment.

6   *Metabolic and nutritional disorders,* such as underactivity of the thyroid gland, may lead to irritability and cognitive dysfunction. Pernicious anemia and serious vitamin B deficiencies produce brain syndrome symptoms. Calcium levels above normal produce apathy and confusion (Eisdorfer & Cohen, 1978).

7   Severe pain, chronic discomfort, or psychological stress of catastrophic intensity may produce symptoms of acute brain disorder.

There is a high immediate death rate in deliriums (about 40 percent), but if patients survive the acute period, many can resume normal functioning if they receive prompt, adequate treatment. If proper treatment is not given, a potentially reversible organic brain syndrome may become chronic. Since it is not always clear which brain syndromes will be chronic, one strategy is to assume that *all* are potentially reversible. Reversibility can be assessed only after attempts to treat the condition are made, and the individual either responds or not. In the next chapter we will review various modes of intervention used to treat the pathological conditions discussed in this chapter.

SUMMARY

1   *Psychopathology, abnormal behavior, mental disorder,* and *maladaptive behavior* are all terms used to indicate inner personality or outer behavioral patterns that deviate from commonly accepted standards of healthy, adaptive behavior and that have harmful consequences for the self or others.

2   A developmental perspective stresses the ways psychopathological behavior may reflect specific patterns of strength and vulnerability at various life periods. According to this perspective, abnormal behavior may result when the individual is unable to deal with the emerging potentials of the next period or when the social world does not provide necessary facilitation. A developmental perspective is often used to explore maladaptive behaviors in earlier life, but it has not yet been extensively used for psychopathologies of later life.

3   Two major kinds of explanations are offered for abnormal behavior. Biological or *organic* factors include chemical imbalances, lesions or structural damage to the central nervous system, or specific vulnerabilities to particular stresses. Biological factors may develop because of inheritance or as a result of environmental conditions. *Psychosocial* explanations emphasize the ways in which individual responses to special environments shape abnormal behavior. Psychosocial factors may include childhood traumas; parental deprivation; pathogenic parent–child relationships; pathogenic family structures; or special frustrations, conflicts, and pressures. Biological and psychosocial factors are interdependent in ways that research is gradually making clearer.

4   Mental health may be assessed for varied reasons, from the desire to achieve further self-growth to the determining of legal competence for one's own actions. The most common system for assessing individual psychopathology is the DSM III. Current diagnostic systems are probably less useful for older adults than for younger adults; however, they are useful for describing major forms of abnormal behavior.

5   Individuals with a *neurotic disorder* characteristically adopt defensive behaviors designed to avoid or lessen anxiety. The neurotic individual has a faulty evaluation of reality and a tendency to avoid rather than cope with stress. Neurotic patterns are maintained even though they are self-defeating and maladaptive. Recognized forms of neuroses include *anxiety, psychosexual,* and *somatoform* disorders.

6   *Affective disorders* are those in which a single mood of extreme depression or manic elation prevails. *Depression* involves feelings of personal worthlessness, lack of hope about the future, and disturbances in various biological functions. Depression may arise from a biologically based predisposition or vulnerability, particularly in the most severe cases. In addition, psychosocial factors are clearly implicated. Stressful events involving loss or disappointment are especially likely to cause depression in persons who are vulnerable because of early-life or current deprivations. Suicide is a serious risk in severe depressions. Depression may alternate with *manic* states of extreme elation and optimism. Depressions are often self-correcting and respond well to varied treatments.

7   *Psychosomatic disorders* are physical disorders in which psychological factors play a major causative role. The psychological processes are similar to those in neuroses. Stress acts upon a vulnerable part of the body to produce real physical change.

8   *Substance use disorders* involve excessive psychological or physiological reliance upon a substance. Alcohol is the most commonly abused substance in Western societies. The unfortunate symptoms of alcoholism may result from excessive intake of alcohol or an unusual intolerance for alcohol. In addition to alcohol virtually any substance that chemically alters mood or perceptual processes can be used to excess. Patterns of substance abuse differ among younger and older adults; treatment efforts must be responsive to such patterns.

9   Serious distortions of thought characterize *schizophrenic disorders*. Schizophrenic disorders have been noted in every culture; they probably involve biological predispositions interacting with psychosocial factors. *Paranoid distortions*—attributing to other people motivations that do not, in fact, exist—may be part of schizophrenic disorders. Few (if any) effective interventions have been found for schizophrenia and paranoia.

10   Organic mental disorders are those caused by changes in the brain. However, even when basic impairments are organic, there are usually important nonorganic (functional) aspects of psychopathology as well. Organic mental disorders are a particular hazard of late life. Brain damage does not necessarily result in seriously altered behavior. An individual who has slow, progressive deterioration, good coping styles, and a familiar supportive environment may show minimal effects. Brain syndromes may be acute and reversible or chronic and irreversible. Much progress is needed in finding ways to maximize the functioning of organically impaired individuals.

CHAPTER FOURTEEN

INTERVENTIONS

Intervention means a coming or being between, an interference in the affairs of others. In psychology it involves doing something systematically and intentionally to alter a relationship in ways that are likely to have a positive outcome with regard to some problem of psychological functioning.

This chapter will identify some of the major challenges for people who plan, carry through, or receive interventions designed to affect psychological functioning during adulthood. Our primary focus will be on interventions designed to affect mental health. These challenges include defining the problem, identifying the probable causes of the problem, understanding intervention options, selecting and implementing appropriate intervention strategies, evaluating outcomes, and determining policies about interventions.

A DEVELOPMENTAL PERSPECTIVE ON INTERVENTION

As we have seen, psychological problems may be related to age in that they are brought about by internal and external events that are likely to occur at certain

ages or stages of adult development. Most adults develop an "expected time-table" of normal life events and experience minimal distress when the changes occur when and as anticipated. In part, the view of the expected life course is based on information about life events provided by experts and the mass media; this information can be regarded as a form of "preventive intervention," designed to help adults plan ahead to avert problems. Interventions may be necessary when an event occurs off-time, either earlier or later than anticipated.

Resources—including both formal and informal external support and personal resources—may also vary with age. The woman widowed at 55 has many years of coping with life changes, and she may have developed strengths not evident at 30.

Problems and resources may be age-linked because of particular cohort effects. For example, many people now assume it is both necessary and desirable for women to remain economically self-supporting throughout adulthood. If women do, in fact, arrange their lives with an eye to ensuring their economic independence, the next generations of women may have different problems and options in middle age than past generations. Another cohort difference is seen in the willingness to define personal problems in terms of mental health. Americans who are now older adults seldom define a personal problem in mental-health terms, nor are they likely to utilize mental-health services. In contrast, about 44 percent of adults 20–49 years old in 1976 defined personal problems in mental-health terms (Kulka & Tamir, 1978). The ways individuals define their problems influence the kinds of interventions they will seek out or accept. Thus, for example, we can expect that the demand for mental-health services appropriate for older adults will increase as the current cohorts of young and middle-aged adults grow older.

Before describing various kinds of intervention options, we will summarize some of the most salient issues at various phases of normal adult development, suggesting some of the ways interventions are developmentally appropriate.

Intervention in Young Adulthood

The main goal of intervention in young adulthood is promoting positive development. Young adults are confronted, often abruptly, with many developmental tasks that have lifelong consequences—clarifying their own values and goals, selecting and preparing for a career, and satisfying needs for intimacy and parenting. In addition, young people renegotiate their relationships with parents as they establish themselves in adult commitments and responsibilities. Young adults are more likely than middle-aged or older adults under 65 to have stressful experiences such as marital strain, divorce, or being fired or having to withdraw from employment (Pearlin & Radabaugh, 1979).

Youths who go directly from high school to work enter young adulthood at earlier ages than those who attend college and thus may be subject to somewhat different strains. Young people attending college use that time and experience to explore career and intimacy options. The following list is an example of the kinds of questions used to help young people assess their alternatives; these questions may be equally appropriate at other life phases when adults are contemplating changes:

1   What is motivating the search or the change?
2   What are my needs, wants, and interests?
3   What do I like to do? What do I like to learn?
4   What is available? What are the opportunities?
5   What are my abilities and skills?
6   What preparation do I need?
7   What are my priorities?
8   What are my short-term and long-term goals?
9   What are the benefits and costs of several alternatives?
10   What is my best alternative?
11   What do I need to do to carry out my goal?
12   What are the first steps?

Young adults can often benefit from programs designed to ease the strains of dealing with new responsibilities such as marriage, parenting, combining employment and parenting, divorce, unemployment, or career promotions. Young adults who are striving to succeed in careers may benefit from an informal relationship with a mentor, an older, more experienced person who will help them develop their career. The potential importance of mentoring is shown in a survey of prominent men and women executives in the United States, two-thirds of whom reported having a mentor or sponsor during their young adult years. By middle age the group who had mentors earned significantly more money and reported greater career satisfaction and progress than those who did not have mentors (Nugent, 1980).

One risk for young people is that they will be overwhelmed by the pressures involved in the choices they make. For example, young women who parent small children often experience great stress, whether or not they combine parenting with outside employment. Another risk is that young people will not settle on any choices in work, love, or values that they can honor through the young adult period. As a result, they come to middle age without having established themselves as adults by succeeding in the tasks of young adulthood.

Intervention in Middle Adulthood

During the transition into middle adulthood many people reexamine the goals, vocation, mate, lifestyle, and geographical location they chose in young adulthood. Some theorists suggest that early in life we develop a dream of how life is supposed to be, and in mid-life we need to reexamine this dream, either affirming it or rejecting it for another (Levinson, 1978). Often life dreams are constructed without much information about what is required to carry them out. A child may decide to be an actress, a cowboy, a doctor, or a housewife without knowing the real costs and benefits of the choice. Even young adults may not fully appreciate the long-term consequences of such decisions as career and mate selection. In middle age there is a strong need to use one's remaining time well, to do the right things, and to make the right moves *now*. Thus an important area for intervention in middle adulthood is the mid-life crisis, which we have examined in some detail earlier.

Most adults master the transition into middle age and experience themselves as part of the "command generation"—those in charge of important decisions and carrying substantial responsibilities in work and family arenas. Many experience an expansion of life goals and priorities to include more nurturance in men and more assertiveness in women. Marriage relationships may be revised, and the career focus may shift to becoming a mentor. In fact, some large corporations have recently begun to encourage mentoring as a way of dealing with the concerns and problems of their middle-aged employees. After the young adult decades of energetic, productive, competitive work orientation, many middle-aged employees have valuable experience and perspective but feel stressed, bored, or burned out; reduced efficiency and motivation, absenteeism, alcoholism, and depression are consequences that cost corporations billions of dollars yearly. Shifting the emphasis of middle-aged employees somewhat away from competitive productivity and toward developing the talents of younger workers can benefit both generations.

Middle-aged persons often accept substantial responsibility for providing for both growing children and aging parents, and the stresses of being the generation in the middle can be debilitating. Some middle-aged women wish to be more involved in careers than they are and may experience considerable strain in obtaining the desired education, credentials, and job opportunities; other women feel pushed into the labor market by inflation, divorce, or widowhood. Strain is greatest when the individual feels blocked from making desired changes or forced to make undesired changes. Interventions can help make it possible for individuals to match their ambitions with their opportunities.

Some individuals experience middle age as a period of stagnation, decline, and anxiety about aging. For example, there is evidence to suggest that some adults are predisposed to psychological problems at mid-life because of their strong need for positive self-regard and praise (Kernberg, 1976), whereas others are vulnerable because of previously unresolved developmental tasks (Gutmann, 1980).

Intervention in Late Adulthood

Later life is marked by many changes for which intervention is appropriate. Most older individuals continue to function independently. A relatively new challenge is how to make the most of the period in life when people are in relatively good health but are no longer heavily involved in employment and parenting—the young-old phase (Neugarten, 1975). Generally, elders who remain involved in activities that are meaningful to them have higher morale and are more adaptive than those who cannot replace their involvements of the middle years. Thus options should be available for limited employment, volunteer work, continued education, social and recreational pursuits, and so forth. The options must be appropriate for the particular group of elders; some will prefer to play bingo at a local seniors' club, others may want a garden plot, and some may prefer an easily accessible library.

Couples who have been married a long time may wish to revitalize their relationship or deal with problems that they put aside during the busier middle years. Many persons are confronted during later life with the illness or death of a spouse or close relative and can benefit from services that provide support during this period. Older adults who have lost a companion continue to desire the company of others; some court and remarry and could use counseling services (including sexual counseling) sensitized to making the transition into late life remarriage. Many elders must deal with the divorces and remarriages of children and grandchildren.

The greatest risk is poor health. On the average, persons over 65 experience more than twice as many days when activities are restricted because of illness than persons under 65 (U.S. Bureau of the Census, 1979). Various studies have found that 20 to 45 percent of the aged living in the community experience behavioral and emotional disorders significant enough to be labeled psychiatric problems (Eisdorfer & Cohen, 1978). Community surveys summarized by Kay and Bergmann (1980) show that between 5 and 8 percent of the elderly are disabled enough by chronic organic brain syndromes to be unable to care for themselves; 1 to 2 percent of the samples are totally disoriented and need constant care. After the age of 80 approximately 20 percent of elderly show moderate or severe forms of chronic organic brain syndrome. Interestingly, approximately 75 percent of the persons with moderate or severe organic brain syndromes were living at home (like Gramps, in Chapter 13); the rest were living in long-term care institutions.

Elderly persons, who comprise 10 percent of the United States population, make up 30 percent of the population of mental hospitals (Kramer, Taube, & Redick, 1973). Though only 4 to 5 percent of all people over 65 in the United States live in long-term institutions, the percentage increases as age increases. For example, 15 to 20 percent of the elderly in Detroit die in institutions (excluding hospitals), mostly nursing homes (Kastenbaum & Candy, 1973). Many people in nursing homes have a mental disorder or impairment and go to long-term care facilities because they can no longer be cared for at home or because they have no one to care for them.

These figures demonstrate why one of the major challenges for the later years has become how to maintain good physical and mental health. Those providing intervention can help elderly persons, their relatives, and those who care for them deal with the problems associated with failing health.

A normal developmental issue of late life is dealing with death. People may be confronted by the death of others throughout life, but old age inevitably brings each person to the end of his or her own life. This topic will be discussed in detail in Chapter 15.

Various psychotherapeutic interventions appropriate for younger adults are useful with older people as well. It has taken many years to overcome the view that older adults are poor candidates for psychotherapy. However, partly because relatively few older persons have been treated as mental-health patients—elderly persons are only 2 percent of the cases seen at outpatient clinics and 4 percent of those seen at community mental-health centers (Kramer, Taube, & Redick, 1973)—there are considerable problems in the accurate assessment and diagnosis of their problems (Schaie & Schaie, 1977). On the one hand, symptoms of disturbance manifested by an older person are often overlooked by family members or others dealing with the elder or explained by the statement, "He's getting old." At the other extreme, certain behaviors (such as forgetting a name or misplacing car keys) may be interpreted as symptomatic of irreversible brain damage when shown by an older person. The variation of behavior patterns with situation, age, ethnicity, and gender also can lead to diagnostic problems. For example, an elderly individual who recently experienced a personal loss might exhibit excessive body shakiness, poor conversational skills, or psychomotor slowness and poor cognitive performance, and be diagnosed and treated as suffering from organic brain syndrome rather than as depressed because of the loss. Because of all these complex factors the mental-health needs of the elderly in America often go unmet (Gatz, Smyer, & Lawton, 1980).

Insofar as problems and resources are age-linked, interventions must also be developmentally appropriate, based on careful assessment of the strengths and vulnerabilities of the individuals involved. There is considerable disagreement whether the standards for what is "normal" or "pathological" *should* be linked to age or life stage. Nevertheless, it is probably important to recognize that such standards often are applied, implicitly or explicitly, by those involved in intervention. As we discuss intervention, we will try to include developmental perspectives.

DEFINING THE PROBLEM REQUIRING INTERVENTION

The first step in any intervention program is to identify the problem to be remedied. This raises at least three basic questions: Who defines the problem? At what point is a process declared a problem? How does a challenge become a problem?

Defining an event or behavior as problematic means that it cannot be accommodated within the range of usual functioning; adaptive efforts have already failed or are expected to fail in the future unless interventions are applied. "Who defines" is in part a question of power, as several people usually have some stake in defining the problem—the individuals who most directly experience the problem, those who may be called upon to assist in the intervention, and those charged with paying for the intervention. It is important to understand the perspectives of each person with a stake in the definition. Often there is some conflict at this stage, and, if a definition cannot be agreed on, any further efforts to intervene may be difficult.

In the simplest cases all involved agree on the definition of the problem and the fact that it is a problem at that particular point. Difficulties may arise when there is disagreement about whether a problem exists or when one of the interested parties is reluctant to acknowledge an existing problem. For example, adult children may be ambivalent about admitting that an aging parent has serious problems that require intervention (see Chapter 9). The adult child may fear further deterioration and eventual loss of the parent, may be reluctant to become more intensely involved in daily contact with the parent, may have long-standing conflicts with the parent, or may resist what seems like role reversal. The parent, of course, often has similar reluctance to define the situation as serious enough to require outside intervention. Thus both parent and children may delay seeking outside help until the problem is, indeed, very disabling and requires substantial intervention.

Intervention could be sought for many problems. The challenge for all involved is to agree on a statement of the problem to be addressed. If the definition is relatively specific and limited, it may be easier to formulate a reasonable plan of intervention than to attack a broadly defined, wide-scope problem. Intervening to enhance the "quality of life" may be the most ambitious aspiration of all.

IDENTIFYING PROBABLE CAUSES

Once a problem is defined as precisely as possible, it becomes important to find what is causing the problem. In Chapter 13 we focused on the presumed causes of various kinds of psychopathological problems; such statements represent the current thinking and are being revised continually on the basis of further evidence.

Ideally, before establishing an intervention program we would have a good understanding of the usual developmental course of the problem. This includes past predictors of the current problem—what paths lead to this particular problem. In addition, we would be able to project the course of the problem if no intervention is made. Unfortunately, we understand relatively few problems so well. Though some paths are fairly clear for childhood years, there is less adequate evidence about problems over the adult years.

Let us look at several ways of identifying probable causes of a problem.

The Identified-Problem Group

Perhaps the most common strategy is to describe those who are identified as having the problem. We can take all patients in a clinic diagnosed as depressed, or those who come to a clinic to stop smoking, and see what they may have in common in terms of biological, psychological, and social functioning. This method is inadequate for several reasons. Unless the identified-problem group is compared to some other group without the problem, there is no way to differentiate whether the common factors are related to the problem or not. For example, early research indicated that a higher percentage of delinquent boys came from single-parent homes. Later studies showed that many nondelinquent boys from similar neighborhoods also came from single-parent homes. Thus living with one parent could no longer be considered to "cause" delinquent behavior.

Comparison of Problem and Nonproblem Groups

In another common strategy to uncover patterns of probable cause, a *comparison group,* sometimes called a *control group,* is selected, which is as much like the identified-problem group as possible except for the presence of the problem under study. The nondelinquent boys mentioned above are such a comparison group. Deciding on an appropriate comparison group is often difficult. Comparability in terms of sex, social class, ethnicity, or community may be desirable. From a developmental perspective it may be important to have the groups comparable in age or developmental stage.

Once a comparison group is determined, it is compared with the identified-problem group to see which factors can differentiate between the groups. Evidence about differentiation is often based on retrospective data—that is, information about the past as recalled by the respondent. For example, several of the studies cited in Chapter 13 about the precursors of adult depression examined the prevalence of parental loss during childhood among adults who became seriously depressed and/or suicidal, and "normal" adults (Lloyd, 1980). Most of the studies provided some support for a causal link between early parental loss and later depression.

This method of establishing causal connections is flawed, however, because of difficulties in (1) establishing appropriate comparison groups; (2) relying on selective recall, which may be biased by later developments; and (3) establishing whether the relationships observed are, in fact, specific to the identified problem behavior.

Epidemiological Studies

Epidemiology is the study of the distribution and causes of disease or disorder in total, defined populations. It examines conditions associated with variations in the frequency of each disorder and in disorders that are the most common, both at a given point and over time. Longitudinal study of a population can provide important information about how events are linked and at which points problems emerge.

One important decision in epidemiology involves the "total population" to be studied. The population is often selected on the basis of individual characteristics such as age, sex, or social class. Another strategy might be to do epidemiological studies in several well-defined communities (see Warren, 1963).

A longitudinal epidemiological study can delineate patterns of events as they emerge. By studying an entire, identified population, it is possible to chart the prevalence of disorders. Many individuals are available to compare to those who develop problems, and the stability of the relationships between disorders and individual characteristics can be observed. The observations can be used to suggest causal models, which can then be compared to those derived from similar and different communities, and appropriate interventions designed.

Inferences from Treatment Effects

Probable causation may be evaluated partly by the outcome of various interventions. For example, the major question regarding mental health is probably the extent to which psychopathological problems are caused by biological malfunctioning, deficits in the interpersonal sphere, or some interaction between the two factors. One way to establish probable cause is to test the effectiveness of various drug and interpersonal therapies, separately and together. Problems that respond well to drug therapies alone, but not to other kinds of therapies, are presumed to have a strong biological cause. If drug treatments produce no effects, or negative effects, and interpersonal therapies provide a remedy, an interpersonal-deficit model of causation is supported.

UNDERSTANDING INTERVENTION OPTIONS

Intervention can take many forms. We have categorized intervention in terms of goals, areas, techniques, settings, and change agents. Options within each category are summarized in Table 14-1.

Goals of Intervention

Four general goals of intervention are listed in Table 14-1; any particular intervention may entail one or more of these.

Alleviation   One goal is to alleviate or remove an identifiable problem. For example, an elderly person who has gone into shock because of the interaction of multiple medications must first have the drugs removed from his body and his physical functioning stabilized as completely as possible. Psychotherapists may set a goal of reducing pain, as revealed in reported anxiety, distress, anger, aggression, or hostility. Therapists may also set a goal of reducing psychopathology. Such a goal assumes that the patient or client has a definable, diagnosable problem that can be alleviated, remedied, or reduced by intervention. Psychotherapeutic models vary in their emphasis on the manifest behavior as the problem or as the symptom. For example, behavior modifiers treat observable behavior as the target problem, whereas psychodynamically oriented interventionists view behaviors as symptoms of underlying psychopathology. A behavior therapist might try to change shyness or nervousness directly, while another therapist might view shyness and nervousness as symptoms of deeper problems.

Table 14-1   A Framework for Intervention Options

Goals
Alleviation
Compensation
Enrichment
Prevention

Selected areas
Health (e.g., prolonging positive health)
Cognition (e.g., improving memory, intelligence, learning)
Emotions (e.g., improving motivation, reducing anxieties)
Socialization (e.g., strengthening social interactions)
Attitudes and values (e.g., creating a positive outlook and self-attitude)

Techniques
Pharmacotherapies
Psychotherapies
Education and training
Service delivery
Ecological interventions
Legislating social and behavioral change

Settings
Home
Work
Educational
Hospital or institution
Community
Society

Change agents
Self
Family members, friends
Paraprofessionals
Professionals
Administrators
Lawmakers and governmental leaders

Compensation   A second goal may be to compensate for losses contributing to the problem. For example, after stabilizing the general functioning of a person suffering from drug reactions, we may find that she has had some brain damage. Interventions would be designed to compensate for the deficits noted; this might involve simplifying and stabilizing her environment so she could continue to manage in it, or retraining her for lost capacities.

Enrichment   This intervention goal is intended to bring the level of functioning beyond the minimal or "usual." Classes in childbirth for expectant mothers and fathers, Elderhostel programs for older adults who enjoy continuing education and travel, and training programs in managerial effectiveness may have such goals. Psychotherapists may see the goal of therapy as enhancing self-acceptance, self-fulfillment, or self-actualization. Interpersonal adaptability is a target for some therapists and clients. Therapists may focus on helping the client function effectively and comfortably in social settings and interpersonal relationships. This goal might involve helping the person become more intimate, more harmonious in interpersonal contexts, or more or less assertive or submissive.

Prevention   Finally, some interventions are designed to prevent problems from occurring or recurring. Instead of trying to change "deviant" or inappropriate behaviors, preventionists try to take action that will reduce the likelihood or severity of problems before they occur (see Caplan, 1964; Cowen, 1973; Kessler & Albee, 1975). Prevention programs should be based on good evidence about the factors that place individuals or groups at risk for certain kinds of problems. Designing preventive programs is very difficult since data are seldom adequate. The relationship between smoking and cancer has been demonstrated to be credible enough to justify massive preventive programs aimed at reducing the incidence of smoking; there are fewer sociopsychological problems for which the remedy is so clear.

The distinction between prevention and intervention is perhaps becoming less important as intervention programs become more broad-based and multifaceted. For example, a program that combined preventive and treatment goals might include the following:

1   Knowledge dissemination regarding risk factors and treatment resources.
2   Early detection and diagnosis of individuals at risk.
3   Strengthening of the adaptive capacities of individuals at risk.
4   Reduction of pathogenic factors and strengthening of support systems within the environment.
5   Rapid, effective intervention when problems become evident.
6   Concern for long-term as well as short-term consequences of the problem.
7   Containment of the problem's effects.

Any of the kinds of goals described above may be long- or short-term. The goal of detoxifying a person suffering from an acute drug reaction is short-term; informing young adults about the nature of aging in the hope that they will age better than their elders is a very long-term goal.

The goals of intervention often depend partly on the age of the person involved. A young man who suffers multiple fractures and possible brain damage in a car accident is likely to have many interventions available to him; some will have the goal of immediate relief, and others will be designed to compensate for lost or damaged functions. Psychological counseling to deal with his rage, depression, and sense of vulnerability would be part of his therapy. The long-term goal would most likely be to restore the young man to as near his preaccident level of functioning as possible. Rarely does an elderly person have such optimistic goals or the resources allocated to meet such goals. Interventions with elderly persons usually have shorter-term goals of symptom relief and halting or slowing further deterioration.

The goals set and the resources allocated depend, of course, on the values of the goal setters (health professionals, family members, and the afflicted individual) and the resources available. Resources for intervention are always limited; therefore, priorities must be established. It is a matter of much debate, among professionals and politicians, which general goals should have priority and whether age should be relevant in setting goals for intervention programs. We will discuss these issues further when we consider social policy.

Areas of Intervention

Interventions may be directed at different areas of functioning (see Table 14-1). More than one area may be targeted in any particular intervention program, of course, and the goals may include any of those discussed above. The areas of intervention may be age-linked in several ways.

Likelihood   First, the likelihood of a particular area of functioning's becoming problematic may vary with age. For example, cognitive functioning is rarely a serious problem for most of adulthood unless one suffers from a cerebral stroke or brain injury. Research suggests that some minor deterioration in cognitive functioning begins in late middle age (see Chapter 6). Marked cognitive deterioration is a risk associated with late life. As we discussed in Chapters 6 and 13, *most* old people do not become senile. However, most senile people are old, a fact that links age to this particular vulnerability. Decline is greater in some areas of functioning than others and is more pronounced in some individuals than in others (Horn, 1970; Horn & Donaldson, 1976).

On the basis of the evidence, interventions can be designed to slow the rates of decline—for instance, improved diet, exercise, and regular intellectual stimulation. These kinds of interventions may be particularly appropriate for middle-aged and older adults who do not show signs of marked cognitive decline. In addition, interventions are being designed and implemented that expand the individual's range of optimal cognitive functioning (see Labouvie-Vief & Chandler, 1978). Some such programs are directed toward improving performance in skills tested by standardized measures of cognitive functioning; others are oriented toward practical daily living skills (Hoyer, Mishara, & Riedel, 1975; Richards & Thorpe, 1978).

Kinds of Functioning   Within any particular area the kind of functioning defined as problematic or pathological may change with age. These shifting definitions reflect our expectations about what is normal and what should be accomplished at various ages. Recently, Schaie and Schaie (1977) discussed the need to establish criteria for the level or range of functioning characteristic of "normal" age decline as compared to pathological aging. The general rule of thumb—interference with everyday functioning—is likely to imply pathology for a substantial majority of elderly. Older people may tolerate significant physical pain and discomfort as a "normal" accompaniment of aging, whereas younger adults may request—and obtain—intervention for similar pains.

Symptoms   The symptoms that serve to identify problems in particular areas may vary with age. For example, the symptoms of depression are different for adults at various ages (Eisdorfer & Cohen, 1978). Verwoerdt (1976) noted that depression in old age is frequently overlooked because the affective manifestations such as sad feelings, self-deprecatory thoughts, and crying spells are less conspicuous than other symptoms such as psychomotor retardation, impaired attention and memory, somatic symptoms, and loss of energy and initiative. As many of the latter characteristics are attributable to organic brain syndrome or other organic processes, elderly depressed patients are often given an organic brain syndrome diagnosis, are treated accordingly, and then fulfill the prophecy of irreversible decline.

TECHNIQUES OF INTERVENTION

Interventions can utilize a wide variety of techniques, limited only by the imagination and resources of the intervener. We will discuss some of the major options and consider how they may be relevant to various problems of adult life. Professionals tend to develop expertise in a few techniques; intervention programs can often be enhanced by combining the special perspectives and skills of several intervention specialists.

Pharmacotherapies

Pharmacotherapies are those that use medications to alter the individual's internal biological state in order to effect desired changes. The use of drugs dates back to at least the 6th century B.C., when the extracts of such herbs as hemlock and poppy were used to instill good cheer, courage, or relief from pain (Coleman, 1976). Our reliance on drugs has steadily increased since ancient times, in part as a consequence of increased sophistication about the potential and actual impact of drugs on functioning.

Drug interventions are based on evidence that the problem to be treated is caused by a biological malfunction that can be remedied by physical/chemical means. Such decisions are regarded as the special domain of physicians or others with extensive training in the interaction of drugs and physiological functioning. In the United States such expertise is most often found with psychiatrists, medical doctors specializing in the kinds of disorders discussed in Chapter 13.

In evaluation of any psychopharmacological intervention, several cautions are necessary:

1   Any drug may have multiple effects.

2   Drug effects may vary depending on dosage levels.

3   Drugs do not necessarily activate new behaviors; rather, drugs serve to alter the rate and quality of ongoing behavioral processes.

4   Different individuals are affected differently by the same drug at the same dosages, depending on attitudinal factors, expectation, and physiological status.

The effects of drugs are different at different ages. As people grow older, there are physiological changes in metabolism and absorption rate but also decreased drug transport because of reduced arterial blood flow (Eisdorfer & Stotsky, 1977). When drugs are held in the system for a long time, older adults have a greater risk of negative side effects—such as drug intoxication, lethargy, confusion, disorientation, and sensory impairment—than younger adults. Chemotherapies for cancer, for example, are not as effective with older adults as with younger adults, and sometimes the risk of drug toxicity or poisoning is increased with older patients. Many of these same cautions apply to the use of surgical anesthesias with different-aged adults.

Pharmacological interventions must be adapted to the age of the recipient. The following are guidelines with regard to the use of drug therapy with older persons:

1   Psychoactive medications eliminate only the symptoms of emotional or mental stress, not the causes of the distress. Psychopharmacological intervention should be used as an adjunct to other direct forms of psychological, social, or medical intervention.

2   Effective and safe psychopharmacological intervention is related to accurate assessment of the health and physiological status of the person. This includes obtaining information about allergies and currently used medications since many of the acute drug reactions of older people are related to the interactions of two or more drugs (Greenblatt & Shader, 1981). Age-

related physiological changes (such as decrease in body mass, increase in body fat) affect the individual's responsivity to medication. Some drugs cannot be used simultaneously with alcohol (Kapnick, 1978).

3 Psychopharmacological interventions, perhaps more than other forms of intervention, need to be carefully evaluated in terms of the needs of the individual. Medications are often prescribed so as to make psychiatric and nursing home residents more manageable for the staff (Butler & Lewis, 1977). Low to moderate doses may make patients less irritable, anxious, and restless; heavy doses are likely to make them lethargic and out of touch with external reality. In addition, patients may develop serious side effects from prolonged medication. Medications also may be advocated by staff to avoid interacting with the patients or planning appropriate recreational programs.

4 When drugs are needed, simple schedules of usage should be prescribed whenever possible. The user must consume the proper amount at the proper time in order to get the maximum benefit from the medication. Scheduling can get complicated if the person is taking several medications. Further, drug use should be terminated as soon as it is no longer necessary.

Psychotherapy

Psychotherapies rely on some form of interpersonal relationship to restore or enhance functioning. Although more than 140 different approaches have been identified (Parloff, 1976), they have in common a confiding relationship and a verbal dialogue between the person administering the treatment and the person receiving it. The dialogue is directed at bringing about the desired change in the recipient (often called a patient or a client). The length of the relationship, the number and kinds of individuals involved, the treatment goals, the content of the interactions, and the desired style of interaction vary considerably. The variations reflect the training and ideology of the therapist, the personal and situational characteristics of the person seeking help, and the social-psychological characteristics of the therapy situation.

Every psychotherapy situation is a social situation, and consequently it must be understood in terms of the individuals involved and the setting. The outcome of psychotherapy is related to patient, therapist, and treatment factors (Luborsky, Chandler, Auerback, Cohen, & Bachrach, 1971; Bergin, 1971). Table 14-2 lists some of the individual patient characteristics that are relevant to the course of psychotherapy, as well as some of the therapist characteristics that have been related to outcomes. Studies suggest that, in general, patient factors related to improvement in psychotherapy are psychological health or adequacy of personality functioning before and at the point of diagnosis; absence of schizoid trends (marked withdrawal from others); intelligence; anxiety level; motivation; and educational and social assets. To date there have been very few systematic studies of the particular characteristics of older patients associated with successful outcome. The most important therapist factors are experience, attitude and interest patterns, empathy, and similarity with the patient.

Broadly speaking, three major approaches to psychotherapy are used by contemporary practitioners: psychodynamic, humanistic, and behavioral. Each is derived from a general theory of psychological behavior, and each has many variant forms.

Psychodynamic Therapy: The Pursuit of Insight   Psychoanalysis and some of the other psychodynamic theories are the oldest of the formalized schools or systems of psychotherapy, beginning with Freud (1904) at the turn of the century. Psychodynamic theories include models of adult development reviewed in Chapter 7 and theories about the therapeutic process: What causes disturbed development and what procedures may be useful for maximizing recovery and full functioning.

Analytic therapies are based on the premise that disturbed functioning often occurs because of unconscious conflicts: The individual strives both to express and to refrain from expressing some wish or action. As long as the desire

Table 14–2   Patient and Therapist Characteristics

Characteristics that the target individual (patient)
brings to the treatment setting:

Physical health status
Current medications (if any)
Mental status (including cognitive and attentional skills, styles, and strategies)
Affective (or emotional) status (e.g., anxiety, depression)
Language and communication skills
Social and interpersonal skills (e.g., self-esteem, self-concept)
Attitudes, values, and beliefs
Educational level
Marital/family status
Age, ethnicity, gender
Social class (including employment history)
Length, type, and frequency of previous psychiatric contact
Responsiveness to past treatments (if any)
Expectations of outcome

Characteristics that the change agent (therapist)
brings to the treatment setting:

A treatment orientation (e.g., behavioral, psychoanalytic)
Expectations of outcome
Attitudinal and affective factors (e.g., empathy, "agism")
Age, ethnicity, gender
Experience as a change agent

and the conflict remain unconscious, they cannot be subjected to the rational, conscious control of the ego. Therapy thus becomes a process of gradually "loosening" the barriers of repression. In the safety of the therapeutic relationship the person experiences the feared feelings, inpulses, rages, and so on in such a way as to understand them and, ultimately, to master them. This is sometimes referred to as *insight* therapy, reflecting the importance placed on helping the individual understand—at a feeling as well as a cognitive level—his or her patterns of behavior. In particular, the individual is expected to come to appreciate the ways he or she contributes to the problems, often by unconsciously repeating or re-creating the kinds of situations experienced earlier in life.

The analytic therapist relies heavily on transference to help the patient understand recurrent patterns of behavior. *Transference* is the phenomenon of displacing feelings, fantasies, idealizations, and the like about one person onto another person; in the therapy situation that other person is typically the therapist. In other words, it is assumed that the patient often responds to the therapist *as if* the therapist were the patient's mother, father, wife, and so on. The patient and the therapist can then analyze those interactions as representations of important, enduring behavioral styles rather than temporary responses to the analyst.

Both younger and older patients often unconsciously perceive the analyst as parent, and patients often sexualize the therapeutic relationship, distorting the therapist's friendly interest into an erotic one. Older patients may be more likely than younger ones to respond to the therapist as a child or a sibling (Hiatt, 1975).

Older patients may arouse different patterns of *countertransference*, the therapist's unconscious reactions to the patient. A therapist who is younger than the patient may respond as if the patient were a parent and consequently overidealize or devalue the older patient (Goldfarb, 1964). Countertransference is undoubtedly an issue in all therapy relationships, but psychoanalytic therapy openly acknowledges this risk and challenges the therapist to be alert for his or her own biases so they do not impede accurate perception of the patient. The patient's primary protection is the therapist's willingness and ability to monitor his or her own responses during the therapeutic situation and to modify behavior in behalf of the patient.

In addition to analyzing transference, the therapist notes patterns of *resistance*, those themes the patient tries to avoid discussing. Resistance is considered to belie especially important internal conflicts. In order to get at such unconscious material, the patient is encouraged to speak freely, even when thoughts do not seem to be "rationally" ordered, and to report dreams and semiconscious thoughts. All such apparently illogical and random information is presumed to be ordered by the idiosyncratic, unconscious logic of the patient. The therapist is, then, a "detective" and a guide. The challenge is to discern the patterns that can reveal the unique meanings of the troubling behavior for this individual. In order to reveal the hidden conflicts, the therapist lets the patient experience anxiety without reassurance that everything will be all right. Anxiety is taken as an important clue to underlying problems.

The process involved in psychodynamic therapy can be very demanding for both patient and therapist. The extreme is classic psychoanalysis, in which the patient and analyst commit themselves to uncovering the "core issues" that lie behind the reported disturbances in behavior. Analysis may involve hourly sessions three to five times a week for several years; as such, it represents one of the more intensive—and expensive—intervention efforts.

Modifications of intensive psychoanalysis have been developed and used successfully. Brief psychotherapy of 10 to 40 sessions has been used, applying analytic therapy techniques to specific focal problems rather than attempting a more general personality restructuring (Malan, 1963, 1976a); we will discuss brief therapy further when we consider evaluating interventions later in this chapter. Some therapists, meeting a patient once or twice weekly, place less emphasis on uncovering and reworking the roots of the problem and more on understanding how current conflicts contribute to the identified problem. Others emphasize the importance of the therapist's understanding the dynamic nature of the patient's problems, even if the therapist primarily provides support or assistance and does not push for insight by the patient.

Although Freud did not believe that psychoanalysis was a useful therapy for anyone over 40, later therapists have disagreed and have documented the potential for profound personality change in the older person (Blum & Tross, 1980). However, relatively little research has been done on psychodynamic treatment of the elderly (Blum & Tross, 1980). Some therapists emphasize that quite traditional modes may be effective with older patients. Older people are very heterogeneous; some will have the ego strength and interest necessary to succeed in rigorous insight-oriented therapies, and some will not (Kahana, 1979). Other analytic therapists suggest the selective use of insight-oriented approaches combined with supportive therapies as more appropriate for older patients.

Humanistic Psychotherapy: Supportive Facilitation   Humanistic therapies are based on the assumption that people have the freedom to control their own behavior. A humanistic psychotherapist serves primarily as counselor, guide, and facilitator as the individual reflects upon his or her own problems, makes choices, and decides what action to take. The therapist tries to lower the patient's anxiety by supporting the ways the client reports and resolves the problems. Although supportive therapy is not aimed at leading the troubled person toward insight, individuals may, in fact, gain substantial insight into their own behavior patterns as they discuss them with the therapist.

Humanistic or supportive therapies may be appropriate throughout adulthood. Some psychoanalytic therapists recommend supportive therapy for patients who lack the motivation or the ego strength to benefit from traditional analytic techniques, particularly the elderly who suffer from cognitive impairments or substantial loss of social supports (Goldfarb, 1956, 1969; Weinberg,

1976). Supportive therapy may include guidance in planning activities that bolster self-esteem, imparting a sense of hopefulness about the person's immediate distress, and helping the person obtain community assistance. In these respects the "activist" stance taken with older patients represents a considerable modification of the more neutral, interpretative stance taken by the psychoanalyst.

Behavioral Therapies: Modifying Behavior   A third major form of psychotherapeutic intervention systematically applies principles of learning to the modification of maladaptive behaviors. The assumption is that maladaptive behaviors are learned; more desirable behaviors can be learned by the manipulation of environmental contingencies. The therapist helps the patient define the behavior pattern to be changed and establishes a program of reinforcements designed to gradually modify the behavior. The ultimate goal is for the individual to monitor and control his or her own behavior.

Behavioral therapies use several techniques in changing behaviors.

Extinction involves removing reinforcement for an undesired behavior. For example, an aide in a nursing home may complain about a patient's messing with his food during mealtimes. After discussing the variety of interactions the aide has with the patient, the therapist discovers that the only time the aide pays attention to the patient is when the patient is messing with his food; "good" (that is, orderly and quiet) patients are ignored by the staff. The intervener helps establish a program whereby the aide ignores the patient when he is messing with his food but tries to chat with him when he is behaving "reasonably." This procedure uses the technique of reinforcement as well as the principle of extinction.

Positive reinforcement is used systematically to shape behavior. Anything that increases the likelihood of a behavior's occurring is considered reinforcing; individuals vary in what will serve as an effective reinforcer. The aide in the example above was relying on the fact that personal attention is reinforcing for most people. Tangible reinforcers, such as candy, cigarettes, money, or tokens may be used with children or individuals who have severely limited cognitive or emotional functioning. The goal is to develop responses that will ultimately prove self-rewarding because the behavior leads to social and intrinsic rewards.

Systematic desensitization is used when an individual avoids anxiety by withdrawing from a situation. The patient must learn to experience the situation as nonpainful, or even rewarding. Wolpe (1969) devised a method to train clients to remain calm and relaxed in situations that previously produced anxiety. First, the individual is trained to relax. Second, the individual constructs an "anxiety hierarchy," ordered in terms of how much anxiety is aroused when the patient is in various situations. Finally, when the client is completely relaxed, the therapist describes the least threatening situation of the hierarchy and has the client imagine it. Progressively more threatening situations are described until the client reports feeling anxious. Treatment is terminated for that session and continued at another time when the client is fully relaxed. The goal of this progressive densensitization procedure is for the client to remain relaxed even when imagining—and ultimately experiencing—the situations that previously aroused the greatest anxiety.

Cognitive restructuring focuses on changing the individual's thoughts about him- or herself. The client is helped to identify unrealistic and untrue thoughts about him- or herself and directed toward experiences that demonstrate how the cognitive perceptions are faulty. For example, a client may complain, "Nobody likes me." The therapist may instruct the client to attend a party and then report in detail how different people responded to him. The client would come to admit that, while some ignored or rejected him, others had offered clues of being attracted to him.

Behavioral therapies have been shown to be effective for some problems and some people at all ages. They are especially valuable for changing discrete, identifiable maladaptive behaviors, such as phobias. They are also useful for modifying behaviors of individuals who may be unavailable or unwilling to participate in more dynamic, insight-oriented therapies. For example, even fairly deteriorated residents of nursing homes or psychiatric hospitals may respond to well-carried-through behavioral change programs. One challenge is to establish and maintain the consistent programs of reinforcement necessary to modify behaviors; when this can be done, it may be the only intervention that succeeds.

Group Psychotherapies   Therapies based on analytic-insight, humanistic-supportive, or behavior modification principles may be carried out with groups as well as with individuals. Various techniques have been developed that are used specifically with groups.

Group psychotherapies may be appropriate for all age groups, depending on the problems and the participants. Yalom and Terrazas (1968) suggested some of the characteristics of group psychotherapy: (1) setting realistic goals for the individual and group, (2) increasing patient interaction, (3) focusing on patient strengths, and (4) building group cohesiveness. The main benefits of group psychotherapy appear to be in two areas: (1) fostering expressive and meaningful interpersonal interaction, and (2) developing and sharing realistic self-goals and self-descriptions. For instance, the older client in a group at a day treatment center might discuss the emotional and practical advantages and disadvantages of moving toward a more independent residential arrangement. Other topics for discussion might be dealing with personal loss, loneliness, or feelings of obsolescence. Burnside (1978), Liederman, Green, and Liederman (1967), and Wolff (1971) have all been advocates of group psychotherapy with the elderly. Hartford (1980) warns against the misuse of groups to pressure old people into conforming to group goals that they do not truly accept.

Does Psychotherapeutic Intervention Work?   Several excellent reviews of aging and mental health recently have been published (Birren & Sloane, 1980; Butler & Lewis, 1982; Storandt, Siegler, & Elias, 1978; Verwoerdt, 1976). As in many other health-related areas, psychiatrists, psychologists, and

Although most psychotherapy is a two-person process, a skilled therapist can often create a group process that is helpful to all participants. Group therapy may be appropriate at any age.

others who provide mental-health services are faced with the issue of account-ability.

Accountability refers to the process whereby professionals are rewarded on the basis of the quantity and quality of services they provide. Eysenck (1952) was perhaps the first to draw attention to the need for systematic evaluation of the effects of psychotherapy. On the basis of the therapeutic outcome of more than 8,000 adult patients, Eysenck observed that "roughly two-thirds of a group of neurotic patients will recover or improve to a marked extent within about two years of the onset of their illness, whether they are treated by means of psychotherapy or not. . . . The figures fail to support the hypothesis that psy-chotherapy facilitates recovery from neurotic disorders" (pp. 322–323).

It is surprising that it has taken over 25 years and numerous studies (for instance, Bergin, 1966, 1971; Eysenck, 1966; Kiesler, 1966, 1971; Luborsky, 1954; Strupp & Bergin, 1969; Truax & Carkhuff, 1967) to establish that the question "Does psychotherapy work?" is too broad to be answered systemati-cally. For example, Bergin (1971) concluded that psychotherapy "has had an average effect that is modestly positive. It is clear, however, that the averaged grouped data on which this conclusion is based obscure the existence of a mul-tiplicity of processes occurring in therapy, some of which are now known to be either unproductive or actually harmful" (p. 263). Eysenck's critique and the subsequent debate over the effectiveness of psychotherapy has led to several important methodological and conceptual advancements. Most important, it encouraged disillusionment with studies in which qualitatively different types of therapies are broadly compared (that is, comparing therapy X or therapy Y with no therapy).

In recent years clinical researchers have tried to identify the elements that are critical to successful psychotherapy. "Does psychotherapy work?" is no longer asked; rather, the question is now "Under what conditions and with what type of therapist (or therapy) will this type of client with these problems be changed?" The basic belief is that, although a wide variety of effective techniques exists, there are only a handful of very effective combinations where the therapist and patient are compatible in terms of the presenting problems, personality, age, sex, race, and so forth. A systematic and prescriptive patient–therapist matching approach avoids the pitfalls associated with myths that patients, therapists, and treatments are interchangeable or that it is sufficient to match patients and therapists only on the basis of age or sex. It is especially important to be responsive to the wide range of interindividual variation present in elderly patients, who may have very little in common beyond a certain number of years since birth (Hoyer, 1974).

Education and Training

Another major technique of intervention uses education and training to alter or prevent maladaptive behavior. Information about problems that may be encountered or are being experienced is provided, with the expectation that the individual will use the information in beneficial ways. Specific skills needed to cope effectively with the problem may be taught.

For example, classes in preparing for retirement may include information about money management, health care in later years, and normal stresses associated with changing patterns of work and leisure. Individuals with particular health problems may need to learn new methods of salt-free cooking, lifting heavy objects, or lip reading. A retirement preparation or retirement adjustment program may also include supportive counseling.

Education and training may be appropriate interventions for many adults, although the format and educational techniques may have to be revised for older learners. The traditional classroom situation with teacher-as-expert is offensive and threatening to many adults, particularly those who never felt adequate in school and whose daily adult life has not included formal instruction. Education may evoke painful memories of evaluation. Programs that allow the individual to proceed at his or her own pace, minimize evaluation, meet at a neutral place such as a local church or neighborhood club, and use television or magazines as instructional media may be effective in such cases.

On the other hand, individuals with more formal education (for instance, college entrance) are more likely to continue involvement with education as adults. The cohorts of those who are now old are unlikely to have high levels of formal education, and they respond less well to such intervention. However, as the relatively well educated cohorts of middle-aged become older, they will (presumably) continue to respond to educational opportunities. There are already hundreds of educational programs serving the young-old, offering alternatives to boredom, a sense of enrichment, and opportunities for social interaction.

Service Delivery

Another major technique of intervention is the delivery of services. *Services* are substitutes for activities that individuals normally perform for themselves. When an individual can no longer perform some usual function, functioning in other areas is often affected as well. The provision of services can restore overall functioning.

Many services are delivered in the home. For example, if a single mother living alone with her small child fractures her hip and is immobilized, her physical problem quickly leads to other problems. If she cannot shop or cook, she and the child will suffer at least short-term nutritional deficits, which may lower their resistance to disease and affect their sense of well-being. Her inability to care adequately for the child may lead to depression, and her immobility can increase the feeling of isolation normally relieved by excursions to shops and friends. In this case some of the missing elements could be provided by a visiting homemaker, house cleaner, and shopper. Often a younger woman will have a circle of kin and friends who can provide such services; if not, formal service providers might be called upon.

The goal in this case would be to provide only the kinds and extent of services necessary to restore the individual to normal functioning. The goal becomes more complex when the disabilities are long-term or permanent. Some people, especially the elderly, lose capacities they need to function independently. The alternative to institutionalization becomes a package of services designed to meet their needs. The variety of services available to maintain even frail elderly in their own homes is impressive—visiting nurses, physical therapists, heavy and light housekeeping, cooks or meals delivered at home, "friendly visitors" who may write and mail letters or do errands as well as chat, tele-

When a person loses the ability to perform some usual function, a visiting nurse, housekeeper, cook, or friend may provide the services needed to restore overall functioning or to prevent or to slow further deterioration.

phone calls to check on well-being, and many more. Unfortunately, the necessary services are not always available when needed. And when they are available, service delivery may be difficult. Many people feel ambivalent about the need for long-term services. They may be grateful but at the same time resentful and depressed about their own loss of functioning. They may see service provision as a loss of independence. While some welcome the dependency and the care, many others resist.

At some point service delivered to an individual in the community may become so extensive and expensive that it seems wiser, or more efficient, to provide it in an institutional setting. Homes for the aged, nursing homes, and hospices are facilities where many services are provided. The challenge at all such facilities is to provide only those services essential to the welfare of the individual and not to provide "excess services" that deprive the individual of remaining functional abilities. For example, an elderly person may be able to feed and dress herself, even though she is slow and somewhat sloppy. Excess service would be provided if an attendant fed and dressed her.

Environmental Interventions

Finally, interventionists may focus on the ways larger environmental circumstances affect individual well-being. Interventions may be directed at microenvironmental effects, such as making sure that families with small children have safe, interesting playgrounds nearby, or that residents in housing for the elderly have glare-free rooms, signs that can be read even with visual deficits, and chairs with firm sidearms. The focus may be on the neighborhood, ensuring that needed resources and services are available to all who need them. At a wider level, we may aim for increasing availability of work, money, adequate health care, security from crime and warfare, and respect for all individuals. Such intervention ultimately contributes to the well-being of all.

Settings and Agents for Intervention

As Table 14-1 shows, interventions can occur in varied settings, including home, work, educational institutions, hospitals or other health institutions, a particular community, or the larger society. Obviously, various techniques will be found in different settings.

As became clear during our discussion of intervention techniques, a variety of change agents are used. Most problems are dealt with by the individual and his or her family or friends. When those intervention efforts do not bring the desired outcome, professionals and paraprofessionals may be consulted. Professionals have special training in particular intervention techniques. They may specialize in one age group or apply their approach across all ages.

Relatively few professionals have expertise in dealing with problems of older adults. For example, a national survey of clinical psychologists identified fewer than 400 who were seeing older clients (Dye, 1978). Another survey of psychologists found that a very few older therapists were seeing most of the elderly patients receiving outpatient psychotherapy (Mills, Wellner, & Vanden-Bos, 1979). The figures for other mental-health professionals are not much more encouraging. The implication is that older adults' mental-health needs are not likely to be met adequately by professionals and that further recruitment, training, and retraining are needed to greatly expand the group of professionals who can work effectively with older adults.

Lawmakers and administrators influence interventions by the policies set and the practices followed. For example, national and state lawmakers and administrators substantially intervene in adult lives when they pass and implement regulations governing abortion. Some countries or states provide easily available abortions paid for by public funds as a matter of right; others restrict or forbid abortions except to save the life of the mother. In addition to the general guidelines, laws often require those actually performing abortions to make judgments about whether a woman requesting an abortion meets the stated guidelines; for example, whether the mental or physical health of the mother is at risk if she bears the child. The administrator influences interventions by the kinds of evidence he accepts as meeting the legal requirements; one administrator may, for example, require evidence that a pregnant woman has attempted suicide before allowing an abortion, whereas another may accept the statement of the woman and her family physician that having the child would place substantial stress on her.

EVALUATING THE
OUTCOMES OF INTERVENTION

Reasons for Evaluation

Part of the intervention process is to evaluate the outcome—to see whether the action had the intended results and to check for unanticipated effects. This information can be used to justify the continuation of a successful program, to modify the intervention if necessary, and to test models of causation.

Evaluation may focus on whether therapy is more effective than no treatment or on identification of the most effective modes of therapy for a particular problem. Most intervention evaluation studies have at least two major flaws: (1) The populations studied have not been adequately defined in terms of diagnosis (as discussed in Chapter 13), nor have the procedures for their selection and allocation to treatment been adequately described. (2) The treatments have not been operationally defined, and the techniques used in each treatment have not been specified (Weissman, 1979).

We will illustrate the evaluation of interventions with research on treatments for depression and on the effectiveness of brief psychotherapy. This is, obviously, not an exhaustive or definitive discussion of competing therapies; rather, it is intended to highlight some of the strategies used by careful researchers who are trying to carry through credible intervention research.

An Example of Evaluation: Drug and Psychotherapy Treatments for Depression

Theories of Depression   As we saw in Chapter 13, *depression* describes a broad range of moods and behaviors that produce mild to severely impaired functioning. The symptoms include "blue" moods, with loss of pleasure and interest, sleep and appetite disturbances, suicidal thoughts, loss of energy, feelings of self-reproach, and so on. Depression is one of the most common forms of emotional disturbance and is especially common in old age.

There are many theories about what causes depression (Akiskal & McKinney, 1975). Biological psychiatrists regard depression as a consequence of abnormally low levels of endocrines needed to transmit neural impulses (Lipton & Nemeroff, 1978). Psychoanalytic theory emphasizes the importance of object loss, self-esteem, aggression turned inward, and a conviction that things cannot improve associated with hopelessness. Behavioral theories view depression as learned helplessness in the face of enduring painful conditions that are out of the patient's control; in addition, secondary rewards from the depressed role may substitute for other, more desirable sources of reward. Sociologists see depression as related to the loss of role status and social support systems. Existential psychologists focus on the freedom of humans to choose their goals and projects; they view depression as reflecting loss of meaning and purpose in life.

Research on the outcomes of therapies based on each theory contributes to evaluating the various explanations. The research we will describe is based on biological and behavioral theories of depression.

The Research Team   We will summarize some research designed to evaluate the effects of a 16-week trial therapy period on functioning during that period and one year after completion of therapy (DiMascio, Weissman, Prusoff, Neu, Zwilling, & Klerman, 1979; Weissman, Klerman, Prusoff, Sholomskas, & Padian, 1981). The research was carried out by a team of psychologists and psychiatrists in New Haven and Boston associated with the medical schools at Harvard, Tufts, and Yale universities; two hospitals in Massachusetts; and the Depression Research Unit of the Connecticut Mental Health Center. Various members of the research team have participated in a series of studies on depression. Such sustained, collaborative research in one area is important in accumulating the kinds of expertise and data needed to evaluate interventions.

Subjects   All patients aged 18 to 65 years who came to a mental-health clinic in New Haven or Boston and were diagnosed as having an acute depression were potentially eligible for the study. Some patients were excluded because they had conditions that could obscure the results—those who had another predominant disorder, or who had failed to respond to an earlier course of psychotherapy, or who had been treated or could not be treated with the drug to be used in the research. Ninety-six patients met the criteria for sample inclusion; however, 15 patients refused the treatment assigned within the first week and were dropped from the analysis (and given other treatment). Thus 81 patients entered the therapy evaluation project. One year later 62 of the 81 patients were available for follow-up assessment.

Treatment Options   The patients were assigned randomly to one of four treatment options. This procedure of random assignment is an important aspect of a scientific design because it enables us to assume that the groups do not differ substantially in their initial composition. If the groups do not differ before treatment begins, differences found at future times may be ascribed to treatment effects. (In order to facilitate replication of their research, the therapists prepared a training manual for psychotherapists; this helps meet one of the common criticisms of much psychotherapy research—not having a clear idea of what the treatment was. A training manual in no way guarantees a "standard situation," but it provides more information about the likely range of treatment than a general description of a highly individualized mode of therapy.)

One option was *psychotherapy alone.* The patient had at least one weekly 50-minute session with an experienced psychiatrist. The therapy was interpersonal, focusing on the social context of the depression.

A second option was *pharmacotherapy alone,* with flexible doses of a common antidepressant (amitriptyline hydrochloride). Some studies of drug effects randomly assign half the patients to receive a *placebo,* a pill that looks like the active drug used but contains no active ingredients. This method allows the investigator to see whether it is the chemical or the process of being "treated" that is responsible for observed changes. In this study of depression a placebo condition was not used, as it would have introduced another variable and further reduced the number in each group.

The third option was a *combination* of psychotherapy and pharmacotherapy.

The fourth option consisted of *nonscheduled treatment.* The patients were assigned a psychiatrist whom they could contact whenever they felt a need for treatment. This option served as a "control" group for the treatment groups. The best control could be a no-treatment condition, but ethical, humane, and practical considerations make it difficult to deny or delay treatment to individuals who have sought help. In order to make this a "low-treatment" condition, individuals who requested more than one therapy session a month were removed from the study (but not from treatment).

All treatments were continued for 16 weeks unless the patient became substantially more depressed and required intensive treatment.

Outcome Assessments   All patients were evaluated after 1, 4, 8, 12, and 16 weeks, or at the termination of treatment. The psychologist or psychiatrist who evaluated the patient was not informed which treatment the patient was receiving; this blind assessment is an important part of the design, to avoid biasing the results. One year after the 16-week trial ended, patients were again assessed, by a different clinician who was uninformed about which kind of treatment had been received.

Results   At the termination of therapy the psychotherapy and pharmacotherapy combination had produced the greatest overall symptom reduction; psychotherapy alone and pharmacotherapy alone were about equal; and the nonscheduled treatment had produced the least effect. Although the overall effectiveness of both individual treatments were approximately equal, the two had differential effects on symptoms. Drug therapy was primarily effective in reducing anxiety, sleep disturbances, and somatic complaints, and improving appetite; these improvements occurred early in treatment and were maintained. Psychotherapy effects, which appeared at four to eight weeks, were seen in the areas of depressed mood, recurrent thoughts about suicide, work, interests, and guilt.

One year after the trial treatment ended, the majority of the patients were doing well, 8 percent were chronically depressed, and 12 percent had become seriously depressed and required retreatment. There were no statistically significant differences in the general course of outcome among the four treatment groups. However, patients who had received psychotherapy were functioning significantly better in social and leisure activities, in parenting, as members of the family unit, and in overall adjustment.

Implications   According to the researchers, the results of this investigation demonstrated the relative effectiveness of four kinds of treatment with acutely depressed adult patients. Weekly therapy continued for a maximum of 16 weeks was more effective than unscheduled psychotherapy. Drug therapy had a relatively rapid impact on symptoms of appetite loss and sleeplessness, supporting theories that those aspects of depression have a biological basis. Psychotherapy had effects on mood, work, interests, and suicidal thoughts within the four-month treatment period and, in addition, a long-term positive effect on social functioning. The results from this research support models of depression that emphasize psychosocial causes of some depressive symptoms.

Comments   In discussing the findings from the study, the investigators emphasized the limitations inherent in using a naturalistic long-term follow-up (Weissman et al., 1981). They had no control over the patients during the year after completion of the clinical trial. Many of the patients received other treatments during that period; the researchers inquired about such treatment, but they had no adequate way of assessing the possible impact of experiences during that year.

The research described used a common between-group design. One problem with this design is that results are averaged over individuals, obscuring individual responses to the intervention or treatment. Inferences drawn from group data may not generalize to the individual. The researchers are now identifying the kinds of patients who respond best to different modes of treatment. They noted that some of those eligible for the study refused drugs, and some refused psychotherapy. Other research has indicated that individuals may be more or less sensitive to drug therapies; no doubt the same is true for different forms of psychotherapy. This study compared one variety of psychotherapy with one form of drug therapy; whether the results will generalize to other forms of psychotherapy or pharmacotherapy is an open question.

From a developmental perspective we can note that there were no elderly persons included in this study, nor were any age differences noted. It would be valuable to assess the impact of these interventions with different age and sex groups.

We might also point out that the depression research summarized here used a design with assessment at fixed points in time. Though measurements were made at six different times, that is not enough to capture the ups and downs of behavior change over time.

An Alternative: Intensive Analysis of a Few Cases in Brief Psychotherapy

Sometimes interventions can be evaluated more effectively through the use of intensive analysis of a few cases rather than relying on comparison groups (see Hersen & Barlow, 1976; Kratochwill, 1978). We will illustrate this option with research on brief psychodynamic psychotherapy.

The Technique   Brief psychodynamic psychotherapies have emerged in response to recognition of problems with traditional psychoanalytic therapy and reluctance to rely on either drug or supportive therapies. Long-term reconstructive therapies based on psychoanalytic principles lead to long waiting lists and a high drop-out rate while people wait for therapists. Because many people who could benefit from therapy at the point of crisis drop out while waiting for a therapist and those who remain are apt to have severe, chronic problems, therapists frequently experience relatively poor results, and staff morale in clinics specializing in long-term psychotherapy is low (Malan, 1963).

Brief psychodynamic therapies are intended for use with the range of neurotic problems seen in long-term psychoanalysis. The technique is also similar to psychoanalysis: The therapist carefully provokes the patient's anxiety in the therapy session so that the unconscious conflicts causing the anxiety can be understood and interpreted. The technique differs from traditional psychoanalysis in two important ways, however: The length of the treatment is usually set in advance (from 10 to 40 sessions), and the therapist is much more active in interpreting the patient's behavior.

When brief therapies were begun in the 1950s, many traditional psychoanalysts doubted that the technique would be successful in dealing with any but the mildest forms of disturbance. A team of psychoanalysts at the Tavistock Clinic in London began to evaluate their work with brief psychotherapy to see to what extent it was successful with various kinds of patients; by 1963 David Malan published a report on the first 21 patients seen from 1954 to 1958 (Malan, 1963). Reports published in 1976 presented information on a total of 39 cases, 30 of whom were available for follow-up so outcome could be evaluated (Malan, 1976a, 1976b).

Procedures   Malan pointed out that the evaluation of brief therapy must address three questions: (1) Who is selected for the treatment, and how do selection factors relate to outcome? (2) What techniques are used, and how are techniques related to outcome? and (3) What are the outcomes of the treatment?

Patients were very carefully selected for participation in brief psychotherapy at the Tavistock Clinic; every effort was made to provide a therapist and a mode of therapy most likely to be successful with each patient's problem. Thus the design is not comparable to a random assignment to treatment groups. The prediction in the brief therapy research was that some patients were almost certain to gain from the therapy, some were unlikely to benefit, some were likely to deteriorate, and some were high risks for success. The ability of the therapists to accurately predict outcome in advance is a test of the adequacy of their treatment model.

The first step in selection occurred when a person came to the Tavistock Clinic for treatment. After the first screening interview, some patients were rejected as inappropriate for psychodynamic psychotherapy, including those who had made serious suicide attempts or exhibited other seriously self-destructive behavior; those who were addicted to drugs or were chronic alcoholics; those convinced they were homosexual; and those who had had long-term psychiatric hospitalization, more than one course of electric shock treatment for severe depression, or incapacitating chronic obsessional or phobic symptoms. Patients not rejected by these criteria were intensively evaluated by a team of therapists to assess their suitability for brief therapy. Evidence provided by the initial psychiatric interview, responses to projective tests, and the first therapeutic session were studied by the therapists.

One purpose of the therapists' discussions was to see whether they could define a *basic neurotic conflict* for the patients that could serve as the focus for the brief therapy. This definition included statements about a specific kind of stress to which the patient was vulnerable; what would have to change in order for the patient to be considered recovered; and changes that might make the patient appear to be recovered but that would not really be a recovery. If a basic neurotic conflict could not be identified, the patient was considered a poor candidate for brief psychotherapy.

If a focus for the therapy was identified, the patient was then assessed in terms of motivation for therapy, capacity to form an attachment with the therapist, and rigidity of defenses; patients with low motivation for therapy, no evidence of being able to make emotional contact, or very rigid defenses were rejected as having a high risk of becoming worse in brief therapy. Patients who showed in the initial assessment interviews that they were at least moderately motivated to gain insight into their problems and were able to define their problems in psychological terms (rather than simply blaming them on others) were considered good candidates for brief therapy. The 30 men and women accepted for brief therapy and followed for evaluations ranged in age from 18 to 60 years and were working- and middle-class; some had shown severely maladaptive behavior for many years.

Patients were seen once a week. Therapy techniques were based on standard principles of psychoanalysis whereby the therapist interprets the patient's transference responses—that is, points out how the patient's responses to the therapist, supervisors, spouse, and so forth duplicate earlier relationships with parents.

Evaluation   The outcome of therapy was evaluated statistically and clinically. As Malan and his colleagues point out, "Without valid outcome criteria, much of psychotherapy research is meaningless" (Malan, Rayner, Heath, Bacal, & Balfour, 1976, p. 57). Statistical evaluations were made by having four psychotherapists independently rate the degree to which each patient had met the criteria for maximum improvement established at the beginning of therapy. Outcomes were rated on a 0–3 scale for the first study (reported in Malan, 1963); in the second set of analyses (Malan, 1976a, 1976b) all the cases were scored on a scale of 0 to +4 for improvement and negative scores for patients who got worse, using half-points as well as full points. Judgments were based on evidence about changes at the termination of therapy and at several points up to seven years after therapy terminated. The final outcome score assigned to each case was the mean of the four raters. Agreement between raters was high; for 21 of the 30 cases the difference in judgments was .5 or less.

With this procedure 17 of the 30 patients were judged to be successful, scoring +2 or higher; +2 was selected as a cut-off for success because the therapists decided that improvements less than that were too minimal to be clinically important. Of the 13 judged to be unsuccessful in brief psychotherapy, 3 required prolonged treatment that was eventually successful, 7 received mean scores of +1.00 to +1.99, 2 received mean scores of 0 to +.99, and 1 patient was worse after therapy than before.

The Tavistock researchers also used a clinical approach to evaluating brief psychotherapy. For example, they compared their predictions at the onset of therapy with the outcomes and found that their forecast of which patients would do very well in therapy and which were high risks was largely correct. Some unpredicted failures were accounted for by inadequate assessment procedures, such as neglecting to find out about previous hospitalization or not noticing that the patient refused to consider the interpretations made by the therapist in the first therapy session.

The researchers had several ways to assess the impact of the therapy sessions. They used records of each therapy session to see whether behavior changed following certain kinds of therapy interactions. The researchers also computed a score for the proportion of parent transference interpretations made by a therapist over the course of therapy and found that the more the patient was helped to work through patterns of transference, the more the patient benefited.

This procedure of analyzing the content of the therapy allows the researcher to assess which features of the intervention are most important to the outcome. On the basis of their research and that of other therapists investigating brief dynamic psychotherapy, Malan and his colleagues concluded that "the capacity for genuine recovery in certain neurotic patients is greater than has hitherto been believed" (Malan 1976a, p. 353). Brief therapies need not be used only for mild disorders of recent origin; they have been therapeutic for individuals who have been behaving maladaptively for many years. Malan views the success of brief psychotherapy in reversing long-standing disabilities as the strongest evidence against the argument that observed changes may be the result of processes outside of therapy. He acknowledges, however, that there is little way to evaluate the importance of events outside therapy in producing changes.

The Tavistock brief therapy research did not utilize control groups, although it did explore the possibility of using a group of neurotic patients who received only a diagnostic interview but no therapy as a control group (Malan, Heath, Bacal, & Balfour, 1975). The researchers found that some of the individuals contacted months after the initial interview had made apparently genuine improvements. The therapists decided that the group represented a minimal-therapy (one session) rather than a no-therapy condition, since it was clear from talking with the individuals that some had used the initial interview to gain considerable insight into their difficulties and had been able to change their behavior on the basis of even this minimal contact. Their experience points again to the difficulty in deciding what an appropriate control group might be for some kinds of intervention research.

Many types of single-subject or small-number designs are appropriate for the systematic study of change in an individual's behavior under different conditions. For example, the same individual may respond differently to different treatments for depression.

There are several ways in which the intensive analysis of a few cases may be especially useful for the purposes of intervention. First, developmental change does not occur to everyone in the same way. Results of single-subject or small-number studies serve to refine broad developmental theories and principles derived from comparisions of large groups. Second, not all things occur to everyone. Intensive case studies are useful for studying rare phenomena, and unique treatments can be tried and evaluated for particular individuals.

Single-subject studies, between-group comparisons, and other research designs can all be useful in evaluating the impact of interventions during adulthood. It is the responsibility of the researcher to select the design most appropriate to the state of knowledge, the questions to be answered, the resources available, and the ethical and humane considerations. Well-done intervention research can provide important guidelines for policy makers.

ESTABLISHING
INTERVENTION POLICIES

Policies are guiding principles to be used in establishing and carrying out specific programs. They serve as statements of intent and reflect the value system of those who draw them up. Policy may be made at many levels, and policies established at different levels do not necessarily agree with each other. For example, a neighborhood social-service agency may establish a policy of allocating service dollars to various age groups in the same proportion as clients coming to the agency; if the majority of clients are teenagers, most of the agency resources would be directed toward programs for teens. Such a policy might conflict with the policy of a city-wide funding agency that money should be distributed in proportion to the individuals in each age group living in the community. If the community had a high proportion of elderly, the city board would want that proportion of service money directed toward services for elderly persons, even if they had not sought such services yet.

In this section we will discuss three of the major policy issues in intervention for positive mental health during adulthood: (1) How can we use all levels of the mental-health system? (2) Is age relevant? (3) Should intervention be based on need or entitlement?

The Mental-Health System

In discussing policies for intervention, we can use the vision of the mental-health system developed by a group of researchers involved in longitudinal epidemiological studies. On the basis of their experiences over the years, Sheppard Kellam and Margaret Ensminger (1980) have identified three levels of the mental-health system; intervention options and programs and research strategies are different at each level.

The first level of the mental-health system has a *community* focus. It includes those aspects of service and research related to prevention, early treatment, and many aspects of continued treatment. The concern is with total populations of healthy and ill. An understanding of the cultural, social, and political structure of the community is important as both researchers and service providers may have to become involved in social and political contexts in order to be effective. A preventive mental-health program may involve a policy that a local citizens' board shall be actively involved in the planning and evaluation of the program. Failure to involve the key people in the community may lead to the failure of the program.

The second level includes more traditional *outpatient* settings, such as the mental-health clinic or the private practitioner's office. Policies and services at this level are directed toward the outpatient populations already in need. The research on depression treatment programs discussed earlier was conducted at this level of the mental-health system. Policies set for this level may assume that the individuals who come for treatment represent the ill part of the first-level population. However, there is little evidence to confirm that assumption; there are many factors besides severity of malfunction that affect the reasons individuals move from level one to level two (Mechanic, 1970).

The third level of the mental-health system consists of *hospitals* and similar institutions. The population served is more disturbed and requires extensive professional care.

The goal of a mental-health system should be to develop policies that would provide appropriate interventions at each level. In addition, there is great need for policies and programs that integrate interventions across levels. Thus a program to intervene with depression includes activities at every level, with special attention given to helping individuals move in both directions across the levels. The policies established for various levels of the system reflect prevailing judgments about two key issues: age and entitlement.

Age: Relevant or Irrelevant?

Throughout this book we have argued that one's place in the life course should be considered in understanding individual behavior. This suggests that age may be relevant to intervention policies. On the other hand, Neugarten (1979b) has listed three reasons to be cautious in overemphasizing the importance of age or life stage.

First, the timing of life events is becoming less regular, age is losing its customary social meanings, and the trends are toward the fluid life cycle and an age-irrelevant society. Second, the psychological themes and preoccupations reported by young, middle-aged, and older persons are recurrent ones that appear and reappear in new forms and do not follow a single fixed order. Third, intrapsychic change occurs slowly with age and not in stepwise fashion. (p. 887)

Neugarten's perspective reminds us that, while the presenting problem may appear age-linked, the issues represented may be recurrent ones. Interventions should be relevant to the ways in which the issues are presented at the time. Identity, for example, is reworked throughout adulthood, but the specific issues and options are different in young adulthood, middle age, and old age—as they are also different depending on sex, social class, and ethnicity.

Need versus Entitlement

A central controversy in all social program policy is whether services and supports should be available as a matter of right, because of membership in a particular group, or on the basis of demonstrated need alone.

At the second and third levels of the mental-health system, which serve only those who have already demonstrated need, the issue centers on payment for service rather than need for service. At the first level the controversy may involve the provision of services, particularly in prevention programs directed at all members of a particular group regardless of demonstrated vulnerability.

The current controversy especially involves policies concerning older adults and the extent to which age should be used as a basis for inclusion or exclusion for particular benefits. Such questions have arisen in part because of changes in the life course during the past century. Medical and social advances have resulted in an aging society, in which the large majority of people reach old age, and increasing numbers live to their 80s and 90s. The increased longevity includes lengthened periods of health and vigor but also results in increased numbers of ill and deteriorated persons of advanced age. As Neugarten has stated,

The major problems for social scientists and policy makers are how to improve the lives of present and future older persons, and how, at the same time, to facilitate the changes occurring in the family and in the educational, economic, political and human services systems because of the presence of increasing numbers of older people in the U.S. population [Neugarten, 1979a].

For several decades governmental and social program policies have used chronological age as a marker to qualify for various supportive programs. The number and variety of interventions available specifically for older adults have increased dramatically in the past few decades. Many of the programs are presented as a matter of *entitlement;* that is, all members of a particular group are eligible for benefits—in this case those over a certain age. Neugarten (1979a) argues that, because the great range of differences in functioning and need among adults are not strongly related to age, policies and regulations should not be age-based. Income, health care, housing, and other goods and services should be provided according to need, not according to age. Neugarten also pointed out the difficulties in separating age and need. If policies were restructured on the basis of need, new definitions of need might be necessary. Making such definitions age-specific (or, we might say, age-appropriate) might be regarded as an instance of age discrimination, which, according to recent federal legislation, is illegal unless based on good scientific evidence. It is not at all clear at this time what kinds of age discrimination will come to be regarded as justified, nor which kinds will be based on scientific evidence and which on mere stereotypes.

Advocacy for All

Throughout this book we have stressed the need to work toward maximizing functioning at all phases of life. There are no easy answers as to how that might be accomplished. Our guiding principles remain oriented to the entire life course: We must strive always for the welfare of all rather than act as sole advocates for one age, sex, or racial subgroup. Our understanding about development over the life course must be directed toward establishing policies that balance the needs of all. That represents a considerable challenge, worthy of our best efforts.

Various organizations have proposed statements of the rights of children, the handicapped, mental patients, and others at risk in American society. The general objective of such declarations is to bring about an awareness of the rights of all human beings in society regardless of individual differences and exceptional limitations. In this spirit we have adapted some of the tenets of these formulations, and we propose a "bill of rights" for adults of all ages.

A Bill of Rights for Adults
- The right to affection, love, and respect
- The right to good nutrition and medical care as needed
- The right to privacy
- The right to information and education
- The right to be a useful member of society
- The right to live in a spirit of tranquility and universal fellowship
- The right to these rights regardless of race, color, sex, religion, or national origin

SUMMARY

1   *Intervention* means intentionally altering a relationship in ways that are likely to have a positive outcome with regard to some problem.

2   A developmental perspective emphasizes the ways in which interventions may be designed to reflect the strengths and vulnerabilities characteristic of individuals at various life periods. Many young adults cope with substantial stress associated with multiple life changes, and interventions in young adulthood often focus on helping the person deal with commitments to work, to intimate relationships, and to values. During middle age, commitments made during young adulthood are reassessed. Middle-aged persons bear substantial responsibilities as workers and as providers for growing children and aging parents. Some middle-aged persons are troubled by the emergence of new potentials associated with the opposite sex. In the young-old period, people adapt to a shift in focus from full-time employment and parenting to alternative meaningful uses of time and energy. Many experience loss of longtime companions; some remarry after losing a spouse, and some learn to live alone. Declining health is a major problem in old age, particularly for the minority of elderly who experience deterioration of cognitive abilities and cannot live independently. There is disagreement about the extent to which presumed or demonstrated age-linked differences should be reflected in intervention policies.

3   The intervention process begins with *identification* of the problem. Intervention is more difficult when several persons have conflicting definitions of the problem, or when the problem defined is vague and global.

4   Intervention must be based on a model specifying the probable causes of the identified problem. Causal models may be established on the basis of epidemiological studies, comparisons of problem and nonproblem groups, or responses to different interventions.

5   A wide variety of intervention options may be used. The options vary in terms of goals, areas, techniques, settings, and change agents. The challenge is to select the most appropriate combination for the problem and resources.

6   Areas of intervention may be age-linked in likelihood of a problem's occurring, kinds of functioning affected, and symptoms of the problem.

7   Interventions may be designed to alleviate problems, to compensate for losses, to enrich existing functioning, or to prevent problems. Many intervention programs have multiple goals.

8   Two basic classes of interventions in mental health are pharmacotherapy and psychotherapy. Pharmacotherapy includes the use of drugs designed to change symptoms. Psychotherapies rely on structured interpersonal relations. Three varieties of psychotherapy were summarized: psychodynamic, humanistic, and behavioral. Psychodynamic therapies focus on gaining insight into the unconscious conflicts that produce symptoms disturbing to the patient or to others. Humanistic psychotherapies emphasize the inherent potential for good actions; therapists try to minimize anxiety and encourage their clients' inner potential for growth. Behavioral therapies focus on modifying behavior by helping the client learn more adaptive responses to troubling situations. Each of these therapeutic modes has been demonstrated to be effective with some problems of adulthood.

9   An important component of the intervention process is the evaluation of outcomes. A between-groups design was illustrated by research comparing the effectiveness of drug and psychotherapy treatments for depressed adults. The most effective treatment was regularly scheduled psychotherapy and drug therapy combined. Regular psychotherapy and drug therapy alone were equally effective overall, but affected different symptoms. The least effective treatment was psychotherapy on request. An alternative to comparing groups receiving different treatments is intensive analysis of a few cases. This alternative was illustrated by the evaluation of brief psychodynamic psychotherapy. Patients were carefully selected for brief therapy and evaluation, including assessing the relationship of selection procedures and therapy techniques to outcome. Criteria for successful outcome were established in advance. Brief psychotherapy was successful even with patients with chronic neurotic problems. Success in therapy was greatest for patients who were highly motivated and able to gain insight into their problems and whose therapists made relatively many transference interpretations.

10   Policies are guiding principles to be used in establishing and carrying out specific programs. Policies about interventions in behalf of mental health must be based on an understanding of the different levels of the mental-health system, from community-based programs to specialized psychiatric hospitals.

11   One of the current controversies in social policy is whether interventions should be available as a matter of entitlement on the basis of age or on the basis of demonstrated need alone. The question of age entitlement has become more critical with an aging population. The challenge is to meet the needs of all individuals, regardless of age, sex, or ethnicity—but in ways that are most appropriate in terms of age, sex, and ethnicity.

CHAPTER FIFTEEN

DEATH, DYING, AND MOURNING

Not to laugh, not to lament, not to hate, but to understand.
Spinoza

What do you expect to read about in this chapter? You may be saying to yourself that death is a boring or grim topic and that you are only reading about it because the instructor assigned the chapter for the next test. You may think it is a fearful topic but one that is becoming increasingly popular and public. Or you may think it is a curious topic—one you would like to know more about.

People often have approach–avoidance reactions to the topics of death, dying, and bereavement: We are curious about death, and we deny death. We say it is interesting, but then we avoid thinking about it or discussing it. People are both fascinated and repulsed by horror movies, war, and violence in the news. Death is exciting, fearful, evil, and joyful. It is morbid, black, Halloween, the devil, and rest. Our thoughts and feelings toward death and life are continually changing and paradoxical. Now that you have begun this chapter, be attentive to your feelings as well as your thoughts. Perhaps you can take two sets of notes—one set for the information to be learned and the other for your feelings about the information.

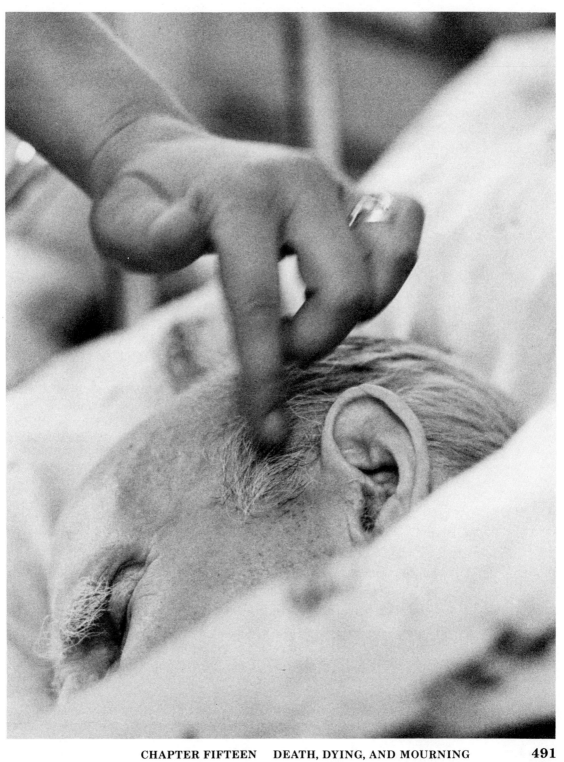

WHAT IS DEATH?

Some Definitions

How would you answer this question? We shall begin our answer in an abstract and safe fashion with a definition from a standard dictionary (*Doubleday Dictionary,* 1975).

Death is:

- the permanent cessation of physical life in a person, animal, or plant;
- the condition of being dead;
- the extinction of anything; destruction.

There are also legal definitions and biological definitions of death. The *biological* definitions are based mainly on the loss of such basic functions as heartbeat, breathing, cephalic reflexes, and brain activity. Although the loss of all these functions is indicative of death, the presence of any one of them is not always indicative of life. Most *legal* definitions of death treat it as the end of total brain function, even though a heartbeat might be present. Most hospitals require the complete absence of both lower (brain stem) and higher (cortical) activity before pronouncing death. It is important to have clear and distinct criteria for determining when death has occurred. The criteria should be simple enough that they can be used unambiguously by physicians and nurses without elaborate equipment. Further, the determination should be permanent (that is, irreversible) and not confusable with other comalike states (Task Force on Death and Dying of the Institute of Society, Ethics, and the Life Sciences, 1972).

To date the most widely accepted set of criteria has been the Report of the Ad Hoc Committee of the Harvard Medical School to Examine the Definition of Brain Death (1968). The criteria are as follows:

1 No spontaneous movements in response to any stimuli (pain, touch, sound, light) and no spontaneous respiration for at least one hour

2 Total unresponsivity to even the most painful stimuli

3 No pupillary responses, eye movements, or blinking; no postural activity, swallowing, yawning, or vocalizing; no motor reflexes whatsoever

4 A flat electroencephalogram for at least 10 minutes

These criteria are to be repeated at least 24 hours later with no change. In order for an individual to be declared dead, all the criteria must be met. There are two exceptions to this working definition: hypothermia (that is, a body temperature below 90° F or 32.2° C) and a high dosage of depressants (barbiturates); both these conditions may mimic death.

Individual and Societal Views of Death

While Gertrude Stein was on her death bed, her longtime companion Alice B. Toklas asked her, "What is the answer?" True to form, Gertrude responded, "What is the question?" The questions are often more interesting than the answers when it comes to death.

Theologians and philosophers have contemplated the meaning of mortality since the beginning of time. In the *Book of the Dead,* for example, the ancient Egyptians expressed their wishes to prolong and review life. Early Greeks and Romans also examined the meanings of being and nonbeing in their early writings (Choron, 1963).

Throughout the history of civilization many different views of death have emerged. Even in cultures that were or are largely death denying, some people bravely confront the various taboos. Herman Feifel was one of the first to publicly break the silence about death and dying in the contemporary social sciences. In his collection of essays on the meaning of death (Feifel, 1959), one of the main themes was the importance of accepting death. Feifel's book included essays by Jung, Tillich, Marcuse, and other philosophers representing a variety of positions.

Until recently, denial and avoidance rather than acceptance have characterized the American view of death. Robert Fulton's (1976) volume on *Death and Identity* reflects the recent attention to the topic of death that seems to be occurring in American society. Nevertheless, our firm resistance to confronting death cannot be overlooked. Ernest Becker (1973) argued that we cannot objectively face our own destruction—at least until the very end. Largely on the basis of the writings of Freud and Kierkegaard, Becker pointed out that we have strong defense mechanisms that protect against recognition of our own insignificance.

Since the "discovery" of death by the social sciences many writers have emphasized the cultural forces more than the psychodynamics that control the human view of death (for example, see Kastenbaum, 1977). Kastenbaum and Aisenberg (1972) use the term *death system* to refer to the way a given culture treats the topic of death. All cultures socialize their members with regard to feelings, attitudes, and actions toward death. In ancient Egypt, for example, some aspects of funerals (such as embalming and burial practices) were not very different from today's rituals of passage, especially for lower- and middle-class people (Hardt, 1979). Other aspects were quite different. For example, family members covered their faces with mud, and some special belongings were placed in the casket with the deceased. The funerals of kings and royal family members were a very different matter. All the people in the country would weep and mourn for 72 days—the time necessary to prepare the body for the journey to the next world. On the 72nd day, the body was placed in a coffin and sailed across a nearby river in a boat. All the people then voted on whether or not the king was "good." If the verdict was positive, the king was buried in an elaborate tomb; otherwise his coffin was dumped into the river (Hardt, 1979).

The funeral industry is a very obvious example of the socialization of death in our society. Jessica Mitford has described the commercial aspects of death in *The American Way of Death* (1969). The funeral industry puts a high cost on the rituals of death. It is difficult to say how much of what is provided by the funeral home is exploitation of the bereaved's vulnerability and how much is what the surviving family and friends really want. In all cases, however, the costs are high.

Death is cheap in some cultures, however, depending on the age and assigned status of the person in question. In some cultures, in fact, the sick and the old do not want to live, and they bury themselves.

In all cultures we come to understand that death is more natural, frequent, and acceptable for the old than for the young. The association of old age and death is probably one major contributor to the stigma of growing older. Our surprise at the following two stories (adapted from newspaper accounts) indicates how strongly we associate death with aging.

On Thursday, December 13, 1979, Penny Valentine died. She suffered from arthritis, cataracts, glaucoma, poor hearing, high blood pressure, poor circulation, decaying teeth, receding gums, weakened muscles, and dry and brittle hair. Penny was only 5 years old. She weighed nine pounds when she died at Children's Hospital, San Diego. Penny had the rare genetic disorder known as Cockayne's Syndrome, which caused her to age 15–20 years for every year she lived.

William Miller probably did not know that he would drop dead of a heart attack during his usual jog around the university area on October 27, 1979. He was 21 years old, a high school track star, a devoted runner, and apparently in excellent health. To himself and to his friends, he had the greatest of chances for a very long life.

Officer MacLaughlin had responded to a call that a man in jogging gear had collapsed on the grass by the field house. The police officer determined that there were no signs of life, and the runner carried no personal identification. The cause of death was initially listed as "undetermined."

Can healthy 21-year-olds just drop dead? The answer is an unassuring "yes." After autopsy the precise cause of death was determined as cardiac arrest caused by idiopathic cardiac hypertrophy. In other words, Bill Miller experienced a heart attack due to an unexplained enlargement of the heart muscle.

The point is that death can occur at any age, even though we tend to think that healthy, active young adults, like children, are exempt. Nevertheless, death is more of a reality for the old than the young and for the unhealthy than for those who are physically and mentally active. As we saw in Chapter 3, the probability of death roughly doubles every seven years after the age of 30.

Individuals of different ages often have different attitudes toward death and dying. Although it has been suggested that older people may have a greater preoccupation with death than younger people, much of the empirical evidence shows that middle-aged people are most fearful about death and older people are less fearful of dying and death (see Feifel & Branscomb, 1973; Kalish, 1976).

Some of the discrepancies among the studies of age differences in death attitudes can be explained by generational differences. People used to have more direct contact with death than they do now. Less than 100 years ago people died at home or in the community, children were not exempt from dying or witnessing death, and funerals were attended by a large segment of the community. Death struck unexpectedly and uncontrollably. In this century we have strengthened our defenses against death. Rates of infant and child mortality are relatively low, older people die in hospitals, and the mortician insulates us from most of the direct contact with the dead person.

The personal response to death is mourning. Because we mourn the loss of many others before confronting our own death, we will consider mourning before reviewing research on the process of dying.

MOURNING

Even though we are more insulated from physical death now than in the past, we are all confronted by loss and change. *Mourning* and *bereavement* refer to the thoughts, feelings, and actions associated with major loss. Usually the terms refer to loss of a spouse, a parent, or a child through death, but they can also refer to feelings of grief related to moving away from home or close friends, loss of a pet, or termination of a deep relationship through divorce. Mourning is an essential adaptive process, enabling us to acknowledge and finally accept changed reality. The mourning process is referred to by some as *grief work* (Parkes & Brown, 1972).

Mourning is most often associated with adapting to death. However, several writers have suggested that the mourning process is a universal response to change and development (Marris, 1974; Pollock, 1961). Mourning is, thus, a "normal" aspect of living. We mourn for people and things that become unavailable to us; we may also mourn changes and losses within ourselves. In this chapter our discussion of mourning focuses on losses of significant human relationships through death.

Mourning and bereavement refer to the thoughts, feelings, and actions associated with major loss. Mourning is a process of adaptation that enables one to acknowledge and finally accept change.

The Challenge of Mourning

Other people are important to us because they help meet our needs. Over time we become deeply attached to those who help us maintain some kind of adaptive balance. When such a person dies, our balance is upset. We must "undo" the previous arrangements and gradually reestablish new relationships with individuals who are present in reality. The reorganization may be felt first in behavior: One no longer buys enough groceries for two people or has someone special to tell important news. More important, however, is the reorganization that must occur internally, in the cognitive and emotional structures. Knowing intellectually that one's spouse is dead does not mean really feeling that he or she will never return. One is not able to invest in a new close relationship until one has genuinely accepted the changed reality. Unfortunately, some individuals never adapt to the loss (Peterson, 1980).

The Process of Mourning

Reorganization at profound levels of feeling takes time. The amount of time seems to depend on the extent of reorganization required and the ability of the individual to do the necessary reworking. Several researchers who have studied the process of mourning identify phases in the process (Averill, 1968; Lindemann, 1944; Parkes, 1970; Pollock, 1961). However, although the phases of mourning usually occur sequentially, progress through them is not necessarily even or predictable. The descriptions below draw heavily on the formulations of Parkes (1970), Pincus (1976), and Pollock (1961).

The First Phase   The first response to death is usually *shock,* with some denial that the death has actually occurred. There may be a profound sense of unreality; a panic response, with shrieking, wailing, or moaning; or a collapse, with paralysis and greatly slowed movement. Such behavior indicates acute regression to a much earlier developmental level (Pollock, 1961).

The first shock response may occur most strongly before actual death, when a person is informed of a hopeless diagnosis for a loved one. In such cases the person may have done a considerable amount of restructuring by the time death actually occurs. It is generally assumed that *anticipating grief* will lessen the intensity of grief after death. However, for chronic illnesses the shorter the time of dying the better the medical prognosis of the survivors (Gerber, Rusalem, Hannon, Battin, & Arkin, 1975). Obviously, the shock to the bereaved is greatest when the death is unexpected.

The Second Phase   During the second phase the individual experiences *grief.* There is a subjective feeling of intense psychic pain. There seem to be strong desires to recover the lost person. In an extreme case the individual may commit suicide in order to "join" the loved one (Pollock, 1976); others may wish to hold the dead one or perform some magic to retrieve the dead. Hallucinations—seeing or hearing the dead person—are common. Early grief is often characterized by hyperactivity, such as hand wringing, hair and clothes pulling, or aimless walking. There may be very primitive animal-like crying (Engel, 1961).

Realizing that nothing can be done, the sufferer becomes very quiet and sighs deeply; muscles become flaccid. Fatigue, exhaustion, and loss of appetite are common. This stage of grief indicates that the mourner is beginning to sense the reality of loss (Pollock, 1961).

Many individuals have fantasies and dreams about the departed. The dead remain "inside," available for imagined conversations. Such responses are common during this phase, and they represent one way of ignoring reality. The person who continues to use such fantasy or daydreams about the dead to ignore or deny reality for several months may have a very difficult time completing the mourning process.

The Third Phase   A more realistic recognition of the loss marks the third phase of the mourning process. The *separation reaction* involves disorganization and despair as the mourner realizes that the dead one is no longer externally present. Anxiety is one response to the danger entailed by the loss. The danger may be realistic threats to security and safety. For example, an older man may be anxious about who will care for him if he cannot walk, shop, or get to the doctor alone. His wife may have made it possible for him to stay out of an institution. Even in the absence of such threats one may feel the loss of an inner sense of security that comes with having a familiar, trusted person available.

In addition, there is often *anger* at being left to endure such pain. Most adults recognize that such anger is irrational. Because they feel uncomfortable being angry with the dead, they may direct this hostility toward physicians, hospital personnel, undertakers, or friends.

Another common response is *guilt,* remorse, and self-accusation. These feelings result because, inevitably, we are imperfect, and even ambivalent, in our love. As Lily Pincus (1976) points out on the basis of her work with mourning, adult responses are rooted in earliest experiences of separation and ambivalence. The infant hates the loved parent when he or she leaves, and the infant must deal with the terror that his rage may kill his parent, who will then be lost forever. "The adult mourner who has lost his loved object forever relives the infantile terror that his hate and lack of love have brought about the loss" (Pincus, 1976, p. 118).

Thus guilt is linked to ambivalence. There is frequently, perhaps always, guilt at the death of an important person. The guilt may be based on legitimate regrets about what one did not say or do for the dead. Other feelings about being responsible or negligent reflect totally irrational beliefs. Such feelings can persist for a long time and may be a source of continuing despair.

For example, Mrs. E was bereft when her husband died of a second heart attack at 89. She recounted the events of that day over and over, each time chastising herself for allowing him to go to his law office instead of requiring him to take a nap. The heart attack that evening seemed to prove to her that she had been negligent in protecting him. Her guilt was intensified because she could not express any of her anger at her husband for ignoring her pleas and medical advice, even though his actions left her a widow.

Guilt may lead to an idealization of the dead. As we noted in our discussion of adapting to widowhood (Chapter 12), Lopata (1979) found that many widows idealized their late husbands. Idealizing the dead is a denial of ambivalence: The dead had no flaws, and our feelings toward them are only positive. It is a way of making restitution for harm we may fear we caused while the beloved was alive.

The Fourth Phase   The *reorganization* phase begins the recovery process. An important part of reorganization is *identification* with the lost person. The mourner may take on the mannerisms, habits, conversational style, concerns, and even the illness of the deceased. Such behavior "gives comfort to the mourner, makes him feel close to the deceased, and thus mitigates somewhat the pain of loss" (Pincus, 1976, p. 121). Through identification the lost person becomes part of the self; once the dead person is internalized in this way, he or she cannot be lost. The survivor has changed to incorporate the beloved. Identification thus represents a filling up, a replenishing of the self, in order to become a stronger, better-integrated, more separate person (Pincus, 1976). As this occurs, the reality and finality of the external loss is accepted.

In the reorganization phase the survivor rearranges many aspects of life. As decisions are made, living arrangements altered, and pleasures enjoyed without the lost person, the individual comes to realize that other sources of support and love are available. These alternatives do not exactly substitute for the lost person; they are different but valued on their own. The bereavement process can come to an end when the individual can love again and can accept the new beloved not as a substitute for the dead person but as unique and worthy of love.

Pincus and others stress the *regression* involved in mourning, a return to earlier childish and infantile ways of feeling and behaving. Many people are bewildered and frightened by regression, particularly because throughout the mourning process periods of regression may alternate with periods of great maturity and self-discipline. The mourner needs sympathy and loving acceptance during periods of regression (Pincus, 1976).

Outcomes of Mourning

George Pollock is a psychoanalyst who has studied the process of mourning as revealed in historical and anthropological accounts (1970, 1975a), studies of gifted and creative individuals (1975a, 1978a), and psychotherapy patients (1978b). He believes that the mourning process and outcome possibilities are similar for response to deaths and responses to less drastic changes, though the responses to change may be very abbreviated. Pollock identifies four kinds of outcomes of the mourning process.

Normal resolution of the mourning process leads to creative activity, creative reinvested living, and creative products. The energy that was previously invested in the lost person is freed up, and the individual who has internalized the lost person can use those new capacities for different—creative—enterprises. Pollock has been particularly impressed with the evidence that a common outcome of the mourning process for gifted scientists, artists, and writers is a great piece of work (Pollock, 1978b). Less gifted individuals may show their creative outcome in a new relationship, the ability to feel joy, and satisfaction with new accomplishments.

Unfortunately, mourning may become *arrested* at any phase. Grief work may not be completed, and the reality of the loss may not be accepted. Grief work may be repressed for many years; Pincus (1976) relates case histories of individuals with problems related to unresolved losses from 5 to 40 years before therapy. Individuals may block all feelings in order not to deal with the pain of grief; obviously, this has repercussions in other areas of life.

The mourning process may result in more total *regression* to an earlier stage of development. While some regression is a typical part of mourning, individuals who have not really matured beyond an early stage may return to functioning at that stage when distressed. This is a particular risk for those who have lost a parent during childhood; a loss during adulthood may reactivate the buried memories of that trauma and reveal the developmental deficiencies.

Finally, the loss may result in *pathological* mourning processes such as severe and prolonged depression or apathy, strong illogical fears, and a strong, continued sense of unreality.

From time to time events occur that remind the mourner of his or her loss. Pollock has studied what are referred to as *anniversary reactions,* recurring responses to an emotionally significant event. In mild form they are common; the survivor may feel sad and think about the lost one as the yearly markers come and go. Some anniversary reactions are severe, however; suicides and homocides are especially likely to occur on an anniversary of an important loss. Pollock believes that anniversary reactions always indicate some form of incompleted mourning.

Pathological responses seem to be more likely when the death was unexpected and/or suicidal; when the survivor had complex and inconsistent feelings toward the deceased; and when the survivor is shy, timid, and without other emotional supports (Hinton, 1972).

Factors Affecting the Mourning Process

Two major factors influence the mourning process: what is lost, and when it is lost. The "what" refers to the nature of the relationship. Relationships are defined partly by formal connections—mothers, brother, wife, grandchild, and so on. Relationships are also defined by individual psychological meanings and patterns. The impact of any loss depends on the psychological development of the mourner. We will very briefly review some of the differences in mourning various losses.

Loss of a Parent Children and adolescents need parents, and the loss of a parent during these years usually has lifelong consequences. As we saw in Chapter 13, the loss of a parent during childhood is often associated with adult adjustment difficulties. The difficulties may emerge on anniversaries. For example, one study found that, among patients who had lost a parent, first admission to a mental hospital was especially likely to occur at the age of the parent at death. Emotional problems also may be more marked when a person's oldest child is the age the person was when his or her parent died (Pollock, 1962). These anniversary reactions indicate unresolved mourning.

Most parents die after their children are adults. Parental death may still be difficult, however, even when the death is seen realistically as the timely and natural end to a good life. When a parent dies, we lose any further opportunity to receive the kind of parenting we may have yearned for; to resolve any rage, anger, or resentment; or to show our parent how much we need or love him or her. Moreover, our earliest fears of abandonment are reactivated. Our parent no longer stands between us and the ultimate danger—death. Many mourning rituals recognize the special importance of parental loss by providing distinctive mourning procedures to mark parental death (Pollock, 1972).

Loss of a Child   Grief over the death of a child may be intense, and the loss may never be accepted. The "natural" sequence of events is for the parent to predecease the child; thus a child's death is always felt to be an affront to nature. The loss is especially traumatic when sudden and unexpected; parents of ill children have opportunities to do anticipatory grieving (Sahler, 1978). The grief may be intense even for an abortion, stillbirth, or neonatal death, since the process of attachment begins when life is felt within the womb (Grobstein, 1978).

Grandparents may also be profoundly affected by the death of a grandchild. They grieve for the grandchild, for their son or daughter, and for themselves (Hamilton, 1978). They should be included in whatever help is provided with mourning.

Loss of a Sibling   The death of a brother or sister during childhood may have important consequences for adult functioning. Sibling rivalry is commonplace during childhood (and often throughout adulthood); when a loved competitor dies, the child often assumes, subconsciously, that his own rivalry, jealousy, or strength "killed" the sibling. When these feelings are not resolved, surviving siblings may be plagued in adulthood with guilt over their own survival and success, a need to fail and an inability to succeed, and rage at the parents for "allowing" the brother or sister to die (Pollock, 1978a).

However, the loss of a sibling may also inspire great achievements, in an effort to make up for the missing family members. For example, Mariette was an extremely energetic woman who maintained a close, care-giving relationship with her two parents, as well as tending the family business and caring for her husband and sons. She explained that her own parents had twin boys who died shortly after birth, and Mariette had to "do the work of three."

With the death of a spouse—a major change in adult life—the survivor often behaves less maturely than usual during mourning. After mourning, some individuals become more mature and take on qualities of the dead spouse.

Loss of a Spouse   The death of a spouse is a major change in adult life, with special potentials for both maturity and regression. We discussed adaptation to this change in Chapter 12. Here we will focus on how the particular marriage relationship affects mourning, drawing on the work of Pincus (1976).

Some marriages are based on a complementary relationship in which the partners developed distinct roles. The partners may be very dependent on each other for support and suffer a severe sense of loss at the death of one. However, Pincus found that, after a period of mourning, the

> *bereaved not only appeared to have gained in strength but all expressed in words and deeds that they felt stronger, liberated, freed, more themselves, more able to cope with life than they ever had been while their partners were alive.... They made one feel that [their spouse] had stood in the way of their own growth, had robbed them of their potential for maturity (p. 78).*

This outcome of mourning makes sense when we understand that marriage partners may project their own characteristics onto the other. The "strong" partner in a marriage may seem so strong and competent because he (or she) projects his weakness and dependence onto the other, while the "weak" partner in turn projects her (or his) own strength onto the other. When the "strong" partner dies, the "weak" and "dependent" person may gain strength, if he or she can withdraw the projections from the dead and become a more independent person. The survivor must learn to take over some of the attitudes and characteristics that had been vital to their joint lives together. Therapy may be useful in helping the survivor do this.

The mourning process may be different in marriages based on identification, where the couples cannot tolerate separation and have always been unsure of their own identities. Partners in such relationships may have great difficulty even surviving the death of the other. For example, the mortality rate of surviving spouses is as much as 40 percent higher than average during the first six months after the death of a spouse (Carpenter & Wylie, 1974; Hinton, 1967; Rees & Lutkins, 1967).

Because Pincus's observations are drawn from couples in therapy, she has less to say about mourning in relationships where both partners are stronger than in marriages based on projection and identification. Presumably, the mourning process is more likely to be completed successfully when both partners have a strong positive sense of self apart from the other.

Personal Death   Eventually, we face our own death. By this time most people have mourned other losses. This ultimate loss, of life itself, is a very special challenge. It, too, is avoided, mourned, and finally accepted. We will discuss the way individuals confront death in more detail later in this chapter.

UNDERSTANDING DEATH

Time and Death

The relationship between time and death is important in our attempts to understand all the meanings of death. One fundamental aspect of this relationship is the individual's perception of time left to live (Kastenbaum & Aisenberg, 1972). The basic question is, "When do you think you will die?" If you think you have 50 more years to live, then you view life very differently than someone who has five years or only five days left to live. As we saw in Chapter 8, several investigators have attempted to use the concept of "time remaining" as a predictor of various developmental phenomena (Bortner & Hultsch, 1972; Kastenbaum & Aisenberg, 1972).

In relation to death the passage of time cannot always be measured by a clock or a calender. Time is the experience of life; one can live a lifetime in five minutes or five days. We have already mentioned that death helps us to conceptualize the meanings of life. Although life is often viewed as an accumulation of experience, time provides the opportunity to experience.

What if your time to live were to become more limited than you currently anticipate? What would you do and not do if you had only one more day to live: read, think, walk, sail, ski, sit? Would you want to be alone? What would be different? To confront these questions honestly is a challenge and an opportunity to give greater meaning to the lifetime remaining.

Death and Personal Causation

When the physical causes of death elude us, we tend to look for psychological or personal antecedents. Psychological explanations and causes of death are affirmed when death follows personal crises more closely than would be expected by chance. Kastenbaum and Costa (1977) have recently reviewed some of the personal events that occur shortly before death. Marriage partners dying close in time, cases of the "will to live" and "will to die," sudden death in concentration camps and prisoner of war camps, and death related to the belief that one cannot help oneself or change an undesirable situation all suggest that death can have nonphysical causes. Rowland (1977) has reviewed the evidence suggesting that three events—involuntary relocation in institutions, death of a loved one, and retirement—serve to increase vulnerability to death.

Increased Vulnerability   Institutional relocation or "transfer trauma" involves many factors and types of moving. For example, a parent or grandparent could be involuntarily admitted to an institution, relocated from one institution to another, or involuntarily moved from one part of an institution to another. Aldrich and Mendkoff (1963) found that when 182 nursing home patients were moved for the purpose of administrative reorganization, the mortality rate rose. The mortality rate was high in the first three months after the relocation and then gradually returned to the normal rate. Since residents were moved regardless of health and were moved to a facility of equal or better quality, the authors concluded that relocation in itself increased the probability of death.

Markus, Blenkner, Bloom, and Downs (1972) found that residents in poor health are more vulnerable to the effects of forced relocation than are physically healthier residents. When older people are well prepared for relocation, when they have some choice in the move, and when the relocation is perceived as desirable, mortality is diminished or eliminated (Bourestrom & Tars, 1974; Rowland, 1977).

Death of a loved one is also associated with an increased likelihood of death, especially in late adulthood. The mortality rate for widows and widowers is highest during the first six months of bereavement (Rowland, 1977). Loss of a parent or significant sibling in late life is also a predictor of mortality.

Retirement is not always a stressful or forced transition for older people, as we saw in Chapter 11. Depending on the meaning of retirement for the individual, one's relationship to work, and other factors, retirement can be a positive, stress-reducing event. When retirement is a voluntary decision on the part of the worker, and when it is a planned and prepared-for event, it is not lethal. However, when individuals are forced to retire and they have nothing to substitute for the activity and meaning work provided, they are more vulnerable to death.

The term *holiday syndrome,* like *anniversary reaction,* has been used to describe the relationship between significant yearly events and the timing of death. Indeed, there are seasonal variations in the timing of death, as well as fewer deaths associated with significant dates in a person's life (Baltes, 1977; Marriot & Harshbarger, 1973; Rebok & Hoyer, 1979). The days immediately following Christmas Day and New Year's Day show the highest frequencies of death. For Jewish people in New York and Budapest there is a decrease in death rate before Yom Kippur and an increase after the holiday (Phillips & Feldman, 1973). There is also a relationship between month of birth and month of death; individuals are less likely to die in the month preceding their birth and more likely to die in the month following birth (Phillips & Feldman, 1973). It seems as though some people have a "will to live" that helps to bring them through, or at least up to, significant holidays, birthdays and anniversaries, and other meaningful events. Other people may "will to die" on or before a holiday that reminds them of how alone they are.

Although there is a growing body of evidence showing the role of nonphysical factors in the timing of death, Kastenbaum and Costa (1977) point out that there is no such thing as a "purely physical" or a "purely psychological" death. All deaths involve biological, social, and emotional processes. All lives terminate in lifelessness. We measure life and death physically (by heartbeat or brain death), but psychosocial as well as biomedical risk factors are related to the timing of death.

Psychosocial Predictors   Some work is being done on identifying specific psychosocial or lifestyle factors predictive of death. One important area of research is coronary-prone behavior, such as that discussed in Chapter 12 (see Rosenman, Brand, Jenkins, Friedman, Straus, & Wurm, 1975). The Rosenman et al. study found that Type A individuals had 2.37 times as many heart attacks as Type B individuals. When group differences in age, serum cholesterol level, smoking frequency, and blood pressure are taken into account, Type A subjects exhibited 1.97 times the rate of heart attacks of Type B subjects (Brand, 1978).

Lifestyle factors are also predictive of five of the other six leading causes of death in the United States (Siegler, Nowlin, & Blumenthal, 1980). Table 15-1 lists the main causes of death; cigarette smoking, improper diet, poor coping strategies, insufficient exercise, alcohol and drug abuse, loneliness, and other lifestyle factors are associated with such diseases as cancer, diabetes mellitus, cirrhosis of the liver, and arteriosclerosis (Siegler et al., 1980; Pomerleau, 1979).

Dr. James J. Lynch, a specialist in behavioral medicine at the University of Maryland Medical School, has argued that loneliness can lead to early coronary disease and death for the single, widowed, and divorced (Lynch, 1977). For subjects ranging in age from 15 to 64 years, Lynch has reported the following statistics:

- For white males per 100,000 population 176 married men died of heart attacks compared with 362 single men.

- For nonwhite males per 100,000 population 142 married men and 298 divorced men died of heart disease.

- For white females per 100,000 population 44 married women and 67 widows died of heart disease.

- For nonwhite females per 100,000 population 83 married women and 165 widows died of heart disease.

Table 15-1   Leading Causes of Death in the United States (1977)

Rank	Cause of death	Number of deaths[1]	Death rate per 100,000 population
1	Heart diseases	718,900	332.3
2	Cancer	386,700	178.7
3	Stroke	181,900	84.1
4	Accidents	103,200	47.7
	Motor vehicles	(49,500)	(22.9)
	Other	(53,800)	(24.9)
5	Influenza and pneumonia	51,200	23.7
6	Diabetes mellitus	33,000	15.2
7	Cirrhosis of the liver	30,800	14.3
8.5	Arteriosclerosis	28,800	13.3
8.5	Suicide	28,700	13.3
10	Diseases of early infancy	23,400	10.8

[1]Total number of deaths in 1977 = 1,899,600.

Source: Adapted from U.S. Bureau of the Census, *Statistical Abstract of the United States: 1979* (100th edition). Washington, D.C., 1979, p. 76.

According to Lynch (1977), for all the leading causes of death—including heart diseases, cancer, suicide, cirrhosis of the liver, rheumatic fever, pneumonia, diabetes mellitus, tuberculosis, and syphilis—the single, widowed, and divorced have significantly higher death rates than married people—white and nonwhite, male and female, young and old. As we have seen, interpersonal relationships clearly serve many important functions for all adults, providing intimacy, support, power and control, and a feeling of belongingness (Candy, 1977; Lowenthal & Haven, 1968; Pearson, 1980).

CONFRONTING DEATH

Stages of Dying

Elisabeth Kübler-Ross did not know that her stage-wise description of the dying process was to become so widely known. As a new instructor in psychiatry at the University of Chicago in the early 1960s, she simply wanted to cover material that would be stimulating to medical students. She selected the topic of death and dying because it was one that everyone would need to deal with sooner or later. One day she followed her lecture with a "live" interview with a 16-year-old leukemia patient. The experience was a very significant one for the class, the patient, and Kübler-Ross; she continued to use terminal patients as "informants" for many years thereafter.

On the basis of interviews with over 200 terminal patients Kübler-Ross observed that many patients went from an initial reaction of shock and disbelief to a level or stage of acceptance of death. This stage-wise progression is described below (Kübler-Ross, 1969):

- *Stage 1: Denial.* Denial, shock, and disbelief are the first reactions to being informed of a serious, life-terminating illness. According to Kübler-Ross, few patients maintain this stance to the end.

- *Stage 2: Anger.* After denial, the patient often becomes nasty, demanding, difficult, and hostile. Asking and resolving the question "Why me?" can help the patient reduce resentment.

- *Stage 3: Bargaining.* In this stage the patient wants more time and asks for favors to postpone death. The bargaining may be carried out with the physician or, more frequently, with God. Kübler-Ross gives the example of a dying woman who asked to be relieved of her severe pain just for one day so that she could attend her son's wedding. The woman promised that if she could just see her son married, she would then be able to die in peace. She was taught self-hypnosis to control the pain and was permitted to leave the hospital for one day. She did not want to return. "Dr. Ross," she said, "don't forget, I have another son."

- *Stage 4: Depression.* Depression is a signal that the acceptance process has really begun. Kübler-Ross has referred to this stage as *preparatory grief*—the sadness is related to impending loss.

- *Stage 5: Acceptance.* Now the person has taken care of unfinished business. The patient has relinquished the unattainable and is now ready to die. He or she will want to be with close family members, usually a wife or husband and children; children want to be with their parents. The presence of someone warm, caring, and accepting is desired at this time, but verbal communication may be totally unnecessary.

Dying Trajectories

Some *thanatologists* (those who study the death process) have argued that there is little justification for a stage theory of death and dying. In fact, Kübler-Ross (1974) herself has pointed out that some individuals can be in more than one stage at the same time and that some individuals do not exhibit these stages or this sequence of stages. Schulz and Aderman (1974) have reported that some terminal patients persist in one pattern of adjustment until death; others vary their emotions frequently and unpredictably.

Alternatives to the stage approach give emphasis to an individual's expectations of death. That is, we have an idea of how much longer we are going to live, and we plan our life within this interval (Pattison, 1977). Our actual life span may be either shorter or longer than what we expect. A *death crisis* is an unanticipated change in the amount of time left to live. For example, our *dying trajectory* (expected time of death) can be shortened by days, months, or decades because of serious accident or disease.

Pattison (1977) calls the interval between the death crisis and the actual time of death the *living–dying interval.* This interval can be divided into three phases: (1) the acute phase; (2) the chronic living–dying phase; and (3) the terminal phase.

During the *acute phase* a maximum anxiety or fear level is reached. Individuals simply cannot stay at this peak level of anxiety for very long; soon defense mechanisms and other cognitive and emotional resources serve to reduce high anxiety. The acute phase corresponds to Kübler-Ross's stages of denial, anger, and bargaining. The initial denial reaction to the "crisis knowledge of death" may be immobilization and depersonalization. For example, the patient may say, "This is not really happening to me." High anxiety and fear follow this realization that it is, in fact, happening.

In the second phase, *chronic living–dying,* anxiety begins to diminish. Once this happens, the individual can start to face the reality of death in a way that is consistent with his or her personal integrity, dignity, and self-esteem. Several questions need to be realistically addressed during the chronic living–dying phase (Diggory & Rothman, 1961):

- What changes will occur to my body?
- What will happen to my body after I die?
- What will happen to my "self" after I die?
- What will happen to my family and friends as I die and afterward?
- What about my future plans?

In addressing these questions, the dying person experiences both fear and anxiety. Fear is a state of agitation or threat brought about by a specific danger or pain (anticipated or experienced), whereas anxiety is a generalized feeling of agitation or threat having unknown causes. The fear of the person in the living–dying phase is a specific fear, but it is a fear of the unknown. Existing psychological terminology is often inadequate in attempts to describe the experience of dying.

Rituals provide a way of dealing with the unknown. The socialization practices of a family, a culture, and a society help the dying person face death with calmness and courage. During the living–dying phase the dying person is rational as well as fearful and anxious, realizing that others have died and that everyone must die sooner or later. The individual begins to accept death gracefully. The dying person knows that others in the family and society have accepted these losses of body, self, and loved ones. Cultures differ in their models of death and bereavement, but the function of tradition and death rituals is the same across cultures—to give the dying and the bereaved something to believe in and something to do (Kalish, 1976).

Pattison's third and final phase of the experience of dying is the *terminal phase*. The dying person now begins his or her final social and emotional withdrawal from life. The person has very little energy and mainly wants comfort and caring. Often there is no clear distinction between this phase and the living–dying phase, especially if the dying person gradually gives up expectations to live. The person still desires to live but no longer expects that death is going to go away.

Death Anxiety

Why do we fear death? Why are we anxious about our own death? In recent years researchers have begun to examine the nature of death anxiety. Some investigators have developed tests and questionnaires to assess death anxiety (Templer, 1972). Other writers (for example, Pattison, 1977; Schulz, 1978) have identified areas of fear and anxiety that people commonly face when thinking about death or adjusting to their own death. The major fears are:

- Suffering and pain
- Loss of body

- Loss of self-control
- Loss of identity
- The unknown
- Loneliness
- Sorrow
- Regression

To understand what it is like to experience dying, it is important to see the interrelationships among these categories of fear. For example, many dying patients do report a strong fear of suffering and pain. Technically, suffering is a type of pain that has no specific cause or location, whereas pain is a relatively localized cognitive and sensory experience. Fear of suffering and pain in relation to death is usually a fear of the unknown; that is, "Will death be painful?"

Another example of overlapping fears involves becoming and being a hospital patient. Nurses and doctors come into "your room" at any time to do what they need to do to "your body." Loss of privacy and invasions of personal and intrapersonal space bring about losses in dignity and self-esteem. In addition, we feel bad when we perceive ourselves as looking bad. Although the patient may intellectually accept the surgical removal of a malignant body part, for example, it is also necessary to accept the hard fact that he or she is now physically different.

Fears of regression and loss of self-control are also interrelated (Rebok & Hoyer, 1979). The person has a view of self that he or she has struggled to develop since birth; now it is necessary to fight against a regression into selflessness. With the weakening of physical and emotional strengths, thoughts of regression and withdrawal may be especially frightening to the dying individual. The question is, "Must I relinquish my identity and my strength?" Losses of self-control and self-efficacy are related to feelings of helplessness and depression (Bandura, 1977; Seligman, 1975).

Although we may never be able to fully accept our own death until we are convinced that it is imminent, Robert Neale (1973) has posed some questions that sometimes aid the adjustment process.

1 Have you ever seen a person die? What were your feelings?
2 Have you ever been in a situation where you thought you were soon going to die? What were your feelings?
3 How was death presented to you when you were a child?
4 How many funerals have you attended? What were they like?

Some other questions and exercises that are designed to increase your death awareness and acceptance are as follows (see Koestenbaum, 1976):

1 Write your own obituary.
2 Plan your own death and funeral.
3 What circumstances would help to make your own death acceptable?
4 Is death the worst thing that could happen to you?
5 What circumstances help to make the death of others acceptable?

LIFE, DEATH, AND LIFE AFTER DEATH

Elisabeth Kübler-Ross argues in her book *Death: The Final Stage of Growth* (1975) that death is a natural and integral part of life; it is not a disease or an enemy to be conquered. Death is inevitable, and, by accepting its inevitability, we can use our lifetime meaningfully and productively. Death rarely occurs without some warning. The warning, no matter how brief, is a signal to grow—to learn honestly who we are. In the face of death we come to terms with who we really are. All facades must fall. What has been achieved must be accepted, and what has not been attained must be relinquished.

Kastenbaum (1977) has also observed that death can be a healthy companion to life. With death as an increasingly familiar comrade as we grow older, we are urged to live fully in the present rather than in the past or future. The familiar saying "Live each day as if it were your last" partially captures this death-accepting perspective on life. What would you be doing differently if this were your last day? What is your unfinished business? To confront these questions honestly is a difficult challenge, but it is also an opportunity to enhance the meaning of our present life—whether we have 2 or 60 years left to live on this earth.

Kübler-Ross has directly aided many dying patients by helping them to accept death and to fully experience their time remaining. Recently, she has adopted the view that spiritual life continues after the body is dead. Dr. Raymond Moody, a physician, has also raised the question of life after death in his book *Life after Life* (1975). On the basis of interviews with people who have had close calls with death, Moody has identified universal themes in what it is like to die. Consider, for example, the following case:

George McCabe died—or so it seemed. He had been informed that the operation would entail certain risk, and just as the anesthesia was wearing off, his heart went into a fibrillation and stopped beating. After a few moments he began to leave his body and was looking down upon it. As he continued his upward journey to somewhere, things were getting brighter. He was travelling through a light-flooded tunnel. He was seeing his past life in a clear, coherent vision, he was about to reach. . . .

And then he was brought back. He had been resuscitated at the last possi-

minute. He was certain that he had died. He was given a glimpse of life after death.

Similar experiences have been documented by Moody (1975, 1977) and by Siegel (1980). People who have been "brought back" just after being pronounced dead often recall the experience of leaving their body, of their life quickly passing in front of them. People also report feelings of warmth, peace, and serenity; seeing a bright light or a being of light at the end of a tunnel; hearing noises; and meeting others as they die. Using evidence from evolutionary biology, anthropology, and psychology, Siegel (1980) has argued that life-after-death images are a kind of universal hallucination that all humans experience when they are near death.

Some people at first resent being brought back to life. For most people the experience of dying and then living again gives a new and more positive outlook on life. Many individuals change their patterns of living, and some commit themselves to deep spiritualism.

A Gallup poll in 1978 found that 70 percent of the people in the United States believe in an afterlife. Even if perceptions of life after death are inaccurate or unfounded, such views may very well be adaptive in this life. A belief in an afterlife can be looked at as a form of death denial—a predisposition to deny the devastating condition of total nonbeing.

PLANNING FOR DEATH

Looking Ahead

Planning for death is logical—and emotionally difficult. We are willing to plan most aspects of our future except death. To plan one's death may seem "morbid" or "scary," but such planning is very helpful to survivors and provides the family with an opportunity to share openly feelings about death. The Lutheran Brotherhood has published a guide for survivors (Figure 15-1) that includes most of the important questions to be dealt with when someone dies:

1   Do you wish heroic measures and/or artificial means to be used to sustain your life?

2   Who should be notified at the time of your death (family, funeral home, friends, employers, cemetery, unions, fraternal and professional organizations, Social Security office, attorney, insurance agents, etc.)?

3   What kind of funeral service do you want?

4   Where should the service (if any) be (a church, a funeral home, or your home)?

Figure 15–1   Guidance for survivors. © 1975. Used by permission.

PREPARING FOR DEATH

Guidance for survivors

The most difficult day of one's life is, for many, the day a loved one dies. And added to it is the necessity of doing many things. Pre-planning can help immeasurably. This form may be used to aid in such planning. In addition, the values that one holds in life can be made to "live on" through designated gifts to be made available upon one's death.

I do ☐ do not ☐ wish to have unusual measures or artificial means used to sustain my life when death is imminent.

I do ☐ do not ☐ wish to give my eyes or other organs to another person for transplant purposes; I do ☐ do not ☐ wish to give my body for medical research or training. (In both cases authorization must be made in writing. Special forms are available for this purpose from various organizations.)

I do ☐ do not ☐ wish an autopsy to be performed if permission for it is requested.

At the time of my death please notify those listed below. (List may include pastor, funeral home, relatives, employer, friends and co-workers, cemetery, unions and fraternal and professional organizations, Social Security office, veterans administration office, attorney, newspapers, insurance agent, etc.)

Name & identification	Telephone	Address (if needed)

(Attach extra sheet if needed)

I wish earth burial ☐; mausoleum entombment ☐; cremation ☐, with ashes to be ─────────────────

Cemetery name, location and lot numbers ─────────────────────────

Preferences regarding marker: ──────────────────────────────

I desire that a funeral service ☐ or memorial service ☐ be held at ─────────── with ☐ or without ☐ reviewal of my body.

Further plans for such a service have been discussed with ─────────────────and are attached (include casketbearers, organist, vocalists, favorite music, and type of service).

I prefer that any memorial gifts be designated for organizations and institutions most meaningful to me and my family such as: ───────────────────────────────

───

───

───

Biographical information:

Born (place and date)_____

Father's name_____

Mother's name_____

Date baptized_____ Date confirmed_____

Church_____

Place and date of marriages and to whom:_____

_____

_____

Children (if not all listed on other side):_____

_____

_____

(Attach a brief biography —) including schools, memberships, places of employment, accomplishment, etc.

Valuable records:

Location of birth certificate_____ marriage certificate_____

Veteran's identification No._____ Location of discharge papers_____ VA office to notify_____

Social Security No._____ Location of office_____

Location of will and / or trust_____

Location of safe deposit box_____

(Attach a list of other valuables — including stocks, bonds, deeds, etc.)

Bank accounts (name, location, type)

_____

_____

_____

_____

_____

Pension benefits (employers to notify):

_____

_____

Insurance policies:

Company or Society	Contract or Policy No.	Amount	Representative or Agent

Outstanding loans and credit obligations (attach dated listing and bring up to date each year).

These seem to be the wisest and most prudent decisions at this time. However, I expect my survivors to use good judgment in making necessary changes.

Signature_____ _____

Address_____

Keep this form in a safe but accessible place and inform several people close to you of its existence.
You may need to prepare extra copies.

1578-1

5 Do you wish earth or mausoleum burial, or cremation?

6 Do you wish to prepurchase a cemetery lot? Where?

7 Do you wish a grave marker? What should it say?

8 Do you wish to donate any of your body parts for medical research or training?

9 Do you permit autopsy if requested by the hospital?

10 What special arrangements should be made if you die away from home?

Euthanasia

In Chapter 3 we referred to bioethics, a field of study combining biological and technological knowledge with human values. *Euthanasia,* the act or practice of killing for reasons of mercy, is a bioethical issue in today's society.

The word *euthanasia* is derived from the Greek *eu,* meaning good, and *thanatos,* meaning death. The term can refer to many different aspects of dying and death. *Passive* (or negative) *euthanasia* refers to allowing a person to die by not using available interventions. For example, a "Code 90" on a patient's hospital chart means that nothing is to be done to prolong life artificially other than trying to comfort the patient. *Active* (or positive) *euthanasia,* deliberately shortening a person's life, has three forms. First, the patient can voluntarily carry out his own her own death. This sometimes happens in hospital settings with the aid of a physician, nurse, or family member, but more frequently individuals who choose to end their own life will do so outside of a hospital. A second type of active euthanasia is when the individual decides that his or her life should be ended when specified circumstances occur, with the timing of death left to the discretion of the person who is responsible for his or her welfare. For example, a person may not wish to live if he is not conscious; this wish can be written in advance. The Euthanasia Education Council has developed the "Living Will" for this purpose (see Figure 15-2). A third type of active euthanasia involves ending a person's life without his or her permission (mercy killing); this is often done when a person is in great pain and there is virtually no hope of recovery.

There are social as well as ethical issues to be considered with regard to euthanasia. When asked in a Gallup poll whether a physician should be legally allowed to end the life of a person with an incurable disease, 36 percent of the population in 1950 and 53 percent in 1973 said *yes.* Though practicing physicians generally accept passive euthanasia, many do not support the idea of mercy killing; 59 percent of practicing physicians said that they would perform passive euthanasia when authorized by the patient, but only about 25 percent indicated that they would practice active euthanasia even if it were legalized (Laws, 1971). In the same survey it was reported that 90 percent of fourth-year medical students agreed with passive euthanasia; about 50 percent favored active euthanasia (if legalized).

TO MY FAMILY, MY PHYSICIAN, MY LAWYER, MY CLERGYMAN
TO ANY MEDICAL FACILITY IN WHOSE CARE I HAPPEN TO BE
TO ANY INDIVIDUAL WHO MAY BECOME RESPONSIBLE FOR MY HEALTH, WELFARE OR
AFFAIRS

Death is as much a reality as birth, growth, maturity and old age—it is the one certainty of life. If the time comes when I, _____ can no longer take part in decisions for my own future, let this statement stand as an expression of my wishes, while I am still of sound mind.

If the situation should arise in which there is no reasonable expectation of my recovery from physical or mental disability, I request that I be allowed to die and not be kept alive by artificial means or "heroic measures". I do not fear death itself as much as the indignities of deterioration, dependence and hopeless pain. I, therefore, ask that medication be mercifully administered to me to alleviate suffering even though this may hasten the moment of death.

This request is made after careful consideration. I hope you who care for me will feel morally bound to follow its mandate. I recognize that this appears to place a heavy responsibility upon you, but it is with the intention of relieving you of such responsibility and of placing it upon myself in accordance with my strong convictions, that this statement is made.

Signed _____

Date _____

Witness _____

Witness _____

Copies of this request have been given to _____

_____

_____

_____

The ethical arguments in favor of euthanasia center on two propositions (Dyck, 1974):

1   There is such a thing as a life that is not worth living or maintaining.

2   There is dignity in the capacity to control one's life and death.

The main argument against euthanasia is "Thou shalt not kill" under any circumstances. The position is to protect life without exception so that there is no precedent to extend euthanasia to groups such as the defenseless, the senile aged, and the nonproductive (Kieffer, 1979). Health professionals often distinguish between acts of omission (that permit death) and acts of commission (that cause death). Many feel that under some circumstances (for instance, when there is no hope of recovery) acts of omission are warranted (Baer, 1978).

Fletcher (1974) has argued that birth control and death control represent similar bioethical issues. To be logically and ethically consistent, life *in utero* and life *in extremis* must be considered of the same value. The questions that are raised are major philosophical issues: What is a human life? When does it begin? When does it end?

WORKING WITH THE DYING

Nurses, physicians, clergy, counselors, and others who are experienced in working with the dying often describe a common pattern of adjustment and can recognize an individual's level or stage of adjustment. In addition to the commonalities or universals of dying and death, however, there are always unique individual differences. Hinton (1967), for example, observed the following:

1 Patients who had previously coped well with adversity were less dependent, less anxious, less irritable, and showed less social withdrawal in the face of death.

2 Decisive people were more cognizant of the reality of their illness than less decisive individuals.

3 Individuals who perceived their lives as fulfilled and satisfied approached death with acceptance.

4 Dying individuals who had happy and successful marriages showed less depression and anxiety.

In sum, a positive attitude toward death was associated with strong coping skills, decisiveness, and a satisfying and fulfilled life. The severity of organic damage and the attitudes of the physician and family are also important factors in adjustment.

The family is the first and usually the most important creator of the individual's attitude toward dying and death. If the family is accepting, then it is easier for the dying person to accept death.

Many fear the process of dying more than death (Feifel, 1959; Hinton, 1967). According to Feifel, this is because dying is associated with suffering and dependency. When patients were asked about how they wished to die, 90 percent hoped that death would occur peacefully and swiftly.

Should a patient be told that he or she is dying? Changing answers to this question over the past few years indicate an increasingly direct approach to death in contemporary society. Feifel reported in 1963 that 60–90 percent of the physicians interviewed favored not telling the patient. Today most physicians favor a gentle but honest approach, as long as it is in the best interests of the patient (Schulz, 1978).

Experienced professionals who work with the dying favor an honest treatment of the topic with the patient (Saunders, 1976). Patients greatly appreciate the physician's honesty. It gives them time to review their life and to prepare for death. Most patients seem to know when they are dying, and they are relieved when others are also aware of their state and are willing to confront it (Kastenbaum, 1977; Weisman, 1972). Dying patients show less depression, deviant behavior, and blame of others when they are encouraged to discuss their concerns (Langone, 1972). The task of the attending staff is a more rewarding one when there is openness and the fear of dying alone is reduced. Often the issue is not what to tell the patient, but rather letting the patient tell the staff members. The task is to listen and facilitate expression of feelings and thoughts.

Kübler-Ross addressed many of the common questions about death and dying in her book *Questions and Answers on Death and Dying* (1974). For example:

Question: *How would you answer an 86-year-old grandmother when she states "I wish I would die," or "I want to jump off the bridge." She is in restraints in a nursing home.*

Answer: *If I were in restraints in a nursing home at age 86, I would also jump off a bridge, if I had the energy to do so. Has anybody ever tried taking her off the restraints, putting her in a wheelchair, and taking her for a walk in the garden? These little services to old people can make their lives, if not pleasant, then at least a bit more bearable. (p. 151)*

People who work with the dying are concerned that the process be as peaceful as possible. Kübler-Ross (1969) points out that what the dying individual really needs is a warm, supportive, caring listener.

Professionals as well as family members may simply want to withdraw from the dying individual. Some professionals say that in order to be a warm and supportive listener, one has to have accepted one's own mortality. In working with the dying, one is reminded of the reality of one's own death.

When we are close to a dying person, we may desperately want that person to be at peace—to die comfortably. What if the dying person feels pain, a denial, a resentment? We charge ourselves with the task of cheering up the dying person, but such maneuvers probably reflect our need to comfort and reassure *ourselves* (Kastenbaum, 1977).

Increasing recognition of the needs of dying patients has led to the development of *hospices,* special environments designed to meet the needs of terminally ill people and their families and closest friends. While the goal of a hospital is to prolong life, the hospice's goals are to make the dying patient as comfortable as possible and to help family members and close friends deal with the death. The hospice movement, which began in England (Saunders, 1976), is based on the belief that patients can die with autonomy and dignity if provided with the appropriate setting and services.

Care of the patient is directed at alleviating pain before it becomes severe. Giving patients a mixture of morphine, cocaine, and gin—known as a Brompton's cocktail—in small doses throughout the day allows the patient to remain relatively pain-free and to maintain a clear mind.

The hospice treats the patient and the family together. Visiting hours are unrestricted so family members can be with the patient as much as the patient desires. Family members are encouraged to perform practical services for the patient, such as preparing special meals or taking the ill person out for a ride. Counseling is available to family members or close friends to help them deal with their feelings during the periods preceding and following the patient's death.

Hospices have met a need for people who want an option between the medically expert but often impersonal care of the hospital and personalized but exhausting home care for dying persons. In addition, hospices can provide a personalized, caring environment for individuals without family or close friends to care for them. Their success depends in part on the willingness of people to work closely with dying patients and their families, and on the relative costs of the services provided. Hospice services are currently less expensive than hospitalization, a fact that may contribute to their success.

SUMMARY

1   Death is an inevitable part of life. There are many definitions of death, though most include the loss of such basic functions as heartbeat, breathing, cephalic reflexes, and brain activity.

2   All cultures socialize their members with regard to feelings, attitudes, and actions toward death, and all develop rituals to mark the transition from living-with-us to joining-the-dead.

3   Current research suggests that middle-aged people fear death the most. Old people are less concerned about death, though they often fear a prolonged and painful period of dying. Such age differences may reflect developmental shifts, indicating that the elderly have been reconciled to the realities of the life course. Such findings may also reflect generational or historical effects, since direct experience with death is less common now than in earlier times.

4   Mourning and bereavement refer to the thoughts, feelings, and actions involved in dealing with major loss. Mourning entails the final acceptance of changed reality. Some researchers see creativity as the normal outcome of completed mourning, as energy formerly invested in the past is freed for reinvestment in new activities or new relationships.

5   An individual often passes through several phases of mourning, though progress may be uneven or incomplete. Shock and denial are followed by intense and then deep grief. During the separation–reaction phase anxiety, anger, guilt, and idealization are commonly experienced. Reorganization and resolution of mourning occur as the individual acknowledges and accepts the finality of the change, integrates aspects of the lost person, and becomes able to commit him- or herself to new relationships.

6   The process of mourning is affected by what is lost and when it is lost. The losses of parents, siblings, spouse, or child all have somewhat distinctive consequences for the survivor. The consequences also depend a great deal on the psychological maturity of the survivor and the quality of the severed relationship.

7   Death may be caused or hastened by nonphysical forces such as personal crises; on the other hand, death may be delayed by a strong will to live. Lifestyle factors such as cigarette smoking, improper diet, poor coping strategies, insufficient exercise, alcohol and drug abuse, and loneliness are associated with life-threatening diseases and earlier deaths than would otherwise be predicted.

8   Kübler-Ross and Pattison are two researchers who have suggested stages of dying. Denial, anger, bargaining, depression, and acceptance may or may not follow sequentially. Many individuals fear the pain and losses of competence and control that may accompany dying. Generally, those who have dealt well with earlier crises cope relatively well with dying.

9   There is considerable debate about how death relates to life. One view is that accepting ultimate personal death allows individuals to live fully before dying. Some propose that spiritual life continues after death. Belief in life after death may be adaptive for the living.

10   Individuals can plan for their own death. Some groups have published guides for personal planning; such guides are especially helpful to the survivors who will carry out the arrangements after death.

11   Euthanasia, the right to choose death, is a bioethical issue in today's society. It can take either active or passive form.

12   Those who work effectively with individuals who are dying and those who survive recognize both the common patterns of mourning and the distinct individual styles of coping with loss. The most critical skill is listening to both the dying person and the survivors and helping the mourners express their feelings and thoughts as these evolve over the process of mourning. Hospices are facilities especially created to care for terminally ill people and their families. Such programs are one way to deal with a common life experience.

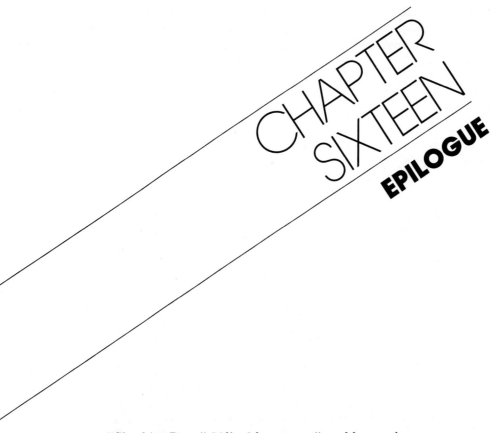

CHAPTER SIXTEEN
EPILOGUE

*"Cheshire Puss," [Alice] began . . . "would you please
tell me which way I ought to go from here?"
"That depends on where you want to get to," said the cat.*
                              Alice in Wonderland

SOME BASIC THEMES

Developmental psychology is a continuously evolving discipline. As times
change, so do our ideas of what constitutes the dimensions of development.
Science does not progress in a vacuum. Scientists, professors, service providers,
and the recipients or consumers of their work are affected by the prevailing
social, political, and economic climate, their own developmental level, and other
covert and overt personal and societal influences. The writers of this book acknowledge the subtle as well as the not so subtle influence of such sources,
maintaining the following basic themes and principles in our discussion:

   1. *A life-span developmental orientation.* Even though our primary cover-
age has been the adult years, we have implied throughout this book that, to

fully understand any part of the life cycle, one must be cognizant of what has gone before and what will follow. Further, we have opted for an active-interactive model of development that takes into account social forces, a developing individual, and the continuous interplay of social and intrapersonal factors.

2. *A social sciences orientation.* Although primary emphasis has been given to development from a psychological perspective, we have incorporated knowledge from all the social sciences wherever applicable. Much of the knowledge base in psychogerontology has evolved from the need to solve the practical problems facing older people in contemporary American society. We have built on this base in an effort to encourage the development of sound theory, research, and application in the social sciences. Psychology, sociology, and biology have provided the fundamental concepts and tools for discovery and interpretation.

3. *A process-centered approach.* The book does not provide pat answers so much as ways of thinking about events and issues in adult life. Some of the information about adult development and aging is best organized by developmental stages (young adulthood, middle adulthood, late adulthood), whereas other information is clearest when it is conceptualized and presented topically (intelligence, personality, memory, perception). There are advantages and disadvantages to each type of organization. When development is presented as a stage-wise process, there is a tendency to overlook the transitions and continuities from one stage or era to the next. When a topic like memory or personality is discussed as it develops and changes throughout the adult years, there is a tendency to overlook the relationship of that concept to other dimensions that are changing simultaneously and interdependently. Although we have used both approaches in order to encourage the greatest latitude in thinking about adult development, our emphasis was on organizing knowledge by processes that change throughout adulthood.

4. *A contemporary American focus.* It was beyond our capacities as well as the space limitations of this book to present a truly universal cross-cultural approach to adult development. Consequently, we focused on current patterns in the United States. There are many important cultural variations in adult development that were not covered in this text.

Most books on adult development and aging would have ended with the chapter on Death, Dying, and Mourning. We felt it was important not to end with death, but to do some "crystal ball gazing" and address the future.

We can understand and predict adult developmental trends when we are aware of the various developmental models that guide contemporary research and theory. First we shall review such models, and then we will show how models lead to predictions about development.

MODELS OF DEVELOPMENT

Models of adult development are designed to communicate, explain, or predict. They can be built at several different levels of detail.

General Models

A general model postulates a few broad factors and a set of gross relationships among those factors. For example:

$$\text{Development} = \text{Environmental change} \times \text{Heredity factors}$$

General models give relatively little attention to identifying the specific mechanisms of environmental change and heredity and how specific subfactors might interact. Baltes and Goulet (1970) proposed an expansion of an E (environment) x H (heredity) model by identifying the following primary, developmental antecedents: immediate environmental events, past environmental influences, inherited genetic factors, and the interrelationships among all these factors. Schaie's (1965) model, although more concerned with how to assess factors than the one proposed by Baltes and Goulet, is another example of a general model. As we saw in Chapter 1, Schaie's factors were chronological age, cohort, and time of measurement.

Recently, Baltes and his colleagues have proposed a new general model of life-span development that acknowledges three generic sources of developmental change (Baltes, Reese, & Lipsitt, 1980):

1   *Normative developmental influences.* These are the universal forces of biological and maturational development.

2   *Culture- or cohort-specific developmental influences.* These are social and biological forces that are typical of development at a certain point in historical time (for instance, being born in the 1930s or the 1980s).

3   *Individualized developmental influences.* These are influences that affect one individual or a group of individuals, but not others. This category can also include the individual's unique perception of events and experiences.

Elder (1979) has argued that normative developmental influences serve an important function for adults in guiding expectations and aspirations. We need to anticipate and prepare for major life events and developmental tasks. Accepting age norms is essential to accepting the dignity of development and aging; when the aged desire youthfulness or agelessness, and when the young do not desire to become old, the dignity of adult development and aging is obscured.

Specific developmental models postulate detailed links between a dependent variable and its antecedents. A good example is Bandura's (1977) self-efficacy model, in which expectations of personal effectiveness determine an individual's strength of coping and adaptation. Expectations of personal efficacy are derived from four principal sources of information: performance accomplishments, vicarious experience, verbal persuasion, and physiological states. These major sources of information are then broken down even further. According to Bandura, self-instruction or self-monitoring is one way of inducing performance accomplishments; observation and modeling of others' behavior are the methods of inducing vicarious experience; suggestion and instruction are techniques of verbal persuasion; and relaxation training, biofeedback, and desensitization (counterconditioning of an emotional response incompatible with fear) are examples of techniques to change physiological state.

Developmental simulations can be designed to estimate and describe specific patterns of age change through knowledge of the effects of various antecedents on various response systems and their interactions. An example is Baltes and Nesselroade's (1973) simulation of interindividual and intraindividual changes in adult intelligence (see Chapter 6). Simulations take multiple antecedents and multiple response systems into account simultaneously. The worth of any simulation outcome depends on the reliability of the information that is entered into the prediction (see Wohlwill, 1973).

Another type of specific developmental model, Markov analysis, is useful in describing development when a future behavior is determined by a current behavioral state and a set of transitional probabilities (Hoyer, 1978). Suppose there are three ways of responding to a situation (A, B, or C). Also suppose that, of those who made response A last time, 70 percent will again respond A, 20 percent will respond B, and 10 percent will respond C (see Table 16-1). The response switching rates provide a basis for predicting future behavior.

One of the most challenging—and most ignored—design problems in developmental psychology involves the continuous interaction of organisms. Markov analysis can be used for conceptualizing the continuously changing interaction between two individuals or systems (Gottman & Notarius, 1978). For example, in one study using Markov analysis Jaffe and Feldstein (1970) recorded at fixed time intervals an "A" whenever one person was speaking and a "B" whenever another person was speaking. They defined three possible states of dialogue:

- A—person 1 speaking
- B—person 2 speaking
- C—neither person 1 nor person 2 speaking

It was not necessary to define a condition of two people speaking simultaneously, since it was too infrequent to analyze. Having described a system with three states (A, B, or C), they then constructed a transition matrix similar to that in

Table 16–1 An Example of Markov Analysis

	To		
	A	B	C
From A	.70	.20	.10
B	.17	.33	.50
C	.00	.50	.50

Table 16-1, showing the probability of person 1 saying something after person 2 says something. Following this model, several matrices and sets of conditional probabilities can be constructed to represent different types of communication—for example, the social interaction between a grandparent and grandchild.

Specific models of development, like general models, are concerned with description and explanation, but they go on to postulate and test specific cause–effect relationships among dependent and independent variables (see Chapter 1). However, not all models fall neatly into a general or specific category, which suggests that there is a continuum of generality and specificity.

INTERPRETATIONS OF ADULT DEVELOPMENTAL RESEARCH

Consider the following:

1 Human beings are instinctively self-oriented.
2 Society teaches the developing individual what is good.
3 Human beings are basically socially oriented.
4 Society corrupts the developing individual.

Which (if any) of the above statements is (are) true? Such statements are oversimplifications, yet they often express or reflect a world view that guides people in daily life. According to Reese and Overton (1970), world views influence the kind of research one might undertake and how the researcher and others might interpret the findings of research.

There is great variation in how we interpret any fact or experience. Consider death, for example: It is the inevitable end of life, the end of development. Is there anything good about it? Can you imagine life without death? Death is an essential aspect of life and development. Concepts of time, love, and work would be much different (not necessarily better) in a deathless universe. Life draws its special value from the fact that it is perishable; life is precious because there is death. Death therefore affects the developmental interpretations of all people, not only a person who is dying.

In addition to the health-related and medical advancements that have been stimulated by the desire to conquer aging and death, many individuals in various fields have done their greatest work in reaction to a compressed or shortened life span. Aspirations and self-development are related to the view one takes toward personal time remaining.

To accept death as part of the life course is different from seeing it as "life taken away." Similarly, to accept other naturally occurring age-related changes as integral parts of the life course and not as "increasing incapacitations" is a realistic and beneficial viewpoint. Much can be learned through discussion with older persons about development and death. Someone who genuinely accepts developmental change is able to communicate a sense of confidence in life and in the developmental future. As Erikson (1963) writes, "... healthy children will not fear life if their elders have integrity enough not to fear death" (p. 269).

Three final points need to be made with regard to interpreting developmental change in adulthood:

1   Psychological and biological decline and death are associated with aging by probability; death and decline can occur at any age.

2   The two points of maximum development within the life course development are birth and death.

3   There are many age-related losses, but there are also many competencies that are strengthened throughout life.

DIMENSIONS OF ADULT DEVELOPMENT AND AGING

When we look back over the important advancements of this century, new products and new technologies are usually first to come to mind. However, there have also been important advancements related to the quality of adult life. A longer and healthier life span, increased knowledge and competency, a more positive conception of aging and old age, and a greater concern for all human rights are current areas of advancement in American society.

Perhaps the most consistently striking idea throughout this book was the negative stereotype of aging. The perceived decline associated with aging was consistently greater than the actual extent of age-related loss. Negative stereotypes of aging were especially prevalent in the areas of intelligence, perception, and personality. There is now a concern in research for identifying the qualitative differences among different developmental levels in adulthood rather than focusing on motivationally based declines. Many age-related losses are outweighed by age-related gains in experience, judgment, stability, and wisdom. Examples of the highest levels of intellectual, personal, and technical competency are found in older adults. Most presidents and supreme court justices, and many senators, congressional representatives, and leaders in business, education, labor, and the arts are older adults. Such examples of high competency in old age have led Neugarten (1974) and others to distinguish between the young-old and the old-old, as we saw in Chapter 2. The young-old, between the ages of 55 and 75–80, serve many significant functions in society, including leadership. They also serve as models of integrity, generativity, wisdom, and support and create a confidence that humans will not only survive but prevail.

Figure 16-1 Dimensions of adult development and aging.

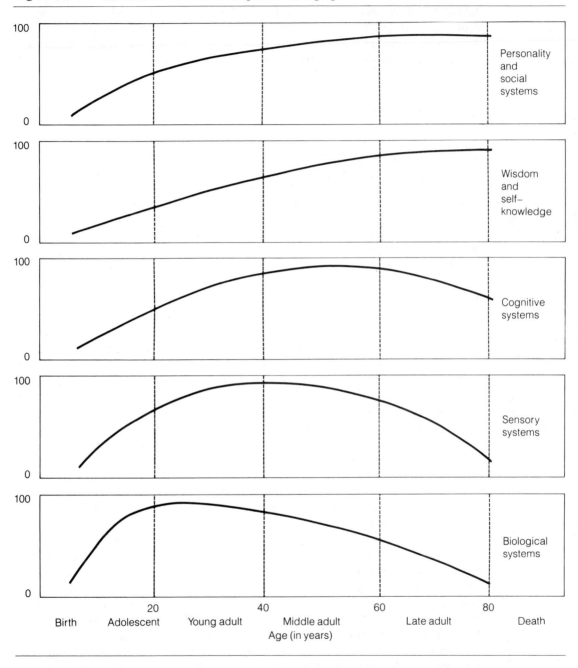

In Figure 16-1 we review some of the major changes that occur during adult development and aging. Note that some systems, especially those with a strong biological basis, show decline, whereas other systems, especially those determined by experience, show age-related gains. Some aspects of each system are biologically based, some are experientially based, and some are based on a nature–nurture interaction; the extent of decline within the whole system depends on the relative contributions of nature and nurture factors.

DEVELOPMENTAL FORECASTING

Psychology, sociology, and other social sciences are not the only fields concerned with prediction. Economists, meteorologists, environmentalists, geologists, and politicians, for instance, are also interested in prediction. Some of the general forecasting methods used by people in these various fields apply to predicting human behavior. The following questions are guidelines:

1. *How reliable is the sample of behavior on which we are basing our predictions?* As we saw in Chapter 1, reliability refers to internal consistency within a test or behavior sample. Some individuals are more consistent than others, and they are probably likely to remain consistent over time (Bem & Allen, 1974).

2. *Is what is measured representative of the phenomena we are trying to predict?* We may not always know in advance how development will be expressed. While we might be interested in predicting personality change, intellectual change, or mental or physical health, the dimensions along which we measure these characteristics will change over time. This kind of change is often seen in longitudinal studies, where the test instruments that were used at the outset become obsolete as more reliable and valid instruments develop. The best approach to this question is to try to obtain a relatively thorough assessment of present behaviors so as to maximize the chances that these behaviors will represent future functioning.

3. *How far ahead are we trying to forecast?* What will you be like at age 65? The closer you are to age 65, the more accurate your answer to this question should be. Not only is the answer based on more information, but the opportunity for change is less in a smaller prediction interval.

4. *Is the rate of change or development different at different points in the life cycle?* Some evidence suggests that the rate of biological change varies as we grow older (Shock, 1977). *Biological reserve capacity* indicates the ratio of the amount that any organ or organism can optimally function to its average functional level under normal conditions. For example, in young adulthood the heart is able to beat 4 times faster than it usually does but only about twice as fast under peak exertion in late adulthood. Thus reserve capacity indicates how far out of the normal range of functioning the organism can go without malfunctioning. Biological reserve capacities might be as high as 4:1 in young adulthood and as low as 1.5:1 in very late life.

The concept of reserve capacity may be useful not only to the understanding of health development and change but also to the description of intellectual, social, and other aspects of psychological development. Recall that some investigators in the area of adult intelligence were interested in "testing the limits" of optimal performance at different age levels (Labouvie-Vief & Gonda, 1976; Labouvie-Vief et al., 1974). Plasticity or intraindividual variability has been found to be a characteristic that remains relatively stable over the adult life cycle (Schultz, Kaye, & Hoyer, 1980).

5. *How stable are the factors that affect behavior over time?* There are developmental periods (such as adolescence or late senescence) when intraindividual change occurs relatively rapidly and dramatically. However, it is reasonable to argue that the amount of intraindividual change will be less in times of societal or cultural stability. An understanding of development thus depends on having good measures of both behavior and the environment and how they change, independently and interactively, over time. Only recently has some work been done on developing a taxonomy of the functional environment for different-aged adults (Schaie, 1978; Scheidt & Schaie, 1978).

6. *Are intraindividual predictions more accurate than interindividual predictions?* This is a complex research question and one that overlaps with some of the issues raised above. Kluckholn and Murray (1949) wrote that every man is, in certain respects, (1) like all other men, (2) like some other men, and (3) like no other man. One search is for the commonalities that all people share—the universal processes of development that affect all humans, perhaps all living creatures, throughout life. Another approach is to seek to understand each individual as a whole system—for instance, to systematically study your best friend, your parents, a child, or yourself.

The problem of learning how "every man is like some other men" as well as how each is different from all others is of special interest to developmental psychologists, as the field of developmental psychology grew out of the comparative study of individuals and species.

Self-Development:
Does Any of This Apply to You?

Development takes place within the individual within the family (for instance, emotional development), and within a social and societal context (for instance, career development, cohort and generational factors). Some aspects of the research presented in this book apply only to some people and other aspects apply to everyone. Sex differences, cohort differences, ethnic differences, and the fact that each person is unique in some respect serve to limit the applicability of the information presented.

However, humans appear to be the only living organisms that can (or choose to) look into the future and plan (or try to plan) their lives, the lives of others, and the world of the future. Therefore, it is relevant to ask whether the knowledge of adult development and aging in general applies to your own development and planning.

Self-knowledge, the first step in self-development, is useful not only for future planning but also for understanding the present world. It is important to take the time to reflect on your own development at any age. Who you are today is an outcome of your past experience, and tomorrow depends on today. Be deliberate in your own development. Our position in writing this book is that development involves a continuing lifelong search for self-understanding.

It is important that we be aware of and responsive to the dramatic aspects of self-development. Self-development is dramatic if it has three characteristics:

1   Development must be novel within the person's experience. Not every aspect of development needs to be novel, but some important aspects must be new.

2   The activity of development must be perceived as important.

3   The outcome of development must be in doubt, and the person must feel that he or she will determine the outcome.

This dramatic aspect touches on the role of *crisis* in adult development. Recall that, from a dialectical perspective, crisis leads to growth. Crisis often means that what we expected to happen has not or will not occur. The usual reaction to crisis is a desire to get things back to "normal." However, people develop in part as a result of crises, and they rarely if ever return to their precrisis state. Humans are often at their best in the face of crisis; thus crises can be perceived as challenges to growth. At each stage of adult development there are new crises and responsibilities, and different aspects of personality, cognition, and so forth develop. Past crises and how we have handled them have greatly influenced who we are now.

Often it is the outcome that determines whether or not a certain event was a positive contributor to development. In childhood, development can be associated with growth in size or an increase in skills and competencies. Adult development involves growth in specialization and in integration. Adults are able to limit their own development trajectories through their aspirations. Young adults can project themselves 30 or 50 years into the future, but it is probably unreasonable for an older adult to make such long-range projections. Self-development for young adults involves the integration of long-range aspirations into present behavior, whereas for an older adult it means the integration of short-range aspirations with past and present behavior.

Self-Health

Individuals are beginning to be aware that they are largely responsible for their own developmental states, especially their own physical and mental health. In Chapter 3 it was pointed out that many of the infectious diseases that plagued earlier generations have been totally or practically eliminated. We are left with diseases related to lifestyle, diet, exercise, nutrition, and environmental quality. These are risk factors that individuals control for themselves.

There has been a profound consciousness raising in regard to self-health, or "wellness," in American society in recent years. As we saw in Chapter 3, wellness is not just the absence of disease, but reflects a positive, ongoing approach on the part of the individual to stay healthy and become healthier.

Not all physicians support the self-health movement. Some say their patients just don't want to know about or be responsible for their own health. However, all adults in modern societies should know at least the symptoms and risk factors associated with major diseases such as cancer and heart disease. Self-care should be not a replacement for but an adjunct to a physician's treatment.

Personal Control

What do the following have in common?

- Alcohol
- Cigarettes
- Coffee
- Cola drinks
- Overeating
- Sleep
- Television
- Work

The common factors are that almost all adults have experience with these activities or things, and that many adults have become strongly dependent on one or more of them. The term *addict* brings to mind a hard-core user or an abuser of drugs or alcohol, yet there are many legal and socially acceptable "soft" addictions that can be equally harmful to health and the quality of ordinary life and thus to an individual's self-development. *Soft addictions* are excessive or obsessive habits that interfere with effective daily living; *hard addictions* have both physiological and psychological components that interfere with effective living.

Addictions involve loss of personal control such that a specific substance or activity controls the person. The thing or activity somehow provides an escape from anxiety, reality, others, or oneself. Frumkes (1980) has identified some of the factors associated with vulnerability to addiction:

- Low levels of frustration tolerance and impulse control
- High levels of chronic anxiety, pressure, and repressed hostility

- High levels of denial of reality (a cool, calm external denial that anything is ever wrong)

- High levels of narcissism (often a facade for insecurity)

- High levels of interpersonal alienation and high fear of interpersonal dependence (which can lead to dependence on other types of support or crutches)

Whether or not a thing or an activity is an addiction depends on the extent to which it affects the individual's quality of life. If an "addicted" individual perceives what he or she is doing as helpful or essential rather than harmful, change in behavior is unlikely.

Some "addictions" can enhance the quality of life. William Glasser, director of the Reality Therapy Institute in Fresno, California, has described a *positive addiction* as (Frumkes, 1980):

- Something you do for about an hour each day or on a regular basis

- Something that is not too easy or too hard

- Something that can be done alone or with someone else

- Something that is valuable—physically, mentally, or spiritually

- Something that improves with self-paced practice

For some people jogging or other sports activities, hobbies, gardening, or meditation are positive addictions.

Do We or Can We Know How Society Will Change?

Some dimensions of adult development and aging change in a relatively logical and predictable sequence. For example, in Chapter 3 we discussed predictable biological aging processes that affect all humans. The rate of senescent change differs from one individual to the next because of genetic factors, developmental history, diet, health status, and environmental and lifestyle factors, but the sequence of senescence is the same for all.

To what extent can we predict social development? What are the causes or antecedents of social development? What will social conditions for middle-aged and older adults be like 25 and 50 years from now?

It is easier to predict the biological future than the social future. Thomas Kuhn (1962) and other philosophers of science have criticized the intuitive notion that scientific knowledge and disciplines progress in an orderly incremental fashion. Nevertheless, it is very likely that progress will continue to be made in the general areas of physical and mental health care and medical-surgical intervention. However, the *rate* of progress on these fronts may soon reach a point of diminishing returns; as we saw in Chapter 3, even if all diseases were eliminated, the average human life span would increase by only 10 to 15 years.

In Chapters 7 and 8 we discussed various frameworks for ordering age-related personality and social changes. Current views of adult personality and social development give emphasis to its multidimensionality. In other words, a multitude of internal and external factors bring about changes in our social behavior, and these changes are expressed along many different dimensions.

Because of the increasing importance of having a national policy for the aged and the aging in the United States, several writers (for example, Beattie, 1976; Neugarten, 1975) have made forecasts about the social and political climate for the future elderly. Peterson, Powell, and Robertson (1976), in an article titled "Aging in America: Toward the Year 2000," made the following predictions:

1   The aged will receive a more equitable portion of the society's resources.
2   A comprehensive national policy for the aged will be stated by the federal government.
3   Older people as a group or voting bloc will exert a more powerful role in politics and legislative decision making.
4   Mandatory retirement will be totally eliminated.

There have been some gains along these dimensions in recent years. Elias Cohen (1976), however, challenged the projections made by Peterson and his colleagues on the basis of the supporting evidence. Cohen pointed out that as a country we have not as yet met the mandates of the Older Americans Act that was signed into law on July 14, 1965. Some of the objectives of this law were for all older Americans to have the following:

1   An adequate income
2   The best possible mental and physical health care
3   Adequate housing
4   Opportunity for employment without discrimination
5   Opportunity for retirement with dignity, honor, and health
6   Community support services as needed
7   Benefit from gerontological research knowledge
8   Pursuit of meaningful activity
9   Freedom, independence, and the free exercise of individual initiative.

It was clear from the findings of the 1981 White House Conference on Aging that these goals and objectives have not as yet been met and that there is still a large gap between what is ideal and what is real for older people in American society. We can only hope that, as more people become old, more people will act on these objectives and the quality of life in old age will improve.

How Will Psychogerontology Change in the Future?

The first scientists were artists. As the quantity of knowledge and the technology of inquiry grew, it was necessary for scientists to specialize. Knowledge was then organized into disciplines, with each developing its own distinct traditions, domains, methods, and languages. Universities as well as governmental agencies have generally maintained the separation of disciplines by constructing departments of biology, psychology, sociology, and so forth. Since departments representing academic disciplines are usually the budgetary units of higher education, disciplines often compete with each other, with little incentive for cooperative and collaborative inquiry.

Two recent and opposing trends go beyond disciplinary barriers. First, with the tendency of science to go from the general to the specific some disciplinary barriers disappear. For example, hybrid fields, such as psychobiology and sociobiology, are emerging. Much of the new knowledge that has been presented in this book derives from these and other hybrid fields such as bioethics. These fields can be specified even further as developmental psychobiology or life-span bioethics.

At the same time, there is a second trend toward greater generality or breadth through multidisciplinary inquiry. Gerontology can be considered a *multidiscipline* in which biologists, psychologists, sociologists, and many other specialists contribute their expertise to the concerns of developing adults and the quality of their lives. This trend reflects the tendency in science toward application. According to a multidisciplinary model, the contributions of each discipline to aging are maximized when combined with other disciplines.

In other words, as new basic knowledge and effective applications accumulate over time, there is both unification and differentiation of the traditional disciplines. The boundaries as well as the substance of disciplines seem to develop and change as readily as people do. Disciplinary identities, however broad or narrow, should serve to enhance rather than restrict the understanding of development and aging processes.

We need to deemphasize disciplinary "tribalism" and encourage both interdisciplinary (for example, developmental biostatistics) and multidisciplinary (for instance, architects and psychologists working together on housing for the aged) ventures. However, we also must not underestimate the significance of basic research as the foundation of what we know and what we do. There is pressure on scientists to show the relevance of their research to ordinary life. Economic pressure for relevance comes from the private and public agencies that provide the monies for scientific research endeavors. The funding priorities of the various supporting agencies necessarily guide the activities of researchers. One of the difficulties with this system is that it is often difficult for nonexperts to see the merits of research in highly technical areas. Not long ago U.S. Senator William Proxmire began presenting what he called the "Golden Fleece Awards" to researchers whose work seemed particularly wasteful of "taxpayers' money." However, scientific work that appears irrelevant at first to a nonscientist may have a large payoff by providing a cure or a technology that saves or improves lives in some way. Fortunately, Senator Proxmire acknowledged some of his short-sightedness when he retracted one of his Golden Fleece Awards.

The greatest opportunities for disciplinary, interdisciplinary, and multidisciplinary advances are likely to occur in the area of interventions. Many careers offer opportunities to influence the lives of adults in positive directions. In Chapter 14 we spoke of change agents, the people who bring about positive change. Precise roles and identities will evolve more clearly as technology and theory in gerontology evolve. It is an encouraging indication of progress in any field when independent research disciplines begin to work with each other on important problems of mutual concern.

In a recent book Horace Judson (1980) observed that the functions of science and art in society are becoming increasingly similar. The creative processes of science and art are also becoming more similar because of the advancing technologies of art and the rise of aesthetics and ethics in science. There are scientific as well as nonscientific or artistic aspects to the field of adult development and aging. Foremost would be an interest in working with people and a sensitivity, curiosity, and concern regarding who they are, who they have been, and who they will become. Perhaps this is an artistic sensitivity. Second would be a command of current knowledge and experience that could be creatively brought to bear on important, unanswered questions that affect the lives of adults—this is science. *Psychogerontology* is the art and the science of understanding the changes that occur to individuals as they grow older.

CONCLUSION

All things change. Developmental change in single-celled organisms might be easier to understand than the development processes of human adults. Much is known, and much is not known. Much has been done, and much more needs to be done.

- For the scientist: There are many questions and hypotheses to be proposed and studied.

- For the practitioner: There are many needs and services to be provided and improved.

- For the artist: There are many ways to portray the developing individual in a developing society; the images are continuously changing.

- For all of us: There is an adulthood to experience and develop.

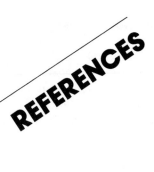

REFERENCES

Abrahams, J. P. Psychological correlates of cardiovascular disease. In M. F. Elias, B. E. Eleftheriou, & P. K. Elias (Eds.), *Special review of experimental aging research: Progress in biology.* Bar Harbor, Maine: Experimental Aging Research Inc., 1976.

Abrahams, J. P., Hoyer, W. J., Elias, M. F., & Bradigan, B. Gerontological research in psychology published in the *Journal of Gerontology,* 1963–1974: Perspectives and progress. *Journal of Gerontology,* 1975, *30,* 668–673.

Achenbach, T. *Research in developmental psychology: Concepts, strategies, methods.* Riverside, N. J.: The Free Press, 1978.

Adam, J. Sequential strategies and the separation of age, cohort, and time of measurement contributions to developmental data. *Psychological Bulletin,* 1978, *85,* 1309–1316.

Adams, B. *Kinship in an urban setting.* Chicago: Markham, 1968.

Adams, C., & Turner, B. Sexuality in old age. Paper presented at 1st annual meeting of the Northeastern Gerontological Society, Newport, R.I., May 1981.

Ad Hoc Committee of the Harvard Medical School to Examine the Definition of Brain Death. A definition of irreversible coma. *Journal of the American Medical Association,* 1968, *205,* 337–340.

Agnew, H. W., Webb, W. B., & Williams, R. L. Sleep patterns in late middle aged males: An EEG study. *Electroencephalography and Clinical Neurophysiology,* 1967, *23,* 168–171.

Ahammer, I. M. Social-learning theory as a framework for the study of adult personality development. In P. Baltes & W. Schaie (Eds.), *Life-span developmental psychology: Personality and socialization.* New York: Academic Press, 1973.

Akiskal, H., & McKinney, W., Jr. Overview of recent research in depression. *Archives of General Psychiatry,* 1975, *32,* 285–305.

Albert, M. L., Feldman, R. C., & Willis, A. L. The subcortical dementia of progressive supranuclear palsy. *Journal of Neurology, Neurosurgery, & Psychiatry,* 1974, *37,* 121–130.

Aldous, J., & Hill, R. Social cohesion, lineage type, and intergenerational transmission. *Social forces,* 1965, *43,* 471–482.

Aldrich, C., & Mendkoff, E. Relocation of the aged and disabled: A mortality study. *Journal of the American Geriatrics Society,* 1963, *11,* 185–194.

Alpaugh, P. K., & Birren, J. E. Variables affecting creative contributions across the adult life span. *Human Development,* 1977, *20,* 240–248.

American Psychiatric Association. *Diagnostic and statistical manual of mental disorders* (DSM II). Washington, D. C.: American Psychiatric Association, 1968.

American Psychiatric Association. *Diagnostic and statistical manual of mental disorders* (DSM III) (3rd ed.). Washington, D. C.: American Psychiatric Association, 1980.

Anders, T. R., Fozard, J. L., & Lilliquist, T. D. Effects of age upon retrieval from short-term memory. *Developmental Psychology,* 1972, *6,* 214–217.

Anderson, J. R., & Bower, G. H. *Human associative memory.* New York: Wiley, 1973.

Angrist, S. A. The study of sex roles. *Journal of Social Issues,* 1969, *15,* 215–232.

Antliff, A. R., & Young, W. C. Internal secretory capacity of the abdominal testis in the guinea pig. *Endocrinology,* 1957, *61,* 121–127.

Arenberg, D. Cognition and aging: Verbal learning, memory, and problem solving. In C. Eisdorfer & M. P. Lawton (Eds.), *Psychology of adult development and aging.* Washington, D. C.: American Psychological Association, 1973.

Arenberg, D. A longitudinal study of problem solving in adults. *Journal of Gerontology,* 1974, *29,* 650–658.

Arens, D. Widowhood and well-being: An interpretation of sex differences. Paper presented at the 32nd annual meeting of the Gerontological Society, Washington, D. C., November 1979.

Ariès, P. *Centuries of childhood.* New York: Knopf, 1962.

Arlin, P. K. Cognitive development in adulthood: A fifth stage? *Developmental Psychology,* 1975, *11,* 602–606.

Arlin, P. K. Toward a metatheoretical model of cognitive development. *International Journal of Aging and Human Development,* 1976, *7,* 247–253.

Armentrout, J. A. Bender Gestalt recall: Memory measure or intelligence estimate? *Journal of Clinical Psychology,* 1976, *32,* 832–834.

Atchley, R. C. Dimensions of widowhood in later life. *Gerontologist,* 1975, *11,* 176–178.

Atchley, R. C. *Social forces in later life* (2nd ed.). Belmont, Calif.: Wadsworth, 1977.

Atchley, R. C. Aging and suicide: Reflection of the quality of life? Proceedings of the second conference on the epidemiology of aging, March 1977, Bethesda, Md. NIH Publication No. 80–969. Washington, D.C.: U.S. Department of Health and Human Services, 1980. (a)

Atchley, R. C. *The social forces in later life* (3rd ed.). Belmont, Calif.: Wadsworth, 1980. (b)

Atkeson, B. M. Differences in the magnitude of the simultaneous and successive Muller-Lyer illusions from age 20 to 79 years. *Experimental Aging Research,* 1978, *4,* 55–66.

Atkinson, R. C., & Shiffrin, R. M. Human memory: A proposed system and its control processes. In K. W. Spence & J. T. Spence (Eds.), *Advances in the psychology of learning and motivation: Advances in research and theory* (Vol. 2). New York: Academic Press, 1968.

Averill, J. R. Grief: Its nature and significance. *Psychological Bulletin,* 1968, *6,* 721–748.

Averill, J. R. Personal control over aversive stimuli and its relationship to stress. *Psychological Bulletin,* 1973, *80,* 286–303.

Baddeley, A. D. *The psychology of memory.* New York: Basic Books, 1976.

Baddeley, A. D., & Warrington, E. K. Amnesia and the distinction between long- and short-term memory. *Journal of Verbal Learning and Verbal Behavior,* 1970, *9,* 176–189.

Baer, L. S. *Let the patient decide: A doctor's advice to older persons.* Philadelphia: Westminster Press, 1978.

Bahrick, H. P., Bahrick, P. O., & Wittlinger, R. P. Fifty years of memory for names and faces: A cross-sectional approach. *Journal of Experimental Psychology: General,* 1975, *104,* 54–75.

Bain, A. *The senses and the intellect.* London: Parker, 1886. (Originally published in 1855.)

Baird, L. *The graduates.* Princeton, N. J.: Educational Testing Service, 1973.

Baird, L. Entrance of women to graduate and professional education. Paper presented at meeting of American Psychological Association, Washington, D.C. September 1976. Cited in R. Barnett & G. Baruch, *The competent woman.* New York: Halstead/Wiley Press, 1978.

Bakan, D. *The duality of human existence.* Chicago: Rand McNally, 1966.

Bakshy, J. Men's perceptions of the achieving female: A thematic analysis of affiliative and instrumental role functioning. Unpublished doctoral dissertation, Illinois Institute of Technology, Chicago, 1977.

Baltes, M. M. On the relationship between significant yearly events and time of death: Random or systematic distribution? *Omega,* 1977, *8,* 165–172.

Baltes, M. M., & Baltes, P. B. The ecopsychological relativity and plasticity of psychological aging. *Zeitschrift fur Experimentelle und Angewandte Psychologie,* 1977, *24,* 179–197.

Baltes, P. B. Longitudinal and cross-sectional sequences in the study of age and generation effects. *Human Development,* 1968, *11,* 145–171.

Baltes, P. B., Cornelius, S. W., Nesselroade, J. R., & Willis, S. L. Integration versus differentiation of fluid/crystallized intelligence in old age. *Developmental Psychology,* 1980, *16,* 625–635.

Baltes, P. B., & Goulet, L. R. Status and issues of life-span developmental psychology. In L. R. Goulet & P. B. Baltes (Eds.), *Life-span developmental psychology: Research and theory.* New York: Academic Press, 1970.

Baltes, P. B., & Goulet, L. R. Exploration of developmental variables by manipulation and simulation of age differences in behavior. *Human Development,* 1971, *14,* 149–170.

Baltes, P. B., & Labouvie, G. V. Adult development of intellectual performance: Description, explanation, and modification. In C. Eisdorfer & M. P. Lawton (Eds.), *Psychology of adult development and aging.* Washington, D. C.: American Psychological Association, 1973.

Baltes, P. B., & Nesselroade, J. R. Developmental analysis of individual differences on multiple measures. In J. R. Nesselroade & H. W. Reese (Eds.), *Life-span developmental psychology: Methodological issues.* New York: Academic Press, 1973.

Baltes, P. B., Reese, H. W., & Lipsitt, L. P. Life-span developmental psychology. *Annual Review of Psychology,* 1980, *31,* 65–110.

Baltes, P. B., Reese, H. W., & Nesselroade, J. R. *Life-span developmental psychology: Introduction to research methods.* Monterey, Calif.: Brooks/Cole, 1977.

Baltes, P. B., & Schaie, K. W. The myth of the twilight years. *Psychology Today,* 1974, *7,* 35–40.

Baltes, P. B., & Schaie, K. W. On the plasticity of intelligence in adulthood and old age: Where Horn and Donaldson fail. *American Psychologist,* 1976, *31,* 720–725.

Baltes, P. B., Schaie, K. W., & Nardi, A. H. Age and experimental mortality in a seven-year longitudinal study of adult cognitive behavior. *Developmental Psychology,* 1971, *5,* 18–26.

Baltes, P. B., & Willis, S. L. Enhancement of intellectual functioning in old age: Penn State Adult Development and Enrichment Project (ADEPT). In F. I. M. Craik & S. E. Trehub (Eds.), *Aging and cognitive processes.* New York: Plenum, 1980.

Bandura, A. Self-efficacy: Toward a unifying theory of behavioral change. *Psychological Review,* 1977, *84,* 191–215.

Barber, C. An experience in middle adulthood: The transition to the empty nest. Paper presented at the National Conference on Aging and Families, Brigham Young University, Provo, Utah, May 1979.

Bard, M., & Sutherland, A. M. Psychological impact of cancer and its treatment: IV. Adaptation to radical mastectomy. *Cancer,* 1965, *8,* 656–672.

Barnett, R. C., & Baruch, G. K. *The competent woman: Perspectives on development.* New York: Halstead/Wiley, 1978.

Barrett, C. J. Women in widowhood: Review essay. *Signs: Journal of Women in Culture and Society,* 1977, *2,* 856–868.

Barrett, C. J., & Schneweis, K. An empirical search for stages of widowhood. Paper presented at the annual scientific meeting of the Gerontological Society, New York, October 1976.

Barrows, C. H., & Roeder, L. M. Nutrition. In C. Finch and L. Hayflick (Eds.), *Handbook of the biology of aging.* New York: Van Nostrand Reinhold, 1977.

Bart, P. Depression in middle-aged women: Some sociocultural factors. Unpublished doctoral dissertation, University of California, Los Angeles, 1967. (University Microfilms No. 68–7452).

Bart, P. Depression in middle-aged women. In V. Gornick and B. K. Moran (Eds.), *Women in sexist society.* New York: New American Library, 1971.

Bartlett, F. C. *Remembering.* Cambridge, England: Cambridge University Press, 1932.

Baude, A. Public policy and changing family patterns in Sweden 1930–1977. In J. Lipman-Blumen & J. Bernard (Eds.), *Sex roles and social policy.* Beverly Hills, Calif.: Sage Publications, 1979.

Beattie, W. Aging and the social services. In R. H. Binstock & E. Shanas (Eds.), *Handbook of aging and the social sciences.* New York: Van Nostrand Reinhold, 1976.

Becker, E. *The denial of death.* New York: Free Press, 1973.

Becker, H., & Strauss, A. Careers, personality, and adult socialization. Reprinted in B. L. Neugarten (Ed.), *Middle age and aging.* Chicago: University of Chicago Press, 1968, pp. 311–320.

Bell, A., & Weinberg, M. *Homosexualities: A study of diversity among men and women.* New York: Simon & Schuster, 1978.

Bell, R. *Marriage and family interaction* (5th ed.). Homewood, Ill.: Dorsey Press, 1979.

Bell, S. G. Expectations of marriage and motherhood: Was it ever enough? A historical study of women in middle age. Summarized in R. Barnett & G. Baruch, *The competent woman.* New York: Halstead/Wiley, 1978.

Bellucci, G., & Hoyer, W. J. Feedback effects on the performance and self-reinforcing behavior of elderly and young adult women. *Journal of Gerontology,* 1975, *30,* 456–460.

Bem, D. J., & Allen, A. On predicting some of the people some of the time: The search for cross-situational consistencies in behavior. *Psychological Review,* 1974, *81,* 506–520.

Bem, S. L. The measurement of psychological androgyny. *Journal of Consulting & Clinical Psychology,* 1974, *47,* 155–162.

Bengtson, V. L., Kasschau, P. L., & Ragan, P. K. The impact of social structure on aging individuals. In J. E. Birren & K. W. Schaie (Eds.), *Handbook of the psychology of aging.* New York: Van Nostrand Reinhold, 1977.

Bengtson, V. L., & Kuypers, J. A. Generational influences and the developmental stake. *Aging and Human Development,* 1971, *2,* 249–260.

Bengtson, V. L., & Troll, L. E. Youth and their parents: Feedback and intergenerational influences in socialization. In R. Lerner & G. Spanier (Eds.), *Child influences on marital and family interaction: A life span perspective.* New York: Academic Press, 1978.

Berardo, F. M. Widowhood status in the U.S.: A perspective on a neglected aspect of the family life cycle. *Family Coordinator,* 1968, *17,* 191–203.

Berardo, F. M. Survivorship and social isolation: The case of the aged widower. *Family Coordinator,* 1970, *19,* 11–25.

Bergin, A. E. Some implications of psychotherapy research for therapeutic practice. *Journal of Abnormal Psychology,* 1966, *71,* 235–246.

Bergin, A. E. The evaluation of therapeutic outcomes. In A. E. Bergin & S. L. Garfield (Eds.), *Handbook of psychotherapy and behavior change.* New York: Wiley, 1971.

Bergman, M., Blumenfeld, V. G., Casardo, D., Dash, B., Levitt, H., & Margulies, M. K. Age-related decrement in hearing for speech: Sampling and longitudinal studies. *Journal of Gerontology,* 1976, *31,* 533–538.

Berlyne, D. E. Knowledge and stimulus-response psychology. *Psychological Review,* 1954, *61,* 245–254.

Berlyne, D. E. *Conflict, arousal, and curiosity.* New York: McGraw-Hill, 1960.

Bernard, J. *Academic women.* University Park, Penn.: Pennsylvania State University Press, 1964.

Bernard, J. *The future of marriage.* New York: Bantam Books, 1973.

Bernard, J. *Women, wives, mothers: Values and options.* Chicago: Aldine, 1975.

Bernard, J. Policy and women's time. In J. Lipman-Blumen & J. Bernard (Eds.), *Sex roles and social policy.* Beverly Hills, Calif.: Sage Publications, 1979.

Bijou, S. W., & Baer, D. M. *Child development, Vol. 1: A systematic and empirical theory.* New York: Appleton-Century-Crofts, 1961.

Birkhill, W. R., & Schaie, K. W. The effect of differential reinforcement of cautiousness in intellectual performance among the elderly. *Journal of Gerontology,* 1975, *30,* 578–582.

Birnbaum, J. A. Life patterns and self-esteem in gifted family-oriented and career-oriented women. In M. Mednick, S. Tangri, & L. Hoffman (Eds.), *Women and achievement: Social and motivational analyses.* Washington, D. C.: Hemisphere, 1975.

Birnbaum, N., & Kimmel, H. D. *Biofeedback and self-regulation.* Hillsdale, N. J.: Erlbaum, 1979.

Birren, J. E. (Ed.). *Handbook of aging and the individual.* Chicago: University of Chicago Press, 1959.

Birren, J. E. *The psychology of aging.* Englewood Cliffs, N. J.: Prentice-Hall, 1964.

Birren, J. E. Translations in gerontology—From lab to life: Psychophysiology and speed of response. *American Psychologist,* 1974, *29,* 808–816.

Birren, J. E., Butler, R. N., Greenhouse, S. W., Sokoloff, L., & Yarrow, M. (Eds.). *Human aging: A biological and behavioral study.* Washington, D. C.: U.S. Government Printing Office, 1963.

Birren, J. E., Casperson, R. C., & Botwinick, J. Age changes in pupil size. *Journal of Gerontology,* 1950, *5,* 267–271.

Birren, J. E., & Renner, V. J. Research on the psychology of aging. In J. E. Birren & K. W. Schaie (Eds.), *Handbook of the psychology of aging.* New York: Van Nostrand Reinhold, 1977.

Birren, J. E., & Sloane, R. B. (Eds.). *Handbook of mental health and aging.* Englewood Cliffs, N.J.: Prentice-Hall, 1980.

Blau, F. D. Women in the labor force: An overview. In J. Freeman (Ed.), *Women: A feminist perspective* (2nd ed.). La Jolla, Calif.: Mayfield, 1979.

Blau, Z. S. Old age in a changing society. New York: Franklin Watts, 1973.

Blauner, R. Death and social structure. *Psychiatry,* 1966, *29,* 378–394.

Blenkner, M. Social work and family relationships in late life with some thoughts on filial maturity. In E. Shanes & G. Strieb (Eds.), *Social structure in the three generation family.* Englewood Cliffs, N.J.: Prentice-Hall, 1965.

Block, J. Some enduring and consequential structures of personality. In A. I. Rabins, J. Aronoff, A. Barclay, & R. Zucker (Eds.), *Further explorations in personality.* New York: Wiley, 1981.

Block, J., in collaboration with N. Haan. *Lives through time.* Berkeley, Calif.: Bancroft Books, 1971.

Bloom, B. L., Asher, S. J., & White, S. W. Marital disruption as a stressor: A review and analysis. *Psychological Bulletin,* 1978, *85,* 867–894.

Blum, J. E., & Tross, S. Psychodynamic treatment of the elderly: A review of issues in theory and practice. In C. Eisdorfer (Ed.), *Annual review of gerontology and geriatrics* (Vol. 1). New York: Springer, 1980.

Blumberg, R. L. A paradigm for predicting the position of women: Policy implications and problems. In J. Lipman-Blumen & J. Bernard (Eds.), *Sex roles and social policy.* Beverly Hills, Calif.: Sage Publications, 1979.

Bock, E., & Webber, I. L. Suicide among the elderly: Isolating widowhood and mitigating alternatives. *Journal of Marriage and the Family,* 1979, February, 24–30.

Bondareff, W. The neural basis of aging. In J. E. Birren & K. W. Schaie (Eds.), *Handbook of the psychology of aging.* New York: Van Nostrand Reinhold, 1977.

Bondareff, W. Synaptic atrophy in the senescent hippocampus. *Mechanisms of Aging and Development,* 1979, *9,* 163–171.

Boone, J. A., & Adesso, V. J. Racial differences on a black intelligence test. *Journal of Negro Education,* 1974, *43,* 429–436.

Booth, A. Sex and social participation. *American Sociological Review,* 1972, *37,* 183–192.

Booth, A., & Hess, B. Cross-sex friendship. *Journal of Marriage and the Family,* 1974, *39,* 38–47.

Bortner, R. W., & Hultsch, D. F. Personal time perspective in adulthood. *Developmental Psychology,* 1972, *7,* 98–104.

Boston Women's Health Book Collective. *Our bodies, our selves* (2nd ed.). New York: Simon & Schuster, 1976.

Boston Women's Health Book Collective. *Our selves and our children.* New York Random House, 1977.

Botwinick, J. *Cognitive processes in maturity and old age.* New York: Springer, 1967

Botwinick, J. Intellectual abilities. In J. E. Birren & K. W. Schaie (Eds.), *Handbook of the psychology of aging.* New York: Van Nostrand Reinhold, 1977.

Botwinick, J. *Aging and behavior.* New York: Springer, 1978.

Botwinick, J., & Kornetsky, C. Age differences in the acquisition and extinction GSR. *Journal of Gerontology,* 1960, *15,* 83–84.

Botwinick, J., & Siegler, I. C. Intellectual ability among the elderly: Simultaneous cross-sectional and longitudinal comparisons. *Developmental Psychology,* 1980, *16,* 49–53.

Botwinick, J., & Storandt, M. *Memory, related functions, and age.* Springfield, Ill.: Charles C. Thomas, 1974.

Bourestrom, N., & Tars, S. Alterations in life patterns following nursing home relocation. *Gerontologist,* 1974, *14,* 506–510.

Bouvier, L., Atlee, E., & McVeigh, F. *The elderly in America.* Washington, D.C.: Population Reference Bureau, 1975.

Boyd, R. The valued grandparent: A changing social role. *Living in a multigenerational family.* Occasional Papers in Gerontology No. 3. University of Michigan–Wayne State, Institute of Gerontology, 1969.

Bradburn, N. *The structure of psychological well-being.* Chicago: Aldine, 1969.

Brand, R. J. Coronary prone behavior as an independent risk factor for coronary heart disease. In T. M. Dembroski, S. M. Weiss, S. G. Haynes, & M. Heinlab (Eds.), *Coronary prone behavior.* New York: Springer-Verlag, 1978.

Braun, H. W., & Geiselhart, R. Age differences in the acquisition and extinction of the conditioned eyelid response. *Journal of Experimental Psychology,* 1959, *57,* 386–388.

Brazier, M. A. B., & Finesinger, J. E. Characteristics of the normal electroencephalogram. I. A study of the occipital cortical potentials in 500 normal adults. *Journal of Clinical Investigations,* 1944, *23,* 303–311.

Breytspaak, L. Achievement and the self-concept in middle age. In E. Palmore (Ed.), *Normal aging II.* Durham, N. C.: Duke University Press, 1974.

Brinley, J. F. Cognitive sets and accuracy of performance in the elderly. In A. T. Welford & J. E. Birren (Eds.), *Behavior, aging and the nervous system.* Springfield, Ill.: Charles C. Thomas, 1965.

Britton, J., & Britton, J. O. *Personality changes in aging: A longitudinal study of community residents.* New York: Springer, 1972.

Broadbent, D. E. *Perception and communication.* London: Pergamon, 1958.

Broadbent, D. E. The hidden preattentive processes. *American Psychologist,* 1977, *32,* 109–118.

Brody, H. Structural changes in the aging nervous system. In H. T. Blumenthal (Ed.), *Interdisciplinary topics in gerontology,* Vol. 7. Basel: Karges, 1970.

Brody, H. Aging of the vertebrate brain. In M. Rockstein (Ed.), *Development and aging in the nervous system.* New York: Academic Press, 1973.

Brody, H., & Vijayashankar, N. Anatomical changes in the nervous system. In C. E. Finch & L. Hayflick (Eds.), *Handbook of the biology of aging.* New York: Van Nostrand Reinhold, 1977.

Bromley, D. B. Some experimental tests of the effect of age on creative intellectual output. *Journal of Gerontology,* 1956, *11,* 74–82.

Bromley, D. B. *The psychology of human aging.* Baltimore, Md.: Penguin, 1966.

Brown, A. L. The development of memory: Knowing, knowing about knowing, and knowing how to know. In H. W. Reese (Ed.), *Advances in child development and behavior* (Vol. 10). New York: Academic Press, 1975.

Brown, G., & Harris, T. *Social origins of depression: A study of psychiatric disorder in women.* New York: The Free Press, 1978.

Brown, J. A note on the division of labor by sex. *American Anthropologist,* 1970, *72,* 1074–1978.

Bruner, J. S., & Taguri, R. The perception of people. In G. Lindzey (Ed.), *Handbook of social psychology.* Reading, Mass.: Addison-Wesley, 1954.

Brunner, L. S., & Suddarth, D. S. *Textbook of medical-surgical nursing.* New York: Lippincott, 1975.

Buell, S. J., & Coleman, P. D. Dendritic growth in the aged human brain and failure of growth in senile dementia. *Science,* 1979, *206,* 854–856.

Buhler, C. The curve of life as studied in biographies. *Journal of Applied Psychology,* 1935, *19,* 405–409.

Bultena, G. L. Structural effects on the morale of the aged: A comparison of age-segregated and age-integrated communities. In J. Gubrium (Ed.), *Late life: Communities and environmental policy.* Springfield, Ill.: Charles C. Thomas, 1974.

Bunk, B. Sexually-open marriages: Ground rules for countering potential threats to marriage. *Alternative Lifestyles,* 1980, *3,* 312–328.

Burgess, E., Locke, B., & Thomas, D. *The family: From institution to companionship.* New York: American Book Company, 1963.

Burnside, I. M. Group work with the mentally impaired elderly. In I. Burnside (Ed.), *Working with the elderly: Group processes and techniques.* North Scituate, Mass.: Duxbury Press, 1978.

Buss, A. R. A general developmental model for inter-individual differences, intra-individual differences, and intra-individual changes. *Developmental Psychology,* 1974, *10,* 70–78.

Busse, E. W. A physiological, psychological and sociological study of aging. In E. Palmore (Ed.), *Normal aging.* Durham, N.C.: Duke University Press, 1970.

Butler, R. The life review: An interpretation of reminiscence in the aged. *Psychiatry,* 1963, *26,* 65–76.

Butler, R., & Lewis, M. *Aging and mental health: Positive psychosocial approaches* (3rd ed.). St. Louis, Mo.: C. V. Mosby, 1982.

Byrne, R. W. Memory in complex tasks. Unpublished doctoral dissertation. Cambridge University (England), 1976.

Bytheway, W. R. Aging and sociological studies of the family. Paper presented at the annual colloquium of the Social Science Research Division, International Association of Gerontology, Ystad, Sweden, September 1977.

Cameron, P. Masculinity/femininity of the generations: As self-reported and as stereotypically appraised. *International Journal of Aging and Human Development,* 1976, *7,* 143–151.

Campbell, A., Converse, P., & Rogers, W. *The quality of American life.* New York: Russell Sage Foundation, 1976.

Campbell, D. T. On the conflicts between biological and social evolution and between psychology and moral tradition. *American Psychologist,* 1975, *30,* 1103–1126.

Candy, S. A. A comparative analysis of functions of friendship in six age groups of men and women. Unpublished doctoral dissertation. Wayne State University, 1977.

Canestrari, R. E. Paced and self-paced learning in young and elderly adults. *Journal of Gerontology,* 1963, *18,* 165–168.

Caplan, G. *Principles of preventive psychiatry.* New York: Basic Books, 1964.

Caplan, G. *Support systems and community mental health: Lectures on concept development.* New York: Behavioral Publications, 1974.

Caplow, T. *The sociology of work.* Minneapolis: University of Minnesota Press, 1954.

Carlson, R. Sex differences in ego functioning: Exploratory studies of agency and communion. *Journal of Consulting and Clinical Psychology,* 1971, *37,* 267–277.

Carpenter, J. O., & Wylie, C. M. On aging, dying, and denying. *Public Health Reports,* 1974, *89,* 403–407.

Cath, S. J. Individual adaptation in the middle years: A testing of faith in self and object constancy. *Journal of Geriatric Psychiatry,* 1976, *9,* 19–40.

Cattell, R. B., and Scheier, I. H. *The meaning and measurement of neuroticism and anxiety.* New York: Ronald Press, 1961.

Cauna, N. The effects of aging on the receptor organs of the human dermis. In W. Montagna (Ed.), *Advances in biology of skin, Vol. VI: Aging.* New York: Pergamon Press, 1965.

Cermak, L. S. The contribution of a "processing" deficit to alcoholic Korsakoff patients' memory disorder. In I. M. Birnbaum & E. S. Parker (Eds.), *Alcohol and memory.* Hillsdale, N. J.: Erlbaum, 1977.

Cermak, L. S. Memory as a processing continuum. In L. W. Poon, J. L. Fozard, L. S. Cermak, D. L. Arenberg, & L. W. Thompson (Eds.), *New Directions in memory and aging.* Hillsdale, N. J.: Erlbaum, 1980.

Cermak, L. S., & Butters, N. The role of interference and encoding in the short-term memory deficits of Korsakoff patients. *Neuropsychologia,* 1972, *10,* 89–96.

Cherry, E. C. Some experiments on the recognition of speech, with one and two ears. *Journal of the Acoustical Society of America,* 1953, *25,* 975–979.

Chessler, P. *Women and madness.* Garden City, N.Y.: Doubleday, 1972.

Chinoy, E. *Automobile workers and the American dream.* Garden City, N. Y.: Doubleday, 1955.

Chiriboga, D. A., & Cutler, L. Stress and adaptation: Life-span perspectives. In L. W. Poon (Ed.), *Aging in the 1980s: Psychological issues.* Washington, D.C.: American Psychological Association, 1980.

Chodorow, N. *The reproduction of mothering.* Berkeley: University of California Press, 1978.

Choron, J. *Death and Western thought.* New York: Collier, 1963.

Chown, S. M. Age and the rigidities. *Journal of Gerontology,* 1961, *16,* 353–362.

Chown, S. M. Personality and aging. In K. W. Schaie (Ed.), *Theory and methods of research on aging.* Morgantown, W. Va.: West Virginia University Library, 1968.

Christenson, C. V., & Gagnon, J. H. Sexual behavior in groups of older women. *Journal of Gerontology,* 1965, *20,* 351–356.

Clark, L. E., & Knowles, J. B. Age differences in dichotic listening performance. *Journal of Gerontology,* 1973, *28,* 173–178.

Clark, M., & Anderson, B. G. *Culture and aging: An anthropological study of older Americans.* Springfield, Ill.: Charles C. Thomas, 1967.

Clay, V. *Women: Menopause and middle age.* Pittsburgh, Pa.: KNOW, Inc., 1977.

Clayton, V., & Birren, J. E. Age and wisdom across the life-span: Theoretical perspectives. In P. B. Baltes & O. G. Brim, Jr. (Eds.), *Life-span development and behavior* (Vol. 3). New York: Academic Press, 1980.

Clayton, V., & Overton, W. F. Concrete and formal operational thought processes in young adulthood and old age. *International Journal of Aging and Human Development,* 1976, *7,* 237–245.

Cleary, A. Test bias: Prediction of grades of Negro and White students in integrated colleges. *Journal of Educational Measurement,* 1968, *5,* 115–124.

Cleveland, W. P., and Gianturco, D. Remarriage probability after widowhood: A retrospective method. *Journal of Gerontology,* 1976, *31,* 99–103.

Cohen, E. S. Comment: Editor's note. *Gerontologist,* 1976, *16,* 270–275.

Cohen, G. Language comprehension in old age. *Cognitive Psychology,* 1979, *11,* 412–429.

Cohler, B., & Grunebaum, H. Mothers, grandmothers, and daughters: Personality and child care in three-generation families. New York: Wiley, 1981.

Cole, J., & Gutmann, D. The later life of Druze women: A TAT investigation. *Totus Homo,* 1977, *7,* 23–38.

Coleman, J. C. *Abnormal psychology and modern life* (5th ed.). Chicago: Scott, Foresman, 1976.

Coleman, J. C., Butcher, J. N., & Carson, R. C. *Abnormal psychology and modern life* (6th ed.). Glenview, Ill.: Scott, Foresman, 1980.

Collett, L., & Lister, D. Fear of death and fear of dying. *Journal of Psychology,* 1969, *72,* 179–181.

Comalli, P. E., Jr. Life-span changes in visual perception. In L. R. Goulet & P. B. Baltes (Eds.), *Life-span developmental psychology.* New York: Academic Press, 1970.

Comfort, A. *The biology of senescence.* New York: Holt, Rinehart and Winston, 1956.

Comfort, A. (Ed.). *The joy of sex: A cordon bleu guide to lovemaking.* New York: Crown, 1972.

Constantinople, A. Masculinity-femininity: An exception to a famous dictum. In F. Denmark (Ed.), *Women: A PDI research reference work* (Vol. I). New York: Psychological Dimensions, Inc., 1976.

Cooper, I. S. *Living with chronic neurologic disease.* New York: Norton, 1976.

Coren, S., & Girgus, J. S. Density of human lens pigmentation: In vivo measures over an extended age range. *Vision Research,* 1972, *12,* 343–346.

Corso, J. F. *The experimental psychology of sensory behavior.* New York: Holt, Rinehart and Winston, 1967.

Corso, J. F. Sensory processes and age effects in normal adults. *Journal of Gerontology,* 1971, *26,* 90–105.

Corso, J. F. Auditory perception and communication. In J. E. Birren & K. W. Schaie (Eds.), *Handbook of the psychology of aging.* New York: Van Nostrand Reinhold, 1977.

Costa, P. T., & McCrae, R. R. Age differences in personality structure revisited: Studies in validity, stability, and change. *International Journal of Aging and Human Development,* 1977, *8,* 261–275.

Costa, P. T., & McCrae, R. R. Objective personality assessment. In M. Storandt, I. C. Siegler, & M. F. Elias (Eds.), *The clinical psychology of aging.* New York: Plenum Press, 1978.

Costa, P. T., & McCrae, R. R. Still stable after all these years: Personality as a key to some issues in aging. In P. B. Baltes & O. G. Brim (Eds.), *Life-span development and behavior* (Vol. 3). New York: Academic Press, 1980.

Costa, P. T., McCrae, R. R., & Arenberg, D. Enduring dispositions in adult males. *Journal of Personality and Social Psychology,* 1980, *38,* 793–800.

Cottrell, F., & Atchley, R. C. *Women in retirement: A preliminary report.* Oxford, Ohio: Scripps Foundation, 1969.

Covin, T. M., & Covin, J. N. Comparability of Peabody and WAIS scores among adolescents suspected of being mentally retarded. *Psychological Reports,* 1976, *39,* 33–34.

Cowan, P., Cowan, C., Coie, J., & Coie, L. In L. Newman & W. Miller (Eds.), *The first child and family formation.* Durham, N. C.: University of North Carolina Press, 1978.

Craik, F. I. M. Age differences in human memory. In J. E. Birren & K. W. Schaie (Eds.), *Handbook of the psychology of aging.* New York: Van Nostrand Reinhold, 1977.

Craik, F. I. M., & Lockhart, R. S. Levels of processing: A framework for memory research. *Journal of Verbal Learning and Verbal Behavior,* 1972, *11,* 671–684.

Craik, F. I. M., & Masani, P. A. Age and intelligence differences in coding and retrieval of word lists. *British Journal of Psychology,* 1969, *60,* 315–319.

Craik, F. I. M., & Tulving, E. Depth of processing and the retention of words in episodic memory. *Journal of Experimental Psychology: General,* 1975, *104,* 268–294.

Crandall, R. *Gerontology: A behavioral science approach.* Reading, Mass.: Addison-Wesley, 1980.

Critchley, M. Aging of the nervous system. In E. V. Cowdry (Ed.), *Problems of aging.* Baltimore, Md.: Williams and Wilkins, 1942.

Cuber, J., & Harroff, P. *The significant Americans.* New York: Appleton-Century-Crofts, 1965.

Cumming, E., & Henry, W. *Growing old: A process of disengagement.* New York: Basic Books, 1961.

Cumming E., & Schneider, D. M. Sibling solidarity: A property of American kinship. *American Anthropologist,* 1961, *63,* 498–507.

Cunningham, W. R. Speed, age, and qualitative differences in cognitive functioning. In L. W. Poon (Ed.), *Aging in the 1980s: Psychological issues.* Washington, D. C.: American Psychological Association, 1980.

Daniels, P., & Weingarten, P. Later first-time parenthood: The two sides of the coin. Working paper No. 7. Wellesley, Mass.: Wellesley College Center for Research on Women, October 1979.

Davis, E. E. Are adolescents anti-society oriented? *Intellect,* 1973, *102,* 62–64.

Dawkins, R. Selective neurone death as a possible memory mechanism. *Nature,* 1971, *229,* 117–118.

Delprato, D. J. The reactional biography concept: Early contributions to a perspective for the psychology of aging. *Human Development,* 1980, *23,* 314–322.

Dement, W., & Kleitman, N. The relation of eye movements during sleep to dream activity. *Journal of Experimental Psychology,* 1957, *53,* 539.

Demming, J. A., & Pressey, S. L. Tests indigenous to the adult and older years. *Journal of Counseling Psychology,* 1957, *4,* 144–148.

Denney, D. R., & Denney, N. W. The use of classification for problem solving: A comparison of middle and old age. *Developmental Psychology,* 1973, *9,* 275–278.

Denney, N. W. Evidence for developmental change in categorization criteria for children and adults. *Human Development,* 1974, *17,* 41–53.

Denney, N. W. Problem solving in later adulthood: Intervention research. In P. B. Baltes & O. G. Brim (Eds.), *Life-span development and behavior.* New York: Academic Press, 1979.

Denney, N. W., & Cornelius, S. Class inclusion and multiple classification in middle and old age. *Developmental Psychology,* 1975, *11,* 521–522.

Denney, N. W., & Denney, D. R. Modeling effects on the questioning strategies of the elderly. *Developmental Psychology,* 1974, *10,* 458.

Denney, N. W., & Lennon, M. L. Classification: A comparison of middle and old age. *Developmental Psychology,* 1972, *7,* 210–213.

Dennis, W. Creative productivity between ages of 20 and 80 years. *Journal of Gerontology,* 1966, *21,* 1–8.

De Vries, H. A. Physiology of exercise and aging. In D. S. Woodruff & J. E. Birren (Eds.), *Aging: Scientific perspectives and social issues.* New York: Van Nostrand Reinhold, 1975.

Diggory, J. C., & Rothman, D. Z. Values destroyed by death. *Journal of Abnormal and Social Psychology,* 1961, *63,* 205–210.

DiMascio, A., Weissman, M., Prusoff, B., Neu, C., Zwilling, M., & Klerman, G. Differential symptom reduction by drugs and psychotherapy in acute depression. *Archives of General Psychiatry,* 1979, *36,* 1450–1456.

Dinnerstein, D. *The mermaid and the minotaur: Sexual arrangements and human malaise.* New York: Harper & Row, 1977.

Dobson, J. F. *Ancient education and its meaning to us.* New York: Longmans, Green, 1932.

Dohrenwend, B., & Dohrenwend, B. S. Sex differences and psychiatric disorders. *American Journal of Sociology,* 1976, *81,* 1447–1454.

Domey, R. G., McFarland, R. A., & Chadwick, E. Dark adaptation as a function of age and time: II. A derivation. *Journal of Gerontology,* 1960, *15,* 267–279.

Dooghe, G., & Vanderleyden, L. Loneliness of old widows and married women. Paper presented at meeting of the European Social Science Research Committee, the International Association of Gerontology, Ystad, Sweden, September 1977.

Doubleday Dictionary. Garden City, N.Y.: Doubleday, 1975.

Douglas, K., & Arenberg, D. Age changes, cohort differences, and cultural change on the Guilford-Zimmerman Temperament Survey. *Journal of Gerontology,* 1978, *33,* 737–747.

Douvan, E., & Adelson, J. *The adolescent experience.* New York: Wiley, 1966.

Doyle, K. O., Jr. Theory and practice of ability testing in ancient Greece. *Journal of the History of the Behavioral Sciences,* 1974, *10,* 202–212.

Drachman, D., & Leavitt, J. Memory impairment in the aged: Storage versus retrieval deficit. *Journal of Experimental Psychology,* 1972, *93,* 302–308.

Du Bois, P. H. A test-dominated society: China 1115 B.C.—1905 A.D. In L. J. Barnette (Ed.), *Readings in psychological tests and measurements.* Homewood, Ill.: Dorsey, 1968.

Dunbar, F. *Psychosomatic diagnosis.* New York: Harper & Row, 1943.

Duncan, O. D. A socioeconomic index for all occupations. In A. J. Reiss, Jr. (Ed.), *Occupations and social status.* New York: Free Press, 1961.

Dyck, A. An alternative to the ethic of euthanasia. In R. H. Wilhams (Ed.), *To live and to die: When, why, and how.* New York: Springer-Verlag, 1974.

Dye, C. J. Psychologists' role in the provision of mental health care for the elderly. *Professional Psychology,* 1978, *9,* 38–49.

Dykhuizen, D. Evolution of cell senescence, atherosclerosis and benign tumors. *Nature,* 1974, *251:* 616–618.

Ebbinghaus, H. *Memory.* New York: Dover, 1964. (Originally published as *Uber das gedachtnis.* Leipzig, 1885.)

Eichorn, D. H., Clausen, J. A., Haan, N., Honzik, M. P., & Mussen, P. (Eds.), *Present and past in middle life.* New York: Academic Press, 1981.

Eisdorfer, C., Axelrod, S., & Wilkie, F. L. Stimulus exposure time as a factor in serial learning in an aged sample. *Journal of Abnormal and Social Psychology,* 1963, *67,* 594–600.

Eisdorfer, C., & Cohen, D. The cognitively impaired elderly: Differential diagnosis. In M. A. Storandt, I. C. Siegler, & M. F. Elias (Eds.), *The clinical psychology of aging.* New York: Plenum Press, 1978.

Eisdorfer, C., Nowlin, J., & Wilkie, F. Improvement of learning in the aged by modification of autonomic nervous system activity. *Science,* 1970, *170,* 1327–1329.

Eisdorfer, C., & Stotsky, B. A. Intervention, treatment, and rehabilitation of psychiatric disorders. In J. E. Birren & K. W. Schaie (Eds.), *Handbook of the psychology of aging.* New York: Van Nostrand Reinhold, 1977.

Eisdorfer, C., & Wilkie, F. Stress, disease, aging, and behavior. In J. E. Birren & K.

W. Schaie (Eds.), *Handbook of the psychology of aging*. New York: Van Nostrand Reinhold, 1977.

Eisner, D. A., & Schaie, K. W. Age change in response to visual illusions from middle to old age. *Journal of Gerontology,* 1971, *26,* 146–150.

Elder, G. H. Historical change in life patterns and personality. In P. B. Baltes & O. G. Brim (Eds.), *Life-span development and behavior* (Vol. 2). New York: Academic Press, 1979.

Elias, M. F., & Elias, P. K. Motivation and activity. In J. E. Birren & K. W. Schaie (Eds.), *Handbook of the psychology of aging*. New York: Van Nostrand Reinhold, 1977.

Elias, M. F., & Kinsbourne, M. Age and sex differences in the processing of verbal and non-verbal stimuli. *Journal of Gerontology,* 1974, *29,* 162–171.

Eliot, A. Did Monet see what he thought he saw? *The Atlantic Monthly,* 1973, 108–111.

Emmerich, W. Socialization and sex-role development. In P. B. Baltes and K. W. Schaie (Eds.), *Life-span developmental psychology: Personality and socialization.* New York: Academic Press, 1973

Engel, G. L. Sudden and rapid death during psychological stress: Folklore or folk wisdom. *Annals of Internal Medicine,* 1971, *79,* 771–782.

English, H. B., & English, A. C. *A comprehensive dictionary of psychological and psychoanalytical terms.* New York: David McKay, 1958.

Erikson, E. H. *Young man Luther.* New York: Norton, 1958.

Erikson, E. H. *Childhood and society* (2nd ed.). New York: Norton, 1963.

Erikson, E. H. *Identity: Youth and crisis.* New York: Norton, 1968.(a)

Erikson, E. H. Womanhood and inner space. In E. Erikson (Ed.), *Identity: Youth, and crisis.* New York: Norton, 1968.(b)

Erikson, E. H. *Gandhi's truth.* New York: Norton, 1969.

Erikson, E. H. Once more on the inner space: Letter to a former student. In J. Strouse (Ed.), *Women and analysis.* New York: Grossman/Viking Press, 1974.

Erikson, R. C., & Scott, M. L. Clinical memory testing: A review. *Psychological Bulletin,* 1977, *84,* 1130–1149.

Eysenck, H. J. The effects of psychotherapy: An evaluation. *Journal of Consulting Psychology,* 1952, *16,* 319–324.

Eysenck, H. J. *The effects of psychotherapy.* New York: International Science Press, 1966.

Eysenck, M. W. Age differences in incidental learning. *Developmental Psychology,* 1974, *10,* 936–941.

Fallot, R. D. The impact on mood of verbal reminiscing in later adulthood. *International Journal of Aging and Human Development,* 1980, *10,* 385–400.

Fanestil, D. D., & Barrows, C. H. Aging in the rotifer. *Journal of Gerontology,* 1965, *20,* 462–469.

Fasteau, M. F. *The male machine.* New York: Dell, 1976.

Fehr, L. J. Piaget and S. Claus: Psychology makes strange bedfellows. *Psychological Reports,* 1976, *39,* 740–742.

Feifel, H. (Ed.). *The meaning of death.* New York: McGraw-Hill, 1959.

Feifel, H., & Branscomb, A. B. Who's afraid of death? *Journal of Abnormal Psychology,* 1973, *81,* 282–288.

Feinberg, I. Changes in sleep cycle patterns with age. *Journal of Psychiatric Research,* 1974, *10,* 283–306.

Feinberg, I., & Carlson, V. R. Sleep variables as a function of age in man. *Archives of General Psychiatry,* 1968, *18,* 239–250.

Ferguson, T. Dealing with potential stress: A day in the life of Joe and Roscoe. *Medical Self-Care,* 1978, No. 5, 11.

Finch, C. E., & Hayflick, L. (Eds.). *Handbook of the biology of aging.* New York: Van Nostrand Reinhold, 1977.

Fink, H. F. The relationship of time perspective to age, institutionalization and activity. *Journal of Gerontology,* 1957, *12,* 414–417.

Firestone, S. *The dialectic of sex: The case for feminist revolution.* New York: Morrow, 1970.

Fitzgerald, J. M. Learning and development: Mutual bases in a dialectical perspective. *Human Development,* 1980, *23,* 376–382.

Flavell, J. H. Cognitive changes in adulthood. In L. R. Goulet & P. B. Baltes (Eds.), *Life-span developmental psychology: Research and theory.* New York: Academic Press, 1970.

Flavell, J. H. Stage-related properties of cognitive development. *Journal of Cognitive Psychology,* 1971, *2,* 421–453.

Flavell, J. H. *Cognitive development.* Englewood Cliffs, N.J.: Prentice-Hall, 1977.

Flavell, J. H., & Wellman, H. M. Metamemory. In R. V. Karl, Jr., & J. W. Hagen (Eds.), *Perspectives on the development of memory and cognition.* Hillsdale, N. J.: Erlbaum, 1977.

Fletcher, J. The "right" to live and the "right" to die. *The Humanist,* 1974, *34,* 15.

Fogarty, M., Rapoport, R., & Rapoport, R. *Sex, career, and family.* Beverly Hills, Calif.: Sage Publications, 1971.

Foley, J. M., & Murphy, D. M. Sex role identity in the aged. Paper presented at 30th annual scientific meeting of the Gerontological Society, San Francisco, November 1977.

Fox, J. H. Effects of retirement and former work life on women's adaptation in old age. *Journal of Gerontology,* 1977, *32,* 196–202.

Fozard, J. L. The time for remembering. In L. W. Poon (Ed.), *Aging in the 1980s: Psychological issues.* Washington, D.C.: American Psychological Association, 1980.

Fozard, J. L., & Popkin, S. J. Optimizing adult development: Ends and means of an applied psychology of aging. *American Psychologist,* 1978, *33,* 975–989.

Fozard, J., & Thomas, J. Psychology of aging: Basic findings and their psychiatric applications. In J. G. Howells (Ed.), *Modern perspectives in the psychiatry of old age.* New York: Brunner-Mazel, 1975.

Fozard, J. L., Wolf, E., Bell, B., McFarland, R. A., & Podolsky, S. Visual perception and communication. In J. E. Birren & K. W. Schaie (Eds.), *Handbook of the psychology of aging.* New York: Van Nostrand Reinhold, 1977.

Fredricksen, N. Toward a taxonomy of situations. *American Psychologist,* 1972, *27,* 114–123.

Freeman, J. Women: A feminist perspective (2nd ed.). Palo Alto, Calif.: Mayfield, 1979.

Freud, A. *Ego and the mechanisms of defense* (Rev. ed.). New York: International Universities Press, 1967.

Freud, S. On psychotherapy. In *Collected papers* (Vol. 1). London: Hogarth Press, 1953. (Originally published, 1904.)

Freud, S. *The origin of psychoanalysis: Letters to Wilhelm Fliess, drafts and notes, 1897–1902* (M. Bonaparte, A. Freud, & E. Kris, Eds.). New York: Basic Books, 1954.

Freud, S. A difficulty in the path of psychoanalysis. In J. Strachey (Ed. and trans.), *Standard edition of the complete psychological works of Sigmund Freud,* Vol. 17. London: Hogarth, 1955. (Originally published, 1917.)

Freud, S. Mourning and melancholia. In P. Rieff (Ed.), *General psychological theory: Papers on metapsychology.* New York: Collier Books, 1963. (Originally published, 1917.)

Freud, S. *New introductory lectures on psychoanalysis* (James Strachey, trans.). New York: Norton, 1965. (Originally published, 1933.)

Friedman, M., & Rosenman, R. *Type A behavior and your heart.* New York: Knopf, 1974.

Friend, R. Gayging: Adjustment and the older gay male. *Alternative Lifestyles,* 1980, *3,* 231–248.

Fries, J. F. Aging, natural death, and the comparison of morbidity. *New England Journal of Medicine,* 1980, *303,* 130–135.

Frieze, I. H. Women's expectations for and causal attributions of success and failure. In M. Mednick, S. Tangri, & L. Hoffman (Eds.), *Women and achievement: Social and motivational analysis.* New York: Hemisphere-Halstead, 1975.

Frumkes, L. B. High risk addiction. *Harper's Bazaar,* March 1980, 88–94.

Fullerton, A. M., & Smith, A. D. Age-related differences in the use of redundancy. *Journal of Gerontology,* 1980, *35,* 729–735.

Fulton, R. *Death and identity.* Bowie, Md.: The Charles Press, 1976.

Furry, C. A., & Baltes, P. B. The effect of age differences in ability-extraneous performance variables on the assessment of intelligence in children, adults, and the elderly. *Journal of Gerontology,* 1973, *28,* 73–80.

Gadpaille, W., with L. Freeman. *The cycles of sex.* New York: Scribner's, 1975.

Gardner, E. *Fundamentals of neurology* (3rd ed.). Philadelphia: Saunders, 1958.

Gardner, E. F., & Monge, R. H. Adult age differences in cognitive abilities and educational background. *Experimental Aging Research,* 1977, *3,* 337–383.

Gatz, M., Smyer, M. A., & Lawton, M. P. The mental health system and the older adult. In L. W. Poon (Ed.), *Aging in the 1980s: Psychological issues.* Washington, D. C.: American Psychological Association, 1980.

Gelles, R. J. Child abuse as psychopathology: A sociological critique and formulation. *American Journal of Orthopsychiatry,* 1973, *43,* 611–621.

Gerber, I., Rusalem, R., Hannon, N., Battin, D., & Arkin, A. Anticipatory grief and aged widows and widowers. *Journal of Gerontology,* 1975, *30,* 225–229.

Gerth, H. H., & Mills, C. W. *From Max Weber: Essays in sociology.* New York: Oxford University Press, 1946.

Giambra, L. M. Adult male daydreaming across the life-span: A replication, further analyses, and tentative norms based upon retrospective reports. *International Journal of Aging and Human Development,* 1977, *8,* 197–228.

Giambra, L. M., & Arenberg, D. Problem solving, concept learning, and aging. In L.

W. Poon (Ed.), *Aging in the 1980s: Psychological issues.* Washington, D. C.: American Psychological Association, 1980.

Gibbs, J. C. The meaning of ecologically oriented inquiry in contemporary psychology. *American Psychologist,* 1979, *34,* 127–139.

Gilford, R., & Black, D. The grandchild–grandparent dyad: Ritual or relationship. Paper presented at 25th annual scientific meeting of the Gerontological Society, San Juan, Puerto Rico, December 1972.

Ginsberg, H., & Oppler, S. *Piaget's theory of intellectual development* (2nd ed.). Englewood Cliffs, N. J.: Prentice-Hall, 1979.

Gladis, M., & Braun, H. Age differences in transfer and retroaction as a function of intertask response similarity. *Journal of Experimental Psychology,* 1958, *55,* 25–30.

Glenn, N. Psychological well being in the post-parental stage: Some evidence from national surveys. *Journal of Marriage and the Family,* 1975, *37,* 105–110.

Glenn, N., & Weaver, C. Attitudes toward premarital, extramarital, and homosexual behavior in the United States in the 1970's. *Journal of Sex Research,* 1979, *15*(2), 108–118.

Glick, I., Weiss, R. S., & Parkes, C. M. *The first year of bereavement.* New York: Wiley, 1974.

Glick, P. Remarriage: Some recent changes and variations. *Journal of Family Issues,* 1980, *1,* 455–478.

Goldberg, H. *The hazards of being male: Surviving the myth of masculine privilege.* New York: Signet Books/New American Library, 1976.

Goldfarb, A. J. The rationale for psychotherapy with older persons. *American Journal of Medical Science,* 1956, *237,* 181–185.

Goldfarb, A. J. Patient–doctor relationship in treatment of aged persons. *Geriatrics,* 1964, *19,* 18–23.

Goldfarb, A. J. The psychodynamics of dependency and the search for aid. In R. A. Kalish (Ed.), *The dependencies of old people.* Ann Arbor: University of Michigan Institute of Gerontology, 1969.

Goldstein, K. M., & Blackman, S. *Cognitive style: Five approaches and relevant research.* New York: Wiley-Interscience, 1978.

Goodman, E. *Turning points.* New York: Doubleday, 1979.

Gordon, C., Gaitz, C., & Scott, J. Leisure and lives: Personal expressivity across the life-span. In R. Binstock & E. Shanas (Eds.), *Handbook of aging and the social sciences.* New York: Van Nostrand Reinhold, 1976, 310–341.

Gornick, V., & Moran, B. K. (Eds.). *Woman in sexist society: Studies in power and powerlessness.* New York: Mentor/New American Library, 1971.

Gottman, J. M., & Notarius, C. Sequential analyses of observational data using Markov chains. In T. R. Kratochwill (Ed.), *Single subject research: Strategies for evaluating change.* New York: Academic Press, 1978.

Gould, R. L. The phases of adult life: A study in developmental psychology. *American Journal of Psychiatry,* 1972, *129,* 521–531.

Gould, R. L. Adult life stages: Growth toward self tolerance. *Psychology Today,* 1975, *8,* 74–78.

Gould, R. L. *Transformations: Growth and change in adult life.* New York: Simon & Schuster, 1978.

Gould, S. J. Our allotted lifetimes. *Natural History,* 1978, *87,* 34–41.

Goulet, L. R., & Baltes, P. B. (Eds.). *Life-span developmental psychology: Research and theory.* New York: Academic Press, 1970.

Gove, W. R. Adult sex roles and mental illness. In F. Denmark (Ed.), *Women* (Vol. I). New York: Psychological Dimensions, Inc., 1976.

Gove, W. R., & Tudor, J. F. Adult sex roles and mental illness. *American Journal of Sociology,* 1973, *78,* 812–835.

Granick, S., & Friedman, A. S. The effect of education on the decline of test performance with age. *Journal of Gerontology,* 1967, *22,* 191–195.

Granick, S., & Friedman, A. S. Educational experience and the maintenance of intellectual functioning by the aged. In L. F. Jarvik, C. Eisdorfer, & J. E. Blum (Eds.), *Intellectual functioning in adults.* New York: Springer, 1973.

Granick, S., Kleban, M. H., & Weiss, A. D. Relationships between hearing loss and cognition in normally hearing aged persons. *Journal of Gerontology,* 1976, *31,* 434–440.

Granick, S., & Patterson, R. D. *Human aging, II: An eleven year biomedical and behavioral study.* Washington, D. C.: U. S. Government Printing Office, 1971.

Green, D. M., & Swets, J. A. *Signal detection theory and psychophysics.* New York: Wiley, 1966.

Green, R. F. Age-intelligence relationship between ages sixteen and sixty-four. *Developmental Psychology,* 1969, *1,* 618–627.

Greenblatt, D. J., & Shader, R. I. Pharmacokinetics in old age: Principles and problems of assessment. In L. Jarvik, D. Greenblatt, & D. Harman (Eds.), *Pharmacology of the aged.* New York: Raven Press, 1981.

Grobstein, R. The effect of neonatal death on the family. In O. J. Sahler (Ed.), *The child and death.* St. Louis, Mo.: C. V. Mosby, 1978.

Grzegorczyk, P. B., Jones, S. W., & Mistretta, C. M. Age-related differences in salt taste acuity. *Journal of Gerontology,* 1979, *34,* 834–840.

Gubrium, J. F. Being single in old age. *International Journal of Aging and Human Development,* 1975, *6,* 29–41.

Guilford, J. P. Intelligence: 1965 model. *American Psychologist,* 1966, *21,* 20–26.

Guilford, J. P. *The nature of human intelligence.* New York: McGraw-Hill, 1967.

Gurian, B., & Cantor, M. Mental health and community support systems for the elderly. In G. Usdin & C. Fofling (Eds.), *Aging: The process and the people.* New York: Bruner/Mazel, 1978.

Gutmann, D. L. An exploration of ego configurations in middle and later life. In B. L. Neugarten and Associates, *Personality in middle and later life.* New York: Atherton Press, 1964.

Gutmann, D. L. Mayan aging: A comparative TAT study. *Psychiatry,* 1966, *23,* 246–259.

Gutmann, D. L. Aging among the highland Maya: A comparative study. *Journal of Personality and Social Psychology,* 1967, *7,* 28–35.

Gutmann, D. L. Navajo dependency and illness. In E. Palmore (Ed.), *Predictions of life-span.* Lexington, Mass.: D. C. Heath, 1971.(a)

Gutmann, D. L. The hunger of old men. *Trans-Action,* 1971, *9,* 55–66.(b)

Gutmann, D. L. Ego psychological and developmental approaches to the retirement crises in men. In F. M. Carp (Ed.), *Retirement*. New York: Behavioral Publications, 1972.

Gutmann, D. L. Men, women, and the parental imperative. *Commentary,* 1973, *56,* 59–64.

Gutmann, D. L. Alternatives to disengagement: Aging among the highland Druze. In R. LeVine (Ed.), *Culture and personality: Contemporary readings.* Chicago: Aldine, 1974.

Gutmann, D. L. Parenthood: A key to the comparative study of the life cycle? In N. Datan & L. Ginsberg (Eds.), *Life-span developmental psychology: Normative life crises.* New York: Academic Press, 1975.

Gutmann, D. L. Individual adaptation in the middle years: Developmental issues in the masculine mid-life crisis. *Journal of Geriatric Psychiatry,* 1976, *9,* 41–59.

Gutmann, D. L. The cross-cultural perspective: Notes toward a comparative psychology of aging. In J. E. Birren & K. W. Schaie (Eds.), *Handbook of the psychology of aging.* New York: Van Nostrand Reinhold, 1977.

Gutmann, D. L. Psychoanalysis and aging: A developmental view. In S. I. Greenspan & G. H. Pollock (Eds.), *The course of life: Psychoanalytic contributions toward understanding personality development. Vol. 3: Adulthood and the aging process.* Washington, D.C.: U. S. Government Printing Office, 1980.

Gutmann, D. L., Grunes, J., & Griffin, B. The clinical psychology of later life: Developmental paradigm. In N. Datan & N. Lohmann (Eds.), *Life-span developmental psychology: Transitions of aging.* New York: Academic Press, 1980.

Guttman, D. L., and Kassem, K. Aging and traditionalism: A study of the highland Druze. *Gerontology,* 1975, *1,* 3–13.

Haan, N., & Day, D. A longitudinal study of change and sameness in personality development: Adolescence to later adulthood. *International Journal of Aging and Human Development,* 1974, *5,* 11–39.

Hagestad, G. Role changes in adulthood: The transition to the empty nest. Unpublished manuscript, Committee on Human Development, University of Chicago, 1977.

Hagestad, G. Patterns of communication and influence between grandparents and grandchildren in a changing society. Paper presented at the World Congress of Sociology, Sweden, 1978.

Hall, P. Cycladelate in the treatment of cerebral arteriosclerosis. *Journal of the American Geriatric Society,* 1976, *24,* 41–44.

Hallstrøm, T. *Mental disorder and sexuality in the climacteric: A study in psychiatric epidemiology.* Göteborg, Sweden: Akademiforlaget, 1973.

Hamilton, J. Grandparents as grievers. In O. J. Sahler (Ed.), *The child and death.* St. Louis, Mo: C.V. Mosby, 1978.

Hansen, J. C., & Putnam, B. A. Feminine role concepts of young women. *Sex Roles,* 1978, *4,* 127–130.

Hardt, D. V. *Death: The final frontier.* Englewood Cliffs, N.J.: Prentice-Hall, 1979.

Harkins, E. B. Effects of empty nest transition on self-report of psychological and physical well-being. *Journal of Marriage and the Family,* 1978, *40,* 549–556.

Harkins, S. W., & Chapman, C. R. Detection and decision factors in pain perception in young and elderly men. *Pain,* 1976, *2,* 253–264.

Harkins, S. W., & Chapman, C. R. The perception of induced dental pain in young and elderly women. *Journal of Gerontology,* 1977, *32,* 428–435.

Harkins, S. W., Chapman, C. R., & Eisdorfer, C. Memory loss and response bias in senescence. *Journal of Gerontology,* 1979, *34,* 66– 72.

Harrell, T. W., & Harrell, M. S. Army general classification test scores for civilian occupations. *Educational and Psychological Measurement,* 1945, *5,* 231–239.

Harris, Louis, and Associates. *The myth and reality of aging in America.* Washington, D. C.: National Council on the Aging, 1975.

Harris, M. *Cell culture and somatic variation.* New York: Holt, Rinehart and Winston, 1964.

Hartford, M. The use of group methods for work with the aged. In J. Birren & R. Sloane (Eds.), *Handbook of mental health and aging.* Englewood Cliffs, N.J.: Prentice-Hall, 1980.

Hartman, W., & Fithian, M. *Treatment of sexual dysfunction: A bio-psycho-social approach.* Long Beach, Calif.: Center for Marital and Sexual Studies, 1972.

Harvey, C., & Bahr, H. Widowhood, morale, and affiliation. *Journal of Marriage and the Family,* 1974, *36,* 97–106.

Hauser, P. M. Aging and world-wide population change. In R. H. Binstock & E. Shanas (Eds.), *Handbook of aging and the social sciences.* New York: Van Nostrand Reinhold, 1977.

Havighurst, R. J. *Developmental tasks and education* (3rd ed.). New York: David McKay, 1972.

Hayflick, L. Aging under glass. *Experimental Gerontology,* 1970, *5,* 291–303.

Hayflick, L. The longevity of cultured human cells. *Journal of the American Geriatrics Society,* 1974, *22,* 1–6.

Hayflick, L. The cellular basis for biological aging. In C. E. Finch & L. Hayflick (Eds.), *Handbook of the biology of aging.* New York: Van Nostrand Reinhold, 1977.

Hayflick, L. The cell biology of human aging. *Scientific American,* 1980, *242,* 58–66.

Hayslip, B., & Sterns, H. L. Age differences in relationships between crystallized and fluid intelligences and problem solving. *Journal of Gerontology,* 1979, *14,* 404–414.

Heath, D. What meaning and effects does fatherhood have for the maturing of professional men? *Merrill-Palmer Quarterly,* 1972, *24,* 265–278.

Heglin, H. J. Problem solving set in different age groups. *Journal of Gerontology,* 1956, *11,* 310–317.

Helmreich, R. Self-esteem and social behavior. In B. Wolman (Ed.), *International encyclopedia of neurology, psychiatry, psychoanalysis and psychology.* New York: Van Nostrand Reinhold, 1977.

Hemminki, E., & Heikkila, J. Elderly people's compliance with prescriptions and quality of medication. *Scandinavian Journal of Social Medicine,* 1975, *3,* 87–92.

Henker, Fred, III. Male climacteric. In J. G. Howells (Ed.), *Modern perspectives in the psychiatry of middle age.* New York: Brunner-Mazel, 1981.

Hennig, M., & Jardim, A. *The managerial woman.* New York: Doubleday/Anchor, 1977.

Hensel, H. Electrophysiology of cutaneous thermal receptors. In D. R. Kenshalo (Ed.), *The skin senses.* Springfield, Ill.: Charles C. Thomas, 1968.

Herman, G. E., Warren, L. R., & Wagener, J. W. Auditory lateralization: Age differences in sensitivity to dichotic time and amplitude cues. *Journal of Gerontology,* 1977, *32,* 187–191.

Herr, J., & Weakland, J. *Counseling elders and their families: Practical techniques for applied gerontology.* New York: Springer, 1979.

Herrmann, D. J. How people answer memory questionnaires: A theory of memory introspection. Paper presented at a conference for psychologists of upstate New York, Colgate University, Hamilton, N.Y., October 1979.

Hersen, M., & Barlow, D. H. *Single case experimental designs: Strategies for studying behavior change in the individual.* New York: Pergamon, 1976.

Hertzog, C. Applications of signal detection theory to the study of psychological aging: A theoretical view. In L. W. Poon (Ed.), *Aging in the 1980s: Psychological issues.* Washington, D. C.: American Psychological Association, 1980.

Hess, B. Friendship. In M. W. Riley, M. Johnson, & A. Foner (Eds.), *Aging and society, Vol. 3: A sociology of age stratification.* New York: Russell Sage Foundation, 1972.

Hess, B., & Waring, J. Changing patterns of aging and family bonds in later life. *Family Coordinator,* 1978, *27,* 303–313. (a)

Hess, B., & Waring, J. Parent and child in later life: Rethinking the relationship. In R. Lerner & G. Spanier (Eds.), *Child influences on marital and family interaction: A life-span perspective.* New York: Academic Press, 1978. (b)

Hiatt, H. Dynamic psychotherapy of the aged. In J. H. Masserman (Ed.), *Handbook of psychiatric therapies.* New York: Science House, 1975.

Higgins, D. Themes of middle age. Unpublished transcripts of group interviews with middle-class women. On file with M. Huyck, Illinois Institute of Technology, Chicago, 1976.

Higgins, D. Self-concept and its relation to everyday stress in middle-aged women: A longitudinal study. Unpublished doctoral dissertation, Illinois Institute of Technology, 1977.

Hilgard, E. *Divided consciousness: Multiple controls in human thought and action.* New York: Wiley, 1977.

Hilgard, E. R., & Bower, G. H. *Theories of learning.* New York: Appleton-Century-Crofts, 1975.

Hill, R., Foote, N., Aldous, J., Carlson, R., & MacDonald, R. *Family development in three generations.* Cambridge, Mass.: Schenkman, 1970.

Hinton, J. M. *Dying.* Baltimore, Md.: Penguin, 1967.

Hinton, J. M. *Death* (2nd ed.). Baltimore, Md.: Penguin, 1972.

Hoffman, L. W., & Hoffman, M. The value of children to parents. In J. T. Fawcett (Ed.), *Psychological perspectives on population.* New York: Basic Books, 1973.

Holland, T. R., & Holt, N. Prisoner intellectual and personality correlates of offense severity and recidivism probability. *Journal of Clinical Psychology,* 1975, *31,* 667–672.

Holstrom, L. L. *The two-career family.* Cambridge, Mass.: Schenkman, 1972.

Holte, A. The interaction of social-cognitive and physiological determinants of perimenopausal "symptoms." Paper presented at workshop on sociological, psychological and anthropological aspects of the menopause, 2nd International Congress on the Menopause, Jerusalem, Israel, July 1978.

Hooper, F. H., Fitzgerald, J. M., & Papalia, D. E. Piagetian theory and the aging process: Extensions and speculations. *Aging and Human Development,* 1971, *2,* 3–20.

Horn, J. L. Organization of data on life-span development of human abilities. In L. R. Goulet & P. B. Baltes (Eds.), *Life-span developmental psychology: Research and theory.* New York: Academic Press, 1970.

Horn, J. L., & Cattell, R. B. Refinement and test of the theory of fluid and crystallized intelligence. *Journal of Educational Psychology,* 1966, *57,* 253–270.

Horn, J. L., & Donaldson, G. On the myth of intellectual decline in adulthood. *American Psychologist,* 1976, *31,* 701–719.

Horn, J. L., & Donaldson, G. Faith is not enough: A response to the Baltes-Schaie claim that intelligence does not wane. *American Psychologist,* 1977, *32,* 369–373.

Hornblum, J. N., & Overton, W. F. Area and volume conservation among the elderly: Assessment and training. *Developmental Psychology,* 1976, *12,* 68–74.

Horner, M. S. Toward an understanding of achievement related conflicts in women. *Journal of Social Issues,* 1972, *28,,* 157–175.

Horowitz, A. Families who care: A study of natural supports of the elderly. Paper presented at the 31st annual scientific meeting of the Gerontological Society, Dallas, November 1978.

Howe, L. K. *Pink collar workers: Inside the world of women's work.* New York: Putnam, 1977. New York: Avon, 1978.

Howell, J. T. *Hard living on Clay Street: Portraits of blue collar families.* Garden City, N. Y.: Doubleday/Anchor, 1973.

Howells, J. G. (Ed.). *Modern perspectives in the psychiatry of middle age.* New York: Brunner-Mazel, 1981.

Hoyenga, K. B., & Hoyenga, K. T. *The question of sex differences: Psychological, cultural and biological issues.* Boston: Little, Brown, 1979.

Hoyer, W. J. Aging as intraindividual change. *Developmental Psychology,* 1974, *10,* 821–826.

Hoyer, W. J. Design considerations in the assessment of psychotherapy with the elderly. Paper presented at the 31st annual scientific meeting of the Gerontological Society, Dallas, November 1978.

Hoyer, W. J. (Ed.). Conceptions of learning and the study of life-span development: A symposium. *Human Development,* 1980, *23,* 361–399.

Hoyer, W. J. Information processing, knowledge acquisition, and learning: Developmental perspectives. *Human Development,* 1980, *23,* 389–399.

Hoyer, W. J., Labouvie, G. V., & Baltes, P. B. Modification of response speed and intellectual performance in the elderly. *Human Development,* 1973, *16,* 233–242.

Hoyer, W. J., Mishara, B. L., & Riedel, R. G. Problem behaviors as operants: Applications with elderly individuals. *Gerontologist,* 1975, *15,* 452–456.

Hoyer, W. J., & Plude, D. J. Attentional and perceptual processes in the study of cognitive aging. In L. W. Poon (Ed.), *Aging in the 1980s: Psychological issues.* Washington, D. C.: American Psychological Association, 1980. (a)

Hoyer, W. J., & Plude, D. J. Aging and the allocation of attentional resources. Paper presented at a symposium on aging and visual function. National Academy of Sciences, Washington, D. C., May 1980. (b)

Hoyer, W. J., Rebok, G. W., & Sved, S. M. Effects of varying irrelevant information on adult age differences in problem solving. *Journal of Gerontology,* 1979, *34,* 553–560.

Hoyt, L. Determinants of aged female sexuality. Paper presented at 33rd annual scientific meeting of the Gerontological Society, San Diego, Calif., November 1980.

Hughes, C. P. The differential diagnosis of dementia in the senium. In K. Nandy (Ed.), *Senile dementia: A biomedical approach.* New York: Elsevier/North-Holland Biomedical Press, 1978.

Hultsch, D. F. Adult age differences in the organization of free recall. *Developmental Psychology,* 1969, *1,* 673–678.

Hultsch, D. F. Adult age differences in free classification and free recall. *Developmental Psychology,* 1971, *4,* 338–342.

Hultsch, D. F. Learning to learn in adulthood. *Journal of Gerontology,* 1974, *29,* 302–308.

Hultsch, D. F. Adult age differences in retrieval: Trace-dependent and cue-dependent forgetting. *Developmental Psychology,* 1975, *11,* 197–201.

Hultsch, D. F., & Hickey, T. External validity in the study of human development: Theoretical and methodological issues. *Human Development,* 1978, *21,* 76–91.

Hunt, M. *The world of the formerly married.* New York: McGraw-Hill, 1966.

Hunt, M. *Sexual behavior in the 1970s.* Chicago: Playboy Press, 1974.

Huston-Stein, A., & Baltes, P. B. Theory and methods in life-span developmental psychology: Implications for child development. In K. W. Reese (Ed.), *Advances in child development and behavior.* New York: Academic Press, 1976.

Huyck, M. H. Age norms and career lines among military officers. Unpublished doctoral dissertation, University of Chicago, 1969.

Huyck, M. H. *Growing older.* Englewood Cliffs, N.J.: Prentice-Hall, 1974.

Huyck, M. H. (Ed.). Women and achievement: A life cycle perspective. Symposium presented at the 28th annual scientific meeting of the Gerontological Society. Louisville, Ky., October 1975.

Huyck, M. H. Sex and the older woman. In L. Troll, J. Israel, & K. Israel (Eds.), *Looking ahead: A woman's guide to the problems and joys of growing older.* Englewood Cliffs, N. J.: Prentice-Hall, 1977.

Information Please Almanac. New York: Information Please Publishing, 1979.

Inglis, J. Effects of age on responses to dichotic stimulation. *Nature,* 1962, *194,* 1101.

Inglis, J. Memory disorder. In C. G. Costello (Ed.), *Symptoms of psychopathology.* New York: Wiley, 1970.

Inglis, J., & Caird, W. K. Age differences in successive responses to simultaneous stimulation. *Canadian Journal of Psychology,* 1963, *17,* 98–105.

Irish, D. P. Sibling interaction: A neglected aspect in family life research. *Social Forces,* 1964, *42,* 279–288.

Israel, J. Confessions of a 45-year-old feminist. In L. Troll, J. Israel, & K. Israel (Eds.), *Looking ahead: A woman's guide to the problems and joys of growing older.* Englewood Cliffs, N. J.: Prentice-Hall, 1977.

Jackson, J. But where are the men? *Black Scholar,* 1971, *3,* 30–41.

Jacobs, S. S., & Shin, S. H. Interrelationships among intelligence, product dimension of Guilford's model and multilevel measure of cognitive functioning. *Psychological Reports*, 1975, *37*, 903–910.

Jaffe, J., & Feldstein, S. *Rhythms of dialogue.* New York: Academic Press, 1970.

Jaggar, A., & Struhl, P. (Eds.). *Feminist frameworks: Alternative theoretical accounts of the relations between women and men.* New York: McGraw-Hill, 1978.

Jakubczak, L. F. Effects of testosterone propionate on age differences in mating behavior. *Journal of Gerontology*, 1964, *19*, 458–461.

James, W. *The principles of psychology.* New York: Holt, Rinehart and Winston, 1890.

Jaques, E. Death and the mid-life crisis. *International Journal of Psychoanalysis*, 1955, *46*, 502–514.

Jarvik, L. F. Thoughts on the psychobiology of aging. *American Psychologist*, 1975, *30*, 576–583.

Jarvik, L. F., & Falek, A. Intellectual stability and survival in the aged. *Journal of Gerontology*, 1963, *18*, 173–176.

Jaslow, P. Employment, retirement, and morale among older women. *Journal of Gerontology*, 1976, *31*, 212–218.

Jaszmann, L., van Lith, N. D., & Zaat, J. C. A. The perimenopausal symptoms: The statistical analysis of a survey, parts A and B. *Medical Gynecology and Society*, 1969, *4*, 268–276.

Jaynes, J. *The origin of consciousness in the breakdown of the bicameral mind.* Boston: Houghton Mifflin, 1977.

Jencks, C. *Inequality.* New York: Basic Books, 1972.

Jencks, C., Bartlett, S., Corcorin, M., Crouse, J., Eaglesfield, D., Jackson, G., McClelland, K., Mueser, P., Olneck, M., Schwartz, J., Ward, S., & Williams, J. *Who gets ahead? The determinants of economic success in America.* New York: Basic Books, 1979.

Jernigan, T. L., Zatz, L. M., Feinberg, I., & Fein, G. The measurement of cerebral atrophy in the aged by computed tomography. In L. W. Poon (Ed.), *Aging in the 1980s: Psychological issues.* Washington, D. C.: American Psychological Association, 1980.

Johnson, R. Psychodynamic and developmental considerations of the childless older woman. Unpublished doctoral dissertation, Northwestern University, 1981.

Judson, H. F. *The search for solutions: An introduction to the art of discovery.* New York: Holt, Rinehart and Winston, 1980.

Jung, C. G. The stages of life (1933). In J. Campbell (Ed.), *The Portable Jung.* New York: Viking, 1971.

Jury, M., & Jury, D. *Gramps.* New York: Grossman, 1976.

Kagan, J., & Moss, H. A. *Birth to maturity: A study in psychological development.* New York: Wiley, 1962.

Kahana, B., & Kahana, E. Grandparenthood from the perspective of the developing grandchild. *Developmental Psychology*, 1970, *13*, 98–105.

Kahana, E. & Coe, R. Perceptions of grandparenthood by community and institutionalized aged. *Proceedings of 77th Annual Convention, American Psychological Association*, 1969, *4*, 735–736.

Kahana, R. J. Strategies of dynamic psychotherapy with the wide range of older patients. *Journal of Geriatric Psychiatry,* 1979, *12,* 71–101.

Kalish, R. A. Death and dying in a social context. In R. H. Binstock & E. Shanas (Eds.), *Handbook of aging and the social sciences.* New York: Van Nostrand Reinhold, 1976.

Kallmann, F. J., Feingold, L., & Bondy, E. Comparative adaptational, social and psychometric data on life histories of senescent twin pairs. *American Journal of Human Genetics,* 1951, *3,* 65–73.

Kallmann, F. J., & Jarvik, L. F. Individual differences in constitution and genetic background. In J. E. Birren (Ed.), *Handbook of aging and the individual.* Chicago: University of Chicago Press, 1959.

Kangas, J., and Bradway, K. Intelligence at middle age: A thirty-eight year follow-up. *Developmental Psychology,* 1971, *5,* 333–337.

Kanter, R. M. *Men and women of the corporation.* New York: Basic Books, 1977.

Kaplan, H. B., & Pokorny, A. P. Aging and self attitude: A conditional relationship. *International Journal of Aging and Human Development,* 1970, *1,* 241–250.

Kaplan, H. S. *The new sex therapy.* New York: Brunner-Mazel, 1974.

Kaplan, H. S. *Disorders of sexual desire and other new concepts and techniques in sex therapy.* New York: Brunner-Mazel, 1979.

Kaplan, M. Toward a theory of leisure for social gerontology. In R. Kleemeier (Ed.), *Aging and leisure.* New York: Oxford University Press, 1961.

Kapnick, P. Organic treatment of the elderly. In M. Storandt, I. Siegler, & M. Elias (Eds.), *The clinical psychology of aging.* New York: Plenum Press, 1978.

Kart, C. S., Metress, E. S., & Metress, J. F. *Aging and health: Biologic and social perspectives.* Menlo Park, Calif.: Addison-Wesley, 1978.

Kastenbaum, R. J. *Death, society, and human experience.* St. Louis, Mo.: C.V. Mosby, 1977.

Kastenbaum, R. J., & Aisenberg, R. *The psychology of death.* New York: Springer, 1972.

Kastenbaum, R. J., & Candy, S. The four per cent fallacy: A methodological and empirical critique of extended care facility population statistics. *International Journal of Aging and Human Development,* 1973, *4,* 15–21.

Kastenbaum, R. J., & Costa, P. T. Psychological perspectives on death. *Annual Review of Psychology,* 1977, *8,* 225–249.

Katchadourian, H. A., & Lundes, D. T. *Fundamentals of human sexuality.* New York: Holt, Rinehart and Winston, 1975.

Katz, J., Herbert, W., Gallagher, T. F., & Hellman, L. Stress, distress, and ego defenses: Psychoendocrine response to impending breast tumor biopsy. In A. Monet & R. Lazarus (Eds.), *Stress and coping: An anthology.* New York: New York University Press, 1977.

Kay, D. W. K. The epidemiology of brain deficit in the aged: Problems in patient identification. In C. Eisdorfer & R. O. Friedel (Eds.), *The cognitively and emotionally impaired elderly.* Chicago: Medical Yearbook Publishers, 1977.

Kay, D. W. K., & Bergmann, K. Epidemiology of mental disorders among the aged in the community. In J. Birren & R. Sloane (Eds.), *Handbook of mental health and aging.* Englewood Cliffs, N.J.: Prentice-Hall, 1980.

Kedar, H. S., & Shanan, J. The phenomenological structure of the life-span from adolescence to senescence as spontaneously reported by different age-sex groups. Paper presented at 10th International Congress of Gerontology, Jerusalem, Israel, July 1975.

Kellam, S., & Ensminger, M. Theory and method in child psychiatric epidemiology. In F. Earls (Ed.), *Studying children epidemiologically* (Vol. 1). New York: Neale Watson Academic Publishers, 1980.

Kellam, S., Ensminger, M., & Turner, J. Family structure and the mental health of children. *Archives of General Psychiatry,* 1977, *34,* 1012–1022.

Kelly, J. The aging male homosexual: Myth and reality. *Gerontologist,* 1977, *17,* 328–332.

Kerchkoff, A. C. Norm-value clusters and the strain toward consistency among older married couples. In I. Simpson & J. McKinney (Eds.), *Social aspects of aging.* Durham, N.C.: Duke University Press, 1966.

Kernberg, O. *Borderline conditions and psychological narcissism.* New York: Aronson, 1976.

Kessler, M., & Albee, G. W. Primary prevention. *Annual Review of Psychology,* 1975, *26,* 557–592.

Kieffer, G. H. *Bioethics: A textbook of issues.* Reading, Mass.: Addison-Wesley, 1979.

Kiesler, D. J. Some myths of psychotherapy research and the search for a paradigm. *Psychological Bulletin,* 1966, *65,* 110–136.

Kiesler, D. J. Experimental designs in psychotherapy research. In A. E. Bergin & S. L. Garfield (Eds.), *Handbook of psychotherapy and behavior change.* New York: Wiley, 1971.

Kimmel, D. C. Adult development and aging: A gay perspective. *Journal of Social Issues,* 1978, *34,* 113–130.

Kimmel, D. C. Life history interviews of aging gay men. *International Journal of Aging and Human Development,* 1979–80, *10,* 239–248.

Kinsey, A. C., Pomeroy, W. B., & Martin, C. *Sexual behavior in the human male.* Philadelphia: Saunders, 1948.

Kinsey, A. C., Pomeroy, W. B., Martin, C. E., & Gebhard, P. H. *Sexual behavior in the human female.* Philadelphia: Saunders, 1953.

Kleemeier, R. W. Intellectual change in the senium, or death and the IQ. Presidential Address, American Psychological Association, New York, August 1961.

Kleemeier, R. W. Intellectual change in the senium. *Proceedings of the Social Statistics Section of the American Statistical Association,* 1962, *1,* 290–295.

Kleiman, G. R. Age and clinical depression: Today's youth in the twenty-first century. *Journal of Gerontology,* 1976, *31,* 318–323.

Kline, D. W., & Baffa, G. Differences in the sequential integration of form as a function of age and interstimulus interval. *Experimental Aging Research,* 1976, *2,* 333–343.

Kline, D. W., & Orme-Rogers, C. Examination of stimulus persistence as the basis for superior visual identification performance among older adults. *Journal of Gerontology,* 1978, *33,* 76–81.

Kline, D. W., & Schieber, F. What are the age differences in visual sensory memory? *Journal of Gerontology,* 1981, *36,* 86–89.

Kline, D. W., & Szafran, J. Age differences in backward monoptic masking. *Journal of Gerontology,* 1975, *30,* 307–311.

Kluckholn, C., & Murray, H. A. (Eds.). *Personality in nature, society, and culture.* New York: Knopf, 1949.

Knapp, M. Predicting the dimensions of life satisfaction. *Journal of Gerontology,* 1976, *31,* 595–604.

Knox, A. B. *Adult development and learning: A handbook on individual growth and competence in the adult years for education and the helping professions.* San Francisco: Jossey-Bass, 1977.

Kobasa, S. Stressful life events, personality, and health: An inquiry into hardiness. *Journal of Personality and Social Psychology,* 1979, *37,* 1–11.

Koestenbaum, P. *Is there an answer to death?* Englewood Cliffs, N.J.: Prentice-Hall, 1976.

Koff, T. H. *Hospice: A caring community.* Cambridge, Mass.: Winthrop, 1980.

Kogan, N., & Wallach, M. A. Age changes in values and attitudes. *Journal of Gerontology,* 1961, *16,* 272–280.

Kohlberg, L. A cognitive-developmental analysis of children's sex-role concepts and attitudes. In E. E. Maccoby (Ed.), *The development of sex differences.* Stanford, Calif.: Stanford University Press, 1966.

Kohlberg, L. Stage and sequence: The cognitive-developmental approach to socialization. In D. A. Goslin (Ed.), *Handbook of socialization theory and research.* Chicago: Rand McNally, 1969.

Kohlberg, L. Continuities in childhood and adult moral development revisited. In P. B. Baltes & K. W. Schaie (Eds.), *Life-span developmental psychology.* New York: Academic Press, 1973.

Kohlberg, L. Continuities in childhood and adult moral development revisited. In L. Kohlberg & E. Turiel (Eds.), *Moralization, the cognitive development approach.* New York: Holt, Rinehart and Winston, 1974.

Kohn, R. R. Human disease and aging. *Journal of Chronic Diseases,* 1963, *5,* 16.

Komarovsky, M. *Dilemmas of masculinity: A study of college youth.* New York: Norton, 1976.

Konigsmark, B. W., & Murphy, E. A. Volume of the ventral cochlear nucleus in man: Its relationship to neuronal population and age. *Journal of Neuropathology and Experimental Neurology,* 1972, *31,* 304–316.

Korchin, S. J., & Basowitz, H. The judgment of ambiguous stimuli as an index of cognitive functioning in aging. *Journal of Personality,* 1956, *25,* 81–95.

Kosa, J., & Schommer, C. O. Sharing the home with relatives. *Marriage and Family Living,* 1960, *22,* 129–131.

Koval, P. O. *The woman alone.* New York: Quadrangle, 1973.

Kramer, M., Taube, C. A., & Redick, R. W. Patterns of use of psychiatric facilities by the aged: Past, present, and future. In C. Eisdorfer & M. P. Lawton (Eds.), *Psychology of adult development and aging.* Washington, D.C.: American Psychological Association, 1973.

Kratochwill, T. R. (Ed.). *Single subject research: Strategies for evaluating change.* New York: Academic Press, 1978.

Kreps, J. The economy and the aged. In R. H. Binstock & E. Shanas (Eds.), *Handbook of aging and the social sciences.* New York: Van Nostrand Reinhold, 1976.

Kübler-Ross, E. *On death and dying.* New York: Macmillan, 1969.

Kübler-Ross, E. *Questions and answers on death and dying.* New York: Macmillan, 1974.

Kübler-Ross, E. (Ed.). *Death: The final stage of growth.* Englewood Cliffs, N.J.: Prentice-Hall, 1975.

Kuhlen, R. G. Social change: A neglected factor in psychological studies of the lifespan. *School and Society,* 1940, *52,* 14–16.

Kuhn, T. S. *The structure of scientific revolutions.* Chicago: University of Chicago Press, 1962.

Kuiper, P. *The neuroses: A psychoanalytic survey.* New York: International Universities Press, 1972.

Kulka, R. A., & Tamir, L. Patterns of help-seeking and formal support. Paper presented at the 31st annual scientific meeting of the Gerontological Society, Dallas, November 1978.

Kunkel, S. Sex differences in adjustment to widowhood. Paper presented at the 32nd annual scientific meeting of the Gerontological Society, Washington, D.C., November 1979.

Kupperman, H. S., Wetchler, B. B., & Blatt, M. H. Contemporary therapy of the menopausal syndrome. *Journal of the American Medical Association,* 1959, *171,* 1627–1637.

Kushner, R. Breast cancer. *Proceedings of the Conference on Health Issues of Older Women: A Projection to the Year 2000.* Stony Brook, N.Y.: Health Sciences Center, State University of New York, 1981.

Kutner, B. *Five hundred over sixty: A community survey on aging.* New York: Sage Foundation, 1956.

Kuypers, J., & Trute, B. The older family as the locus of crisis intervention. *Family Coordinator,* 1978, *27,* 405–411.

Kvale, S. Memory and dialectics: Some reflections on Ebbinghaus and Mao Tse-tung. *Human Development,* 1975, *18,* 205–222.

LaBarba, R. C., Klein, M. L., White, J. L., & Lazar, J. Effects of early cold stress and handling on the growth of Ehrlich carcinoma in BALB/C mice. *Developmental Psychology,* 1970, *2,* 312–313.

LaBerge, D. Attention and the measurement of perceptual learning. *Memory and Cognition,* 1973, *1,* 268–276.

Labouvie-Vief, G. Toward optimizing cognitive competence. *Educational Gerontology,* 1976, *1,* 75–92.

Labouvie-Vief, G. Adult cognitive development: In search of alternative interpretations. *Merrill-Palmer Quarterly,* 1977, *23,* 227–263.

Labouvie-Vief, G. Beyond formal operations: Uses and limits of pure logic in life-span development. *Human Development,* 1980, *23,* 141–161.

Labouvie-Vief, G., & Chandler, M. J. Cognitive development and life-span developmental theory: Idealistic versus contextual perspectives. In P. B. Baltes (Ed.), *Lifespan development and behavior* (Vol. 1). New York: Academic Press, 1978.

Labouvie-Vief, G., & Gonda, J. N. Cognitive strategy training and intellectual performance in the elderly. *Journal of Gerontology,* 1976, *31,* 327–332.

Labouvie-Vief, G., Hoyer, W. J., Baltes, P. B., & Baltes, M. Operant analyses of intellectual behavior in old age. *Human Development,* 1974, *17,* 259–272.

Lachman, J. L., Lachman, R., & Thronesbery, C. Metamemory through the adult life-span. *Developmental Psychology,* 1979, *15,* 543–551.

Lake, A. *Our own years: What women over 35 should know about themselves.* New York: Women's Day/Random House, 1979.

Langone, J. *Death is a noun.* Boston: Little, Brown, 1972.

Lansing, A. K. General biology of senescence. In J. E. Birren (Ed.), *Handbook of aging and the individual.* Chicago: University of Chicago Press, 1959.

Larson, R. Thirty years of research on the subjective well-being of older Americans. *Journal of Gerontology,* 1978, *33,* 109–125.

Larsson, T., Sjögren, T., & Jacobson, G. Senile dementia: A clinical, socio-medical, and genetic study. *Acta Psychiatrica Scandinavica,* 1963 (Supplements, *167*), 38–49.

Laurence, M. W. A developmental look at the usefulness of list categorization as an aid to free recall. *Canadian Journal of Psychology,* 1967, *21,* 153–165.(a)

Laws, E. H. Views on euthanasia. *Journal of Medical Education,* 1971, *46,* 540–542.

Lawton, M. P. Competence, environmental press, and the adaptation of older people. In P. G. Windley and G. Ernst (Eds.), *Theory development in environment and aging.* Washington, D. C.: Gerontological Society, 1975.

Layton, B. Perceptual noise and aging. *Psychological Bulletin,* 1975, *82,* 875–883.

Lazarus, R., Averill, J. R., & Opton, E. M., Jr. The psychology of coping: Issues of research and assessment. In G. V. Coelho, D. A. Hamburg, & J. E. Adams (Eds.), *Coping and adaptation.* New York: Basic Books, 1974.

Lear, M. W. Is there a male menopause: Or, what is going on when the glands, the genes, the mind and culture conspire? *The New York Times Magazine,* January 28, 1973. Reprinted in M. Huyck, *Growing older.* Englewood Cliffs, N. J.: Prentice-Hall, 1974.

Le Blanc, A. F. Time orientation and time estimation as a function of age. *Journal of Genetic Psychology,* 1969, *115,* 187–194.

Lehman, H. C. *Age and achievement.* Princeton, N. J.: Princeton University Press, 1953.

Lehner, G. F. J., & Gunderson, E. K. Height relationships on the draw-a-person test. *Journal of Personality,* 1953, *21,* 392–399.

Leifer, M. Psychological changes accompanying pregnancy and motherhood. *Genetic Psychology Monographs,* 1977, *95,* 55–96.

Leifer, M. *Psychological effects of motherhood: A study of first pregnancy.* New York: Praeger, 1980.

Le Masters, E. Parenthood as crisis. *Marriage and Family Living,* 1957, *19,* 352–355.

Lenski, G. *Power and privilege: A theory of social stratification.* New York: McGraw-Hill, 1966.

Leon, G. R., Gillum, B., Gillum, R., & Gouze, M. Personality stability and change over a 30 year period—Middle age to old age. *Journal of Consulting and Clinical Psychology,* 1979, *47,* 517–524.

Lerner, R. M. *Concepts and theories of human development.* Reading, Mass.: Addison-Wesley, 1976.

Lerner, R. M., & Spanier, G. B. (Eds.). Child influences on marital and family interaction: A life-span perspective. New York: Academic Press, 1978.

Le Shan, L. Mobilizing the life force. *Annals of the New York Academy of Science,* 1969, *164,* 846–861.

Levin, R., & Levin, A. Sexual pleasure: The surprising preferences of 100,000 women. *Redbook* magazine, September 1975, 51–58.

Levine, R. V., & Megargee, E. I. Prediction of academic success with the MMPI and Beta Intelligence Test in a correctional institute. *Catalog of Selected Documents in Psychology,* 1975, *5* (ms. 1129), 343.

Levinson, D. Middle adulthood in modern society: A sociopsychological view. In G. DiRenzo (Ed.), *We the people: Social change and social character.* Westport, Conn.: Greenwood Press, 1977.

Levinson, D., Darrow, C. M., Klein, E. B., Levinson, M. H., & McKee, B. The psychosocial development of men in early adulthood and the mid-life transition. In D. F. Ricks, A. Thomas, & M. Roff (Eds.), *Life history research in psychopathology* (Vol. 3). Minneapolis: University of Minnesota Press, 1974.

Levinson, D., with Darrow, C., Klein, E., Levinson, M., & McKee, B. *The seasons of a man's life.* New York: Knopf, 1978.

Levy, S. M., Derogatis, L. R., Gallagher, D., & Gatz, M. Intervention with older adults and the evaluation of outcome. In L. W. Poon (Ed.), *Aging in the 1980s: Psychological issues.* Washington, D. C.: American Psychological Association, 1980.

Lewis, R. A. Transitions in middle-age and aging families: A bibliography from 1940 to 1977. *The Family Coordinator,* 1978, *27,* 457–476.

Lewis, S. *Main street.* New York: Harcourt, Brace, and World, 1920.

Lieberman, M. A. Adaptive processes in late life. In N. Datan & L. Ginsberg (Eds.), *Life-span developmental psychology: Normative life crises.* New York: Academic Press, 1975.

Lieberman, M. A. Social and psychological determinants of adaptation. *International Journal of Aging and Human Development,* 1978, *9,* 115–126.

Liebeskind, J. C., & Paul, L. A. Psychological and physiological mechanisms of pain. *Annual Review of Psychology,* 1977, *28,* 41–60.

Liederman, P. C., Green, R., & Liederman, V. R. Outpatient group therapy with geriatric patients. *Geriatrics,* 1967, *22,* 148–153.

Lindemann, E. Symptomatology and management of acute grief. Reprinted in A. Monat and R. Lazarus (Eds.), *Stress and coping: An anthology.* New York: Columbia University Press, 1977.

Lipman-Blumen, J., & Bernard, J. (Eds.). *Sex roles and social policy: A complex social science equation.* Beverly Hills, Calif.: Sage Publications, 1979.

Lipton, M., & Nemeroff, C. The biology of aging and its role in depression. In G. Usdin & C. Hofling (Eds.), *Aging: The process and the people.* New York: Brunner-Mazel, 1978.

Livson, F. Patterns of personality development in middle-aged women: A longitudinal study. *International Journal of Aging and Human Development,* 1976, *7,* 107–115.(a)

Livson, F. Coming together in the middle years: A longitudinal study of sex role convergence. Unpublished paper presented at the 29th annual scientific meeting of the Gerontological Society, New York City, October 1976.(b)

Livson, F. Coming out of the closet: Marriage and other crises of middle age. In L. Troll, J. Israel, & K. Israel (Eds.), *Looking ahead: A woman's guide to the problems and joys of growing older.* Englewood Cliffs, N. J.: Prentice-Hall, 1977.

Livson, F. Paths to psychological health in the middle years: Sex differences. In D. Eichorn, J. Clausen, N. Haan, M. Honzik, & P. Mussen (Eds.), *Present and past in middle life.* New York: Academic Press, 1981.

Lloyd, C. Life events and depressive disorder reviewed. I: Events as predisposing factors. *Archives of General Psychiatry,* 1980, *37,* 529–535.

Loftus, E. F., & Zanni, G. Eyewitness testimony: The influence of the wording of a question. *Bulletin of the Psychonomic Society,* 1975, *5,* 86–88.

Lopata, H. Z. *Occupation: Housewife.* New York: Oxford University Press, 1971.(a)

Lopata, H. Z. Widows as a minority group. *The Gerontologist,* 1971, *2,* 67–77.(b)

Lopata, H. Z. *Widowhood in an American city.* Cambridge, Mass.: Schenkman, 1973.

Lopata, H. Z. *Women as widows: Support systems.* New York: Elsevier North-Holland, 1979.

Lorden, R., Atkeson, B. M., & Pollack, R. H. Differences in the magnitude of the Delboeuf Illusion and Usnadze Effect during adulthood. *Journal of Gerontology,* 1979, *34,* 229–233.

Lorge, I. Aging and intelligence. *Journal of Chronic Diseases,* 1956, *4,* 131–139.

Lowenthal, M. F., & Chiriboga, D. Transition to the empty nest: Crises, challenge, or relief? *Archives of General Psychiatry,* 1972, *26,* 8–14.

Lowenthal, M. F., & Chiriboga, D. Social stress and adaptation. Toward a life-course perspective. In C. Eisdorfer & M. P. Lawton (Eds.), *The psychology of adult development and aging.* Washington, D. C.: American Psychological Association, 1973.

Lowenthal, M. F., & Haven, C. Interaction and adaptation: Intimacy as a critical variable. *American Sociological Review,* 1968, *33,* 20–30.

Lowenthal, M. F., Thurnher, M., & Chiriboga, D., and associates. *Four stages of life.* San Francisco: Jossey-Bass, 1975.

Luborsky, L. A. A note on Eysenck's article, "The effects of psychotherapy: An evaluation." *British Journal of Psychology,* 1954, *45,* 129–131.

Luborsky, L. A., Chandler, M., Auerback, A. H., Cohen, J., & Bachrach, H. M. Factors influencing the outcome of psychotherapy: A review of quantitative research. *Psychological Bulletin,* 1971, *75,* 145–185.

Luchins, A. S. Mechanization in problem solving. *Psychological Monographs,* 1942, *54,* 1–95.

Ludeman, K. The sexuality of the older person: Review of the literature. *Gerontologist,* 1981, *21,* 203–208.

Lynch, J. J. *The broken heart.* New York: Basic Books, 1977.

McDonough, C. An examination of causal attribution, emotional expressiveness, and body image as indices of adjustment to mastectomy. Unpublished doctoral dissertation, Illinois Institute of Technology, 1979.

McFarland, R. A., & Fisher, M. B. Alterations in dark adaptation as a function of age. *Journal of Gerontology,* 1955, *10,* 424–428.

McGeer, E., & McGeer, P. L. Neurotransmitter metabolism in the aging brain. In R. D. Terry & S. Gershon (Eds.), *Neurobiology of aging.* New York: Raven Press, 1976.

McGrath, J. Settings, measures, and themes: An integrative review of some research on social psychological factors in stress. In A. Monat & R. Lazarus (Eds.), *Stress and coping.* New York: Columbia University Press, 1977.

McKain, W. C., Jr. A new look at older marriages. *The Family Coordinator,* 1972, *21,* 61–70.

McKenzie, S. C. *Aging and old age.* Glenview, Ill.: Scott, Foresman, 1980.

Maas, H. S., & Kuypers, J. A. *From thirty to seventy.* San Francisco: Jossey-Bass, 1974.

Macklin, E. Nontraditional family forms: A decade of research. *Journal of Marriage and the Family,* 1980, *42,* 905–922.

Mack, J. L., & Carlson, N. J. Conceptual deficits and aging: The category test. *Perceptual and Motor Skills,* 1978, *46,* 123–128.

Maddi, S. *Personality theories: A comparative analysis* (3rd ed.). Homewood, Ill.: Dorsey Press, 1976.

Maddox, G. Persistence of life style among the elderly: A longitudinal study of patterns of social activity in relation to life satisfaction. In B. L. Neugarten (Ed.), *Middle age and aging.* Chicago: University of Chicago Press, 1968.

Maddox, G., & Wiley, J. Scope, concepts, and methods in the study of aging. In R. Binstock & E. Shanas (Eds.), *Handbook of aging and the social sciences.* New York: Van Nostrand Reinhold, 1976.

Malan, D. H. *A study of brief psychotherapy.* New York: Plenum, 1963.

Malan, D. H. *The frontier of brief psychotherapy; An example of the convergence of research and clinical practice.* New York: Plenum Medical Books, 1976.(a)

Malan, D. H. *Toward the validation of dynamic psychotherapy.* New York; Plenum, 1976.(b)

Malan, D. H., in collaboration with Rayner, E. M., Heath, E. S., Bacal, H. A., & Balfour, F. H. The psychodynamic assessment of outcome. In D. H. Malan, *The frontier of brief psychotherapy.* New York: Plenum Medical Books, 1976.(c)

Malan, D. H., Heath, E. S., Bacal, H. A., & Balfour, F. H. Psychodynamic change in untreated neurotic patients. II. Apparently genuine improvements. *Archives of General Psychiatry,* 1975, *32,* 110.

Malloy, J. T. *The woman's dress for success book.* New York: Warner Books, 1977.

Mandler, G. *Mind and emotion.* New York: Wiley, 1975.

Mannheim, K. *Essays on the sociology of knowledge* (P. Kecskemeti, trans.). New York: Oxford University Press, 1952.

Maoz, B. *The perception of menopause in five ethnic groups in Israel.* Doctoral dissertation, Kupat Holim Health Insurance of The Federation of Labour, Eretz, Israel, 1973.

Maoz, B., Dowty, N., Antonovsky, A., & Wijsenbeck, H. Female attitudes to menopause. *Social Psychiatry,* 1970, *5,* 35–40.

Markus, E., Blenkner, M., Bloom, M., & Downs, T. Some factors and their association with post-relocation mortality among institutionalized aged persons. *Journal of Gerontology,* 1972, *27,* 376–382.

Marriot, C., & Harshbarger, D. The hollow holiday: Christmas, a time of death in Appalachia. *Omega,* 1973, *4,* 259–266.

Marsh, G. R., & Thompson, L. W. Psychophysiology of aging. In J. E. Birren & K. W. Schaie (Eds.), *Handbook of the psychology of aging.* New York: Van Nostrand Reinhold, 1977.

Martin, C. Sexual activity in the aging male. In J. Money & H. Musaph (Eds.), *Handbook of sexology.* New York: Elsevier/North-Holland Biomedical Press, 1977.

Marx, M. H., & Hillix, W. A. *Systems and theories in psychology* (3rd ed.). New York: McGraw-Hill, 1979.

Mason, S. E. The effects of orienting tasks on the recall and recognition performance of subjects differing in age. *Developmental Psychology,* 1979, *15,* 467–469.

Masters, W. H., & Johnson, V. *Human sexual response.* Boston: Little, Brown, 1966.

Masters, W. H., & Johnson, V. *Human sexual inadequacy.* Boston: Little, Brown, 1970.

Matarazzo, J. D. *Wechsler's measurement and appraisal of adult intelligence* (5th ed.). Baltimore, Md.: Williams and Wilkins, 1972.

Matthews, S. *The social world of old women: Management of self-identity.* Beverly Hills, Calif.: Sage Publications, 1979.

May, R. *Love and will.* New York: Norton, 1969.

Meacham, J. A. The development of memory abilities in the individual and society. *Human Development,* 1972, *15,* 205–228.

Meacham, J. A., & Singer, J. Incentive effects in prospective remembering. *Journal of Psychology,* 1977, *97,* 191–197.

Mead, G. H. Mind, self, and society from the standpoint of a social behaviorist. In C. W. Morris (Ed.), *The works of George Herbert Mead* (Vol. 1). Chicago: University of Chicago Press, 1934.

Mead, M. *Male and female.* New York: Morrow, 1949.

Mears, F., & Gatchel, R. *Fundamentals of abnormal psychology.* Chicago: Rand McNally, 1979.

Mechanic, D. Problems and prospects in psychiatric epidemiology. In E. H. Hare & J. K. Wing (Eds.), *Psychiatric epidemiology.* New York: Oxford University Press, 1970.

Mednick, M. T., Tangri, S. S., & Hoffman, L. W. (Eds.). *Women and achievement: Social and motivational analyses.* New York: Halstead/Wiley, 1975.

Melrose, J., Welsh, O. L., & Luterman, D. M. Auditory responses in selected elderly men. *Journal of Gerontology,* 1963, *18,* 267–270.

Melzack, R., & Wall, P. D. Pain mechanisms: A new theory. *Science,* 1965, *150,* 971–979.

Mergler, N. Flexibility of attention in young and elderly adults as a function of degree of training and task difficulty. Unpublished doctoral dissertation, Syracuse University, 1977.

Messick, S. Test validity and the ethics of assessment. *American Psychologist,* 1980, *35,* 1012–1027.

Miller, A. Reactions of friends to divorce. In P. Bohannan (Ed.), *Divorce and after.* New York: Doubleday/Anchor, 1968.

Miller, B. C., & Olsen, D. Typology of marital interaction and contextual characteristics: Cluster analysis of the I.M.C. Unpublished paper on file at the Minnesota Family Study Center, University of Minnesota, Minneapolis, 1978.

Miller, E., & Lewis, P. Recognition memory in elderly patients with depression and dementia: A signal detection analysis. *Journal of Abnormal Psychology,* 1977, *86,* 84–86.

Miller, M. *Suicide after sixty: The final alternative.* New York: Springer, 1979.

Mills, D. H., Wellner, A. J., & VandenBos, G. R. The national register survey: The first comprehensive study of all licensed/certified psychologists. In C.A. Liesler, N. W. Cummings, & G. R. VandenBos (Eds.), *Psychology and national health insurance: A sourcebook.* Washington, D. C.: American Psychological Association, 1979.

Milner, B. Memory and the medial temporal regions of the brain. In K. H. Pribram & D. E. Broadbent (Eds.), *Biology of memory.* New York: Academic Press, 1970.

Mischel, W. *Personality and assessment.* New York: Wiley, 1968.

Mitford, J. *The American way of death.* New York: Fawcett-World, 1969.

Monagle, R. D., & Brody, H. The effects of age upon the main nucleus of the inferior olive in the human. *Journal of Comparative Neurology,* 1974, *155,* 61–66.

Monat, A., & Lazarus, R. (Eds.). *Stress and coping: An anthology.* New York: Columbia University Press, 1977.

Money, J., & Ehrhardt, A. A. *Man and woman, boy and girl.* Baltimore, Md.: Johns Hopkins University Press, 1972.

Moody, R. *Life after life.* New York: Bantam, 1975.

Moody, R. *Reflections on life after life.* New York: Bantam, 1977.

Morgan, M. *The total woman.* New York: Pocket Books/Simon & Schuster, 1973.

Morris, J. *Conundrum.* New York: Signet/New American Library, 1974.

Moss, H. A., & Sussman, E. J. Constancy and change in personality development. In O. G. Brim, Jr., & J. Kagan (Eds.), *Constancy and change in human development.* Cambridge, Mass.: Harvard University Press, 1980.

Murphy, E. B., Silber, E., Coehlo, G. V., Hamburg, D. A., & Greenberg, I. Development of autonomy and parent–child interaction in later adolescence. *American Journal of Orthopsychiatry,* 1963, *33,* 643–652.

Murphy, M. D., Sanders, R. E., Gabriesheski, A. S., & Schmitt, F. A. Metamemory in the aged. *Journal of Gerontology,* 1981, *36,* 185–193.

Murray, H. A. *Explorations in personality: A clinical and experimental study of fifty men of college age.* New York: Oxford University Press, 1938.

Murray, J. Family structure in the preretirement years. *Almost 65: Baseline data from the retirement history study.* Washington, D. C.: U. S. Department of Health, Education and Welfare, 1976.

Murrell, K. F. H. The effects of extensive practice on age differences in RT. *Journal of Gerontology,* 1970, *25,* 268–274.

Murstein, B. I. Mate selection in the 1970s. *Journal of Marriage and the Family.* 1980, *42,* 777–792.

National Council on the Aging. *The myth and reality of aging in America.* Study conducted for NCOA by Louis Harris and Associates, Washington, D.C., 1975.

National Council on the Aging. *Fact book on aging: A profile of America's older population.* Washington, D.C.: National Council on the Aging, 1978.

Neale, R. E. *The art of dying.* New York: Harper & Row, 1973.

Neisser, U. *Cognitive psychology.* New York: Appleton-Century-Crofts, 1967.

Neisser, U. *Cognition and reality.* San Francisco: W. H. Freeman, 1976.

Neiswander, M., & Birren, J. E. Love over the life-span: Models and a methodological inquiry. Paper presented at 26th annual scientific meeting of the Gerontological Society, Miami, Florida, October 1973.

Neugarten, B. L. The awareness of middle age. In B. L. Neugarten (Ed.), *Middle age and aging.* Chicago: University of Chicago Press, 1968.

Neugarten, B. L. Personality and the aging process. *Gerontologist,* 1972, *12,* 9–15.

Neugarten, B. L. Personality change in late life: A developmental perspective. In C. Eisdorfer & M. P. Lawton (Eds.), *The psychology of adult development and aging.* Washington, D.C.: American Psychological Association, 1973.

Neugarten, B. L. Age groups in American society and the rise of the young-old. *Annals of the American Academy of Political and Social Sciences,* 1974, *415,* 187–198.

Neugarten, B. L. The future and the young-old. *Gerontologist,* 1975, *15,* 4–9.

Neugarten, B. L. Personality and aging. In J. E. Birren & K. W. Schaie (Eds.), *Handbook of the psychology of aging.* New York: Van Nostrand Reinhold, 1977.

Neugarten, B. L. Policy for the 1980s: Age or need entitlement? Paper prepared for the conference "Aging: Agenda for the eighties," sponsored by the *National Journal,* November 29–30, 1979, Washington, D.C.(a)

Neugarten, B. L. Time, age, and the life cycle. *American Journal of Psychiatry,* 1979, *136,* 887–894.(b)

Neugarten, B. L., and associates. *Personality in middle and late life.* New York: Arno, 1980. (Originally published, 1964).

Neugarten, B. L., & Datan, N. Sociological perspectives on the life cycle. In P. B. Baltes & K. W. Schaie (Eds.), *Life-span developmental psychology: Personality and socialization.* New York: Academic Press, 1973.

Neugarten, B. L., & Hagestad, G. O. Age and the life course. In R. H. Binstock & E. Shanas (Eds.), *Handbook of aging and the social sciences.* New York: Van Nostrand Reinhold, 1976.

Neugarten, B. L., Havighurst, R. J., & Tobin, S. The measurement of life satisfaction. *Journal of Gerontology,* 1961, *16,* 134–143.

Neugarten, B. L., Havighurst, R. J., & Tobin, S. S. Personality and patterns of aging. In B. L. Neugarten (Ed.), *Middle age and aging.* Chicago: University of Chicago Press, 1968.

Neugarten, B. L., Moore, J. W., & Lowe, J. C. Age norms, age constraints, and adult socialization. *American Journal of Sociology,* 1965, *70,* 710–717.

Neugarten, B. L., & Peterson, W. A. A study of the American age-grade system. *Proceedings of the Fourth Congress of the International Association of Gerontology,* 1957, *3,* 497–502.

Neugarten, B. L., & Weinstein, K. The changing American grandparent. *Journal of Marriage and the Family,* 1964, *26,* 199–204.

Neugarten, B. L., Wood, N., Kraines, R., & Loomis, B. Women's attitudes toward the menopause. *Vita Humana,* 1963, *6,* 140–151.

Netter, F. H. *CIBA collection of medical illustrations.* New York: CIBA, 1962.

Newberry, P. Working wives and housewives: Do they differ in mental status and social adjustment? *American Journal of Orthopsychiatry,* 1979, *49,* 282–291.

Nisbett, R. E., & Wilson, T. D. Telling more than we can know: Verbal reports on mental processes. *Psychological Review,* 1977, *84,* 231–259.

Nock, S. L. The family life cycle: Empirical or conceptual tool? *Journal of Marriage and the Family,* 1979, *41,* 15–26.

Nowak, C. Does youthfulness equal attractiveness? In L. Troll, J. Israel, & K. Israel (Eds.), *Looking ahead: A woman's guide to the problems and joys of growing older.* Englewood Cliffs, N.J.: Prentice-Hall, 1977.

Nugent, B. The corporate mentor. *Republic Scene,* 1980, *2,* 50–57.

Nydegger, C. N. Late and early fathers. Paper presented at the 26th annual scientific meeting of the Gerontological Society, Miami, October 1973.

Obrist, W. D. Cerebral physiology of the aged: Influence of circulatory disorder. In C. M. Gaitz (Ed.), *Aging and the brain.* New York: Plenum Press, 1972.

Obrist, W. D., & Bissell, L. F. The electroencephalogram of aged patients with cardiac and cerebral vascular disease. *Journal of Gerontology,* 1955, *10,* 315–330.

Obrist, W. D., & Busse, E. W. The electroencephalogram in old age. In W. P. Wilson (Ed.), *Application of electroencephalography in psychiatry.* Durham, N.C.: Duke University Press, 1965.

Odom, R. D., & Guzman, R. D. Developmental hierarchies of dimensional salience. *Developmental Psychology,* 1972, *6,* 271–287.

Odom, R. D., & Lemond, C. M. The recall of relevant and incidental dimensional values as a function of perceptual salience, cognitive set, and age. *Journal of Experimental Child Psychology,* 1975, *19,* 524–535.

Offenbach, S. I. A developmental study of hypothesis testing and cue selection strategies. *Developmental Psychology,* 1974, *10,* 484–490.

Offer, D., & Sabshin, M. *Normality: Theoretical and clinical concepts of mental health.* New York: Basic Books, 1966.

Omenn, G. S. Behavior genetics. In J. E. Birren & K. W. Schaie (Eds.), *Handbook of the psychology of aging.* New York: Van Nostrand Reinhold, 1977.

O'Neill, N., & O'Neill, G. *Open Marriage: A new life style for couples.* New York: Evans, 1972.

Orlofsky, J. L. Sex-role orientation, identity formation, and self-esteem in college men and women. *Sex Roles,* 1977, *3,* 561–575.

Ostfeld, A., & Gibson, D. (Eds.). *Epidemiology of aging.* Bethesda, Md.: National Institutes of Health, 1975.

Overton, W. F., & Reese, H. W. Models of development: Methodological implications. In J. R. Nesselroade & H. W. Reese (Eds.), *Life-span developmental psychology: Methodological issues.* New York: Academic Press, 1973.

Oyer, H. J., & Oyer, E. J. Social consequences of hearing loss for the elderly. *Allied Health and Behavioral Sciences,* 1978, *2,* 123–138.

Palmore, E. The relative importance of social factors in predicting longevity. In E. Palmore & F. Jeffers (Eds.), *Prediction of life-span: Recent findings.* Lexington, Mass.: D.C. Heath, 1971.

Panek, P. E., Barrett, G. V., Sterns, H. L., & Alexander, R. A. A review of age changes in perceptual information processing ability with regard to driving. *Experimental Aging Research,* 1977, *3,* 387–449.

Papalia, D. E., & Bielby, D. D. Cognitive functioning in middle and old age adults. *Human Development,* 1974, *17,* 424–443.

Papanek, H. The two person career. *American Journal of Sociology,* 1973, *78,* 852–872.

Parkes, C. M. "Seeking" and "finding" a lost object. *Social Science and Medicine,* 1970, *4,* 187–201.

Parkes, C. M., & Brown, R. Health after bereavement: A controlled study of young Boston widows & widowers. *Psychosomatic Medicine,* 1972, *34,* 449–461.

Parloff, M. B. Shopping for the right therapy. *Saturday Review,* 1976, *3,* 14–20.

Parsons, T., & Bales, R. *Family, socialization, and interaction process.* Glencoe, Ill.: Free Press, 1955.

Pastalan, L. A., Mautz, R. K., & Merrill, J. The simulation of age-related losses: A new approach to the study of environmental barriers. In W. F. E. Preiser (Ed.), *Environmental design research* (Vol. 1). Stroudsberg, Pa.: Poroden, Hutchinson, and Ross, 1973.

Pastorello, T. The differential impact of familial and nonfamilial close social relationships on morale in late life. Presented at the 27th annual scientific meeting of the Gerontological Society, Portland, Oregon, October 1974.

Pattison, E. M. *The experience of dying.* Englewood Cliffs, N.J.: Prentice-Hall, 1977.

Pearlin, L. Sex roles and depression. In N. Datan & L. Ginsberg (Eds.), *Life-span developmental psychology: Normative life crises.* New York: Academic Press, 1975.

Pearlin, L. The life cycle and life strains. Paper presented at annual scientific meeting of the American Sociological Association, Boston, August 1979.

Pearlin, L., & Johnson, J. Marital status, life strains, and depression. *American Sociological Review,* 1977, *42,* 704–715.

Pearlin, L., & Lieberman, M. Social sources of emotional distress. In R. Simmons (Ed.), *Research in community and mental health.* Greenwich, Conn.: JAI Press, 1979.

Pearlin, L., & Radabaugh, C. Age and stress: Perspectives and problems. In M. Fiske (Ed.), *Time and transitions.* San Francisco: Jossey-Bass, 1979.

Pearlin, L. I., & Schooler, C. The structure of coping. *Journal of Health and Social Behavior,* 1978, *19,* 2–21.

Pearson, R. E. Support: A central concept in counseling. Paper presented at the annual scientific meeting of the National American Personnel and Guidance Association, Atlanta, March 1980.

Peck, R. C. Psychological developments in the second half of life. In B. L. Neugarten (Ed.), *Middle age and aging.* Chicago: University of Chicago Press, 1968.

Peplau, L., Cochran, S., Rook, K., & Padesky, C. Loving women: Attachment and autonomy in lesbian relationships. *Journal of Social Issues,* 1978, *34,* 7–27.

Perlmutter, M. What is memory aging the aging of? *Developmental Psychology,* 1978, *14,* 330–345.

Person, E. Sexuality as the mainstay of identity: Psychoanalytic perspectives. *Signs: Journal of Women in Culture and Society,* 1980, *3,* 605–630.

Peterson, D. A., Powell, C., & Robertson, L. Aging in America: Toward the year 2000. *Gerontologist*, 1976, *16*, 264–269.

Peterson, J. A. Leisure without guilt. In V. I. Boyack (Ed.), *Time on our hands.* Los Angeles: The Ethel Percy Andrus Gerontology Center, University of Southern California, 1973.

Peterson, J. A. Social-psychological aspects of death and dying and mental health. In J. Birren & R. Sloane (Eds.), *Handbook of mental health and aging.* Englewood Cliffs, N.J.: Prentice-Hall, 1980.

Peterson, L. R., & Peterson, M. J. Short-term retention of individual items. *Journal of Experimental Psychology*, 1959, *58*, 193–198.

Pfeiffer, E. Psychopathology and social pathology. In J. E. Birren & K. W. Schaie (Eds.), *Handbook of the psychology of aging.* New York: Van Nostrand Reinhold, 1977.

Pfeiffer, E., & Busse, E. W. Mental disorders in later life: Affective disorders; paranoid, neurotic, and situational reactions. In E. W. Busse & E. Pfeiffer (Eds.), *Mental illness in later life.* Washington, D.C.: American Psychiatric Association, 1973.

Pfeiffer, E., & Davis, G. C. The use of leisure time in middle life. *Gerontologist*, 1971, *11*, 87–95.

Pfeiffer, E., Verwoerdt, A., & Wang, M. Sexual behavior in aged men and women. *Archives of General Psychiatry*, 1968, *19*, 753–758.

Phillips, D. P., & Feldman, K. A. A dip in deaths before ceremonial occasions: Some new relationships between social integration and mortality. *American Sociological Review*, 1973, *38*, 678–696.

Piaget, J. *The mechanisms of perception.* New York: Basic Books, 1969.

Piaget, J., & Inhelder, B. *Memory and intelligence.* London: Routledge and Kegan Paul, 1973.

Pietropinto, A., & Simenauer, J. *Husbands and wives: A nationwide survey of marriage.* New York: Times Books, 1979.

Pincus, L. *Death and the family: The importance of mourning.* New York: Pantheon Books, 1976.

Pitt, B. *Psychogeriatrics.* London: Churchill Livingston, 1974.

Plude, D. J., & Hoyer, W. J. Adult age differences in visual search as a function of stimulus mapping and processing load. *Journal of Gerontology*, 1981, *36*(5), 598–604.

Polivy, J. Psychological effects of mastectomy on a woman's feminine self concept. *Journal of Nervous and Mental Disease*, 1977, *164*, 77–82.

Pollack, R. H., & Zetland, F. A. A translation of the measurement of visual illusions in children by Alfred Binet. *Perceptual and Motor Skills*, 1965, *20*, 917–930.

Pollock, G. Mourning and adaptation. *International Journal of Psycho-Analyses*, 1961, *42*, 341–361.

Pollock, G. Childhood parent and sibling loss in adult patients: A comparative study. *Archives of General Psychiatry*, 1962, *7*, 295–305.

Pollock, G. Anniversary reactions, trauma, and mourning. *Psychoanalytic Quarterly*, 1970, *39*, 347–371.

Pollock, G. On mourning and anniversaries: The relationship of culturally constituted defense systems to intra-psychic adaptive processes. *Israel Annals of Psychiatry-related Disciplines,* 1972, *10,* 9–40.

Pollock, G. Mourning and memorialization through music. *Annals of Psychoanalysis,* 1975, *3,* 423–436.(a)

Pollock, G. On mourning, immortality, and utopia. *Journal of American Psychoanalytic Association,* 1975, *23,* 334–362.(b)

Pollock, G. Manifestations of abnormal mourning: Homicide and suicide following the death of another. *Annals of Psychoanalysis,* 1976, *4,* 225–249.

Pollock, G. On siblings, childhood sibling loss, and creativity. *Annals of Psychoanalysis,* 1978, *6,* 443–481.(a)

Pollock, G. Process and affect: Mourning and grief. *International Journal of Psychoanalysis,* 1978, *59,* 255–276. (b)

Pomerleau, O. F. Behavioral medicine: The contribution of the experimental analysis of behavior to medical care. *American Psychologist,* 1979, *34,* 654–663.

Poon, L. W., & Fozard, J. L. Speed of retrieval from long-term memory in relation to age, familiarity, and datedness of information. *Journal of Gerontology,* 1978, *33,* 711–717.

Posner, M. I., & Boies, S. J. Components of attention. *Psychological Review,* 1971, *78,* 391–408.

Potter, V. R. *Bioethics.* Englewood Cliffs, N.J.: Prentice-Hall, 1971.

Powers, E. A., and Bultena, G. Sex differences in intimate friendships of old age. *Journal of Marriage and the Family,* 1976, *38,* 739–747.

Price, L. J., Fein, G., & Feinberg, I. Neuropsychological assessment of cognitive function in the elderly. In L. W. Poon (Ed.), *Aging in the 1980s: Psychological issues.* Washington, D. C.: American Psychological Association, 1980.

Price-Bonham, S., & Balswick, J. O. The noninstitutions: Divorce, desertion, and remarriage. *Journal of Marriage and the Family,* 1980, *42,* 959–972.

Pringle, M. L. K. *Deprivation and education.* New York: Humanities Press, 1965.

Prill, H. J. Menopause und klimakterische symptome. *München Medizinische Wochenschrift,* 1964, *49,* 2246–2251.

Rabbitt, P. M. A. Grouping of stimuli in pattern recognition as a function of age. *Quarterly Journal of Experimental Psychology,* 1964, *16,* 172–176.

Rabbitt, P. M. A. An age-decrement in the ability to ignore irrelevant information. *Journal of Gerontology,* 1965, *20,* 233–238.

Rabbitt, P. M. A. Changes in problem solving ability in old age. In J. E. Birren & K. W. Schaie (Eds.), *Handbook of the psychology of aging.* New York: Van Nostrand Reinhold, 1977.

Rado, S. *Adaptational Psychodynamics.* New York: Science House, 1969.

Ramey, J. W. Intimate groups and networks: Frequent consequences of sexually open marriage. *Family Coordinator,* 1975, *24,* 515–530.

Ramey, J. W. *Intimate friendships.* Englewood Cliffs, N. J.: Prentice-Hall, 1976.

Ramsdell, D. A. The psychology of the hard-of-hearing and the deafened adult. In H. Davis & S. R. Silverman (Eds.), *Hearing and deafness.* New York: Holt, Rinehart and Winston, 1970.

Raphael, S., & Robinson, M. The older lesbian: Love relationships and friendship patterns. *Alternative Lifestyles,* 1980, *3,* 207–229.

Rapoport, R., & Rapoport, R. *Leisure and the family life cycle.* Boston: Routledge and Kegan Paul, 1975.

Rapoport, R., & Rapoport, R. *Dual-career families re-examined: New integrations of work and family.* New York: Harper & Row, 1976.

Rapoport, R., Rapoport, R., & Strelitz, Z., with Kew, S. *Fathers, mothers, and society: Toward new alliances.* New York: Basic Books, 1977.

Raven, J. C. *Progressive matrices: Sets A, B, C, D, & E.* London: Lewis, 1938.

Rebok, G. W. Adult age differences in problem solving as a function of perceptual salience level. Unpublished doctoral dissertation, Syracuse University, 1977.

Rebok, G. W., & Hoyer, W. J. Clients nearing death: Behavioral treatment perspectives. *Omega,* 1979, *10,* 191–201.

Reedy, M. N. Age and sex differences in personal needs and the nature of love: A study of happily married young, middle-aged, and older adult couples. Unpublished doctoral dissertation, University of Southern California, 1977.

Rees, J. N., & Botwinick, J. Detection and decision factors in auditory behavior of the elderly. *Journal of Gerontology,* 1971, *26,* 133–136.

Rees, W. D., & Lutkins, S. G. Mortality of bereavement. *British Medical Journal,* 1967, *4,* 13–16.

Reese, H. W. Models of memory development. *Human Development,* 1976, *19,* 291–303.

Reese, H. W., & Overton, W. F. Models of development and theories of development. In L. R. Goulet & P. B. Baltes (Eds.), *Life-span developmental psychology: Theory and research.* New York: Academic Press, 1970.

Reinert, G. Comparative factor analytic studies of intelligence throughout the human life-span. In L. R. Goulet & P. B. Baltes (Eds.), *Life-span developmental psychology.* New York: Academic Press, 1970.

Reitan, R. M. The relation of the trail making test to organic brain damage. *Journal of Consulting Psychology,* 1955, *19,* 393–394.

Reitan, R. M., & Davison, L. A. *Clinical neuropsychology: Current status and applications.* New York: Winston/Wiley, 1974.

Report of the Ad Hoc Committee of the Harvard Medical School to Examine the Definition of Brain Death. *Journal of the American Medical Association,* 1968, *205,* 337–340.

Restak, R. M. *The brain: The last frontier.* Garden City, N. Y.: Doubleday, 1979.

Richards, W. S., & Thorpe, G. L. Behavioral approaches to the problems of later life. In M. Storandt, I. Siegler, & M. Elias (Eds.), *The clinical psychology of aging.* New York: Plenum, 1978.

Riegel, K. F. Dialectic operations: The final period of cognitive development. *Human Development,* 1973, *16,* 346–370.

Riegel, K. F. Adult life crises: A dialectic interpretation of development. In N. Datan & L. H. Ginsburg (Eds.), *Life-span developmental psychology: Normative life crises.* New York: Academic Press, 1975.(a)

Riegel, K. F. (Ed.). *The development of dialectical operations.* Basel, Switzerland: Karger, 1975.(b)

Riegel, K. F. The dialectics of human development. *American Psychologist,* 1976, *31,* 689–700.

Riegel, K. F. History of psychological gerontology. In J. E. Birren & K. W. Schaie (Eds.), *Handbook of the psychology of aging.* New York: Van Nostrand Reinhold, 1977.

Riegel, K. F., & Riegel, R. M. Development, drop, and death. *Developmental Psychology,* 1972, *6,* 306–319.

Riley, M. W. Age strata in social systems. In R. H. Binstock & E. Shanas (Eds.), *Handbook of aging and the social sciences.* New York: Van Nostrand Reinhold, 1976.

Riley, M. W., & Foner, A. (Eds.). *Aging and society: An inventory of research findings.* New York: Russell Sage, 1968.

Riley, M. W., Johnson, M., & Foner, A. *Aging and society: A sociology of age stratification.* New York: Russell Sage, 1972.

Roberts, W. L., & Roberts, A. Factors in lifestyles of couples married over 50 years. Paper presented at 28th annual scientific meeting of the Gerontological Society, Louisville, Ky., October 1975.

Robertson, J. Significance of grandparents: Perceptions of young adult grandchilren. *Gerontologist,* 1976, *16,* 137–140.

Robertson, J. Grandmotherhood: A study of role conceptions. *Journal of Marriage and the Family,* 1977, *39,* 165–174.

Rockstein, M. Heredity and longevity in the animal kingdom. *Journal of Gerontology,* 1958, *13,* 7–12.

Rockstein, M., & Sussman, M. *Biology of aging.* Belmont, Calif.: Wadsworth, 1979.

Roffwarg, H. P., Munzio, J. N., & Dement, W. C. Ontogenetic development of the human sleep-dream cycle. *Science,* 1966, *152,* 604–619.

Rogers, J. C., Keyes, B. J., & Fuller, B. J. Solution shift performance in the elderly. *Journal of Gerontology,* 1976, *31,* 670–675.

Rollin, B. *First, you cry.* New York: Lippincott, 1976.

Rollins, B. & Thomas, D. Parental support, power, and control techniques in the socialization of children. In W. Burr, R. Hill, F. I. Nye, & I. Reiss (Eds.), *Contemporary theories about the family* (Vol. 1). *Research-based theories.* New York: Free Press, 1979.

Roper Organization, Inc. *The 1980 Virginia Slims American women's opinion poll.* Storrs, Conn.: The Roper Center, University of Connecticut, 1980.

Rosenfeld, A. *Prolongevity.* New York: Avon, 1976.

Rosenkrantz, P., Vogel, S., Bee, H., Broverman, D., & Broverman, I. Sex-role stereotypes and self-concepts in college students. *Journal of Consulting and Clinical Psychology,* 1968, *32,* 287–295.

Rosenman, R. H., Brand, R. J., Jenkins, C. D., Friedman, M., Straus, R., & Wurm, M. Coronary heart disease in the western collaborative group study: A final follow-up experience to eight and one-half years. *Journal of the American Medical Association,* 1975, *233,* 872–877.

Rosenwaks, Z. Estrogen replacement therapy. *Proceedings of the Conference on Health Issues of Older Women: A Projection to the Year 2000.* Stony Brook, N.Y.: School of Allied Health Professions, State University of New York, 1981.

Rosow, I. Status and role change through the life-span. In R. H. Binstock & E. Shanas

(Eds.), *Handbook of aging and the social sciences.* New York: Van Nostrand Reinhold, 1976.

Ross, E. Effects of challenging and supportive instructions on verbal learning in older persons. *Journal of Educational Psychology,* 1968, *59,* 261–266.

Rossi, A. Barriers to the career choice of engineering, medicine, or science among American women. In J. Mattfield & C. G. Van Aken (Eds.), *Women in the scientific professions.* Cambridge, Mass.: MIT Press, 1965.

Rossi, A. Sex equality: The beginning of ideology. *The Humanist,* 1969, *29,* 3–6.

Rossman, I. Human aging changes. In I. M. Burnside (Ed.), *Nursing and the aged.* New York: McGraw-Hill, 1976.

Rostand, J. *Humanly possible.* New York: Saturday Review Press, 1973.

Rotter, J. B. Generalized expectancies for internal versus external control of reinforcement. *Psychological Monographs,* 1966, *80* (Whole No. 609).

Rovee, C. K., Cohen, R. Y., & Shlapak, W. Life-span stability in olfactory sensitivity. *Developmental Psychology,* 1975, *11,* 311–318.

Rowland, K. F. Environmental events predicting death for the elderly. *Psychological Bulletin,* 1977, *84,* 349–372.

Rubenstein, S. L. *Prinzipien und wege der entwicklung der psychologie.* Berlin: Akademie Verlag, 1963.

Rubin, L. B. *Worlds of pain: Life in the working class family.* New York: Basic Books, 1976.

Ryder, R. Husband–wife dyads versus married strangers. *Family Process,* 1968, *7,* 233–238.

Ryder, R., & Goodrich, D. W. Married couples' response to disagreement. *Family Process,* 1966, *5,* 30–42.

Sacher, G. A. Longevity, aging, and death: An evolutionary perspective. *Gerontologist,* 1978, *18,* 112–119.

Sacher, G. A., & Duffy, P. H. Genetic relation of life-span to metabolic rate for inbred mouse strains and their hybrids. *Federal Proceedings,* 1979, *38,* 184–188.

Safilios-Rothschild, C. Across-cultural examination of woman's marital, educational and occupational options. *Acta Sociologica,* 1971, *14,* 96–113.

Safilios-Rothschild, C. Sexuality, power, and freedom among "older" women. In L. Troll, J. Israel, & K. Israel (Eds.), *Looking ahead: A woman's guide to the problems and joys of growing older.* Englewood Cliffs, N.J.: Prentice-Hall, 1977.

Sahler, O. J. *The child and death.* St. Louis, Mo.: Mosby, 1978.

Sanders, R. E., Sanders, J. A. C., Mayes, G. J., & Sielski, K. A. Enhancement of conjunctive concept attainment in older adults. *Developmental Psychology,* 1976, *12,* 485–486.

Sarason, S. B. *Work, aging, and social change: Professionals and the one life–one career imperative.* New York: Free Press, 1977.

Sarbin, T. R. Ontology recapitulates philology: The mythic nature of anxiety. *American Psychologist,* 1968, *23,* 411–418.

Sataloff, J. & Vassalo, L. Hard-of-hearing senior citizens and the physician. *Geriatrics,* 1966, *21,* 182.

Saunders, C. The moment of truth: Care of the dying person. In E. Pearson (Ed.),

Death and dying: Current issues in the treatment of the dying person. Cleveland: Case Western Reserve University, 1969.

Saunders, C. St. Christopher's hospice. In E. S. Shneidman (Ed.), *Death: Current perspectives.* Palo Alto, Calif.: Mayfield, 1976.

Sawhill, I. The economics of discrimination against women: Some new findings. *Journal of Human Resources,* 1973, *8.*

Scanzoni, J. Contemporary marriage types: A research note. *Journal of Family Issues,* 1980, *1,* 125–140.

Scanzoni, L., & Scanzoni, J. *Men, women, and change: A sociology of marriage and family.* New York: McGraw-Hill, 1976.

Schaie, K. W. Rigidity-flexibility and intelligence: A cross sectional study of adult life span from 20 to 70 years. *Psychological Monographs,* 1958, *72* (9, Whole No. 462).

Schaie, K. W. A general model for the study of developmental problems. *Psychological Bulletin,* 1965, *64,* 92–107.

Schaie, K. W. A reinterpretation of age related changes in cognitive structure and functioning. In L. R. Goulet & P. B. Baltes (Eds.), *Life-span developmental psychology.* New York: Academic Press, 1970.

Schaie, K. W. Quasi-experimental research designs on the psychology of aging. In J. E. Birren & K. W. Schaie (Eds.), *Handbook of the psychology of aging.* New York: Van Nostrand Reinhold, 1977.

Schaie, K. W. External validity on the assessment of intellectual development in adulthood. *Journal of Gerontology,* 1978, *33,* 695–701.

Schaie, K. W. The primary mental abilities in adulthood: An exploration in the development of psychometric intelligence. In P. B. Baltes & O. G. Brim, Jr. (Eds.), *Life-span development and behavior* (Vol. 2). New York: Academic Press, 1979.

Schaie, K. W., & Labouvie-Vief, G. V., Generational versus ontogenetic components of change on adult cognitive behavior: A fourteen-year cross-sequential study. *Developmental Psychology,* 1974, *10,* 305–320.

Schaie, K. W., Labouvie-Vief, G. V., & Barrett, T. J. Selective attrition effects on a fourteen-year study of adult intelligence. *Journal of Gerontology,* 1973, *28,* 328–334.

Schaie, K. W., Labouvie, G. V., & Buech, B. U. Generational and cohort-specific differences in adult cognitive functioning: A fourteen-year study of independent samples. *Developmental Psychology,* 1973, *9,* 151–166.

Schaie, K. W., & Parham, I. A. Stability of adult personality: Fact or fable? *Journal of Personality and Social Psychology,* 1976, *34,* 146–158.

Schaie, K. W., & Parham, I. A. Cohort sequential analysis of adult intellectual development. *Developmental Psychology,* 1977, *13,* 649–653.

Schaie, K. W., & Schaie, J. P. Clinical assessment and aging. In J. E. Birren & K. W. Schaie (Eds.), *Handbook of the psychology of aging.* New York: Van Nostrand Reinhold, 1977.

Schaier, A. H. & Cicirelli, V. G. Age differences in humor comprehension and appreciation in old age. *Journal of Gerontology,* 1976, *31,* 577–582.

Scheidt, R. J., & Schaie, K. W. A taxonomy of situations for an elderly population: Generating situational criteria. *Journal of Gerontology,* 1978, *33,* 848–857.

Schludermann, E., & Zubek, J. P. Effect of age on pain sensitivity. *Perceptual Motor Skills,* 1962, *14,* 295–301.

Schmitz-Scherzer, R. Longitudinal change in leisure behavior of the elderly. *Contributions to Human Development,* 1976, *3,* 127–136.

Schneirla, T. C. The concept of development in comparative psychology. In D. B. Harris (Ed.), *The concept of development.* Minneapolis: University of Minnesota Press, 1957.

Schonfield, D. Translations in gerontology—From lab to life: Utilizing information. *American Psychologist,* 1974, *29,* 796–801.

Schonfield, D., & Robertson, E. A. Memory storage and aging. *Canadian Journal of Psychology,* 1966, *20,* 228–236.

Schonfield, D., & Stones, M. J. Remembering and aging. In J. F. Kihlstrom & F. J. Evans (Eds.), *Functional disorders of memory.* Hillsdale, N.J.: Erlbaum, 1979.

Schonfield, D., & Wegner, L. Age limitation of perceptual span. *Nature,* 1975, *253,* 377–378.

Schopler, E. Changing parental involvement in behavioral treatment. In M. Rutter & E. Schopler (Eds.), *Autism: A reappraisal of concepts and treatments.* New York: Plenum, 1978.

Schuknecht, H. F. *Pathology of the ear.* Cambridge, Mass.: Harvard University Press, 1974.

Schultz, N. R., Jr. Spontaneous flexibility and rigidity in adulthood and old age: A multitrait-multimethod analysis. Unpublished doctoral dissertation, Syracuse University, 1977.

Schultz, N. R., Jr., Dineen, J. T., Elias, M. F., Pentz, C. A., & Wood, W. G. WAIS performance for different age groups of hypertensive and control subjects during the administration of a diuretic. *Journal of Gerontology,* 1979, *34,* 246–253.

Schultz, N. R., Jr., & Hoyer, W. J. Feedback effects on spatial egocentrism on old age. *Journal of Gerontology,* 1976, *31,* 72–75.

Schultz, N. R., Jr., Hoyer, W. J., & Kaye, D. B. Trait anxiety, spontaneous flexibility, and intelligence in young and elderly adults. *Journal of Consulting and Clinical Psychology,* 1980, *48,* 289–291.

Schultz, N. R., Jr., Kaye, D. B., & Hoyer, W. J. Intelligence and spontaneous flexibility in adulthood and old age. *Intelligence,* 1980, *4,* 219–231.

Schulz, R. *The psychology of death, dying, and bereavement.* Reading, Mass.: Addison-Wesley, 1978.

Schulz, R., & Aderman, D. Clinical research and the "stages of dying." *Omega,* 1974, *5,* 137–143.

Sears, R. Sources of life satisfaction of the Terman gifted men. *American Psychologist,* 1977, *32,* 119–128.

Seelbach, W. Correlates of aged parents' filial responsibility expectations and realizations. *Family Coordinator,* 1978, *27,* 341–349.

Seligman, B. S. On work, alienation, and leisure. *American Journal of Economics and Sociology,* 1965, *24,* 337–360.

Seligman, M. E. P. *Helplessness.* San Francisco: W. H. Freeman, 1975.

Selye, H. *The stress of life.* New York: McGraw-Hill, 1956.

Selye, H. Stress and aging. *Journal of the American Geriatrics Society,* 1970, *18,* 660–681.

Selye, H. *The stress of life* (rev ed.). New York: McGraw-Hill, 1976.

Shanas, E. Family responsibility and the health of older people. *Journal of Gerontology,* 1960, *15,* 408–411.

Shanas, E., Townsend, P., Wedderburn, D., Friis, H., Milhoj, P., & Stenhouwer, J. *Old people in three industrial societies.* New York: Atherton Press, 1968.

Shanas, E. Family-kin networks and aging in cross-cultural perspective. *Journal of Marriage and the Family,* 1973, *35,* 505–511.

Shanas, E. Social myth as hypothesis: The case of family relations of old people. *Gerontologist,* 1979, *19,* 3–9.

Shanas, E., & Sussman, M. (Eds.). *Family, bureaucracy, and the elderly.* Durham, N.C.: Duke University Press, 1977.

Shearer, M. R., & Shearer, M. L. Sexuality and sexual counseling in the elderly. *Clinical Obstetrics and Gynecology,* 1977, *20,* 197–210.

Sheehy, G. *Passages: Predictable crises of adult life.* New York: E. P. Dutton, 1976.

Sheppard, H. L., & Rix, S. E. *The graying of working America: The coming crisis in retirement-age policy.* New York: Free Press/Macmillan, 1977.

Sherif, M., & Sherif, C. *Social psychology.* Evanston, Ill.: Harper & Row, 1969.

Sherman, E. D., & Robillard, E. Sensitivity to pain in the aged. *Canadian Medical Association Journal,* 1960, *83,* 944–947.

Shiffrin, R. M. The locus and role of attention in memory systems. In P. M. A. Rabbitt & S. Dornic (Eds.), *Attention and performance.* New York: Academic Press, 1975.

Shock, N. W. System integration. In C. E. Finch & L. Hayflick (Eds.), *Handbook of the biology of aging.* New York: Van Nostrand Reinhold, 1977. (a)

Shock, N. W. Biological theories of aging. In J. E. Birren & K. W. Schaie (Eds.), *Handbook of the psychology of aging.* New York: Van Nostrand Reinhold, 1977. (b)

Sholl, D. A. *The organization of the cerebral cortex.* London: Methuen, 1956.

Shostak, A., & Gomberg, W. *Blue collar world: Studies of the American worker.* Englewood Cliffs, N.J.: Prentice-Hall, 1964.

Siegel, R. K. The psychology of life after death. *American Psychologist,* 1980, *35,* 911–931.

Siegler, I. C. The terminal drop hypothesis: Fact or artifact. *Experimental Aging and Research,* 1975, *1,* 169–185.

Siegler, I. C., & Botwinick, J. A long-term longitudinal study of intellectual ability of older adults: The matter of selective subject attention. *Journal of Gerontology,* 1979, *34,* 242–245.

Siegler, I. C., George, L. K., & Okun, M. A. A cross-sequential analysis of adult personality. *Developmental Psychology,* 1979, *15,* 350–351.

Siegler, I. C., Nowlin, J. B., & Blumenthal, J. A. Health and behavior: Methodological considerations for adult development and aging. In L. W. Poon (Ed.), *Aging in the 1980's: Psychological issues.* Washington, D.C.: American Psychological Association, 1980.

Silverstone, B., & Hyman, H. *You and your aging parent.* New York: Pantheon, 1976.

Simon, A. The neuroses, personality disorders, alcoholism, drug use and misuse, and crime in the aged. In J. E. Birren & R. B. Sloane (Eds.), *Handbook of mental health and aging.* Englewood Cliffs, N.J.: Prentice-Hall, 1980.

Sinnott, J. D. Everyday thinking and Piagetian operativity in adults. *Human Development,* 1975, *18,* 430–443.

Sjostrom, K. P., & Pollack, R. H. The effect of simulated receptor aging on two types of visual illusions. *Psychonomic Science,* 1971, *23,* 147–148.

Smith, A. D. Adult age differences in cued recall. *Developmental Psychology,* 1977, *13,* 326–331.

Smith, E. R., & Miller, F. D. Limits on perception of cognitive processes: A reply to Nisbett and Wilson. *Psychological Review,* 1978, *85,* 355–362.

Smith, M. E. Delayed recall of previously memorized material after fifty years. *Journal of Genetic Psychology,* 1963, *102,* 3–4.

Smith-Rosenberg, C. The female world of love and ritual: Relations between women in nineteenth-century America. *Signs: Journal of Women in Culture and Society,* 1975, *1,* 1–30.

Sontag, S. The double standard of aging. *Cosmopolitan,* 1972, *174,* 208–223.

Spanier, G. B., & Lewis, R. A. Marital quality: A review of the seventies. *Journal of Marriage and the Family,* 1980, *42,* 825–839.

Spanier, G. B., Sauer, W., & Larzelere, R. An empirical evaluation of the family life cycle. *Journal of Marriage and the Family,* 1979, *41,* 27–38.

Spearman, C. *The abilities of man: Their nature and measurement.* New York: Macmillan, 1927.

Spence, D., & Lonner, T. The "empty nest": A transition within motherhood. *Family Coordinator,* 1971, *20,* 369–375.

Spence, J. T., & Helmreich, R. L. *Masculinity and femininity: Their psychological dimensions, correlates, and antecedents.* Austin: University of Texas Press, 1978.

Sperling, G. The information available in brief visual presentations. *Psychological Monographs,* 1960, *74* (Whole No. 11).

Spielberger, C. D. Anxiety as an emotional state. In C. D. Spielberger (Ed.), *Anxiety: Current trends in theory and research.* New York: Academic Press, 1972.

Spieth, W. Slowness of task performance and cardiovascular diseases. In A. T. Welford & J. E. Birren (Eds.), *Behavior, aging, and the nervous system.* Springfield, Ill.: Charles C. Thomas, 1965.

Spiro, M. *Gender and culture: Kibbutz women revisited.* Durham, N.C.: Duke Universtity Press, 1979.

Spoor, A. Presbycusis values in relation to noise induced hearing loss. *International Audiology,* 1967, *6,* 48–57.

Sporakowski, M., & Hughston, G. Prescription for happy marriage: Adjustments and satisfactions of couples married for 50 or more years. *Family Coordinator,* 1978, *27,* 321–327.

Spreitzer, E., & Riley, L. E. Factors associated with singlehood. *Journal of Marriage and the Family,* 1974, *36,* 533–542.

Staines, G. et al. Alternative methods for measuring sex discrimination in occupational incomes. In F. Denmark & R. Wesner (Eds.), *Women* (Vol. I). New York: Psychological Dimensions, Inc., 1976.

Steele, B. F., & Pollock, C. B. A psychiatric study of parents who abuse infants and small children. In R. E. Helfer & C. H. Kempe (Eds.), *The battered child* (2nd ed.). Chicago: University of Chicago Press, 1980.

Steinman, A. A study of the concept of the feminine role of 51 middle-class American families. *Genetic Psychology Monographs,* 1963, *67,* 275–352.

Steinman, A., & Fox, D. Male-female perceptions of the female role in the United States. *Journal of Psychology,* 1966, *64,* 265–276.

Steinman, A., Fox, D., & Levi, J. Shared values about women's role within and across cultures in the United States, Peru, and Argentina. *International Understanding,* 1964, *2,* 13–17.

Sternbach, R. A. *Pain patients: Traits and treatment.* New York: Academic Press, 1974.

Sternberg, R. J. The nature of mental abilities. *American Psychologist,* 1979, *34,* 214–230.

Sternberg, S. Memory scanning: Mental processes revealed by reaction time experiments. *American Scientist,* 1969, *57,* 421–457.

Stevens-Long, J. *Adult life.* Palo Alto, Calif.: Mayfield, 1979.

Stewart, R., Guest, F., Stewart, G., & Hatcher, R. *My body, my health: The concerned woman's guide to gynecology.* New York: Wiley, 1979.

Stierlin, H. *Separating parents and adolescents.* New York: New York Times Book Co., 1974.

Stinnett, N., Collins, J., & Montgomery, J. Marital need satisfaction of older husbands and wives. *Journal of Marriage and the Family,* 1970, *32,* 428–434.

Stoller, R. J. *Sex and gender.* New York: Science House, 1968.

Storandt, M. *Senile dementia: The challenge of the 21st century.* Division 20 Presidential address, American Psychological Association meeting, Montreal, August 1980.

Storandt, M., Siegler, I. C., & Elias, M. F. (Eds). *The clinical psychology of aging.* New York: Plenum, 1978.

Storck, P. A., Looft, W. R., & Hooper, F. H. Interrelationships among Piagetian tasks and traditional measures of cognitive abilities in mature and aged adults. *Journal of Gerontology,* 1972, *27,* 461–465.

Stoyva, J., & Kamiya, J. Electrophysiological studies of dreaming as the prototype of a new strategy on the study of consciousness. *Psychological Review,* 1968, *75,* 192–205.

Strehler, B. *Time, cells, and aging.* New York: Academic Press, 1962.

Streib, G. F. Social stratification and aging. In R. H. Binstock & E. Shanas (Eds.), *Handbook of aging and the social sciences.* New York: Van Nostrand Reinhold, 1976.

Streib, G. F., & Schneider, C. J. Retirement in American society. Ithaca, N.Y.: Cornell University Press, 1971.

Streib, G. F., & Thompson, W. The older person in a family context. In C. Tibbetts (Ed.), *Handbook of social gerontology.* Chicago: University of Chicago Press, 1960.

Strong, E. K. *Vocational interests of men and women.* Stanford, Calif.: Stanford University Press, 1943.

Strong, E. K. Permanence of interest scores of 22 years. *Journal of Applied Psychology,* 1951, *35,* 89–91.

Strouse, J. *Women and analysis: Dialogues on psychoanalytic views of femininity.* New York: Viking/Grossman, 1974.

Strupp, H. H., & Bergin, A. E. Some empirical and conceptual bases for coordinated research on psychotherapy: A critical review of issues, trends, and evidence. *International Journal of Psychiatry,* 1969, *7,* 18–90.

Super, D. E. *The psychology of careers.* New York: Harper & Row, 1957.

Surwillo, W. W. The relation of simple response time to brain wave frequency and the effects of age. *Electroencephalography and Clinical Neurophysiology,* 1963, *15,* 105–114.

Sussman, M. B. Relationships of adult children with their parents in the United States. In E. Shanas & G. Streib (Eds.), *Social structure and the family: Generational relations.* Englewood Cliffs, N.J.: Prentice-Hall, 1965.

Sussman, M. B. Incentives and family environment for the elderly. Final report to the Administration on Aging, Washington, D.C. Mimeo, 1976.

Szalai, A. Women's time: Women in the light of contemporary time-budget research. In G. Streatfield (Ed.), *Women and the future.* Guildford, Surrey (England): IFC Science and Technology Press, 1975; Binghamton, N.Y.: Center for Integration Studies, 1975.

Talland, G. A. Three estimates of the word span and their estimates over the adult years. *Quarterly Journal of Experimental Psychology,* 1965, *17,* 301–307.

Tangri, S. S. Determinants of occupational role innovation among college women. *Journal of Social Issues,* 1972, *28,* 177–199.

Task Force on Death and Dying of the Institute of Society, Ethics, and the Life Sciences. Refinements on criteria for the determination of death: An appraisal. *Journal of the American Medical Association,* 1972, *221,* 48–53.

Taub, H. A. Paired associates learning as a function of age, rate, and instructions. *Journal of Genetic Psychology,* 1967, *111,* 41–46.

Taub, H. A. Aging and free recall. *Journal of Gerontology,* 1968, *23,* 466–468.

Taub, H. A. Memory span, practice, and aging. *Journal of Gerontology,* 1973, *28,* 335–338.

Taub, H. A. Coding for short-term memory as a function of age. *Journal of Genetic Psychology,* 1974, *125,* 309–314.

Taub, H. A. Comprehension and memory of prose by young and old adults. *Experimental Aging Research,* 1979, *5,* 3–13.

Taub, H. A., & Greiff, S. Effects of age on organization and recall of two sets of stimuli. *Psychonomic Science,* 1967, *7,* 53–54.

Templer, D. The construction and validation of a death anxiety scale. *Journal of General Psychology,* 1972, *82,* 165–177.

Terry, R. D., & Wisniewski, H. Ultrastructure of senile dementia and of experimental analogs. In C. Gaitz (Ed.), *Aging and the brain,* New York: Plenum Press, 1973.

Terry, R. D., & Wisniewski, H. Structural and chemical changes of the aged human brain. In S. Gershon & A. Raskin (Eds.), *Aging, Vol. 2: Genesis and treatment of psychological disorders in the elderly.* New York: Raven Press, 1975.

Terry, R. D., & Wisniewski, H. Structural aspects of aging in the brain. In C. Eisdorfer & R. O. Friedel (Eds.), *The cognitively and emotionally impaired elderly.* Chicago: Medical Yearbook Publishers, 1977.

Thomas, L. *Lives of a cell.* New York: Bantam, 1974.

Thomas, W. I., & Znaniecki, F. W. *The Polish peasant in Europe and America.* New York: Knopf, 1918.

Thorndike, E. L., Bregman, E. O., Cobb, M. B., & Woodyard, E. *The measurement of intelligence.* New York: Teachers College, 1927.

Thurstone, L. L., & Thurstone, T. G. *Factorial studies of intelligence.* Chicago: University of Chicago Press, 1941.

Thurstone, T. G. *Manual for the SRA primary mental abilities.* Chicago: Science Research Associates, 1958.

Tibetan Book of the Dead (W. Y. Evans-Wentz, trans.). New York: Causeway Books, 1973.

Tidball, M. E. Perspective on academic women and affirmative action. *Educational Record,* 1973, *4*, 130–135.

Till, R. E. Age-related differences in binocular backward masking with visual noise. *Journal of Gerontology,* 1978, *33*, 702–710.

Timiras, P. *Developmental physiology and aging.* New York: Macmillan, 1972.

Titchener, E. B. The postulates of a structural psychology. *Philosophical Review,* 1898, *7*, 449–465. Summarized in W. Dennis (Ed.), *Readings on the history of psychology.* New York: Appleton-Century-Crofts, 1948.

Tobin, S. S. Old people. In H. Maas (Ed.), *Review of research in the social services.* New York: National Association of Social Workers, 1978.

Tobin, S. S., & Kulys, R. The family and services. In Eisdorfer, C. (Ed.), *Annual review of gerontology and geriatrics.* New York: Springer, 1980.

Toffler, A. *Future shock.* New York: Random House, 1970.

Tomlinson, B. E., Blessed, J., & Roth, M. Observations on the brains of demented old people. *Journal of Neurological Sciences,* 1970, *11*, 205–242.

Torrance, E. P. *Torrance tests of creative thinking: Verbal form A and B.* Princeton, N.J.: Personnel Press, 1966.

Treas, J. Family support systems for the aged: Some social and demographic considerations. *Gerontologist,* 1977, *17*, 486–491.

Treas, J., & Van Hilst, A. Marriage and remarriage rates among older Americans. *The Gerontologist,* 1976, *16*, 132–136.

Treisman, A. M. Contextual cues in selective listening. *Quarterly Journal of Experimental Psychology,* 1960, *12*, 242–248.

Treisman, A. M. Strategies and models of selective attention. *Psychological Review,* 1969, *76*, 282–299.

Tresmer, D., & Pleck, J. Sex-role boundaries and resistance to sex-role change. In F. Denmark & R. Wesner (Eds.), *Women* (Vol. 1). New York: Psychological Dimensions, Inc., 1976.

Troll, L. E. The salience of members of three-generation families for one another. Paper presented at American Psychological Association meeting, Honolulu, September 1972.

Troll, L. E. *Early and middle adulthood.* Monterey, Calif.: Brooks/Cole, 1975.

Troll, L. E. Intergenerational relationships. In N. Datan & N. Lohmann (Eds.), *Life-span developmental psychology: Transitions of aging.* New York: Academic Press, 1980.

Troll, L. E., & Bengtson, V. Generations in the family. In W. Burr, R. Hill, I. Nye, & I. Reiss (Eds.), *Contemporary theories about the family.* New York: Free Press, 1979.

Troll, L. E., Miller, S. J., & Atchley, R. C. *Families in later life.* Belmont, Calif.: Wadsworth, 1979.

Troll, L. E., & Turner, B. Secular trends in sex roles and the family of later life. Paper presented at Ford Foundation conference, Merrill-Palmer Institute, Detroit, October 1976.

Truax, C. B., & Carkhuff, R. R. *Toward effective counseling and psychotherapy: Training and practice.* Chicago: Aldine, 1967.

Tulving, E. Episodic and semantic memory. In E. Tulving & W. Donaldson (Eds.), *Organization of memory.* New York: Academic Press, 1972.

Tulving, E., & Thompson, D. M. Encoding specificity and retrieval processes in episodic memory. *Psychological Review,* 1973, *80,* 352–373.

Turner, B. The self concepts of older women. *Research on Aging,* 1979, *1,* 464–480.

Turner, B. Sex-related differences in aging. In B. B. Wolman & G. Stricker (Eds.), *Handbook of developmental psychology.* Englewood Cliffs, N.J.: Prentice-Hall, 1981.

Turner, B., Tobin, S., & Lieberman, M. Personality traits as predictors of institutional adaptation among the aged. *Journal of Gerontology,* 1972, *27,* 61–68.

Turner, B., & Turner, C. Evaluations of women and men among black and white college students. *Sociological Quarterly,* 1974, *15,* 442–456.

Turner, C., & Turner, B. Perception of the occupational opportunity structure, socialization to achievement, and career orientation as related to sex and race. *Proceedings of the 79th Annual Convention of the American Psychological Association,* 1971.

Turvey, M. On peripheral and central processes in vision: Inferences from an information-processing analysis of masking with patterned stimuli. *Psychological Review,* 1973, *80,* 1–52.

U.S. Bureau of the Census. *Subject report: Marital status.* Washington, D.C.: U.S. Government Printing Office, 1972.

U.S. Bureau of the Census. *Statistical abstract of the United States: 1979* (100th ed.). Washington, D.C.: U.S. Government Printing Office, 1979.

U.S. Department of Health, Education and Welfare. *Excerpts from Health, United States, 1975.* Washington, D.C.: DHEW, PHS, Health Resources Administration, National Center for Health Services Research of the National Center for Health Statistics, 1976.

U.S. fact book: The statistical abstract of the U.S. (97th ed.). New York: Grosset & Dunlap, 1977.

United States National Health Survey. *Monocular-binocular visual acuity of adults.* (Public Health Service Publication No. 100, Series 11, No. 30). Washington, D.C.: U.S. Government Printing Office, 1968.

Vaillant, G. *Adaptation to life.* Boston: Little, Brown, 1977.

VanKeep, P., & Freebody, P. (Eds.). The menstrual cycle and missing menstruation. Conference held at the International Health Foundation and the Transnational Family Research Institute, Geneva, Switzerland, 1972.

Verillo, R. T. Age-related changes in the sensitivity to vibration. *Journal of Gerontology,* 1980, *35,* 185–193.

Veroff, J., Feld, S. C., & Gurin, G. Dimensions of subjective adjustment. *Journal of Abnormal and Social Psychology,* 1962, *64,* 192–205.

Verwoerdt, A. *Clinical geropsychiatry.* Baltimore, Md.: Williams and Wilkins, 1976.

Verwoerdt, A., Pfeiffer, E., & Wang, H. S. Sexual behavior in senescence: Changes in sexual activity and interest of aging men and women. *Journal of Geriatric Psychiatry,* 1969, *2,* 163–180.

Videbeck, R. E., & Knox, A. B. Alternative participatory responses to aging. In A. M. Rose & W. A. Peterson (Eds.), *Older people and their social world.* Philadelphia: F. A. Davis, 1965.

Vinick, B. Remarriage in old age. *Family Coordinator,* 1978, *27,* 359–363.

Von Hentig, H. The sociological function of the grandmother. *Social Forces,* 1945–46, *24,* 389–392.

Wachowski, D., & Bragg, H. Open marriage and marital adjustment. *Journal of Marriage and the Family,* 1980, *42,* 57–62.

Wallace, D. J. The biology of aging. *Journal of the American Geriatrics Society,* 1977, *25,* 104–111.

Wallach, M. A., & Kogan, N. *Modes of thinking in young children.* New York: Holt, Rinehart and Winston, 1965.

Walsh, D. A. Age differences in central perceptual processing: A dichoptic backward masking investigation. *Journal of Gerontology,* 1976, *31,* 178–185.

Walsh, D. A., & Baldwin, M. Age differences in integrated semantic memory. *Developmental Psychology,* 1977, *13,* 509–514.

Walsh, D. A., Till, R. E., & Williams, M. Age differences in peripheral visual processing: A monoptic backward masking investigation. *Journal of Experimental Psychology: Human Perception and Performance,* 1978, *4,* 232–243.

Wang, H. S., & Busse, E. W. EEG of healthy old persons—A longitudinal study: I. Dominant background activity and occcipital rhythm. *Journal of Gerontology,* 1969, *24,* 419–426.

Wapner, S., Werner, H., & Comalli, P. E., Jr. Perception of part–whole relationships in middle and old age. *Journal of Gerontology,* 1960, *15,* 412–416.

Warner, L., & Lunt, P. *The social life of a modern community.* New Haven, Conn.: Yale University Press, 1941.

Warren, R. L. *The community in America.* Chicago: Rand McNally, 1963.

Watson, C. G., & Klett, W. G. The Henmon-Nelson, Cardall-Miles, Slosson and Quick Tests as predictors of WAIS IQ. *Journal of Clinical Psychology,* 1975, *31,* 310–313.

Weale, R. A. *The aging eye.* New York: Harper & Row, 1963.

Weale, R. A. On the eye. In A. T. Welford & J. E. Birren (Eds.), *Aging, behavior, and the nervous system.* Springfield, Ill.: Charles C. Thomas, 1965.

Webb, J. L., Urner, S. C., & McDaniels, J. Physiological characteristics of a champion runner: Age 77. *Journal of Gerontology,* 1977, *32,* 286–290.

Webb, W. B. *Sleep: An experimental approach.* New York: Macmillan, 1968.

Wechsler, D. *Manual for the Wechsler adult intelligence scale.* New York: Psychological Corporation, 1955.

Wegner, D., & Vallacher, R. *Implicit psychology.* New York: Oxford University Press, 1977.

Weinbach, E. C., & Garbus, J. Oxidative phosphorylation in mitochondria from aged rats. *Journal of Biological Chemistry,* 1959, *234,* 412–417.

Weinberg, J. On adding insight to injury. *Gerontologist,* 1976, *16,* 6–10.

Weiner, B., Frieze, J., Kukla, A., Reed, L., Rest, S., & Rosenbaum, R. *Perceiving the causes of success and failure.* New York: General Learning, 1971.

Weisenberg, M. Pain and pain control. *Psychological Bulletin,* 1977, *84,* 1008–1044.

Weisman, A. D. *On dying and denying: A psychiatric study of terminality.* New York: Behavioral Publications, 1972.

Weiss, A. D. Sensory functions. In J. E. Birren (Ed.), *Handbook of aging and the individual.* Chicago: University of Chicago Press, 1959.

Weiss, L., & Lowenthal, M. F. Life course perspectives on friendship. In M. Lowenthal, M. Thurnher, D. Chiriboga, and associates, *Four Stages of Life.* San Francisco: Jossey-Bass, 1975.

Weissman, M. The psychological treatment of depression: Evidence for the efficacy of psychotherapy alone, in comparison with, and in combination with pharmacotherapy. *Archives of General Psychiatry,* 1979, *36,* 1261–1269.

Weissman, M., Klerman, G., Prusoff, B., Sholomskas, D., & Padian, N. Depressed outpatients: Results one year after treatment with drugs and/or interpersonal psychotherapy. *Archives of General Psychiatry,* 1981, *38,* 51–55.

Weisstein, N. Psychology constructs the female. In V. Gornick & B. K. Moran (Eds.), *Woman in sexist society.* New York: Basic Books, 1971.

Welford, A. T. Motor performance. In J. E. Birren and K. W. Schaie (Eds.), *Handbook of the psychology of aging.* New York: Van Nostrand Reinhold, 1977.

Whanger, A. D., & Wang, H. S. Clinical correlates of the vibratory sense in elderly psychiatric patients. *Journal of Gerontology,* 1974, *29,* 39–45.

White, R. W. Motivation reconsidered: The concept of competence. *Psychological Review,* 1959, *66,* 297–333.

White, R. W. *The enterprise of living.* New York: Holt, Rinehart and Winston, 1972.

White, R. W. *Lives in progress* (3rd ed.). New York: Holt, Rinehart and Winston, 1975.

Wilder, M. Home care for persons 55 years and over: United States, July 1966 to June 1968. *Vital and Health Statistics,* Series 10 (Whole No. 73), 1972.

Wilhamson, E. G. *Vocational counseling.* New York: McGraw-Hill, 1965.

Wilkie, F., & Eisdorfer, C. Intelligence and blood pressure of the aged. *Science,* 1971, *172,* 959–962.

Williams, J. H. *Psychology of women: Behavior in a biosocial context.* New York: Norton, 1977.

Willis, S. L., & Baltes, P. B. Intelligence in adulthood and aging: Contemporary issues. In L. Poon (Ed.), *Aging in the 1980s: Psychological issues.* Washington D.C.: American Psychological Association, 1980.

Wilson, E. O. *Sociobiology: The new synthesis.* Cambridge, Mass.: Harvard University Press, 1975.

Wilson, E. O. *Sociobiology: The abridged version.* Cambridge, Mass.: Belknap/Harvard University Press, 1980.

Wimer, R. E., & Wigdor, B. T. Age difference in retention of learning. *Journal of Gerontology,* 1958, *13,* 291–295.

Windley, P. G., & Scheidt, R. J. Person-environment dialectics: Implications for competent functioning in old age. In L. W. Poon (Ed.), *Aging in the 1980s: Psychological issues.* Washington, D.C.: American Psychological Association, 1980.

Winkelman, R. K. Nerve changes in aging skin. In W. Montagna (Ed.), *Advances in the biology of the skin.* New York: Pergamon, 1965.

Woehrer, C. Cultural pluralism in American families: The influence of ethnicity on social aspects of aging. *Family Coordinator,* 1978, *27,* 329–339.

Wohlwill, J. F. Methodology and research strategy in the study of developmental change. In L. R. Goulet & P. B. Baltes (Eds.), *Life span developmental psychology: Research and theory.* New York: Academic Press, 1970.

Wohlwill, J. F. *The study of behavioral development.* New York: Academic Press, 1973.

Wolff, K. Rehabilitating geriatric patients. *Hospital and Community Psychiatry,* 1971, *22,* 8–11.

Wolpe, J. *The practice of behavior therapy.* New York: Pergamon, 1969.

Wood, V., & Robertson, J. The significance of grandparenthood. In J. Gubrium (Ed.), *Time, roles, and self in old age.* New York: Human Science Press, 1976.

Woodrow, K. M., Friedman, G. D., Siegelaub, A. B., & Collen, M. F. Pain tolerance: Differences according to age, sex, and race. *Psychosomatic Medicine,* 1972, *34,* 548–556.

Woodruff, D. S. Biofeedback control of the EEG alpha rhythm and its effect on reaction time on the young and old. Unpublished doctoral dissertation, University of Southern California, 1972.

Woodruff, D. S. A physiological perspective of the psychology of aging. In D. S. Woodruff & J. E. Birren (Eds.), *Aging: Scientific perspectives and social issues.* New York: Van Nostrand Reinhold, 1975.

Woodruff, D. S., & Birren, J. E. Age changes and cohort differences in personality. *Developmental Psychology,* 1972, *6,* 252–259.

Woods, N. F., & Earp, J. L. Women with cured breast cancer: A study of patients in North Carolina. *Nursing Research,* 1978, *27,* 279–285.

Work in America. Report of a special task force to the Secretary of Health, Education and Welfare. Cambridge, Mass: MIT Press, 1973.

World almanac and book of facts 1981. New York: Newspaper Enterprise Association, 1981.

Wozniak, R. H. A dialectic paradigm for psychological research: Implications drawn from the history of psychology in the Soviet Union. *Human Development,* 1975, *18,* 18–34.

Yalom, I. D., & Terrazas, F. Group therapy for psychiatric elderly patients. *American Journal of Nursing,* 1968, *68,* 1690–1694.

Yankelovich, Skelly, & White, Inc. *Raising children in a changing society: The General Mills American Family Report, 1976–77.* Minneapolis, Minn.: General Mills, Inc., 1977.

Youssef, N., & Hartley, S. F. Demographic indicators of the status of women in various societies. In J. Lipman-Blumen & J. Bernard (Eds.), *Sex roles and social policy.* Beverly Hills, Calif.: Sage, 1979.

Youssen, S. R., & Levy, V. M., Jr. Developmental changes in predicting one's own span of short-term memory. *Journal of Experimental Child Psychology,* 1975, *19,* 502–508.

Zaccaria, J. *Theories of occupational choice and vocational development.* Boston: Houghton Mifflin, 1970.

Zaks, P. M., & Labouvie-Vief, G. Spatial perspective taking and referential communication skills in the elderly: A training study. *Journal of Gerontology,* 1980, *35,* 217–224.

Zelinski, E. M., Gilewski, M. J., and Thompson, L. W. Do laboratory tests relate to self-assessment of memory ability in the young and old? In L. W. Poon, J. L. Fozard, L. S. Cernak, O. Arenberg, and L. W. Thompson (Eds.), *New Directions in Memory and Aging.* Hillsdale, N. J.: Erlbaum, 1980.

Zemen, W. Neuronal ceroid storage disease. *Journal of Neuropathology and Experimental Neurology,* 1974, *33,* 1–12.

NAME INDEX

Abrahams, J. P., 99, 174
Achenbach, T., 6
Adam, J., 14
Adams, B., 322
Adams, C., 315
Adelson, J., 237
Aderman, D., 507
Adesso, V. J., 173
Agnew, H. W., 97
Aisenberg, R., 493, 503
Akiskal, H., 476
Albee, G. W., 461
Albert, M. L., 443
Aldous, J., 270, 274, 276
Aldrich, C., 503
Alexander, R. A., 121
Allen, A., 528
Alpaugh, P. K., 191
Anders, T. R., 140
Anderson, B. G., 322, 324
Anderson, J. R., 151
Angrist, S. A., 45, 237
Antliff, A. R., 95
Antonovsky, A., 384
Arenberg, D., 145, 149, 150, 187, 188, 189, 231, 233
Arens, D., 393
Aries, P., 2
Arkin, A., 497
Arlin, P. K., 182, 183, 190
Armentrout, J. A., 173
Asher, S. J., 421

Atchley, R. C., 273, 274, 286, 287, 349, 350, 351, 352, 371, 393, 433, 434
Atkeson, B. M., 113
Atkinson, R. C., 140, 141
Atleigh, E., 28
Auerback, A. H., 465
Averill, J. R., 86, 496
Axelrod, S., 145

Bacal, H. A., 482
Bachrach, H. M., 465
Baddeley, A. D., 123, 141, 156
Baffa, G., 125
Bahr, H., 393
Bahrick, H. P., 140
Bahrick, P. O., 140
Bain, A., 122
Baird, L., 346
Bakan, D., 237, 257
Bakshy, J., 363
Baldwin, M., 142, 151
Bales, R., 50
Balfour, F. M., 481, 482
Baltes, M. M., 8, 86, 185, 504, 529
Baltes, P. B., 5, 6, 8, 14, 16, 17, 144, 169, 170, 171, 178, 179, 180, 181, 185, 186, 523, 524, 529
Bandura, A., 509, 523
Barber, C., 285
Bard, M., 397
Barlow, D. H., 479

Barnett, R. C., 330, 332, 346, 360, 362
Barrett, C. J., 393, 396
Barrett, C. V., 121
Barrett, T. J., 175
Barrows, C. H., 86, 87, 117
Bart, P., 285, 384, 385
Bartlett, F. C., 150, 151
Baruch, G. K., 330, 332, 346, 360, 362
Basowitz, H., 128, 129
Battin, D., 497
Baude, A., 50
Beattie, W., 533
Becker, E., 493
Bee, H., 237
Bell, A., 308, 318
Bell, B., 108
Bell, R., 317, 321, 324, 325, 360
Bell, S. G., 301, 307, 309, 310
Bellucci, G., 178
Bem, D. J., 528
Bem, S. L., 238
Bengtson, V. L., 38, 40, 62, 64, 274, 284
Berardo, F. M., 393
Bergin, A. E., 465, 471
Bergman, M., 114
Bergmann, K., 455
Berlyne, D. E., 192, 193
Bernard, J., 54, 292, 296, 298, 393
Birkhill, W. R., 186
Birnbaum, J. A., 251
Birnbaum, N., 99
Birren, J. E., 18, 23, 26, 72, 90, 97, 111, 125, 183, 184, 191, 231, 326, 470
Bissell, L. F., 99
Black, D., 288
Blackman, S., 400
Blatt, M. H., 382
Blau, F. D., 47
Blau, Z. S., 323
Blauner, R., 391
Blenkner, M., 290, 502
Block, J., 233, 234, 235, 239, 240
Bloom, B. L., 421
Blum, J., 468
Blumberg, R. L., 48
Blumenfeld, V. G., 114
Blumenthal, J. A., 505
Bock, E., 393

Boies, S. J., 123
Bondareff, W., 77, 79, 80, 81
Bondy, E., 442
Boone, J. A., 173
Booth, A., 324
Bortner, R. W., 503
Botwinick, J., 16, 85, 97, 111, 115, 125, 128, 140, 143, 144, 145, 146, 147, 149, 150, 162, 174, 175, 179, 192
Bourestrom, N., 504
Bouvier, L., 28
Bower, G. H., 140, 151
Boyd, R. R., 276, 277, 289
Bradburn, N., 380
Bradigan, B., 174
Bradway, K., 17
Bragg, H., 325
Brand, R. J., 505
Branscomb, A. B., 495
Braun, H. W., 144, 149
Brazier, M.A.B., 99
Bregman, E. O., 168
Breytspaak, L., 250
Brinley, J. F., 128
Britton, J., 228, 235, 236, 379
Britton, J. O., 228, 235, 236, 379
Broadbent, D. E., 124, 125
Brody, H., 77, 80
Bromley, D. B., 12, 191
Broverman, D., 237
Broverman, I., 237
Brown, A. L., 154
Brown, G., 281, 431, 432
Brown, R., 495
Bruner, J. S., 400
Brunner, L. S., 120
Buech, B. U., 175
Buell, S. J., 79
Bultena, G. L., 324
Bunk, B., 325
Burnside, R. M., 443, 488
Busse, E. W., 16, 99, 437
Butcher, J. N., 412, 419, 420, 422, 424, 430, 435, 436, 438
Butler, R., 25, 90, 152, 434, 446, 465, 470
Butters, N., 156
Byrne, R. W., 141
Bytheway, W. R., 273

Caird, W. K., 126, 155
Cameron, P., 51, 238
Campbell, A., 251
Campbell, D. T., 101
Candy, S. A., 455, 506
Canestrari, R. E., 145
Cantor, M., 409
Caplan, G., 408, 461
Caplow, T., 344
Carkhuff, R. R., 471
Carlson, J. J., 188
Carlson, P., 237, 270, 274, 276
Carlson, V. R., 97
Carpenter, J. O., 502
Carson, R. C., 412, 419, 420, 422, 424,
    430, 435, 436, 438
Casardo, D., 114
Casperson, R. C., 111
Cattell, R. B., 169, 170, 177
Cauna, N., 118
Cermak, L. S., 156
Chadwick, E., 111
Chandler, M. J., 182, 462, 464
Chapman, C. R., 120, 157
Cherry, E. C., 124
Chessler, P., 48
Chinoy, E., 347
Chiriboga, D. A., 86, 240, 241, 243, 244,
    250, 251, 255, 281, 285
Chodorow, N., 279
Choron, J., 493
Chown, S. M., 191, 237
Christenson, C. V., 94
Cicirelli, V. G., 184
Clark, L. E., 126
Clark, M., 322, 324
Clay, V., 381, 382, 383, 386
Clayton, V., 183, 184
Cleary, A., 173
Cleveland, W. P., 316
Cobb, M. B., 168
Cochran, S., 308
Coe, R., 288
Coehlo, G. V., 283
Cohen, D., 442, 443, 446, 455, 463
Cohen, E. S., 533
Cohen, G., 142
Cohen, J., 465

Cohen, R. Y., 116
Cohler, B., 281, 284, 287, 288
Coie, J., 280
Coie, L., 280
Coleman, J. C., 412, 419, 420, 422, 424,
    430, 435, 436, 438, 464
Coleman, P. D., 79
Collen, M. F., 120
Collins, J., 320
Comalli, P. E., Jr., 113
Comfort, A., 88, 315
Constantinople, A., 45
Converse, P., 251
Cooper, I. S., 76
Coren, S., 110
Cornelius, S., 171, 189
Corso, J. F., 111, 114, 115, 439
Costa, P. T., 230, 231, 232, 233, 235, 244,
    254, 255, 258, 261, 503, 504, 517
Cottrell, F., 352
Covin, J. N., 173
Covin, T. M., 173
Cowan, C., 280
Cowan, P., 280
Cowen, E. L., 461
Craik, F. I. M., 123, 139, 140, 142, 143,
    146, 147, 150
Crandall, R., 393
Critchley, M., 77
Cuber, J., 312
Cumming, E., 403
Cunningham, W. R., 170
Cutler, L., 86

Daniels, P., 203, 225
Darrow, C. M., 12, 221, 222, 248, 252,
    454
Dash, B., 114
Datan, N., 180
Davis, E. E., 321
Davis, G. C., 371
Davison, L. A., 76, 90
Dawkins, R., 77
Day, D., 244
Delprato, D. J., 100
Del Vento Bielby, D., 182, 183
Dement, W., 97, 98

Demming, J. A., 187
Denney, D. R., 189
Denney, N. W., 189
Dennis, W., 191
Derogatis, L. R., 25
DeVries, H. A., 93
Diggory, J. C., 507
DiMascio, A., 476
Dineen, J. T., 99, 178
Dinnerstein, D., 49, 278
Dobson, J. F., 162
Dohrenwend, B., 48
Dohrenwend, B. S., 48
Domey, R. G., 111
Donaldson, G., 462
Dooghe, G., 394
Douglas, K., 233
Douvan, E., 237
Downs, T., 504
Dowty, N., 384
Doyle, K. O., Jr., 162
Drachman, D., 147
Du Bois, P. H., 162, 164
Duffy, P. H., 85
Dunbar, F., 436
Duncan, O. D., 58
Dyck, A., 515
Dye, C. J., 475
Dykhuizen, D., 85

Earp, J. L., 399
Ebbinghaus, H., 138
Ehrhardt, A. A., 44, 51
Eisdorfer, C., 86, 89, 90, 145, 151, 178,
    442, 443, 446, 455, 463, 464
Eisner, D. A., 113
Elder, G. H., 181, 523
Elias, M. F., 95, 99, 126, 174, 178, 470
Elias, P. K., 99, 174, 178, 470
Eliot, A., 132
Emmerich, W., 51
Engel, G., 86, 497
English, A. C., 6
English, H. B., 6
Ensminger, M., 483
Erikson, E. H., 12, 52, 155, 205, 206, 208,
    213, 214, 215, 256, 279, 526

Eysenck, H. J., 471
Eysenck, M. W., 143

Falek, A., 180
Fallot, R. D., 152
Fanestil, D. D., 86, 87
Fasteau, M. F., 48
Fehr, L. J., 182
Feifel, H., 493, 495, 515
Fein, G., 76, 96
Feinberg, I., 76, 96, 97
Feingold, L., 442
Feld, S. C., 250
Feldman, K. A., 504
Feldman, R. C., 443
Feldstein, S., 524
Ferguson, T., 401, 402
Finch, C. E., 25, 81
Finesinger, J. E., 99
Fink, H. F., 152
Firestone, S., 50
Fisher, M. B., 110, 111
Fithian, M., 315
Fitzgerald, J. M., 182, 193
Flavell, J. H., 10, 154, 181, 182
Fletcher, J., 516
Fogarty, M., 47, 238, 281, 341, 353, 360
Foley, J. M., 240, 241
Foner, A., 63, 250
Foote, N., 270, 274, 276
Fox, D., 46, 240
Fox, J. H., 365
Fozard, J. L., 8, 108, 140, 141, 146, 177,
    240, 244
Fredricksen, N., 185
Freebody, P., 381, 385
Freeman, J., 50
Freud, A., 405
Freud, S., 205, 303, 466
Friedman, A. S., 175
Friedman, G. D., 120
Friedman, M., 401, 505
Friend, R., 318
Fries, J. F., 88
Frieze, I. H., 332
Friis, H., 276, 292
Frumkes, L. B., 531, 532

Fuller, B. J., 188
Fullerton, A. M., 151
Fulton, R., 493
Furry, C. A., 186

Gabriesheski, A. S., 155
Gadpaille, W., 51, 304
Gagnon, J. H., 94
Gaitz, C., 240
Gallagher, D., 25
Gallagher, T. F., 397
Gardner, E., 118
Gardner, E. F., 187
Gatchel, P., 419, 425
Gatz, M., 25, 456
Gebhard, P. H., 94, 566
Geiselhart, R., 144
Gelles, R. J., 281
George, L. K., 233
Gerber, I., 497
Gerth, H. H., 40
Giambra, L. M., 187, 189, 239, 241
Gianturco, D., 316
Gibbs, J. C., 185
Gibson, D., 28
Gilewski, M. J., 155
Gilford, R., 288
Gillum, B., 237
Gillium, R., 237
Ginsberg, H., 246
Girgus, J. S., 110
Gladis, M., 149
Glenn, N., 285, 325
Glick, I., 316, 394
Glick, P., 301
Goldberg, H., 48, 49
Goldfarb, A. J., 416, 467, 468
Goldstein, K. M., 400
Gomberg, W., 336
Gonda, J. N., 177, 186, 529
Goodman, E., 356, 357, 358
Goodrich, D. W., 274
Gordon, C., 240, 367, 369, 370
Gornick, V., 50
Gottman, J. M., 524
Gould, R. L., 248, 253, 300, 358
Gould, S. J., 87

Goulet, L. R., 5, 144, 171, 523
Gove, W. R., 48
Granick, S., 27, 115, 175
Green, D. M., 115
Green, R., 470
Green, R. F., 175
Greenberg, I., 283
Greenblatt, D. J., 464
Greenhouse, S. W., 90
Greiff, S., 145, 150
Griffin, B., 199, 204, 259, 260, 417
Grobstein, R., 501
Grunebaum, H., 281, 284, 287, 288
Grunes, J., 199, 204, 259, 260, 417
Grzegorczyk, P. B., 116
Gubrium, J. F., 322
Guest, F., 314
Guilford, J. P., 166, 167, 191
Gunderson, E. K., 249, 250
Gurian, B., 409
Gurin, G., 250
Gutmann, D. L., 49, 51, 66, 198, 199,
    200, 202, 204, 240, 242, 243, 245,
    257, 259, 260, 282, 287, 313, 316,
    404, 417, 454
Guzman, R. D., 128

Haan, N., 244
Hagestad, G. O., 64, 66, 67, 288
Hall, P., 442
Hallstrom, T., 384, 385
Hamburg, D. A., 283
Hamilton, J., 501
Hannon, N., 497
Hansen, J. C., 240
Hardt, D. V., 493, 494
Harkins, E. B., 285
Harkins, S. W., 120, 157
Harrell, M. S., 177
Harrell, T. W., 177
Harris, L., 271, 322, 350, 352, 370, 380
Harris, M., 83
Harris, T., 281, 431, 432
Harroff, P., 312
Harshbarger, D., 504
Hartford, M., 470
Hartley, S. F., 47, 50

Hartman, W., 315
Harvey, C., 393
Hatcher, R., 314
Hauser, P. M., 34
Haven, C., 268, 506
Havighurst, R. J., 218, 365, 380, 404
Hayflick, L., 25, 81, 82, 83, 85, 88
Hayslip, B., 188
Heath, D., 283
Heath, E. S., 481, 482
Heglin, H. J., 127
Heikkila, J., 446
Hellman, L., 397
Helmreich, R. L., 237, 238, 241, 242, 250, 251
Hemminki, E., 446
Henker, F., III, 387
Hennig, M., 243, 363
Henry, W., 403
Hensel, H., 119
Herman, G. E., 126, 127
Herr, J., 443
Hersen, M., 479
Hertzog, C., 115, 157
Hess, B., 276, 277, 324
Hess, E., 324
Hiatt, H., 467
Higgins, D., 285, 286, 312
Hilgard, E. R., 137, 140
Hill, R., 270, 274, 276
Hillix, W. A., 123
Hinton, J. M., 500, 502, 516
Hoffman, L. W., 279, 362
Hoffman, M., 279
Holland, T. R., 173
Holstrom, L. L., 48
Holt, N., 173
Holte, A., 384, 385, 386
Hooper, F. H., 182, 189
Horn, J. L., 169, 170, 171, 189, 462
Hornblum, J. N., 182
Horner, M. S., 363
Horowitz, A., 292
Howe, L. K., 334, 356, 359
Howell, J. T., 336
Hoyenga, K. B., 237, 240
Hoyenga, K. T., 237, 240
Hoyer, W. J., 16, 18, 29, 86, 91, 123, 125, 126, 130, 131, 132, 144, 146, 186,

Hoyer, W. J. *(Continued)*
188, 191, 463, 472, 504, 509, 524, 529
Hoyt, L., 314
Hughes, C. P., 75, 156
Hughston, G., 320
Hultsch, D. F., 146, 503
Hunt, M., 311, 315, 317, 325
Huston-Stein, A., 5
Huyck, M. H., 66, 313, 363
Hyman, H., 292

Inglis, J., 126, 155, 157
Inhelder, B., 151
Irish, D. P., 322
Israel, J., 248

Jackson, J., 299
Jacobs, S. S., 173
Jacobson, G., 442
Jaffe, J., 524
Jaggar, A., 49, 50
Jakubczak, L. F., 95
Jardim, A., 243
Jarvik, L. F., 85, 180
Jaslow, P., 359
Jaszmann, L., 385
Jaynes, J., 137
Jencks, C., 173
Jenkins, C. D., 505
Jernigan, T. L., 76
Johnson, J., 310
Johnson, M., 63
Johnson, R., 418
Johnson, V., 93, 94
Jones, S. W., 116
Judson, H. F., 535
Jung, C. G., 200, 257, 313
Jury, D., 443
Jury, M., 443

Kagan, J., 16
Kahana, B., 288
Kahana, E., 288
Kahana, R. J., 468
Kalish, R. A., 495, 508
Kallmann, F. J., 85, 442

Kamiya, J., 97
Kangas, J., 17
Kanter, R. M., 340
Kantor, J. R., 100
Kaplan, A., 165
Kaplan, H. B., 250
Kaplan, H. S., 306, 307, 314, 315
Kaplan, M., 365
Kapnick, P., 465
Kart, C. S., 89
Kasschau, P. L., 38, 40, 62, 64
Kassem, K., 198
Kastenbaum, R. J., 455, 493, 503, 504, 510, 517
Katchadowrian, H. A., 94
Katz, J., 397
Kay, D. W. K., 441, 455
Kaye, D. B., 176, 191, 529
Kedar, H. S., 65
Kellam, S., 272, 483
Kelly, J., 318
Kerckhoff, A. C., 352
Kernberg, O., 454
Kessler, M., 461
Kew, S., 281, 282
Keyes, B. J., 188
Kieffer, G. H., 101, 516
Kiesler, D. J., 471
Kimmel, D. C., 318, 319
Kimmel, H. D., 99
Kinsey, A. C., 56, 94, 305, 314, 325
Kleban, M. H., 115
Kleemeier, R. W., 180
Klein, E. B., 12, 221, 222, 248, 252, 454
Klein, M. L., 87
Kleitman, N., 97
Klerman, G., 476, 478
Klett, W. G., 173
Kline, D. W., 125, 126, 139
Kluckholn, C., 529
Knapp, M., 380
Knowles, J. B., 126
Knox, A. B., 230, 250, 267, 369
Kobasa, S., 401
Koestenbaum, P., 509
Kogan, N., 190, 249
Kohlberg, L., 45, 246, 247
Kohn, R. R., 88
Komarovsky, M., 240

Konigsmark, B. W., 77
Korchin, S. J., 128, 129
Kornetsky, C., 144
Kosa, J., 292
Koval, P. O., 395
Kraines, R., 384
Kramer, M., 455, 456
Kratochwill, T. R., 18, 479
Kreps, J., 25
Kübler-Ross, E., 506, 507, 510, 517
Kuhlen, R. G., 175
Kuhn, T. S., 532
Kuiper, P., 249
Kulka, A., 332
Kulka, R. A., 452
Kulys, R., 292
Kunkel, S., 393
Kupperman, H. S., 382
Kushner, R., 397
Kutner, B., 276
Kuypers, J. A., 16, 244, 251, 277
Kvale, S., 155

LaBarba, R. C., 87
LaBerge, D., 131
Labouvie, G. V., 16, 185, 186
Labouvie-Vief, G., 8, 169, 174, 175, 177, 178, 182, 185, 186, 463, 529
Lachman, J. L., 154
Lachman, R., 154
Lake, A., 381
Landers, A., 318
Langone, J., 517
Larson, R., 380
Larsson, T., 442
Laurence, M. W., 147
Laws, E. H., 514
Lawton, M. P., 185, 456
Layton, B., 123, 125
Lazar, J., 87
Lazarus, R. S., 86, 399
Lazelere, R., 273
Lear, M. W., 387
Leavitt, J., 147
Le Blanc, A. F., 152
Lehman, H. C., 191
Lehner, G. F. J., 249, 250
Leifer, M., 280, 416

Lemond, C. M., 128
Lennon, M. L., 189
Lenski, G., 47
Leon, G. R., 237
Lerner, R. M., 5
Le Shan, L., 87
Levi, J., 240
Levine, R. V., 173
Levinson, D., 12, 221, 222, 240, 248, 252, 313, 348, 454
Levinson, M. H., 12, 221, 222, 248, 252, 454
Levitt, H., 114
Levy, S. M., 25
Levy, V. M., Jr., 154
Lewis, M., 25, 152, 434, 446, 465, 470
Lewis, P., 157, 158
Lewis, R. A., 312
Lewis, S., 56
Lieberman, M. A., 400, 408, 409, 439
Liebeskind, J. C., 119
Liederman, P. C., 470
Liederman, V. R., 470
Lilliquist, T. D., 140
Lindemann, E., 496
Lipman-Blumen, J., 54
Lipsitt, L. P., 180, 523
Lipton, M., 476
Livson, F., 233, 239, 250, 251, 255, 256, 257, 258, 313
Lloyd, C., 458
Lockhart, R. S., 142
Loftus, E. F., 151
Looft, W. R., 189
Loomis, B., 384
Lopata, H. Z., 316, 355, 356, 389, 390, 391, 393, 394, 498
Lorden, R., 113
Lorge, I., 187
Lowe, J. C., 65
Lowenthal, M. F., 86, 240, 241, 243, 244, 250, 251, 255, 268, 281, 285, 303, 312, 313, 323, 324, 506
Luborsky, L. A., 465, 471
Ludeman, K., 94
Lum, M., 504
Lundes, D. T., 94
Lunt, P., 55

Luterman, D. M., 114
Lutkins, S. G., 502
Lynch, J. J., 505, 506

Maas, H. S., 16, 244, 251, 320
MacDonald, R., 270, 274, 276
Machlin, E., 325
Mack, J. L., 188
Maddox, G., 23, 25, 404
Malan, D. H., 468, 479, 480, 481, 482
Malloy, J. T., 53
Mandler, G., 137
Mannheim, K., 137
Maoz, B., 384
Margulies, M. K., 114
Markus, E., 504
Marriot, C., 504
Marsh, G. R., 90, 99
Martin, C., 314
Martin, C. E., 56, 94
Marx, M. H., 123
Masani, P. A., 147
Mason, S. E., 143
Masters, W. M., 93, 94, 305, 306, 314, 315, 325
Matarazzo, J. D., 17, 165, 175
Matthews, S., 391
Mautz, R. K., 106
May, R., 266, 301
Mayes, G. J., 178
McCrae, R. R., 230, 231, 232, 233, 235, 244, 254, 255, 258, 261
McDaniels, J., 92
McDonough, C., 397
McFarland, R. A., 108, 110, 111
McGeer, E., 81
McGeer, P. L., 81
McGrath, J., 399
McKain, W. C., Jr., 318
McKee, B., 12, 221, 222, 248, 252, 454
McKenzie, S. C., 119
McKinney, W., Jr., 476
McVeigh, F., 28
Meacham, J. A., 153, 155
Mead, M., 46
Mears, F., 419, 424
Mechanic, D., 484

Mednick, M. T., 362
Megargee, E. I., 173
Melrose, J., 114
Melzack, R., 119
Mendkoff, E., 501
Mergler, N., 130
Merrill, J., 106
Messick, S., 172
Mettress, E. S., 89
Mettress, J. F., 89
Milhoy, P., 276, 292
Miller, A., 310
Miller, E., 157, 158
Miller, F. D., 137
Miller, M., 434
Miller, S. J., 273, 274, 286, 287
Mills, C. W., 40
Mills, D. H., 474
Milner, B., 156
Mischel, W., 400
Mishara, B. L., 144, 463
Mistretta, C. M., 116
Mitford, J., 494
Monagle, R. D., 77
Monat, A., 399
Money, J., 44, 51
Monge, R. H., 187
Montgomery, J., 320
Moody, R., 508, 511
Moore, J. W., 65
Moran, B. K., 50
Morris, J., 42
Moss, H. A., 16, 233, 244
Munzio, J. N., 97, 98
Murphy, D. M., 240, 241
Murphy, E. A., 77
Murphy, E. B., 283
Murphy, M. D., 155
Murray, H. A., 266, 332, 529
Murray, J., 271
Murrell, K. F. H., 177
Murstein, B. I., 301

Naudi, A. H., 16, 179
Neale, R. E., 509
Neisser, U., 106, 130, 137
Neiswander, M., 326

Nemeroff, C., 476
Nesselroade, J. R., 6, 14, 17, 169, 170,
    171, 181
Neu, C., 476
Neugarten, B. L., 13, 64, 65, 66, 67, 180,
    198, 219, 220, 237, 241, 244, 248,
    249, 255, 285, 288, 311, 312, 343,
    380, 384, 401, 404, 455, 484, 485,
    526, 533
Newberry, P., 359
Nisbett, R. E., 137
Nock, S. L., 273
Notarios, C., 524
Nowak, C., 248
Nowlin, J. B., 178, 505
Nugent, B., 453
Nydegger, C. N., 66

Obrist, W. D., 99
Odom, R. D., 128
Offenbach, S. I., 188
Offer, D., 414
Okun, M. A., 233
Olson, D., 303
Omenn, G. S., 80
O'Neill, G., 325
O'Neill, N., 325
Oppler, S., 246
Opton, E. M., Jr., 86
Orlofsky, J. L., 251
Orme-Rogers, C., 125
Ostfeld, A., 28
Overton, W. F., 7, 182, 183, 525
Oyer, E. J., 121
Oyer, H. J., 121

Padesky, C., 308
Padian, N., 476, 478
Palmore, E., 335
Panek, P. E., 121
Papalia, D. E., 182, 183
Papanek, H., 358
Parham, I. A., 169
Parkes, C. M., 394, 495, 496, 497
Parloff, M. B., 465
Parsons, T., 50

Pastalan, L. A., 106
Pastorello, T., 324
Patterson, R. D., 27
Pattison, E. M., 507, 508
Paul, L. A., 119
Pearlin, L., 46, 285, 310, 394, 405, 407, 409, 452
Pearson, R. E., 506
Peck, R. C., 217
Pentz, C. A., 99, 178
Peplau, L., 308
Perlmutter, M., 153
Person, E., 304
Peterson, D. A., 533
Peterson, J. A., 369, 496
Peterson, L. R., 140, 156
Peterson, M. J., 140, 156
Peterson, W. A., 64, 65
Pfeiffer, E., 86, 314, 319, 371, 437, 439, 441, 443, 445
Phillips, D. P., 504
Piaget, J., 113, 151, 183
Pietropinto, A., 302, 325
Pincus, L., 497, 498, 499, 501
Pitt, B., 431, 446
Plick, J., 324
Plude, D. J., 91, 126, 131, 132, 146, 177
Podolsky, S., 108
Pokorny, A. P., 250
Polivy, J., 396, 397
Pollack, C. B., 281
Pollack, R. H., 106, 111, 113
Pollock, G., 495, 496, 497, 499, 501, 503
Pomerleau, O. F., 505
Pomeroy, W. B., 56, 94
Poon, L. W., 177
Popkin, S. J., 8
Posner, M. I., 123
Postman, L., 142
Potter, V. R., 100
Powell, C., 533
Powers, E. A., 324
Pressey, S. L., 187
Price, L. J., 76
Price-Bonham, S., 309
Pringle, M. L. K., 420
Prill, H. J., 385
Prusoff, B., 476, 478
Putnam, B. A., 240

Rabbitt, P. M. A., 123, 125, 188
Radabaugh, C., 285, 452
Rado, S., 264
Ramey, J. W., 325
Ramsdell, D. A., 126
Raphael, S., 318, 319
Rapoport, R., 47, 48, 238, 281, 282, 366, 367, 369
Rapoport, R., 48, 281, 282, 362, 366, 367, 369
Raven, J. C., 189
Rayner, E. M., 481
Rebok, G. W., 86, 123, 125, 130, 188, 504, 509
Redick, R. W., 455, 456
Reed, L., 332
Reedy, M. N., 326
Rees, J. N., 115
Rees, W. D., 500
Reese, H. W., 6, 7, 14, 17, 136, 180, 181, 523, 524
Reinert, G., 169, 170
Reitan, R. M., 76, 90
Renner, V. J., 23, 29, 72, 97
Rest, S., 332
Restak, R. M., 100
Richards, W. S., 463
Riedel, R. G., 144, 463
Riegel, K. F., 7, 8, 16, 23, 137, 155, 179, 180, 183
Riley, L. E., 321
Riley, M. W., 63, 66, 67, 250
Roberts, A., 320
Roberts, W. L., 320
Robertson, E. A., 147
Robertson, J., 288
Robertson, L., 533
Robillard, E., 120
Robinson, M., 318, 319
Rockstein, M., 74, 79, 80, 82, 83, 84, 85, 111, 114, 115
Roeder, L. M., 117
Roffwarg, H. P., 97, 98
Rogers, J. C., 188
Rogers, W., 251
Rollins, B., 279, 398
Rook, K., 308
Rosenbaum, R., 332
Rosenfeld, A., 83, 84

Rosenkrants, P., 237
Rosenman, R. H., 401, 505
Rosenwaks, Z., 386
Rosow, I., 43, 380
Ross, E., 178
Rossi, A., 251
Rossman, I., 118
Rostand, J., 79
Rothman, D., 507
Rotter, J. B., 249
Rovee, C. K., 116
Rowland, K. F., 86, 503, 504
Rubenstein, S. L., 221
Rubin, L. B., 336
Rusalem, R., 497
Ryder, R., 274, 303

Sabshin, M., 413
Sacher, G. A., 85, 101
Safilios-Rothschild, C., 50, 66, 314, 317
Sahler, O. J., 501
Sanders, J. A. C., 178
Sanders, R. E., 155, 178
Sarason, S. B., 333, 337, 343
Sarbin, T. R., 177
Sataloff, J., 114
Sauer, W., 273
Saunders, C., 517, 518
Sawhill, I., 47
Scanzoni, J., 303
Scanzoni, L., 303
Schaie, J. P., 456, 463
Schaie, K. W., 14, 16, 17, 113, 128, 169, 174, 175, 178, 179, 185, 186, 456, 463, 523, 529
Schaier, A. H., 184
Scheidt, R. J., 174, 185, 529
Scheier, I. H., 177
Schieber, F., 126, 139
Schludermann, E., 120
Schmitt, F. A., 155
Schmitz-Scherzer, R., 369
Schneider, C. J., 351, 352, 365
Schneirla, T. C., 5
Schneweis, K., 396
Schommer, C. O., 292
Schonfield, D., 123, 140, 146, 148, 150

Schooler, C., 405, 407
Schopler, E., 421
Schuknecht, H. F., 114
Schultz, N. R., Jr., 99, 176, 178, 186, 191, 192, 529
Schulz, R., 507, 508, 517
Scott, J., 240
Scott, M. L., 155
Sears, R., 312, 400
Seelbach, W., 290
Seligman, B., 335
Seligman, M. E. P., 86, 145, 509
Selye, H., 75, 87
Shader, R. I., 464
Shanan, J., 65
Shanas, E., 23, 271, 274, 276, 277, 292, 322
Shearer, M. L., 94
Shearer, M. R., 94
Sheehy, G., 12, 222, 225, 248
Sheppard, H. L., 342
Sherif, C., 68
Sherif, M., 68
Sherman, E. D., 120
Shiffrin, R. M., 140, 141
Shin, S. H., 173
Shlapak, W., 116
Shock, N. W., 83, 86, 528
Sholomskas, D., 476, 478
Shostak, A., 336
Siegel, R. K., 511
Siegelaub, A. B., 120
Siegler, I. C., 16, 179, 233, 470, 505
Sielski, K. A., 178
Silber, E., 283
Silverstone, B., 292
Simenauer, J., 302, 325
Simon, A., 437
Singer, J., 153
Sinnot, J. D., 182
Sjogren, T., 442
Sjostrom, K. P., 106
Sloane, R. B., 470
Smith, A. D., 147, 151
Smith, E. R., 137
Smith, M. E., 140, 148
Smith-Rosenberg, C., 323
Smyer, M. A., 456
Sokoloff, L., 90

Sontag, S., 249
Spanier, G. B., 273, 312
Spearman, C., 168
Spence, D., 240
Spence, J. T., 237, 238, 241, 242, 250, 251
Sperling, G., 139
Spielberger, C. D., 178
Spieth, W., 89, 90
Spiro, M., 238, 269
Spoor, A., 114
Sporakowski, M., 320
Spreitzer, E., 321
Staines, G., 47
Steele, B. F., 281
Steinman, A., 46, 240
Stenhouwer, G., 276, 292
Sternbach, R. A., 120
Sternberg, R. J., 165
Sternberg, S., 140
Sterns, H. L., 121, 188
Stevens-Long, J., 113
Stewart, G., 314
Stewart, R., 314
Stierlin, H., 284
Stinnett, N., 320
Stoller, R. J., 44, 51
Stones, M. J., 146, 148, 150
Storandt, M., 75, 140, 147, 156, 470
Storck, P. A., 189
Stotsky, B. A., 464
Stoyva, J., 97
Straus, R., 505
Stehler, B., 74, 80
Streib, G. F., 66, 276, 351, 352, 365
Strelitz, Z., 281, 282
Strong, E. K., 240
Strouse, J., 214
Struhl, P., 49, 50
Strupp, H. H., 471
Suddarth, D. S., 120
Super, D. E., 344
Surwillo, W. W., 99
Sussman, E. J., 233, 244
Sussman, M. B., 74, 79, 80, 82, 83, 111, 114, 115, 277, 289, 292
Sutherland, A. M., 397
Sved, S. M., 123, 125, 130, 188

Swets, J. A., 115
Szafrau, J., 126
Szalai, A., 48

Taguri, R., 400
Talland, G. A., 156
Tamir, L., 452
Tangri, S. S., 338, 362
Tars, S., 502
Taub, H. A., 140, 142, 145, 150
Taube, C. A., 455, 456
Templer, D., 508
Terrazas, F., 470
Terry, R. D., 75, 81, 442
Thomas, D., 279
Thomas, J., 240, 244
Thomas, W. I., 38
Thompson, D. M., 148
Thompson, L. W., 90, 155
Thompson, W., 276
Thorndike, E. L., 168
Thorpe, G. L., 463
Thronesbery, C., 154
Thurner, M., 240, 241, 243, 251, 281
Thurstone, L. L., 168, 169
Thurstone, T. G., 168
Tidball, M. E., 362
Till, R. E., 126
Timiras, P., 87, 108, 118, 119
Titchener, E. B., 123
Tobin, S. S., 276, 290, 292, 380, 404, 439
Toffler, A., 300
Tomlinson, B. E., 442
Torrance, E., 190
Townsend, P., 276, 292
Treas, J., 32, 320, 321
Treisman, A. M., 124, 125
Tresmer, D., 324
Troll, L. E., 48, 273, 274, 278, 284, 286, 287, 300, 309, 313, 315, 316, 320, 322
Tross, S., 468
Truax, C. B., 470
Trute, B., 277
Tudor, J. F., 48
Tulving, E., 141, 142, 143, 148
Turner, B., 48, 242, 248, 249, 250, 251, 313, 315, 354, 439

Turner, C., 242, 354
Turner, J., 272
Turvey, M., 126

Urner, S. C., 92

Vaillant, G., 244, 248, 264, 267, 405, 407
Vallacher, R., 400
VanderBos, G. R., 475
Vanderleyden, L., 394
Van Hilst, A., 320, 321
VanKeep, P., 381, 385
Van Lith, N. D., 385
Vassalo, L., 114
Verillo, R. T., 117
Veroff, J., 250
Verwoerdt, A., 314, 319, 463, 470
Videback, R. E., 369
Vijayashankar, N., 80
Vinick, B., 320
Vogel, S., 237

Wachowski, D., 325
Wagener, J. W., 126, 127
Wall, P. D., 119
Wallace, D. J., 82, 83
Wallach, M. A., 190, 249
Walsh, D. A., 126, 140, 142, 151
Wang, H. S., 99, 118, 319
Wang, M., 314
Wapner, S., 113
Waring, J., 276, 277
Warner, L., 55
Warren, L. R., 126
Warren, R. L., 459
Warrington, E. K., 156
Watson, C. G., 173
Weakland, J., 443
Weale, R. A., 108, 111
Weaver, C., 285, 325
Webb, J. L., 92
Webb, W. B., 96, 97
Webber, I. L., 393
Wechsler, D., 16, 17
Wedderburn, D., 276, 292

Wegner, D., 400
Wegner, L., 140
Weinberg, J., 468, 469
Weinberg, M., 308, 318
Weiner, B., 332
Weingarten, P., 203, 225
Weinstein, K., 198, 288
Weisenberg, M., 119, 120
Weisman, A. D., 517
Weiss, A. D., 114, 115
Weiss, L., 324
Weiss, R. S., 394
Weissman, M., 475, 476, 478
Weisstein, N., 214
Welford, A. T., 124
Wellman, H. M., 154
Wellner, A. J., 475
Whanger, A. D., 118
Welsh, O. L., 114
Werner, H., 113
Wetchler, B. B., 382
White, J. L., 87
White, R. W., 228, 239, 244, 245, 246,
    247, 267, 332
White, S. W., 421
Wigdor, B. T., 149, 150
Wijsenbeck, H., 384
Wilder, M., 292
Wiley, J., 23, 25
Wilkie, F., 86, 89, 90, 145, 178
Williams, J. H., 50, 53
Williams, M., 126
Williams, R. L., 97
Willis, A. L., 443
Willis, S. L., 171, 178
Wilson, E. O., 101, 264
Wilson, T. D., 137
Wimer, R. E., 149, 150
Windley, P. G., 174
Winkelman, R. K., 117
Wittunger, R. P., 140
Woehrer, C., 275
Wohlwill, J. F., 522
Wolf, E., 108
Wolff, K., 471
Wolpe, J., 469
Wood, N., 384
Wood V., 288

Wood, W. G., 99, 178
Woodrow, K. M., 120
Woodruff, D. S., 97, 99, 236
Woods, N. F., 399
Woodyard, E., 168
Wozniak, R. H., 221
Wurm, M., 505
Wylie, C. M., 502

Yalom, I. D., 470
Yankelovich, Skelly, and White, Inc.,
    282
Yarrow, M., 90
Young, W. C., 95

Youssef, N., 47, 50
Youssen, S. R., 154

Zaat, J. C. A., 385
Zaccaria, J., 343, 344
Zaks, P. M., 178
Zannie, G., 151
Zatz, L. M., 76
Zelinski, E. M., 155
Zemen, W., 80
Zetland, F. A., 111
Znaniecki, F. W., 38
Zubek, J. P., 120
Zwilling, M., 476

SUBJECT INDEX

Acceptance of death, 507
Accommodation in vision, 109
Accountability, 471
Achievement motivation, 332
Activity theory, 403
Adaptation:
  changes requiring, 380
  cognitive factors affecting, 399–401
  coping strategies and, 404–408
  definition of, 376
  Kansas City studies, 401–404
  male climacteric and, 387–388
  mastectomy and, 396–399
  measures of, 379–380
  menopause and, 380–385
  nonnormative changes and, 378
  normative changes and, 378
  other transient life crises and, 399
  personality and, 401
  social resources and, 408–409
  successful transitions in, 378–379
  widowhood and, 388–396
Adaptiveness, 243–245
Addictions:
  alcoholism and, 437–438
  drug abuse and, 437–438
  hard, 531
  positive, 532
  soft, 531
Adolescence, 51, 233–234, 346, 367–368
Adult Development and Enrichment
  Project, 176

Advocacy, 486, 532–534
Affective disorders, 431–435
Affiliation, 267–268
Age:
  sex-role differentiation and, 51–52
  social status and, 63–67
  stereotypes of, 247–249, 526
  as a variable in research, 19–22
Age-by-treatment interaction, 21
Age changes, 15
Age concepts:
  biological age, 26
  chronological age, 25–26
  functional age, 26
  psychological age, 26
  social age, 26–27
Age differences, 15
Age discrimination, 67
Age-irrelevancy, 219–220, 225
Age norms and behavior, 65–66, 180–
  181, 247–249, 378, 458, 523
Age politics, 35, 533
Age stereotypes, 526
Age structure, 32–33
Aging:
  affiliation and, 267
  health and, 80–97
  love and, 266–267
  memory and, 143–149
  personality and, 231–247
  retirement and, 349–352, 364–365
  work and, 343

Aging parents, 289–293
Aging population:
  age structure, 32–33
  demographics, 27–29
  life expectancy, 29–30
  longevity, 30–32
  societal consequences, 32–35
Agism, 67
Alcoholism, 437–438
Alzheimer's disease, 75, 441–442
Amnesia, 156
Androgyny, 238
Anger in dying, 506
Anniversary reactions in bereavement,
  500–504
Anticipation interval in learning, 145
Anticipatory grief, 497
Anxiety:
  cancer and, 398
  coping strategies and, 404–405
  ego-defense mechanisms and, 405–
    408
  psychopathology and, 424–430
Arteriosclerosis, 89, 156, 505
Associationism, 136
Associative learning, 149
Atherosclerosis, 89. *See also* Arteriosclerosis
Attentional processes, 123–125
Auditory processing. *See* Hearing
Autoimmunity:
  aging and, 74
  cancer and, 74
Baltimore Study of Aging, 231–233
Bandura's social learning theory, 523–
  524
Bargaining as stage of dying, 506
Behavioral change, 17
Behavior disorders, 414, 417
Behaviorism, 137
Behavior medicine, 436, 505
Behavior therapy:
  cognitive restructuring, 470
  extinction, 469
  learning and, 144–145
  positive reinforcement and, 469
  systematic desensitization, 469–470
Bereavement, 495–502
Berkeley Guidance Study, 16, 233–235

Bill of rights for adults, 486
Bioethics, 100
Biological age, 26, 72, 382–383
Biological reserve capacity, 528–529
Biological sex, 43, 45
Blood pressure, 89–90
Brain activity:
  biofeedback and, 99
  death and, 490
  psychomotor slowing and, 99
  sleep and, 96–97
Brain death, 492
Breasts, 398
Brief psychotherapy, 479
Cancer, 74, 88, 396–399, 505–506
Cardiovascular system, 88–90
Careerists, 360
Careers:
  advancement in, 337
  aging and, 343
  selection of, 346–349
  social status and, 337
  Super's theory of, 344–345, 347, 354
  women and, 360–362
Cataracts, 110
Cautiousness, 155
Cellular theories of senescence, 82–83
Central nervous system, 76–81
Cerebrovascular accidents, 88–89, 442,
  505
Childhood and Society (Erikson), 205
Childlessness:
  Gutman's theory and, 204
  Havighurst's theory and, 219
Chronic brain syndromes, 443–445
Chronological age, 26
Classical conditioning, 144
Climacteric:
  females and, 381–383
  males and, 387–388
Close relationships:
  brothers and sisters, 322
  friends, 323–324
  homosexuality, 242, 308, 318–319
  lovers, 325–326
  marriage, 296–321
  parent-child, 278–293
Cognition:
  hearing loss, 115

intelligence and, 167, 181–184
memory and, 137, 151
perception and, 122, 130–132
regression of, 183
schemata and, 151
Cognitive-behavioral therapies, 470
Cognitive development, 181–184, 527
Cognitive processes in adaptation, 399–401
Cognitive regression, 183
Cognitive rigidity, 190–192
Cognitive style, 400
Cohabitation, 325
Cohort:
   development and, 13–14
   intelligence and, 174–175, 180
   personality and, 242
   self-development and, 529
   work and, 340–342
Cohort-specific developmental influences, 180–181, 523
Competence-performance distinction, 186
Computerized axial tomography, 76
Concept learning, 187
Concrete operations, 182
Conditioning:
   classical, 144
   operant, 144
Convergent thinking, 167
Coronary prone behavior, 505–506
Creativity, 190–191
Crisis:
   developmental dialectics and, 7, 530
   intellectual development and, 183
   in personality development, 221–225
   mastectomy and, 396
   widowhood and, 388–396
Critical flicker frequency, 111
Cross-sectional method, 15
Crystallized intelligence, 170–171
Cue overload and memory, 147
Curiosity, 190, 192–193

Dark adaptation, 110–111
Data collection strategies:
   cross-sectional, 15

longitudinal, 15
sequential, 17
time lag, 17
Death:
   anxiety and, 508–509
   avoidance of, 490
   causes of, 505
   definitions of, 492–493
   development and, 525–526
   divorce and, 506
   euthanasia and, 514–516
   holiday syndrome and, 504
   life after death, 510–511
   mourning and, 496–502
   personal causation and, 503–506
   planning for, 511–514
   psychosocial predictors and, 504
   societal views of, 493–495
   stages of, 506–507
   time and, 503
   trajectories and, 507–508
Death system, 493–494
Delirium, 446
Dementia. See Senile dementia
Demography, 27–35
Denial:
   bereavement and, 497
   of death, 490, 493, 506, 509
   as stage of dying, 506
Dependency ratio, 33–34
Depression:
   aging and, 431–435
   causes of, 431–432
   memory loss in, 157–158
   mid-life crisis and, 260
   personality and, 260
   theories of, 476
   treatment of, 434–435, 477–478
Depth of processing, 142
Developmental change:
   directionality of, 12–13
   interindividual differences, 18
   intraindividual, 17
   qualitative, 10
   quantitative, 10
   rate of, 12–13
Developmental forecasting, 528–529
Developmental paradigms, 6, 523–525

Diabetes:
    brain syndromes and, 446
    death and, 505–506
Diagnosis:
    of affective disorders, 431–435
    of alcoholism and drug abuse, 426,
        437–438
    of anxiety disorders, 424–425
    of depression, 431–432
    of dissociative disorders, 425
    DSM III, 423–429
    of neurotic disorders, 424, 425
    of organic mental disorders, 427, 440–
        447
    of personality disorders, 428
    of psychosexual disorders, 425, 430–
        431
    of psychotic disorders, 438–440
    of schizophrenic disorders, 427
    of somatoform disorders, 435–437
Diagnostic and Statistical Manuals
        (DSM II and DSM III), 423–430
Dialectical paradigm, 7
Dialectical theory:
    definition of, 220–221
    intelligence and, 183
    Levinson's theory and, 221–225
Dipsomania, 437
Directionality of development, 12, 13,
        528
Discrimination:
    agism and, 67
    defined, 42
    ethnicity and, 61
    racism and, 62
    sexism and, 46–48, 61
    stereotypes and, 61–62
Disengagement, 349–352, 403–404
Divergent thinking:
    cognitive flexibility and, 191–192
    creativity and, 190–191
    in Guilford's theory, 167
Diversive curiosity, 193
Divorce, 219, 309, 315, 506
Dreaming, 96–97
Drug abuse, 437–438, 465
Dual career marriage, 362
Dying trajectories, 507–508

Ear, 112–115
EEG (Electroencephalography):
    indicating death, 492
    sleep waves, 96–97
    slowing of brain wave activity, 96–99
Ego defense mechanisms, 243–245, 405–
        408
Ejaculation, 93, 306, 315
Elderly population:
    characteristics of, 27–32
    dependency ratio and, 33
    growth of, 29–30
    institutionalization and, 455, 483–484
    social consequences of, 32–35
Employment patterns, 341
Empty nest, 284–285
Encoding specificity, 147–148
Epidemiology, 422, 458–459
Episodic memory, 141
Epistemic curiosity, 193
Erikson's theory:
    concept of mutuality, 206
    critique of, 216–217
    developmental energy, 216
    ego challenges, 207–215
        autonomy vs. doubt and shame,
            209
        basic trust vs. mistrust, 208
        ego diffusion or confusion, 213
        ego identity vs. role diffusion, 211–
            214
        ego integrity vs. dispair, 215
        generativity vs. stagnation, 215
        industry vs. inferiority, 210–211
        initiative vs. guilt, 209
        intimacy vs. isolation, 215
    of Individual and Society, 206–207
    psychosocial life cycle and, 12, 204–
        217
Estrogen, 386
Ethnicity:
    assessment, 59–60
    discrimination and, 61–62
    identity and, 60–61
    social policies and, 62–63
Euthanasia, 514–516
Excitement phase of sexual responsive-
        ness, 93, 305

Exercise:
   aging and, 92–93
   heart rate and, 93
   reserve capacity and, 528, 532
Experimental research, 19–23
Extended family, 272
External validity, 172, 174
Extramarital sexual behavior, 325–326
Extroversion, 231–232
Eye:
   aging of, 108–113
   anatomy of, 109

Factor analysis, 165, 169–170
Families:
   career women and, 360–362
   as caregivers, 275–276
   contact among family members, 273–274
   cultural variability of, 275
   housewives in, 355–359
   influencing factors on, 276–277
   life cycle of, 272–273, 367
   parent-child relations and, 278–293
   psychopathology and, 420–421
   retirement and, 352, 364–365
   as social institutions, 268–271
   structure of, 272
Fatherhood, 283
Feminism, 50
Fidelity in marriage, 325–326
Filial maturity, 290
Fluid intelligence, 170–171
Formal operations, 182–183
Fovea, 108
Freud's theory:
   ego-defense mechanisms, 405–408
   psychoanalysis and, 466–468
   three-part structure of personality, 205–206
   unconscious motivation, 205
   views of instincts, 206–207
Functional age, 26
Functional disorders, 418
Functionalist sex differentiation, 50
Funerals, 493–494

Gay, 307–309, 318–319
Gender identity, 44–45, 51, 429
General developmental model, 17–18, 523
Generational stake, 274
Genetic theories of senescence, 84–85
Gerontology, 23–25, 534
Gestalt psychology, 136–137
Grandparenting, 286–289
Grief, 316, 395–396, 497
Group psychotherapies, 470
Guilford's structure of intellect model, 166–168
Gustation. *See* Taste and smell
Gutman's theory:
   critique of, 202–204
   depression and, 316
   developmental psychopathology and, 417, 454
   ego mastery styles and, 199, 202–203, 313
   gender shifts and, 51, 66, 200
   of male and female patterns, 200, 243, 245, 404
   mid-life crisis and, 200
   nature-nurture and, 199
   parental imperative and, 49, 200–204, 282
   species life cycle and, 198

Harvard criteria of brain death, 492–493
Havighurst's theory:
   age-graded life cycle and, 217–220
   critique of, 219–220
   developmental tasks and, 218–219
Hayflick's limit, 83
Health:
   aging and, 88–91
   personality and, 505
   physical fitness and, 92–93
   preventive care and, 91–93
   psychological health, 256–261
   wellness and, 91
Hearing:
   aging and, 113–115
   ear anatomy, 112, 114
   presbycusis and, 113

Hearing *(Continued):*
  tinnitus and, 114
Hearing aids, 121
Heart disease, 88–90, 505
Homogamy, 301
Homosexuality, 242, 271, 307–308, 318–
  319, 431
Hospice, 518
Housewife role, 356–357
Humanistic psychotherapy, 468–469
Humor comprehension, 184
Hypertension, 88–90, 505
Hypochondriasis, 436–437
Hysterectomy, 381

Iconic memory, 139
Identity development:
  in Erikson's theory, 212, 213, 215, 216
Information processing, 122–125, 136,
  138, 141, 142, 146
Insomnia, 97
Inspection interval in learning, 145
Institutionalization:
  aging and, 455
  mental health, 483–484
  relocation and, 503–504
Integrity of personality, 208, 215–216,
  405, 525–526
Intellectual plasticity, 164, 168, 178–179,
  529
Intelligence (162–194):
  age-graded influences and, 180–181
  anxiety and, 177–178
  cohort and, 174–175, 180
  context and, 184–187
  definitions of, 164–165
  educational level and, 175–176
  measures of, 164–169, 188
  modifiers of, 174–181
  nonnormative influences and, 180–
  181
  occupation and, 176–177
  problem finding and, 183
  self-knowledge and, 184
  structure of, 165
  terminal drop and, 179–180
  theories of, 166–170, 181–183

Intelligence testing:
  history of, 162–163
  psychometrics and, 165
  reliability and, 162–163, 172
  validity and, 162–163, 172–174
Intelligence theories:
  cognitive development, 182–184
  crystallized and fluid intelligence,
    170–171
  dialectical operations, 183
  general factor theory, 168
  integration-differentiation-dedifferen-
    tiation, 169–170
  primary mental abilities, 168–169
  structure of intellect, 166–168
Interactionism, 21, 196
Interests and leisure time, 365–366
Interference in learning, 149
Interindividual variation, 18, 527
Intervention:
  agents of, 474–475
  areas of, 462–463
  definitions of, 449
  education and, 472
  evaluation of, 475–483
  goals of, 459–462
  intelligence and, 189–190
  in late adulthood, 454–456
  memory and, 158
  in middle adulthood, 453–454
  policies and, 483–486
  problems of, 456–459
  research designs and, 8, 458–459
  service delivery and, 473
  settings of, 474–475
  techniques of, 460, 463–474
  in young adulthood, 452–453
Intimacy:
  Erikson's theory and, 215, 256
  love and, 266
Intraindividual change, 17, 529
Introspection, 137
Irreversibility and reversibility:
  of dementia, 441, 447
  and health, 91–93
  and intelligence, 189–190
  and memory loss, 157–158
  of senescence, 74–75, 97, 99–100

Ischemia, 99
Isolation:
    Erikson's theory and, 215

Job enrichment, 337
Job involvement, 343–365
Job satisfaction, 332–335
Job selection, 333, 346, 347
Jogging, 92–93
Journal of Gerontology, 24

Kansas City Studies:
    analysis of data in, 404
    disengagement theory in, 403–404
    personality types identified in, 403
    summary of, 401
Knowledge explosion, 191
Kohlberg's theory, 45, 246–247
Korsakoff's syndrome, 156
Kübler-Ross stages of dying, 506–507,
        510

Learning:
    associative learning, 149
    conditioning and, 144
    interference and, 149–150
    memory and, 143
    preparedness, 145–146
    response learning, 149
Leisure:
    age changes in, 369–371
    balancing work and, 371–372
    definition of, 330, 365
    developmental stages of, 367–369
    theories of, 365–367
Lens, 108–109
Lesbian, 307–309, 318–319
Levinson's theory:
    critique of, 224–225
    eras and transitions, 222–225
    life structure, 222
    stages of, 12, 454
Life-after-life, 510–511
Life expectancy, 29–30
Life-review, 152–153

Life-satisfaction, 256–261, 403–404
Life-span:
    average length of, 27–35
    changes in, 29–30
    developmental study of, 4, 520–522
    factors affecting, 30–32
    maximum, 88
Life-span developmental psychology, 4,
        520, 522
Life-style and personality, 256–261, 403
Lipofuscan, 80
Living-dying interval, 507
Living Will, 515
Locus of control, 249
Longevity, 30–32
Longitudinal method, 15–16, 235
Long-term memory, 138, 140–141
Love:
    capacity to, 266–267
    forms of, 266

Maladaptive behavior, 412, 416
Markov analysis, 524
Marriage:
    developmental issues in, 300
    expectations and, 299
    fidelity and, 325–329
    in middle adulthood, 311–318
    in old age, 319–321
    social-historical factors and, 299
    strain in, 298
    in young adulthood, 301–310
Masculinity-Femininity, 45–46
Masking, 126
Mastectomy:
    adjustment phases of, 396–398
    coping with, 396
    impact of, 399
    men's feelings about, 398
Mate selection, 301–302
Mechanistic paradigm, 7
Memory (134–158):
    aging and, 146–155
    clinical aspects 155–158, 441–442
    depth of processing and, 142–143
    encoding and retrieval, 146–147
    interference in, 149

Memory, *(Continued)*
  learning and, 143–146
  models of, 138–143
  search of, 140
  types of:
    encoding and retrieval, 146–147
    primary (short-term) memory, 138, 140
    prospective memory, 153
    recall and recognition, 147
    reconstructive memory, 150–152
    retrospective memory, 153
    secondary (long-term) memory, 138, 410–411
    semantic and episodic memory, 141–142
    sensory memory, 139
Memory interference:
  proactive interference, 149
  retroactive interference, 149
Menopause:
  definition of, 381
  facilitating adaptation to, 386–387
  men's responses to, 385–386
  outcomes of, 382
  social and psychological conditions of, 384–385
  symptoms and complaints in, 382–384
Mental health:
  development and, 415–418
  normality and, 414
Mental health systems, 483–484
Mentor, 362, 454
Metamemory, 153–154
Mid-life crisis, 252–261, 312, 348
Models of development:
  dialectical, 7
  general, 17, 18, 522–523
  mechanistic, 7
  organismic, 7
  specific, 523–525
Moral development:
  definition of, 245
  Kohlberg's stages of, 246, 247
  moral behavior, 245, 246
Mourning and bereavement:
  definition of, 495
  loss of child and, 501
  loss of parent and, 500

Mourning and bereavement:
  (Continued)
  loss of sibling and, 501
  loss of spouse and, 502
  outcomes of, 499–500
  process of, 496–499
Murray's theory:
  affiliation and, 266
  succorance and, 266

Nature and nurture, 5, 199
Neurofibrillary tangling, 80
Neurological plasticity, 79
Neuronal loss, 76, 442–443
Neuroticism, 231, 232
Nonnormative developmental influences, 180–181, 378, 523
Normative Aging Study, 231–233
Normative developmental influences, 180–181, 378, 523
Nuclear family, 272
Nutrition, 80, 91–92, 116–117, 446, 473, 505, 531

Oakland Growth Study, 233–234, 256
Occupational inheritance, 344
Occupations. *See* Careers; Work
Older Americans Act, 533
Olfaction. *See* Smell, sense of
Ontogeny, 17
Openness to experience, 231–233
Operant conditioning, 144
Organic brain syndrome (OBS), 440–447
Organic mental disorders:
  Alzheimer's disease, 441–442
  cerebrovascular variants of, 442
  congestive heart failure and, 446
  delirium and, 446
  drug intoxication and, 446
  hypoglycemia, 446
  Jakob-Crutzfeld disease, 443
  nutritional disorders and, 446
  organic brain syndrome, 440–441
  pain and, 446
  Pick's disease, 443
  reversible brain syndromes, 445–447
  senile dementia, 441–443
  subcortical variants of, 442–443

Organic mental disorders: *(Continued)*
  treatment of, 443–445
Organismic paradigm, 7
Orgasmic phase of sexual responsive-
    ness, 93, 306

Pain:
  acute brain syndrome and, 446
  aging and, 119–121
  gate-control theory of, 119
Paradigms, 5–8
Paranoid disorders, 439–440
Paraphilias, 430
Parent-child relations:
  development and, 278–293
  psychopathology and, 420–421
Parenting:
  delaying of, 219
  generativity and, 215
  parental imperative and, 49, 200–204,
    282
  pathology and, 420–421
  standards of, 245
Passages (Sheehy), 12, 222
Pathogenic families, 420–421
Perception:
  aging and, 130–133
  attention and, 123–125
  cognition and, 130–132
  definitions of, 122
  information processing and, 122–123
  masking and, 126
  sensation and, 106–126
Perceptual curiosity, 192
Perceptual noise, 125
Perceptual preference, 128–130
Perceptual processing:
  bottom-up, 131–132
  top-down, 131–132
Perceptual rigidity, 127–128
Personal control, 503–504, 531–532
Personal death, 502
Personality:
  assessing changes and stability in,
    228, 230, 233, 234, 235
  cohort effect on, 236, 242
  continuity in, 236
  definition of, 228

Personality: *(Continued)*
  ethnic and cultural differences of, 242
  life experiences and, 243
  self-concept and, 247–252
  sex-typed characteristics of, 237, 242,
    250–252, 256–261
  stability in, 233
  tests of, 234
Personal memory, 150–153
Pharmacotherapies, 463–465
Phobias, 430
Physical fitness, 92–93
Piaget's theory, 151, 181–182
Plateau phase of sexual responsiveness,
    93
Pleiotropy, 85
Population trends, 27–35
Positive mental health, 414
Preoperational thought, 182
Preparatory grief, 507
Preparedness for learning, 141–142
Presbycusis, 113
Presbyopia, 110
Primary mental abilities, 168–169
Principled moral behavior, 246–247
Problem finding, 183
Problem solving, 188–190
Psychoanalysis, 466–468
Psychodynamic therapy:
  countertransference, 467
  psychoanalysis, 466–467
  resistance, 467
  transference, 467
Psychogerontology, 25, 534–535
Psychological age, 26
Psychologically healthy men, 257–261
Psychologically healthy women, 256–261
Psychopathology:
  biological explanations of, 418–419
  development and, 415–418
  diagnosis of, 423–447
  family influences and, 420–421
  in later life, 417
  psychosocial explanations of, 419–420
Psychosexual disorders, 430–431
Psychosocial theories of development:
  Erikson, 204–217
  Gutman, 198–204
  Havighurst, 217–220

Psychosocial theories of development:
(Continued)
Levinson, 221–225
Riegel, 221
Psychosomatic disorders, 436–437
Psychotherapy, 465–472
Psychotic disorders, 438–440

Qualitative change, 10, 183
Quantitative change, 10
Quasi-experimental designs, 21

Racism, 61–62
Radical feminists, 50
Rate of development, 12, 13, 528
Recall, 147
Recognition memory, 147
Reconstructive memory, 150–153
Refractory period in sexual responsive-
ness, 93, 306, 315
Rehearsal of memory, 138, 141
Reinert's integration-differentiation-
dedifferentiation model, 169–170
Relaxation, 330, 365–372
Reliability, 22, 172, 528
Relocation mortality, 503–504
Remarriage, 220, 317
Reminiscence, 152–153
REM sleep, 96–97
Research methods:
descriptive, 19–20
experimental, 19–22
Markov analysis, 524
quasi-experimental, 21
Resolution phase of sexual responsive-
ness, 93, 306
Response persistence, 127
Retina, 108–109
Retirement:
men and, 349–352
women and, 364–365
Reversible brain syndromes, 445–447
Riegel's dialectic operations theory, 183
Rigidity:
cognitive, 190–192
perceptual, 127–128
Rituals of dying, 506

Schizophrenia, 438–439
Selective attrition, 179
Self-concept:
adaptation and, 391
age identification and, 247–249
self-esteem and, 249
Self-efficacy, 509, 523
Self-esteem:
depression and, 231
personality and, 249–252
widowhood and, 391
work and, 332
Self-health, 530–531
Self-knowledge, 184, 529–530
Semantic memory, 141
Senescence:
brain, 76–82
defined, 74–75
memory and, 155
reversal of, 97–100
senile dementia and, 75
theories of, 82–87
Senile dementia, 75, 89, 156–157, 441–
443
Sensation:
aging and, 106–122
definition of, 104–122
information processing and, 122–126
Sensorimotor operations, 182
Sensory loss:
aging and, 104–121
perceptual noise and, 125
practical consequences of, 121–122
stimulus persistence and, 125
Sequential data collection strategies:
general developmental model and, 17
intelligence and, 174–175
Sex differences:
female climacteric, 381–383
male climacteric, 387–388
widowhood and, 392–394
Sex print, 304–305
Sex-role differentiation:
aging and, 51–52
biological basis, 49
consequences of, 45–47
feminism and, 50–51
functionalism and, 50

Sex-role differentiation: *(Continued)*
  mental health and, 48
  power and, 47
  privilege and, 48
  social policy and, 52–54
  work and, 338–340, 346–365
Sex-typed characteristics:
  mid-life crisis and, 256–261
  personality and, 237–242
  self-esteem and, 250–252
Sexual behavior, 93–95, 303–307, 313–315
Sexuality:
  Erikson's theory and, 207, 213, 214
  Freud's theory and, 207
Short-term memory, 138, 140
Signal detection analysis, 115, 157–158
Simulation strategies, 106–108, 171, 522
Single subject research designs, 18, 482–483
Sleeping and dreaming, 96–97
Smell, sense of, 115–117
Social age, 26–27
Social clock, 247–249
Socialist feminists, 50
Social status:
  age as a characteristic of, 63–68
  ascribed vs. achieved, 40
  defined, 40
  ethnicity, 59–63
  individual development and, 38–68
  sex as a characteristic of, 43–53
  socioeconomic status, 54–58
  stratification systems, 40
Sociobiology, 100
Socioeconomic status:
  membership qualifications, 55–56
  mobility and change, 56–57
  self-perceptions of, 55
  social class systems, 54
  social policy and, 58–59
  women and, 58
Spearman's general factor theory of intelligence, 168
Stage models of development, 9, 10, 11, 12, 215
Stages of mourning, 496–499
State-trait anxiety, 178

Step-parenting, 271
Stereotypes:
  age and, 63–67
  defined, 41
  ethnicity and, 61–62
Stimulus persistence, 125
Stratification systems:
  age stratification, 66–67
  defined, 40
Stress, 415, 421–422
Stress theory of aging, 86–87
Stroke, 89, 442, 505
Suicide, 431–435
Superego, 205–206
Super's theory, 344–345
Support systems, 408–409, 506
Synaptic changes, 81–82
Systematic observation, 19

Taste and smell, 115–117
Terminal drop, 179–180
Testosterone, 387–388
Test-retest:
  in longitudinal research, 15–16
  reliability and, 172
Thanatology, 507–508
Thermoregulation, 119
Thurstone's primary mental abilities, 168–169
Time-lag, 17
Time of measurement changes, 15, 532–533
Touch, 117–118
Tranquilizers, 438
Transference and countertransference, 467
Transient schemic attacks, 89, 441
Two-person career, 357–358
Type A (coronary-prone behavior), 505

Unemployment, 340–342
Universal ethics, 246–247

Validity:
  concurrent, 172–173

Validity: *(Continued)*
    construct, 172
    content, 172
    defined, 22, 172
    external, 172, 174
    predictive, 172–173, 528
Values clarification, 247
Vision:
    accommodation, 109–110
    cataracts, 110
    critical flicker frequency, 111
    dark adaptation, 110–111
    illusions, 111–113
    presbyopia, 110
    visual acuity, 108–109
Visual acuity, 108–109
Visual illusions, 111–113
Vocational development, 344–349

Wear-and-tear of senescence, 86–87
Wellness, 91
Widowers, 316, 393
Widowhood:
    aging and, 316

Widowhood: *(Continued)*
    common problems in, 395–396
    incidence of, 388–389
    mourning and, 498
    other factors affecting, 391–394
    outcomes of, 394–395
    women's resources in, 389–391
Widows, 316, 388–396
Wisdom, 183, 348, 526, 527
Work:
    advancement in, 337
    aging and, 343
    definition of, 330
    housewife role of, 355–359
    meanings of, 332, 333, 342
    retirement from, 349–352, 364–365
    satisfactions and burdens in, 333–335
    selection of, 346, 347
    sex differences in, 338–340, 346–365
    social status of, 335–337
    socioeconomic factors and, 340–342
    Super's theory of, 344–345, 347, 354
Work ethic, 342–343
Work force, 335–343
Working with the dying, 516–518